Assessment in

About the Editors

Yael Benyamini, PhD, is Professor at the Bob Shapell School of Social Work, Tel Aviv University (Israel). She attained her PhD in Health and Social Psychology at Rutgers University (USA). She teaches assessment in her master's- and doctoral-level methodology courses and has a long record of research on self-regulation and the role of perceptions of health and illness in chronic diseases, women's health issues, and health promotion, including the development and adaptation of research instruments for specific health contexts. She has authored over 70 journal articles and book chapters and is an elected honorary fellow of the European Health Psychology Society.

Marie Johnston, PhD, is Emeritus Professor of Health Psychology in the College of Life Sciences and Medicine at the University of Aberdeen (UK). She gained her degrees and training in Aberdeen, Hull, and Oxford (UK). She is an ex-president and elected honorary fellow of the European Health Psychology Society, honorary fellow of the British Psychological Society, and fellow of the Academy of Medical Sciences. She taught behavioral sciences to medical students for 25 years in addition to undergraduate and postgraduate psychology courses. Her research interests focus on theory, methods (including measurement), and interventions to achieve health- and disability-related behavior change. She has published over 200 peer-reviewed journal articles as well as books and other publications.

Evangelos C. Karademas, PhD, is Associate Professor of Clinical Health Psychology at the Department of Psychology, University of Crete (Greece). He was trained and obtained his PhD in Health Psychology at the University of Athens (Greece). He teaches undergraduate and postgraduate health psychology courses at the universities of Crete and Athens. His research interests include adaptation to chronic illness, self-regulation, quality of life, and CBT interventions. He has authored more than 60 peer-reviewed journal articles as well as several book chapters.

Psychological Assessment – Science and Practice

Each volume in the series *Psychological Assessment – Science and Practice* presents the state-of-the-art of assessment in a particular domain of psychology, with regard to theory, research, and practical applications. Editors and contributors are leading authorities in their respective fields. Each volume discusses, in a reader-friendly manner, critical issues and developments in assessment, as well as well-known and novel assessment tools. The series is an ideal educational resource for researchers, teachers, and students of assessment, as well as practitioners.

Psychological Assessment – Science and Practice is edited with the support of the European Association of Psychological Assessment (EAPA).

Editor-in-Chief: Anastasia Efklides, Greece
Editorial Board: Itziar Alonso-Arbiol, Spain; Tuulia M. Ortner, Austria; Willibald Ruch, Switzerland; Fons J. R. van de Vijver, The Netherlands

Psychological Assessment – Science and Practice, Vol. 2

Assessment in Health Psychology

Edited by
Yael Benyamini, Marie Johnston, and Evangelos C. Karademas

hogrefe

Library of Congress Cataloging in Publication information for the print version of this book is available via the Library of Congress Marc Database under the LC Control Number 2015952378

Library and Archives Canada Cataloguing in Publication

Assessment in health psychology/edited by
Yael Benyamini, Marie Johnston, and Evangelos C. Karademas.

(Psychological assessment--science and practice ; vol. 2)
Includes bibliographical references and index.
Issued in print and electronic formats.
ISBN 978-0-88937-452-2 (paperback).--ISBN 978-1-61676-452-4 (pdf).--
ISBN 978-1-61334-452-1 (html)

    1. Clinical health psychology. 2. Clinical health psychology--Methodology.
3. Clinical health psychology--Practice. 4. Health--Psychological aspects. I. Karademas,
Evangelos, author, editor II. Benyamini, Yael, 1959-, author, editor III. Johnston, Marie,
1944-, author, editor IV. Series: Psychological assessment--science and practice vol. ; vol. 2

R726.7.A87 2015   616.001'9   C2015-906584-4
                                                                 C2015-906585-2

2016 © by Hogrefe Publishing
http://www.hogrefe.com

PUBLISHING OFFICES
USA: Hogrefe Publishing Corporation, 38 Chauncy Street, Suite 1002, Boston, MA 02111
                Phone (866) 823-4726, Fax (617) 354-6875; E-mail customerservice@hogrefe.com
EUROPE: Hogrefe Publishing GmbH, Merkelstr. 3, 37085 Göttingen, Germany
                Phone +49 551 99950-0, Fax +49 551 99950-111; E-mail publishing@hogrefe.com

SALES & DISTRIBUTION
USA: Hogrefe Publishing, Customer Services Department,
                30 Amberwood Parkway, Ashland, OH 44805
                Phone (800) 228-3749, Fax (419) 281-6883; E-mail customerservice@hogrefe.com
UK: Hogrefe Publishing, c/o Marston Book Services Ltd., 160 Eastern Ave., Milton Park,
                Abingdon, OX14 4SB, UK
                Phone +44 1235 465577, Fax +44 1235 465556; E-mail direct.orders@marston.co.uk
EUROPE: Hogrefe Publishing, Merkelstr. 3, 37085 Göttingen, Germany
                Phone +49 551 99950-0, Fax +49 551 99950-111; E-mail publishing@hogrefe.com

OTHER OFFICES
CANADA: Hogrefe Publishing, 660 Eglinton Ave. East, Suite 119-514, Toronto, Ontario, M4G 2K2
SWITZERLAND: Hogrefe Publishing, Länggass-Strasse 76, CH-3000 Bern 9

Hogrefe Publishing
Incorporated and registered in the Commonwealth of Massachusetts, USA, and in Göttingen, Lower Saxony, Germany

No part of this book may be reproduced, stored in a retrieval system or transmitted, in any form or by any means, electronic, mechanical, photocopying, microfilming, recording or otherwise, without written permission from the publisher.

Printed and bound in Germany

ISBN 978-0-88937-452-2 (print) • ISBN 978-1-61676-452-4 (PDF) • ISBN 978-1-61334-452-1(EPUB)
http://doi.org/10.1027/00452-000

Table of Contents

Part I: Introduction

Chapter 1   Introduction 3
            Evangelos C. Karademas, Yael Benyamini, and Marie Johnston

Part II: Domains Assessed

Chapter 2   Social Cognitions in Health Behaviour 19
            Mark Conner

Chapter 3: Self-Efficacy and Outcome Expectancies 31
            Ralf Schwarzer and Aleksandra Luszczynska

Chapter 4: Illness Representations... 45
            Linda D. Cameron, Arturo Durazo, and Holly M. Rus

Chapter 5: Health Behavior 60
            Aleksandra Luszczynska and Martin Hagger

Chapter 6: Patient–Physician Communication and Patient Satisfaction 73
            Kelly B. Haskard-Zolnierek and Summer L. Williams

Chapter 7: Adherence to Medical Advice 86
            Julie A. Chambers and Ronan E. O'Carroll

Chapter 8: Stress and Stressors 103
            Daryl B. O'Connor and Eamonn Ferguson

Chapter 9: Coping 118
            Benjamin H. Gottlieb

Chapter 10: Social Support 131
            Thomas A. Wills, Erin O'Carroll Bantum, and Michael G. Ainette

Chapter 11: Pain and Pain Behavior 147
            Kim E. Dixon

Chapter 12: Health Outcomes: Functional Status 160
            Marie Johnston and Diane Dixon

Chapter 13: Self-Rated Health... 175
            Yael Benyamini

Chapter 14: Quality of Life 189
            Karen Morgan and Hannah McGee

Chapter 15: Psychological Adjustment 201
            Timothy R. Elliott and Norma A. Erosa

Chapter 16: Neuropsychological Assessment 213
            Ruchika Shaurya Prakash, Alisha L. Janssen, and Heather M. Derry

Chapter 17: Biological and Physiological Measures in Health Psychology 227
Suzanne C. Segerstrom, Dorothée Out, Douglas A. Granger, and Timothy W. Smith

Part III: Assessment Methods and Issues

Chapter 18: Ecological Momentary Assessment 241
Derek W. Johnston

Chapter 19: Reporting Behaviour Change Interventions and Techniques 252
Susan Michie and Caroline E. Wood

Chapter 20: Cultural Adaptation of Measures 265
Sofía López-Roig and María-Ángeles Pastor

Chapter 21: Assessment in Children 278
Deborah Christie

Chapter 22: Qualitative Assessment.. 290
Felicity L. Bishop and Lucy Yardley

Part IV: Conclusion

Chapter 23: Assessment: Moving Beyond Association to Explanation and Intervention   305
Howard Leventhal, Danielle E. McCarthy, Emily Roman, and Elaine A. Leventhal

Chapter 24: Measurement Issues in Health Psychology 320
Marie Johnston, Yael Benyamini, and Evangelos C. Karademas

Contributors 335
Subject Index 339

Part I
Introduction

Chapter 1
Introduction

Evangelos C. Karademas[1], Yael Benyamini[2], and Marie Johnston[3]

[1]Department of Psychology, University of Crete, Greece
[2]Bob Shapell School of Social Work, Tel Aviv University, Israel
[3]Aberdeen Health Psychology Group, Institute of Applied Health Sciences, University of Aberdeen, UK

As early as the beginning of the 1980s, it was pointed out that effective measurement and assessment are a sine qua non for the advancement of health psychology and the development of rigorous and successful theories and applications (Karoly, 1985; Keefe & Blumenthal, 1982). Properly developed, reliable, and well-validated assessment instruments and sound measurement procedures are needed for (a) the assessment of health status and the consequences of illness on quality of life and functioning; (b) the examination of the type and the strength of the association between well-being and other variables, including stress, health behaviours, and personal and social characteristics; and the assessment of the ability of a theoretical model or a construct to explain and predict health- and illness-related reactions, as well as the evaluation of the effectiveness of an intervention programme. Although frequently ignored, assessment and advancement in assessment lie at the heart of the scientific knowledge developed in each discipline, including health psychology, and of its contribution to human welfare.

From the early simplified ways of assessing mortality rates (as a first health indicator) in pre-industrial societies to the sophisticated methods of assessing health-related behaviours, cognitions, emotions, and an array of health indices at the present time, assessment has come a long way (McDowell, 2006). However, the progress in the assessment of health-related phenomena depends on the definition: How we assess health, illness, and psychological factors related to health and illness is influenced by the ways we understand and represent *health*, while at the same time our understanding of health is influenced by the ways we assess it. This bi-directional effect between health psychology history and theory, on the one hand, and assessment, on the other, guides the evolution of basic and applied science in health psychology.

The Roots and Development of Health Psychology

It is noteworthy that the history of health psychology is often reflected in the history of assessment in the field, and vice versa. Therefore, in order to better understand this link, a brief description of the roots and the history of health psychology is required.

The roots of health psychology go very deep (Friedman & Adler, 2011). From the ancient world of the Greeks and the Romans, through the philosophy and practice of the medieval ages and the Renaissance, and to the modern era, a long line of philosophers, physicians, and other practitioners have raised questions and issues that still challenge health psychology. As

Friedman and Adler (2011) point out, the modern field of health psychology has emerged and was influenced by an array of intellectual trends in the understanding of health that appeared during the history of human science, but especially by those developed in the 19th and 20th centuries. The development in the areas of biology, medicine, and psychology during the last two centuries has also significantly contributed to the development of health psychology.

In fact, health psychology has evolved as a 20th-century discipline related to many other disciplines and its roots can be detected in several fields (Friedman & Adler, 2011; Johnston, Weinman, & Chater, 2011). First, the work of Sigmund Freud and his students in the fields of psychoanalysis and psychosomatic medicine (e.g., Alexander, 1950; Marty & M'Uzam, 1963; McDougall, 1974) brought forth the role of psychological factors in the causation and progress of somatic symptoms and linked certain psychological processes to bodily manifestations and illnesses. By the 1970s, behaviour modification and therapy had demonstrated that methods based on psychological theory could be clinically effective (O'Leary & Wilson, 1975; Yates, 1970). Second, medical sociology and medical anthropology, and social science in general, contributed to the understanding of the social, cultural, and sociodemographic aspects of health and illness and of the human reactions to these (e.g., Kleinman, 1988; Parsons, 1958). It was Viktor von Weizsäcker, the founder of medical anthropology, for example, who underlined the significance of the patient–physician interaction and attempted to describe the relation between physiological and psychological phenomena (von Weizsäcker, 1949). Third, medical and clinical psychologists became involved in assessment and treatment based on psychological theory in hospitals and in primary care settings where the line between physical and mental health was more blurred. This enhanced their collaboration with other health professionals and advanced knowledge about medical science and medical care as well as its caveats, and also strengthened the interest of psychologists in physical health issues. Additionally, psychologists were increasingly involved in the teaching and training of medical students. They taught about behavioural factors in health and health care and were frequently involved in providing communication skills training aimed at increasing adherence to medical regimens and patient satisfaction. In the UK, publication of projects conducted with medical students created a body of health psychology research evidence (Johnston et al., 2011). Another area of psychology that was influential was social psychology:

> Social psychologists frequently used the health domain to test theoretical propositions, such as the relations between beliefs, attitudes and behaviour (e.g., Fishbein & Azjen, 1975), resulting in a body of evidence and theory development in factors that can predict health behaviour. (Johnston et al., 2011, p. 890)

The disciplines of epidemiology and public health reported research evidence that raised issues concerning long-term care and put great emphasis on the role of personal lifestyle as well as on that of the community in health promotion. Consider, for example, the impact of the Framingham Study in defining the role of psychological factors in chronic illness (e.g., Haynes, Levine, Scotch, Feinleib, & Kannel, 1978) or in the use of advanced statistics in health sciences (e.g., Wu & Ware, 1979). Johnston et al. (2011) also noted the importance of this evidence:

> Epidemiological evidence of the importance of behavioural factors in health: such as the link between reduced smoking behaviour and rates of lung cancer (Doll et al., 2004), as well as the early results from the Alameda County Study (Housman & Dorman, 2005), underlining the potential for behaviour change as a method of enhancing health. (p.890)

Overall, the issues raised by these scientific areas affected the rationale and the range of research and professional practice efforts undertaken by the founders of health psychology and their successors.

Finally, the emerging disciplines of psychophysiology and psychoneuroimmunology (PNI) were based on an understanding of how psychological and physiological factors interact, particularly in the cardiovascular (Steptoe, 2007) and immune (Ader & Cohen, 1975) systems. In the 1980s, the first diagnoses of HIV/AIDS added urgency and momentum to the development of behaviour change interventions to address prevention and, later, to enhance adherence to medications controlling viral load.

Besides the impact of other disciplines, several movements have contributed to the emergence of health psychology. Pickren and Degni (2011) highlighted the role of the American 19th- and early-20th-century emphasis on personal health and well-being as well as on the effects of mental factors and personal behaviour on maintaining and improving health. The same authors also underlined the contribution to the development of health psychology of the works of Hans Selye on general adaptation syndrome (e.g., Selye, 1956) and of George Engel on the biopsychosocial model (e.g., Engel & Schmale, 1972), the rapid growth of psychology and, especially, clinical psychology after World War II, and the acknowledgement in the 1960s that the primary causes of mortality and disability are chronic conditions, such as cardiovascular disease and cancer (for a detailed recounting of the history of the development of health psychology, we refer the reader to Pickren & Degni, 2011).

Furthermore, a crucial aspect of the intellectual roots of health psychology can be traced to the biopsychosocial model (Friedman & Adler, 2011). This model was based on the work of several researchers and theorists in the fields of stress, social perception, and autonomic and immune systems, including Meyer, Cannon, Selye, Janis, Lazarus, Miller, Ader, and Cohen (Friedman & Adler, 2011; Rodin & Stone, 1987). The model was presented by George L. Engel in his 1977 article in *Science* and detailed in his 1980 article in the *American Journal of Psychiatry* (Engel, 1980). In general, the model posits that, in contrast to the traditional biomedical model and away from a mechanistic understanding of health and illness, not only biological, but also psychological (i.e., cognition, emotion, and behaviour), social, and cultural factors play a crucial role in the onset and the progression of a disease and in patients' adaptation to illness. Although not without criticism (e.g., McLaren, 2009), the biopsychosocial model has become a very popular concept and a paradigm for health psychology in terms of both theory and practice.

The factors that guided the development of health psychology and the intellectual roots of the field, which were very briefly described here, as well as the adoption of the biopsychosocial model are reflected in the definition of the discipline. Not only the original definition by Matarazzo (1980), but also the modern definitions of health psychology (e.g., Belar & Deardorff, 2009; Friedman & Adler, 2011) or Johnston's (1994) simpler definition of health psychology as "the study of psychological and behavioural processes in health, illness and health care" (p. 114) emphasize the extensiveness of the psychosocial processes that are related to health and illness and the significance of understanding these processes in order to promote health and facilitate adaptation to illness.

In the same line, health psychologists' research scope and practice have grown to such an extent that they currently refer to a large number of health-related phenomena including stress and coping, health behaviour, health promotion, adaptation to illness, communication and decision making within the health-care system, illness management and relevant interventions, psychological factors affecting health and illness, social and cultural determinants of health, quality of life, patients' and professionals' mental health and well-being, psychoneuroimmunology, and several others. All these are reflected in the assessment domains and processes employed in health psychology, as we will describe in the following sections.

The Context and Purpose of Assessment in Health Psychology

Assessment in health psychology is often a complicated task and depends on the purpose of the assessment. It demands an extensive knowledge of theory and of the existing assessment methods and tools as well as their psychometric properties. It also requires flexibility in the application of this knowledge, especially when new questions and theoretical models are examined. In any case, a sound assessment of the concepts employed in any study is a prerequisite for valid results and conclusions.

Assessments may be conducted in order to:

1. Reach a clinical decision, for example, about initiation or change of an intervention programme, about eligibility for a programme, about referral to a different agency;
2. Describe a population, for example, the patients of a clinic, the participants in a study;
3. Predict outcomes, for example, health behaviours predicting later health, affectivity predicting coping with stressful medical procedures; and
4. Test theory, for example, whether scientific evidence supports or contradicts the theory, whether a theory explains the behaviour of a single individual or organization.

In each case, good assessment is fundamental. Assessments may be descriptive and qualitative (see Chapter 22 in this volume) or may require quantitative measurement.

At the core of the measurement process lies Stevens' definition of measurement as "the assignment of numbers to aspects of objects or events according to one or another rule of convention" (Stevens, 1968, p. 850), provided, however, that these numbers (e.g., a scale) represent a meaningful and clear attribute/construct (Judd & McClelland, 1998). In this case, there is evidence that respondents can make remarkably consistent and accurate numerical estimates of phenomena, even when they are subjective and the comparisons between the numbers of the scale are more or less abstract (McDowell, 2006).

With respect to health psychology, we require assessment and measurement of a wide range of constructs. The biopsychosocial model of health entails biological, psychological, and sociocultural processes that should all be integrated in research and practice. Thus, assessment in health psychology includes a variety of domains, such as physical–biological factors, cognitive and emotional phenomena, behaviours, social variables, the health-care system, social networks, and the social–cultural context. The assessment of these domains demands the use of several methods and sources of information, including health-care records and other archival data, clinical and pathophysiological indices, physiological measures, interviews, observation (e.g., of behaviour), automatic electronic recordings, diaries, standardized tests, and, of course, self-report questionnaires.

According to Smith (2003), this wide range of assessment domains in health psychology can be organized into three overlapping areas: (a) health behaviour and prevention, which includes the relationship between a diversity of health-related behaviours (from smoking and physical activity to the use of seat belts and vaccination) and health outcomes, as well as the theoretical models and the corresponding intervention programmes developed to facilitate health behaviour modification; (b) stress and health (or psychosomatics), which incorporates the effort to define which bio-psychological factors are involved in medical illness (e.g., stress, emotions, personality, social factors) and in what ways, as well as the interventions to minimize the impact of relevant detrimental influences; (c) psychosocial aspects of medical illness and care, which refers to adaptation to illness, to the impact of illness on functioning, well-being, and quality of life and the factors involved in this process, to the characteristics and the factors related to the health-care system, as well as to the interventions aimed at facilitating patients' adaptation to illness and improving their well-being. Likewise, Johnston, French, Bonetti, and Johnston (2005) noted that assessment in health psychology refers to three main clusters of questions concerning: (a) the psychological and behavioural indices of the status or amount of health, illness and health care; (b) the psychological and behavioural consequences of health, illness and health care; (c) the psychological or behavioural factors that may act as predictors or explanations of health, illness and health care. To this complexity, one should add the different levels of analysis (e.g., individual, couple/family, group, social, psychological, biological) that are often incorporated in the same assessment efforts.

Health psychologists have to manoeuvre through this farrago of assessment domains and methods, which very often is quite a challenging task. Yet, the roots and the history of health psychology may also prove to be a great advantage towards a more effective assessment process. In other words, the knowledge and the experience transferred to health psychology by its interdisciplinary origins may provide the pledge and also the context for successfully overcoming assessment difficulties. As Smith (2011) notes, health psychology has drawn from concepts and methods in other fields of psychology (e.g., reliability, validity), as well as other scientific areas, including biomedical sciences (e.g., heart rate, immune function), medicine (e.g., disease indices), public health (e.g., sensitivity, specificity), and social sciences (e.g., social deprivation indices). Thus, health psychology can also benefit from the accumulated knowledge and experience gained in these areas regarding assessment processes. In addition, the collaboration of health psychologists with experts coming from other psychology fields or other sciences in a diversity of contexts (from hospitals to schools and research centres) facilitates the improvement and refinement of the assessment processes being used in health psychology. Several examples of this are provided throughout this volume.

Key Issues in Assessment

Assessment is subject to a number of potential challenges that may affect the conduct of the assessment and may influence results. The choice of assessment method, including its length and burden, intelligibility, sensitivity, and relevance to the population assessed may affect the motivation of participants. The quality and relevance of data obtained may be affected by the mode of assessment: by interview, face-to-face or by telephone, direct observations, self-report (e.g., in questionnaires or diaries), electronically (e.g., online or by smart phone), or automatically (e.g., ambulatory heart rate or physical activity monitoring).

The context of assessment (e.g., whether for clinical or research purposes, whether the participants have consented and/or are volunteers, whether assessed individually or in groups) may additionally impact on ethical issues as well as completion of the assessment. Respondents' fatigue, motivation, negative emotions, personal biases, and interests may further affect the quality of the assessment.

Another issue of importance refers to the applicability of a measure to the population under study. For instance, measures that apply to patients with chronic pain may not be suitable for acute pain, while measures addressed to patients may not be appropriate for their partners – an issue particularly relevant to studies with dyadic data. One should also consider whether the possible norms or cut-off points of a measure apply to every population or not, whether a full or a short version of a measure fits better the respondents' needs or the situation, etc. Age, sex, and culture are also important matters to be considered in this regard.

Key Issues in Quantitative Assessment

Besides these issues, assessment tools per se are often subject to flaws that do not permit an accurate estimation of the construct being assessed. As McDowell (2006,) puts it, "someone learning archery must first learn how to hit the center of the target, and then to do it consistently" (p. 30). This is also true with any assessment tool in use: It needs to be accurate, valid, and reliable. However, as a full discussion of these issues is beyond the scope of this chapter, only a short presentation of the necessary properties of an assessment tool is made here. For a more detailed presentation and discussion of these issues, we refer the reader to Anastasi (1968), Nunnally (1978), Meier (1994), Smith (2011), as well as to the American Psychological Association relevant edition (APA, 1985).

Three properties are all necessary for the instruments, which are used to assess a specific construct or quality in an accurate way: reliability, validity, and sensitivity. Reliability refers to the overall consistency of a measure; that is, its ability to produce similar results across time, individuals, or observers. Validity is commonly defined as the extent to which a measure actually assesses the construct or quality that it is intended to assess. Finally, sensitivity refers to the ability of a measure to discriminate degrees of difference between individuals, populations, or situations.

Reliability

Typically, four methods are used to evaluate the reliability (or consistency) of an assessment tool:

1. Internal consistency, which indicates the degree to which each item of a measure is related to the other items of this measure. In other words, it indicates the extent to which all of the items reflect the same construct or concept. The most frequently used test to assess internal consistency is Cronbach's α coefficient (Cronbach, 1951). This coefficient reflects the average of the correlations between all possible split halves of a set of items. A high level of internal consistency, although a prerequisite, is not sufficient to indicate that a scale is unidimensional (i.e., it assesses a single construct or concept). For instance, the α coefficient can be influenced by the number of the items included in a scale: too many may increase the strength of the coefficient, whereas too few may decrease it. Furthermore, several researchers have seriously questioned the use of the α coefficient as an adequate or even accurate way to estimate reliability (e.g., Peters, 2014; Raykov, 1997). New methods that can provide more accurate reliability estimates have recently been developed. For instance, Sijtsma (2009) has proposed the use of the greatest lower bound, McDonald (1999) the use of the ω coefficient, Revelle and Zinbarg (2009) the use of the ω total, and Raykov (2004) the use of the ρ coefficient. In general, these coefficients are based on hierarchical factor models and not on the inter-item correlations, as is the case with Cronbach's α. Also, Cronbach's α depends on certain assumptions (e.g., that each variable contributes equally to the factor), whereas the afore-mentioned indices do not and, therefore,

may estimate reliability more accurately. Finally, where measures have been developed to have a hierarchical or cumulative structure and use scaling reflecting this structure, item response theory methods, such as Rasch or Mokken methods, are necessary to assess internal consistency.
2. Test–retest reliability indicates the degree to which a measure gives similar scores when repeated across time. Although a high test–retest reliability (expressed in correlation coefficients) is essential for a good assessment tool, it is not always relevant. There are certain constructs (e.g., mood, pain) that are expected to change over time. In these cases, high test–retest reliability may be a serious limitation.
3. Inter-rater reliability indicates the level of agreement between raters, judges, observers, or interviewers.
4. Alternative form reliability refers to the extent to which two forms of the same measure give the same result. It is relevant when two comparable versions of a measure, which are administered to the same (group of) individuals, are needed for theoretical or research reasons. It is seldom necessary to use this type of reliability in health psychology.

Reliability is a critical issue for the measures used in psychological research. Low reliability may lead to underestimations of the actual relations between two measures, may negatively affect statistical power and the observed effect sizes, and may produce wrong null results and affect multivariate and mediational analysis. Furthermore, while a measure may be reliable without being valid, reliability is a prerequisite for validity. For all these reasons, researchers should be sensitive to the reliability of the measures they intend to use.

Validity

Validity is the link between a measure and the construct that this measure is intended to assess. Therefore, a clear and well-developed definition and theory detailing this construct and its relationships to other constructs is critical for the evaluation of the overall validity of the relevant measure (West & Finch, 1997).

Content validity refers to the extent that the items/questions of a measure are relevant and representative of the themes described in the construct it is intended to assess, and is essential before construct validity can be achieved. Content validity has frequently been evaluated in terms of face validity, that is, the validity of a measure is inferred from the comments of experts or users who examine whether the items of a measure appear to measure the intended concept. Sometimes, more formal focus groups or in-depth interviews may be used to evaluate the content validity of a new instrument (McDowell, 2006). However, recently new methods of assessing content validity quantitatively have been proposed. The method of discriminant content validation (DCV) can be applied to measures before using them to assess participants. It gives a transparent, quantitative index of the extent to which a measure assesses the proposed construct and is distinguishable from other constructs in the theory or assessment protocol (Johnston et al., 2014).

Construct validity, which is an overarching type of validity, refers to whether a measure behaves in a way consistent with the theoretical schemes of the construct being assessed. A well-developed theory is expected to describe and define a specific construct in a precise way as well as to indicate the relations between this construct and others either coming from the same theoretical model or not. Thus, a high construct validity requires stronger relations between multiple measures of the same construct (i.e., convergent construct validity) and weaker relations with measures of different constructs (i.e., discriminant construct validity).[1] Factor analysis, which identifies strongly inter-correlated groups of items within a larger scale or questionnaire, is often used to evaluate construct validity but may be misleading unless content validity has been established. A large body of evidence regarding the associations of a measure is often necessary in order to establish the construct validity of an assessment instrument.

Construct validity also entails criterion validity, the extent to which a new measure is related to the present (concurrent) or future (predictive criterion validity) score of an already existing measure, which is used as a criterion of validity (e.g., a gold standard measure of the same construct). Alternatively, criterion validity may be assessed as the extent to which the measure differentiates between groups of persons known to vary on the variable(s) being assessed (also known as the *known groups* validity).

Sensitivity and Other Issues

Sensitivity refers to the extent to which an assessment tool can measure/detect (even small) changes over time. This is especially important for longitudinal studies as well as for the evaluation of the effectiveness of an intervention programme. Sensitivity also refers to the extent to which an assessment tool can differentiate between individuals or populations. Therefore, although validity and reliability are crucial, they are not sufficient when a sensitive measure is needed.

Several of the issues raised above may be addressed with the use of classical test theory (CTT; e.g., factor analysis) or procedures related to item response theory (IRT). Both approaches apply to multi-item or multi-indicator measures but make different assumptions about how the items within the measure are related. In CCT, it is assumed that each item works in the same way as other items; whereas in IRT, items may give information at different levels of difficulty of the construct investigated and with different degrees of sensitivity. It is beyond our scope to present these procedures in detail. However, we will try to briefly present them.

Factor analysis is probably the most frequently used method to evaluate the structure of a measure. There are two types of factor analysis: (a) exploratory, which seeks to identify the underlying structure of a set of items/variables, and (b) confirmatory, which is used to examine whether the structure of a measure corresponds to a hypothesized model (by the researcher or the theory) or one known from previous research. Exploratory factor analysis (EFA) is typically used with new or understudied measures, or when the researcher has no clear hypothesis regarding the factors measured by a specific instrument. Confirmatory factor analysis (CFA) can be used when a specific prediction of the structure of a measure is available. Sometimes, a confirmatory factor analysis follows an initial exploratory one.

IRT and the associated Rasch and Mokken models have been less used in health psychology as a method for designing, analysing, and scoring measures. IRT is based on the principle that each item included in a measure may be sensitive at different levels of the construct, that is, they may be more or less extreme, or more or less difficult. Therefore, IRT treats the difficulty of each item as information important for the scaling purpose and process (Bond & Fox, 2001; Schmidt & Embretson, 2003). Because IRT takes into account both the characteristics of the

---

1 It should be stressed that not all researchers agree that theory is important for the development or the evaluation of a measure. These researchers follow the well-known and influential tradition of operationalism. For an excellent discussion of the issues concerning the operationalism and the post-operationalism approaches and the role of the advances in the philosophy of science in this debate, we refer the reader to Strauss and Smith (2009).

scale (items) and the respondent, it is already regarded as a superior method for addressing complex aspects of content validity, for reducing the number of items included in a measure, and for increasing the overall quality of a measure. An example of the application of both CTT and IRT can be found in Pollard, Dixon, Dieppe, and Johnston (2009).

Two further methods are used in measurement evaluation, namely, *clinimetrics* and signal detection theory (SDT). SDT is generally used to quantify the ability to differentiate between information-bearing stimuli and random patterns that distract from the information. In psychology, SDT can be used to measure decision making under conditions of uncertainty and, thus, it is useful for evaluating the criterion validity and the sensitivity of a measure (McFall, 2005; Smith, 2011).

Clinimetrics was initially proposed as a "subset of clinical epidemiology" (Feinstein, 1987) and the items included in a measure were those found to be predictive of a critical outcome. Examples include the Apgar score used to assess infants, and cardiac risk scores, which combine information about behavioural risk factors such as smoking with clinical measures such as cholesterol levels. They represent a different way of evaluating the quality of a measure (e.g., does not regard internal consistency as a necessary property of a measure).

There is much concern whether clinimetrics, as opposed to psychometrics, is a truly useful or even a unique/distinct contribution to the assessment process (see, e.g., Streiner, 2003). Still, several researchers believe that clinimetrics is a useful approach to *metrics*, as it may facilitate doctors' involvement in assessment issues and also emphasize what is really important in clinical practice and research (e.g., de Vet, Terwee, & Bouter, 2003).

Is There a Need for a New Book on Assessment in Health Psychology?

There are a number of reasons that render the collection and coding of existing knowledge and experience regarding assessment in health psychology a crucial task. These reasons include: (a) the expanding field of health psychology and the need to cover an extended area of topics ranging from health status to health behaviours and beliefs, (b) the increasing number of studies and intervention programmes developed within the context of health psychology, (c) the collaboration between health psychologists and experts from other psychology fields and other sciences and the need to bring good health psychological measures to these research and clinical contexts, (d) the geometrical growth in the assessment tools being published, (e) the need, above all, for sound assessment processes that will permit health psychology to achieve and further promote its goals in terms of theory building, research and clinical practice.

So far, the topic of assessment in health psychology has been addressed in a number of chapters included in health psychology or behavioural medicine publications. Also, certain editions (e.g., Bowling, 2001, 2004; McDowell, 2006) include descriptions of a significant number of specific measures concerning health and illness. Nonetheless, chapters can provide only a brief or limited illustration of the topic, while the existing publications lack a particular focus on health psychology, as they concentrate on specific topics and do not cover many crucial areas for the field (e.g., illness cognitions or health behaviours).

In addition, there are several websites that present assessment tools. However, some of them refer only to particular themes, such as quality of life or mental health (e.g., http://www.qolid.

org and http://www.wiley.com/legacy/products/subject/reference/salek_index.html that include a great number of measures but only regarding quality of life); some sites offer large numbers of measures concerning the broader field of psychology (e.g., http://www.psychtesting.org.uk and http://www.assessmentpsychology.com); others focus on a specific measure (e.g., http://www.uib.no/ipq/, which is dedicated to the Illness Perception Questionnaire and its various forms). The well-known and broadly used portfolio of *Measures in Health Psychology* edited by Johnston, Wright, and Weinman in 1995 provided a wide range of measures with separate booklets for each domain of measurement in health psychology. It used a format entirely different from a typical textbook as it included the measures in a format that could be used in research and practice. However, it needs updating. It does not address recent and crucial developments in assessment (e.g., issues related to the cultural adaptation of measures or new assessment methods). Further, with Internet access to measurement instruments and their updating, provision of the actual measures is no longer necessary or desirable.

For the reasons enumerated here, we believe that there is need for a new integrated publication that will fill the lack of a major edition, particularly focusing on assessment in health psychology and also presenting current knowledge and issues relevant to the breadth of this field. Therefore, we decided to publish *Assessment in Health Psychology*, which aspires to be a comprehensive resource for all those interested in assessment in health psychology.

Purpose and Intended Audience for This Book

Assessment in Health Psychology seeks to provide accurate and in-depth knowledge on issues related to assessment as well as on specific measures used in health psychology research and practice. This volume is intended to serve two important purposes. The first major purpose is to present and discuss the appropriate assessment methods and/or instruments for specific areas that are central for health psychologists (e.g., illness cognitions, quality of life, and pain). The second purpose is to describe the conceptual and methodological bases for assessment in health psychology, including important issues in health psychology assessment (e.g., translation and validation across languages/cultures), as well as recent progress in methods (e.g., ecological momentary assessment, self-report vs. other methods of assessing behaviour and health). A unique feature of this volume is its emphasis on the bidirectional link between theory and assessment.

Assessment in Health Psychology is intended for a broad audience. First, it is addressed to the very large number of master's and doctoral students in health psychology. In the US, more than 45 programmes offer training just in health psychology (related areas and fields are not included; http://www.health-psych.org/LandingEducation.cfm, accessed September 9, 2014), while there are about 40 accredited postgraduate (master's and doctoral) professional training programmes in the UK (http://www.bps.org.uk/bpslegacy/ac?frmAction=results & Course_IDs_Selected=&CourseType=PG&Search_Type=NC&OrderBy=NAME&OrderDir =ASC&INSTITUTION_NUMBER=&TRAINING_COMMITTEE=DHPTC, accessed September 9, 2014). Numerous other programmes across Europe and the world offer training in health psychology. All of these graduate students who are interested in (a) a thorough update of the progress made in assessing health and illness related issues and (b) in a discussion of emerging and/or controversial issues may find this edition very helpful for their research and intervention efforts.

We anticipate the book being useful also to researchers from other disciplines including clinical psychology, rehabilitation, as well as health promotion, health behaviour change, public health, and health services research. In the interdisciplinary collaborations, the book should prove useful in enabling good communication between disciplines about measures used in the collaboration.

Furthermore, given that *Assessment in Health Psychology* is intended to provide state-of-the-art knowledge about assessment methods and instruments in several areas, as well as to put an emphasis on the bidirectional link between theory and assessment, it can also serve as a reference source for health policymakers and health-care practitioners. Finally, we believe that this edition will be very helpful for all those who teach health psychology in their work with their students.

Structure of the Book

For these goals to be achieved, *Assessment in Health Psychology* brings together top experts with noteworthy involvement in their field of expertise who will present the current trends in assessment and measurement. Their long experience and contribution in health psychology-related research and practice ensure an integrated and thorough presentation of all topics covered in the edition. We are grateful to them for accepting our invitation to contribute.

Assessment in Health Psychology consists of 24 chapters organized in four main sections. This introduction is the first section. Sixteen chapters constitute the second part of the volume, which refers to assessment issues and measures used in domains relevant to health psychology. A broad range of domains are covered, including, for example, quality of life, health behaviours, beliefs about health and illness, neuropsychological assessment, coping, pain, and social support.

The third part of the book comprised five chapters. These refer to critical and/or novel aspects of assessment in health psychology. Specifically, the topics of ecological momentary assessment, reporting behaviour change interventions and techniques, issues related to the cultural adaptation of measures, qualitative assessment, and assessment in children are presented and discussed in this part. The final part consists of two chapters. The first of these considers how assessment might be used in explanation and intervention. The final chapter addresses issues and concerns often raised throughout this volume and proposes basic considerations for developing measures in health psychology.

Each chapter is structured in the following manner: In a short introduction, the theoretical/conceptual background of the topic under discussion is briefly presented. Its relevance to health psychology research and practice is also noted. Next, a presentation is made of what is measured and why, as well as of the possible difficulties and challenges of assessment in this particular area. The description of the main instruments in the domain follows with notes regarding their psychometric properties. Instructions about how to obtain open-access measures are also given here. Finally, an illustration of the use of the measures under discussion in research and/or practice, as well as authors' comments about these instruments, concludes each chapter.

This volume is not intended to prescribe which assessment tool or method is suitable for each specific case or cause. This lies with the reader, either a researcher or a practitioner, who is aware of the details and the needs of the particular study or application. It is our hope, nevertheless, that *Assessment in Health Psychology* will provide a thorough record of available assessment tools and methods used in health psychology, facilitate relevant quests, and, thus, make easier the work of all those who are interested in the matter. We hope you will enjoy reading and using *Assessment in Health Psychology*.

References

Ader, R., & Cohen, N. (1975). Behaviorally conditioned immunosuppression. *Psychosomatic Medicine, 37*, 333–340. http://doi.org/10.1097/00006842-197507000-00007

Alexander, F. (1950). *Psychosomatic medicine: Its principles and applications*. New York, NY: Norton.

American Psychological Association. (1985). *Standards for educational and psychological testing*. Washington, DC: Author.

Anastasi, A. (1968). *Psychological testing*. New York, NY: Macmillan.

Belar, C. D., & Deardorff, W. W. (2009). *Clinical health psychology in medical settings: A practitioner's guidebook* (2nd ed.). Washington, DC: American Psychological Association. http://doi.org/10.1037/11852-000

Bond, T. G., & Fox, C. M. (2001). *Applying the Rasch model: Fundamental measurement in the human sciences*. Mahwah, NJ: Erlbaum.

Bowling, A. (2001). *Measuring disease: A review of disease specific quality of life measurement scales* (2nd ed.). London, UK: Open University Press.

Bowling, A. (2004). *Measuring health: A review of quality of life measurement scales* (3rd ed.). London, UK: Open University Press.

Cronbach, L. J. (1951). Coefficient alpha and the internal structure of tests. *Psychometrika, 16*, 297–334. http://doi.org/10.1007/BF02310555

de Vet, H. C. W., Terwee, C. B., & Bouter, L. M. (2003). Variance and dissent. A reply to: Clinimetrics and psychometrics: Two sides of the same coin. *Journal of Clinical Epidemiology, 56*, 1146–1147. http://doi.org/10.1016/j.jclinepi.2003.08.010

Engel, G. L. (1977). The need for a new medical model: A challenge for biomedicine. *Science, 196*, 129–136. http://doi.org/10.1126/science.847460

Engel, G. L. (1980). The clinical application of the biopsychosocial model. *American Journal of Psychiatry, 137*, 535–544. http://doi.org/10.1176/ajp.137.5.535

Engel, G. L., & Schmale, A. H. (1972). Conservation-withdrawal: A primary regulatory process for organismic homeostasis. In R. Porter & J. Knight (Eds.), *Physiology, emotion & psychosomatic illness. Ciba Foundation Symposium 8* (pp. 57–85). Amsterdam, The Netherlands: Elsevier-Excerpta Medica.

Feinstein, A. R. (1987). *Clinimetrics*. New Haven, CT: Yale University Press.

Friedman, H. S., & Adler, N. E. (2011). The intellectual roots of health psychology. In H. F. Friedman (Ed.), *The Oxford handbook of health psychology* (pp. 3–14). Oxford, UK: Oxford University Press.

Haynes, S. G., Levine, S., Scotch, N., Feinleib, M., & Kannel, W. B. (1978). The relationship of psychosocial factors to coronary heart disease in The Framingham Study. I. Methods and risk factors. *American Journal of Epidemiology, 107*, 362–383.

Johnston, M. (1994). Current trends in health psychology. *The Psychologist, 7*, 114–118.

Johnston, M., Dixon, D., Hart, J., Glidewell, L., Schröder, C., & Pollard, B. (2014). Discriminant content validity (DCV): A quantitative methodology for assessing content of theory-based measures, with illustrative applications. *British Journal of Health Psychology, 19*, 240–257. http://doi.org/10.1111/bjhp.12095

Johnston, M., French, D. P., Bonetti, D., & Johnston, D. (2005). Assessment and measurement in health psychology. In S. Sutton, A. Baum, & M. Johnston (Eds.), *The SAGE handbook of health psychology* (pp. 360–401). London, UK: Sage.

Johnston, M., Weinman, J., & Chater, A. (2011, December). 25 Years of health psychology in the BPS. *The Psychologist, 24*, Part 12, 890–892.

Johnston, M., Wright, S., & Weinman, J. (1995). *Measures in health psychology: A user's portfolio*. Windsor, UK: NFER-Nelson.

Judd, C. M., & McClelland, G. H. (1998). Measurement. In D. T. Gilbert, S. T. Fiske, & G. Lindzey (Eds.), *Handbook of social psychology* (Vol. 2, pp. 180–232). Boston, MA: McGraw-Hill.

Karoly, P. (Ed.). (1985). *Measurement strategies in health psychology*. New York, NY: Wiley.

Keefe, F. J., & Blumenthal, J. A. (Eds.). (1982). *Assessment strategies in behavioral medicine*. New York, NY: Grune and Stratton.

Kleinman, A. (1988). *The illness narratives: Suffering, healing and the human condition*. New York, NY: Basic Books.

Marty, P., & M'Uzam, M. (1963). La pensée opératoire [Operational thought]. *Revue Française de Psychoanalise, 27*, 345–356.

Matarazzo, J. D. (1980). Behavioral health and behavioral medicine: Frontiers for a new health psychology. *American Psychologist, 35*, 807–817. http://doi.org/10.1037/0003-066X.35.9.807

McDonald, R. P. (1999). *Test theory: A unified treatment*. Mahwah, NJ: Erlbaum.

McDougall, J. (1974). The psychosoma and the psychoanalytic process. *International Review of Psycho-Analysis, 1*, 437–459.

McDowell, I. (2006). *Measuring health: A guide to rating scales and questionnaires* (3rd ed.). Oxford, UK: Oxford University Press. http://doi.org/10.1093/acprof:oso/9780195165678.001.0001

McFall, R. M. (2005). Theory and utility – key themes in evidence based assessment: Comment on the special section. *Psychological Assessment, 17*, 312–323. http://doi.org/10.1037/1040-3590.17.3.312

McLaren, N. (2009). *Humanizing psychiatry*. Ann Arbor, MI: Loving Healing Press.

Meier, S.T. (1994). *The chronic crisis in psychological measurement and assessment: A historical survey*. San Diego, CA: Academic Press.

Nunnally, J. O. (1978). *Psychometric theory*. New York, NY: McGraw-Hill.

O'Leary, K. D., & Wilson, G. T. (1975). *Behavior therapy: Application and outcome*. Englewood Cliffs, NJ: Prentice-Hall.

Parsons, T. (1958). Definitions of health and illness in the light of American values and social structure. In E. G. Jaco (Ed.), *Physicians, patients, and illness: Sourcebook in behavioral science and medicine* (pp. 165–187). Glencoe, IL: Free Press.

Peters, G.-J. Y. (2014). The alpha and the omega of scale reliability and validity. *The European Health Psychologist, 16*, 56–69.

Pickren, W. E., & Degni, S. (2011). A history of the development of health psychology. In H. F. Friedman (Ed.), *The Oxford handbook of health psychology* (pp. 15–41). Oxford, UK: Oxford University Press.

Pollard, B., Dixon, D., Dieppe, P., & Johnston, M. (2009). Measuring the ICF components of impairment, activity limitation and participation restriction: An item analysis using classical test theory and item response theory. *Health and Quality of Life Outcomes, 7*, 41.

Raykov, T. (1997). Scale reliability, Cronbach's coefficient alpha, and violations of essential tau-equivalence with fixed congeneric components. *Multivariate Behavioral Research, 32*, 329–353. http://doi.org/10.1207/s15327906mbr3204_2

Raykov, T. (2004). Point and interval estimation of reliability for multiple-component measuring instruments via linear constraint covariance structure modeling. *Structural Equation Modeling, 11*, 342–356. http://doi.org/10.1207/s15328007sem1103_3

Revelle, W., & Zinbarg, R. E. (2009). Coefficients alpha, beta, omega, and the glb: Comments on Sijtsma. *Psychometrica, 74*, 145–154. http://doi.org/10.1007/s11336-008-9102-z

Rodin, J., & Stone, G. (1987). Historical highlights in the emergence of the field. In G. C. Stone, S. Weiss, J. D. Matarazzo, N. E. Miller, J. Rodin, C. D. Belar, ... J. F. Singer (Eds.), *Health psychology: A discipline and a profession* (pp. 15–26). Chicago, IL: University of Chicago Press.

Schmidt, K. M., & Embretson, S. E. (2003). Item response theory and measuring abilities. In J. A. Schinka & W. Velicer (Eds.), *Comprehensive handbook of psychology, Vol. 2: Research methods* (pp. 429–446). Hoboken, NJ: Wiley.

Selye, H. (1956). *The stress of life*. New York, NY: McGraw-Hill.

Sijtsma, K. (2009). On the use, the misuse, and the very limited usefulness of Cronbach's alpha. *Psychometrika, 74*, 107–120. http://doi.org/10.1007/s11336-008-9101-0

Smith, T. W. (2003). Health psychology. In J. A. Schinka & W. Velicer (Eds.), *Comprehensive handbook of psychology, Vol. 2: Research methods* (pp. 241–270). Hoboken, NJ: Wiley.

Smith, T. W. (2011). Measurement in health psychology research. In H. F. Friedman (Ed.), *The Oxford handbook of health psychology* (pp. 42–72). Oxford, UK: Oxford University Press.

Steptoe, A. (2007). Psychophysiological contributions to behavioral medicine and psychosomatics. In J. T. Cacioppo, L. G. Tassinary, & G. Bernston (Eds.), *The handbook of psychophysiology* (3rd ed., pp. 723–751). New York, NY: Cambridge University Press.

Stevens, S. S. (1968). Measurement, statistics, and the schemapiric view. *Science, 161*, 849–856. http://doi.org/10.1126/science.161.3844.849

Strauss, M. E., & Smith, G. T. (2009). Construct validity: Advances in theory and methodology. *Annual Review of Clinical Psychology, 5*, 1–25.

Streiner, D. L. (2003). Clinimetrics vs. psychometrics: an unnecessary distinction. *Journal of Clinical Epidemiology, 56*, 1142–1145. http://doi.org/10.1016/j.jclinepi.2003.08.011

von Weizsäcker, V. (1949). Psychosomatische Medizin [Psychosomatic medicine]. *Psyche, 3*, 331–341.

West, S. G., & Finch, J .F. (1997). Personality measurement: Reliability and validity issues. In R. Hogan, J. Johnson, & S. Briggs (Eds.), *Handbook of personality psychology* (pp. 143–164). Dallas, TX: Academic Press.

Wu, M., & Ware, J. H. (1979). On the use of repeated measurements in regression analysis with dichotomous responses. *Biometrics, 35*, 513–521. http://doi.org/10.2307/2530355

Yates, A. J. (1970). *Behavior therapy*. New York, NY: Wiley.

Part II
Domains Assessed

Chapter 2

Social Cognitions in Health Behaviour

Mark Conner

School of Psychology, University of Leeds, UK

Introduction

The psychological determinants of health behaviours have been an important focus of health psychology for a number of years. The behaviour-specific thoughts and feelings that an individual has about a particular health behaviour have received particular attention (Conner & Norman, 1996, 2005, 2015). These are commonly referred to as social cognitions (or health cognitions). Part of the justification for a focus on social cognitions has been that they represent modifiable determinants of health behaviour that can be targeted in interventions to improve health outcomes. Rather than being examined as individual social cognitions, research has tended to focus on groups of social cognition variables as specified by models such as the theory of planned behaviour, the health belief model, protection motivation theory, and social cognitive theory (Conner & Norman, 2005). These models suggest that the thoughts and feelings I have now about a behaviour will predict whether I perform that behaviour in the future (partly because they inform my current decision or intention to perform that behaviour and partly because that decision plus those thoughts and feelings impact on the performance of the behaviour when the opportunity to act presents itself). This chapter first briefly describes the content of these theories. Second, it focuses on the assessment of key social cognitions as identified by these theories. This is done in relation to general principles guiding the appropriate development of measures rather than highlighting specific existing measures to use. This is because the social cognitions are nearly always developed as behaviour-specific measures that vary as a function of the behaviour being studied (and to some extent based on the population under study). Third, a short conclusion summarises the chapter and discusses future directions.

Key Social Cognition Models

The key social cognitions models include the health belief model (HBM; e.g., Abraham & Sheeran, 2005; Janz & Becker, 1984), protection motivation theory (PMT; e.g., Maddux & Rogers, 1983; Norman, Boer, & Seydel, 2005), theory of reasoned action/theory of planned behaviour (TRA/TPB; e.g., Ajzen, 1991; Conner & Sparks, 2005), and social cognitive theory (SCT; e.g., Bandura, 2000; Luszczynska & Schwarzer, 2005). These models will be briefly described here (see Chapter 3 in this volume for further details on SCT). There is significant overlap between the models in terms of the key health cognitions they identify, which will become apparent as we consider measures of the key social cognitions.

Health Belief Model

The HBM posits that health behaviour is determined by two cognitions: perceptions of illness threat and evaluation of behaviours to counteract this threat. Threat perceptions are based on two beliefs: the perceived *susceptibility* of the individual to the illness ("How likely am I to get ill?"); and the perceived *severity* of the consequences of the illness for the individual ("How serious would the illness be?"). Similarly, evaluation of possible responses involves consideration of both the potential benefits of and barriers to action. Together these four beliefs are thought to determine the likelihood of the individual performing a health behaviour. The specific action taken is determined by the evaluation of the available alternatives, focusing on the benefits or efficacy of the health behaviour and the perceived costs or barriers of performing the behaviour. Individuals are assumed to be most likely to follow a particular health action if they believe themselves to be susceptible to a particular condition that they also consider to be serious, and believe that the benefits outweigh the costs of the action taken to counteract the health threat. Two further cognitions usually included in the model are cues to action and health motivation. Cues to action are assumed to include a diverse range of triggers to the individual taking action, which may be internal (e.g., physical symptom) or external (e.g., mass media campaign, advice from others) to the individual (Janz & Becker, 1984). Health motivation refers to more stable differences between individuals in the value they attach to their health and their propensity to be motivated to look after their health.

Protection Motivation Theory

In PMT the primary determinant of performing a health behaviour is protection motivation or intention to perform a health behaviour. Protection motivation is determined by two appraisal processes: threat appraisal and coping appraisal. Threat appraisal is based on a consideration of perceptions of susceptibility/vulnerability to the illness and severity of the health threat in a very similar way to the HBM. Coping appraisal involves the process of assessing the behavioural alternatives that might diminish the threat. This coping process is itself assumed to be based upon two components: the individual's expectancy that carrying out a behaviour can remove the threat (*action–outcome efficacy*), and a belief in one's capability to successfully execute the recommended courses of action (*self-efficacy*).

Theory of Planned Behaviour

The TPB specifies the factors that determine an individual's decision to perform a particular behaviour. Importantly this theory added perceived behavioural control to the earlier TRA (Ajzen & Fishbein, 1980). The TPB proposes that the key determinants of behaviour are *intention* to engage in that behaviour and perceived behavioural control over that behaviour. As in the PMT, intentions in the TPB represent a person's motivation or conscious plan or decision to exert effort to perform the behaviour. Perceived behavioural control (PBC) is a person's expectancy that performance of the behaviour is within his/her control (perceived control) and confidence that he/she can perform the behaviour (perceived confidence) and is similar to

Bandura's (1982) concept of self-efficacy. In the TPB, intention is assumed to be determined by three factors: attitudes, subjective norms, and PBC. Attitudes are the overall evaluations of the behaviour by the individual as positive or negative (and sometimes split into affective and instrumental attitudes). Subjective norms are a person's beliefs about whether significant others think he/she should engage in the behaviour (and sometimes split into injunctive norms and descriptive norms). PBC is assumed to influence both intentions and behaviour because we rarely intend to do things we know we cannot and because believing that we can succeed enhances effort and persistence and so makes successful performance more likely.

Attitudes are based on behavioural beliefs (or outcome expectancies), that is, beliefs about the perceived outcomes of a behaviour. In particular, they are a function of the likelihood of the outcome occurring as a result of performing the behaviour (e.g., "How likely is this outcome?") and the evaluation of that outcome (e.g., "How good or bad will this outcome be for me?"). It is assumed that an individual will have a limited number of consequences in mind when considering a behaviour. This outcome expectancy framework is based on Fishbein's (1967) earlier summative model of attitudes. Subjective norm is based on beliefs about salient others' approval or disapproval of whether one should engage in a behaviour (e.g., "Would my best friend want me to do this?") weighted by the *motivation to comply* with each salient other on this issue (e.g., "Do I want to do what my best friend wants me to do?"). Again it is assumed that an individual will only have a limited number of referents in mind when considering a behaviour. PBC is based on control beliefs concerning whether one has access to the necessary resources and opportunities to perform the behaviour successfully (e.g., "How often does this facilitator/inhibitor occur?"), weighted by the perceived power, or importance, of each factor to facilitate or inhibit the action (e.g., "How much does this facilitator/inhibitor make it easier or more difficult to perform this behaviour?"). These factors include both internal control factors (information, personal deficiencies, skills, abilities, emotions) and external control factors (opportunities, dependence on others, barriers). As for the other types of beliefs, it is assumed that an individual will only consider a limited number of control factors when considering a behaviour.

Social Cognitive Theory

In SCT, behaviour is held to be determined by three factors: goals, outcome expectancies, and self-efficacy. Goals are plans to act and can be conceived of as intentions to perform the behaviour (see Luszczynska & Schwarzer, 2005). Outcome expectancies are similar to behavioural beliefs in the TPB but here are split into physical, social, and self-evaluative depending on the nature of the outcomes considered. Self-efficacy is the belief that a behaviour is or is not within an individual's control and is usually assessed as the degree of confidence the individual has that he/she could still perform the behaviour in the face of various obstacles (and is similar to PBC in the TPB). Bandura (2000) recently added socio-structural factors to his theory. These are factors assumed to facilitate or inhibit the performance of a behaviour and affect behaviour via changing goals. Socio-structural factors refer to the impediments or opportunities associated with particular living conditions, health systems, and political, economic, or environmental systems. This component of the model incorporates perceptions of the environment as an important influence on health behaviours.

Key Social Cognitions

The overlap between the aforementioned models in the social cognitions they describe as being key should be apparent. For example, intention, self-efficacy (or PBC), and attitude or outcome expectancies appear in several models. A number of authors would consider these to be the key social cognitions determining health behaviours (e.g., Norman & Conner, 2005). Several other social cognitions are also widely used and worthy of consideration. Norms, susceptibility and severity, and benefits and barriers fall into this category. Cues to action in the HBM and socio-structural factors in the SCT tend to be less widely used and the measures of these constructs have not been well specified. Similarly, health motivation is less widely used and unlike other social cognitions is not specified in relation to particular behaviours (see Abraham & Sheeran, 2005). In the subsequent sections we look at the assessment of these key social cognitions (i.e., intention, self-efficacy/PBC, attitude/outcome expectancies, norms, susceptibility and severity, benefits and barriers).

Principle of Compatibility

One consideration in developing social cognition measures that has been particularly applied in relation to the TPB is the principle of compatibility (Ajzen, 1988). This principle is that each social cognition and behaviour has the four elements (sometimes summarised by the mnemonic *TACT*) of target, action, context, and time, and states that correspondence between social cognitions and behaviour will be greatest when both are measured at the same degree of specificity with respect to each element (see Ajzen & Fishbein, 2005, for a recent discussion). Hence, any behaviour consists of (a) an action (or behaviour), (b) performed on or toward a target or object, (c) in a particular context, (d) at a specified time or occasion. For example, a person concerned about oral hygiene (a) brushes (b) her teeth (c) in the bathroom (d) every morning after breakfast. In the study of health behaviours it is usually the repeat performance of a single behaviour (e.g., teeth brushing) or general class of behaviours (e.g., healthy eating) across contexts and times that we wish to predict (Ajzen, 1988). Social cognitions and behaviour will be most strongly related when both are assessed at the same level of specificity with regard to these four elements.

Other General Principles

The following sections set out the measurement of key social cognitions. Common to the development of many of these measures are pilot work and procedures to avoid bias and maximise reliability and validity. Pilot work often involves researchers conducting semi-structured interviews with 20 or 30 potential participants to generate the content of each measure (e.g. the salient outcomes to measure in outcome expectancies). Such pilot work can also be used to test the understanding of items in order to avoid biased responses. For example, it is common practice to reverse the wording of approximately half the items measuring a construct to reduce bias among those simply marking one end of all items regardless of content. Piloting can also ensure adequate variability in responses, which is essential if the items are to measure variations in the construct across individuals. Various standard procedures for assessing reliability and validity should also be employed. For example, the face validity of items should be judged by experts in this area of measurement. Internal reliability of items (i.e., a weighted measure of the correlation among items after recoding negatively worded items) should be assessed using Cronbach's α and should normally be above 0.6.

Measuring Intentions

Intentions are key components of the PMT, TPB, and SCT. They capture the motivational factors that influence a behaviour, how hard people are willing to try, how much effort they would exert to perform the behaviour (Ajzen, 1991, p. 181), or the self-instructions individuals give themselves to act (Triandis, 1977). There has been some variation in how the intention construct has been assessed. Common measures include behavioural intentions (e.g., "I intend to perform behaviour x"), self-predictions (e.g., "How likely is it that you will perform behaviour x?"), and behavioural desires (e.g., "I want to perform behaviour x"). In their review of the TPB, Armitage and Conner (2001) noted that the majority of studies they reviewed employed mixed measures of intention (combining measures of intention, self-prediction and/or desire). Conner and Sparks (2005) recommend a number of standard wordings that incorporate the same level of specificity with respect to action, target, context, and time frame as used in the behaviour measure. For example:

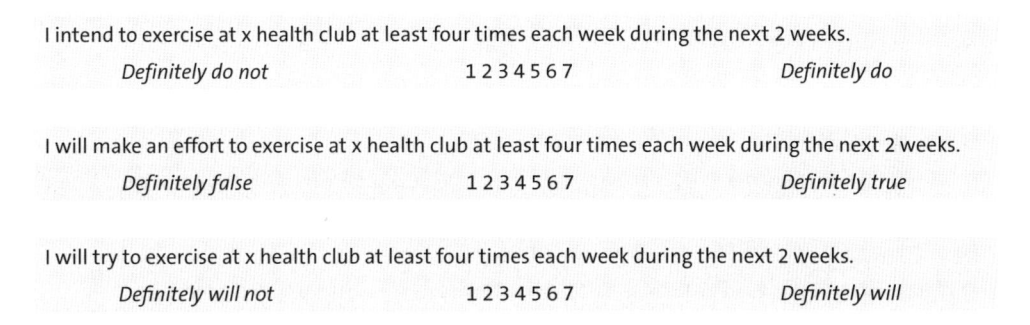

I intend to exercise at x health club at least four times each week during the next 2 weeks.
    Definitely do not   1 2 3 4 5 6 7   *Definitely do*

I will make an effort to exercise at x health club at least four times each week during the next 2 weeks.
    Definitely false   1 2 3 4 5 6 7   *Definitely true*

I will try to exercise at x health club at least four times each week during the next 2 weeks.
    Definitely will not   1 2 3 4 5 6 7   *Definitely will*

Other terms commonly used in place of *intend* or *try* include *plan, expect,* and *want.* Generally these measures show high levels of internal reliability (Cronbach's $\alpha > 0.80$).

Measuring Perceived Behavioural Control/Self-Efficacy

Ajzen and Madden (1986) defined perceived behavioural control (PBC) as "the person's belief as to how easy or difficult performance of the behavior is likely to be" (p. 457). However, the items used to tap PBC included both perceptions of difficulty and perceptions of control over the behaviour. Ajzen (2002a) argues that PBC can be considered as a second-order construct that consists of two components that can be labelled *perceived confidence and perceived controllability.* The perceived confidence component of PBC "deals with the ease or difficulty of performing a behavior, with people's confidence that they can perform it if they want to do so" (Ajzen, 2002b). Ajzen (2002a) has suggested that this component of PBC can be tapped by items tapping the perceived difficulty of the behaviour (e.g., "For me to quit smoking would be …" – *very difficult–very easy*) and the perceived confidence the individual has that he/she can perform the behaviour (e.g., "I am confident that I could quit smoking" – *definitely false–definitely true*). Ajzen (2002b) suggests that the perceived control component of PBC "involves people's beliefs that they have control over the behavior, that performance or non-performance of the behavior is up to them". Ajzen suggests this component of PBC can be tapped by items tapping the perceived control over performance of the behaviour (e.g., "How much control do you believe you have over quitting smoking?" – *no control–complete control*; "It is mostly up to me whether I quit smoking" – *strongly disagree–strongly agree*). Reviews of the increasing numbers of studies measuring perceived confidence and perceived control tend to find the former to be more predictive of intentions and behaviour (e.g., McEachan, Lawton, Taylor, Harrison, & Conner, 2015).

Another issue in relation to the PBC component of the TPB is the assessment of underlying control beliefs. Ajzen (1991) suggests that control beliefs "assess the presence or absence of requisite resources and opportunities" (p. 196). These beliefs are assumed to be based upon various forms of previous experience with the behaviour (see Conner & Sparks, 2005, for more detailed consideration of how to measure control beliefs in relation to health behaviours).

Typical items used to measure PBC would be the following (Conner & Sparks, 2005):

How much control do you have over whether you exercise for at least 20 min, three times per week for the next fortnight?
No control　　　　　　　　　1 2 3 4 5 6 7　　　　　　　　*Complete control*

I feel in complete control of whether I exercise for at least 20 min, three times per week for the next fortnight.
Completely false　　　　　　　1 2 3 4 5 6 7　　　　　　　　*Completely true*

For me to exercise for at least 20 min, three times per week for the next fortnight will be...
Very easy　　　　　　　　　　1 2 3 4 5 6 7　　　　　　　　*Very difficult*

I am confident that I can exercise for at least 20 min, three times per week for the next fortnight.
Strongly disagree　　　　　　　1 2 3 4 5 6 7　　　　　　　　*Strongly agree*

The first two items would tap perceived control and the second two perceived confidence.

The overlap in definition of PBC, and the perceived confidence component in particular, with self-efficacy is striking. Bandura (1977) defines self-efficacy as "the conviction that one can successfully execute the behaviour required to produce the outcomes" (p. 192). Standard measures of self-efficacy tend to focus on confidence that one can perform a behaviour despite varying impediments (e.g., "I am confident that I could quit smoking even if all my friends smoke" – *definitely false–definitely true*; "I am confident that I could quit smoking even if I felt tempted to smoke" – *definitely false–definitely true*). Chapter 3 in this volume deals with measuring self-efficacy in more detail.

Measuring Attitudes and Outcome Expectancies

In the TRA/TPB, attitudes towards behaviours are measured by semantic differential scales (Osgood, Suci, & Tannenbaum, 1957). Two components of attitudes are commonly distinguished: instrumental or cognitive attitudes (e.g., desirable–undesirable, valuable–worthless) and experiential or affective (e.g., pleasant–unpleasant, interesting–boring) attitudes (see Ajzen & Fishbein, 2005; Crites, Fabrigar, & Petty, 1994), with many studies using a combination of the two to measure attitudes (McEachan et al., 2015). For example, we might tap attitudes using the following measure (Conner & Sparks, 2005):

My taking regular physical activity over the next 6 months would be:

Harmful	1 2 3 4 5 6 7	Beneficial
Foolish	1 2 3 4 5 6 7	Wise
Unpleasant	1 2 3 4 5 6 7	Pleasant
Unenjoyable	1 2 3 4 5 6 7	Enjoyable
Bad	1 2 3 4 5 6 7	Good

Typically four to six such differentials are used and these tend to show high internal reliability ($\alpha > 0.9$). Such combined measures tend to include overall evaluation items (e.g., bad–good) as well as instrumental (e.g., worthless–valuable; harmful–beneficial; unimportant–important) and experiential (e.g., unpleasant–pleasant; unenjoyable–enjoyable; unsatisfying–satisfying) items (Ajzen, 2002b). Measures designed to tap one or more of these components of attitude need to include the appropriate semantic differentials.

Alternatively, attitudes may be assessed by simply asking the respondent more direct questions about their attitudes (see Ajzen & Fishbein, 1980, p. 55). For example:

My attitude towards my exercising at x health club is ...

Extremely unfavourable	1 2 3 4 5 6 7	Extremely favourable
Extremely negative	1 2 3 4 5 6 7	Extremely positive

Outcome expectancies are a key determinant of health behaviours in models like the SCT and TRA/TPB. In the TRA/TPB they are labelled *behavioural beliefs* and assumed to determine attitudes that in turn influence intentions. In SCT they are labelled *outcome expectancies* (with several types distinguished) and directly influence intentions. Such outcome expectancies are measured in a standard way (described later). The content of the outcome expectancies is the salient outcomes of the behaviour. For example, in PMT action–outcome expectancies focus on whether the behaviour will change the health threat (e.g., "Stopping smoking will reduce my chance of getting cancer" – *strongly disagree–strongly agree*). In SCT the salient outcomes focus on physical outcomes (e.g., "If I use condoms I would avoid health problems, such as chlamydia" – *strongly disagree–strongly agree*), social outcomes (e.g., "If I use condoms my partner might be happy that I take care of him/her" – *strongly disagree–strongly agree*), and self-evaluative outcomes (e.g., "If I use condoms I will feel proud of myself" – *strongly disagree–strongly agree*). In the TRA/TPB, modally salient outcomes are derived from pilot studies with a representative sample of individuals drawn from the population of interest. The pilot studies typically consist of semi-structured interviews or questionnaire studies in which participants are asked to list the characteristics, qualities, and attributes of the object or behaviour (Ajzen & Fishbein, 1980, pp. 64–71). For example, participants are asked: "What do you see as the advantages and disadvantages of [behaviour]?" The most frequently mentioned (modal) outcomes are then used in the final questionnaire, with commonly between six and 12 outcomes being employed.

Usually *likelihood* and *evaluation* are assessed for each salient outcome. Outcome likelihood (or belief strength) assesses the subjective probability that a particular outcome will be a consequence of performing the behaviour. Such items commonly use response formats such as *unlikely–likely, improbable–probable*, or *false–true*. Outcome evaluations assess the overall evaluation of that outcome and are generally responded to on *bad–good* response formats (Ajzen & Fishbein, 1980).

Conner and Sparks (2005) give the following examples:

Belief Strength

My taking regular physical activity would make me feel healthier.
  Unlikely   1 2 3 4 5 6 7   Likely

My taking regular physical activity would make me lose weight.
  Unlikely   1 2 3 4 5 6 7   Likely

Outcome Evaluation

Feeling healthier would be ...
  Bad   1 2 3 4 5 6 7   Good

Losing weight would be ...
  Bad   1 2 3 4 5 6 7   Good

Internal reliability data for such measures are not usually reported since they are probably best considered as formative rather than reflective indicators. In addition, the fact they are multiplicatively combined (i.e., Σ Belief strength × Outcome evaluation) makes appropriate scaling a complex issue.

Measuring Norms

Norm refers to the perceived influence of others. In the TRA/TPB this is labelled *subjective norm* and described as a "person's ... perception that most people who are important to him think he should or should not perform the behavior in question" (Ajzen & Fishbein, 1980, p. 57) and a "person's perception of the social pressures put on him to perform or not perform the behavior in question" (p. 6). In the TRA/TPB, subjective norms have been traditionally measured as injunctive norms (i.e., what we perceive others to believe that we should do) as they concern the social approval of others that motivates action through social reward/punishment. More recently, norm measures in the TPB have also included descriptive norms, which are perceptions of what others do (Cialdini, Reno, & Kallgren, 1990). Ajzen and Fishbein (2005) suggested that both injunctive norms and descriptive norms be considered indicators of the same underlying concept, social pressure or norms. Norms might be conceived as a higher-order factor with injunctive and descriptive norms as lower-order measures. There is a relatively low correlation between the two (Rivis & Sheeran, 2003, report $r=.38$ for injunctive norm and descriptive norm).

In the TRA/TPB, norms are generally assessed in relation to those people who are important to the individual rather than specifying the particular groups. The particular groups are only specified in the normative beliefs that are assumed to underlie norms. However, not all research follows this convention with measures specifying both general groups (e.g., people who are important to me) and more specific groups (e.g., my family) and individuals (e.g., my best male friend). Normative beliefs can be considered as one specific form of outcome expectancy (as does SCT). Miniard and Cohen (1981) point out that within the TRA/TPB the impact of another person's behaviour can equally be assessed as a behavioural belief (e.g., "Using a condom would please my partner") or a normative belief (e.g., "My partner thinks I should use a condom").

Conner and Sparks (2005) suggest the following items to tap injunctive norms:

Most people who are important to me think I ...
        Should   1 2 3 4 5 6 7   Should not
... take regular physical activity over the next 6 months.

People who are important to me would ...
        Approve   1 2 3 4 5 6 7   Disapprove
... of my taking regular physical activity over the next 6 months.

People who are important to me want me to take regular physical activity over the next 6 months.
        Likely   1 2 3 4 5 6 7   Unlikely

Conner and Sparks (2005) also suggest the following items to tap descriptive norms:

Most of my friends exercise regularly.
       Strongly disagree   1 2 3 4 5 6 7   Strongly agree

Most of my family members exercise regularly.
       Strongly disagree   1 2 3 4 5 6 7   Strongly agree

Again the value of internal reliability data for such measures is unclear since they are probably best considered as formative rather than reflective indicators of the norms' construct.

Measuring Susceptibility and Severity, Benefits and Barriers

Susceptibility, severity, benefits, and barriers are constructs measured in the HBM (and in the PMT for susceptibility/vulnerability and severity). Abraham and Sheeran (2005) and Norman et al. (2005), respectively, provide useful overviews of the HBM and PMT and measurement of the constructs they contain. Perceived susceptibility/vulnerability measures tend to focus on the individual's chances of experiencing the health threat at some point in the future (e.g., "My chances of developing breast cancer in the future are … very low/very high"). Some studies ask respondents to consider their vulnerability on the basis of their current and past behaviour (e.g., "Considering my present and past behaviour my chances of getting health problems from binge drinking are very high"). An alternative approach is to ask respondents to provide vulnerability ratings if a recommended behaviour is not performed (e.g., "If left untreated, what are the chances that your child's visual impairment will affect his/her reading ability?").

Table 2.1. Items tapping susceptibility, severity, benefits, and barriers in a study of breast self-examination (adapted from Champion 1984)

Susceptibility/vulnerability	
1	My chances of getting breast cancer are great.
2	My physical health makes it more likely that I will get breast cancer.
3	I feel that my chances of getting breast cancer in the future are good.
...	
Cronbach's α = 0.78 (6 items)	
Severity	
1	The thought of breast cancer scares me.
2	When I think about breast cancer I feel nauseous.
3	If I had breast cancer my career would be endangered.
...	
Cronbach's α = 0.70 (12 items)	
Benefits	
1	Doing breast self-exams prevents future problems for me.
2	I have a lot to gain by doing breast self-exams.
3	Breast self-exams can help me find lumps in my breast.
...	
Cronbach's α = 0.61 (5 items)	
Barriers	
1	It is embarrassing for me to do monthly breast exams.
2	In order for me to do monthly breast exams I have to give up quite a bit.
3	Breast self-exams can be painful.
...	
Cronbach's α = 0.76 (8 items)	

Severity items typically focus on the physical severity of the health threat (e.g., "How serious a health problem is a heart attack?"). However, other aspects of the seriousness of the health threat have been considered including the potential impact on psychological well-being (e.g., "Even if I was infected by HIV, I would still lead a happy life") and involvement in normal activities (e.g., "I see this injury as a serious threat to my sport/exercise involvement").

Benefit items (e.g., "Doing breast self-exams prevents future problems for me") often include both medical and psychosocial benefits of engaging in health-promoting behaviours. While barrier items ("Breast self-exams are time consuming") include practical barriers to performing the behaviour (e.g., time, expense, availability, transport, waiting time) as well as psychological costs associated with performing the behaviour (pain, embarrassment, threat to well-being or lifestyle and livelihood). Champion (1984) provides a useful example of how to develop HBM measures such as benefits, barriers, susceptibility, and severity in relation to breast self-examination (see Table 2.1 for example items). The first step involves generating items that purport to measure HBM components. This can be partly based on previous HBM studies or pilot work with relevant respondents in order to determine respondents' perceptions of the health threat and beliefs about the behaviour in an open-ended manner (Abraham & Sheeran, 2005). Champion (1984) developed a set of items for each HBM component but then retained only those items that at least six out of eight expert judges agreed represented the constructs in question (Table 2.1).

Conclusions

The reliable and valid assessment of social cognitions can be the basis of research to further our understanding of the determinants of health behaviours and provide appropriate targets for interventions designed to change these behaviours. Based on the most important social cognition models used in relation to health behaviours (i.e., health belief model, protection motivation theory, theory of planned behaviour/reasoned action, social cognitive theory) several key social cognition variables were examined. These were intention, self-efficacy (or PBC), attitude or outcome expectancies, norms, susceptibility and severity, and benefits and barriers. In each case, principles for measurement were considered. Internal reliability data can be usefully reported for most of these measures. Test–retest reliability can also be useful when reported over limited periods (e.g., periods over which the measures might not be expected to change). Discriminant validity (correlation between different social cognitions) is also a useful focus, although it tends to be given limited attention in social cognition research. The predictive validity of the constructs in predicting behaviour appears to vary markedly as a function of the population and behaviour under study. These aspects of reliability and validity might usefully be given further attention in the assessment of social cognitions about health behaviours.

References

Abraham, C., & Sheeran, P. (2005). The health belief model. In M. Conner & P. Norman (Eds.), *Predicting health behaviour: Research and practice with social cognition models* (2nd ed., pp. 28–80). Maidenhead, UK: Open University Press.

Ajzen, I. (1988). *Attitudes personality and behavior*. Milton Keynes, UK: Open University Press.

Ajzen, I. (1991). The theory of planned behavior. Special Issue: Theories of cognitive self-regulation. *Organizational Behavior and Human Decision Processes, 50*, 179–211.

Ajzen, I. (2002a). Perceived behavioural control, self-efficacy, locus of control, and the theory of planned behaviour. *Journal of Applied Social Psychology, 32*, 1–20. http://doi.org/10.1111/j.1559-1816.2002.tb00236.x

Ajzen, I. (2002b). *Constructing a TPB Questionnaire: Conceptual and methodological considerations*. Retrieved from http://www.people.umass.edu/aizen/pdf/tpb.measurement.pdf

Ajzen, I., & Fishbein, M. (1980). *Understanding attitudes and predicting social behavior*. Englewood-Cliff, NJ: Prentice-Hall.

Ajzen, I., & Fishbein, M. (2005). The influence of attitudes on behavior. In D. Albarracin, B. T. Johnson, & M. P. Zanna. (Eds.), *Handbook of attitudes and attitude change: Basic principles* (pp. 173–221). Mahwah, NJ: Erlbaum.

Ajzen, I., & Madden, T. J. (1986). Prediction of goal directed behavior: Attitudes, intentions and perceived behavioral control. *Journal of Experimental Social Psychology, 22*, 453–474. http://doi.org/10.1016/0022-1031(86)90045-4

Armitage, C. J., & Conner, M. (2001). Efficacy of the theory of planned behaviour: A meta-analytic review. *British Journal of Social Psychology, 40*, 471–499. http://doi.org/10.1348/014466601164939

Bandura, A. (1977). Self-efficacy: Toward a unifying theory of behavioural change. *Psychological Review, 84*, 191–215. http://doi.org/10.1037/0033-295X.84.2.191

Bandura, A. (1982). Self-efficacy mechanism in human agency. *American Psychologist, 37*, 122–147. http://doi.org/10.1037/0003-066X.37.2.122

Bandura, A. (2000). Exercise of human agency through collective efficacy. *Current Directions of Psychological Science, 9*, 75–8. http://doi.org/10.1111/1467-8721.00064

Champion, V. L. (1984). Instrument development for health belief model constructs. *Advances in Nursing Science, 6*(3), 73–85.

Cialdini, R. B., Reno, R. R., & Kallgren, C. A. (1990). A focus theory of normative conduct: Recycling the concept of norms to reduce littering in public places. *Journal of Personality and Social Psychology, 58*, 1015–1026. http://doi.org/10.1037/0022-3514.58.6.1015

Conner, M. T., & Norman, P. (Eds.). (1996). *Predicting health behaviour: Research and practice with social cognition models*. Milton Keynes, UK: Open University Press.

Conner, M., & Norman, P. (Eds.). (2005). *Predicting health behaviour: Research and practice with social cognition models* (2nd ed.). Maidenhead, UK: Open University Press.

Conner, M., & Norman, P. (Eds.). (2015). *Predicting and changing health behaviour* (3rd ed.). Maidenhead, UK: Open University Press.

Conner, M., & Sparks, P. (2005). The theory of planned behaviour and health behaviours. In M. Conner & P. Norman (Eds.), *Predicting health behaviour* (pp. 170–222). Buckingham, UK: Open University Press.

Crites, S. L., Fabrigar, L. R., & Petty, R. E. (1994). Measuring the affective and cognitive properties of attitudes: Conceptual and methodological issues. *Personality and Social Psychology Bulletin, 20*, 619–634. http://doi.org/10.1177/0146167294206001

Fishbein, M. (1967). Attitude and the prediction of behavior. In M. Fishbein (Ed.), *Readings in attitude theory and measurement* (pp. 477–492). New York, NY: Wiley.

Janz, N. K., & Becker, M. H. (1984). The health belief model: A decade later. *Health Education Quarterly, 11*, 1–47. http://doi.org/10.1177/109019818401100101

Luszczynska, A., & Schwarzer, R. (2005). Social cognitive theory. In M. Conner & P. Norman (Eds.), *Predicting health behaviour: Research and practice with social cognition models* (2nd ed., pp. 127–169). Maidenhead, UK: Open University Press.

Maddux, J. E., & Rogers, R. W. (1983). Protection motivation and self-efficacy: A revised theory of fear appeals and attitude change. *Journal of Experimental Social Psychology, 19*, 469–479. http://doi.org/10.1016/0022-1031(83)90023-9

McEachan, R. R. C., Lawton, R. J., Taylor, N. J., Harrison, R., & Conner, M. (2015). *A meta-analysis of the extended Theory of Planned Behavior as applied to prospective studies of health behaviors*. Manuscript in preparation.

Miniard, P. W., & Cohen, J. B. (1981). An examination of the Fishbein-Ajzen behavioural-intentions model's concepts and measures. *Journal of Experimental Social Psychology, 17*, 309–339. http://doi.org/10.1016/0022-1031(81)90031-7

Norman, P., & Conner, M. (2005). Predicting and changing health behaviour: Future directions. In M. Conner & P. Norman (Eds.), *Predicting health behaviour: Research and practice with social cognition models* (2nd ed., pp. 324–371). Maidenhead, UK: Open University Press.

Norman, P., Boer, H., & Seydel, E. R. (2005). Protection motivation theory. In M. Conner & P. Norman (Eds.), *Predicting health behaviour: Research and practice with social cognition models* (2nd ed., pp. 81–126). Maidenhead, UK: Open University Press.

Osgood, C. E., Suci, G. J., & Tannenbaum, P. H. (1957). *The measurement of meaning*. Urbana, IL: University of Illinois Press.

Rivis, A., & Sheeran, P. (2003). Descriptive norms as an additional predictor in the theory of planned behaviour: A meta-analysis. *Current Psychology, 22*, 218–233. http://doi.org/10.1007/s12144-003-1018-2

Triandis, H. C. (1977). *Interpersonal behavior*. Monterey, CA: Brooks/Cole.

Chapter 3
Self-Efficacy and Outcome Expectancies

Ralf Schwarzer[1] and Aleksandra Luszczynska[2]

[1]Institute for Positive Psychology and Education, Faculty of Health Sciences,
Australian Catholic University, Strathfield, NSW, Australia
[2]Trauma, Health, & Hazards Center, University of Colorado at Colorado Springs, CO, USA

Social Cognitive Theory

In his landmark book *Social Foundations of Thought and Action: A Social Cognitive Theory*, Bandura (1986) developed the social cognitive theory (SCT) of human functioning based on his earlier social learning theory and his pioneering article on perceived self-efficacy (Bandura, 1977). This work has been crowned by the 1997 volume *Self-Efficacy: The Exercise of Control* (Bandura, 1997). SCT has been applied to diverse areas such as school achievement, emotional disorders, mental and physical health, career choice, and socio-political change.

According to the theory, human motivation and action are regulated by forethought. This anticipatory control mechanism involves expectations that might refer to outcomes of undertaking a specific action. The theory outlines two core constructs that influence behaviour. The first factor is perceived self-efficacy, which is concerned with people's beliefs in their capabilities to perform a specific action required to attain a desired outcome. Outcome expectancies, the other core construct of SCT, reflect perceptions about the possible consequences of their actions.

Perceived Self-Efficacy

Perceived self-efficacy is concerned with individuals' beliefs in their capability to exercise control over challenging demands and their own functioning. Expectations of self-efficacy are self-regulatory cognitions that determine whether instrumental actions will be initiated, how much effort will be expended, and how long it will be sustained in the face of obstacles and failures. Self-efficacy has an influence on preparing for action because self-related cognitions are a major ingredient in the motivation process. Self-efficacy levels can enhance or impede motivation. Persons with low self-efficacy harbour pessimistic thoughts about their likely accomplishments and personal development. Self-efficacy can also be directly related to behaviour. Perceived self-efficacy represents the confidence that one can employ the skills necessary to resist temptation, cope with stress, and mobilize one's resources required to meet the situational demands. Self-efficacy beliefs affect the amount of effort to change risk behaviour and the persistence to continue striving in the face of barriers and setbacks that may undermine motivation.

Self-efficacy is based on different sources (Bandura, 1997). First, self-efficacy beliefs can be enhanced through personal accomplishment or mastery, as far as success is attributed internally and can be repeated. A second source is vicarious experience. When a role model that is similar to the individual successfully masters a difficult situation, social comparison processes can enhance self-efficacy beliefs. Third, self-efficacy beliefs can also be changed through verbal persuasion by others (e.g., a health educator reassures a patient that she will certainly adhere to a demanding dietary regimen, due to her competence). The last source of influence is emotional arousal, that is, the person may experience no apprehension in a threatening situation and, as a result, may feel capable of mastering the situation. These four informational sources vary in strength and importance in the order presented here, with personal mastery being the strongest source of self-efficacy (Warner, Schüz, Knittle, Ziegelmann, & Wurm, 2011). A meta-analysis has examined sources of self-efficacy by comparing the effects of various intervention techniques upon self-efficacy for physical activity (Ashford, Edmunds, & French, 2010).

Compared with similar constructs such as self-esteem, self-concept, or locus of control, the essential distinction between these and self-efficacy lies in three aspects: (a) self-efficacy implies an internal attribution (a person is the cause of the action), (b) it is prospective, referring to future behaviours, and (c) it is an operative construct, which means that this cognition is proximal to the critical behaviour. A rich resource on self-efficacy is available at http://www.uky.edu/~eushe2/Pajares/self-efficacy.html.

Phase-Specific Self-Efficacy

Perceived self-efficacy has been found to be important at all stages of health behaviour change (Bandura, 1997), but it does not always constitute exactly the same construct. Its meaning depends on the particular situation of individuals who may be more or less advanced in the change process. The distinction between action self-efficacy, coping self-efficacy, and recovery self-efficacy has been brought up by Marlatt, Baer, and Quigley (1995) in the domain of addictive behaviours. The rationale for the distinction between several phase-specific self-efficacy beliefs is that during the course of health behaviour change, different tasks have to be mastered, and that different self-efficacy beliefs are required to master these tasks successfully. For example, a person might be confident in his or her capability to be physically active in general (i.e., high action self-efficacy), but might not be very confident to resume physical activity after a setback (low recovery self-efficacy).

Preaction self-efficacy (also called *action self-efficacy* or *task self-efficacy*) refers to the first phase of the process, in which an individual does not yet act, but develops a motivation to do so. It is an optimistic belief during the preactional phase. Individuals high in preaction self-efficacy imagine success, anticipate potential outcomes of diverse strategies, and are more likely to initiate a new behaviour. Those with less self-efficacy imagine failure, harbour self-doubts, and tend to procrastinate. While preaction self-efficacy is most instrumental in the motivation phase, the two following constructs are most instrumental in the subsequent volition phase and can, therefore, also by summarized under the heading of *volitional self-efficacy*. Maintenance self-efficacy represents optimistic beliefs about one's capability to cope with barriers that arise during the maintenance period. (The equivalent term *coping self-efficacy* has also been used in a different sense in the trauma context; therefore, we now prefer the term *maintenance self-efficacy*.) A new health behaviour might turn out to be much more difficult to adhere to than expected, but a self-efficacious person responds confidently with better strategies, more effort, and prolonged persistence to overcome such hurdles. Once an action has been taken, individuals with high maintenance self-efficacy invest more effort and persist longer than those who are less self-efficacious.

Recovery self-efficacy addresses the experience of failure and recovery from setbacks. If a lapse occurs, individuals can fall prey to the *abstinence violation effect*, that is, they attribute their lapse to internal, stable, and global causes, dramatize the event, and interpret it as a full-blown relapse (Marlatt et al., 1995). High self-efficacious individuals, however, avoid this effect by attributing the lapse to an external high-risk situation and by finding ways to control the damage and to restore hope. Recovery self-efficacy pertains to one's conviction to get back on track after being derailed. The person trusts his/her competence to regain control after a setback or failure and to reduce harm (Luszczynska, Mazurkiewicz, Ziegelmann, & Schwarzer, 2007; Ochsner, Scholz, & Hornung, 2013).

This distinction between phase-specific self-efficacy beliefs has proven useful in various domains of behaviour change. Preaction self-efficacy tends to predict intentions, whereas maintenance self-efficacy tends to predict behaviours. Individuals who have recovered from a setback need different self-beliefs than those who maintain their levels of activity (Scholz, Sniehotta, & Schwarzer, 2005). There is evidence for phase-specific self-efficacy beliefs in the domain of exercise behaviour (i.e., task self-efficacy, coping self-efficacy, and scheduling self-efficacy; Rodgers, Murray, Courneya, Bell, & Harber, 2009). Phase-specific self-efficacy differed in the effects on various preventive health behaviours such as breast self-examination (Luszczynska & Schwarzer, 2003), dietary behaviours (Ochsner et al., 2013), and physical activity (Scholz et al., 2005).

Outcome Expectancies

Outcome expectancies, the other key construct in SCT, are beliefs about the consequences of one's action. Physical, social, affective, and self-evaluative outcome expectancies have been distinguished (Bandura, 1997). One's behaviour may provoke bodily changes, responses from others, or feelings about oneself. Together with self-efficacy they influence mainly goal setting and, more indirectly, also goal pursuit.

While perceived self-efficacy refers to personal action control or agency, outcome expectancies pertain to the perception of possible behavioural consequences. Outcome expectancies can be organized along three dimensions: (a) area of consequences, (b) positive or negative consequences, and (c) short-term or long-term consequences. Areas of consequences can be split into three factors (Dijkstra, Bakker, & De Vries, 1997). Physical outcome expectations, such as expectations of discomfort or disease symptoms, refer to the anticipation of what will be experienced after behaviour change takes place. These include both the short- and long-term effects of behaviour change. For example, immediately after quitting smoking, an ex-smoker might observe a reduction of coughing (positive consequence) and a higher level of muscle tension (negative consequence). In the long run, an ex-smoker might expect lower susceptibility to respiratory infections (positive consequence) but an increased susceptibility to weight gain (negative consequence). Social outcome expectancies refer to anticipated social responses after behaviour change. Smokers might expect disapproval from friends who continue to smoke, or, positively, they might expect their family to congratulate them on quitting smoking. In the long run, ex-smokers might expect that they will increase their chances to find and maintain an attractive partner or a better job. Self-evaluative and affective outcome expectations refer to the anticipation of emotional experience, such as being ashamed, being proud of oneself, or being satisfied, due to internal standards. These affective outcome expectancies may be the more salient ones when it comes to intention formation and behaviour (Conner, Rhodes, Morris, McEachan, & Lawton, 2011; Gellert, Ziegelmann, & Schwarzer, 2012). An example of an emotional outcome expectancy is anticipated regret ("If I do not use a condom tonight, then I will regret it tomorrow").

In addition to being aware of a health threat, people also need to understand the links between their preventive actions and subsequent outcomes. These outcome expectancies can be the most influential beliefs in the motivation to change. The term *outcome expectancies* is used in SCT (Bandura, 1986). The equivalent term *pros and cons* is used in the transtheoretical model (Prochaska & DiClemente, 1983), where it represents the decisional balance when people contemplate whether to adopt a novel behaviour or not. In the reasoned action approach (Fishbein & Ajzen, 2010) the corresponding term is *behavioural beliefs* that act as precursors of attitudes.

The pros and cons represent positive and negative outcome expectancies. A smoker may find more good reasons to quit ("If I quit smoking, then my friend will like me much more") than reasons to continue smoking ("If I quit, I will become more tense and irritated"). This imbalance in favour of positive outcome expectancies will not lead directly to action, but it can help to generate the intention to quit. Outcome expectancies can also be understood as means–ends relationships, indicating that people know proper strategies to produce the desired effects.

Outcome expectancies encourage the decision to change one's behaviour. People weigh the pros and cons of a certain behaviour, which means that they harbour positive and negative outcome expectancies. Depending on this decisional balance they may develop an intention to act or an intention not to act.

The perceived contingencies between actions and outcomes need not be explicitly worded; they can also be rather diffuse mental representations, loaded with emotions. Social cognition models are often misunderstood as being rational models that deal with cold cognitions. By contrast, health behaviour change, to a large degree, is an emotional process that turns into a cognitive one only after people have been asked about their thoughts and feelings, thus making them aware of what is going on emotionally.

Assessment Principles

It is most important to achieve a proper wording of test items to avoid overlap with other constructs. For this purpose, exploratory studies on respondent-generated statements are helpful. *Outcome expectancies* have been assessed by free association in a study on alcohol consumption (Reich & Goldman, 2005). Participants were asked to free associate to the phrase, "Alcohol makes me ….," and they also reported their amount of alcohol intake. Depending on the level of consumption, different types of outcome expectancies were prevalent. The heaviest drinkers gave more positive and arousing responses (e.g., alcohol makes me more sociable) than did lighter drinkers, who gave more negative and sedating responses referring, for example, to compromised health and emotions.

The free association paradigm is appropriate in the more exploratory phase of research. Most researchers prefer to use brief scales that provide sufficiently valid quantitative information. There are some rules of thumb in assessing outcome expectancies and perceived self-efficacy. To simplify test construction, one can keep in mind that outcome expectancies are best worded

	Action	Non-action
Positive outcomes	If I use a condom, we will be protected	If I don't use a condom, it feels better
Negative outcomes	If I use a condom, I feel awkward	If I don't use a condom, I take a risk

Figure 3.1. Positive and negative outcome expectancies for action and non-action

with *if–then* statements, and self-efficacy items as confidence statements. The semantic structure of outcome expectancies is: "If ... (a behaviour), then ... (consequences)." An example of a positive outcome expectancy is: "If I reduce my dietary fat intake, I will become slim." An example of a negative one is: "If I reduce my dietary fat intake, I cannot enjoy my favourite desserts any longer."

Another point of consideration is whether one wants to balance positive and negative outcome expectancies and whether to look at both sides of the coin: to behave and not to behave, as illustrated in Figure 3.1.

In many cases, it may be redundant to address all four cells of Figure 3.1 when designing a scale to assess outcome expectancies. In some cases, however, it may be useful because action and non-action can constitute quite different constructs. For example, sedentary behaviours (watching TV, reading, doing desk work, etc.) represent more than simply not being physically active. Therefore, assessing physical activity along with sedentary behaviours and their corresponding outcome expectancies broadens the scope of the investigation.

For *self-efficacy*, a semantic rule is: "I am confident that I can ... (perform an action), even if ... (a barrier)." An example of a self-efficacy item is: "I am confident that I can skip desserts even if my family continues to devour them in my presence." This semantic rule need not be applied rigidly, but might serve as a useful heuristic. A comprehensive book chapter with detailed guidelines on the construction of various kinds of self-efficacy measures has been provided by Bandura (2006). He also introduces a variety of possible response formats. Some examples include scales from 0 to 100. There is no general recommendation for the choice of response formats. Most research uses Likert-type formats (1 to 4, 1 to 5, or 1 to 6). This applies to the measurement of self-efficacy as well as outcome expectancies.

It is desirable to assess a variety of (a) barriers that might arise if an individual tries to change a behaviour, and (b) outcome expectancies, both positive and negative. Individuals face various social, personal, and environmental obstacles. For example, they have many reasons why they should quit smoking or why they find it better to continue. Therefore, questionnaire items should refer to multiple possible barriers and outcomes that are specific for a health behaviour. Following these general rules, researchers usually develop their own measures that suit their particular research context.

When it comes to addictive behaviours, there are two basic methods to design a risk behaviour self-efficacy scale. One is to confront the individual with a list or hierarchy of tempting situations and to assess situation-specific self-efficacy in line with these demands. The second approach aims at the restricted use of substances, asking participants whether in general they feel competent to control the behaviour in question (irrespective of specific risk situations). In the domain of smoking, for example, the first method has been chosen by Colletti, Supnick, and Payne (1985) and by Velicer, DiClemente, Rossi, and Prochaska (1990). Dijkstra and DeVries (2000) elaborated a smoking self-efficacy scale that reflects different barriers that might arise during adoption, maintenance, and recovery after lapses. For example, barriers pertaining to emotional states (e.g., being stressed), social situations (e.g., seeing someone enjoying a smoke), or lack of skills (e.g., telling smokers to quit smoking during a party) might occur during the maintenance period. The second approach was chosen by Godding and Glasgow (1985), Shiffman et al. (2000), and Gwaltney et al. (2002) to assess smoking self-efficacy.

Measurement Examples

In the following sections, we will address a number of health behaviours, and give some examples for outcome expectancies and self-efficacy within each of these behaviours. These items can be used directly for future research and readers are encouraged to modify and adjust these items to their own research context. Self-efficacy scales have been developed for all kinds of health behaviours (see http://dccps.cancer.gov/brp/constructs/self-efficacy/index.html).

Dietary Outcome Expectancies and Dietary Self-Efficacy

Dietary outcome expectancies pertain to the perceived possible consequences of dietary behaviours. For each specific behaviour (e.g., eating five portions of fruit and vegetables) there may be various outcomes, positive and negative ones, and these outcomes may be categorized in terms of different areas such as health, fitness, social approval, or affective consequences.

In the study by Godinho, Alvarez, and Lima (2013), the positive outcome expectancy measure started with, "If I ate five portions of fruit and vegetables a day..." and was followed by four consequences that constitute the items of the scale: "I would improve my health," "I would feel satisfaction and pleasure," I would feel better," and "I would prevent cardiovascular diseases." Whether one forms a reliable sum score (in this case Cronbach's $\alpha=0.79$) or decides to analyse items separately depends on the psychometric nature of the instrument and the purpose of the study.

In the study by Hankonen, Absetz, Kinnunen, Haukkala, and Jallinoja (2013), outcome expectations were measured with a general stem "If I eat healthy food – low-fat, low-salt, lots of vegetables – the consequences are …" followed by four physical well-being expectation items (e.g., "I won't suffer from weight problems," "I have more energy," "I am in better physical shape," $\alpha=0.76$); two inconvenience expectation items (e.g., "I have to go through a lot of trouble in pondering what to eat," "Buying the right products is inconvenient," $\alpha=.55$); two social punishment expectation items (e.g., "Friends think I am feminine/womanish," "My friends will mock me," $\alpha=0.65$); and two bad taste expectation items (e.g., "Food will not taste good," "Food will taste better" [reversed], $\alpha=0.63$). In this case, the author has decided not to build a total score but rather four subscales, as the idea was to examine different facets of outcome expectancies.

Measures of self-efficacy for dietary behaviours address beliefs about the ability to perform a lifestyle change. These behaviours may be defined broadly (i.e., healthy food consumption) or in a more narrow way (i.e., fruit intake, salt avoidance, or consumption of high-fibre food). The measurement of dietary self-efficacy aims at statements that include control over the temptation to eat too much or to choose the wrong foods. Items can include particular foods, such as "I am certain that I can eat five portions of fruits and vegetables per day," or can refer to self-regulatory efforts, such as "I am confident that I can resist my craving for chocolate." Some instruments target very specific components of nutrition, such as fat intake in specific populations.

In the study by Godinho et al. (2013), dietary self-efficacy included four items (Cronbach's $\alpha=0.87$). The first item was: "I believe I can eat five or more portions of fruit and vegetables a day," and for the next three items this stem was followed by barriers: "…even if I have to establish a detailed plan not to forget to eat fruit and vegetables," "…even if I am too tired and not willing to prepare and/or eat fruit and vegetables," and "…even if I have to overcome my habit of not eating much fruit and vegetables."

A brief scale to measure nutrition self-efficacy has been developed by Schwarzer and Renner (2000). The scale refers to barriers that arise while developing the motivation to initiate health behaviour change (e.g., "How certain are you that you could overcome the following barriers?" "I can manage to stick to healthful food, even if I have to rethink my entire way of nutrition"). The items also refer to the barriers that are specific for later behavioural maintenance (e.g., "I can manage to stick to healthful food, even if I do not receive a great deal of support from others when making my first attempts").

Also in the study by Ochsner et al. (2013), a distinction was made between motivational and volitional self-efficacy. Motivational self-efficacy was assessed by three items such as "I am confident that I can change my dietary habits." Volitional (= maintenance) self-efficacy was measured with four items such as "I am confident that I can maintain a low-fat diet on a long-term basis even if I cannot see any positive changes immediately."

Physical Exercise Outcome Expectancies and Self-Efficacy

Exercise outcome expectancies pertain to the perceived possible consequences of physical activity or exercise. For each specific behaviour (e.g., swimming laps every morning) there may be various outcomes, positive and negative ones, and these outcomes may be categorized in terms of different areas such as health, fitness, social approval, or affective consequences.

Positive outcome expectancies (pros) can be assessed, for example, with the stem, "If I engage in physical activity at least three times per week for 20 min…" followed by pros such as "…then I feel better afterwards," or "…then I meet friendly people," whereas negative outcome expectancies (cons) use the same stem but may be followed by cons such as "…then every session would cost me a lot of money," or "…then I would be financially depleted" (Gellert et al., 2012).

The scope of the chosen physical activity determines the scope of the assessment of outcome expectancies and other constructs. If the study deals with activity in general, then the items must correspond to the same level of generality. If the study deals with a specific behaviour such as weekly frequency of walking, then all items must address the pros (and cons, if desired) of walking, and it is recommended to include multiple dimensions of consequences, affective, social, and physical ones.

The measurement of exercise self-efficacy may relate to a specific task, such as "I am certain that I can run for half an hour without stopping, even uphill." Or the target behaviour is not directly specified in favour of explicit barriers, as in the context of patient education (Lorig et al., 1996): "How confident are you that you can exercise without making symptoms worse?".

Perceived motivational and volitional self-efficacy can be composed of items such as the following. Motivational self-efficacy (task self-efficacy) refers to the goal-setting phase and can be measured with the stem, "I am certain…" followed by items such as "…that I can be physically active on a regular basis, even if I have to mobilize myself," or "…that I can be physically active on a regular basis, even if it is difficult" (Lippke, Fleig, Pomp, & Schwarzer, 2010). Volitional self-efficacy refers to the goal-pursuit phase. It can be subdivided into maintenance self-efficacy and recovery self-efficacy. Maintenance self-efficacy has been measured with the stem, "I am capable of strenuous physical exercise on a regular basis…" followed by barriers such as "…even if it takes some time until it becomes routine," or "…even if I need several attempts until I will be successful" (Lippke et al., 2010). Items on recovery self-efficacy can be worded: "I am confident that I can resume a physically active lifestyle, even if I have relapsed several times," "I am confident that I am able to resume my regular exercises after failures to pull myself together," or "I am confident that I can resume my physical activity, even when feeling weak after an illness" (Schwarzer, Luszczynska, Ziegelmann, Scholz, & Lippke, 2008; see also Parschau et al., 2013). A similar approach was taken by Murray and Rodgers (2012).

Dental Hygiene Outcome Expectancies and Self-Efficacy

Dental hygiene is mainly performed as brushing or flossing one's teeth more than once a day. Individuals may not be motivated to do so because they lack sufficient positive outcome expectancies. Outcome expectancies can be assessed with positive or negative items such as: "If I floss my teeth frequently on a daily basis: (a) then friends and parents will see that I am a clean person; (b) then I will have healthy teeth for most of my life; (c) then I will feel good with beautiful teeth all the time; (d) then it takes too much extra time."

On the other hand, one can compose items that refer to not performing the behaviour followed by negative outcomes. This is the same as conditional risk perception as in the following examples: "If I don't floss my teeth frequently: (a) then I risk getting gum or periodontal diseases; (b) then I might lose some teeth prematurely; (c) then I might have bad smell from my mouth; (d) then I need not purchase dental floss."

When it comes to self-efficacy, the barrier here is not the technical difficulty but rather the regular performance that is not easy for some people. In the following examples, the first items refer to task self-efficacy before acting whereas the next items pertain to maintenance self-efficacy while flossing. "Please think about the few days before adopting your new flossing habit: 'I am confident that I can frequently floss my teeth: (a) even if it is time consuming; (b) even if others do not floss their teeth'. Please think about the few days after adopting your new flossing habit: 'I am confident that I can frequently floss my teeth regularly on a long-term basis: (a) even when I cannot see any positive changes immediately; (b) even when I am in a hurry; (c) even when it takes a long time to become part of my daily routine'" (examples are from Gholami, Knoll, & Schwarzer, 2014; and Schwarzer, Antoniuk, & Gholami, 2014).

Alcohol Consumption Outcome Expectancies and Self-Efficacy

When drinking alcohol, people expect positive as well as negative outcomes. Positive ones consist of social and stress-reducing outcomes such as feeling sociable or relaxed. Negative ones can be related to impaired physical or mental health. In a free-association paradigm, Reich and Goldman (2005) compiled a list with the 30 most frequent alcohol expectancies from people with different drinking levels. Glock and Krolak-Schwerdt (2013) used these responses and ordered them into three categories. One contained three statements referring to negative illness-related alcohol expectancies (i.e., "Alcohol makes me feel sick"). The other two categories each comprised five statements indicating depression-related expectancies (i.e., "Alcohol makes me feel depressed"), and positive socially related alcohol expectancies (i.e., "Alcohol makes me sociable").

Assessing one's self-efficacy to reduce alcohol consumption follows the same pattern as in the previous examples. Items can target a highly specific behaviour such as, "I am certain that I can refuse a drink tonight when my buddies offer it to me." Or it can be less specific (Schwarzer, 2001) such as, "I am certain that I can control myself to: (a) reduce my alcohol consumption; (b) not drink any alcohol at all; (c) drink only on special occasions." This area of research can be further subdivided into controlled drinking self-efficacy, drinking refusal self-efficacy, and abstinence self-efficacy. A systematic literature review on interventions to increase self-efficacy in the context of addiction behaviours has also been provided by Hyde, Hankins, Deale, and Marteau (2008).

Smoking Cessation Outcome Expectancies and Self-Efficacy

In the same line as for the other behaviours, one can design outcome expectancy statements for action (quit smoking) or non-action (continue smoking) as well as for distinct positive and negative outcomes (see Figure 3.1). Examples: "If I quit smoking, then my mother will be happy. If I don't quit smoking, then I can better control my weight. If I quit smoking, then I don't know what to do with my hands. If I don't quit smoking, then my friend does not like to kiss me." The classic smoking self-efficacy measurement is the scale by Colletti et al. (1985). They developed the 17-item Smoking Self-Efficacy Questionnaire (SSEQ), an instrument designed to measure self-efficacy for resisting the urge to smoke. Confidence to overcome barriers (i.e., smoking cessation self-efficacy) can predict attempts to quit smoking (Dijkstra & DeVries, 2000). Nicotine abstinence of self-quitters depends on various demographic, physiological, cognitive, and social factors, but only a few factors are common predictors of maintaining abstinence. These are physiological factors, such as lower nicotine dependence, longer duration of previous abstinence, and, as a cognitive factor, high perceived smoking cessation self-efficacy (see Ockene et al., 2000). In a study by Gwaltney et al. (2001), the Relapse Situation Efficacy Questionnaire (RSEQ) was developed. Results showed that both context-specific and unidimensional measures of self-efficacy were relevant. Context-specific factors included negative affect, positive affect, restrictive situations (to smoking), idle time, social-food situations, low arousal, and craving. Some smoking cessation self-efficacy scales were composed in a multidimensional manner. In one study (Dijkstra & De Vries, 2000), the following five subscales were constructed: Situational Self-Efficacy, eight items ("Imagine you are engaging in a quit attempt. Are you able to refrain from smoking when you are going out with friends?"); Skill Self-Efficacy, nine items ("Are you able to divert yourself when you feel like smoking?"); Relapse Self-Efficacy, five items ("Are you able to maintain your quit attempt when you have been refraining from smoking for one month, but you light a cigarette?"); Try Self-Efficacy, five items ("Are you able to smoke fewer cigarettes a day?").

Condom Use Outcome Expectancies and Self-Efficacy

In a study on young Portuguese men (Carvalho, Alvarez, Barz, & Schwarzer, 2014), positive outcome expectancies of condom use were measured by four items (e.g., "When I use a condom, I feel safe," "When I use a condom I feel that I'm protecting my partner"), emphasizing the emotional aspects of this behaviour. The internal consistency of this measure was $\alpha = 0.77$.

Negative outcome expectancies can be of the type, "If I use a condom, I feel awkward." But one can also design items for non-action (see Figure 3.1) such as: "If I don't use a condom, it feels better" or "If I don't use a condom, I take a risk."

In the same study (Carvalho et al., 2014), maintenance self-efficacy was measured by seven items asking men to evaluate their confidence in maintaining condom use when faced with barriers. Example items were: "I think I can maintain the systematic use of condoms even if I am under the influence of substances (drugs and/or alcohol)" and "I believe I can maintain the systematic use of condoms, even if my partner is very attractive." The internal consistency was $\alpha = 0.87$. Brafford and Beck (1991) have developed the Condom Use Self-Efficacy scale, consisting of 28 items describing an individual's feelings of confidence about being able to purchase and use condoms.

Detection Behaviours Outcome Expectancies and Self-Efficacy

Health behaviours can be distinguished in terms of prevention and detection. Preventive behaviours (e.g., diet and exercise) can be performed to prevent the onset of disease, whereas detection behaviours are performed to identify early symptoms of a disease (e.g., screening for cancer or tooth decay).

Some studies provide evidence that both outcome expectancies and perceived self-efficacy were the best joint predictors of the intention to engage in regular breast cancer detection behaviours (Meyerowitz & Chaiken 1987; Seydel, Taal, & Wiegman, 1990). One can design outcome expectancy statements for action (screening) or non-action (not screening) as well as for distinct positive and negative outcomes. Examples: "If I attend the screening session, then I feel I have done whatever is possible." "If I don't attend the screening session, then I save the time." "If I attend the screening session, then I have to endure the inconvenience." "If I don't attend the screening session, then I have to live in uncertainty."

An example of a breast self-examination (BSE) self-efficacy scale was developed by Luszczynska and Schwarzer (2003). Additionally, the authors divided BSE self-efficacy into those referring to forming an intention (preaction BSE self-efficacy) and those referring to the maintenance of BSE (maintenance BSE self-efficacy). The scale had satisfactory reliability ($\alpha = 0.81$ and 0.77) and a two-factorial structure: preaction self-efficacy – "I am able to perform breast self-examination regularly: (a) even if I will have to make a detailed plan describing how to remember about breast self-examination; (b) even if I will have to rethink my behaviours and opinions concerning breast self-examination; (c) even if I will have to overcome my different habit of non-examination." Maintenance self-efficacy: "Imagining that you make an attempt to perform regular breast self-examination, do you think that you will procrastinate and reschedule it?" – "I am able to perform it regularly: (a) even if I need a long time to develop necessary routines; (b) even if I have to try several times before it works."

Research Illustrating the Use of Outcome Expectancies and Self-Efficacy

In this section we will briefly discuss one research finding about outcome expectancies and one finding on self-efficacy. Hankonen et al. (2013) made an attempt to identify a broader range of social cognitive determinants of dietary intentions and behaviours by elaborating on different kinds of outcome expectancies. In a structural equation model, they specify four outcome expectancies as predictors of the behavioural intention. They use separate models to predict the intention to avoid fat consumption and the intention to eat fruit and vegetables.

In the final model to predict the intention to avoid fat, two of the four outcome expectancies are dominant: Avoiding fat is perceived as promoting physical well-being, but the trade-off is that fatty foods taste good (Figure 3.2). This is an example of the joint use of detailed positive and negative outcome expectancies, however, at the expense of parsimony. One could also generate sum scores of all positive and all negative outcome expectancies, which reduces the number of predictors. Moreover, in some studies we have found that negative outcome expectancies are rather understood as barriers while acting, making this a post-intentional construct. In such cases, the most parsimonious solution is to use only one positive outcome expectancy sum score as a predictor of intentions.

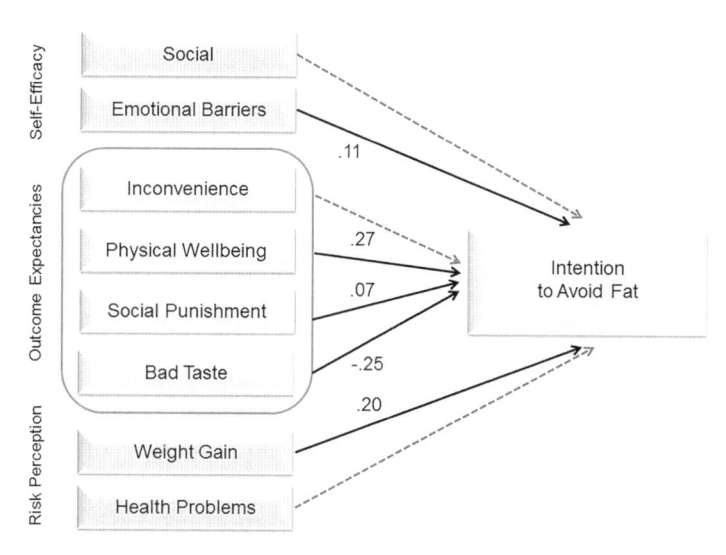

Figure 3.2. Predicting dietary intentions by outcome expectancies (see also Hankonen et al., 2013).

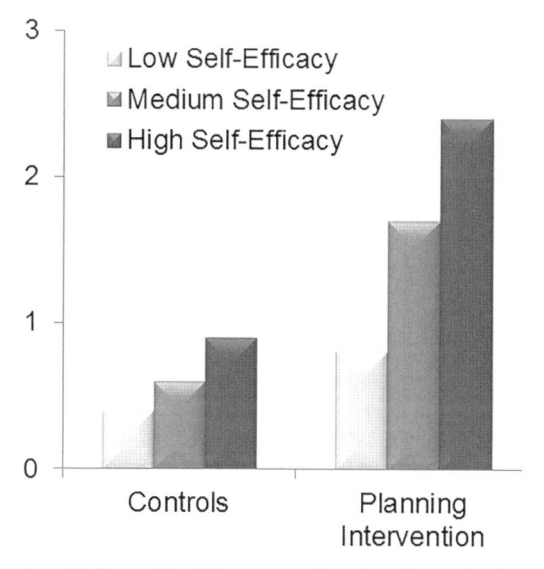

Figure 3.3. Physical activity self-efficacy moderates the relationship between experimental conditions exercise frequency (see also Luszczynska et al., 2011).

In the second example (Figure 3.3), exercise self-efficacy turned out to moderate the relationship between experimental conditions and the outcome that here was the number of physically active sessions per week (Luszczynska, Schwarzer, Lippke, & Mazurkiewicz, 2011). This means that those participants who were initially quite optimistic about their capability to change their physical activity levels were the ones to have benefitted most from the planning intervention.

Conclusion

Two key constructs from SCT (Bandura, 1997, 2006) were selected because they are used very often in health behaviour research. We have briefly described the theory and discussed assessment principles before presenting numerous measurement examples and research findings. As a conclusion, the health psychologist should keep a number of inter-related factors in mind. These refer to stability, generality, and context.

First, when studying health behaviour change, one should not look for stable dispositions that are assessed with standard measures. Instead, one should rather consider change-sensitive assessment tools. Usually, a few content-valid items are appropriate for such a purpose.

Second, a low level of generality is typically preferred by health behaviour researchers. This means that the assessment tools are highly situation-specific and address a narrow range of behaviours. In other words, statements can focus, for example, on the frequency and duration of walking or fruit intake, instead of asking for a healthy lifestyle. The more specific the range of a construct, the lower the number of items generated, if one wants to avoid redundancy.

Third, it should not be the easy availability of standard measures in the literature that determines their choice, but rather the unique demands of a particular research context. Validity is not a lasting internal property of a scale that can be carried unharmed from one research context to the next one. The actual setting may demand adjustment of items or rewriting of statements from scratch. To facilitate such a procedure, we have suggested some semantic rules that are likely to produce content-valid items.

References

Ashford, S., Edmunds, J., & French, D. P. (2010). What is the best way to change self-efficacy to promote lifestyle and recreational physical activity? A systematic review with meta-analysis. *British Journal of Health Psychology, 15*(2), 265–288. http://doi.org/10.1348/135910709X461752

Bandura, A. (1977). Self-efficacy: Toward a unifying theory of behavioral change. *Psychological Review, 84*(2), 191–215. http://doi.org/10.1037/0033-295X.84.2.191

Bandura, A. (1986). *Social foundations of thought and action*. Englewood Cliffs, NJ: Prentice-Hall.

Bandura, A. (1997). *Self-efficacy: The exercise of control*. New York, NY: Freeman.

Bandura, A. (2006). Guide for creating self-efficacy scales. In F. Pajares & T. Urdan (Eds.), *Self-efficacy beliefs of adolescents* (pp. 307–338). Greenwich, CT: Information Age Publishing.

Brafford, L. J., & Beck, K. H. (1991). Development and validation of a condom self-efficacy scale for college students. *Journal of the American College Health, 39*(5), 219–225. http://doi.org/10.1080/07448481.1991.9936238

Carvalho, T., Alvarez, M. J., Barz, M., & Schwarzer, R. (2014). Preparatory behavior for condom use among heterosexual young men: A longitudinal mediation model. *Health Education and Behavior*. Advance online publication. http://doi.org/10.1177/1090198114537066

Colletti, G., Supnick, J. A., & Payne, T. J. (1985). The Smoking Self-Efficacy Questionnaire (SSEQ): Preliminary scale development and validation. *Behavioral Assessment, 7*(3), 249–260.

Conner, M., Rhodes, R. E., Morris, B., McEachan, R., & Lawton, R. (2011). Changing exercise through targeting affective or cognitive attitudes. *Psychology & Health, 26*(2), 133–149. http://doi.org/10.1080/08870446.2011.531570

Dijkstra, A., Bakker, M., & De Vries, H. (1997). Subtypes within a sample of precontemplating smokers: a preliminary extension of the stages of change. *Addictive Behaviors, 22*(3), 327–337. http://doi.org/10.1016/S0306-4603(96)00054-8

Dijkstra, A., & Vries, H. D. (2000). Self-efficacy expectations with regard to different tasks in smoking cessation. *Psychology and Health, 15*(4), 501–511. http://doi.org/10.1080/08870440008402009

Fishbein, M., & Ajzen, I. (2010). *Predicting and changing behavior: The reasoned action approach.* New York, NY: Psychology Press.

Gellert, P., Ziegelmann, J. P., & Schwarzer, R. (2012). Affective and health-related outcome expectancies for physical activity in older adults. *Psychology & Health, 27*(7), 816–828. http://doi.org/10.1080/08870446.2011.607236

Gholami, M., Knoll, N., & Schwarzer, R. (2014). *A brief self-regulatory intervention increases dental flossing in adolescent girls.* Manuscript submitted for publication.

Glock, S., & Krolak-Schwerdt, S. (2013). Changing outcome expectancies, drinking intentions, and implicit attitudes toward alcohol: A comparison of positive expectancy-related and health-related alcohol warning labels. *Applied Psychology: Health & Well-Being, 5*(3), 332–347. http://doi.org/10.1111/aphw.12013

Godding, P. R., & Glasgow, R. E. (1985). Self-efficacy and outcome expectations as predictors of controlled smoking status. *Cognitive Therapy and Research, 9*(5), 583–590. http://doi.org/10.1007/BF01173011

Godinho, C. A., Alvarez, M. J., & Lima, M. L. (2013). Formative research on HAPA model determinants for fruit and vegetable intake: Target beliefs for audiences at different stages of change. *Health Education Research, 28*(6), 1014–1028. http://doi.org/10.1093/her/cyt076

Gwaltney, C. J., Shiffman, S., Normal, G. J., Paty, J. A., Kassel, J. D., Gnys, M. H., … Balabanis, M. (2001). Does smoking abstinence self-efficacy vary across situations? Identifying context-specificity within the Relapse Situation Efficacy Questionnaire. *Journal of Consulting and Clinical Psychology, 69*(3), 516–527. http://doi.org/10.1037/0022-006X.69.3.516

Gwaltney, C. J., Shiffman, S., Paty, J. A., Liu, K. S., Kassel, J. D., Gnys, M., & Hickcox, M. (2002). Using self-efficacy judgments to predict characteristics of lapses to smoking. *Journal of Consulting and Clinical Psychology, 70*(5), 1140–1149. http://doi.org/10.1037/0022-006X.70.5.1140

Hankonen, N., Absetz, P., Kinnunen, M., Haukkala, A., & Jallinoja, P. (2013). Toward identifying a broader range of social cognitive determinants of dietary intentions and behaviors. *Applied Psychology: Health & Well Being, 5*(1), 118–135. http://doi.org/10.1111/j.1758-0854.2012.01081.x

Hyde, J., Hankins, M., Deale, A., & Marteau, T. M. (2008). Interventions to increase self-efficacy in the context of addiction behaviours: A systematic literature review. *Journal of Health Psychology, 13*(5), 607–623. http://doi.org/10.1177/1359105308090933

Lippke, S., Fleig, L., Pomp, S., & Schwarzer, R. (2010). Validity of a stage algorithm for physical activity in participants recruited from orthopedic and cardiac rehabilitation clinics. *Rehabilitation Psychology, 55*, 398–408. http://doi.org/10.1037/a0021563

Lorig, K., Stewart, A., Ritter, P., González, V., Laurent, D., & Lynch, J. (1996). *Outcome measures for health education and other health care interventions.* Thousand Oaks, CA: Sage.

Luszczynska, A., Mazurkiewicz, M., Ziegelmann, J. P., & Schwarzer, R. (2007). Recovery self-efficacy and intention as predictors of running or jogging behavior: A cross-lagged panel analysis over a two-year period. *Psychology of Sport and Exercise, 8*(2), 247–260. http://doi.org/10.1016/j.psychsport.2006.03.010

Luszczynska, A., & Schwarzer, R. (2003). Planning and self-efficacy in the adoption and maintenance of breast self-examination: A longitudinal study on self-regulatory cognitions. *Psychology & Health, 18*(1), 93–108. http://doi.org/10.1080/0887044021000019358

Luszczynska, A., Schwarzer, R., Lippke, S., & Mazurkiewicz, M. (2011). Self-efficacy as a moderator of the planning-behaviour relationship in interventions designed to promote physical activity. *Psychology and Health, 26*(2), 151–166. http://doi.org/10.1080/08870446.2011.531571

Marlatt, G. A., Baer, J. S., & Quigley, L. A. (1995). Self-efficacy and addictive behavior. In A. Bandura (Ed.), *Self-efficacy in changing societies* (pp. 289–315). New York, NY: Cambridge University Press.

Meyerowitz, B. E., & Chaiken, S. (1987). The effect of message framing on breast self-examination attitudes, intentions, and behavior. *Journal of Personality and Social Psychology, 52*(3), 500–510. http://doi.org/10.1037/0022-3514.52.3.500

Murray, T., & Rodgers, W. (2012). The role of socioeconomic status and control beliefs on frequency of exercise during and after cardiac rehabilitation. *Applied Psychology: Health and Well Being, 4*, 49–66. http://doi.org/10.1111/j.1758-0854.2011.01061.x

Ochsner, S., Scholz, U., & Hornung, R. (2013). Testing phase-specific self-efficacy beliefs in the context of dietary behaviour change. *Applied Psychology: Health and Well Being, 5*(1), 99–117. http://doi.org/10.1111/j.1758-0854.2012.01079.x

Ockene, J. K., Emmons, K. M., Mermelstein, R. J., Perkins, K. A., Bonollo, D. S., Voorhees, C. C., & Hollis, J. F. (2000) Relapse and maintenance issues for smoking cessation. *Health Psychology, 19*, 17–31. http://doi.org/10.1037/0278-6133.19.Suppl1.17

Parschau, L., Fleig, L., Koring, M., Lange, D., Knoll, N., Schwarzer, R., & Lippke, S. (2013). Positive experience, self-efficacy, and action control predict physical activity changes: A moderated mediation analysis. *British Journal of Health Psychology, 18*(2), 395–406. http://doi.org/10.1111/j.2044-8287.2012.02099.x

Prochaska, J. O., & DiClemente, C. C. (1983). Stages and processes of self-change of smoking: Toward an integrative model of change. *Journal of Consulting and Clinical Psychology, 51*(3), 390–395. http://doi.org/10.1037/0022-006X.51.3.390

Reich, R. R., & Goldman, M. S. (2005). Exploring the alcohol expectancy memory network: The utility of free associates. *Psychology of Addictive Behaviors, 19*(3), 317–325. http://doi.org/10.1037/0893-164X.19.3.317

Rodgers, W. M., Murray, T. C., Courneya, K. S., Bell, G. J., & Harber, V. J. (2009). The specificity of self-efficacy over the course of a progressive exercise programme. *Applied Psychology: Health & Well-Being, 1*, 211–232. http://doi.org/10.1111/j.1758-0854.2009.01012.x

Scholz, U., Sniehotta, F. F., & Schwarzer, R. (2005). Predicting physical exercise in cardiac rehabilitation: The role of phase-specific self-efficacy beliefs. *Journal of Sport & Exercise Psychology, 27*(2), 135–151.

Schwarzer, R. (2001). Autoefficacia e comportamenti salutogenici [Self-efficacy and health behaviours]. In G. V. Caprara (Ed.), *La valutazione dell'autoefficacia. Costrutti e strumenti. Centro Studi Erickson, Trento* (pp. 173–184). Gardolo di Trento, Italy: Erickson.

Schwarzer, R., Antoniuk, A., & Gholami, M. (2014). A brief intervention changing oral self-care, self-efficacy, and self-monitoring. *British Journal of Health Psychology*. Advance online publication. http://doi.org/10.1111/bjhp.12091

Schwarzer, R., Luszczynska, A., Ziegelmann, J. P., Scholz, U., & Lippke, S. (2008). Social-cognitive predictors of physical exercise adherence: Three longitudinal studies in rehabilitation. *Health Psychology, 27*(1S), S54–S63. http://doi.org/10.1037/0278-6133.27.1(Suppl.).S54

Schwarzer, R., & Renner, B. (2000). Social-cognitive predictors of health behavior: Action self-efficacy and coping self-efficacy. *Health Psychology, 19*(5), 487–495. http://doi.org/10.1037/0278-6133.19.5.487

Seydel, E., Taal, E., & Wiegman, O. (1990). Risk-appraisal, outcome and self-efficacy expectancies: Cognitive factors in preventive behaviour related to cancer. *Psychology and Health, 4*(2), 99–109. http://doi.org/10.1080/08870449008408144

Shiffman, S., Balabanis, M. H., Paty, J. A., Engberg, J., Gwaltney, C. J., Liu, K. S., ... Paton, S.M. (2000). Dynamic effects of self-efficacy on smoking lapse and relapse. *Health Psychology, 19*(4), 315–323. http://doi.org/10.1037/0278-6133.19.4.315

Velicer, W. F., DiClemente, C. C., Rossi, J. S., & Prochaska, J. O. (1990). Relapse situations and self-efficacy: An integrative model. *Addictive Behaviors, 15*(3), 271–283. http://doi.org/10.1016/0306-4603(90)90070-E

Warner, L. M., Schüz, B., Knittle, K., Ziegelmann, J. P., & Wurm, S. (2011). Sources of perceived self-efficacy as predictors of physical activity in older adults. *Applied Psychology: Health and Well-Being, 3*(2), 172–192. http://doi.org/10.1111/j.1758-0854.2011.01050.x

Chapter 4

Illness Representations

Linda D. Cameron[1,2], Arturo Durazo[1], and Holly M. Rus[1]

[1]School of Social Sciences, Humanities, and the Arts, University of California, Merced, CA, USA
[2]School of Psychology, The University of Auckland, New Zealand

Introduction

An *illness representation* is a schema or set of cognitions about the subjective experience of an illness or health threat. Other terms for this construct include *explanatory model, mental model, illness narrative, illness perceptions,* and *beliefs about illness.* The importance of illness representations in guiding illness-related behaviours and experiences has long been recognized by medical anthropologists (e.g., Kleinman, 1980), sociologists (e.g., Cockerham, 1981), psychosomatic researchers (e.g., Engel, 1960), and health psychologists (e.g., Leventhal, Meyer, & Nerenz, 1980). Measures of illness representation have evolved largely through applications of three theoretical frameworks: explanatory models of illness, the common-sense model (CSM) of the self-regulation of health, and stress and cognitive appraisal theories.

Early anthropological research by Arthur Kleinman and colleagues explored explanatory models of illness across many cultures and social groups. This research revealed distinctive structures for these mental models, with attributes reflecting beliefs about the symptoms, causes, timeline, consequences, and control through treatments (Kleinman, 1980, 1988). That this common set of attributes is found across cultures suggests a universal need to understand these features of an illness experience.

Howard Leventhal, in developing the CSM, integrated theories of cognition, emotion, and self-regulation into a model that delineates the structure and contents of illness representations and their central role in guiding emotional responses and behaviours in the management of health conditions (Leventhal, Brissette, & Leventhal, 2003; Leventhal et al., 1980). Drawing on the explanatory models research, Leventhal proposed that illness representations include the attributes of identity (including illness label and associated symptoms), cause, timeline, consequences, and control/cure. These illness representations are elicited by internal or external stimuli (e.g., a somatic sensation or a media message) and their activation guides the use of action plans for controlling the health threat. Appraisals of the effectiveness of these actions guide revisions of the representations and action plans. This cognitive system operates in parallel and interacts with the emotional system, in which representations of emotional experiences such as fear guide the use of procedures for regulating them, with appraisals of coping outcomes shaping further emotions and actions.

The CSM also delineates two levels of information processing: abstract, conceptual processes involving linguistic forms of information, and concrete-experiential processes involving perceptual and image-based information and memories. Representations include both conceptual and concrete-experiential contents, and these contents can differentially influence emotional and behavioural reactions (Cameron & Chan, 2008). Another feature of a representation is its coherence, or the extent to which attributes and their links with protective actions are understandable and make sense. High coherence can reduce emotional distress caused by confusion and increase motivations to engage in treatment plans.

Stress and cognitive appraisal theories used to develop illness representation measures generally construe illness as a potential stressor and specify appraisals influencing stress responses. For example, the theory of cognitive appraisal of stress (Lazarus & Folkman, 1984) delineates primary appraisals of the potential for harm or loss and secondary appraisals of resources available to meet the demands as determinants of appraisals of potential health threats as threatening or challenging. These threat or challenge appraisals trigger emotional responses (e.g., distress or relief) and guide coping efforts. Related theories identify the roles of beliefs about helplessness (e.g., Abramson, Metalsky, & Alloy, 1989), acceptance (Hayes, Jacobson, Follette, & Dougher, 1994), and benefits arising from stressful experiences (Park, 1998). Researchers have developed tools to assess a mix of these illness appraisals (Browne et al., 1988; Evers et al., 2001; Weir, Browne, Roberts, Tunks, & Gafni, 1994).

Interestingly, relatively little cross-talk or synthesis of explanatory models research and research guided by the CSM and cognitive appraisal theories has occurred over the past two decades, apparently due to the evolution of these theoretical perspectives in different social science disciplines. Cultural anthropologists and medical sociologists typically rely on the explanatory models framework and associated measures, which are primarily qualitative or mixed-methods tools. These measures generally follow an *emic* approach in that they are designed to elicit illness beliefs and experiences as construed by the actors themselves (Harris, 1976). By contrast, most health psychology and public health researchers have used the CSM or cognitive appraisal theories and associated measures, most of which are quantitative in nature. These psychological theories generally follow an *etic* approach in that they measure phenomena and schematic attributes identified through the perspective of the scientist (Harris, 1976). Thus, despite strong similarities in theoretical construals of illness representations by explanatory models and the CSM (and, to a lesser extent, cognitive appraisal theories), the research paths have remained primarily parallel, with findings presented in different journals and conferences and with limited exchanges of insights across disciplinary boundaries. There is considerable potential to synthesize and accelerate illness representations research through greater sharing of measures and findings across disciplines.

Assessment/Measurement Issues

Several assessment considerations can guide the selection and adaptation of measures of illness representations to fit with study aims and contexts. These issues include the relative utility of qualitative or quantitative approaches, considerations for assessing representations of illness risk, options for assessing mental imagery contents of illness representations, and the conceptual distinctiveness of illness representation measures from outcome measures.

Qualitative Versus Quantitative Approaches

Qualitative and quantitative methods for assessing illness representations have their respective advantages and limitations. Qualitative approaches provide rich accounts of representations and experiences while allowing unanticipated beliefs to emerge (see Chapter 22, this volume). Common limitations include a reliance on lengthy interviews, extensive time and effort for interview transcription and analysis, and potential for researcher bias in conducting interviews and interpreting data. Quantitative measures can provide standardized assessments that are easily administered even for large samples. They are limited, however, in their ability to capture complexities in illness beliefs, unique beliefs, and the full meanings of beliefs within the sociocultural contexts. Social and cultural frames can alter the meaning of a questionnaire item and how it is interpreted, leading individuals from different social contexts to respond to it in different ways (see Chapter 20, this volume).

Qualitative approaches have tended to dominate anthropological and sociological research on illness representations whereas quantitative methods have dominated recent health psychology and public health research. Yet both sets of tools are applicable and relevant across these disciplines. Researchers can enhance their scientific endeavours by taking a mixed-methods approach and utilizing a combination of qualitative and quantitative tools.

Representations of Illness Versus Illness Risk

Illness representations form the basis of representations of illness risk and so, guided by theory, illness representation measures can be adapted to assess illness risk representations (Cameron, 2008). According to the CSM, individuals generate illness risk representations by matching illness representation attributes with attributes of the self. For example, beliefs about one's likelihood of skin cancer arise from comparing illness attributes of cause (e.g., excessive sun exposure), identity (e.g., black moles), and timeline (e.g., it develops in middle age) with self attributes (e.g., "I've had many sunburns"; "I have some black moles"; "I am in my 40s"). Severity beliefs arise from comparing attributes of consequences (e.g., skin cancer leads to skin disfigurement) and control (surgery can cure it) with beliefs about their importance (e.g., personal impact of disfigurement) and access to control measures (e.g., ability to obtain surgery). Risk representations thus include the contents appraised when generating estimates of likelihood and severity. Perceived likelihood and severity are established predictors of protection motivations, but attempts to alter them through messages about risk levels (e.g., "Your risk for skin cancer is 14%, not 2%") generally fail. A more successful approach for changing risk perceptions might be to target the representational contents on which they are based. Interventions targeting the contents of risk representations can alter risk perceptions and, in turn, protective intentions and behaviour (Lee, Cameron, Wünsche, & Stevens, 2011). The impact of these interventions could best be evaluated by assessing changes in representational contents rather than changes in perceived likelihood.

Measures of Mental Images

To date, researchers have focused primarily on conceptual contents of representations through their reliance on text-based measures assessing agreement with conceptual beliefs. Increasingly, however, researchers are developing techniques for measuring image-based contents of representations. The CSM's delineation of conceptual and concrete-experiential processes highlights the distinctiveness of conceptual contents such as linguistically based beliefs ("My high cholesterol is causing my heart disease") versus experientially based contents such as images (e.g., a mental picture of clogged arteries) and perceptual memories (e.g., memories of viewing cholesterol test results). Linguistic and image-based information are encoded and processed within distinctive memory systems (Cameron & Chan, 2008); compared to linguistic information, image-based information is more closely linked with emotional systems and more accessible to recall. Images stored in illness representations are thus likely to be more powerful in triggering emotions and influencing protective behaviours.

Conceptual Distinctiveness With Outcome Measures

When using illness representation measures, researchers must examine their conceptual overlap with outcome measures. For example, quality-of-life measures often include items about specific symptoms and pain, illness distress, social consequences, and limitations in activity. Their overlap with items in identity, emotional representation, and consequence subscales could lead to artificially inflated associations between representational attributes and quality of life (see Chapter 14, this volume) or functional health outcomes (see Chapter 9, this volume).

Main Instruments

In this section, we present primary measures of illness representations. We focus first on tools guided by explanatory models theory (Table 4.1), followed by measures guided by the CSM and then measures guided by stress and cognitive appraisal theories (Table 4.2). We then consider illness-specific measures and measures of specific attributes and mental images.

Measures Guided by the Explanatory Models Framework

Kleinman's Explanatory Models Approach

Kleinman (1980) developed an interview consisting of eight open-ended questions:

- What do you think has caused your problems?
- Why do you think it started when it did?
- What do you think your sickness does to you?
- How severe is your sickness? Will it have a long or short course?
- What kind of treatment do you think you should receive?
- What are the most important results you hope to receive from this treatment?
- What are the chief problems your sickness has caused for you?
- What do you fear most about your sickness?

This set of questions has been used in individual interviews and focus groups to explore a wide variety of physiological and mental health conditions. Examples include explanatory models of overweight and its health risks held by White, Black, and Hispanic women (Allan, 1998) and of diabetes held by Mexican American women (Luyas, Kay, & Solomons, 1991).

Explanatory Model Interview Catalogue (EMIC)

The EMIC is a semi-structured interview offering a mixed methods approach for assessing illness representations (Weiss et al., 1992). The interview includes four sections: (a) patterns of distress, focusing on illness-related problems such as symptoms and lifestyle consequences; (b) perceived causes; (c) help-seeking and treatment, focusing on efforts to seek care from health providers and others; and (d) general illness beliefs, focusing on broader beliefs about illness. Each section starts with a vignette to clarify the focus of the questions, continues with open-ended questions and directed probes, and concludes with a question about the most important aspects (e.g., most troubling symptom or most important cause). Responses are coded using content-analytic techniques. Researchers can also calculate prominence scores for use in quantitative analyses. For example, in a study of explanatory models of drug addiction held by French migrants and non-migrants with drug dependence (Taieb et al., 2012), prominence scores for categories (e.g., withdrawal symptoms) were calculated to range from 0 (not mentioned) to 7 (mentioned spontaneously with emphasis and listed as the most important aspect; e.g., most troubling symptom). Analyses revealed that, compared with non-migrants, migrants reported fewer symptoms and more attributions of their addiction to magical and religious factors.

The EMIC has been used to assess representations of numerous illnesses such as leprosy, somatoform disorders, and psychiatric disorders in more than a dozen cultures. Its length and complexity limit its feasibility for use in large-scale studies and surveys.

Short Explanatory Model Interview (SEMI)

The SEMI was developed as a shorter alternative to the EMIC for use in large-scale studies (Lloyd et al., 1998). It assesses mental illness representations and has been used primarily with patients attending mental health consultations. The SEMI differs from the EMIC in that it has structured questions rather than guidelines for questions. The interview is thus more standardized across participants but less likely to elicit unanticipated representational beliefs. It consists of five sections: (a) personal background, including cultural beliefs; (b) nature of the problem, including the label; reason for consultation; causes; consequences; and severity of physical, psychological, social and occupational effects; (c) help-seeking, including contacts with health services; (d) interaction with health practitioners, including roles, expectations, and satisfaction with care; and (d) illness beliefs, assessed with three vignettes about common disorders (phobia, depression, and somatization), each followed by open-ended questions about one's beliefs about the illness.

The SEMI has been used to evaluate explanatory models of mental disorders held by individuals in many cultures, including residents in India (Saravanan et al., 2007) and East Timor (Silove et al., 2008). Although shorter than the EMIC, each interview still takes 30–45 min to complete. Most studies have used the SEMI to acquire descriptive findings on illness representations and have not examined whether specific beliefs predict behaviours or outcomes, and so evidence of predictive validity is lacking. The SEMI has not yet been adapted for use in assessing representations of physical illnesses. It could easily be adapted for this purpose, although new vignettes would be needed for the illness belief section.

McGill Illness Narrative Interview (MINI)

The MINI is a semi-structured interview initially designed to explore representations of medically unexplained symptoms (Groleau, Young, & Kirmayer, 2006) and later adapted to assess representations of physical conditions (Young & Kirmayer, 2006). It assesses three facets of

Table 4.1. Interview instruments guided by explanatory models theory

Measure name Authors	Type of interview	Representational facets (number of questions)	Average completion time	Quantitative scoring (inter-rater reliability)
Kleinman's Explanatory Models Approach Kleinman & Seeman (2000)	Qualitative (ethnographic): semi-structured interview or focus groups	Eight questions on five facets: aetiology (1), time of onset (1), pathophysiology (3), course of illness (1), treatment (2)	1–2 hrs	Relies on strict text and/or theme coding guided by the five facets. (κ = .61–.98)
Explanatory Model Interview Catalogue (EMIC) Weiss et al. (1992)	Mixed methods, semi-structured interview	Patterns of distress[a], causes[a], help-seeking and treatment[a], general illness beliefs[a]	2.5 hrs	Responses are coded for content analysis. Codes can be used to generate prominence scores. (κ = .60–1.0)
Short Explanatory Model Interview (SEMI) Lloyd et al. (1998)	Structured interview, including three vignettes about common disorders	Personal background[a], nature of the problem[a], help-seeking behaviours[a], interaction with health provider[a], illness beliefs[a]	30–45 min	Responses are coded for content analysis. (κ ≥ .70)
McGill Illness Narrative Interview (MINI) Groleau, Young, & Kirmayer (2006)	Semi-structured interview	Facets: explanatory models, prototypes, chain-complexes Sections: narrative (7), prototype narrative (8), explanatory model (16), help-seeking and service use (9), impact of illness (8)	2 hrs	Narratives are analysed for contents (e.g., themes) or structure (e.g., modes of reasoning) using qualitative techniques. (Inter-rater reliability not reported)
Barts Explanatory Model Inventory (BEMI) Rüdell et al. (2009)	Mixed methods: BEMI-I (Interview) BEMI-C (Checklist)	BEMI-I: identity (3), cause (6), timeline (3), consequences (5), cure/control (11) BEMI-C: symptoms (42), causes (38), consequences (22), treatments (19)	BEMI-I: 20 min BEMI-C: 15 min	BEMI-I: coding of *present/not present* for 23 themes. BEMI-C: responses of *present/not present*. BEMI-I and BEMI-C responses are summed into scores for each of the 23 themes. (κ > .80)

Note. [a]Guidelines are used, with numbers of open-ended questions and probes varying across studies and interviewees.

Table 4.2. Illness representation measures guided by the common-sense model and stress and cognitive appraisal theories

Measure Authors	Subscales (number of items)	Scoring	Evidence of reliability	Representative evidence of validity
Illness Perception Questionnaire-Revised (IPQ-R) Moss-Morris et al. (2002)	Identity (14+), timeline acute/chronic(6), timeline cyclical (4), consequences (6), personal control (6), treatment control (5), illness coherence (5), emotion representation (6), cause (18+)	Identity: yes/no responses are summed. Others: 5-point Likert scales	Internal consistency (subscales): α = 0.79–0.89. Test–retest: 3 weeks: r = .46–88 6 months: r = .35–.82	Construct validity: PCA yielded predicted factors with item loadings = .51–.86. Known groups validity: Acute versus chronic pain patients reported differences on all attributes. Discriminant validity with positive and negative affect. Predictive validity: For a multiple sclerosis sample, illness representations accounted for variance in illness dysfunction (15%), physical fatigue (27%), and mental fatigue (20%).
Brief Illness Perception Questionnaire (Brief IPQ) Broadbent et al. (2006)	Consequences (1), timeline (1), personal control (1), treatment control (1), identity (1), concern (1), emotional response (1), understanding (1), cause (1)	Cause: free-response listing of the three most important causes. All other items: 10-point scale	Test–retest: 3 weeks: r = .35–.82 6 weeks: r = .42–.75	Convergent validity: Items correlate with relevant IPQ-R subscales, r = .2–.54. For asthma patients, items correlate with asthma morbidity subscales, r = .18–.42. Predictive validity: For a myocardial infarction sample, Brief-IPQ at discharge predicted cardiac anxiety and quality of life 3 months later. Identity predicted rehabilitation attendance. Concern and treatment control predicted slower return to work.
Assessment of Illness Risk Representations (AIRR) Cameron (2008)	Identity (23), cause (8), timeline (3), personal control–prevent (3), personal control–cure (3), treatment control (3), consequences: shortened life, pain, psychosocial (10), imagery (1), imagery positivity (5), imagery vividness (5)	Identity: Σ [Feature (0 or 1) × Risk of feature (0–4)] Cause: Σ [Cause (0–3) × History] Imagery: free response of five images Others: 5- to 10-point scales	Internal consistency of subscales: α = 0.56–0.79. Test–retest: 4 weeks: r = .36–.85	Convergent validity: Subscales correlate meaningfully with likelihood, severity and worry measures. Predictive validity: Identity risk beliefs predicted skin self-examination intentions; timeline risk and skin symptom imagery predicted clinical exam intentions; personal control–cure, imagery positivity and imagery vividness predicted prevention intentions. Skin symptom imagery interacted with worry to predict all three intentions; having a skin symptom image and higher worry predicted greater intentions.
Meaning of Illness Questionnaire (MIQ) (Revised) V1: Weir et al., (1994) V2: Downe-Wambolt et al. (2006)	Impact (V1: 5, V2: 6)[a], burdened (V1: 8, V2: 3), meaning (V1: 4; V2: 5)[a], managing (V1: 6; V2: 3), vulnerability (V1: 4)	7-Point Likert scales	Internal consistency of subscales: V1: not reported V2: α = 0.64–0.81	Construct validity: PCA yielded predicted factors, but V1 and V2 differ in the number of factors and the items loading onto them. Known groups validity: V1 subscales (except vulnerability) differentiate between groups identified as poorly and well-adjusted to their illness. Predictive validity: V2 managing and impact subscales predicted quality of life in lung cancer patients.
Illness Cognitions Questionnaire (ICQ) Evers et al. (2001)	Helplessness (6); acceptance (6); disease benefits (6)	4-Point Likert scales	Internal consistency of subscales: α = 0.84–0.91	Construct validity: PCA yielded predicted factors with item loadings = .65–.85. Convergent validity: Subscales are up to moderately correlated with relevant health, personality, coping, and social support measures. Predictive validity: Over 1 year, helplessness predicted increases in functional disability and disease impact; acceptance predicted decreases in disease activity, physical complaints, and negative mood; and disease benefits predicted increases in positive mood.

Note. V1 = Revised Version 1; V2 = Revised Version 2; PCA = principal components analyses. [a]Subscale labels vary slightly across V1 and V2 representations: (a) explanatory models, defined as schemata incorporating causal attributions and models of specific processes or mechanisms; (b) prototypes, which give meaning to illnesses through analogies with other events (e.g., "My father died of heart disease and so I worry about getting heart disease"); and (c) chain complexes, in which a sequence of events surrounding an illness experience are linked without explicit causal connections (e.g., "After I started my new job, my back went out and I've had back pain ever since"). Chain complexes represent implicit learning and procedural knowledge. When brought to awareness, they are elaborated so that they "make sense" and then assimilated into an explanatory model or prototype.

The MINI consists of five sections: (a) the narrative, in which the participant shares the story of the illness experience; (b) prototype narrative, in which the participant describes how the experience is similar to or different from past illness experiences or those of other people; (c) explanatory model narrative, targeting representational attributes identified by Kleinman; (d) help seeking, targeting experiences with health services and treatments; and (e) impact of illness, targeting the effects of the illness on one's life, coping efforts, and coping resources. Transcripts are qualitatively analysed for structure (e.g., temporal structure, modes of reasoning) and contents (e.g., themes, images, metaphors). The MINI has been translated into at least 10 languages and used to explore mental models of diabetes, scleroderma, depression, and other conditions (http://www.mcgill.ca/tcpsych/research/cmhru/mini).

Barts Explanatory Model Inventory (BEMI)

The BEMI was designed as a brief tool with sensitivity to detect culturally variable beliefs about mental illness (Rüdell, Bhui, & Priebe, 2009). It was developed through a thematic analysis of narrative accounts of mental distress from members of over 35 cultural groups. The analysis yielded 23 themes across the five representational attributes. For example, three identity themes emerged: somatic identity, mental identity, and behavioural identity. The BEMI starts with an interview (BEMI-I) about beliefs about identity, cause, timeline, consequences, and control/cure. Responses are coded for the presence of contents reflecting the 23 themes. The second part, the BEMI-Checklist (BEMI-C), includes checklists for symptoms, causes, consequences and treatments (response options are *present* or *not present*). BEMI-I and BEMI-C responses are summed to generate scores for the 23 themes. Only a few studies have used the BEMI to date, but it is a promising tool with evidence of concurrent validity with the IPQ-R and other measures (Rüdell, 2014). It has been used to reveal cultural variations in representations of mental disorders (Rüdell et al., 2009) and to predict health services and adherence (Rüdell, 2014). It has not yet been adapted to assess physical illness representations, but there is clear potential for doing so.

Measures Guided by the Common-Sense Model

Illness Perceptions Questionnaire-Revised (IPQ-R)

The IPQ-R (Moss-Morris et al., 2002), an adaptation and extension of the Illness Perceptions Questionnaire (IPQ; Weinman, Petrie, Moss-Morris, & Horne, 1996), includes 73 items within three sections. The first section assesses identity and includes a set of symptoms tailored to the specific illness and cultural context. Respondents indicate the symptoms experienced since their illness started (*yes/no*) and whether they relate to their illness (*yes/no*); sums of the latter responses reflect the number of symptoms attributed to the illness. The second section includes items, rated for agreement on 5-point Likert scales, for timeline (acute/chronic, cyclical), consequences, control (personal, treatment), coherence, and emotional representation. The third section assesses causal attributions with items tailored to the illness and cultural context and a rank-ordering of the three most important causes. The rated items are analysed individually or factor-analysed to identify clusters representing attributional constructs (e.g., psychological attributions) for that illness and cultural context. In the first and third sections, the number of items varies based on how they are tailored for the specific illness and context.

The IPQ-R has been translated into over 18 languages and used for numerous illness conditions (http://www.uib.no/ipq). Confirmatory factor analyses generally validate the factor structure (Brink, Alsen, & Cliffordson, 2011; Dempster & McCorry, 2012), although authors have identified minor modifications such as item removal to improve the model fit. Ashley and colleagues (2013) used IPQ-R responses from individuals with cancer to test the factor structure using both confirmatory factor analyses and Rasch models. Both sets of analyses showed adequate fit and unidimensionality within each subscale, although fit was achieved or improved after deleting three items: personal control item, "There is a lot which I can do to control my symptoms/side effects"; timeline-acute/chronic item, "My illness will improve in time"; and coherence item, "The symptoms/side effects of my treatment are puzzling to me."

The IPQ-R has also been adapted for use with caregivers (Olsen, Berg, & Wiebe, 2008). These adaptations also enable researchers to explore discrepancies in representations held by patients and their caregivers The subscales can be adapted to measure beliefs about the patient's condition (e.g., how much control the patient has over the condition) or the caregiver's experience (e.g., how much control the caregiver has over the patient's condition). Another adaptation, the Revised Illness Perception Questionnaire-Healthy Version (Figueiras & Alves, 2007), measures representations of illnesses held by people who do not have them. It can be used to explore illness beliefs of at-risk individuals and measure changes in beliefs in response to health promotion interventions.

Brief Illness Perceptions Questionnaire (Brief IPQ)

The Brief IPQ was designed for use when researchers want to minimize response burden and assessment time (Broadbent, Petrie, Main, & Weinman, 2006). It includes a single item for each of nine facets: identity, timeline, consequences, personal control, treatment control, coherence, concern (construed as a combination of cognitive and emotional components), emotional representation, and cause. The authors suggest that, in some cases, the first nine items can be summed to generate scores reflecting the threat of the illness. Caution is warranted, however, as internal consistency is often low.

Both theoretical criticisms and empirical findings from a talk-aloud study, in which individuals articulated their thoughts as they completed the Brief IPQ, challenge its content validity (van Oort, Schroder, & French, 2011). Theoretically, content validity is likely limited in that it measures the strength of illness appraisals (e.g., the identity item, "How much do you experience symptoms of your illness?") rather than specific representational contents (e.g., "My breathlessness and irregular heartbeats are signs of my heart condition"). Content validity is limited in that each item is designed to measure a general summary belief and not all aspects of each construct. Empirically, the talk-aloud study participants had difficulty interpreting and responding to the identity, cause, personal control, emotional representation, and coherence items. van Oort and colleagues suggested changes to items to resolve some of the problems, but they note that it remains to be determined whether this approach of using single items to assess representational attributes is inherently flawed.

Assessment of Illness Risk Representations (AIRR)

The AIRR was adapted from the IPQ-R to assess representations of illness risk using the CSM principle that risk beliefs arise from matching attributes of illness representations with attributes of the self (Cameron, 2008). It includes measures of identity risk (beliefs that one's characteristics and symptoms put one at risk for an illness) and causal risk (beliefs that one has experiences and factors that cause an illness), in which individuals' ratings of having specific features (e.g., pale skin) or history/experiences (e.g., family history of skin cancer) are multiplied by associated ratings of how much they put a person at risk (e.g., for skin cancer). The products are summed to generate identity risk scores and causal risk scores. Additional subscales include timeline risk ("How likely is it that a person your age would get skin cancer now – at this age?"), personal control over prevention, personal control over cure, treatment control, consequences, and imagery contents (described in a later section). The AIRR has been adapted to assess risk representations of skin cancer (Cameron, 2008), heart disease (Lee et al., 2011), and diabetes (Durazo & Cameron, 2015). The latter two versions include a coherence subscale.

Measures Guided by Stress and Cognitive Appraisal Theories

Meaning of Illness Questionnaire (MIQ)

The MIQ assesses illness appraisals hypothesized to guide coping efforts. The original 30-item measure (Browne et al., 1988) includes five subscales: impact of illness (e.g., on daily activities), type of stress (e.g., as a harm or threat), degree of stress (e.g., requires change in commitments, stamina), positive attitude/control (e.g., hope, challenge), and expectancy/reoccurrence (e.g., one expected the illness, expects recurrence). Research revealing problems with its factor structure led to two revised versions. The first revision (Weir et al., 1994) derived from factor analyses of MIQ data from a chronic pain sample that revealed five factors: adverse impact, burdened, manageable, meaning, and vulnerability. The second revision (Downe-Wamboldt, Butler, & Coulter, 2006) derived from analyses of data from lung cancer patients and family members, in which only 17 items loaded onto four factors: impact, burdened, meaning/expectation, and managing. Both revised versions have been shown to predict outcomes, but the variability in factor structure across samples raises concerns about consistency in construct validity.

Illness Cognition Questionnaire (ICQ)

The ICQ focuses on three sets of cognitions expected to elicit emotional responses that influence coping responses and psychosocial adjustment (Evers et al., 2001). It includes subscales for these three sets of cognitions: illness acceptance (e.g., "I have learned to live with my illness"), perceived benefits (e.g., "Dealing with my illness has made me a stronger person"), and helplessness (e.g., "My illness limits me in everything that is important to me"). The factor structure has been confirmed with various samples; for example, individuals with multiple sclerosis, chronic pain, and chronic fatigue (Evers, et al., 2001; Lauwerier et al., 2010). The subscales have been found to predict coping and outcomes; for example, acceptance and helplessness were shown to predict coping (e.g., wishful thinking about being healthy, palliative coping through self-soothing), emotional well-being, and physical functioning in a cardiac sample (Karademas & Hondronikola, 2010).

Illness-Specific and Component-Specific Measures of Representations

The measures discussed thus far were designed to be adaptable for measuring representations of any illness. Measures that assess representations of specific illnesses are also available. Other measures assess specific representational attributes, such as control beliefs or causal beliefs. In this section, we briefly review two examples of such measures.

The Asthma Illness Representation Scale (AIRS©; Sidora-Arcoleo, Feldman, Serebrisky, & Spray, 2010) is an example of an illness-specific measure. It was developed through interviews with parents of children with asthma using Kleinman's explanatory models approach, along with interviews of health-care professionals. The 37-item measure includes five subscales: treatment expectations, attitudes about medication use, facts about asthma (e.g., "Inhaled steroids work by fighting inflammation in the lungs"), nature of symptoms (e.g., "Asthma symptoms are unpredictable"), and emotional aspects of medication use. Subscale scores are used individually and also summed to reflect the degree of congruence with the medical model of asthma. The AIRS© also includes subscales of the parent–provider relationship and beliefs about seeking treatment in situations of inadequate symptom control. This type of illness-specific measure can be advantageous in providing a contextualized measure of a specific illness (e.g., asthma) for a specific group (e.g., parents).

The Fear-Avoidance Beliefs Questionnaire (Waddell, Newton, Henderson, Somerville, & Main, 1993) is an example of a measure of specific representational attributes. It assesses beliefs about causes and consequences of pain conditions that indicate catastrophizing and potentially lead to phobic behaviour. The 16-item measure includes two subscales: fear-avoidance beliefs about work and fear-avoidance beliefs about physical activity. The subscales have been shown to predict work loss and disability in individuals with chronic back pain (Crombez, Vlaeyan, Heuts, & Lysens, 1999) and to demonstrate responsivity to (chiropractic) treatment (Staerkle et al., 2004). This type of measure is advantageous when specific attributes have been identified as primary targets for assessment and intervention.

Measures of Images in Illness Representations

Several approaches for assessing imagery contents of illness and illness risk representations are gaining in their application within the field. One approach involves having participants draw or artistically represent these images. For example, the Draw-An-Event Test has been used to assess risk representations created by media messages about alcohol (Stacy, Ames, & Leigh, 2004). Another technique involves participants drawing pictures of their conditions. These drawings can reveal unique beliefs not readily accessed through text-based measures. For example, drawings by individuals with Cushing's disease unexpectedly revealed beliefs that their body size changed dramatically during the illness and did not return to the original size after treatment (Tiemensma et al., 2012). Art toolkits containing pens, modelling clay, and other materials are also used to explore mental images of illnesses. For example, breast cancer survivors used art toolkits to portray their mental images of their cancer (Harrow, Wells, Humphris, Taylor, & Williams, 2008). Some women displayed creature-like images (e.g., a jellyfish with tentacles spreading through the body) whereas others had substance-like images (e.g., as hard, inert lumps). Women with creature-like images reported relatively greater distress and more intrusive thoughts about cancer.

These art tools can yield pictorial information about mental images, but their utility is limited. Limitations include participant reluctance to complete them due to embarrassment about one's artistic abilities, difficulties in creating accurate depictions, the time and effort required and the potential for researchers to code the images inaccurately.

An alternative approach is to collect written reports of mental images. The AIRR includes an imagery subscale in which respondents list five images associated with an illness. They then rate each image on its vividness and negative–positive valence. Use of this subscale to explore representations of skin cancer risk (Cameron, 2008), heart disease risk (Lee et al., 2011), and breast cancer (Cameron & Rogers, 2015) has shown that most mental images fall into the CSM attribute categories of identity, cause, timeline, consequences, and control/cure. Moreover, specific images uniquely predict distress and behaviour motivations. For example, adults reporting skin symptom images (e.g., large mole or crusty sore) in combination with high cancer worry report greater intentions to engage in sun protection and skin self-examinations (Cameron, 2008). Further to Harrow et al. (2008), breast cancer survivors with creature-like images tend to report high worry of recurrence (Cameron & Rogers, 2015). Advantages of this tool include high acceptability and applicability for survey and intervention research as it is completed quickly and scored easily. Yet it is limited in its ability to capture all potentially important features (e.g., object and background details).

Comments and Conclusion

Explanatory models and the CSM remain the dominant theoretical perspectives guiding assessments of illness representations, with additional measures based on stress and cognitive appraisal theories. In health psychology, the development of the IPQ and IPQ-R in particular stimulated rapid growth in illness representations research. Numerous studies reveal how they influence illness management, communications with health-care providers, quality of life, and health outcomes. Numerous reviews provide summaries of this research as related to illnesses in general (Baines & Wittkowski, 2013; Hagger & Orbell, 2003) and to specific conditions such as diabetes (Gherman et al., 2011) and heart disease (Goulding, Furze, & Birks, 2010).

We conclude with suggestions for future directions in illness representation assessment and research. First, we encourage researchers to combine tools guided by explanatory models theory with measures based on the CSM and cognitive appraisal theories to further integrate these research fields and accelerate the pace of science on illness representations. Research could explore how representational contents delineated by explanatory models theory and the CSM shape beliefs targeted by cognitive appraisal measures. With the ICQ, for example, beliefs of serious consequences, high symptom load, low control, low coherence, and negative emotional representations might predict greater helplessness and lower acceptance.

Another direction for future research is to develop quantitative measures of culturally specific representational beliefs. For example, recognition of Hispanic beliefs of *susto* as a cause of illness and *fatalismo* as shaping control beliefs led to the development of measures of these beliefs (Durazo & Cameron, 2015). With the rapid pace of migration worldwide creating challenges for health providers to care for individuals with diverse cultures, there is a critical need for research on culturally shaped representations. Measures of representations of caregivers, illness risk representations, and imagery contents also offer new opportunities for advancing research. Finally, the future will see more trials of interventions for changing illness and risk representations. Use of mixed methods approaches can foster rich insights on how interventions change representations and, in turn, behaviours and outcomes.

References

Abramson, L. Y., Metalsky, G. I., & Alloy, L. B. (1989). Hopelessness depression: A theory-based subtype of depression. *Psychological Review, 96*, 358–372.

Allan, J. (1998). Explanatory models of overweight among African American, Euro-American, and Mexican American women. *Western Journal of Nursing Research, 20*, 45–66. http://doi.org/10.1177/019394599802000104

Ashley, L., Smith, A. B., Keding, A., Jones, H., Velikova, G., & Wright, P. (2013). Psychometric evaluation of the Revised Illness Perception Questionnaire in cancer patients: Confirmatory factor analysis and Rasch analysis. *Journal of Psychosomatic Research, 75*, 556–562.

Baines, T., & Wittkowski, A. (2013). A systematic review of the literature exploring illness perceptions in mental health utilising the self-regulation model. *Journal of Clinical Psychology in Medical Settings, 20*, 263–274.

Broadbent, E., Petrie, K. J., Main, J., & Weinman, J. (2006). The brief illness perception questionnaire. *Journal of Psychosomatic Research, 60*, 631–637. http://doi.org/10.1016/j.jpsychores.2005.10.020

Brink, E., Alsen, P., & Cliffordson, C. (2011). Validation of the revised illness perception questionnaire (IPQ-R) in a sample of persons recovering from myocardial infarction – the Swedish version. *Scandinavian Journal of Psychology, 52*, 573–579.

Browne, G. B., Byrne, C., Roberts, J., Streiner, D., Fitch, M., Corey, P., & Arpin, K. (1988). The Meaning of Illness Questionnaire: Reliability and validity. *Nursing Research, 37*, 368–373.

Cameron, L. D. (2008). Illness risk representations and motivations to engage in protective behavior: The case of skin cancer risk. *Psychology and Health, 23*, 91–112.

Cameron, L. D., & Chan, C. (2008). Designing health communications: Harnessing the power of affect, imagery, and self-regulation. *Social and Personality Psychology Compass, 2*, 262–282. http://doi.org/10.1111/j.1751-9004.2007.00057.x

Cameron, L. D., & Rogers, L. (2015). *Mental images of breast cancer and fears of recurrence*. Manuscript in preparation.

Cockerham, W. (1981). Medical sociology. *International Review of Modern Sociology, 11*, 231–250.

Crombez, G., Vlaeyan, J. W. S., Heuts, P. H. T. G., & Lysens, R. (1999). Fear of pain is more disabling than pain itself: Evidence on the role of pain-related fear in chronic back pain disability. *Pain, 80*, 329–340. http://doi.org/10.1016/S0304-3959(98)00229-2

Dempster, M., & McCorry, N. K. (2012). The factor structure of the revised illness perception questionnaire in a population of esophageal cancer survivors. *Psycho-Oncology, 21*, 524–530.

Downe-Wamboldt, B., Butler, L., & Coulter, L. (2006). The relationship between meaning of illness, social support, coping strategies, and quality of life for lung cancer patients and their family members. *Cancer Nursing, 29*, 111–119.

Durazo, A., & Cameron, L. D. (2015). *Diabetes risk representations held by multiethnic young adults as predictors of protection and behavior*. Manuscript in preparation.

Engel, G. L. (1960). A unified concept of health and disease. *IRE Transations on Medical Electronics, ME–7*, 48–57.

Evers, A. W., Kraaimaat, F. W., van Lankveld, W., Jongen, P. J., Jacobs, J. W., & Bijlsma, J. W. (2001). Beyond unfavorable thinking: The Illness Cognition Questionnaire for chronic diseases. *Journal of Consulting and Clinical Psychology, 69*, 1026–1036.

Figueiras, M. J., & Alvers, N. (2007). Lay perceptions of serious illnesses: An adapted version of the Revised Illness Perceptions Questionnaire (IPQ-R). *Psychology & Health, 22*, 143–158. http://doi.org/10.1080/14768320600774462

Gherman, A., Schnur, J., Montgomery, G., Sassu, R., Veresiu, I., & David, D. (2011). How are adherent people more likely to think? A meta-analysis of health beliefs and diabetes self-care. *The Diabetes Educator, 37*, 392–408.

Goulding, L., Furze, G., & Birks, Y. (2010). Randomized controlled trials of interventions to change maladaptive illness beliefs in people with coronary heart disease: Systematic review. *Journal of Advanced Nursing, 66*, 946–961.

Groleau, D., Young, A., & Kirmayer, L. J. (2006). The McGill Illness Narrative Interview (MINI): An interview schedule to elicit meanings and modes of reasoning related to illness experience. *Transcultural Psychiatry, 43*, 671–691.

Hagger, M. S., & Orbell, S. (2003). A meta-analytic review of the common-sense model of illness representations. *Psychology & Health, 18*, 141–184.

Harris, M. (1976). History and significance of the emic/etic distinction. *Annual Review of Anthropology, 5*, 329–350. http://doi.org/10.1146/annurev.an.05.100176.001553

Harrow, A., Wells, M., Humphris, G., Taylor, C., & Williams, B. (2008). "Seeing is believing, and believing is seeing": An exploration of the meaning and impact of women's mental images of their breast cancer and their potential origins. *Patient Education and Counseling, 73*, 339–346. http://doi.org/10.1016/j.pec.2008.07.014

Hayes, S. C., Jacobson, N. S., Follette, V. M., & Dougher, M. J., (Eds.). (1994). *Acceptance and change: Content and context in psychotherapy*. Reno, NV: Context Press.

Karademas, E. C., & Hondronikola, I. (2010). The impact of illness acceptance and helplessness to subjective health, and their stability over time: A prospective study in a sample of cardiac patients. *Psychology, Health & Medicine, 15*, 336–346.

Kleinman, A. (1980). *Patients and healers in the context of culture: An exploration of the borderland between anthropology, medicine, and psychiatry (Vol. 3)*. Berkeley, CA: University of California Press.

Kleinman, A. (1988). *The illness narratives: Suffering, healing, and the human condition*. New York, NY: Basic Books.

Kleinman, A., & Seeman, D. (2000). Personal experience of illness. In G. L. Albrecht, R. Fitzpatrick & S. Scrimshaw (Eds.), *Handbook of social studies in health and medicine* (pp. 230–242). London, UK: Sage.

Lauwerier, E., Crombez, G., Van Damme, S., Goubert, L., Vogelaers, D., & Evers, A. W. (2010). The construct validity of the Illness Cognition Questionnaire: The robustness of the three-factor structure across patients with chronic pain and chronic fatigue. *International Journal of Behavioral Medicine, 17*, 90–96. http://doi.org/10.1007/s12529-009-9059-z

Lazarus, R. S., & Folkman, S. (1984). *Stress, appraisal and coping*. New York. NY: Springer.

Lee, T., Cameron, L. D., Wünsche, B., & Stevens, C. (2011). A randomized trial of computer-based communications using imagery and text information to alter representations of heart disease risk and motivate protective behaviour. *British Journal of Health Psychology, 16*, 72–91.

Leventhal, H., Brissette, I., & Leventhal, E. A. (2003). The common-sense model of self-regulation of health and illness. In L. D. Cameron & H. Leventhal (Eds.), *The self-regulation of health and illness behaviour* (pp. 42–65). London, UK: Routledge.

Leventhal, H., Meyer, D., & Nerenz, D. (1980). The common sense model of illness danger. In S. Rachman (Ed.), *Medical psychology (Vol. 2*, pp. 7–30). New York, NY: Pergamon.

Lloyd, K. R., Jacob, K. S., Patel, V., St. Louis, L., Bhugra, D., & Mann, A. H. (1998). The development of the Short Explanatory Model Interview (SEMI) and its use among primary-care attenders with common mental disorders. *Psychological Medicine, 28*, 1231–1237. http://doi.org/10.1017/S0033291798007065

Luyas, G. T., Kay, M., & Solomons, H. C. (1991). An explanatory model of diabetes. *Western Journal of Nursing Research, 13*, 681–697. http://doi.org/10.1177/019394599101300602

Moss-Morris, R., Weinman, J., Petrie, K., Horne, R., Cameron, L., & Buick, D. (2002). The revised illness perception questionnaire (IPQ-R). *Psychology & Health, 17*, 1–16.

Olsen, B., Berg, C., & Wiebe, D. J. (2008). Dissimilarity in mother and adolescent illness representations of type 1 diabetes and negative emotional adjustment. *Psychology & Health, 23*, 113–129. http://doi.org/10.1080/08870440701437343

Park, C. L. (1998). Stress-related growth and thriving through coping: The roles of personality and cognitive processes. *Journal of Social Issues, 54*, 267–277.

Rüdell, K. (2014). *Predicting health resource utilization and professional advice for mental distress: A three months cohort study*. Manuscript submitted for publication.

Rüdell, K., Bhui, K., & Priebe, S. (2009). Concept, development and application of a new mixed method assessment of cultural variations in illness perceptions: Bart's Explanatory Model Inventory. *Journal of Health Psychology, 14*, 336–347. http://doi.org/10.1177/1359105308100218

Saravanan, B., Jacob, K. S., Johnson, S., Prince, M., Bhugra, D., & David, A. S. (2007). Belief models in first episode schizophrenia in South India. *Social Psychiatry and Psychiatric Epidemiology, 42*, 446–451. http://doi.org/10.1007/s00127-007-0186-z

Sidora-Arcoleo, K., Feldman, J., Serebrisky, D., & Spray, A. (2010). Validation of the asthma illness representation scale (AIRS©). *Journal of Asthma, 47*, 33–40. http://doi.org/10.3109/02770901003702832

Silove, D., Bateman, C., Brooks, R. T., Fonseca, C. A. Z., Steel, Z., Rodger, J., ... Bauman, A. (2008). Estimating clinically relevant mental disorders in a rural and an urban setting in postconflict Timor Leste. *Archives of General Psychiatry, 65*, 1205–1212. http://doi.org/10.1001/archpsyc.65.10.1205

Stacy, A., Ames, S., & Leigh, B. (2004). An implicit cognition assessment approach to relapse, secondary prevention, and media effects. *Cognitive and Behavioral Practice, 11*, 139–149.

Staerkle, R., Mannion, A. F., Elfering, A., Junge, A., Semmer, N. K., Jacobshagen, N., ... Boos, N. (2004). Longitudinal validation of the fear-avoidance beliefs questionnaire (FABQ) in a Swiss-German sample of low back pain patients. *European Spine Journal, 13*, 332–340. http://doi.org/10.1007/s00586-003-0663-3

Taieb, O., Chevret, S., Moro, M. R., Weiss, M. G., Biadi-Imhof, A., Reyre, A., & Baubet, T. (2012). Impact of migration on explanatory models of illness and addiction severity in patients with drug dependence in a Paris suburb. *Substance Use & Misuse, 47*, 347–355. http://doi.org/10.3109/10826084.2011.639841

Tiemensma, J., Daskalakis, N. P., van der Veen, E. M., Ramondt, S., Richardson, S. K., Broadbent, E., ... Kaptein, A. A. (2012). Drawings reflect a new dimension of the psychological impact of long-term remission in Cushing's syndrome. *Journal of Clinical Endocrinology and Metabolism, 97*, 3123–3131. http://doi.org/10.1210/jc.2012-1235

van Oort, L., Schroder, C., & French, D. P. (2011). What do people think about when they answer the Brief Illness Perception Questionnaire? A 'think-aloud' study. *British Journal of Health Psychology, 16*, 231–245. http://doi.org/10.1348/135910710X500819

Waddell, G., Newton, M., Henderson, I., Somerville, D., & Main, C. J. (1993). A Fear-Avoidance Beliefs Questionnaire (FABQ) and the role of fear-avoidance beliefs in chronic low back pain and disability. *Pain, 52*, 157–168.

Weinman, J., Petrie, K. J., Moss-Morris, R., & Horne, R. (1996). The Illness Perception Questionnaire: A new method for assessing the cognitive representation of illness. *Psychology & Health, 11*, 431–445. http://doi.org/10.1080/08870449608400270

Weir, R., Browne, G., Roberts, J., Tunks, E., & Gafni, A. (1994). The Meaning of Illness Questionnaire: Further evidence for its reliability and validity. *Pain, 58*, 377–386.

Weiss, M. G., Doongaji, D. R., Siddhartha, S., Wypij, D., Pathare, S., Bhatawdekar, M., ... Fernandes, R. (1992). The Explanatory Model Interview Catalogue (EMIC): Contribution to cross-cultural research methods from a study of leprosy and mental health. *The British Journal of Psychiatry, 160*, 819–830. http://doi.org/10.1192/bjp.160.6.819

Young, A., & Kirmayer, L. J. (2006). Illness narrative interview protocols. *Transcultural Psychiatry, 43*, 671–691.

Chapter 5

Health Behavior

Aleksandra Luszczynska[1,2] and Martin Hagger[3]

[1]Trauma, Health, & Hazards Center, University of Colorado at Colorado Springs, CO, USA
[2]SWPS University of Social Sciences and Humanities, Wroclaw, Poland
[3]Faculty of Health Sciences, Curtin University, Bentley, Perth, WA, Australia

Introduction

The spectrum of health-related behaviors is extremely broad and includes: health-enhancing behaviors such as physical activity participation and healthy nutrition; health-protective behaviors such as vaccination participation, cancer screening behaviors, and condom use; avoidance of health-compromising actions such as smoking, consuming alcohol over recommended thresholds, and illicit drug intake; and behaviors related to illness diagnosis and treatment such as adherence to treatment and rehabilitation regimes. Changing health-related behaviors is often the primary aim of health promotion because of the close link between health-related behavior and adaptive health-related outcomes. A focus on identifying modifiable health-related behaviors, therefore, has the potential to make substantial differences to public health (Abraham, Kok, Shaalma, & Luszczynska, 2011).

Uptake and adherence to health-related behaviors is the result of complex direct, indirect, and interactive effects of individual, social, and environmental factors (Abraham et al., 2011). Health psychologists are particularly interested in the modifiable psychological factors involved in the effortful self-regulation of behavior (Hagger, Wood, Stiff, & Chatzisarantis, 2009). Factors that are shown to be related to health behavior are viable targets for interventions on the premise that changing the psychological factor will lead to a concomitant change in behavior. Alongside this, it is important to evaluate the effectiveness of interventions that target these factors in changing the psychological measures of the factors as well as evoking a change in behavior. As a consequence, the precision and accuracy of measures of psychological factors and behavioral outcomes are paramount in order to produce valid evidence for the effects. Finally, health behaviors are measured in multiple fields in health psychology, including stress, health promotion, as well as chronic and infectious diseases issues.

A fundamental feature of health behavior assessment is determining the content and frequency of the behavior. Measures should allow the determination of the precise action and how many times it was carried out over a given period. Typical methods of assessment include self-reports, observation, biomarker-based measurement, sensor-based assessment, and records of the use of institutions/facilities (e.g., pharmacy-based adherence measures, the use of access passes to physical activity facilities). Strengths and weaknesses of the assessment methods are determined by their validity, reliability, specificity in terms of the target population, cost, feasibility, and acceptability for respondents and practitioners. Given the paramount importance of measurement validity and precision in health behavior research, the purpose of the current chapter is to provide an overview of well-established and emerging methods of health behavior assessment, in the context of their strengths and weaknesses.

Measurement Issues

Self-Reports of Health Behavior

Measurement Overview

Self-report is considered the most practical method for behavior assessment in large, population-based studies and is usually the method of choice (Helmerhorst, Brage, Warren, Besson, & Ekelund, 2012). Self-report measures include diaries or logs, questionnaires, surveys, and recall interviews. For several health behaviors there are multiple self-report measures available. For example, there are at least 130 physical activity questionnaires, many of which have been evaluated in terms of their psychometric properties and concurrent and predictive validity against other measures considered more objective (Helmerhorst et al., 2012). In terms of validity, indices of behavior-obtained self-report measures are usually moderately correlated with sensor- or biomarker-based measurement. For example, correlation coefficients ranging from .30 to .40 are found in studies of physical activity assessment (Foley, Maddison, Olds, & Ridley, 2012). On average, self-reports of such behaviors as physical activity often have good reliability (Helmerhorst et al., 2012). Further, newer self-report measures of physical activity do not necessarily perform better in terms of validity than older ones (Helmerhorst et al., 2012).

Self-reports of health behavior vary in terms of format. In *global self-reports of health behavior* individuals are asked to indicate how many times (or how often) they performed the target behavior within a period (e.g., 2 weeks). Counting number of cigarettes (e.g., "On average, how many cigarettes do you smoke per day?"), alcoholic drinks, types of food consumed, and pills taken (Shiffman, 2009) are good examples. *Time-line follow-back (TLFB) self-reports* gather information on behavior during a preselected period that can cover anywhere from the previous 7 days up to the previous 12 months. A calendar is used to structure the report, and personal (birthdays, parties) as well as common (holidays, major news events) landmarks are used as memory aides to assist the recall strategy and engage autobiographical memory (Menon, 1994).

End-of-the-day recall of 24 hours refers to the reported number of behavioral acts during the previous day. For example, *24-hr recall* of food intake measures would include listing in detail all food and drinks people consumed in the previous 24 hours (Wrieden, Peace, & Barton, 2003). As the time span covered by recall is relatively short, the memory bias is less likely to affect the accuracy of the report. In general, self-administered food frequency questionnaires, including lists of foods and indications of frequency of consumption over a short period (preferably with use of photographs estimating portion sizes), pose a low burden on respondents (Wrieden et al., 2003). Procedures for measuring energy and nutrient intake are based on food recall or food identification such that an appropriate item can be chosen from lists/tables, accounting for the frequency with which each food is eaten, and the portion size of each food item can be quantified (Rutishauser & Black, 2002).

Another form of self-report, called *multiple pass*, aims at reducing memory bias and is most often used to assess dietary behavior. It consists of several stages (or passes) of free recall of food intake, with multiple probing questions aimed at gathering detailed information in the final stage. Multiple pass allows the participant to revisit and check behavioral information. In the *first pass* (i.e., first stage of the self-report) a quick list of foods consumed is obtained from the participant; in the *second pass*, information about the snacks consumed (including time and place) is recorded. The *third pass* prompts for foods that may have been forgotten, followed by reviewing portion sizes (Wrieden et al., 2003).

Self-report of food intake poses specific problems as it needs to account for the wide variety and content of foods consumed as well as the frequency of the behavior. Thus, self-reports may be accompanied by *estimated food records*. These records are likely to involve (a) weighing each and every item of food/drink prior to consumption to obtain precise estimation of portion sizes, or (b) food records using other means of quantification, such as food photographs or the use of household measures such as cups (Wrieden et al., 2003).

Participant-Related Issues

In general, self-reports of health behavior are prone to errors attributable to tendencies to misreport, due to a need for approval or affirmation bias, or to cognitive limitations, due to comprehension or recall (Helmerhorst et al., 2012). The validity of self-report measures in the general population should not be extrapolated to populations that may be at risk of misreporting such as elderly populations that may have difficulties when it comes to recall of action (Helmerhorst et al., 2012).

Global self-reports in which the participant is asked to estimate the average occurrence of behavior may be biased because, instead of engaging in systematic counting, respondents base their answers on broad heuristics such as *digit bias* – the tendency to cluster around rounded values (Shiffman, 2009). Self-reports of behavior covering longer periods are susceptible to memory-related biases related to storage and retrieval failures (Menon, 1994). Written diary data reports provide daily records of behavior and may suffer from compliance-related bias: Participants may backfill diaries en masse, even if they are electronically prompted, in order to present compliance (Shiffman, Stone, & Hufford, 2008).

Both TLFB and end-of-the-day recall may be affected by memory and digit bias (Shiffman, 2009). Further, research showed that global and TLBF reports may show systematic over-reporting due to unconscious biases, especially for frequently and habitually performed behaviors (Shiffman, 2009). Further, TLFB reports exhibit only modest correlations with other methods considered more objective such as ecological momentary assessment (Shiffman, 2009).

The reliability and validity of self-reports are also affected by the age of the respondent. Younger children up to the age of 9 years may provide less valid data than older children and adolescents (Helmerhorst et al., 2012). By contrast, self-reports of health-compromising behaviors, such as smoking, may be particularly biased in older adults (cf. Morabia, Bernstein, Curtin, & Berode, 2001). This effect may be not only due to a memory bias, but also due to high risk perception and the related tendency to misreport socially undesirable behaviors (Morabia et al., 2001).

Behavior-Related Issues

Socially undesirable and illegal behaviors also tend to be underreported in interviewer-administered questionnaires, compared with self-administered measures, which in turn provide lower rates than computer-assisted measures (Brener, Billy, & Grady, 2003). Measures requiring the recall of food and drink consumed may suffer from bias in recording foods considered healthy and desirable and those considered unhealthy and undesirable, with over- and under-reporting occurring, respectively (Wrieden et al., 2003). Women tend to underreport fat intake (−12%) and individuals of both genders tend to report 5% less energy intake compared with observational measures, particularly if they are overweight (Wrieden et al., 2003).

Self-reports about habitual behaviors may be less valid, as they are cognitively challenging, because habits tend to be performed with a relative lack of awareness (Brener et al., 2003). Several other issues may be specific for the complex and frequently performed behaviors, such as food intake. For example, the primary limitation of 24-hr recall is that recording consumption for a single day is seldom representative of a person's usual intake due to day-to-day variation (Wrieden et al., 2003). The estimation of a portion size or the number of alcohol units in alcoholic beverages may be difficult for many respondents and thus lead to measurement error, even in compliant respondents. Using household measures or photographs taken by the respondent to evaluate portions prior to eating a meal poses a burden on the respondents (Wrieden et al., 2003).

The validity of self-report measures is also affected by cognitive and situational factors, but the size of the effect of these factors varies across behaviors. For example, reports of drinking and illicit drug use may be biased because individuals may be unable to remember actions that occurred while they were under the influence of the abused substances (Brener et al., 2003). The validity of self-report measures of food intake depends on the study population, with less reliable findings among individuals with eating disorders, those who are dieting, obese individuals, and those who use unhealthy methods of weight control (Brener et al., 2003).

Measure-Specific Issues

Questionnaires covering longer periods (e.g., weeks) may result in under- of over-estimation of health behavior. For example, people are prone to underestimate food intake when using food frequency questionnaires compared with 24-hr reports (Brener et al., 2003). Long and detailed self-reports may result in lower compliance and low agreement rates, thus a systematic error in the data obtained (Helmerhorst et al., 2012).

Measurement of behavior is also limited by inconsistencies in the type of self-report measure used across countries or cultures, which limits the direct comparability of the results. However, there are self-report measures that are able to overcome these limitations, such as the Health Behavior in School-Aged Children survey, which did so by means of extensive work on protocols, translations, and constant adjustments to changing social environments (Roberts et al., 2007). To date, only self-report surveys have provided cross-national data allowing for analyses of changes in health behaviors across multiple countries over last three decades (Roberts et al., 2007)

Intervention-Related Effects

Research on misreporting food consumption suggests that self-reports suffer from *observation effects* (Wrieden et al., 2003). For example, eating behaviors change when individuals are asked to record their intake (Wrieden et al., 2003). In fact, there is a growing literature demonstrating that completing self-report surveys alone lead to changes in behavior, albeit with relatively small effect sizes. This is also known as the mere-measurement effect (Godin et al., 2010). Furthermore, participation in health behavior change interventions may affect self-report measures of behavior. For example, in an intervention study, Natarajan et al. (2010) found that among all participants of the study the validity of 24-hr dietary recall improved at follow-up compared with baseline. The effects were attributed to better practice in the recognition of portion sizes during the course of the study (Natarajan et al., 2010). Interestingly, intervention participants significantly altered their reporting of actual dietary intake if they were notified that the 24-hr recall would be conducted on that day. The need to present oneself as compliant with the intervention was likely to affect the measurement. Unscheduled 24-hr reports could alleviate the issue of anticipated measurement, but they are likely to result in a low response rate (Natarajan et al., 2010).

Ecological Momentary Assessment (EMA) of Health Behavior

Measurement Overview

Self-reports tend to miss the effects of daily events and circumstances and are insensitive to changes over time and across contexts. To aid these issues, the ecological momentary assessment approach to behavior measurement uses repeated collection of real-time data and microprocesses in behavior change (Kuntsche & Labhart, 2013b; Shiffman et al., 2008). Recording takes place when an individual is prompted to report as the behavior happens but also at random times during the day. Repeated assessment (e.g., every 30 min, several times a day, once a day) provides opportunity for evaluating within-subject changes in behavior, appearing over time and across contexts (Shiffman et al., 2008). Health behavior assessment with EMA usually shows high validity when compared with biomarkers (Shiffman, 2009; see also Chapter 18 in this volume).

Limitations of the Use of EMA in Behavior Assessment

Before application of EMA in patient populations in which symptoms or treatment procedures may interfere with providing data by means of EMA, the feasibility and acceptability for the target patient group should be tested (Shiffman et al., 2008). Compliance with event-oriented protocols of EMA (e.g., engagement in a behavior such as snacking, alcohol intake as a prompt to record) is very difficult to verify. Further, measurement reactivity, observed in research on self-monitoring, is also a limitation of EMA (Shiffman et al., 2008). Individuals who intend to change their behavior may be prone to behavior changes due to the acts of monitoring their behavior with EMA. Thus, employing EMA may constitute a behavior-change technique.

Sensor-Based Assessment

Measurement Overview

Technological developments offer sensor-based options to obtain measures of complex behavior. Some of these methods have only been commercially available for just over a decade, therefore information about their validity is relatively limited.

Accelerometers detect acceleration in one, two, or three directions and thus allow determination of the quantity and intensity of movements. Systematic reviews suggest that triaxial accelerometers and multisensor devices are significantly more accurate than uniaxial devices (Van Remoortel et al., 2012). Testing of accelerometers alone and accelerometers combined with other sensors has revealed good validity (Van Remoortel et al., 2012). Pedometers provide assessment of steps, estimated distance travelled, and energy expenditure. In general, a lower accuracy of step count may be expected when the speed of movements is slow, whereas the distance measurement is affected by stride length and accuracy in counting steps (Crouter, Schneider, Karabulut, & Bassett, 2003). Integrated multisensory systems use a combination of accelerometer and other sensors that evaluate body responses, such as heart rate (Van Remoortel et al., 2012).

Wearable cameras with a point-of-view lens offer a stand-alone or a complementary measure. They provide real-life observations instead of observations conducted in a laboratory. Such cameras may record food consumption, alcohol intake, or physical activity. Wearable cameras, such as the SensCam, passively capturing wide-angle images, may be worn around the neck (Doherty et al., 2013). They take pictures every 20 s and in response to movement, ambient temperature, and light (Doherty et al., 2013). They may be used as a complementary measurement for self-reports. Preliminary research showed that compared with 24-hr multiple pass recalls, sensor-equipped cameras show 17% additional food items and 12% higher energy intake (Gemming, Doherty, Kelly, Utter, & Mhurchu, 2013). Sensor-equipped cameras improve the sensitivity and specificity of the data obtained by means of accelerometers (Kerr et al., 2013). For example, up to 72% of behaviors classified as sedentary using accelerometers turned out to be standing without movement or standing with movement (e.g., standing doing yoga conditioning exercises) when concurrent data obtained with sensor-equipped cameras were analyzed (Kerr et al., 2013). Wearable cameras may offer the best available methods to categorize the environmental context (e.g., with or without social interactions) and the type of activity in real-life conditions (Doherty et al., 2013).

Measurement based on a global positioning system (GPS) may be considered as a complementary method to study the location of healthy behaviors. A bluetooth GPS data logger device may be worn on the waist, for example, with an accelerometer (Maddison et al., 2010). It provides the time, date, speed, altitude, and location at preset intervals (Maddison et al., 2010).

Limitations of Sensor-Based Assessment of Health Behavior

The use of accelerometers to measure physical activity in people with chronic health problems has not been widely investigated (Van Remoortel et al., 2012). A major limitation of accelerometry is the measurement of physical activity among patients moving slowly due to their health condition, such as chronic heart disease, pulmonary diseases, back pain, or diabetes related to obesity (Van Remoortel et al., 2012). Unfortunately, studies have shown that accelerometers tend to underestimate total energy expenditure in the case of slow walking, as measured with indirect calorimetry (Van Remoortel et al., 2012). The same weakness of accelerometers may apply to evaluating sedentary behaviors. Behaviors involving standing with movement may be classified as sedentary (Kerr et al., 2013). When measuring cycling, accelerometers may also provide values indicating sedentary activity (Kerr et al., 2013), whereas driving in a car may be recorded as nonsedentary behavior (Kerr et al., 2013). Specific populations, such as toddlers and slowly moving adults, may be tested only after developing adjusted cut-off points.

The measurement conducted with sensor-equipped cameras is likely to yield a nontrivial amount of missing data, for example, when participants want to protect their privacy (Doherty et al., 2013). The cameras also have an option to review the images and delete any content that participants do not want to disclose to the researchers (Doherty et al., 2013).

Categorizing data obtained with sensor-equipped cameras may be time consuming and expensive, as the content of images must be analyzed visually by the researcher in order to categorize recorded behaviors (Doherty et al., 2013). In addition, it may provide data difficult to categorize when the participants are in the dark (Doherty et al., 2013). GPS units have a measurement error depending on the available satellites, meteorology, and physical obstructions, with frequent errors larger than 15 m (Maddison et al., 2010). A greater amount of measurement error and missing data are expected with indoor versus outdoor wear (Maddison et al., 2010).

Biomarker-Based Assessment

Measurement Overview

Biochemical measures are often considered the gold standard in behavior assessment or validation studies because they are believed to be less susceptible to bias than other available techniques such as memory bias and adherence to protocols. However, many biomarker-based measures involve drawing blood samples or providing urine samples, which are considered relatively invasive or intrusive of respondents' privacy. The invasiveness of biomarker measurement varies, with methods relying on saliva or breath analysis representing noninvasive assessments (Morabia et al., 2001).

Measures of expired carbon monoxide (CO) with breathalyzer instruments provide information about recently smoked cigarettes. The half-life time for CO varies from 3 to 8 hrs (cf. Morabia et al., 2001), therefore breathalyzers offer an assessment of short-term exposure to tobacco. Longer-time biomarkers include assessment of cotinine levels in saliva, with a half-life of 5–15 days (cf. Morabia et al., 2001).

The assessment of adherence to medication by means of analyses of biological assays of active drugs, drug metabolites, or other markers in blood, urine, or other bodily fluids, which confirm active drug ingestion, is usually moderately related to self-report (Simoni et al., 2006). Drug assay evaluation with urinalysis and analysis of saliva, sweat, and hair can be used as a measure of illegal drug use (Brener et al., 2003). However, even urinalysis tends to produce a moderate percentage of false-negative results for the use of illicit substances such as marijuana (Brener et al., 2003).

Blood lipid profiles, vitamin C, and carotenoid measures may be used as nutrition or energy intake measures in healthy populations. They are applied also in research on validity of self-reports or in diet-related illness studies. In general, plasma markers have a high validity and are strongly related to intake measures relying on laboratory-based observation of intake (Natarajan et al., 2006). The associations between plasma carotenoid levels and 24-hr recalls or food frequency questionnaires are moderate, ranging from 0.39 to 0.52, with the highest associations found for 24-hr recalls (Natarajan et al., 2006). Compared to plasma measures, the error variance in self-report may be as high as 50% (Natarajan et al., 2006).

Limitations of Assessing Behavior With Biomarkers

In general, biomarker-based measurement provides little information about behavior patterns changing over time. In many cases, biomarkers are influenced by several individual and environmental factors, which are hard to assess in noninvasive and low-cost studies on behavior change (Natarajan et al., 2006). Biomarkers of nutrition behavior are influenced by such factors as body mass or smoking status (Natarajan et al., 2006). Relying solely on a selected biomarker as the indicator of nutrition behavior poses some risks, as the physiological effects of food depend not only on the level of specific compounds, but also on their combination and other macronutrient content.

Further, measuring fruit and vegetable intake by means of biomarkers creates particular difficulties. Most biomarkers have a short half-life and, therefore, measure very recent intake (Kuhnle, 2012). The use of the most popular biomarkers such as vitamin C and carotenoids is also problematic. For example, when using vitamin C as a biomarker of fruit and vegetable intake, a portion of green pepper is equivalent to 20 portions of carrots, but if carotenoids are used as a biomarker, one portion of carrots is equivalent to more than 45 portions of green peppers (Kuhnle, 2012).

In the case of smoking assessment, a single biomarker may be not sufficient to provide reliable behavioral information because smoking is a discontinuous process and biomarkers measure different components of the exposure to tobacco smoke (Morabia et al., 2001). Misclassification of smokers based on one biomarker may be as high as 12% (Morabia et al., 2001). Measures of expired CO provide information about recently smoked cigarettes (cf. Morabia et al., 2001). Thus, CO would be high and cotinine in saliva would be low in a light smoker who smoked shortly before the measurement was taken.

The assessment of cotinine in saliva is also affected by the intake of foods such as almonds, broccoli, and cabbage, which form cyanohydrins upon digestion, a substance that is detoxified to cotinine (Morabia et al., 2001). Thus, to obtain a high validity of a combined application of CO and cotinine in saliva, researchers exclude individuals who report eating food that forms cyanohydrins (Morabia et al., 2001). Nutrition-related systematic dropout may be expected; such dropout presents a problem in longitudinal research.

Other Types of Assessment

Behavior assessment involving direct observation by a trained experimenter may be conducted when self-report or EMA are difficult to administer and other methods such as biomarker-based assessments are not feasible. In last decade, direct observation-based methods seem to be used less frequently, and may often be replaced with sensor-based measurement providing photographic documentation of behavior (e.g., with sensor-equipped cameras). Direct observation is conducted by a trained observer who is present during all the occasions the behavior occurs (e.g., food intake, alcohol consumption) and registers the behavior with charts including the characteristics of behavior, time, and environment (Simmons & Reuben, 2000). It takes place during a defined period (e.g., 3 days). Observation was used in research on older adults in assisted-living facilities, individuals with disabilities, or toddlers (cf. Simmons & Reuben, 2000). Compared to photography-based methods, direct observation was a valid measure of food intake among older adults (Simmons & Reuben, 2000). Using this measurement, Simmons and Reuben (2000) were able to identify 53% of nursing home residents who eat less than three quarters of prepared food portions.

Proxy reports involve reporting behavior of another person, provided by a nonprofessional observer. Usually, the observer is a person spending longer periods with the one observed, for example, a family member (Harakeh, Engels, de Vries, & Scholte, 2006). Most frequently, proxy reports are used to evaluate behavior among young children (aged 0–7 years old) who lack the cognitive skills to provide EMA or self-report of behavior (Börnhorst et al., 2013). Proxy reports have reduced validity if behavior is performed when the child is not under parental control, leading to unintentional misreporting (Börnhorst et al., 2013)

When proxy reports provide assessment of adolescents' or adults' behavior, the proxy measure may use the same wording as self-reports. For example, in research on adolescent smoking, parents were asked to complete identical questionnaires as those completed by the adolescents (Harakeh et al., 2006). Proxy reports of parents are only weakly-to-moderately related to adolescents' self-reports on smoking. Reports of both parents had a stronger association with self-reports of younger adolescents compared with those of older adolescents (Harakeh et al., 2006). By contrast, proxy reports of parental smoking provided by adolescents reflected strong agreement with self-reported smoking in parents (Harakeh et al., 2006).

Pharmacy-based adherence measures allow the calculation of medication possession ratio (compared with number of days prescribed), pill count (a proportion of number of pills dispensed to time between pick-ups), and pill pick-up (picking up before the previous supplies finish; McMahon et al., 2011). Systematic reviews suggest that in the case of adherence to antiretroviral therapy, this measurement strategy may be more accurate than self-report when validated against viral load (McMahon et al., 2011). Pharmacy-based adherence measures are used for patients receiving long-term treatment. Pharmacy-based assessments seem to be sensitive measures, distinguishing patients who self-report perfect adherence but do not show drug intake when biomarkers-based assessment is used (Simoni et al., 2006).

Examples of Assessment

Self-report measures include single-item assessment, such as *global measure of cigarette smoking* (cigarettes per day [CPD]). Respondents are asked to provide information about, "How many cigarettes per day do you currently smoke?" (Lewis-Esquerre et al., 2005), or "On average, how many cigarettes do you smoke per day" (Shiffman, 2009). As with many self-report measures, the global CPD measure has moderate or limited validity when compared with biomarkers, but reasonable validity when compared with other self-report measures (Lewis-Esquerre et al., 2005). This low-burden one-item measure can be easily incorporated into complex research, treatment, or diagnostic procedures.

The Internet-Based Cell Phone-Optimized Assessment Technique (ICAT) is an example of EMA of health behavior (Kuntsche & Labhart, 2013a, 2013b). In line with a study protocol, at respective time points participants receive a short message service (SMS) with a hyperlink to the questionnaires. An ICAT-based measure of alcohol consumption, including seven questions (location, people present, the number of standard drinks of four types of alcohol, and current mood during the previous 60 min) confirmed the validity and high feasibility of the ICAT (Kuntsche & Labhart, 2013a). Half of the participants provided their responses within 25 min of the dispatch of the SMS invitation. Retention rates were very high, with 80% participating in 30 daily assessments and 40–70% of the questionnaires sent each day returned (Kuntsche & Labhart, 2013a). The ICAT had high acceptability rates; it is a low-burden assessment, with less than 1 min used to complete the measurement (Kuntsche & Labhart, 2013a).

Among sensor-based assessment methods, a triaxial accelerometer is considered one of the best measures for evaluating physical activity in healthy adolescents and adults. It provides information about vector magnitude units, energy expenditure, and activity intensity levels (Van

Remoortel et al., 2012). The most extensively validated accelerometers include ActiGraph (previously known as CSA or MTI) and Tracmor. Both devices show reasonable associations with biochemical measures of energy expenditure (Plasqui & Westerterp, 2007).

HIV viral load measurement represents an example of a biomarker-based measure of several health behaviors in people living with HIV (Naar-King et al., 2009). In particular, viral load depends on adherence to antiretroviral treatment and behaviors that may result in infections with the other types of HIV than the type carried by the respondent. Those behaviors include intravenous drug use and engaging in unprotected sex. Viral load tests evaluate the amount of genetic material of HIV (HIV-RNA) in blood samples. The measurement is a standard procedure for all HIV patients and it is taken every 1–6 months, depending on the type of treatment and immune response to it (Naar-King et al., 2009).

Examples of Research Illustrating the Use of Health Behavior Measures

The global CPD measure (one-item self-reported smoking behavior) was used to evaluate the main outcome (cigarette smoking) in a randomized controlled trial testing the effects of implementation intentions (planning) on smoking behavior among 172 adolescents and young adults, smoking on average 11.41 cigarettes a day at baseline and intending to reduce nicotine intake (Webb, Sheeran, & Luszczynska, 2009). The intervention produced a significant effect on the number of cigarettes smoked, assessed with the global CPD measure, in particular among individuals with weak or moderate smoking habits (Webb et al., 2009). As individuals with weak habits smoke a very limited number of cigarettes per day, it may be assumed that the use of biomarker-based measures could have low feasibility in this study. Those who smoke rarely may show negligible salivary cotinine levels but may present high CO levels if they smoked recently. Alternatively, smoking could be measured with EMA. However, the participants who intended to reduce smoking could be prone to behavior changes due to the acts of monitoring their behavior with EMA (Shiffman et al., 2008). Therefore, the use of EMA could interact with the intervention and thus affect the results.

The ICAT-based alcohol intake measure (Kuntsche & Labhart, 2013a) was used to evaluate the role of pre-drinking behavior in predicting negative consequences of alcohol intake (Labhart, Graham, Wells, & Kuntsche, 2013). Pre-drinking involves consumption of alcohol in a private dwelling (e.g., at home) or in a public place (e.g., public park), before drinkers go to a drinking establishment or location where more alcohol is expected to be consumed. Data were collected for 5 weeks among 183 young adults who provided information on 1,441 evenings, for a total of 7,828 assessments. Respondents received six text messages on 3 days per week. Those who engaged in pre-drinking consumed significantly more drinks (7.12) per evening than those who did not engage in pre-drinking (4.22), and they were more likely to suffer from at least one aversive outcome after drinking (24% vs. 14%, respectively). Overall, pre-drinking was a very strong predictor of the total consumption during one evening and of adverse outcomes.

ActiGraph accelerometers were used in a study aiming at the identification of patterns and locations of joint activity in parent–child dyads, which provided opportunities for parental modeling (Dunton et al., 2013). Participants wore the device for seven continuous days on the right hip (Dunton et al., 2013). The location of activity was measured with GPS devices. Of 407 eligible dyads who agreed to take part, 291 dyads provided sufficient amount of matched data. Joint parent–child moderate-to-vigorous physical activity occurred in residential locations (35%) or indoor commercial facilities (retail stores, gyms), whereas open spaces (parks, gardens) were used for only 20% of time (Dunton et al., 2013).

Biomarker-based assessment may pose a low burden on participants who anyway are required to participate regularly in biomarkers measurement due to a chronic illness. For example, HIV viral loads are regularly evaluated to monitor the progress of disease among people living with HIV. Viral load changes result from several behaviors, such as exposure to HIV by means of unprotected sex or intravenous drug use as well as adherence to prescribed medication (Naar-King et al., 2009). HIV viral load was applied as the main outcome of a behavior change intervention for adolescents living with HIV (Naar-King et al., 2009). In this randomized controlled trial, young people ($N=186$) were assigned to either standard specialty care or a four-session individual motivational interviewing intervention, delivered over 10 weeks. Viral loads were measured up to 6 months after the completion of the intervention (9 months after the baseline). Results indicated a reduction of viral load among intervention participants treated with antiretroviral drugs (from $M=3.03$ at baseline to $M=2.89$ at the last follow-up) compared with controls treated with antiretroviral drugs who did not participate in the intervention (from $M=3.27$ to $M=3.37$; Naar-King et al., 2009).

Comments and Conclusions

The decision to use a specific method to assess health-related behavior may be influenced by the validity of the measure, its acceptability by the participants, and feasibility in terms of the study outcomes and protocols. Most measures suffer from limitations in at least one of these areas. A multimeasurement approach may seem beneficial, as this approach showed an incremental validity of the assessment. However, in some cases, the increase in accuracy may be small, questioning whether the advantages of using multiple measures outweigh the time, money, and invasiveness required. The acceptability of behavior measures to practitioners and respondents is seldom evaluated. A closer look at acceptability is especially important and relevant to research conducted in specific populations such as toddlers or individuals with intellectual disabilities.

Health psychology research and practice usually rely on self-reported measurement of health-related behavior. Notably, many self-report behavior measures have substantive limitations often attributable to their low or moderate validity against more objective measures. The advantages of self-report measures include their low costs, minimal training required for administration by participants, practitioners, or experimenters, relatively low participant burden, relatively high compliance, and relatively low missing data (Lewis-Esquerre et al., 2005). Unfortunately, there are few studies comparing different methods of measuring health behavior in terms of their validity, together with evaluations of cost, acceptability, and feasibility.

Acknowledgments

The contribution of the first author was supported by the Foundation of Polish Science, Master Program.

References

Abraham, C., Kok, G., Schaalma, H. P., & Luszczynska, A. (2011). Health promotion. In P. R. Martin, F. M. Cheung, M. C. Knowles, M. Kyrios, L. Littlefield, J. B. Overmier, & J. M. Prieto (Eds.), *Handbook of applied psychology* (pp. 83–111). Chichester, UK: Wiley.

Börnhorst, C., Huybrechts, I., Ahrens, W., Eiben, G., Michels, N., Pala, V., … Pigeot, I. (2013). Prevalence and determinants of misreporting among European children in proxy-reported 24-h dietary recalls. *British Journal of Nutrition, 109*, 1257–1265. http://doi.org/10.1017/S0007114512003194

Brener, N. D., Billy, J. O.G., & Grady, W. R. (2003). Assessment of factors affecting the validity of self-reported health-risk behaviors among adolescents: Evidence from the scientific literature. *Journal of Adolescent Health, 33*, 436–457. http://doi.org/10.1016/S1054-139X(03)00052-1

Crouter, S. E., Schneider, P. L., Karabulut, M., & Bassett, D. R. (2003). Validity of 10 electronic pedometers for measuring steps, distance, and energy cost. *Medicine & Science in Sports & Exercise, 35*, 1455–1460. http://doi.org/10.1097/00005768-200305001-01571

Doherty, A. R., Kelly, P., Kerr, J., Marshall, S., Oliver, M., Badland, H., … Foster, C., (2013). Using wearable cameras to categorise type and context of accelerometer-identified episodes of physical activity. *International Journal of Behavioral Nutrition and Physical Activity, 10*, 22. http://doi.org/10.1186/1479-5868-10-22

Dunton, G. F., Liao, Y., Almanza, E., Jerrett, M., Spruijt-Metz, D., & Pentz, M. A. (2013). Locations of joint physical activity in parent–child pairs based on accelerometer and GPS monitoring. *Annals of Behavioral Medicine, 45*(Suppl. 1), S162–S172. http://doi.org/10.1007/s12160-012-9417-y

Foley, L., Maddison, R., Olds, T., & Ridley, K. (2012). Self-report use-of-time tools for the assessment of physical activity and sedentary behaviour in young people: systematic review. *Obesity Reviews, 13*, 711–722. http://doi.org/10.1111/j.1467-789X.2012.00993.x

Gemming, L., Doherty, A., Kelly, P., Utter, J., & Mhurchu, C. N. (2013). Feasibility of a SenseCam-assisted 24-h recall to reduce under-reporting of energy intake. *European Journal of Clinical Nutrition, 67*, 1095–1099. http://doi.org/10.1038/ejcn.2013.156

Godin, G., Sheeran, P., Conner, M., Delage, G., Germain, M., Bélanger-Gravel, A., … Naccache, H. (2010). Which survey questions change behavior? Randomized controlled trial of mere measurement interventions. *Health Psychology, 29*, 636–644. http://doi.org/10.1037/a0021131

Hagger, M. S., Wood, C., Stiff, C., & Chatzisarantis, N. L. D. (2009). The strength model of self-regulation failure and health-related behavior. *Health Psychology Review, 3*, 208–238. http://doi.org/10.1080/17437190903414387

Harakeh, Z., Engels, R. C. M. E., de Vries, H., & Scholte, R. H. J. (2006). Correspondence between proxy and self-reports on smoking in a full family study. *Drug and Alcohol Dependence, 84*, 40–47. http://doi.org/10.1016/j.drugalcdep.2005.11.026

Helmerhorst, H. J. F., Brage, S., Warren, J., Besson, H., & Ekelund, U. (2012). A systematic review of reliability and objective criterion-related validity of physical activity questionnaires. *International Journal of Behavioral Nutrition and Physical Activity, 9*, 103. http://doi.org/10.1186/1479-5868-9-103

Kerr, J., Marshall, S. J., Godbole, S., Chen, J., Legge, A., Doherty, A. R., … Foster, C. (2013). Using the SenseCam to improve classifications of sedentary behavior in free-living settings. *American Journal of Preventive Medicine, 44*, 290–296. http://doi.org/10.1016/j.amepre.2012.11.004

Kuhnle, G. C. (2012). Nutritional biomarkers for objective dietary assessment. *Journal of the Science of Food and Agriculture, 92*, 1145–1149. http://doi.org/10.1002/jsfa.5631

Kuntsche, E., & Labhart, F. (2013a). ICAT: Development of an internet-based data collection method for ecological momentary assessment using personal cell phones. *European Journal of Psychological Assessment, 29*, 140–148. http://doi.org/10.1027/1015-5759/a000137

Kuntsche, E., & Labhart, F. (2013b). Using personal cell phones for ecological momentary assessment. An overview of current developments. *European Psychologist, 19*, 3–13. http://doi.org/10.1027/1016-9040/a000127

Labhart, F., Graham, K., Wells, S., & Kuntsche, S. (2013). Drinking before going to licensed premises: An event level analysis of pre-drinking, alcohol consumption and adverse consequences. *Alcoholism: Clinical and Experimental Research, 37*, 284–291. http://doi.org/10.1111/j.1530-0277.2012.01872.x

Lewis-Esquerre, J. M., Colby, S. M., Tevyaw, T. O., Eaton, C. A., Kahler, C. W., & Monti, P. M. (2005). Validation of the timeline follow-back in the assessment of adolescent smoking. *Drug and Alcohol Dependence, 79*, 33–43. http://doi.org/10.1016/j.drugalcdep.2004.12.007

Maddison, R., Jiang, Y., Vander Hoorn, S., Exeter, D., Mhurchu, C. N., & Dorey, E. (2010). Describing patterns of physical activity in adolescents using global positioning systems and accelerometry. *Pediatric Exercise Science, 22*, 392–407.

McMahon, J. H., Jordan, M. R., Kelley, K., Bertagnolio, S., Hong, S. Y., Wanke, C. A., … Elliott, J. H. (2011). Pharmacy adherence measures to assess adherence in antiretroviral therapy: Review of literature and implications for treatment monitoring. *Clinical Infectious Diseases, 52*, 493–506. http://doi.org/10.1093/cid/ciq167

Menon, G. (1994). Judgments of behavioral frequencies: Memory search and retrieval strategies. In N. Schwarz & S. Sudman (Eds.), *Autobiographical memory and the validity of retrospective reports* (pp. 161–172). New York, NY: Springer.

Morabia, A., Bernstein, M. S., Curtin, F., & Berode, M. (2001). Validation of self-reported smoking status by simultaneous measurement of carbon monoxide and salivary thiocyanate. *Preventive Medicine, 32*, 82–88. http://doi.org/10.1006/pmed.2000.0779

Naar-King, S., Parsons, J. T., Murphy, D. A., Chen, X., Harris, R., & Belzer, M. E. (2009). Improving health outcomes for youth living with the human immunodeficiency virus: A multisite randomized trial of a motivational intervention targeting multiple risk behaviors. *Archives of Pediatric and Adolescent Medicine, 163*, 1092–1098. http://doi.org/10.1001/archpediatrics.2009.212

Natarajan, L., Flatt, S. W., Sun, X., Gamst, A. C., Major, J. M., Rock, C. L., … Pierce, J. P. (2006). Validity and systematic error in measuring carotenoid consumption with dietary self-report instruments. *American Journal of Epidemiology, 163*, 770–778. http://doi.org/10.1093/aje/kwj082

Natarajan, L., Pu, M., Fan, J., Levine, R. A., Patterson, R. E., Thomson, C., … Pierce, J. P. (2010). Measurement error of dietary self-report in intervention trials. *American Journal of Epidemiology, 172*, 819–287. http://doi.org/10.1093/aje/kwq216

Plasqui, G., & Westerterp, K. R. (2007). Physical activity assessment with accelerometers: An evaluation against doubly labeled water. *Obesity, 15*, 2371–2379. http://doi.org/10.1038/oby.2007.281

Roberts, C., Currie, C., Samdal, O., Currie, D., Smith, R., & Maes, L. (2007). Measuring the health and health behaviors of adolescents through cross-national survey research: Recent developments in the Health Behavior in School-aged Children (NBSC) study. *Journal of Public Health, 15*, 179–186. http://doi.org/10.1007/s10389-007-0100-x

Rutishauser, I. H. E., & Black, A. E. (2002). Introduction to human nutrition. In M. Gibney, H. Vorster, & F. J. Kok (Eds.), *The nutrition society textbook series* (pp. 225–248) Oxford, UK: Blackwell.

Shiffman, S. (2009). How many cigarettes did you smoke? Assessing cigarette consumption by global report, time-line follow-back, and ecological momentary assessment. *Health Psychology, 28*, 519–526. http://doi.org/10.1037/a0015197

Shiffman, S., Stone, A. A., & Hufford, M. R. (2008). Ecological momentary assessment. *Annual Review of Clinical Psychology, 1*, 1–32. http://doi.org/10.1146/annurev.clinpsy.3.022806.091415

Simmons, S. F., & Reuben, D. (2000). Nutritional intake monitoring for nursing home residents: A comparison of staff documentation, direct observation, and photography methods. *Journal of the American Geriatric Society, 48*, 209–213. http://doi.org/10.1111/j.1532-5415.2000.tb03914.x

Simoni, J. M., Kurth, A. E., Pearson, C. R., Pantalone, D. W., Merrill, J. O., & Frick, P. A. (2006). Self-report measures of antiretroviral therapy adherence: A review with recommendations for HIV research and clinical management. *AIDS Behavior, 10*, 227–245. http://doi.org/10.1007/s10461-006-9078-6

Van Remoortel, H., Giavedoni, S., Raste, Y., Burtin, C., Louvaris, Z., Gimeno-Santos, E., … Troosters, T. (2012). Validity of activity monitors in health and chronic disease: A systematic review. *International Journal of Behavioral Nutrition and Physical Activity, 9*, 84. http://doi.org/10.1186/1479-5868-9-84

Webb, T. L., Sheeran, P., & Luszczynska, A. (2009). Planning to break unwanted habits: habit strength moderates implementation intention effects on behaviour change. *British Journal of Social Psychology, 48*, 507–523. http://doi.org/10.1348/014466608X370591

Wrieden, W., Peace, H., & Barton, K., (2003). *A short review of dietary assessment methods used in National and Scottish Research Studies*. Aberdeen, UK: Food Standards Agency in Scotland.

Chapter 6
Patient–Physician Communication and Patient Satisfaction

Kelly B. Haskard-Zolnierek[1] and Summer L. Williams[2]

[1]Department of Psychology, Texas State University, San Marcos, TX, USA
[2]Department of Psychology, Westfield State University, Westfield, MA, USA

Introduction

The delivery of medical care involves not only technical skill and expertise but also interpersonal skills, such as good communication and empathy. The art of medicine has received extensive research attention in recent years, especially as it relates to outcomes of medical care. In particular, effective physician–patient communication is associated with numerous outcomes of clinical significance, such as patient satisfaction (Ong, de Haes, Hoos, & Lammes, 1995) and patient adherence (Zolnierek & DiMatteo, 2009). Patient satisfaction is the most frequently assessed outcome measure in studies of the effects of physician–patient communication (Ong et al., 1995).

Health psychology researchers may be particularly interested in physician–patient communication and patient satisfaction as these are central constructs in health services research investigations into quality of health care and efforts to improve health care. For those who work in the practice of health psychology, communication skills are an increasing area of emphasis in medical schools and residency training programs. Health psychologists may be potential instructors and assessors of communication skills in such settings. In addition, patient satisfaction is frequently used in hospitals and other health-care settings as a measure of quality of health care; thus, those in practice may be involved in such measurement efforts or in using the findings to make system-level changes.

Assessment/Measurement Issues in Physician–Patient Communication

Communication Channels: Verbal and Nonverbal Communication

Researchers in the field of physician–patient communication have assessed both verbal (e.g., information gathering, decision making) and nonverbal (e.g., voice tone, eye contact, body positioning and gestures, facial expressions) communication, although nonverbal communication has historically received less research attention (Beck, Daughtridge, & Sloane, 2002; Henry, Fuhrel-Forbis, Rogers, & Eggly, 2012).

What Is Communicated: Socioemotional and Instrumental Communication

Researchers have often categorized physician–patient communication into two broad areas: socioemotional or affective communication and instrumental or task-oriented communication (Ben-Sira, 1980; Bensing & Dronkers, 1992). Socioemotional/affective communication began to receive research attention in the 1970s and 1980s when evidence indicated that patients valued the interpersonal facets of their medical care as much as their physicians' technical skills (DiMatteo, Friedman, & Taranta, 1979; DiMatteo, Hays, & Prince, 1986; DiMatteo, Taranta, Friedman, & Prince, 1980). Measured socioemotional communication behaviors include expressions of friendliness or concern, expressions of empathy, inviting the patient to discuss psychological or social issues, being reassuring or supportive, discussing nonmedical issues (small talk), and exchanging pleasantries such as introducing oneself and referring to the patient by name. Measurement might also include nonverbal behaviors such as smiling, actively listening, or touching the patient.

Instrumental/task-oriented communication is primarily verbal, but may also be written, such as in patient leaflets, and comprises information seeking, information giving, and information verifying (Cegala, 1997) and typically emphasizes the discussion of biomedical topics (Roter et al., 1997). Instrumental utterances include counseling the patient, discussing test results, discussing medications or giving directions, explaining a diagnosis, and asking history-taking questions, among others. Other scholars have suggested that two general styles of communication, affiliation and control, are demonstrated by physicians in medical interactions (Buller & Buller, 1987). According to the group of scholars who penned the Kalamazoo Consensus Statement, essential tasks of communication in a typical medical visit involve: (a) building a relationship/developing rapport, (b) opening the discussion, (c) collecting information, (d) understanding where the patient is coming from, (e) giving information, (f) coming to agreement on the diagnosis and treatment plan, and (g) providing closure (Makoul, 2001).

How Physician–Patient Communication Data Are Collected

These different categories and elements of communication are measured to understand the aspects of the interpersonal interaction between physician and patient and how this communication affects different outcomes, such as patient satisfaction, patient adherence, physician satisfaction, and patient health outcomes. In studies of the relationship of communication and patient satisfaction, communication is typically assessed by trained observers. Medical visit interactions are most often audiotaped, videotaped, and/or transcribed and are infrequently assessed in real time. Regardless of whether the assessment is conducted in real time or not, it is an analysis of the actual interaction, not self-reports of the physician, the patient, or both.

Type of Assessment

The most common methods of measurement of communication are termed *rating* and *coding*. Rating, involves an observer or judge's subjective judgment of communicative behavior (e.g., physician warmth on a Likert-type scale), whereas coding is considered to be a more objective measure of occurrence of defined behaviors (e.g., number of reassuring/comforting statements over the course of a medical visit; Haskard, Williams, DiMatteo, Rosenthal et al., 2008). A rating approach assesses communicative behaviors globally, typically focusing on affective or expressive behaviors. Thus, for example, a researcher could *code* or count the number of times a patient asks questions in a clinical encounter, or a researcher could *rate* or judge the extent to which a patient seemed involved and questioning over the course of a clinical encounter. Some researchers prefer rating to coding for study of affective behavior as it can demonstrate higher validity since it does not require assumptions about the implications of coded behaviors (Rosenthal, 1966; Siminoff & Step, 2011). A coding system is also referred to as an *interactional analysis system* (e.g., Roter Interaction Analysis System [RIAS]), and such systems contain a number of communication categories in which every utterance is assigned to discrete categories. Other less frequently used approaches to studying the medical encounter include checklist-based methods and conversation analysis (Maynard & Heritage, 2005), which is a sociological approach to the analysis of medical visit communication. Description of these is beyond the scope of the present chapter.

Challenges of Measuring Physician–Patient Communication

There are several major challenges in the measurement of physician–patient communication. One is the logistics of assessing provider–patient communication. Frequently, physician–patient communication is not measured by live observers but is rather videotaped, audiotaped, or transcribed (all of which can be quite time-consuming). Later, verbal or nonverbal behavior (or sometimes both) is assessed. Assessing vocal tone, for example, involves a process called *content-filtering*, in which audiotaped interactions are edited and the frequencies of sound associated with words are removed (Haskard, Williams, DiMatteo, Heritage, & Rosenthal, 2008). Observers must be trained, which can be quite time-intensive for more complex coding schemes.

Establishing Validity and Reliability

Establishing validity in the area of physician–patient communication involves demonstrating predictive or concurrent validity, in that communication should have real-world relevance in its correlations with outcomes such as patient satisfaction, patient adherence, and patient health outcomes, among others. Criterion validity would ideally be measured to assess if the numerous measures of communication are measuring the same phenomena; unfortunately, this type of validity is rarely assessed. Most studies use multiple observers as raters/coders, and interrater reliability or rater/coder agreement must be assessed with appropriate levels of reliability demonstrated.

Choosing a Measurement Instrument

Several scholars have noted there is a lack of agreement by researchers in the field on what aspects of communication are important to measure, as evidenced by the diversity of coding measurement systems that exist (Beck et al., 2002). The first study to examine provider–patient communication systematically and relate it to patient satisfaction was published in 1968 (Korsch, Gozzi, & Francis, 1968). A 1988 review of the measures used in this literature reported 28 analysis systems used in 61 studies (Roter, Hall, & Katz, 1988). According to the review authors, many of these measures were created by the researchers for use in their own study or set of studies conducted by their research group. A more recent review (Boon & Stewart, 1998) described 44 total instruments, 28 of which were used for measuring communication in research endeavors. The RIAS, which was developed in the late 1970s, is the most widely used interactional analysis system (Roter & Larson, 2002) and has been used in numerous studies of physician–patient communication conducted all over the world.

Brief Description of Main Measures of Physician–Patient Communication

In the area of physician–patient communication, several thorough reviews document and provide an overview of numerous measures available for use in this field, and we refer the interested reader to these reviews for more information on measures that are not described here (Boon & Stewart, 1998; Ong et al., 1995; Roter & Hall, 1989). In addition, Henry and colleagues conducted a thorough review of the association between nonverbal communication and patient outcomes, including satisfaction, which describes measures used and relevant findings (Henry et al., 2012). In Table 6.1, we offer an overview of the most frequently used interaction analysis system (the RIAS), as well as several others that have been frequently used (the Davis Observation Code [DOC] and the Bales Interaction Process Analysis). The RIAS provides a list of categories of communication used by both physician and patient and is applicable to a range of medical care settings. Trained coders assess the communication of both provider and patient using audiotapes or videotapes. The DOC measures the content of physician–patient interactions related to both diagnosis and treatment of disease and health promotion endeavors in videotapes or live interactions, and it requires trained coders. The Bales method (a precursor of the RIAS) focuses on measuring instrumental behavior and information exchange behaviors and was first developed to code transcripts but can also be used to code audiotapes or videotapes (using trained coders).

There are other less frequently used rating scale approaches and nonverbal measurement approaches (Hall, Roter, & Rand, 1981; Haskard, Williams, DiMatteo, Rosenthal et al., 2008). Some of the more commonly used/more reliably rated items (that are used in various scales such as the RIAS, among others) include the following: angry, sympathetic/kind/warm, dominant/controlling, anxious/worried/nervous. They are commonly rated on a verbal rating scale and listed in a bipolar or unipolar format. The Bayer Global Rating Scale includes eight physician items, four patient items, and two items about the interaction between the two (Haskard, Williams, DiMatteo, Rosenthal et al., 2008); a sample item is "The physician connected with the patient as a person." This measure produces four subscales of physician and patient behavior that are related to both instrumental and socioemotional communication aspects. For readers interested in measurement of physicians' nonverbal sensitivity (i.e., physician's skill at recognizing and understanding patients' nonverbal cues indicate of affective, cognitive or physical states), we refer to the Profile of Nonverbal Sensitivity (Rosenthal, Hall, DiMatteo, Rogers, & Archer, 1979).

Numerous authors have used a global ratings approach to assess nonverbal behavior of physicians and patients. Hall and colleagues' work (Hall et al., 1981) is considered a classic paper examining the relationship between affective communication and outcomes, including patient satisfaction, whereas the work of Haskard and colleagues (Haskard et al., 2008) is a more recent example.

Table 6.1. Measures of physician–patient communication

Name	Number of items	Reliability	Validity	Subscales	How to obtain
Roter Interaction Analysis System (RIAS; Roter & Larson, 2002)	34 categories of communication (physician); 28 categories of communication (patient)	0.85 Interrater (across multiple studies conducted by Roter and colleagues) (Roter & Larson, 2002)	Predictive validity demonstrated (facets of communication predicting patient and physician satisfaction, malpractice claims, patient recall of information, among others)	Instrumental: giving directions, asking questions, giving information; counseling Socioemotional: social behavior, verbal attentiveness, showing concern, negative talk	http://www.riasworks.com/index.html
Davis Observation Code (Callahan & Bertakis, 1991)	20 categories in checklist format	Agreement between raters = 83% (Boon & Stewart, 1998)	Face validity (Boon & Stewart, 1998)	Six clusters of physician behavior: technical, health behavior, addiction, patient activation, preventive services, and counseling	See Callahan & Bertakis (1991)
Bales Interaction Process Analysis	12 categories	0.91 (Inui et al., 1982)	Convergent validity – correlated with patient adherence, patient satisfaction, some correlation with RIAS (Boon & Stewart, 1998)	Two domains: task and socioemotional	See Bales (1951)

Assessment/Measurement Issues in Patient Satisfaction

Definition of Construct

Patient satisfaction is one clinical outcome that has received extensive research attention in relation to physician–patient communication. As patients have become consumers of health care, patient satisfaction has been recognized as one critical aspect of quality of care.

Definition and Facets of Patient Satisfaction

According to Ware and colleagues (Ware, Snyder, Wright, & Davies, 1983), patient satisfaction ratings "capture a personal evaluation of care that cannot be known by observing care directly" (p. 247). These authors suggested these ratings of care include the patient's preferences, the patient's expectations, and the actual medical care experienced. Indeed, this construct and its measures may reflect patient perceptions of the physician's communication or the interpersonal quality of care. Different researchers define (and therefore measure) the construct in different ways. Two meta-analyses of the patient satisfaction literature grouped articles into the following domains of satisfaction: overall, access to care, cost of care, overall quality, humaneness, competence, amount of information given by provider, physical facility, provider attention to patient psychosocial issues, continuity of care, and outcome of care (Hall & Dornan, 1988a, 1988b).

Data Collection Methods

Patient satisfaction is measured by self-report either by phone, mail, or in-person interview or survey. One widely used measure (the Patient Satisfaction Questionnaire) assesses general or global satisfaction with care, and satisfaction with individual elements of care including technical quality, interpersonal manner, communication, financial aspects, time spent with doctor, and accessibility and convenience (Marshall & Hays, 1994; Ware, Snyder, & Wright, 1976). Patient satisfaction is measured as an indicator of quality of care, and, for the purposes of this review, as an outcome of physician–patient communication, suggesting that effective communication may be linked to greater patient satisfaction.

Measurement Challenges

There are several possible challenges in measurement of patient satisfaction. Some of the major concerns of such measures include the following: concern with whether patients have the technical/medical knowledge to assess their medical care (Manary, Boulding, Staelin, & Glickman, 2013), concern with high reported levels of satisfaction across studies (Williams, Coyle, & Healy, 1998), and concern with bias in patient recall of their medical care experiences (Aharony & Strasser, 1993), among others. One researcher expressed concerns with lack of standardization, low reliability and unknown validity of instruments, and lack of theoretical basis of instruments (Pascoe, 1983).

Brief Description of Main Measures of Patient Satisfaction

Overview

In the area of patient satisfaction, particularly as related to physician–patient communication, one frequently used measure is the Patient Satisfaction Questionnaire (PSQ; Ware et al., 1976). The original measure contains 80 items and subsequent versions include the PSQ-III (50 items) and the PSQ-18. We describe the PSQ-18 (Marshall & Hays, 1994). The Medical Interview Satisfaction Scale (MISS; Wolf, Putnam, James, & Stiles, 1978) measures satisfaction with a particular interaction with a physician. There are numerous measures of satisfaction designed to measure and improve quality of care. One well-known measure is the Consumer Assessment of Healthcare Providers and Systems (CAHPS), which includes surveys of satisfaction with clinicians, hospital care, and other dimensions of health care. The CAHPS measure of clinicians and groups will be described here (Dyer, Sorra, Smith, Cleary, & Hays, 2012). These measures are presented in Table 6.2.

Table 6.2. Measures of patient satisfaction

Name	Number of items	Reliability	Validity	Subscales	How to obtain
Patient Satisfaction Questionnaire-18 (PSQ-18)	18	0.72 (average across subscales)	Convergent validity (strong correlations with 50-item version of measure (PSQ-III)	General satisfaction, technical quality, interpersonal manner, communication, financial aspects, time spent with doctor, and accessibility and convenience	This measure is freely available through the RAND Corporation website: http://www.rand.org/health/surveys_tools/psq.html
Medical Interview Satisfaction Scale (MISS-29; Wolf et al., 1978; developed for use in British general practice consultations)	29	0.93 for total scale	Predictive validity (significant correlations with clinically related physician and patient behaviors)	Distress relief, communication comfort, rapport, and compliance intent	See Wolf et al. (1978)
Medical Interview Satisfaction Scale-21 (modification of MISS; Meakin & Weinman, 2002; developed based on examination of psychometric properties and refinement of MISS-29)	21	0.67–0.92 internal consistency (range across subscales)	Construct validity (significant correlations between scores on the MISS-21 and aspects of patient satisfaction with past visits)	Same as MISS	See Meakin & Weinman (2002)
Consumer Assessment of Healthcare Providers and Systems – Clinician and Group Surveys (CG-CAHPS; Dyer et al., 2012)	28 nondemographic items (assessment of a single visit)	Acceptable individual-level internal consistency, reliability, and practice site level reliability (> 0.70)	Construct validity (significant correlations between composites and single global rating items from the same scale)	Three composites: (1) courteous/helpful staff, (2) doctor communication, and (3) access to care	Public access measures available through the Agency for Health Care Research and Quality website: https://cahps.ahrq.gov/surveys-guidance/cg/instructions/index.html

Establishing Validity and Reliability of Measures

Typically, internal consistency is assessed and established for patient satisfaction measures. Establishment of validity can involve demonstration of predictive validity and convergent validity (in examining correlations between longer and shorter versions of the same scale).

Key Studies and Research Findings of Relevant Measures of Physician–Patient Communication and Patient Satisfaction

An extensive literature documents the relationship between physician–patient communication and patient satisfaction. One review describes findings from studies conducted up to 1998 documenting the relationship between different aspects of communication (information provision, information seeking, relational and affective communication, and the communication style of the physician) and patient satisfaction (Williams, Weinman, & Dale, 1998). It is helpful to review research findings to get a sense of some of the measures described in this chapter. One of the earliest published studies used a modified version of the Bales analysis approach (Korsch et al., 1968). In this study, 800 pediatric physician–parent (patient) interactions were recorded and analyzed. Interviews were conducted after the visits to assess satisfaction, among other outcomes. Findings revealed that on the whole, parents were satisfied with the communication by their children's physicians (76%). However, the researchers in this seminal study reported that patients were more dissatisfied when their physicians lacked warmth/friendliness (i.e., socioemotional communication), and when the parents/patients did not receive clear information and thorough explanation of the child's disease (i.e., instrumental communication).

Numerous studies have applied the RIAS (a reliable and valid measure of communication) to the analysis of the medical visit and relationship between communication and satisfaction. Thus, we report two classic, frequently cited papers. In the first, 550 visits were recorded and analyzed using the RIAS (Bertakis, Roter, & Putnam, 1991). Patient satisfaction was measured using a 43-item scale developed for the study and modified from measures used by past researchers (Inui, Carter, Kukull, & Haigh, 1982; Roter, Hall, & Katz, 1987). Task-directed skill by the physician (instrumental communication) was the strongest predictor of patient satisfaction. Of all of the categories of physician communication measured, communication about psychosocial topics (an aspect of socioemotional communication) was most consistently related to patient satisfaction. Patients were less satisfied when physicians used a dominant tone or talked significantly more than the patient. In another study of the relationship between primary care physicians' communication patterns and patient satisfaction, Roter and colleagues audiotaped 537 primary care visits and analyzed these using the RIAS (Roter et al., 1997). Physician communication categories measured by RIAS were grouped into patterns using cluster analysis: narrowly biomedical, expanded biomedical, biopsychosocial, psychosocial, and consumerist (these are distinct from the socioemotional/instrumental dimensions described earlier in this chapter). The narrowly biomedical type or pattern (communication dominated by physician) was rated by patients as least satisfying (using the aforementioned 43-item scale). The psychosocial pattern (marked by more patient talk, dialogue about social and emotional issues of the patient, and therapeutic role of the physician) was the most satisfying for patients (although occurred less frequently than some of the other patterns of communication).

The DOC has been used to measure communication in numerous studies. In one classic study, the researchers videotaped 100 new patient visits to primary care physicians. Physician behavior was assessed using the DOC and satisfaction was measured with a visit-specific satisfaction questionnaire. Patients were most satisfied when their physicians spent time in the visit discussing health education and effects of treatments the patient was undergoing. Patients were also satisfied with more time spent during the physical exam. Patients were less satisfied when extended time was spent in the history-taking portion of the visit (Robbins et al., 1993).

The PSQ-18 was recently used in a study of the association of affect in content-filtered speech (voice) and patient satisfaction (Haskard, Williams, DiMatteo, Heritage et al., 2008). In one study, a modification of the PSQ-18 was used to assess satisfaction with 61 physicians and 81 nurses in a primary care setting. Affect in voice tone was rated by naïve judges using a rating scale developed for the purposes of the study. Physicians' professional manner in rated voice tone was correlated with patients' overall satisfaction. Also, patients revealed their satisfaction (as measured by a modification of the PSQ) with physicians' competence and personal manner through a more positive tone of voice.

The MISS was used in a questionnaire-based study, which assessed satisfaction and perceptions of patient-centered communication in 865 general practice visits. There was an association between patient satisfaction and communication/partnership behaviors on the part of physicians (i.e., physicians communicated with patients about their concerns, and discussed and came to agreement with them on the diagnosis and treatment; Little et al., 2001).

Comments and Conclusion

As reported here, there are numerous measures available for assessment of both physician–patient communication and patient satisfaction. Thus, the decisions one needs to make include whether to design a new measure for the purposes of one's study or to use an existing measure. The process of developing a reliable and valid measure may be a time-consuming one; subsequently, many researchers may choose an existing measure. If researchers are developing a new measure, they would be advised to establish the reliability and validity of the measure as described in this chapter.

It is important to keep several logistical challenges in mind when embarking on a study of physician–patient communication. Training raters or coders to use these measures is likely necessary, particularly with the coding systems. Collecting interactions to assess involves a decision about medium or channel of communication, verbal or nonverbal, from video-taped, audio-taped, or even content-filtered interactions. This decision will depend on the goals of the study and the aspects of communication the researchers are most interested in. The actual process of rating or coding numerous interactions is also a time-intensive one, so the nature of this process must be taken into account.

In addition, researchers are often concerned that physicians and patients change their behavior because they are being recorded. In fact, physicians and patients become relaxed over the course of recording of the medical visit, and patient privacy is preserved when providers turn the camera or cover the lens during the physical exam (Campbell, Murray, & Sullivan, 1996; Campbell, Sullivan, & Murray, 1995).

Choosing a patient satisfaction measure involves similar consideration of the numerous measures that are used and reflection about which aspects of patient satisfaction a researcher is trying to tap into (e.g., patient satisfaction with the physician's behavior or satisfaction with aspects of the clinic or medical setting, or both).

Future Directions

Despite the call to researchers in the field to agree on a unified theory of physician–patient communication (Beck et al., 2002; Ong et al., 1995; Roter & Hall, 1989), there is no one consistently agreed-upon model of communication in the medical interaction. This affects the measurement process and drives the use of a myriad of instruments to measure different aspects of communication. The field of measurement of physician–patient communication would benefit from agreement on what aspects of communication should be assessed. Regarding patient satisfaction, this is just one of several clinical outcomes of medical care. Some of the most striking findings related to physician–patient communication have been those showing effects on other outcomes, such as clinical outcomes (Kaplan, Greenfield, & Ware, 1989). Researchers in the field should continue to examine the relationship of communication to multiple patient outcomes.

Another important area of communication that can be further explored is effective cross-cultural communication (see Chapter 20 in this volume) and its importance to patient outcomes such as patient adherence and satisfaction. Health-care professionals are increasingly being encouraged to practice culturally sensitive medicine with their patients. Culturally sensitive medicine involves various dimensions of a patient's cultural context such as social class, age, race, ethnicity, and gender, as well as less visible characteristics of the patient such as their health beliefs, values, preferences, and role orientations (Cooper, Beach, Johnson, & Inui, 2006).

There are few studies comparing physician–patient communication with ethnic minority and majority patients; however, there is evidence that disparities exist among these patients in the quality of communication that they receive from health-care providers (Cooper & Roter, 2002; Schouten & Meeuwesen, 2006; Verlinde, De Laender, De Maesschalck, Deveugele, & Willems, 2012). Even fewer studies compare communication of health-care providers with patients of varying socioeconomic backgrounds and insurance status (e.g., in the US, private health insurance, employer-based health insurance, and Medicaid or Medicare). Cultural differences can lead to a host of difficulties in communication between providers and patients, such as lower levels of patient engagement (Johnson, Roter, Powe, & Cooper, 2004) and lower levels of psychosocial affect and rapport-building (Cene, Roter, Carson, Miller, & Cooper, 2009). There are currently training interventions aimed at improving physician–patient communication within culturally sensitive domains (Cene et al., 2009; Cooper et al., 2012) and this will continue to be an area of expansion in the continuing medical education of health-care professionals. Communication training for patients is also key, as teaching them to participate in their care influences physician satisfaction with the medical visit and increases the likelihood that physicians will better understand the needs of their patients (Haskard, Williams, DiMatteo, Rosenthal et al., 2008). Overall, it is evident that communication training for patients and physicians will continue to be at the forefront of clinical practice and education, as the impact on patient outcomes is well established.

References

Aharony, L., & Strasser, S. (1993). Patient satisfaction: What we know about and what we still need to explore. *Medical Care Review, 50*(1), 49–79. http://doi.org/10.1177/002570879305000104

Bales, R. F. (1951). *Interaction process analysis: A method for the study of small groups*. Cambridge, MA: Addison-Wesley.

Beck, R. S., Daughtridge, R., & Sloane, P. D. (2002). Physician-patient communication in the primary care office: A systematic review. *Journal of the American Board of Family Practice, 15*(1), 25–38.

Ben-Sira, Z. (1980). Affective and instrumental components in the physician-patient relationship: An additional dimension of interaction theory. *Journal of Health and Social Behavior, 21*, 170–180. http://doi.org/10.2307/2136736

Bensing, J. M., & Dronkers, J. (1992). Instrumental and affective aspects of physician behavior. *Medical Care, 30*, 283–298. http://doi.org/10.1097/00005650-199204000-00001

Bertakis, K. D., Roter, D. L., & Putnam, S. M. (1991). The relationship of physician medical interview style to patient satisfaction. *Journal of Family Practice, 32*, 175–181.

Boon, H., & Stewart, M. (1998). Patient-physician communication assessment instruments: 1986 to 1996 in review. *Patient Education and Counseling, 35*, 161–176.

Buller, M. K., & Buller, D. B. (1987). Physicians' communication style and patient satisfaction. *Journal of Health and Social Behavior, 28*, 375–388. http://doi.org/10.2307/2136791

Callahan, E. J., & Bertakis, K. D. (1991). Development and validation of the Davis Observation Code. *Family Medicine, 23*(1), 19–24.

Campbell, L. M., Murray, T. S., & Sullivan, F. M. (1996). Videotaping of general practice consultations. *British Medical Journal, 312*, 248. http://doi.org/10.1136/bmj.312.7025.248b

Campbell, L. M., Sullivan, F., & Murray, T. S. (1995). Videotaping of general practice consultations: Effect on patient satisfaction. *British Medical Journal, 311*, 236. http://doi.org/10.1136/bmj.311.6999.236

Cegala, D. J. (1997). A study of doctors' and patients' communication during a primary care consultation: Implications for communication training. *Journal of Health Communication, 2*, 169–194. http://doi.org/10.1080/108107397127743

Cene, C. W., Roter, D. L., Carson, K. A., Miller, E. R., III, & Cooper, L. A. (2009). The effect of patient race and blood pressure control on patient-physician communication. *Journal of General Internal Medicine, 24*(9), 1057–1064. http://doi.org/10.1007/s11606-009-1051-4

Cooper, L. A., Beach, M. C., Johnson, R. L., & Inui, T. S. (2006). Delving below the surface. Understanding how race and ethnicity influence relationships in health care. *Journal of General Internal Medicine, 21*(Suppl. 1), S21–27. http://doi.org/10.1111/j.1525-1497.2006.00305.x

Cooper, L. A., & Roter, D. L. (2002). Patient-provider communication: The effect of race and ethnicity on process and outcomes of healthcare. In B. D. Smedley, A. Y. Stith, & A. R. Nelson (Eds.), *Unequal treatment: Confronting racial and ethnic disparities in healthcare* (pp. 522–593). Washington, DC: National Academies Press.

Cooper, L. A., Roter, D. L., Carson, K. A., Beach, M. C., Sabin, J. A., Greenwald, A. G., & Inui, T. S. (2012). The associations of clinicians' implicit attitudes about race with medical visit communication and patient ratings of interpersonal care. *American Journal of Public Health, 102*, 979–987. http://doi.org/10.2105/AJPH.2011.300558

DiMatteo, M. R., Friedman, H. S., & Taranta, A. (1979). Sensitivity to body nonverbal communication as a factor in practitioner-patient rapport. *Journal of Nonverbal Behavior, 4*(1), 18–26. http://doi.org/10.1007/BF00986909

DiMatteo, M. R., Hays, R. D., & Prince, L. M. (1986). Relationship of physicians' nonverbal communication skill to patient satisfaction, appointment noncompliance, and physician workload. *Health Psychology, 5*, 581–594. http://doi.org/10.1037/0278-6133.5.6.581

DiMatteo, M. R., Taranta, A., Friedman, H. S., & Prince, L. M. (1980). Predicting patient satisfaction from physicians' nonverbal communication skills. *Medical Care, 18*, 376–387.

Dyer, N., Sorra, J. S., Smith, S. a., Cleary, P. D., & Hays, R. D. (2012). Psychometric properties of the Consumer Assessment of Healthcare Providers and Systems (CAHPS(R)) Clinician and Group Adult Visit Survey. *Medical Care, 50*(Suppl.), S28–34. http://doi.org/10.1097/MLR.0b013e31826cbc0d

Hall, J. A., & Dornan, M. C. (1988a). Meta-analysis of satisfaction with medical care: Description of research domain and analysis of overall satisfaction levels. *Social Science and Medicine, 27*, 637–644. http://doi.org/10.1016/0277-9536(88)90012-3

Hall, J. A., & Dornan, M. C. (1988b). What patients like about their medical care and how often they are asked: A meta-analysis of the satisfaction literature. *Social Science and Medicine, 27*, 935–939. http://doi.org/10.1016/0277-9536(88)90284-5

Hall, J. A., Roter, D. L., & Rand, C. S. (1981). Communication of affect between patient and physician. *Journal of Health and Social Behavior, 22*(1), 18–30. http://doi.org/10.2307/2136365

Haskard, K. B., Williams, S. L., DiMatteo, M. R., Heritage, J., & Rosenthal, R. (2008). The provider's voice: Patient satisfaction and the content-filtered speech of nurses and physicians in primary medical care. *Journal of Nonverbal Behavior, 32*, 1–20. http://doi.org/10.1007/s10919-007-0038-2

Haskard, K. B., Williams, S. L., DiMatteo, M. R., Rosenthal, R., White, M. K., & Goldstein, M. G. (2008). Physician and patient communication training in primary care: Effects on participation and satisfaction. *Health Psychology, 27*, 513–522. http://doi.org/10.1037/0278-6133.27.5.513

Henry, S. G., Fuhrel-Forbis, A., Rogers, M. A., & Eggly, S. (2012). Association between nonverbal communication during clinical interactions and outcomes: A systematic review and meta-analysis. *Patient Education and Counseling, 86*, 297–315. http://doi.org/10.1016/j.pec.2011.07.006

Inui, T. S., Carter, W. B., Kukull, W. A., & Haigh, V. H. (1982). Outcome-based doctor-patient interaction analysis: I. Comparison of techniques. *Medical Care, 20*, 535–549. http://doi.org/10.1097/00005650-198206000-00001

Johnson, R. L., Roter, D. L., Powe, N. R., & Cooper, L. A. (2004). Patient race/ethnicity and quality of patient-physician communication during medical visits. *American Journal of Public Health, 94*, 2084–2090. http://doi.org/10.2105/AJPH.94.12.2084

Kaplan, S. H., Greenfield, S., & Ware, J. E., Jr. (1989). Assessing the effects of physician-patient interactions on the outcomes of chronic disease. *Medical Care, 27*(3 Suppl.), S110–127. http://doi.org/10.1097/00005650-198903001-00010

Korsch, B. M., Gozzi, E. K., & Francis, V. (1968). Gaps in doctor-patient communication. 1. Doctor-patient interaction and patient satisfaction. *Pediatrics, 42*, 855–871.

Little, P., Everitt, H., Williamson, I., Warner, G., Moore, M., Gould, C., ... Payne, S. (2001). Observational study of effect of patient centredness and positive approach on outcomes of general practice consultations. *British Medical Journal, 323*, 908–911. http://doi.org/10.1136/bmj.323.7318.908

Makoul, G. (2001). Essential elements of communication in medical encounters: The Kalamazoo consensus statement. *Academic Medicine, 76*, 390–393. http://doi.org/10.1097/00001888-200104000-00021

Manary, M. P., Boulding, W., Staelin, R., & Glickman, S. W. (2013). The patient experience and health outcomes. *New England Journal of Medicine, 368*, 201–203. http://doi.org/10.1056/NEJMp1211775

Marshall, G. N., & Hays, R. D. (1994). *The Patient Satisfaction Questionnaire Short-form (PSQ-18)*. Santa Monica, CA: RAND.

Maynard, D. W., & Heritage, J. (2005). Conversation analysis, doctor-patient interaction and medical communication. *Medical Education, 39*, 428–435. http://doi.org/10.1111/j.1365-2929.2005.02111.x

Meakin, R., & Weinman, J. (2002). The 'Medical Interview Satisfaction Scale' (MISS-21) adapted for British general practice. *Family Practice, 19*, 257–263. http://doi.org/10.1093/fampra/19.3.257

Ong, L. M., de Haes, J. C., Hoos, A. M., & Lammes, F. B. (1995). Doctor-patient communication: A review of the literature. *Social Science and Medicine, 40*, 903–918. http://doi.org/10.1016/0277-9536(94)00155-M

Pascoe, G. C. (1983). Patient satisfaction in primary health care: A literature review and analysis. *Evaluation and Program Planning, 6*(3–4), 185–210. http://doi.org/10.1016/0149-7189(83)90002-2

Robbins, J. A., Bertakis, K. D., Helms, L. J., Azari, R., Callahan, E. J., & Creten, D. A. (1993). The influence of physician practice behaviors on patient satisfaction. *Family Medicine, 25*(1), 17–20.

Rosenthal, R. (1966). *Experimenter effects in behavioral research*. East Norwalk, CT: Appleton-Century-Crofts.

Rosenthal, R., Hall, J. A., DiMatteo, M. R., Rogers, P. L., & Archer, D. (1979). *Sensitivity to nonverbal communication: The PONS Test*. Baltimore, MD: Johns Hopkins University Press.

Roter, D. L., & Hall, J. A. (1989). Studies of doctor-patient interaction. *Annual Review of Public Health, 10*, 163–180. http://doi.org/10.1146/annurev.pu.10.050189.001115

Roter, D. L., Hall, J. A., & Katz, N. R. (1987). Relations between physicians' behaviors and analogue patients' satisfaction, recall, and impressions. *Medical Care, 25*, 437–451. http://doi.org/10.1097/00005650-198705000-00007

Roter, D. L., Hall, J. A., & Katz, N. R. (1988). Patient-physician communication: A descriptive summary of the literature. *Patient Education and Counseling, 12*, 99–119. http://doi.org/10.1016/0738-3991(88)90057-2

Roter, D. L., & Larson, S. (2002). The Roter Interaction Analysis System (RIAS): Utility and flexibility for analysis of medical interactions. *Patient Education and Counseling, 46*, 243–251. http://doi.org/10.1016/S0738-3991(02)00012-5

Roter, D. L., Stewart, M., Putnam, S. M., Lipkin, M., Jr., Stiles, W., & Inui, T. S. (1997). Communication patterns of primary care physicians. *Journal of the American Medical Association, 277*, 350–356. http://doi.org/10.1001/jama.1997.03540280088045

Schouten, B. C., & Meeuwesen, L. (2006). Cultural differences in medical communication: A review of the literature. *Patient Education and Counseling, 64*(1–3), 21–34. http://doi.org/10.1016/j.pec.2005.11.014

Siminoff, L. A., & Step, M. M. (2011). A comprehensive observational coding scheme for analyzing instrumental, affective, and relational communication in health care contexts. *Journal of Health Communication, 16*, 178–197. http://doi.org/10.1080/10810730.2010.535109

Verlinde, E., De Laender, N., De Maesschalck, S., Deveugele, M., & Willems, S. (2012). The social gradient in doctor-patient communication. *International Journal of Equity in Health, 11*, 12. http://doi.org/10.1186/1475-9276-11-12

Ware, J. E., Snyder, M. K., & Wright, W. R. (1976). *Development and validation of scales to measure patient satisfaction with medical care services*. Springfield, VA: National Technical Information Service.

Ware, J. E., Snyder, M. K., Wright, W. R., & Davies, A. R. (1983). Defining and measuring patient satisfaction with medical care. *Evaluation and Program Planning, 6*, 247–263. http://doi.org/10.1016/0149-7189(83)90005-8

Williams, B., Coyle, J., & Healy, D. (1998). The meaning of patient satisfaction: An explanation of high reported levels. *Social Science and Medicine, 47*, 1351–1359. http://doi.org/10.1016/S0277-9536(98)00213-5

Williams, S., Weinman, J., & Dale, J. (1998). Doctor-patient communication and patient satisfaction: A review. *Family Practice, 15*, 480–492. http://doi.org/10.1093/fampra/15.5.480

Wolf, M. H., Putnam, S. M., James, S. a., & Stiles, W. B. (1978). The Medical Interview Satisfaction Scale: Development of a scale to measure patient perceptions of physician behavior. *Journal of Behavioral Medicine, 1*, 391–401. http://doi.org/10.1007/BF00846695

Zolnierek, K. B., & DiMatteo, M. R. (2009). Physician communication and patient adherence to treatment: A meta-analysis. *Medical Care, 47*, 826–834. http://doi.org/10.1097/MLR.0b013e31819a5acc

Chapter 7
Adherence to Medical Advice

Julie A. Chambers and Ronan E. O'Carroll

Department of Psychology, University of Stirling, UK

Background

Adherence to medical advice can be defined as the extent to which patients follow the instructions they are given for treatment for one or more medical conditions, as recommended by their medical practitioner. Adherence to treatment is vital for improved health outcomes yet adherence is often sub-optimal. Poor adherence may be particularly evident in chronic illnesses where patients are required to follow a prolonged and complex medical regime, with the result that many patients may not achieve the full benefits of their treatment (Horne, Weinman, Barber, Elliot, & Morgan, 2005). A comprehensive Cochrane review of adherence interventions determined that developing "effective ways to help people follow medical treatments could have far larger effects on health than any treatment itself" (Haynes, Ackloo, Sahota, McDonald, & Yao, 2008, p. 20).

Adherence behaviour may be better understood by applying Leventhal's common-sense model (CSM) of self-regulation of health and illness (Leventhal, Brissette, & Leventhal, 2003). In this model, a patient holds representations of their illness, based on abstract (e.g., news reports) and concrete (e.g., experience of symptoms) attributions. Patients exhibit a common-sense response to their cognitive and emotional interpretation of their illness by adopting coping behaviour (including adhering to treatment) to contain the threat to their health. Horne (2003) extended the CSM model (see Figure 7.1) by proposing that a patient's perceptions of treatment interact with their illness representations to determine adherence behaviour. For example, the disappearance of symptoms may lead to a perception that the treatment is no longer necessary, whereas continued symptoms may lead to the conclusion that the treatment is ineffective: both assumptions could lead to treatment cessation for difference reasons.

Intentional and Nonintentional Nonadherence

Individuals may consciously choose to ignore medical advice (intentional nonadherence) and/or may intend to adhere, but fail, due to specific circumstances such as forgetting (nonintentional nonadherence). Intentional nonadherence is influenced by a patient's beliefs about their illness and/or treatment (Clifford, Barber, & Horne, 2008), in particular an evaluation of the perceived *necessity* of medication versus *concerns* about possible harmful effects, and represents a conscious choice made by the patient, after deliberation of numerous interacting factors. Nonintentional nonadherence may depend on a patient's ability to develop adequate habitual routines, and is associated with automatic behaviour, triggered by environmental cues.

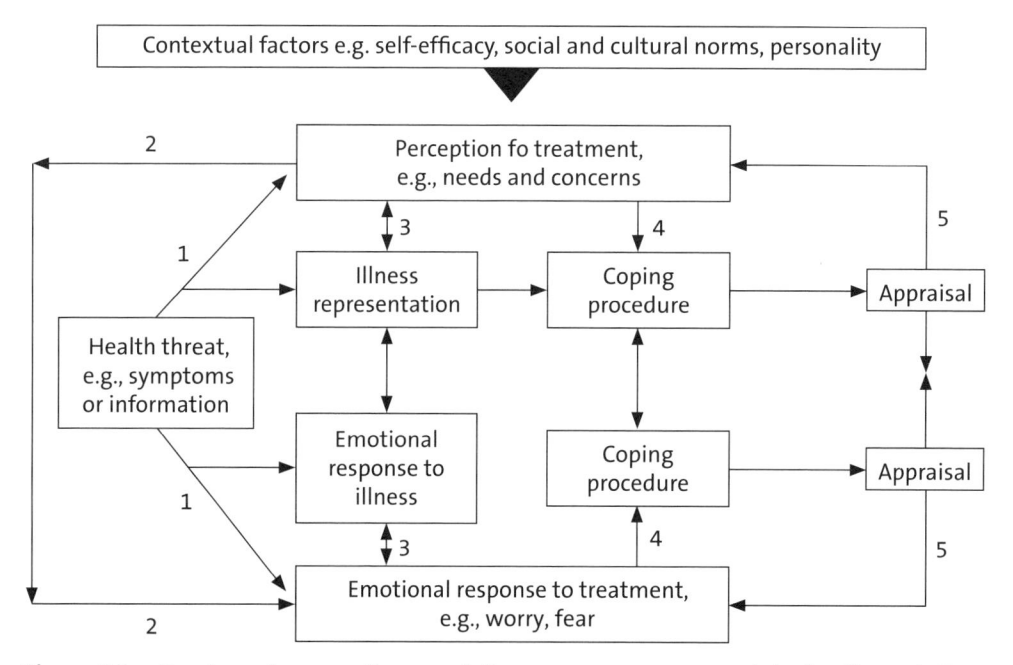

Figure 7.1. Treatment perceptions and the common-sense model of self-regulation. The numbered paths shown in the diagram represent: (1) symptom experiences and information trigger treatment perceptions, depending on attribution of cause – for example, illness attribution reinforces treatment necessity, attribution to side-effects reinforces concerns; (2) parallel processing of cognitive and emotional representations of treatments – for example, "Having to take this treatment worries me"; (3) illness perceptions and treatment beliefs have an internal logic as the individual strives for common-sense coherence; (4) treatment perceptions influence adherence – adherence and nonadherence are both types of coping procedures; (5) the outcome of adherence/nonadherence is appraised with subsequent reinforcement or change in treatment representations. (Reproduced with permission from Horne, R. (2003). Treatment perceptions and self-regulation. In L. D. Cameron & H. Leventhal (Eds.), *The self-regulation of health and illness behavior* (Figure 7.2 and explanatory text on pp. 147–148). Abingdon, UK: Routledge.)

It may be particularly evident in elderly people with cognitive difficulties who are likely to be on long-term, multiple medications for chronic conditions (Hayes, Larimer, Adami, & Kaye, 2009).

Relevance to Health Psychology Research and Practice

If patients often choose to not adhere to treatment, should we, as health professionals, interfere? Surely it is their right to decide whether to follow medical advice or not? The apparent answer is yes; however, for many people, not adhering to treatment may be due to a failure to enact their intention to adhere and/or a consequence of poorly informed decision making. The benefits of adherence (as related to treatment success) are wide-ranging and apply to both the patients themselves and the wider community in terms of fewer symptoms, reduced sick leave, fewer complications, fewer hospitalizations, less disability and hence reduced costs of further treatment and later mortality (Gonzalez & Schneider, 2011). Therefore, increasing adherence to effective treatment is important from a patient, health professional, and societal perspective.

Measuring Adherence to Medical Advice

Adherence to medical advice may cover all aspects of self-management of an illness or condition, as recommended by a health practitioner, including: (a) taking medication (e.g., tablets, injections, inhalers, eye drops) including initiation, persistence, and correct dosing; (b) self-monitoring and/or self-care, for example, checking glucose levels/blood pressure, self-examination (e.g., for lumps or changes in appearance of moles), carrying out physiotherapy exercises; (c) health behaviour (e.g., ceasing smoking, reducing alcohol consumption, exercising, changing diet); (d) losing weight; (e) attending appointments (e.g., medical check-ups, X-rays, follow-up after treatment, dental appointments); (f) hospital discharge (i.e., against medical advice); and (g) participating in screening programmes (e.g., breast cancer, colorectal cancer).

The last four of these behaviours (d–g) can be easily measured, that is, by weighing, checking attendance/discharge records or screening databases, and so these are not covered further in this chapter. There are many available measures of health-related behaviour (item c) that could be used to detect changes in behaviour; this topic is covered in Chapter 5 of this volume. Thus, the present chapter will focus on item a, measurement of adherence to medication, whilst including consideration of item b, self-monitoring and/or self-care.

Why Measure Adherence to Treatment?

Treatment failure resulting from poor adherence leads to significant negative consequences including financial costs (e.g., wasted medication and further treatment), the development of medication-resistant strains (e.g., HIV drugs, antibiotics) and/or can result in health practitioners basing prescribing decisions on inaccurate information (e.g., about the effectiveness of current dose). For some illnesses and/or medications, very high levels of adherence may be necessary to achieve therapeutic benefit (e.g., adherence levels of 95% may be needed to effectively control the HIV virus and reduce infections, hospital stays, and deaths; Paterson et al., 2000). Thus, accurate assessment of adherence to medical advice can be crucial in enabling health practitioners to identify and target patients with sub-optimal adherence who may need intervention.

Interventions aimed at increasing adherence to medical advice have had limited success (Haynes et al., 2008); thus it is important that adherence is accurately measured in order to demonstrate whether a clear effect has occurred and also to permit comparison between studies. If measurement of adherence is poor, then evaluation of the success or otherwise of interventions may be a reflection of the inability of the measure to accurately reflect adherence behaviour, rather than the effectiveness of the intervention itself. In addition, measures should ideally be able to detect both intentional and nonintentional aspects of nonadherence, as these are related to differing underlying causes that require different approaches in order to increase adherence. Thus, accurate, consistent measurement of adherence is essential for researchers and clinicians.

Challenges of Measuring Adherence to Medical Advice

Adherence measurement may be particularly prone to social desirability and/or measurement reactivity effects. Patients may not want their doctors to know that their advice is being modified or ignored, and so choose to provide a favourable (socially desirable) view of their adherence behaviour. As many adherence measures are impossible to administer without the patient's knowledge, patients may also endeavour to increase their adherence during the measurement period (the *mere measurement* effect). Both can lead to biases in conclusions about treatment and/or intervention success. The assessment of adherence in children may be prone to further bias, as the method of measurement is likely to require parental intervention.

Methods of Measuring Treatment Adherence

Many measures of medication adherence focus on whether or not medications have been taken and ignore the fact that some individuals deliberately choose not to take medications as prescribed. Measures of adherence to self-care regimes usually encompass medication adherence alongside behaviours specific to the condition such as checking blood sugar levels in diabetes, but also may include measures of healthy behaviours such as exercising or following dietary recommendations.

Advantages and disadvantages of the types of currently available adherence measures are summarized in Table 7.1. Most of these methods are viewed as indirect, that is, they are a representation of behaviour, rather than a direct measure of the behaviour itself. Apart from *direct observation* (which is impractical in most settings), none of the listed approaches are likely to give a 100% accurate figure on actual ingestion of medication or performance of self-care behaviours. Electronic pill-devices (such as the Medication Event Monitoring System; MEMS® Aardex Ltd., Switzerland) objectively record the date and time of container openings in an electronic chip, which is downloaded to a computer for later analysis; thus they may be less prone to error (such as recall bias) than other methods. However, they are costly and impractical for use except for relatively short periods in research settings.

Pill-count may be an easy, cost-effective way of checking tablet usage, but it can easily be "fixed" by participants (e.g., by pill dumping, that is, discarding untaken medicine prior to visits), and may rely on the participant remembering to bring their medication (e.g., to a pharmacy). Home pill-counts by health practitioners are likely to be the most accurate, but unannounced telephone pill-counts may provide a valid, reliable alternative (Kalichman et al., 2007). The medication possession ratio (MPR; defined as % of doses dispensed or prescribed divided by number of scheduled doses between refills) offers an easy, usually electronic, check of medication obtained by patients; however, this is also open to inaccuracies as patients are known to stock pile medicines (e.g., before a holiday period). *Health practitioner assessment* of medications taken depends on the quality of communication between the health practitioner and patient, and has shown poor validity when compared with other measures of medication adherence. *Assessment of biological markers* (e.g., urine assay) may help identify ingestion of some, but by no means all, medications, and the timing of collection of the assessment medium is crucial. *Clinical outcomes* may be too variable (e.g., blood pressure) or too slow to change (e.g., cholesterol levels) to provide an accurate picture of short-term medication adherence at an individual level. They may also reflect a failure in other factors unrelated to the ingestion of the medicine, such as inadequate dosing or ineffective medication; thus they are unlikely to be reliable as a proxy measure of pill-taking.

Table 7.1. Methods of adherence measurement

Type of measure Adherence measured	How measured	Advantages	Disadvantages/issues
Pill-count Medication	• % Pills missing divided by pills dispensed (home, telephone, clinic, pharmacy)	• Simple to use • Can be consistent across studies • Can be conducted by telephone (relatively inexpensive)	• May rely on access to pill supply for health practitioners or researchers • No information on dosing/whether ingested • Easy to fix (e.g., pill dumping) • May be prone to mere measurement effect • Prescriptions/doses may change during measurement period
Medications prescribed or dispensed Medication	• Electronic data on prescription refills or collection (pharmacy or clinic records) • MPR (medication possession ratio) – medicines prescribed/dispensed by days in period	• Non-invasive, not prone to mere measurement effect • Inexpensive • Can collect long-term data • Easy to collect data on large samples • Can be consistent across studies	• No information on consumption/dosing (e.g., patients who take two tablets one day and none the next) • Patients may not always attend same pharmacy • Patients may stockpile medicines or fail to get prescription refilled
Assay of medicine Medication	• Blood assay • Urine assay • Breath	• Independent measure • Related to ingestion of medicine	• Usually only provides information on very recent ingestion of medicine • Relatively expensive to administer • Intrusive to patient • Depends on metabolism of target medicine • Not feasible for all medications
Electronic measuring devices Medication, limited self-care	• Electronic caps for pill-bottles (e.g., MEMS) • Inhaler devices • Eye drop dispensers • Electronic recording of blood glucose checking	• Objective • Detailed time/date information, allows examination of different patterns of pill-taking, for example, weekends • Continuous data • Suggested as current gold standard	• Expensive (usually one unit per medicine per patient) • No information on ingestion of medicines • May interfere with existing routines (e.g., use of days of the week pill-container) • Pill bottles cumbersome, inconvenient • May not suit all medications

Table 7.1. continued

Type of measure Adherence measured	How measured	Advantages	Disadvantages/issues
Clinical outcome measures *Medication and self-care*	• Blood pressure • Blood levels (e.g., blood sugar levels (glycaemic control), cholesterol levels, INR (warfarin), HIV etc.)	• Independent of researchers • If patients not fore-warned then free from measurement effect	• Remote from adherence • No information about behavioural changes • Not all patients respond in same way to medication; poor clinical outcome may be result of a variety of factors, for example, incorrect prescribing rather than poor adherence • May be costly, intrusive, and need trained personnel to administer • White-coat effect may affect blood pressure readings
Self-report *Medication and self-care*	• Questionnaires • Diaries/logs • Interviews (person or telephone) • Can be administered electronically	• Most-used, convenient • Inexpensive • Can differentiate intentional and nonintentional nonadherence • Can be completed by third parties (e.g., parents, spouse, carer)	• Inaccuracies of recall • Bias of reporting (e.g., social desirability) • Tends to over-report adherence • Prone to mere measurement effect • Prone to ceiling effects
Health professional (HP) reports *Medication and self-care*	• For example, general practitioner's assessment of adherence	• Relatively inexpensive • Independent of patient	• Poor validity • Depends on good HP knowledge of patient
Direct observation *Medication and self-care*	• For example, record of ingestion of medicine by health professional	• May remove social desirability of patient response • Can record actual ingestion of medicine	• Impractical except possibly in hospital settings • Time-consuming • May be intrusive • Dependent on accuracy of recording

The often maligned *self-report* has significant benefits in terms of practicality, relatively low cost, and ease of administration and scoring. However, careful wording is needed to avoid social desirability of responses, and measures should be tested for validity (that they are measuring what they purport to measure) and reliability (across time and different populations). Self-report measures can also differentiate between intentional and nonintentional nonadherence; this is likely to be of particular importance in interventions where different approaches may be required to address these separate aspects of adherence (O'Carroll, Chambers, Dennis, Sudlow, & Johnston, 2013). With the exception of blood glucose testing, adherence to advice for self-care, self-management, or self-examination can only practically be measured by direct observation, health practitioner assessment, or self-report.

A researcher's choice of measure will be influenced by factors such as practicality and cost: Salient features of the types of available measure are compared in Table 7.2. Due to their objectivity, electronic pill-containers are often cited as the gold standard of medication-taking measurement; however, they may be prone to measurement reactivity, so it is advised that they are used in both treatment and control groups, ideally with in a run-in period before intervention. Typically, electronic devices are bulky, cannot be used with patients' own pill-box organizers, and most can only cope with a single medication. Importantly, the unit of measurement is pill-bottle opening, not actual consumption of the target medicine (e.g., patients may dump doses or pocket them to take at a later time). Thus, they are far from being a perfect measure of adherence. Nonetheless, they remain the best available method of getting an accurate picture of the timing and regularity of doses taken (Sutton et al., 2014), whilst following guidelines for their use may help minimize the associated problems (Cook, Schmiege, McCelan, Aargaard, & Kahook, 2012; Riekert & Rand, 2002).

Most measurement methods tend to result in responses that are highly skewed, with a majority of patients reporting high levels of adherence, leading to issues in data analysis. Self-report measures are particularly prone to over-reporting (Berg, Wilson, Ki, & Arnsten, 2012), with many patients reporting 100% adherence[1]. Ceiling effects may be reduced by choosing a longer timeframe (e.g., *past 30 days* rather than *past 7 days*), and/or by phrasing questions to reflect a patient's ability to take medicine (e.g., using qualitative [*excellent, very good*] instead of quantitative [*never, often, always*] responses) rather than actual doses taken (Lu et al., 2008). The skewed nature of adherence measures often leads to the use of arbitrary cut-offs for adherent and nonadherent patients (e.g., 80%, 90%, 100%), which loses valuable information about individuals' levels of adherence and makes it difficult to compare the relative success of adherence interventions. In addition, dichotomising patients as adherent or nonadherent is often based on statistical convenience and not on the relevance of the chosen cut-offs to the medication and/or condition that is being assessed.

Self-Report Measures of Adherence to Treatment and Self-Care

A vast number of self-report measures of adherence are reported in the literature. Several systematic reviews of adherence measures have been conducted, each with specific criteria

---

[1] Self-reported 100% adherence may have many interpretations including: (a) it reflects perfect adherence, (b) the respondent is faking good, and (c) the patient believes they are 100% adherent even though they are not, for example, due to forgetting (or not realising) that they have forgotten to take one or more medication doses.

Table 7.2. Features of types of adherence measure

Type of measure	Measures number of doses taken	Time/date recording	Reasons for non-adherence	Measures persistence	Requires active patient participation	Potential for Measurement Reactivity	Cost	Feasibility in clinical practice
Self-report								
Questionnaire	No	No	Yes	Uncertain[b]	Yes	Yes[b]	Low	Yes
Interview	No	No	Yes	Uncertain[b]	Yes	Yes[b]	Medium	Yes
Diary	Yes[a]	Yes[a]	Yes	Yes[a]	Yes	Yes	Low	Yes
Pill-count								
Home	Yes	No	No[d]	Yes	Yes	Yes[e]	High	No
Pharmacy/clinic	Uncertain[c]	No	No[d]	Yes	Yes	Yes	Medium	Yes
Telephone	Yes	No	No[d]	Yes	Yes	Yes[e]	Medium	Possibly
Medications possessed								
Pharmacy refill	Uncertain[f,g]	No	No	Yes	No	No	Low	Yes[g]
Prescription collection	Uncertain[h]	No	No	Yes	No	No	Low	Yes
Electronic measuring devices	Yes	Yes	No	Yes	Yes	Yes	High	No
Health professional reports	No	No	No	Yes	No	Possibly	Medium	Yes
Direct observation	Yes	Yes[a]	No[d]	Yes	Yes	Yes	High	No
Assay of medicine	No	No	No	Possibly[i]	Yes	Yes[e]	High	Possibly
Clinical outcome measures (e.g., blood pressure, cholesterol)	No	No	No	Possibly[i]	Yes	No	Low to high[i]	Yes

Note. All types of measure except possibly health professional reports could feasibly be used in research settings. All could also be used alongside patients' own pill-box organisers with the exception of current electronic measuring devices.
[a]Depends on consistent recording. [b]Prone to social desirability effect. [c]Relies on patient remembering to bring medication to appointment. [d]Unless combined with interview. [e]Unless unannounced. [f]Patients may stockpile medicines (e.g., before holiday periods). [g]Requires only one pharmacy to be used by patient. [h]Patients may leave prescription unfilled. [i]Depending on measure/medication.

(e.g., Garfield, Clifford, Eliasson, Barber, & Willson, 2011: 58 self-reported measures for medications in routine clinical use; Hearnshaw & Lindenmeyer, 2006: 54 articles measuring adherence to medical advice in diabetes; Nguyen, La Caze, & Cottrell, 2014: 60 articles comprising 43 self-reported measures correlated with comparison measures of medication-taking; Shi et al., 2010: 41 articles comparing self-report measures to electronic monitoring devices; Simoni et al., 2006: 77 studies (1996–2004) assessing adherence in antiretroviral therapy for HIV). These reviews highlight the heterogeneity of developed measures in terms of question wording, adherence cut-off points, and timescales, making comparison between studies extremely difficult. Many self-report measures are only used in the study for which they were developed and/or are only slightly modified from earlier measures; for example, Shea, Misra, Ehrlich, Field, and Francis (1992) added one item to the scale developed by Morisky, Green, and Levine (1986). Some have only been administered via interview and/or may be lengthy to complete. A large number of these reviewed measures fail to assess both intentional and nonintentional nonadherence, and amongst those that do, the relative impact of these different aspects of adherence is rarely examined. Further, existing studies often lack methodological rigour, including a failure to report the validity or reliability of the measures used; and associations with clinical outcomes are often modest. There are fewer measures that assess self-care, self-management, or self-examination behaviours; however, these are subject to many of the same concerns as measures of medication adherence.

Table 7.3 summarises a number of self-report measures of medication adherence and self-care that have been used in more than one research setting and/or evaluated in different patient groups. Advantages and disadvantages are also shown. This is by no means an exhaustive list[2], but all of the included measures comply with the following criteria: (a) development based on existing research and/or sound theoretical concepts; (b questionnaire reported in full, and available as an open access measure or with permission from the author(s); (c) has been psychometrically tested, shown good reliability, and been tested against clinical outcomes; (d) is brief, easy to complete, and easy to administer by both interview and self-report; (e) includes items relating to both intentional and nonintentional nonadherence (except self-care measure); and (f) evidence of use by more than one research group.

Two self-report measures of general medication adherence have been used and psychometrically tested in a wide range of illness contexts and different countries. The Morisky scale (variously called MAS, MMAS, MMAQ) is available in both 4- and 8-item versions (Morisky et al., 1986; Morisky, Ang, Krousel-Wood, & Ward, 2008) and has the advantage of being brief and easy to administer and score. Disadvantages include the limited intentional nonadherence items and that items are scored as *Yes/No*, rather than scaled responses, which would provider richer data. Adherence is generally categorized into nonadherent/adherent, with resultant issues for data analysis (see above).

The Medication Adherence Report Scale (MARS[3]) has been used in 5-item (Horne & Hankins, 2008) and 10-item (Mora et al., 2011) versions (4- and 9-item versions are also reported). Importantly, the introductory wording aims to reduce social desirability bias by normalising nonadherence behaviour. It assesses both nonintentional and intentional nonadherence,

---

2 We should stress that this is not a systematic review; in particular, there may be more recently developed measures that have not yet been extensively tested. We therefore urge prospective users of self-report measures to check the up-to-date literature for recent publication, systematic review, and/or psychometric evaluation of measures that may be pertinent to their particular setting.
3 There are also several other unrelated scales using the acronym MARS including the Medication Adherence Reasons Scale (Unni & Farris, 2015) and the Medication Adherence Rating Scale – Psychosis (MARS-10) (Thompson, Kulkarni, & Sergejew, 2000).

Table 7.3. Self-report adherence measures including psychometric properties as reported in the original study

Measures	Population(s) developed with; type of measure	Subsequent use: patient groups; languages	Development; timeframe of questions; time to complete[a]	Total items (final scale); examples (I=intentional; N=nonintentional)	Validity against other measures[b]	Reliability	Related to clinical outcomes	Advantages (pros)/ disadvantages (cons)
Adherence to Refills and Medications Scale (ARMS) Kripalani, Risser, Gatti, & Jacobson 2009; US	Coronary heart disease patients, antihypertensive medicine N=435; 44% male, 91% African American, mean age=64 years Interview-assisted questionnaire	Diabetes Not clear if translated into other languages	Multidisciplinary team; based on Morisky plus additional items on medication refills. Targeted and tested with low-literacy adults (reading level less than 8th grade) Frequency (none, some, most, all of the time)	12 items (5I, 3N, 4 Refill) I: "How often do you change the dose of your medicines to suit your needs?" N: "How often do you forget to take your medicine when you are supposed to take it more than once a day?"	Compared with: Morisky $r=.65$ 6-month prescription refill (previous to ARMS completion) $r=.32$ 12-month prescription refill (subsequent to ARMS) $r=.29$	Cronbach's α 0.81 Test-retest (3 months) $r=.69$ (control group, $n=93$)	Adherent participants significantly more likely to have controlled diastolic BP ($p<.05$) Systolic and overall BP not significant	Pros: good psychometric testing, good range of questions, low literacy group Cons: I/N not assessed separately, not yet much used or used as self-report questionnaire
Brooks Medication Adherence Scale (BMAS) Brooks et al., 1994; US	Asthma (two studies) Study 1: N=263, 34% male, 36% African American, 47% aged ≥ 50 years Study 2: N=232: similar to first sample Interview	Includes antidepressant medication; HIV Some languages including use in Belgium, Spain	Based on Morisky plus additional items relating to asthma. Two scales: oral medicine/ inhaler Last 3 months: Yes/No	Two 6-item scales (each 3I, 2N, 1 indeterminate): I: "...During the last 3 months... have you ever stopped taking your asthma medicine (using your inhaler) because you felt better?" N: "...have you at times been careless about taking your asthma medicine?"	Medicine and inhaler scales correlated at baseline and 12-month follow-up $.41 < r < .46$ Detected change difference in adherence between intervention and usual-care groups from baseline to 12-month follow-up ($.001 < p < .01$)	Medicine scale: Cronbach's α 0.76–0.80 Inhaler scale: Cronbach's α 0.67–0.75	No association clinician rating of asthma severity and adherence	Pros: brief, assesses both medication and inhaler use Cons: limited items, may not add much to Morisky

Table 7.3. continued

Measures	Population(s) developed with; type of measure	Subsequent use: patient groups; languages	Development; timeframe of questions; time to complete[a]	Total items (final scale); examples (I = intentional; N = nonintentional)	Validity against other measures[b]	Reliability	Related to clinical outcomes	Advantages (pros)/ disadvantages (cons)
Hill–Bone Compliance to High Blood Pressure Therapy Scale Kim, Hill, Bone, & Levine, 2000; US	Hypertension two samples, 100% African American: (1) N = 139, 100% male, mean age = 41 years (2) N = 341, 31% male, mean age = 59 years Interview	Extensive use with hypertension Languages include: Arabic, Korean, Turkish, German	Literature search, experts in hypertensive clinics: 3 domains – appointment keeping, reduced salt, medication adherence High 5th-grade reading level; 5 min to complete Frequency (none, some, most, all of the time)	14 items (8 adherence: 4I, 3N, 1 indeterminate; 6 behaviour [B]) "How often do you... I: ... skip your HBP medicine before you go to the doctor?" N: ... forget to take your HBP medicine?" B: ... eat salty food?"	Content validity checked by experts (one physician, two nurses)	Cronbach's α 0.74–0.84	Controlled BP at 1-year follow-up: r = .21–.16	Pros: covers different aspects of adherence, including self-care, low reading level Cons: needs further validity checking, retained some items with poor psychometric properties
ITAS Chisholm, Lance, Williamson, & Mulloy, 2005; US	Transplant patients N = 244; 67% male, 67% Caucasian, age > 18 years (no further detail) Questionnaire	Transplant patients Some languages including Spanish, also used in Taiwan	Based on MAQ (Morisky) Frequency: none of the time to frequent categorised as 0%, 1–20%, 20–50% more than 50%	4 items (1I, 2N, 1 indeterminate) I: stopped taking immunosuppressant therapy (IST) medication because felt worse N: were careless about taking IST medication	Medication refill rate: r = .57	Cronbach's α 0.81	Immunosuppressant blood serum concentrations: r = .52 Rejection occurrence: r = .25	Pros: good psychometric testing, well-used in specific population Cons: limited intentional/ nonintentional items, may not add much to Morisky

Table 7.3. continued

Measures	Population(s) developed with; type of measure	Subsequent use: patient groups; languages	Development; timeframe of questions; time to complete[a]	Total items (final scale); examples (I = intentional; N = nonintentional)	Validity against other measures[b]	Reliability	Related to clinical outcomes	Advantages (pros)/ disadvantages (cons)
Medication Adherence Report Scale (MARS-10) Horne & Hankins, 2008; Horne & Weinman, 2002; UK Also MARS-A for Asthma (Mora et al., 2011; US)	Asthma, inflammatory bowel disease, diabetes, warfarin users 28 < N < 606; no further information available Questionnaire	Extensive including: asthma, hypertension, COPD, diabetes, inflammatory bowel disease, stroke Languages include: German, Danish, Italian	Adapted from validated questionnaires (earlier version noted as RAM) Frequency (never to always)	MARS: 5 items (4I, 1N); MARS-A: 10 items (9I, 1N) I: "I decide to miss out a dose" N: "I forget to take them"	Compared with Morisky 4-item: r = .23 (N = 84, Asthma community patients) .47 ≤ r ≤ .62 (N = 39–62; hypertension/ diabetes/warfarin)	Cronbach's α 0.83 (N = 197) Test-retest (no information on timescale) r = .97 (N = 43)	Compared with controlled BP (N = 72): Sensitivity[c]: .65 Specificity[c]: .61	Pros: wording designed to limit social desirability; brief, easy to use, much tested, continuous measurement Cons: only one N item; original development and psychometric testing unpublished
Medication Adherence Rating Scale (MARS-10) Psychosis Thompson et al. 2000; Australia	Psychosis n = 66, 23% male, mean age = 33 years; ethnicity not reported Questionnaire	Psychosis Some languages including Cantonese, Norwegian, French	Questions extracted from Drug Attitude Inventory (DAI) and Morisky Yes/No responses	10 items (2I, 2N, 6 attitudes to medication) I: "When you feel better do you sometimes stop taking your medicine?" N: "Do you ever forget to take your medication?"	Compared with Morisky: r = .79 Drug Attitude Inventory: r = .82	Cronbach's α 0.75 Test-retest (2 weeks) r = .72	Blood levels of medication (N = 17): r = .60	Pros: well-tested at development (though small sample), measures attitudes Cons: limited I/N items, adherence items same as Morisky

98 Assessment in Health Psychology

Table 7.3. continued

Measures	Population(s) developed with; type of measure	Subsequent use: patient groups; languages	Development; timeframe of questions; time to complete[a]	Total items (final scale); examples (I = intentional; N = nonintentional)	Validity against other measures[b]	Reliability	Related to clinical outcomes	Advantages (pros)/ disadvantages (cons)
Morisky Medication Adherence Scale (MMAS, MAS, MAQ) Morisky et al., (4-item) 1986; (8-item) 2008; US	Hypertension 4-item: N = 400, 30% male, 91% African American, median age = 54 years 8-item: N = 1,367, 46% male, 77% African American, mean age = 53 years Interview	Very extensive use including type 2 diabetes, HIV, analgesics in cancer, inflammatory bowel disease, anti-coagulants Many languages including: Chinese, Korean, French, Spanish, Thai	Based on theory of reasons for nonadherence; some items reverse-coded to avoid response set bias Timeframe varies with question (8-item: yesterday, past 2 weeks, sometimes, often, ever) – all answered Yes/No	Four items (2I, 2N) and eight items (2I, 3N, 3 behaviour) I: "When you feel better do you sometimes stop taking your medicine?" N: "Do you sometimes forget to take your (high BP) medicine (pills)?" (8-item in brackets)	4-item scale: BP at 6 months: r = .43 and .42 months: r = .58 8-item scale: correlated with 4-item scale r = .64	Cronbach's α 0.61 (4-item); 0.83 (8-item)	BP under control: Sensitivity: .81 (4-item); .93 (8-item) Specificity: .44 (4-item), .53 (8-item)	Pros: most extensively used measure, well-tested, brief, easy-to-use Cons: responses are Yes/No so not continuous data, limited I items
Summary of Diabetes Self-Care Activities measure (SDSCA) Toobert & Glasgow, 1994; US; revised scale: Toobert, Hampson, & Glasgow, 2000; US	Type 2 diabetes N = 105, 37% male, mean age = 67 years; ethnicity not recorded Questionnaire (paper, computer, Internet)	Diabetes – type 1 and 2 Extensive use including Spanish, Portuguese, Chinese, Korean	Designed to assess levels of self-care rather than specific adherence to medical advice in diabetes Revised scale: How many days in past 7 days? (0–7)	Eleven items (4 diet; 3 exercise, 2 blood glucose testing, 1 medication behaviour) I/N: not applicable Revised scale has additional optional items including medication behaviour	Diet versus Block Fat Screener questionnaire r = .23–.25; exercise versus minutes exercising r = .20, class attendance, r = .22, exercise self-monitoring r = .58	Inter-item correlations for scales .20.75 Test–retest (3 months) .30 ≤ r ≤ .58	No – although sensitive to change in intervention versus control group	Pros: well-tested and used; brief, easy to complete Cons: specific diet scale low reliability, medication item dropped from revised version

Note. Permission for use of the above scales should be checked with the authors. BP = Blood pressure; HBP = high BP; COPD = chronic obstructive pulmonary disease.
[a] if reported. [b] Adjusted such that all scores are in the same direction. [c] Sensitivity defined as the number of correctly identified cases of controlled blood pressure detected by high scores on the measure; specificity defined as the number of cases of uncontrolled blood pressure detected by low scores.

although the 5-item version has only one nonintentional item (forgetting). Items are scored as frequency (*never* to *almost always*), and as such continuous scale responses can be calculated. The original development of the scale remains unpublished; permission and results of psychometric testing are available from the author.

Single-item measures of adherence, including Visual Analogue Scales (VAS; i.e., the patient indicates how much medication is taken on a continuous line scaled from 0 to 100%), also have merit in assessing adherence and seem less prone to ceiling effects (Berg et al., 2012). VAS can be framed to varied timescales (such as *generally; last 7 days*). As a single-item question is unlikely to place much additional burden on patients, it could be helpful to include a VAS alongside more detailed questionnaires.

All of the currently available self-report measures have limitations and further development and/or testing is needed to determine whether adherence measurement via self-report can be improved. Measurement may be enhanced by varying the framing of items within the same measure (e.g., frequency of missed doses: *past week, last 3 months, generally*), which may improve validity and help reduce the inherent biases of self-reported adherence (Berg et al., 2012). A recent review of HIV medication adherence sought to address many of these issues by recommending the inclusion of varied elements including a VAS, items relating to intentional and nonintentional nonadherence, and diverse timescales of medication-taking including weekends (Simoni et al., 2006). There could be merit in this approach, but it requires further evaluation.

Comparison of Measures of Adherence and Associations With Clinical Outcome

Despite the fact that there is no currently accepted gold standard for measuring adherence, studies evaluating the validity of adherence measures tend to use either electronic devices, pill-count, or MPR as the reference measure. Agreement between different measures varies enormously, ranging from quite poor to very high agreement (Garfield et al., 2011; Simoni et al., 2006; Wilson, Carter, & Berg, 2009). It has been estimated that self-report scales result in 10–14% higher adherence rates than more objective measures, including pill-counts and/or electronic measures such as MEMS (Shi et al., 2010), probably due to socially desirable responding. In a review of 86 comparisons of self-report against other adherence methods (including pill count, drug levels, and electronic devices), Garber, Nau, Erickson, Aikens, and Lawrence (2004) found that questionnaires and diaries tended to have moderate to high associations with objective adherence measures, whereas interview-administered self-report measures had lower associations, particularly with electronic devices. However, they observed that comparison studies often use inadequate tests of agreement and timescales often vary between the observed measures (e.g., 7 days, past month), which may contribute to poor agreement. Therefore it is difficult to assess the degree to which different measures are accurately measuring adherence to medical advice; at best most methods act as a proxy for adherence behaviour.

Self-report measures are reasonably good at detecting people who may be markedly nonadherent to medication but are less accurate when it comes to assessing high adherence (Horne et al., 2005). Nonetheless, assuming they are used consistently, they are likely to be sensitive to detecting changes in individuals with sub-optimal adherence following intervention. They therefore have merit in both assessing those most in need of intervention, as well as determining the effectiveness of interventions to improve adherence.

A meta-analysis of 63 articles comparing measures of adherence to medical advice and clinical outcomes found that on average 26% more patients experienced good outcomes by adhering than not adhering to their medical regime (DiMatteo, Giordani, Lepper, & Croghan, 2002). Clinical outcomes were best in chronic conditions and poorest for studies assessing adherence to medication, as opposed to adherence to other aspects of medical advice. The best predictor of the adherence–outcome relationship was the sensitivity and/or quality of the adherence measure. The authors concluded that "whenever possible, research should use measures that are continuous instead of dichotomous, use more than one measure of adherence, and include self report" (DiMatteo et al., 2002, p. 806).

Conclusion

There is currently no gold standard method of measuring adherence to medical advice. The choice of method will be guided by issues such as cost, practicality, the need to distinguish intentional versus nonintentional nonadherence, whether dosing/timing information is required, and the appropriateness of the method to the purposes of the intervention.

It has been recommended that using a range of different measures within studies will produce the best chance of generating an accurate picture of actual adherence (Lehmann et al., 2014). Combining multiple assessment methods and/or measuring adherence at multiple time-points may improve validity and reliability; however, this approach is insufficiently tested and requires further evaluation.

References

Berg, K. M., Wilson, I. B., Ki, X., & Arnsten, J. H. (2012). Comparison among antiretroviral adherence questions. *Aids and Behaviour, 16*, 461–468. http://doi.org/10.1007/s10461-010-9864-z

Brooks, C. M., Richards, J. M., Kohler, C. L., Soong, S-J., Martin, B., Windsor, R. A., & Bailey, W. C. (1994). Assessing adherence to asthma medication and inhaler regimens: A psychometric analysis of adult self-report scales. *Medical Care, 3*, 298–307. http://doi.org/10.1097/00005650-199403000-00008

Chisholm, M. A., Lance, C. E., Williamson, G. M., & Mulloy, L. L. (2005). Development and validation of the immunosuppressant therapy adherence instrument (ITAS). *Patient Education and Counseling, 59*, 13–20. http://doi.org/10.1016/j.pec.2004.09.003

Clifford, S., Barber, N., & Horne, R. (2008). Understanding different beliefs held by adherers, unintentional nonadherers, and intentional non-adherers; Application of the Necessity-Concerns Framework. *Journal of Psychosomatic Research, 64*, 41–46. http://doi.org/10.1016/j.jpsychores.2007.05.004

Cook, P., Schmiege, S., McCelan, M., Aargaard, L., & Kahook, M. (2012). Practical and analytic issues in the electronic assessment of adherence. *Western Journal of Nursing Research, 34*, 598–620. http://doi.org/10.1177/0193945911427153

DiMatteo, M. R., Giordani, P. J., Lepper, H. S., & Croghan, T. W. (2002). Patient adherence and medical treatment outcomes: a meta-analysis. *Medical Care, 40*, 794–811. http://doi.org/10.1097/00005650-200209000-00009

Garber, M. C., Nau, D. P., Erickson, S. R., Aikens, J. E., & Lawrence, J. B. (2004). The concordance of self-report with other measures of adherence: A summary of the literature. *Medical Care, 42*, 649–652. http://doi.org/10.1097/01.mlr.0000129496.05898.02

Garfield, S., Clifford, S., Eliasson, L., Barber, N., & Willson, A. (2011). Suitability of measures of self-reported medication adherence for routine clinical use: A systematic review. *BMC Medical Research Methodology, 11*, 149. http://doi.org/10.1186/1471-2288-11-149

Gonzalez, J. S., & Schneider, H. E. (2011). Methodological issues in the assessment of diabetes treatment adherence. *Current Diabetes Reports, 11*, 472–479. http://doi.org/10.1007/s11892-011-0229-4

Hayes, T. L., Larimer, N., Adami, A., & Kaye, J. A. (2009). Medication adherence in healthy elders: Small cognitive changes make a big difference. *Journal of Aging and Health, 21*, 567–580. http://doi.org/10.1177/0898264309332836

Haynes, R., Ackloo, E., Sahota, N., McDonald, H. P., & Yao, X. (2008). Interventions for enhancing medication adherence. *Cochrane Database of Systematic Reviews, 16*(2), CD000011. http://doi.org/10.1002/14651858.CD000011.pub3

Hearnshaw, H., & Lindenmeyer, A. (2006). What do we mean by adherence to treatment and advice for living with diabetes? A review of the literature on definitions and measurements. *Diabetes Medicine, 23*, 720–728. http://doi.org/10.1111/j.1464-5491.2005.01783.x

Horne, R. (2003). Treatment perceptions and self-regulation. In L. D. Cameron & H. Leventhal (Eds.), *The self-regulation of health and illness behaviour* (pp. 138–153). Abingdon, UK: Routledge.

Horne, R., & Hankins, M. (2008). *The Medication Adherence Report Scale (MARS): A new measurement tool for eliciting patients' reports of non-adherence.* London, UK: The School of Pharmacy, University of London.

Horne, R., & Weinman, J. (2002). Self-regulation and self-management in asthma: Exploring the role of illness perceptions and treatment beliefs in explaining non-adherence to preventer medication. *Psychology & Health, 17*(1), 17–32. http://doi.org/10.1080/08870440290001502

Horne, R., Weinman, J., Barber, N., Elliot, R., & Morgan, M. (2005). *Concordance, adherence and compliance in medicine taking.* Report for the National Co-ordinating Centre for NHS Service Delivery and Organisation R & D (NCCSDO). Retrieved from http://www.nets.nihr.ac.uk/__data/assets/pdf_file/0009/64494/FR-08-1412-076.pdf

Kalichman, S. C., Amaral, C. M., Stearns, H., White, D., Flanagan, J., Pope, H., … Kalichman, M. O. (2007). Adherence to antiretroviral therapy assessed by unannounced pill counts conducted by telephone. *Journal of General Internal Medicine, 22*, 1003–1006. http://doi.org/10.1007/s11606-007-0171-y

Kim, M. T., Hill, M. N., Bone, L. R., & Levine, D. M. (2000). Development and testing of the Hill-Bone Compliance to High Blood Pressure Therapy Scale. *Progress in Cardiovascular Nursing, 15*, 90–96. http://doi.org/10.1111/j.1751-7117.2000.tb00211.x

Kripalani, S., Risser, J., Gatti, M. E., & Jacobson, T. A. (2009). Development and evaluation of the Adherence to Refills and Medications Scale (ARMS) among low-literacy patients with chronic disease. *Value in Health, 12*, 118–123. http://doi.org/10.1111/j.1524-4733.2008.00400.x

Lehmann, A., Aslani, P., Ahmed, R., Celio, J., Gauchet, A., Bedouch, P., … Schneider, M. P. (2014). Assessing medication adherence: Options to consider. *International Journal of Clinical Pharmacy, 36*(1), 55–69. http://doi.org/10.1007/s11096-013-9865-x

Leventhal, H., Brissette, I., & Leventhal, E. A. (2003). The common-sense model of self-regulation of health and illness. In L. D. Cameron & H. Leventhal (Eds.), *The self-regulation of health and illness behaviour* (pp. 42–65). Abingdon, UK: Routledge.

Lu, M., Safren, S. a., Skolnik, P. R., Rogers, W. H., Coady, W., Hardy, H., & Wilson, I. B. (2008). Optimal recall period and response task for self-reported HIV medication adherence. *AIDS and Behavior, 12*, 86–94. http://doi.org/10.1007/s10461-007-9261-4

Mora, P. A., Berkowitz, A., Contrada, R. J., Wisnivesky, J., Horne, R., Leventhal, H., & Halm, E. A. (2011). Factor structure and longitudinal invariance of the Medical Adherence Report Scale-Asthma. *Psychology & Health, 26*, 713–727. http://doi.org/10.1080/08870446.2010.490585

Morisky, D. E., Ang, A., Krousel-Wood, M., & Ward, H. J. (2008). Predictive validity of a medication adherence measure in an outpatient setting. *Journal of Clinical Hypertension, 10*, 348–354. http://doi.org/10.1111/j.1751-7176.2008.07572.x

Morisky, D. E, Green, L. W., & Levine, D. M. (1986). Concurrent and predictive validity of a self-reported measure of medication adherence. *Medical Care, 24*, 67–74. http://doi.org/10.1097/00005650-198601000-00007

Nguyen, T., La Caze, A., & Cottrell, N. (2014). What are validated self-report adherence scales really measuring? A systematic review. *British Journal of Clinical Pharmacology, 77*(3), 427–445. http://doi.org/10.1111/bcp.12194

O'Carroll, R. E., Chambers, J. A., Dennis, M., Sudlow, C., & Johnston, M. (2013). Improving adherence to medication in stroke survivors: A pilot randomised controlled trial. *Annals of Behavioral Medicine, 46*, 358–368. http://doi.org/10.1007/s12160-013-9515-5

Paterson, D. L., Swindells, S., Mohr, J., Brester, M., Vergis, E. N., Squier, C., ... Singh, N. (2000). Adherence to protease inhibitor therapy and outcomes in patients with HIV infection. *Annals of Internal Medicine, 133*, 21–30. http://doi.org/10.7326/0003-4819-133-1-200007040-00025

Riekert, K. A., & Rand, C. S. (2002). Electronic monitoring of medication adherence: When is high-tech best? *Journal of Clinical Psychology in Medical Settings, 9*, 25–34. http://doi.org/10.1023/A:1014900328444

Shea, S., Misra, D., Ehrlich, M. H., Field, L., & Francis, C. K. (1992). Correlates of nonadherence to hypertension treatment in an inner-city minority population. *American Journal of Public Health, 82*, 1607–1612. http://doi.org/10.2105/AJPH.82.12.1607

Shi, L., Liu, J., Koleva, Y., Fonseca, V., Kalsekar, A., & Pawaskar, M. (2010). Concordance of adherence measurement using self-reported adherence questionnaires and medication monitoring devices. *Pharmacoeconomics, 28*, 1097–1107. http://doi.org/10.2165/11537400-000000000-00000

Simoni, J. M., Kurth, A. E., Pearson, C. R., Pantalone, D. W., Merrill, J. O., & Frick, P. A. (2006). Self-report measures of antiretroviral therapy adherence: A review with recommendations for HIV research and clinical management. *AIDS and Behavior, 10*, 227–245. http://doi.org/10.1007/s10461-006-9078-6

Sutton, S., Kinmonth, A-L., Hardeman, W., Hughes, D., Boase, S., Prevost, T., ... Farmer, A. (2014). Does electronic monitoring influence adherence to medication? Randomized controlled trial of measurement reactivity. *Annals of Behavioral Medicine, 48*, 293–296. http://doi.org/10.1007/s12160-014-9595-x

Thompson, K., Kulkarni, J., & Sergejew, A. A. (2000). Reliability and validity of a new Medication Adherence Rating Scale (MARS) for the psychoses. *Schizophrenia Research, 42*, 241–247. http://doi.org/10.1016/S0920-9964(99)00130-9

Toobert, D. J., & Glasgow, R. E. (1994). Assessing diabetes self-management: the summary of diabetes self-care activities questionnaire. In C. Bradley (Ed.), *Handbook of psychology and diabetes* (pp. 351–375). Chur, Switzerland: Harwood Academic.

Toobert, D. J., Hampson, S. E., & Glasgow, R. E. (2000). The summary of diabetes self-care activities measure: Results from 7 studies and a revised scale. *Diabetes Care, 23*, 943–950. http://doi.org/10.2337/diacare.23.7.943

Unni, E. J., & Farris, K. B. (2015). Development of a new scale to measure self-reported medication nonadherence. *Research in Social and Administrative Pharmacy, 11*, e133–e143. http://doi.org/10.1016/j.sapharm.2009.06.005

Wilson, I. B., Carter, A. E., & Berg, K. M. (2009). Improving the self-report of HIV antiretroviral medication adherence: Is the glass half full or half empty? *Current HIV/AIDS Reports, 6*(4), 177–186. http://doi.org/10.1007/s11904-009-0024-x

Chapter 8

Stress and Stressors

Daryl B. O'Connor[1] and Eamonn Ferguson[2]

[1]School of Psychology, University of Leeds, UK
[2]School of Psychology, University of Nottingham, UK

What Is Stress?

The study of stress has a long history in the psychological literature and in health research generally (Abraham, Conner, Jones, & O'Connor, 2008). Scientific interest dates back to the First World War, when soldiers were found to exhibit shellshock, an extreme reaction to the trauma of battle that was subsequently acknowledged as a manifestation of post-traumatic stress disorder (Lazarus, 1999). Since this time, stress has become part of everyday vernacular. Two theorists who had a great influence in terms of popularising the concept of stress are Walter Cannon and Hans Selye. Cannon (1932) wrote about the fight-or-flight reaction to describe the human response to threats. Cannon believed that when faced with danger, such as a predator, the human being feels the emotions of fear or anger, the former being linked to an instinct to run away and the latter with the urge to fight.

Hans Selye (1956) built on Cannon's work and described a reaction pattern entitled the general adaptation syndrome (GAS; Selye, 1956). Selye wrote that: "Adaptability and resistance to stress are fundamental prerequisites for life, and every vital organ participates in them" (Selye, 1950, p. 4667). He believed that the basic physiological reaction was generic irrespective of the stressor and depended on the interaction of many of the body's physical systems. In a nutshell, the theory comprises three stages:

1. *Alarm*. This is the immediate reaction whereby stress hormones are released to prepare the body for action (fight or flight).
2. *Resistance*. If stress is prolonged, levels of stress hormones remain high. However, during this period the individual attempts superficially to adapt to the stressor but will still have heightened susceptibility to disease.
3. *Exhaustion*. If the stress continues long enough, the body's defensive resources are used up, leading to illness and ultimately death.

According to Selye, prolonged exposure to a strong stressor will increase an individual's risk of developing health problems, which he described as *diseases of adaptation* (e.g., ulcers). Moreover, he suggested that repeated and long-term exposure to stress will lead to dysfunction of a number of the body's basic systems, such as the immune and metabolic systems. Selye's early approach focused on stress as a physiological reaction and his theory influenced many subsequent researchers. However, Mason (1971) questioned the generality of this approach, arguing that some noxious (stressful) physical conditions do not produce the predicted three stages, alarm, resistance, and ultimately exhaustion responses (e.g., exercise, fasting). More recent approaches have tended to emphasise psychological processes and have recognised that individuals may respond differently (psychologically – appraisals, behaviourally – coping, and physiologically – immune function) to the same stressful events.

Over the last 30 years and beyond, there has been a marked increase in media coverage of stress and as a result this has led to increased research and public awareness. Indeed stress is now the most common cause of long-term sick leave and is frequently shown to be a very important factor accounting for in excess of 10 million working days lost per annum in the UK (Health and Safety Executive, 2013). In 2011/2012, stress accounted for 40% of all cases of work-related illnesses in the UK (i.e., 428,000 cases out of 1,070,000 cases in total). In the US, the impact of stress is also far reaching, with 66% of Americans reporting that that stress is impacting on their physical health and 63% believing the same for their mental health (American Psychological Association, 2012). Nevertheless, the precise definition of what we mean by stress and how it should be measured remains unclear.

There have been three different approaches to the study of stress: the stimulus-based approach; the response-based approach; and the psychological interactional-appraisal approach (Abraham et al., 2008). The stimulus-based approach views stress as a demand on an individual from their environment that produces a strain reaction: the greater the strain, the larger the reaction. This approach assumes that undemanding situations are not stressful. However, monotonous undemanding work environments very often are stressful. The stimulus-based approach is also problematic because it assumes that individuals function both unconsciously and automatically, no consideration is given to the mediating psychological processes (e.g., cognitive appraisal).

The response-based approach mainly considers stress in terms of the general physiological reaction to noxious events in a person's environment such as changes in blood pressure, heart rate, and stress hormones. Again this approach does not account for individual psychological processes. More recent work has adopted an interactional-appraisal or transactional approach in order to explain the stress process. Such theories contribute to our understanding of the variation in responses to similar noxious (or stressful) stimuli by emphasising the importance of the intervening psychological processes.

The development of the transactional approach was spear-headed by Richard Lazarus and Susan Folkman (Lazarus, 1966; Lazarus & Folkman, 1984). They defined stress as "a particular relationship between the person and the environment that is appraised by the person as taxing or exceeding his or her resources and endangering his or her well-being" (Lazarus & Folkman, 1984, p. 19). This suggests that researchers need to look at the environment, the individual's reaction to the environment, and the outcome (which might be in terms of physiological or psychological well-being). Perhaps because of the breadth of issues encompassed within this concept of stress, Lazarus also suggested that the most useful approach would be to regard stress not as a single variable but as a "rubric consisting of many variables and processes" (Lazarus & Folkman, 1984, p. 12). Within this field there are many diverse areas of research that look at relationships between objective or perceived antecedents (or stressors) and a range of physiological, psychological, or behavioural outcomes. The latter may include physiological measures such as cortisol and blood pressure as well as illness outcomes such as the development of cardiovascular disease, measures of work performance or health behaviours, or self-reported outcomes such as depression and anxiety.

Recent theorising by Segerstrom and O'Connor (2012) has built upon these approaches and suggested that identifying where stress is located is important to improve its conceptualisation and assessment. Specifically, in keeping with Lazarus and Folkman, it is argued that stress can be located in the environment, in appraisal or in response (i.e., emotions or physiology);

however, in order to fully understand the stress process, there is a need to investigate how each of these locales interacts. For example, the experience of a major life event, such as unemployment or divorce, is likely to have a knock-on effect on the frequency and intensity of minor daily stressors such as being late for a meeting or having an argument with your partner, and vice versa minor daily stressors may reduce the ability to cope with a major life event; thus the system is reciprocal (Segerstrom & O'Connor, 2012). Both types of stressor are located in the environment; however, the relationship between these events is dynamic, bi-directional, and will change frequently overtime.

In terms of stress being located within the person, this refers to work that has explored the effect of an event in terms of the cognitive appraisals (e.g., Lazarus & Folkman, 1984; Gartland, O'Connor, & Lawton, 2012; Tomaka, Blascovich, Kibler, & Ernst, 1997). Stress appraisals are the interpretations of events in terms of their benefit or harm for the individual. The transactional model of stress posits two dimensions: primary and secondary appraisals (Lazarus & Folkman, 1984). Primary appraisal involves the evaluation of the risks, demands, or challenges of a situation (i.e., high vs. low), while secondary appraisal evaluates the availability of perceived resources and whether anything can be done to alter the outcome of the situation. A major strength of the transactional model of stress is it allows for different people to experience the same noxious event or encounter it differently, as stressful or not.

Key to understanding the appraisal process has to be the role of personality and individual differences. There is a large body of evidence showing that personality traits influence not only how people appraise situations (e.g., Ferguson, Daniels, & Jones, 2006; Ferguson, 2013; O'Connor, Conner, Jones, McMillan, & Ferguson, 2009), but also how they cope with them (Ferguson, 2001). Stress can also be located in responses. This approach defines stress as that which causes distress (Segerstrom & O'Connor, 2012) and is similar to the early response-based approaches whereby stress is defined as strain or by the presence or absence of physiological or psychological change (e.g., evidence of ill-health and/or distress). Once more, personality traits are also likely to influence how people respond physiologically to stress (Chapman et al., 2009; see Ferguson, 2013, for a review) and should be considered a distal influence on the whole stress process. Similar to the other approaches, changes in distress outcomes are likely to have implications for the frequency, intensity, and appraisal of new stressful encounters.

Taken together, a major challenge for stress research is to "appropriately and explicitly locate stress and to understand the effects on other stress *locations*" (Segerstrom & O'Connor, 2012, p. 131). In order to do this, it is imperative that researchers adopt an integrated approach to measurement and ensure that the different locations of stress are assessed using a variety of longitudinal, panel, multi-level, and daily research designs. For example, a major life stressor such as unemployment is likely to lead to an increased number of minor daily stressors (e.g., financial stressors), which are likely to influence appraisals of threat, challenge, and loss, which may generalise to other situations and stressors, thereby resulting in increased levels of psychological distress. However, again, such a cascade will depend on personality. Losing one's job may result in reduced stress (assuming all else is equal in terms of financial constraints) in people who tend to be cautious, methodical, and emotionally stable.

How Is Stress Measured?

We can identify three different types of measures used to study stress in the literature: (a) generic measures of perceived stress, (b) event measures, and (c) cognitive appraisal measures. These are not mutually exclusive. Generic measures of perceived stress aim to capture appraisals of non-event-specific perceptions of stress over the recent past. Event measures examine the experience of major life events, hassles, and single acutely stressful events. Cognitive appraisal measures assess primary (the extent to which an event is appraised as threatening, challenging, or likely to lead to loss) and secondary appraisals (e.g., the extent to which an event is appraised as controllable). We will discuss each of these types of measures later in the chapter.

Life Event Approaches Versus Daily Stressor Approaches

Historically stress researchers have conceptualised stress in terms of the impact of life events (e.g., divorce) and related such measures to physiological, psychological, and behavioural outcomes (e.g., Holmes & Rahe, 1967). The first formal measurement tool was developed by Holmes and Rahe (1967). It was entitled the Social Readjustment Rating Scale and took the form of a 43-event checklist. Central to this tool was the notion that change is stressful and it will require adaptation. Therefore, individuals who are exposed to a larger degree of social readjustment are at greatest risk of disease and ill-health. To this end, in the original Social Readjustment Rating Scale, each event was assigned a weighting known as a life change unit (LCU) reflecting the amount of adjustment required. Holmes and Masuda (1974) described an LCU score of over 150 in 1 year as a life crisis (specifically 150–199 is a mild crisis, 200–299 a moderate crisis, and over 300 a major crisis). During the 1970s, Rahe and colleagues reported a number of studies that showed that high LCU scores were linked to changes in health outcomes such as myocardial infarction (e.g., Rahe & Paasikivi, 1971; Theorell & Rahe, 1971).

The reliability and validity of the life events approach has been heavily criticised together with its focus on major life changes, which are comparatively rare (e.g., Dohrenwend, 2006). Other scales have been developed in order to try to overcome the methodological limitations of the checklist approach. For example, the Life Events and Difficulties Schedule (LEDS) developed by Brown and Harris (1978) employed a semi-structured interview approach where participants described events that are subsequently rated by specially trained individuals.

Nevertheless, these tools ignore the fact that a great deal of stress stems from recurrent day-to-day problems or chronic conditions known as *daily hassles* (Delongis, Coyne, Dakof, Folkman, & Lazarus, 1982; Lazarus & Folkman, 1984). There is a growing body of evidence showing that fluctuations in within-person daily hassles are important in understanding stress-outcome processes (e.g., Affleck, Tennen, Urrows, & Higgins, 1994; Dancey, Taghavi, & Fox, 1998; DeLongis et al., 1982; DeLongis, Folkman, & Lazarus, 1988; Fifield et al., 2004; Kanner, Coyne, Schaefer, & Lazarus, 1981; O'Connor, Jones, Conner, McMillan, & Ferguson, 2008). For example, early work by Kanner et al. (1981) suggested that indices of (life) stress provide no understanding of what actually happens in day-to-day life and it is "day-to-day events that ultimately have proximal significance for health outcomes and whose accumulative impact ... should be assessed" (p. 3). A critical feature of this approach is that, because stress is a process, assessments should be repeated over time. The use of open-ended diaries allows respondents to record day-to-day minor life stressors or hassles that are part of everyday life and have the advantage of not constraining respondents to a limited number of events. Hassles are events, thoughts, or situations that, when they occur, produce negative feelings such as annoyance, irritation, worry, or frustration, and/or make you aware that your goals and plans will be more difficult or impossible to achieve (see Conner, Fitter, & Fletcher, 1999; DeLongis et al., 1982; O'Connor et al., 2008).

The first measure of daily stressors was known as the Hassles Scale (e.g., Kanner et al., 1981) before the shorter Hassles and Uplifts Scale was introduced (DeLongis et al., 1988). The Hassles Scale consisted of 117 items where participants were instructed to indicate the occurrence of any items that "hassled" them in the past month. The revised Hassles and Uplifts Scale was shortened considerably to consist of 53 items and participants were instructed to rate the extent to which each item was a *hassle* and/or an *uplift*. These measures have been widely used in the intervening 25 years; however, they have not gone without criticism (Abraham et al., 2008; Jones & Bright, 2001). For example, by including appraisal of the stressful nature of transactions within measures of hassles, items may be unintentionally measuring psychological distress, thereby potentially confounding stress–outcome relations (Cohen 1986; Dohrenwend, Dohrenwend, Dodson, & Shrout, 1984; Dohrenwend, & Shrout, 1985; Lazarus, DeLongis, Folkman, & Gruen, 1985; Schroeder & Costa, 1984). In addition, a number of researchers have suggested that the 53-item scale is overly burdensome in daily diary designs and have preferred free response approaches whereby participants report up to a maximum of between five and eight hassles each day (e.g., Conner et al., 1999; O'Connor et al., 2008).

Physiological Measures of Stress Activation

Two systems are activated when you experience stress. The first and easiest to activate is the sympathetic adrenal medullary (SAM) system; the second is the hypothalamic–pituitary–adrenal (HPA) axis. According to Clow (2001):

[Activating the SAM system] can be likened to lighting a match whereas activating the HPA axis is like lighting a fire. Lighting a match is easy, has an instant effect and the effect does not last long, whereas lighting a fire takes a lot more effort and its effects last much longer. The HPA axis is only activated in extreme circumstances. (p. 53)

However, when it is activated, cortisol is released from the adrenal glands. Once released, cortisol has several important functions, such as increasing access to energy stores, increasing protein and fat mobilisation, as well as regulating the magnitude and duration of inflammatory responses (Sapolsky, Romero, & Munck, 2000). As such, cortisol is the primary effector hormone of the HPA axis and has received extensive empirical investigation in the area of stress research. Moreover, it has been argued that if the HPA axis is repeatedly activated, the immune, cardiovascular, and endocrine systems are potentially exposed to excessive wear and tear (McEwen, 1998, 2000). Over time, such repetitive activation may contribute to future ill-health by placing excessive pressure on various bodily systems. For these reasons, stress researchers frequently include measures of cortisol as a physiological marker of stress (e.g., O'Connor, Hendrickx, et al., 2009; Schlotz, Hellhammer, Schulz, & Stone, 2004; Vedhara et al., 2003). Detailed consideration of stress biomarkers is beyond the scope of this chapter; nevertheless, researchers ought to include objective physiological measures in future stress and health investigations.

Main Types of Stress Measures

An overview of the main instruments used to measure stress is provided in Table 8.1.

Table 8.1. Brief description of main instruments ordered by type of measure

Title of scale	Author	Number of items/events	Dimensions assessed	Assessment window
Generic measures				
Perceived Stress Scale	Cohen, Kamarck, & Mermelstein (1983)	14, 10, & 4	Global Perceived Stress Score	Past month (but modifiable)
Stress Arousal Checklist	Mackay et al. (1978)	30	Stress Scale, Arousal Scale	At this moment in time
Trier Inventory of Chronic Stress	Schulz, Schlotz, & Becker (2011)	57	Work Overload, Social Overload, Pressure to Perform, Work Discontent, Excessive Demands at Work, Lack of Social Recognition, Social Tensions, Social Isolation, and Chronic Worrying.	Past 3 months
Event measures				
Social Readjustment Rating Scale	Holmes & Rahe (1967)	43	Total Life Change Unit	Past year
Life Events and Difficulties Schedule	Brown & Harris (1978)	N/A events elicited via interview	Ratings of acute (event) and chronic (difficulty) stressors based upon expert ratings following detailed interview and assessment	N/A
Hassles Scale	Kanner et al. (1981)	117	Work, Family, Social Activities, Environment, Practical Considerations, Finances, & Health	Past month
Hassles and Uplifts Scale	DeLongis, Folkman, & Lazarus (1988)	53	Work, Family, Social Activities, Environment, Practical Considerations, Finances, and Health	Today
Single-item Visual Analogue Scale/ Rating Scale	N/A	1	Perceived stress in relation to single event	Variable (depending upon timing of event)
Daily hassles/ stressors – free response format	O'Connor et al. (2008)	N/A	Frequency/intensity of ego-threatening, interpersonal, work-related, and physical	Today
Cognitive appraisal measures				
Stress Appraisal Measure	Peacock & Wong (1990)	28	*Primary appraisals:* Threat, Challenge, Centrality *Secondary appraisals:* Uncontrollable, controllable-by-others, controllable-by-self	Future event (e.g., forthcoming examination)
Appraisal of Life Events	Ferguson, Matthews, & Cox (1999)	16	*Primary appraisals:* Threat, Challenge, Loss	Retrospective events (past 3 months) or current events (right now)
Dimensions of Cognitive Appraisal	Gall & Evans (1987)	19	*Primary appraisals:* Undesirability/Threat, Gain/ Challenge, Need for Information, Familiarity, Need to Accept	Current event

Table 8.1. continued

Title of scale	Author	Number of items/events	Dimensions assessed	Assessment window
Emotion	Folkman & Lazarus (1985)	15	Threat, Challenge, Harm, Benefit	Right now (linked to an event)
Stressor Appraisal Scale	Schneider (2008)	10	*Primary and secondary appraisal*, but no challenge, loss or control items	Future event
Stressor Appraisal Scale – modified	Gartland, O'Connor, & Lawton (2012)	10	*Primary and secondary appraisal*, but no challenge, loss or control items	Past 7 days or today

Generic Measures of Perceived Stress

The most popular global measure of stress is the Perceived Stress Scale (PSS) developed by Cohen, Kamarck, and Mermelstein (1983). This measure was designed to evaluate the degree to which situations in general in one's life are appraised as stressful. The original 14-item scale (PSS 14) and a shorter 10-item (PSS 10) version asks participants to report about their feelings and thoughts during the *last month* in relation to non-specific events. For example, in the last month, "How often have you been upset because of something that happened unexpectedly", and "How often have you been able to control irritations in your life?" In a comparative analysis of the psychometric properties of the 14-item and 10-item scales, Cohen and Williamson (1988) recommended use of the PSS-10 in future research. A 4-item version of the PSS is also available for telephone interviews and large surveys where space or time is a premium (Cohen et al., 1983; Warttig, Forshaw, South, & White, 2013). Both versions of the scales have been found to exhibit good reliability and validity, to outperform life event measures in predicting health outcomes, and have been translated into numerous different languages (Cohen et al., 1983; Cohen & Williamson, 1988).

The Stress Arousal Checklist (SACL) is a short mood adjective checklist originally developed by Mackay, Cox, Burrows, and Lazzarini (1978) and has been used in experimental and field research. It comprises two scales that assess the experience of stress (as negative hedonistic tone) and that of arousal (as activation and alertness). Adjectives in the stress scale include *tense, apprehensive*, and *bothered*, whereas adjectives in the arousal scale include *vigorous, active*, and *alert*. The original version of the SACL contained 45 items but was soon replaced with a much more manageable 30-item version (see Cox & Mackay, 1985). The SACL can be applied to different contexts very easily; however, it is important to bear in mind that it is a measure of activation–deactivation and does not capture the extent to which a person appraises an event or situation as taxing or exceeding his or her resources and endangering his or her well-being.

The Trier Inventory of Chronic Stress (TICS; Schulz, Schlotz, & Becker, 2011) is a new generic 57-item measure of the chronic stress experience and was developed primarily because of the relatively weak relationship often observed between measures of acute (short-term) stress and health and disease outcomes (Schulz et al., 2011). According to the authors, "the design of the questionnaire was based on the following guidelines: subjectivity (measurement of stress experience), chronicity (assessment of chronic stress via a frequency scale), non-specificity (assessment of un-specific demands to be able to assess chronic stress in different groups of individuals or occupations), transparency (items ask for demands that are potentially accessible to the person from their memory) and complexity (retrospective assessment of the frequency of stress over a time window of three months)" (p. 3). The measure has been found to have nine subscales measuring the following types of stress: work overload, social overload, pressure to perform, work discontent, excessive demands at work, lack of social recognition, social tensions, social isolation, and chronic worrying. This appears to be a promising new tool for researchers interested in exploring the links between chronic stress and physical health outcomes. However, further work on its psychometric properties is required before its usefulness can be confirmed.

Evaluation of Generic Measures of Perceived Stress

One criticism that has been levelled at general measures of stress is the extent to which they reflect dispositional factors like negative affectivity or psychopathology and as such associations with outcomes are confounded (Cohen, 1986; Dohrenwend & Shrout, 1985; Dohrenwend et al., 1984; Lazarus et al., 1985; Schroeder & Costa, 1984). Therefore, we suggest that when using these types of measures authors should include a measure of trait negative affect or psychopathology and partial it out in their analyses (Cohen, 1986).

Event Measures of Stress

Measures within this tradition attempt to capture a participant's responses to significant life events (e.g., divorce), a single acutely stressful event (e.g., examination), and daily hassles (e.g., being late for a meeting). This may be achieved by the use of a questionnaire or by a structured interview. These may be generic life events as in the original Holmes and Rahe (1967) work or developed to focus on specific groups such as children (Williamson et al., 2003). In terms of appraisals these may be objective weighting, such as LCUs derived by magnitude estimation, or subjective assessments of how stressful, unpleasant, or uncontrollable the event is.

To our mind, event measures also include assessments of minor daily stressful events or annoyances known as hassles as conceptualised by the original Hassles Scale (Kanner et al., 1981). Items in the 117-item questionnaire covered the content areas of work (e.g., specific work tasks), family (balancing work–family issues), social activities (e.g., unexpected company), the environment (e.g., noise), practical considerations (e.g., misplacing one's keys), finances (e.g., needing money), and health (e.g., being exhausted). Participants are instructed to rate the extent to which they were hassled by each item over the past month and a frequency score and an intensity score are subsequently derived. The 53-item Hassles and Uplifts Scale (DeLongis et al., 1988) was a vastly improved tool as it adopted a daily diary approach and participants were instructed to indicate the extent to which each item had irritated them *today* or made them feel good (i.e., was an uplift).

Appraisals of single acutely stressful events (e.g., an examination; forthcoming surgery) are also an important type of event measure of stress. These measures examine responses to a single event as it unfolds over time. This requires measures that are sensitive to change across the events, over time, and between participants and can be applied to any type of event. As such, generic measures are required here and often include visual analogue or simple rating scales (e.g., "To what extent are you stressed about your forthcoming examinations?"). However, the general cognitive appraisal measures detailed next could all be used in this context.

Evaluation of Event Measures

One major and generic consideration with the assessment of life events and hassles in relation to health is the extent to which they are confounded by psychopathology and personality (Cohen, 1986; Dohrenwend & Shrout, 1985; Dohrenwend et al., 1984; Lazarus et al., 1985; Schroeder & Costa, 1984). Indeed, there is good evidence that life events may confound health (e.g., hospitalisation, dental work) or personality or psychopathology (e.g., problems with a parent). As such, these need to be considered when looking at events and their appraisals. While this debate has raged for many years it is still worth keeping an eye on the events being studied and assessing personality and psychopathology to partial any confounding effects.

In addition, people are often asked to appraise life events they endorse along single dimensions (how unpleasant, how controllable). The use of single items to assess the appraisal raises the issue not only of lack of reliability but also of theoretical concerns that not all dimensions of appraisals (e.g., threat, challenge, loss) are being assessed. We would suggest that authors using such methods at the very least assess a wider range of theoretically relevant appraisals.

Cognitive Appraisal Measures of Stress

As outlined earlier, cognitive appraisal measures of stress are informed by the transactional model of stress (Lazarus & Folkman, 1984). Cognitive stress appraisals are the interpretations of events in terms of their benefit or harm for the individual and the theory posits two dimensions: primary and secondary appraisals (Lazarus & Folkman, 1984).

Situational Versus Psychological Reasoning in Appraisal Measurement

An important question that arises here is the distinction between *situational reasoning* and *psychological reasoning* (Locke & Pennington, 1982). The former refers to judgments about the situation ("It was threatening") and the latter to feeling ("I felt threatened"). One does not necessarily translate to the other. One may observe a sad scene but not feel sad (e.g., seeing someone in need), or know a situation is dangerous but not feel in danger (crossing a busy road). This is partly to do with individual differences and partly to do with coping. If a situation is dangerous, I will not feel danger if I am able to deal with the situation. Thus, measures of appraisals by emotion (psychological reasoning) miss out on how situationally reasoned appraisals ultimately manifest as emotions depending on coping and personality. Thus, ultimately, appraisal measures based on situational and psychological reasoning are needed.

Main Cognitive Appraisal Measures of Stress

The five most frequently used measures are: (a) the Stress Appraisal Measure or SAM (Peacock & Wong, 1990); (b) the Appraisal of Life Events or ALE scales (Ferguson, Matthews, & Cox, 1999); (c) the Dimensions of Cognitive Appraisals (DCA; Gall & Evans, 1987); (d) Emotions (Folkman & Lazarus, 1985); and (f) the Stressor Appraisal Scale (SAS; Schneider, 2008).

Stress Appraisal Measure

The SAM consists of six scales. Three assess primary appraisals (threat, challenge, centrality) and three assess secondary appraisals (uncontrollable, controllable-by-self, and controllable-by-others). Threat assesses the potential for harm or loss; Challenge assesses anticipated gain and growth; and, Centrality the perceived importance of an event for well-being. Uncontrollable refers to a sense of hopelessness; Controllable-by-Others refers to help being available by others; and Controllable-by-Self, to having the skills and ability to do well. Thus, the latter two seem to reflect social support and self-efficacy. This measure has good psychometric properties but there is no reported test–retest reliability. Furthermore, while the SAM shows some cross-cultural factorial validity (Durak & Senol-Durak, 2013), it appears that the centrality and threat factors merge to form a single factor in a five-factor solution. A dispositional version – with four factors (challenge, threat, centrality, and resources) has also been developed (Senol-Durak & Durak, 2013). Finally, the items assess a mixture of psychological and situational reasoning as well as beliefs (e.g., self-efficacy).

Appraisal of Life Events

The ALE scale consists of three primary appraisal scales: Threat, Challenge, and Loss. The Threat scale assesses how threatening and anxiety provoking the situation is; Challenge assesses the potential for growth and learning from the situation, and Loss how sad and depressing the situation is. It focuses solely on psychological reasoning and has good psychometric properties (factorial, reliability, validity). There are cross-cultural translations of the scales, with the factor structure and psychometric properties replicated (Gourounti, Anagnostopoulos, & Vaslamatzis, 2012) – although some studies find that Threat and Loss form a single factor.

Dimensions of Cognitive Appraisals

This measure has five situational reasoning scales assessing: (a) Undesirability/Threat, which assesses threat and lack of positive evaluation; (b) Gain/Challenge, which assesses gain and controllability (which seem to conflate primary and secondary appraisals); (c) Need for Information, which assesses stress and ambiguity; (d) Familiarity, which assesses meaning, familiarity; and (e) Need to Accept, which only has one item and should not be considered a factor and also seems to assess coping rather than appraisals.

Emotions

This measure uses a psychological reasoning approach to identify four emotions for primary appraisals, differentiated into anticipatory and outcome emotions (Folkman & Lazarus, 1985). Anticipatory emotions are threat, referring to fear and anxiety, and challenge, referring to hope and confidence. The outcome emotions are harm, referring to anger and sadness, and benefit, referring to relief and exhilaration.

Stressor Appraisal Scale

Schneider (2008) successfully developed the SAS, which is a measure of anticipatory stress appraisal that assesses primary and secondary appraisal in relation to an upcoming task. Building on this work, Gartland and colleagues (2012) modified the SAS to assess stressor appraisals in relation to the most stressful hassle in the past 7 days and also effectively incorporated this approach into a daily diary format (see Gartland, O'Connor, Lawton, & Ferguson, 2014). This new scale comprises 10 items (primary appraisal = 7 items, secondary appraisal = 3 items) and was found to have good internal reliability, convergent and divergent validity, and can be utilised as a one-off assessment as well as a repeated assessment measure. However, these scales assess general primary appraisal to tap threat and the secondary appraisal measure indexes ability to deal with the demands (akin to self-efficacy). As such, the measures do not contain items tapping challenge, loss, or control. Nevertheless, this is a promising measure but further psychometric development is required.

Evaluating Cognitive Appraisal Measures

A detailed evaluation of cognitive appraisal measures is beyond the scope of this chapter; however, there are a number of key theoretical and psychometric factors that should be considered. For example, is the measure derived theoretically to assess the key dimensions of transactional theory? Does the measure allow for generality of use? That is, is it specific to one situation or class of events or can it be used to assess stress appraisal in a variety of contexts. If the same measure can be used in a variety of contexts then it allows us to compare stress appraisal responses in a more normative way (assuming that any effects of personality are held constant). Measures should also demonstrate the psychometric properties we would expect in any good measure of any psychological process. The measure should show good internal reliability (Cronbach's α of 0.70 or greater) and be stable (showing good test–retest validity) when the measure is used on two occasions to assess the same event. However, given that appraisals are processes, a good measure should also show variation both within and between people to the appraisal of the same event. A measure should also show measurement/factorial validity. That is, factor analytic procedures should be applied (both exploratory and confirmatory) to establish the measure's underlying structure. Finally, the measure should show construct validity (i.e., it is associated with theoretically relevant measures, these may be personality variables, emotions, etc.). A good measure should also show predictive validity (i.e., it is able to predict in a theoretically meaningful way future stress-related outcomes: e.g., mortality, physiological responses).

Future Directions

Recent developments in stress theory have highlighted the importance of worry, rumination, and repetitive thought as important to understanding the stress–disease relationships. Brosschot, Gerin, and Thayer (2006), in their perseverative cognition hypothesis (PCH), have suggested that worry or repetitive thinking may lead to disease by prolonging stress-related physiological activation, amplifying short-term responses, delaying recovery, or reactivating responses after a stressor has been experienced. There is a growing body of evidence that has demonstrated that perseverative cognition is associated with somatic outcomes both cross-sectionally, prospectively, and using daily diary methods (see O'Connor, Walker, Hendrickx,

Talbot, & Schaefer, 2013; Verkuil, Brosschot, Meerman, & Thayer, 2012; Verkuil, Brosschot, Gebhardt, & Thayer, 2010 for a review). This suggests that research on appraisals needs to include indices of rumination in relation to stress appraisal processes. This further highlights the need to assess and consider traits and unconscious processes and to embrace innovative methods and technologies in stress research (e.g., utilising electronic data capture methods together with daily and momentary assessment techniques).

Stress, Appraisals, and the Genomic Age

Research in all areas of psychology is now informed by the behavioural and molecular genetic considerations. There is now growing evidence that cognitive appraisals are under genetic influence (Saudino, Pedersen, Lichtenstein, McClean, & Plomin, 1997) as is the experience of life events (Power et al., 2013). This genetic variation – which is about 20–30% – appears to be fully accounted for by personality (Power et al., 2013; Saudino et al., 1997). This again indicates the importance of including traits in stress research, but also of genetically informed designs (behavioural and molecular or both) when conducting stress research. Finally, it would be useful to know if the associations observed between events, stress appraisal, coping, and specific health outcomes share a common genetic mechanism.

References

Abraham, C., Conner, M., Jones, F., & O'Connor, D. B. (2008). *Health psychology: Topics in applied psychology*. London, UK: Hodder Arnold.
Affleck, G., Tennen, H., Urrows, S., & Higgins, P. (1994). Person and contextual features of daily stress reactivity: Individual differences in relations of undesirable daily events with mood disturbance and chronic pain intensity. *Journal of Personality and Social Psychology, 66*, 329–340. http://doi.org/10.1037/0022-3514.66.2.329
American Psychological Association. (2012). *Stress in America survey*. Retrieved from http://www.apa.org/news/press/releases/stress/2012/impact.aspx
Brosschot, J. F., Gerin, W., & Thayer, J. F. (2006). The perseverative cognition hypothesis: A review of worry, prolonged stress-related physiological activation, and health. *Journal of Psychosomatic Research, 60*, 113–124. http://doi.org/10.1016/j.jpsychores.2005.06.074
Brown, G. W., & Harris, T. O. (1978). *Social origins of depression: A study of depressive disorder in women*. New York, NY: Free Press.
Cannon, W. (1932). *The wisdom of the body*. New York, NY: Norton.
Chapman, B. P., Khan, A., Harper, M., Stockman, D., Fiscella, K., Walton, J., … Moynihan, J. (2009). Gender, race/ethnicity, personality, and interleukin-6 in urban primary care patients. *Brain, Behavior and Immunity, 23*, 636–642. http://doi.org/10.1016/j.bbi.2008.12.009
Clow, A. (2001). The physiology of stress. In F. Jones & J. Bright (Eds.), *Stress: Myth, theory and research* (pp. 47–51). London, UK: Pearson Education.
Cohen, S. (1986). Contrasting the hassles scale and the perceived stress scale: Who's really measuring appraised stress? *American Psychologist, 41*, 716–718. http://doi.org/10.1037/0003-066X.41.6.716
Cohen, S., Kamarck, T., & Mermelstein, R. (1983). A global measure of perceived stress. *Journal of Health and Social Behavior, 24*, 385–396. http://doi.org/10.2307/2136404
Cohen, S., & Williamson, G. M. (1988). Perceived stress in a probability sample of the United States. In S. Spacapan & S. Oskamp (Eds.), *The social psychology of health* (pp. 31–67). Newbury Park, CA: Sage.
Conner, M., Fitter, M., & Fletcher, W. (1999). Stress and snacking: A diary study of daily hassles and between meal snacking. *Psychology & Health, 14*, 51–63. http://doi.org/10.1080/08870449908407313
Cox, T., & Mackay, C. (1985). The measurement of self-reported stress and arousal. *British Journal of Psychology, 76*, 183–186. http://doi.org/10.1111/j.2044-8295.1985.tb01941.x

Dancey, C. P., Taghavi, M., & Fox, R. J. (1998). The relationship between daily stress and symptoms of irritable bowel: A time-series approach. *Journal of Psychosomatic Research, 44*, 537–545. http://doi.org/10.1016/S0022-3999(97)00255-9

DeLongis, A., Coyne, J. C., Dakof, G., Folkman, S., & Lazarus, R. S. (1982). Relationships of daily hassles, uplifts, and major life events to health status. *Health Psychology, 1*, 119–136. http://doi.org/10.1037/0278-6133.1.2.119

DeLongis, A., Folkman, S., & Lazarus, R. (1988). The impact of daily stress on health and mood: Psychological and social resources as mediators. *Journal of Personality and Social Psychology, 54*, 486–495. http://doi.org/10.1037/0022-3514.54.3.486

Dohrenwend, B. P. (2006). Inventorying stressful life events as risk factors for psychopathology: Towards resolution of the problem of intracategory variability. *Psychological Bulletin, 132*, 477–495. http://doi.org/10.1037/0033-2909.132.3.477

Dohrenwend, B. S., Dohrenwend, B. P., Dodson, M., & Shrout, P. E. (1984). Symptoms, hassles, social support and life events: Problem of confounding measures. *Journal of Abnormal Psychology, 93*, 222–230. http://doi.org/10.1037/0021-843X.93.2.222

Dohrenwend, B. P., & Shrout, P. E. (1985). "Hassles" in the conceptualization and measurement of life stress variables. *American Psychologist, 40*, 780–785. http://doi.org/10.1037/0003-066X.40.7.780

Durak, M., & Senol-Durak, E. (2013). The development and psychometric properties of the Turkish version of the stress appraisal measure. *European Journal of Psychological Assessment, 29*, 64–71. http://doi.org/10.1027/1015-5759/a000079

Ferguson, E. (2001). Personality and coping traits: A joint factor analysis. *British Journal of Health Psychology, 6*, 311–325. http://doi.org/10.1348/135910701169232

Ferguson, E. (2013). Personality is of central concern to understand health: Towards a theoretical model for health psychology. *Health Psychology Review, 7*(Suppl. 1), S32–S70. http://doi.org/10.1080/17437199.2010.547985

Ferguson, E., Daniels, K., & Jones, D. (2006). Negatively oriented personality and negative job-characteristics as predictors of future psychological and physical symptoms: A meta-analytic structural modelling approach. *Journal of Psychosomatic Research, 60*, 45–52. http://doi.org/10.1016/j.jpsychores.2005.06.076

Ferguson, E., Matthews, G., & Cox, T. (1999). The appraisal of life events (ALE) scale: Reliability, and validity. *British Journal of Health Psychology, 4*, 97–11. http://doi.org/10.1348/135910799168506

Fifield, J., McQuillan, J., Armeli, S., Tennen, H., Reisine, S., & Affleck, G. (2004). Chronic strain, daily work stress and pain among workers with rheumatoid arthritis: Does job stress make a bad day worse? *Work & Stress, 18*, 275–291. http://doi.org/10.1080/02678370412331324996

Folkman, S., & Lazarus, R. S. (1985). If it changes it must be a process: Study of emotion and coping during three stages of a college examination. *Journal of Personality and Social Psychology, 48*, 150–170. http://doi.org/10.1037/0022-3514.48.1.150

Gall, T. L., & Evans, D. R. (1987). The dimensionality of cognitive appraisal and its relationship to physical and psychological well-being. *Journal of Psychology, 121*, 539–546. http://doi.org/10.1080/00223980.1987.9712682

Gartland, N., O'Connor, D. B., & Lawton, R. (2012). Effects of conscientiousness on the appraisals of daily stressors. *Stress & Health, 28*, 80–86. http://doi.org/10.1002/smi.1404

Gartland, N., O'Connor, D. B., Lawton, R., & Ferguson, E. (2014). Investigating the effects of conscientiousness on daily stress, affect and physical symptom processes: A daily diary study. *British Journal of Health Psychology, 19*(2), 311–328. http://doi.org/10.1111/bjhp.12077

Gourounti, K., Anagnostopoulos, F., & Vaslamatzis, G. (2012). Appraisal of life events scale in a sample of Greek infertile women undergoing fertility treatment: A confirmatory factor analysis. *Midwifery, 28*, 445–450. http://doi.org/10.1016/j.midw.2011.06.010

Health and Safety Executive. (2013). *Stress and psychological disorders in Great Britain 2013*. London, UK: Crown Copyright.

Holmes, T. H., & Masuda, M. (1974). Life change and illness susceptibility. In B. S. Dohrenwend & B. P. Dohrenwend (Eds.), *Stressful life events: Their nature and effects* (pp. 45–72). London, UK: Wiley.

Holmes, T. H., & Rahe, R. H. (1967). The social readjustment rating scale. *Journal of Psychosomatic Research, 11*, 213–218. http://doi.org/10.1016/0022-3999(67)90010-4

Jones, F., & Bright, J. (2001). *Stress: Myth, theory and research*. London, UK: Prentice Hall.

Kanner, A. D., Coyne, J. C., Schaefer, C., & Lazarus, R. S. (1981). Comparison of two modes of stress measurement: Daily hassles and uplifts versus major life events. *Journal of Behavioral Medicine, 4*, 1–39. http://doi.org/10.1007/BF00844845

Lazarus, R. S. (1999). *Stress and emotion: A new synthesis*. London, UK: Springer.

Lazarus, R. S., DeLongis, A., Folkman, S., & Gruen, R. (1985). Stress and adaptational outcomes: The problem of confounded measures. *American Psychologist, 40*, 770–779. http://doi.org/10.1037/0003-066X.40.7.770

Lazarus, R. S., & Folkman, S. (1984). *Stress, appraisal and coping*. New York, NY: Springer.

Locke, D., & Pennington, D. (1982). Reasons and other causes: Their role in attribution processes. *Journal of Personality and Social Psychology, 42*, 212–223. http://doi.org/10.1037/0022-3514.42.2.212

Mackay, C. J., Cox, T., Burrows, G. C., & Lazzarini, A. J. (1978). An inventory for the measurement of self-reported stress and arousal. *British Journal of Social and Clinical Psychology, 17*, 283–284. http://doi.org/10.1111/j.2044-8260.1978.tb00280.x

Mason, J. W. (1971). A re-evaluation of the concept of 'non-specificity' in stress theory. *Journal of Psychiatric Research, 8*, 323–353. http://doi.org/10.1016/0022-3956(71)90028-8

McEwen, B. S. (1998). Protective and damaging effects of stress mediators. *New England Journal of Medicine, 338*, 171–179. http://doi.org/10.1056/NEJM199801153380307

McEwen, B. S. (2000). Allostasis and allostatic load: Implications for neuropsychopharmacology. *Neuropsychopharmacology, 22*, 108–124. http://doi.org/10.1016/S0893-133X(99)00129-3

O'Connor, D. B., Conner, M., Jones, F., McMillan, B., & Ferguson, E. (2009). Exploring the benefits of conscientiousness: An investigation of daily stressors and health behaviors. *Annals of Behavioral Medicine, 37*, 184–196. http://doi.org/10.1007/s12160-009-9087-6

O'Connor, D. B., Hendrickx, H., Dadd, T., Talbot, D., Mayes, A., Elliman, T., … Dye, L. (2009). Cortisol awakening rise in middle-aged women in relation to chronic psychological stress. *Psychoneuroendocrinology, 34*, 1486–1494. http://doi.org/10.1016/j.psyneuen.2009.05.002

O'Connor, D. B., Jones, F., Conner, M., McMillan, B., & Ferguson, E. (2008). Effects of daily hassles and eating style on eating behavior. *Health Psychology, 27*(1 Suppl.), S20–31. http://doi.org/10.1037/0278-6133.27.1.S20

O'Connor, D. B., Walker, S., Hendrickx, H., Talbot, D., & Schaefer, A. (2013). Stress-related thinking predicts the cortisol awakening response and somatic symptoms in healthy adults. *Psychoneuroendocrinology, 38*, 438–446. http://doi.org/10.1016/j.psyneuen.2012.07.004

Peacock, E. J., & Wong, P. T. P. (1990). The stress appraisal measure (SAM): A multidimensional approach to cognitive appraisal. *Stress Medicine, 6*, 227–236. http://doi.org/10.1002/smi.2460060308

Power, R. A., Wingenbach, T., Cohen-Woods, S., Uher, R., Ng, M. Y., Butler, A. W., … McGuffin, P. (2013). Estimating the heritability of reporting stressful life events captured by common genetic variants. *Psychological Medicine, 43*, 1965–1971. http://doi.org/10.1017/S0033291712002589

Rahe, R. H., & Paasikivi, J. (1971). Psychosocial factors and myocardial infarction: An outpatient study in Sweden. *Journal of Psychosomatic Research, 8*, 35–44.

Sapolsky, R. M., Romero, L. M., & Munck, A. U. (2000). How do glucocorticoids influence stress responses? Integrating permissive, suppressive, stimulatory, and preparative actions. *Endocrine Reviews, 21*, 55–89. http://doi.org/10.1210/er.21.1.55

Saudino, K. J., Pedersen, N. L., Lichtenstein, P., McClearn, G. E., & Plomin, R. (1997). Can personality explain the genetic influence in life events? *Journal of Personality and Social Psychology, 72*, 196–206. http://doi.org/10.1037/0022-3514.72.1.196

Schlotz, W., Hellhammer, J., Schulz, P., & Stone, A. A. (2004). Perceived work overload and chronic worrying predict weekend-weekday differences in the cortisol awakening response. *Psychosomatic Medicine, 66*, 207–214. http://doi.org/10.1097/01.psy.0000116715.78238.56

Schneider, T. R. (2008). Evaluations of stressful transactions: What's in an appraisal? *Stress and Health, 24*, 151–158. http://doi.org/10.1002/smi.1176

Schroeder, D. H., & Costa, P. T. (1984). Influence of life event stress on physical illness: substantive effects or methodological flaws? *Journal of Personality and Social Psychology, 46*, 853–863. http://doi.org/10.1037/0022-3514.46.4.853

Schulz, P., Schlotz, W., & Becker, P. (2011). *The Trier Inventory of Chronic Stress (TICS) – Manual (W. Schlotz, Trans.)*. Göttingen, Germany: Hogrefe (Original work published 2004).

Segerstrom, S. C., & O'Connor, D. B. (2012). Stress, health and illness: Four challenges for the future. *Psychology & Health, 27*, 128–140. http://doi.org/10.1080/08870446.2012.659516

Selye, H. (1950). Stress and the general adaptation syndrome. *British Medical Journal, 1*, 1383–1392. http://doi.org/10.1136/bmj.1.4667.1383

Selye, H. (1956). *The stress of life*. New York, NY: McGraw-Hill.

Senol-Durak, E., & Durak, M. (2013). Turkish validation of the dispositional form of the stress appraisal measure. *Education and Science, 37*, 48–63.

Theorell, T., & Rahe, R. H. (1971). Psychosocial factors in myocardial infarction. *Journal of Psychosomatic Research, 15*, 25–31. http://doi.org/10.1016/0022-3999(71)90070-5

Tomaka, J., Blascovich, J., Kibler, J., &Ernst, J. M. (1997). Cognitive and physiological antecedents of threat and challenge appraisal. *Journal of Personality and Social Psychology, 73*, 63–72. http://doi.org/10.1037/0022-3514.73.1.63

Vedhara, K., Miles, J., Bennett, P., Plummer, S., Tallon, D., Brooks, E., ... Farndon, J. (2003). An investigation into the relationship between salivary cortisol, stress, anxiety, and depression. *Biological Psychology, 62*, 89–96. http://doi.org/10.1016/S0301-0511(02)00128-X

Verkuil, B., Brosschot, J. F., Gebhardt, W., & Thayer, J. F. (2010). When worries make you sick: A review of perseverative cognition, the default stress response and somatic health. *Journal of Experimental Psychopathology, 1*, 87–118. http://doi.org/10.5127/jep.009110

Verkuil, B., Brosschot, J. F., Meerman, E. E., Thayer, J. F. (2012). Effects of momentary assessed stressful events and worry episodes on somatic health complaints. *Psychology & Health, 27*, 141–158. http://doi.org/10.1080/08870441003653470

Warttig, S. L., Forshaw, M. J., South, J., & White, A .K. (2013). New, normative, English-sample data for the Short Form Perceived Stress Scale (PSS-4). *Journal of Health Psychology, 18*, 1617–1628. http://doi.org/10.1177/1359105313508346

Williamson, D. E., Birmaher, B., Ryan, N. D., Shiffrin, T. P., Lusky, J. A., Protopapa, J., ... Brent, D. A (2003). The Stressful Life Events Schedule for children and adolescents: Development and validation. *Psychiatry Research, 119*, 225–241. http://doi.org/10.1016/S0165-1781(03)00134-3

Chapter 9
Coping

Benjamin H. Gottlieb

Department of Psychology, University of Guelph, Guelph, ON, Canada

Introduction

From an analytic perspective, the process of coping is a vortex of swirling cognitive and behavioral responses, some of which are highly calculated and strategic, others more reflexive, collectively aimed to return the individual to baseline levels of arousal. When immersed in the process of coping, we are likely to experience intense emotions and physiological sensations of arousal, the pull and expression of our personality and temperament that are strongly activated during crises, the multiple and simultaneous demands imposed by the stressor, and the influence of the social context and norms operating in the situation. In their classic definition, Lazarus and Folkman (1984) define coping as: "Constantly changing cognitive and behavioral efforts to manage specific external and/or internal demands that are appraised as taxing or exceeding the resources of the person" (p. 141). Stated more simply by Carver and Vargas (2011), "Coping is not a special event but is normal behavior that takes place under circumstances of adversity. Stress is the adversity; coping is the attempt to make it go away or to diminish its impact" (p. 181).

To make stress go away we employ a variety of tactics that are strategically aimed to control our emotions and return them to steady state if not a state that improves upon pre-exposure affect, and we do what we can to offset the demands imposed by the hardship at hand. Of course, there are myriad stressors that are unyielding to our efforts to make them actually go away or to reduce their severity. In these instances, the main battle is waged at the emotional level while reserves may still be deployed to address any practical demands that can be diminished. For example, although a serious illness diagnosis cannot be changed, certain lifestyle alterations can be made to optimize disease management and survival time. Moreover, huge quality-of-life benefits can be gained from the psychological confidence and sense of mastery that are nourished by our agency in more controllable stressor domains.

The rapidly evolving field of health psychology is concerned with the application of psychological theories and methods to the assessment, prevention, and treatment of behavior relevant to physical health, illness, and health care. Fundamentally, since health psychologists are concerned with myriad aspects of behavior that affect vulnerability and resistance to illness and disease, much of their work concerns the stress induced by challenges to human adaptation. Indeed, stress-related transactions are strong determinants or inherent elements of most serious illnesses and diseases. Stress can also be produced and regulated when medical intervention is required. The latter includes the stress arising from hospitalization, medical procedures, and interaction between doctor and patient, as well as the stress associated with decision making under conditions of great uncertainty. In short, it is not an exaggeration to conclude that stress is ubiquitous in the biopsychosocial sphere of health, disease, and health care (Ogden, 2012; Sarafino, 1998). Coping follows in the shadow of stress, determining its consequences for health and well-being.

This chapter continues with an exposition of the main constructs in the field of coping, including the cognitive appraisals that shape the extent of stress and the nature of the coping that arise. Typologies of coping responses are reviewed next. They include both generic instruments that can be applied across different stressors, as well as stressor-specific tools that have been developed from discovery-oriented methods of inquiry such as interviews and focus groups. This is followed by a discussion of the main issues that require consideration in the selection of coping measures, and a final section addressing the challenges that lie ahead for coping research in the field of health psychology.

Basic Concepts

Stressors and Coping

It may come as a surprise that it is hard to distinguish coping from ordinary behavior except under conditions that are universally stressful such as natural and technological disasters that place people at high risk of injury and death, or when people undergo major surgery on vital organs that require repair or are affected by cancer. Virtually everyone would agree that these conditions pose a huge threat of both physical and psychological harm, with natural and technological disasters being most stressful because of their suddenness. At least one can prepare for surgery when it is scheduled in advance by gaining as much information about it as possible. Not so for events that are unanticipated, novel, and largely uncontrollable, three stressor properties that multiply the likelihood of resulting stress and intense coping. But not all stressors are event-like in nature, meaning that they have a clear onset and offset.

As Wheaton (1997) points out, stress can arise not only from the occurrence of undesirable events, but also from the non-occurrence of a desired state or status, such as when a couple are unable to conceive or when genetic counseling reveals a strong likelihood of transmitting an inherited disorder to an offspring. Stress can also arise insidiously and proceed in an open-ended way, having no fixed offset, as is the case for dementia that begins with subtle symptoms of memory lapses and losses and follows a downward trajectory that can result in death. Moreover, acute life events can launch lengthy episodes of chronic stress, an example being a hip fracture and hospitalization of an older adult and subsequent deterioration due to neuromuscular atrophy and suboptimal nutrition. Conversely, chronic stressors can host episodes of acute stress, such as the flare-ups that occur to multiple sclerosis and arthritis sufferers and the regimens of chemotherapy that so many cancer patients must endure. In short, the boundary between chronic and acute stressors is not easily demarcated, the more typical scenario being that the two interact and are mutually influential in producing stress.

According to Carver and Vargas (2011) it is the context ("circumstances of adversity," p. 181) that distinguishes coping from the rest of human behavior. Lazarus and Folkman (1984) characterize coping as effortful behavior that is marshaled when demands exceed the individual's resources or usual ways of handling life's challenges. However, they also acknowledge that some ways of coping are so overlearned or scripted as to make them automatic, unremarkable, and built-in features of living. Examples include people who habitually exercise, meditate, pray, or ensure that they are always busy, and on the darker side, people who regularly dull their feelings with alcohol after work, use substances to get through their day, or scapegoat family members for ills that originate elsewhere. No wonder it is such a challenge to assess people's ways of coping; they are not necessarily aware of the resources for resisting stress that are behavioral fixtures in their lives, much less the cognitive coping resources they routinely employ.

Cognitive Appraisals

If coping is not necessarily effortful and co-occurs when adversity strikes, then surely there must be individual differences in reactivity to events such that some people experience more and some less or no stress. Adversity is in the eyes and the resources of the beholders, with some people greeting the event nonchalantly and others reacting with substantial distress. These differences are explained by Lazarus and Folkman's (1984) formulations about the cognitive mediation of stress. They propose an evaluative framework that filters events in terms of their potential for harm, loss, damage, and even benefit – which they label *primary appraisal* – and in terms of the resources available for adjusting or adapting to the event, labeled *secondary appraisal*. This terminology does not connote that one is more important or precedes the other; the two cognitive processes co-occur, are mutually influential, and are in constant flux as the coping episode unfolds.

Secondary appraisal of the resources available to manage the emotional and practical demands of stressors includes the belief that varied types of support and help are available from family, friends, and health-care professionals. This belief is helpful in itself because the perceived availability of a safety net may generate the confidence or self-efficacy to cope. But the belief that support is forthcoming is purely an expectation that has a reassurance function. When network members are actually engaged for help and support, they are providing coping assistance. Hence, the stress-reducing functions of social support lie in its mobilization as a social resource for coping and in its mental representation as a potential resource. This cognitive representation of support places it alongside several other perceived personal resources that can aid and abet the coping process, including high self-esteem, a strong sense of self-efficacy for dealing with adversity, social skills, optimism, and a phlegmatic temperament.

A final distinction bears important implications for measurement. It concerns a decision investigators must make as to whether they aim to capture *situational coping* in specific stressful episodes or *coping styles*, meaning the manner in which the individual usually copes or would cope. Coping styles assume some degree of cross-situational consistency in the manner of coping; examples being individuals who typically engage in support seeking and people who tend to react to tribulations by catastrophizing. When respondents complete a coping inventory preceded by instructions to characterize their usual ways of coping with stressful events, their coping styles are being assessed. When they are asked to rate the extent of their use of coping responses for a particular stressor, situational coping is being assessed. Evidence favoring the existence of coping styles is likely to be more valid when coping is assessed on multiple occasions than when participants are asked to generalize about how they do or would cope. As Aldwin (1994) observes: "How individuals think that they usually cope could be very different from their actual behavior under stress" (p. 113).

Classification and Measurement of Coping Responses: Generic and Stressor-Specific Checklists

Classification of Coping

Coping responses can be classified at three levels of analysis: (a) the specific ways of coping described at the *item* level, (b) the *class* of coping represented by a group of items that have been assigned a common label on the basis of the type of coping they reflect, and (c) the higher-order *mode* of coping that groups the type categories into molar classes that reflect the overall manner or orientation of coping. Although not a comprehensive listing, Table 9.1 displays examples of items that fall into the main classes and modes of coping that underlie the most popular coping checklists. Procedurally, participants typically complete a coping checklist that contains numerous items, rating the extent to which they have employed each item in response to a given stressor. For example, the most widely used Revised Ways of Coping Checklist (RWOC; Vitaliano, Russo, Carr, Maiuro, & Becker, 1985) calls for participants to rate 66 items on a 4-point Likert-type response format that reflects the extent of use of each way of coping.

Table 9.1. Modes, classes, and examples of coping

Mode	Class	Example
Approach/engage	Support seeking	"Talked to someone to find out more"
Approach/engage	Problem solving	"Made a plan and tried to execute it"
Avoid/disengage	Denial	"Went on as if nothing bad had happened"
Avoid/disengage	Withdrawal	"Preferred to keep to myself"
Problem-focused	Direct action	"Did something to try to solve the problem"
Emotion-focused	Religion/spirituality	"Gained spiritual comfort"
Cognitive approach	Positive reinterpretation	"Tried to see something positive"
Cognitive avoidance	Distraction	"Just tried to keep busy"
Behavior approach	Catharsis	"Let my feelings out somehow"
Behavior avoidance	Escape	"Kept clear of reminders of the problem"

The classes of coping that appear in Table 9.1 are derived on either a priori logical grounds or on the basis of a multivariate technique, usually factor or principal components analysis of the item-level responses. It is noteworthy that the solutions that have been generated are unstable across different stressors, different samples, and different checklists, making it impossible to identify a core structure of coping (Skinner, Edge, Altman, & Sherwood, 2003). Moreover, different coping dimensions have emerged from factor analyses of the same measure across stressors and samples (e.g., Cook & Heppner, 1997; Oxlad, Miller-Lewis, & Wade, 2004). These findings explain why attention has been mainly focused on the modes of coping; consensus about the structure of coping exists only at the most general mode level, the level that aggregates different types of coping. These modes refer to central coping tendencies, such as approach versus avoidant coping, a distinction sometimes referred to as engaged versus disengaged coping. As this terminology suggests, approach coping refers to active efforts to directly address stressful demands and the feelings they incur by problem solving or seeking support, for example. Avoidant coping seeks to avoid experiencing thoughts, feelings, sensations, and memories related to the stressor (Skinner et al., 2003). In addition, the overall thrust of coping can be characterized as problem-focused versus emotion-focused (Folkman & Moskowitz, 2004). The problem is that these modes are neater than the ways of coping they subsume, with investigators assigning different types of coping to the same mode depending on the results of an empirical or a priori (rational) filtering process. In one study support seeking appears among the items reflecting problem-focused coping and in another study it appears on the list of emotion-focused items. Clearly, such a high level of classification of the myriad ways of coping serves convenience and simplification, but is otherwise of little intellectual or practical value.

Since coping is expressed not only behaviorally, but also through cognitions that are largely private, there are countless cognitive coping items on all coping checklists. They include thoughts, wishes, reflections, and self-statements that have an important emotion-regulatory function. Examples include acceptance, rumination, self-blame, catastrophizing, and positive reframing (Garnefski, Kraaij, & Spinhoven, 2001). Moreover, because thoughts are so fleeting, abundant, and unremarkable, cognitive coping is far more difficult to record and report than behavioral coping, even when methods to capture them are deployed frequently and almost immediately at the time when they occurred by using the technique of ecological momentary assessment (EMA; Stone & Shiffman, 1994; see also Chapter 18 in this volume).

These disappointing findings have not prevented investigators from employing selected subscales drawn wholesale from checklists without cross-validation or verifying their applicability to a given stressor and sample. Worse yet, the psychometric properties of the subscales are either unknown or poor, the latter evidence raising questions about the appropriateness of traditional measures of reliability and validity. Why should the items contained in any one dimension or type of coping be subjected to an internal reliability analysis that assumes the individuals will also employ the other ways of coping that are classified in that dimension? Why would one expect high test–retest reliability for support-seeking or avoidant behavior when the coping process is so much in flux as demands and appraisals change?

Measures of Coping

Generic Coping Measures

The RWOC is a generic, off-the-shelf inventory that, notionally, is applicable to many different stressors and therefore allows for cross-stressor comparisons of coping. But precisely because it was designed to permit such comparisons, its items are written in general terms, neglecting differences in the type and range of coping responses that are possible for a given stressor, and including ways of coping that may be entirely irrelevant for the same stressor. For example, an item that falls into the coping class called *confrontive coping* states: "Took a big chance or did something very risky." Endorsement of that item does not reveal the nature of the chance that was taken or the nature of the action that was risked. For someone affected by rheumatoid arthritis, coping may have consisted of switching health-care professionals, trying a new medication that may have adverse side effects, or starting a grueling exercise regimen that could exacerbate symptoms. Moreover, from a practice perspective, it is the latter specific expressions of coping, not the generic item, that offer insight into the client's coping and provide a basis for clinical recommendations.

There are several additional generic coping instruments that bear a strong resemblance to the RWOC at the item, type, and mode levels. Because they are too numerous to review here, only the most widely used are covered. They include the COPE Inventory (Carver, Scheier & Weintraub, 1989), the Coping Checklist (CC; Billings & Moos, 1981), the Coping Strategy Indicator (CSI; Amirkhan, 1990), and the Coping Inventory for Stressful Situations (CISS; Endler & Parker, 1990). Details regarding their contents and psychometric properties are contained in Clark, Bormann, Cropanzano, and James (1995) and Schwarzer and Schwarzer (1996). Readers interested in a more penetrating review and critique of types of coping captured by these and other generic tools are referred to Skinner et al. (2003). Given this chapter's broad scope, suffice it to say that the differences among these generic measures have more to do with the number and names of the types of coping they reduce to and their state versus trait orientation than with their coverage of possible coping responses.

For those interested in a more detailed and differentiated assessment of coping, the RWOC and the COPE each contain about 60 items that have yielded eight and 12 subscales, respectively, based on factor analysis. Although labeled differently, they have several subscales in common, including support-seeking and escape/avoidant coping. They also employ similar response formats that gauge the extent to which each way of coping is employed (e.g., the RWOC's format ranges from *not coping in that way at all*, to *used somewhat, used quite a bit*, and *used a great deal*). Moreover, a brief, 28-item version of the COPE has been developed and is widely used because of its greater acceptability to participants and usefulness in clinical and field research (Carver, 1997). It contains 14 subscales composed of two items each, and Carver states that it can be used with three different sets of instructions depending on the investigator's aims (http://www.psy.miami.edu/faculty/ccarver/sclCOPEF.html). Participants can be asked how much they usually cope in each way, thereby tapping dispositional or trait coping styles. Alternatively, they can be asked how much they employed each way of coping over a certain period of time, and they can report their ways of coping with a specific stressor they have been recently or are currently exposed to, thereby tapping state coping. No such options are made available by the authors of the RWOC; their transactional theory requires exclusive application of the RWOC to a specific stressful situation. They even recommend dividing a given stressor into stages of exposure. For example, people scheduled for surgery engage in coping during the preoperative stage when they are anticipating or preparing themselves, then during the immediate recovery stage while still in the hospital, and finally during the recuperation stage that may last for days, weeks, or months and allows for coping to be periodically reassessed.

The remaining generic coping inventories offer more molar assessments and consequently yield more stable factor structures. The CC, CSI, and CISS all yield either two or three broad coping dimensions that include emotion-oriented, task-oriented, and avoidance-oriented coping for the CISS (Endler & Parker, 1990), problem solving, seeking support, and avoidance for the CSI (Amirkhan, 1990), and appraisal-focused coping, problem-focused coping, and emotion-focused coping for the CC (Billings & Moos, 1984). The disadvantage of these tools is that the scores they yield reflect unwieldy and vague second-order coping factors that are little more than diffuse indicators of a general coping orientation. For example, by summing the items that reside on the problem-focused or avoidant coping dimension, one can compare how much reliance is made on each dimension across different stressors, stressor stages, or among participants, but the meaning of the scores remains obscured. A variation of this method of scoring is to calculate proportional coping scores by dividing scores for each mode of coping by the total score for all modes or by dividing the mean score for each mode by the sum of the means for all of the modes. Either method provides information about relative reliance on different modes of coping. The same techniques can be used for the RWOC and the COPE.

Stressor-Specific Coping Measures

Alongside these generic coping checklists are a set of customized coping measures that have been painstakingly designed to capture the multitude of ways of coping that can be employed to manage or adapt to the practical and emotional demands of particular types of stressors. These specialized measures are usually developed inductively by canvassing patients about the varied coping tasks they face and their ways of responding to them, gathering clinical information from practitioners who work with the affected population, and by examining the relevant literatures. An example is the Mental Adjustment to Cancer scale (MAC; Watson et al., 1988), originally consisting of 40 items and then reduced to 33 items (Watson et al., 1994; Watson & Homewood, 2008) that measure five types of coping: (a) fighting spirit, (b) hopelessness/helplessness, (c) anxious preoccupation, (d) fatalism, and (e) avoidance. The latter version also has been reduced to two underlying (higher-order) constructs, one providing a positive adjustment to cancer score and one a negative adjustment to cancer score. Similarly, in the field of pain research, the Coping Strategies Questionnaire (CSQ; Rosenstiel & Keefe, 1983) was developed to assess pain coping, its 48 items yielding eight types that include diverting attention, reinterpreting pain sensations, coping self-statements, ignoring pain, praying and hoping, catastrophizing, increasing activity, and pain behavior. In the field of psycho-oncology, a measure of coping with cancer genetic risk assessment has been developed and includes a matrix of 11 specific stressful demands associated with such genetic testing crossed with eight ways of coping, the content of both axes arising from prior focus groups and clinical contact with people involved in such testing (Phelps et al., 2010).

As just noted, when subjected to factor analysis, these and other stressor-specific coping inventories tend to yield dimensions that differ from those produced by the generic inventories because most of the underlying items reflect the more specialized ways of coping employed by people experiencing that specific stressor. Only the modes of coping are reproduced, but offer far less instruction to practitioners than the stressor-specific types of coping that are highly relevant to the particular stressful demands. It follows that specialized measures of coping, not the generic one-size-fits-all templates, will be far more useful to health psychologists.

Methodological Issues

Whether a generic or specialized coping checklist is employed, the object of coping must be clearly specified. Because most stressors are not unitary in nature but consist of a number of stressful elements or demands, it is critical to ensure that all participants complete the checklist with the same demand in mind. For example, rather than asking participants how they are coping with their diagnosis of cancer, the particular demands that arise ought to be identified, including the existential, practical, social, health-care, and treatment-related demands, and then individually presented as objects of coping. For instance, among the family caregivers of people affected by Alzheimer's disease, coping should be studied in relation to the demands of the hands-on daily care, the management of the affected party's behavior, and the stress associated with their captivity in the caregiver role (Gottlieb & Gignac, 1996). For an excellent example of the process of identifying the constituent stressors of cancer genetic risk assessment and ways of coping with each substressor, see Bennett et al. (2012) and Phelps et al. (2010).

To ensure that participants are all "on the same page" when reporting their coping, consideration should also be given to the stage of stressor exposure and to the timing of the assessment in relation to the stressor exposure. With respect to the former issue, a distinction can be drawn between the anticipation or pre-exposure stage, the actual exposure stage, and the recovery stage. For example, Folkman and Lazarus (1985) studied university students coping with an examination, partitioning this stressor into the preparation phase, the phase when they awaited the results, and the phase when they received their grades. They found that the most prominent coping responses were distinctly different at each stage. More pertinent to the field of health psychology, Oaksford and Frude (2003) examined temporal changes in coping among adult survivors of child sexual abuse. They employed both the RWOC checklist and a grounded theory qualitative analysis of narratives provided by survivors. They discovered that some ways of coping were unique to each method, but that there was an overall pattern of similar findings about how coping differed from the period proximal to exposure to the abuse to the period months and years later. Basically, coping shifted from earlier avoidant responses to later positive framing and growth narratives. The authors conclude that "the ability to use different coping strategies at different points in time, and to use more than one method, may be associated with psychological adjustment" (p. 66). Indeed, a hallmark of coping effectiveness and resilience is its flexible application to different stressors at different stages.

The temporal issue also concerns the time elapsed between stressor exposure and coping assessment. Memory decay and retrospective bias are likely to make reports of coping from people who are actively dealing with breast or prostate cancer quite different from the reports of people who have survived for several years postdiagnosis, largely because the latter already know their health outcome. Complicating matters further, there is evidence that even short-term retrospective accounts of coping do not jibe with coping documented at the time of stressor exposure. Ptacek, Smith, Espe, and Raffety (1994) have demonstrated quite convincingly that coping data collected by checklist on a daily basis for 7 days before a university exam were relatively independent of retrospective reports 5 days after the exam of how the participants had coped during that period. Similar findings were reported 10 years later by Todd, Tennen, Carney, Armeli, and Affleck (2004), who also reviewed additional studies revealing the poor correspondence between daily and retrospective coping methods.

Together, these studies lead to the conclusion that retrospection is not a valid data collection method, that there are numerous biasing factors that can explain this conclusion, and that even new and superior real-time methodologies, such as daily diaries and EMA, cannot bridge the gap between these temporal differences in coping reports. Introduced by Stone and Shiffman (1994), EMA involves interval-based administration of a brief coping checklist that is produced several times by a portable computer over the course of stressor exposure. Daily diaries of coping are similar to EMA (e.g., Keefe et al., 1997; Raffety, Smith & Ptacek, 1997; Tennen & Affleck, 1996); they also solicit ways of coping close to the time they occur, but not as frequently or as expensively as the EMA method.

Unresolved Issues in Coping

Critiques and apologias for the untidy state of affairs concerning the measurement and even the definition of coping abound. In June 2000, a special issue of the *American Psychologist* (Vol. 55, No. 6) contained several influential articles by the field's founding architects. The lead article by the special section's editors begins with the lament that coping research has produced so little and a warning that the field is in danger of collapsing (Somerfield & McCrae, 2000). Presumably, to remedy this morass, the papers that followed offered incisive critiques of research design issues, such as the value of a within-person process-oriented approach to coping, and on ways that coping research could inform clinical practice. In 2004 Austenfeld and Stanton followed up with a paper revealing that certain items that purported to assess emotion-focused coping responses were confounded with certain measures of emotional adjustment, and made an important contribution by identifying the unconfounded items that should be retained in coping checklists.

Coyne and Gottlieb (1996) and Somerfield and McCrae (2000) decried the reactive effects and limited yield of checklists, and suggested using the endorsed items only as superficial markers of a far richer and more complex coping experience. They argued that finer-grain accounts of coping, along with narratives about the goals of employing them, could illuminate the dynamic interplay among the changing demands of stressors, their appraisals, individual differences, and the physical and social contexts in which people are embedded. A practical suggestion was to use a checklist only to flag the ways of coping being employed, and then interview the participants about the items they endorsed in order to gain more exacting accounts of their coping. Indeed, a handful of narrative studies have not only yielded a deeper understanding of the process of coping, but also shown that coping is influenced by the social context and by the individual's goals, values, and cultural heritage (Brannen & Petite, 2008; Chun, Moos, & Cronkite, 2006; Kuo, Roysircar, & Newby-Clark, 2006; Moskowitz & Wrubel, 2000). However, one important limitation of a purely inductive, participant-generated account of coping is that cognitions tend to be missed. Specifically, participants are more aware of the actions they take, including the support they seek, than what they say to themselves and what they privately think. For this reason, the optimal strategy is to interview them about the items that appear on a coping checklist that includes cognitions.

Related Coping Constructs

The preceding developments in the field of coping have had a number of spin-offs that add breadth and value to the field. To gauge people's confidence, both general and stressor-specific measures of *coping self-efficacy* have been published (Chesney, Neilands, Chambers, Taylor, & Folkman, 2006; DiClemente, Carbonari, Montgomery, & Hughes, 1994; Sklar & Turner, 1999). For example, a widely used measure of coping self-efficacy for arthritis, the Arthritis Self-Efficacy Scale (Lorrig & Holman, 1998) has demonstrated strong predictive power for long-term functional benefits. These beliefs in one's own ability to handle the demands of a stressor are likely to come into play in the cognitive process of secondary appraisal when people take stock of the resources available to them. There is evidence that people who are confident that they can adhere to a new lifestyle regimen, manage their illness effectively, and adapt to a new living situation such as a long-term care facility, actually achieve better outcomes than those who are less confident (see also Chapter 3 in this volume).

The unique human capacity to anticipate future events has been drawn into the coping literature as well. Aspinwall (2005, 2011) outlined a variety of preventive and preparatory behaviors and cognitions that ward off threat and position the individual, or at least contribute to the perception of being well provisioned, for dealing with particular imminent stressors. Among other topics, Aspinwall discusses the ways *proactive coping is* applied to advance decision making in medicine and business, and draws critical distinctions among widely studied future-oriented thoughts and feelings such as optimism and hope. Proactive coping can involve resource development and mobilization, strategic planning, and a variety of other cognitive and behavioral preparations for stressful encounters. It is distinguished by its intentional character and its purpose of preventing stressors from occurring that are likely to threaten valued goals or at least blunting their impact. Interventions that provide patients with anticipatory guidance about the surgery they will undergo, the postoperative experience they will have, the side effects they are likely to encounter, and the normative time they will spend in each phase aim to give patients a measure of cognitive control that enables them to generate stress-moderating cognitions and behaviors in advance of their exposure to the ordeal they will undergo. However, based on Miller's (1995) research that distinguishes between two styles of information processing, an important caveat is that people who favor a blunting perceptual style – a style akin to an avoidant orientation – may actually fare worse than those who adopt a monitoring style characterized by their motivation to seek as much information about the imminent stressor as they can. From a clinical perspective, this means that blunters are likely to refuse attending such information sessions or, if required to attend them, are likely to block out the information by distracting themselves or cognitively avoiding the information in another way.

Yet a third offshoot of coping research focuses on the question of its effectiveness. What criteria can be employed to determine the costs and benefits of different ways of coping? Candidate indicators include the duration and degree of pain and suffering, usually gauged with measures of psychiatric symptomatology, and the adverse effects on the body and physiological recovery time, usually gauged by the dopamine and serotonin systems (Taylor, Lerner, Sherman, Sage, & McDowell, 2003) and the speed of return to baseline levels of physiological arousal (Repetti, 1992). Then there are the wider impacts of coping, including its spillover on others in harmful (e.g., alcoholism) and beneficial (e.g., benefit-finding) ways. The latter point raises the question of the appropriate jury for a verdict about *coping's effectiveness*. Gignac and Gottlieb (1996) examined family caregivers' own judgments about their coping effectiveness and compared their association with measures of adjustment to the ways of coping they employed. They found that the caregivers' beliefs about their own effectiveness had more abundant and stronger relationships with their adjustment, complementing the positive effects of favorable self-efficacy beliefs prior to coping.

Conclusion

When Carver and Vargas (2011) observed that "coping is not a special event but is normal behavior that takes place under circumstances of adversity" (p. 181), it is likely that their intent was to demystify this research arena and encourage a more naturalistic perspective on human behaviors that are aimed to maintain or restore equilibrium in emotionally challenging contexts. At certain times, it is, indeed, normal to deny that certain events have occurred, to avoid thinking about them, and to pretend that all is well, just as it is normal at other times to seek the support of family and friends, to believe that things will work out as best they can, and to see opportunity when the alarms of life are sounded. The coping literature has yielded a commendable record of the many different ways we can mobilize our personal and social resources when we run life's gauntlets and encounter its ordeals. We are now well-informed about what people can do to offset the vicissitudes and misfortunes they have instigated or endured at the hands of others or due to fateful events.

However, our understanding of the coping *process* is far more limited. We know precious little about how coping unfolds over time and in relation to the numerous personal and environmental contingencies that affect its trajectory. We continue to launch studies that are cross-sectional in design and usually exploratory rather than based on hypotheses derived from theory. Using generic or stressor-specific checklists, we draw conclusions about coping that are not faithful to its complexity and dynamism because they do not capture the sequential and configurative nature of coping. We take snapshots of coping rather than moving pictures that portray clusters of coping responses that change as a function of appraisals and feedback from earlier responses. And finally, we have little grasp of strategies for promoting improved coping because we know so little about behaviors and cognitions that have proved effective and trainable.

For health psychology practitioners and researchers, the good news is that a combination of checklist-based followed by qualitative interviews of the endorsed items can penetrate more deeply into the ways people come to terms with adversity or surmount it. When available, coping inventories that are stressor-specific should be employed, along with probes about the goals and the perceived effectiveness of the ways of coping that are expressed. Although prescriptions for coping are premature, perhaps even hazardous, familiarity with the varied modes and types of coping that are relevant to different stressors would prove instructive for patients, practitioners, and researchers alike. Patients would learn about coping's variability, acceptability, and functionality for themselves and their associates, while practitioners would come to appreciate ways they can shore up those coping responses that moderate patient stress while supplementing their response repertoire with new strategies that further promote adaptation and instill a stronger sense of self-efficacy. Researchers in the exciting field of health psychology have at their disposal a number of generic and stressor-specific tools for charting the ways people handle the medical alarms of life as well as the relatively enduring diseases and conditions they experience. There is also much room for investigators to craft new measures of coping that are more relevant to patients' diagnoses and the challenges associated with adjustment to their circumstances. Still in its infancy, the study of coping can offer important insights into human resilience and vulnerability both in the face and in the wake of threats to health.

References

Aldwin, C. M. (1994). *Stress, coping and development*. New York, NY: Guilford.
Amirkhan, J. H. (1990). A factor analytically derived measure of coping. The Coping Strategy Indicator. *Journal of Personality and Social Psychology, 59*, 1066–1074. http://doi.org/10.1037/0022-3514.59.5.1066
Aspinwall, L. G. (2005). The psychology of future-oriented thinking: From achievement to proactive coping, adaptation, and aging. *Motivation and Emotion, 29*, 203–235. http://doi.org/10.1007/s11031-006-9013-1
Aspinwall, L. G. (2011). Future-oriented thinking, proactive coping, and the management of potential threats to health and well-being. In S. Folkman (Ed.), *The Oxford handbook of stress, health and coping* (pp. 334–365). New York, NY: Oxford University Press.
Austenfeld, J. L., & Stanton, A. L. (2004). Coping through emotional approach: A new look at emotion, coping, and health-related outcomes. *Journal of Personality, 72*, 1335–1364. http://doi.org/10.1111/j.1467-6494.2004.00299.x
Bennett, P., Phelps, C., Hilgart, J., Hood, K., Brain, K., & Murray, A. (2012). Concerns and coping during cancer genetic risk assessment. *Psycho-Oncology, 21*, 611–617. http://doi.org/10.1002/pon.1938
Billings, A. G., & Moos, R. H. (1981). The role of coping resources in attenuating the stress of life events. *Journal of Behavioral Medicine, 4*, 139–157. http://doi.org/10.1007/BF00844267
Brannen, C., & Petite, K. (2008). Understanding women's caregiving stress. A qualitative application of the ways of coping model. *Journal of Health Psychology, 13*(3), 355–365. http://doi.org/10.1177/1359105307088140
Carver, C. S. (1997). You want to measure coping but your protocol is too long: Consider the brief COPE. *International Journal of Behavioral Medicine, 4*(1), 92–100.
Carver, C. S., Scheier, M. F., & Weintraub, J. K. (1989). Assessing coping strategies: A theoretically based approach. *Journal of Personality and Social Psychology, 56*, 267–283. http://doi.org/10.1037/0022-3514.56.2.267

Carver, C. S., & Vargas, S. (2011). Stress, coping, and health. In H. S. Friedman (Ed.), *The Oxford handbook of health psychology* (pp. 162–188). New York, NY: Oxford University Press.

Chesney, M. A., Neilands, T. B., Chambers, D. B., Taylor, J. M., & Folkman, S. (2006). A validity and reliability study of the coping self-efficacy scale. *British Journal of Health Psychology, 11*, 421–437. http://doi.org/10.1348/135910705X53155

Chun, C. A., Moos, R. H., & Cronkite, R. C. (2006). Culture: A fundamental context for the stress and coping paradigm. In P. T. P. Wong, L. C. J. Wong, & W. J. Lonner (Eds.), *Handbook of multicultural perspectives on stress and coping* (pp. 29–53). New York, NY: Springer.

Clark, K. K., Bormann, C. A., Cropanzano, R. S., & James, K. (1995). Validation evidence for three coping measures. *Journal of Personality Assessment, 65*, 434–455. http://doi.org/10.1207/s15327752jpa6503_5

Cook, S. W., & Heppner, P. P. (1997). A psychometric study of three coping measures. *Educational and Psychological Measurement, 57*, 906–923. http://doi.org/10.1177/0013164497057006002

Coyne, J. C., & Gottlieb, B. H. (1996). The mismeasure of coping by checklist. *Journal of Personality, 64*(4), 959–991. http://doi.org/10.1111/j.1467-6494.1996.tb00950.x

DiClemente, C. C., Carbonari, J. P., Montgomery, R. P., & Hughes, S. O. (1994). The Alcohol Abstinence Self-Efficacy Scale. *Journal of Studies on Alcohol, 55*, 141–148. http://doi.org/10.15288/jsa.1994.55.141

Endler, N., & Parker, J. D. (1990). Multidimensional assessment of coping: A critical evaluation. *Journal of Personality and Social Psychology, 58*, 844–854. http://doi.org/10.1037/0022-3514.58.5.844

Folkman, S., & Lazarus, R. S. (1985). If it changes it must be a process: Study of emotion and coping during three stages of a college examination. *Journal of Personality and Social Psychology, 48*(1), 150–170. http://doi.org/10.1037/0022-3514.48.1.150

Folkman, S., & Moskowitz, J. T. (2004). Coping: Pitfalls and promise. *Annual Review of Psychology, 55*, 745–774. http://doi.org/10.1146/annurev.psych.55.090902.141456

Garnefski, N., Kraaij, V., & Spinhoven, P. (2001). Negative life events, cognitive emotion regulation and depression. *Personality and Individual Differences, 30*, 1311–1327. http://doi.org/10.1016/S0191-8869(00)00113-6

Gignac, M. A., & Gottlieb, B. H. (1996). Caregivers' appraisal of efficacy in coping with dementia. *Psychology and Aging, 11*, 214–225. http://doi.org/10.1037/0882-7974.11.2.214

Gottlieb, B. H., & Gignac, M. A. (1996). Content and domain specificity of coping among family caregivers of persons with dementia. *Journal of Aging Studies, 10*, 137–155. http://doi.org/10.1016/S0890-4065(96)90010-9

Keefe, F. J., Affleck, G., Lefebvre, J. C., Star, K., Caldwell, D. S., & Tennen, H. (1997). Pain coping strategies and coping efficacy in rheumatoid arthritis: A daily process analysis. *Pain, 69*(1–2), 35–42. http://doi.org/10.1016/S0304-3959(96)03246-0

Kuo, B. C. H., Roysircar, G., & Newby-Clark, I. R. (2006). Development of the cross-cultural coping scale: Collective, avoidance, and engagement. *Measurement and Evaluation in Counselling and Development, 39*, 161–181.

Lazarus, R. S., & Folkman, S. (1984). *Stress, appraisal and coping*. New York, NY: Springer.

Lorrig, K., & Holman, H. (1998). Arthritis self-efficacy scales measure self-efficacy. *Arthritis & Rheumatism, 11*, 155–157. http://doi.org/10.1002/art.1790110302

Miller, S. M. (1995). Monitoring versus blunting styles of coping with cancer influence the information patients want and need about their disease. Implications for cancer screening and management. *Cancer, 76*, 167–177. http://doi.org/10.1002/1097-0142(19950715)76:2<167::AID-CNCR2820760203>3.0.CO;2-K

Moskowitz, J. T., & Wrubel, J. (2000, June). *Apples and oranges: Using qualitative and quantitative approaches to coping assessment*. Paper presented at the Annual Meeting of the American Psychological Association, Miami, FL.

Oaksford, K., & Frude, N. (2003). The process of coping following child sexual abuse: A qualitative study. *Journal of Child Sexual Abuse, 12*(2), 41–72. http://doi.org/10.1300/J070v12n02_03

Ogden, J. (2012). *Health psychology: A textbook*. Berkshire, UK: Open University Press.

Oxlad, M., Miller-Lewis, L., & Wade, T. D. (2004). The measurement of coping responses: Validity of the Billings and Moos Coping Checklist. *Journal of Psychosomatic Research, 57*, 477–484. http://doi.org/10.1016/S0022-3999(04)00066-2

Phelps, C., Bennett, P., Jones, H., Hood, K., Brain, K., & Murray, A. (2010). The development of a cancer genetic-specific measure of coping: the GRACE. *Psycho-Oncology, 19*, 847–854. http://doi.org/10.1002/pon.1629

Ptacek, J. T., Smith, R. E., Espe, K., & Raffety, B. (1994). Limited correspondence between daily coping reports and retrospective coping recall. *Psychological Assessment, 6*(1), 41–49. http://doi.org/10.1037/1040-3590.6.1.41

Raffety, B. D., Smith, R. E., & Ptacek, J. T. (1997). Facilitating and debilitating trait anxiety, situational anxiety, and coping with an anticipated stressor: A process analysis. *Journal of Personality and Social Psychology, 72*, 892–906. http://doi.org/10.1037/0022-3514.72.4.892

Repetti, R. L. (1992). Short-term withdrawal as a short-term coping response to daily stressors. In H. S. Friedman (Ed.), *Hostility, coping and health* (pp. 151–166). Washington, DC: American Psychological Association.

Rosenstiel, A. K., & Keefe, F. J. (1983). The use of coping strategies in chronic low back pain patients: Relationship to patient characteristics and current adjustment. *Pain, 17*(1), 33–44. http://doi.org/10.1016/0304-3959(83)90125-2

Sarafino, E. P. (1998). *Health psychology: Biopsychosocial interactions* (3rd ed.). Hoboken, NJ: John Wiley & Sons.

Schwarzer, R., & Schwarzer, C. (1996). A critical survey of coping instruments. In M. Zeidner & N. S. Endler (Eds.), *Handbook of coping. Theory, research, applications* (pp. 107–132). New York, NY: John Wiley & Sons.

Skinner, E. A., Edge, K., Altman, J., & Sherwood, H. (2003). Searching for the structure of coping: A review and critique of category systems for classifying ways of coping. *Psychological Bulletin, 129*, 216–269. http://doi.org/10.1037/0033-2909.129.2.216

Sklar, S. M., & Turner, N. E. (1999). A brief measure for the assessment of coping self-efficacy among alcohol and other drug users. *Addiction, 94*, 723–729. http://doi.org/10.1046/j.1360-0443.1999.94572310.x

Somerfield, M., & McCrae, R. R. (2000). Stress and coping research: Methodological challenges, theoretical advances, and clinical applications. *American Psychologist, 55*, 620–625.

Stone, A. A., & Shiffman, S. (1994). Ecological momentary assessment in behavioral medicine. *Annals of Behavioral Medicine, 16*, 199–202.

Taylor, S. E., Lerner, J. S., Sherman, D. K., Sage, R. M., & McDowell, N. K. (2003). Are self-enhancing cognitions associated with healthy or unhealthy biological profiles? *Journal of Personality and Social Psychology, 85*, 605–615. http://doi.org/10.1037/0022-3514.85.4.605

Tennen, H., & Affleck, G. (1996). Daily processes in coping with chronic pain: Methods and analytic strategies. In M. Zeidner & N. S. Endler (Eds.), *Handbook of coping. Theory, research, applications* (pp. 151–177). New York, NY: Wiley.

Todd, M., Tennen, H., Carney, M., Armeli, S., & Affleck, G. (2004). Do we know how we cope? Relating daily coping reports to global and time-limited retrospective assessments. *Journal of Personality and Social Psychology, 86*, 310–319. http://doi.org/10.1037/0022-3514.86.2.310

Vitaliano, P. P., Russo, J., Carr, J. E., Maiuro, R. D., & Becker, J. (1985). The Ways of Coping Checklist: Revision and psychometric properties. *Multivariate Behavioral Research, 20*(1), 3–26. http://doi.org/10.1207/s15327906mbr2001_1

Watson, M., Greer, S., Young, J., Inayat, Q., Burgess, C., & Robertson, B. (1988). Development of a questionnaire measure of adjustment to cancer: The MAC scale. *Psychological Medicine, 18*, 203–209. http://doi.org/10.1017/S0033291700002026

Watson, M., & Homewood, J. (2008). Mental Adjustment to Cancer Scale: Psychometric properties in a large cancer cohort. *Psycho-Oncology, 17*, 1146–1151. http://doi.org/10.1002/pon.1345

Watson, M., Law, M., Santos, M., Greer, S., Baruch, J., & Bliss, J. (1994). The Mini-MAC: Further development of the Mental Adjustment to Cancer Scale. *Journal of Psychosocial Oncology, 12*(3), 33–45. http://doi.org/10.1300/J077V12N03_03

Wheaton, B. (1997). The nature of chronic stress. In B. H. Gottlieb (Ed.), *Coping with chronic stress* (pp. 43–74). New York, NY: Plenum.

Chapter 10

Social Support

Thomas A. Wills[1], Erin O'Carroll Bantum[1], and Michael G. Ainette[2]

[1]University of Hawaii Cancer Center, Honolulu, HI, USA
[2]Dominican College, Orangeburg, NY, USA

Conceptual Background, Relevance to Health Psychology Research and Practice

Knowledge about the relation of social support to health status originated in several lines of research. Epidemiological studies that included measures of social networks showed that persons with larger networks (family, friends, and community roles) had lower rates of mortality (House, Landis, & Umberson, 1988). Clinical research showed that persons with more emotional support (confiding, understanding, acceptance) had lower rates of depression/anxiety, and that stressful life events had less impact for persons with more support (Cohen & Wills, 1985). This research had strong methodological characteristics including prospective designs, measures with good psychometric properties, and statistical control for alternative explanations of the observed effect of support on health status (Cohen, 2004). It had considerable impact on clinical, community, and public health researchers, bringing recognition to the concept that the nature and extent of a person's social relationships have significant implications for their health status.

In recent years, the body of research on social support and health has continued to grow and elaborate. Findings have been consistent in showing that persons with larger networks and more social support have lower levels of psychological morbidity and less likelihood of mortality (Holt-Lunstad, Smith, & Layton, 2010; Uchino, 2004). Research designs have increased in sophistication so that we now have more understanding of the physiological and psychological pathways that link social support to better health (Cohen & Lemay, 2007; Uchino, 2007). Thus we currently understand more about how social support is related to health status (Wills & Ainette, 2012). However, a number of questions remain to be resolved in this field, and further research with attention to psychometric and methodological issues is needed to promote the translation of social support concepts into prevention and intervention research. In this chapter we discuss issues involved in assessing social networks and social support and discuss a range of measures.

Assessment/Measurement Issues

In this section we provide a brief discussion of central issues for research with the kinds of disease outcomes that are typically of interest to health psychologists, such as heart disease, cancer, or chronic conditions including arthritis and diabetes.

Structural Versus Functional Measures

Measures that assess the size of social networks (technically termed *structural measures*) consist of relatively simple items that ask about the number of friends and family members one has, one's employment status, whether one has roles in community groups (fraternal, service, or sports organizations), and the frequency of interacting with friends and neighbors. Such items are designed to assess the existence of various social connections and are usually summed to produce an index termed *social integration* (Brisette, Cohen, & Seeman, 2000).

By contrast, measures that index the perceived availability of supportive functions (technically termed *functional measures*) are longer, multiple-item inventories that ask about whether there are people who could provide various supportive functions if a problem arises. *Emotional support* (also termed *confidant support* or *intimacy*) is the availability of persons who can be confided in, provide understanding and reassurance, allow expression of concerns and worries, and indicate regard for and acceptance of the person. *Instrumental support* (also termed *tangible or practical support*) is the availability of persons who can provide money, household goods or tools, transportation, and/or assistance with child care or daily chores if needed. *Informational support* (also termed *guidance* or *validation*) means the availability of persons who can provide useful advice and guidance, information about community resources, and/or assistance with problem solving. *Companionship support* (also termed *belonging*) means the availability of persons with whom one can participate in socializing, cultural, or recreational activities (Cohen, Mermelstein, Kamarck, & Hoberman, 1985; Welin, Larsson, Sdvardsudd, Tigblin, & Tibblin, 1992).

Generally, functional measures do not aim to assess the number of people one knows, but rather the extent to which the respondent perceives this kind of support would be available if he/she had a problem. Empirically it is found that structural and functional measures are both related to indices of health status but structural and functional scores are only modestly correlated (Holt-Lunstad et al., 2010). Thus an investigator ideally would include both types of measures but if assessment space is limited, would need to consider the outcome and disease process of his/her research in relation to theory on how social integration and functional support are related to health status (Berkman, Glass, Brissette, & Seeman, 2000; Wills & Ainette, 2012).

Main Effects Versus Buffering Effects

Another issue is how the investigator conceptualizes the way in which social support affects outcomes and therefore which aspects of social support should be assessed. One conception is that social resources operate to influence relatively stable attributes of a person, such as his/her feelings of stability and reliability in connections with a community and his/her perceptions of esteem and identity as a member of a valued group; these would tend to operate irrespective of current stress level. This main-effect model for the effect of support is tapped by structural measures designed to index social integration (Brissette et al., 2000). Alternatively, some problems produce acute elevations in depression or anxiety and problem-solving efforts are needed to resolve the situation, for example, if a family member has a heart attack and is hospitalized. In such situations a variety of supportive functions (emotional support, instrumental support, information about medical treatment and rehabilitation resources) may be most relevant for helping both the patient and his/her family members counter the stressful aspects of the situation. This stress-buffering conception of social resources is tapped by functional measures that assess the extent to which supportive functions are available if needed (Wills & Shinar, 2000). These two aspects are not mutually exclusive and in many situations they may both be relevant for long-term adjustment (e.g., caregiving, unemployment, single parenthood). However, we note that main effects and stress buffering represent different conceptions of the mode of operation of social support, and this issue should be considered in choosing a measure for clinical or community research.

Source of Support

Many different individuals and/or institutions can potentially serve as sources of support in times of distress. Which source of support is most beneficial may depend to some extent on the type of problem, but it is typically found that participants in research studies rate all sources of support highly. Medical professionals are nominated as a major source of support for persons with a life-threatening illness such as cancer, but family members are also rated highly (Stanton, Revenson, & Tennen, 2007). Friends and relatives may be particularly important for persons with chronic role strains (e.g., single parenthood, caregiving for a family member) but other sources of support are also highly regarded. A concept arising from some types of research is a distinction between *close versus diffuse support,* the former tapping close relationships (e.g., spouse) whereas the latter taps a more diffuse set of loose alliances with neighbors, workmates, and community contacts (Wills & Shinar, 2000). Close support seems very relevant for problems that involve intense emotional distress, whereas diffuse support may be very useful for problems such as unemployment where interface with a broad range of social networks is useful. In selecting measures it may be preferable to be inclusive rather than restrictive in the approach to assessing support.

Opposing Networks

Persons may be members of two or more social networks and these networks can have different sets of values about health behaviors. This is most prominently the case with substance use; persons may participate in a peer network that is favorably inclined toward substance use but also participate in other networks (e.g., work, family) whose members are less accepting of substance use (Wills, Forbes, & Gibbons, 2014). In some populations, such as illicit drug users, close relationships may actually be a risk factor if the network members mostly are drug users themselves (Wills & Ainette, 2012). Thus when health behaviors are the focus of a study it is desirable to keep this distinction in mind and conduct preliminary research to determine the networks a client belongs to and the networks members' values about the behavior.

Cultural and Life Span Differences

It has been suggested that there are gender, socioeconomic, and life span differences in support needs, and there is some evidence of cultural differences in the way people seek and receive support (Kim, Sherman, & Taylor, 2008). However, this is generally an understudied aspect of social support research. Although there is evidence that social networks and social support are relevant for health across a broad range of national populations (Wills & Ainette, 2012), there has been little cross-cultural research to explore differences in such effects. Moreover, immigration is a major issue for several parts of the world, but little evidence is available on the comparative social networks and support needs of immigrants versus established-resident populations. Researchers may have a particular opportunity to shed new light on social support processes through research exploring differences between immigrants and established residents.

Assessing Social Integration and Social Support

Here we focus on a selected set of measures relevant to the interests of health psychology researchers. Most have been in the literature for some time but have proven to be valid and are commonly used in current research (see Holt-Lunstad et al., 2010; Wills & Ainette, 2012).

Structural Measures

The aim of structural measures is to index the size of a person's social network and hence the degree of his/her integration in the community. Network measures have been used in epidemiological studies of mortality (Holt-Lunstad et al., 2010; Uchino, 2004) and recently in studies of health-related behaviors (e.g., Christakis & Fowler, 2008; Lakon & Valente, 2012). Structural measures typically are related to outcomes independent of current stress level (i.e., a main-effect relation) although some recent data show buffering effects (Wills & Ainette, 2012).

Simple Network Measures

The Berkman network measure has the longest track record. This measure asks about marital status, sociability (contacts with friends and relatives), membership in a religious organization, and membership in other formal organizations. It yields a 4-point scale (using a weighting approach in the original scoring) that indexes the scope of a person's social connections and has been related to mortality in prospective studies (Berkman & Syme, 1979). The Social Network Index (SNI; Brissette et al., 2000) is a more elaborated measure that asks about the existence of 12 types of social relationships (e.g., with spouse, friends, relatives, neighbors, workmates, community groups) with whom the respondent has contact at least once every 2 weeks. The SNI produces a score on a 12-point scale and has been related to symptomatology and health-relevant behaviors (Cohen & Lemay, 2007).

Social Participation Measures

These measures assess the number of activities that an individual engages in with other persons. For example, Welin and coworkers (1992) administered a checklist asking respondents to indicate on a 3-point scale how often during the past year they had engaged in each of the activities listed. Activities were categorized into home activities (e.g., gardening, hobbies, sauna bathing), outside-home activities (e.g., swimming, skating, berry picking, cinema or theater, viewing sports events), and social activities (e.g., parties, organized sports, visiting friends or relatives, association meetings). Home and social activities were both related to mortality (Welin et al., 1992).

Relationship Networks

A recent approach involves mapping relationship networks (e.g., friends) and examining the spread of behaviors within networks. This approach has proven useful in showing how outcomes such as cigarette smoking, obesity, or happiness are related to connections with network members having similar or contrasted behaviors (Christakis & Fowler, 2008; Fowler & Christakis, 2009; Fujimoto, Unger, & Valente, 2012). This approach has recently been extended to computer-based interactions as well (Huang et al., 2013).

Constructed Social Networks

Support groups have been identified as related to better physical and psychosocial outcomes among cancer patients (Hoyt & Stanton, 2011; Lutgendorf et al., 2012). Though this represents a constructed network instead of an individual's naturally occurring network, because individuals enroll purposively into support groups, by recording online interactions between support-group participants (with their consent) the researcher can obtain information about the number of network members in the support group, who interacts with whom and how frequently, and important details such as reciprocity (whether any two group members reciprocate communications with each other). Through text processing it is also possible to record data about the content of members' online communications, including the affective valence of the communication (i.e., positive mood or negative mood) and whether the communication involves self-disclosure. This opens up the possibility of examining questions about which aspects of interactions with group members are more or less helpful (Lewallen, Owen, Bantum, & Stanton, 2014). This approach enables researchers and clinicians to answer questions about supportive interactions that have not been easily studied in the past.

Functional Measures

Functional measures ask about the extent to which certain supportive functions would be available if a person had a problem. They do not necessarily ask about who could provide the support (though some measures do), instead focusing on the availability of resources provided by other persons that could be helpful for assisting a coping effort. The supportive functions indexed by these measures represent some or all of the four categories outlined previously. Almost all functional measures tap emotional support to some extent, but inventories may also tap some combination of instrumental, informational, and companionship support. Scores for availability of different functions may be correlated, and longer inventories sometimes combine the subscales into a total score for functional support availability (Wills & Shinar, 2000).

Representative functional measures used to assess perceived support with various adult populations are outlined in Table 10.1. In the same table, the authors of each scale are also presented. Scales focused on emotional support include the Older Adults Resource Schedule (OARS), which was developed for older adults. It provides a brief assessment of emotional and instrumental support that can easily be adapted for other populations. The Interview Schedule for Social Interaction (ISSI), developed for general-population samples of adults, taps emotional and instrumental support but is one of the few measures that provides score for both close support (termed *attachment*) and diffuse support (termed *integration*). It was originally constructed as a fairly lengthy interview measure but a briefer version is available. The measure termed Perceived Support Scale for Family and Friends (PSS) taps a mixture of emotional and informational support and has been used both with adolescents and with adults. It has parallel scales for support from family and support from friends (20 items per scale), hence provides an intermediate-length measure useful for samples whose members participate in multiple networks. The Multidimensional Perceived Support Scale (MSPSS) is a brief measure intended to tap satisfaction with emotional support from three sources: family, friends, and significant others. The subscale correlations are substantial and it is usually scored for a single index of perceived support (e.g., Clara, Cox, Enns, Murray, & Torgude, 2003).

Scales with more extensive assessment of supportive functions include the Interpersonal Support Evaluation List (ISEL), which was developed with college students and has subsequently been used with a wide variety of adult populations. It has four subscales (10 items per scale) that correspond to the four functional categories outlined earlier. Subscale correlations are typically lower than for other measures. The Social Provisions Scale (SPS) was developed with a more clinical emphasis but has subsequently been used with several different populations. The scales have somewhat different labels but the functions are conceptually similar to emotional and other types of support. The subscales tend to be highly correlated and the total score is typically used. The Medical Outcomes Study (MOS) Scale was originally developed to assess functional aspects of social support for patients with chronic conditions. This 19-item measure contains the following subscales: emotional and informational support, tangible support, positive interaction, and affection. It was originally used in studies focused on medical patients but has been used in several populations. The Arizona Social Support Interview Schedule (ASSIS) was developed as an interview protocol tapping functional support from nominated network members, so it combines some aspects of both structural and functional approaches to assessment. Different supportive functions are indexed and the measure is usually scored as an overall index of functional support. It includes a scale on negative social interaction (i.e., conflict with one or more network members).

For assessing perceived support among children and adolescents, measures are generally focused on support from parents (see Cauce, Reid, Landesman, & Gonzales, 1990; Sandler, Miller, Short, & Wolchik, 1989) although some research has obtained separate scales for support from parents, peers, and sometimes other sources. The Parental Support and Conflict Scale (PSCS) taps perceived emotional and instrumental support from parents, with a separate scale for conflict with parents (i.e., negative interaction). This measure has been used for ages 9–18 years (e.g., Wills & Cleary, 1996) and is implicated in buffering effects through strong relationships to self-control (Wills & Bantum, 2012). The Survey of Children's Social Support (SCSS) was originally developed for young children (third to fifth graders) and indexes emotional, instrumental, and informational support. It has subscales for support from parents, peers, and teachers; the subscales are moderately correlated and may be combined in a total score for perceived support. This inventory includes a network assessment, ascertaining the number of persons perceived as providing each of three supportive functions. The Barrera Social Support Scales (BSSS) for ages 12–16 years tap satisfaction with social provisions (e.g., esteem enhancement, companionship, guidance) from sources including parents, friends, and siblings, but scales are typically combined for a global score. The measure includes items for social conflict. The Children's Inventory of Social Support (CSSS) is a complex interview measure based on the ASSIS and adapted for children in the age range 8–15 years. It indexes a range of supportive functions provided by various network members (nominated from family and nonfamily members). It provides scores for support from various sources and includes negative interaction.

Table 10.1. Functional social support measures

Measure	Author	Items[a]	Reliability[b]	Comments
Perceived-support measures for adults				
ASSIS	Barrera et al., 1981	n.a.	0.88 (full scale)	Network-based measure on emotional, Instrumental, informational support
ISEL	Cohen et al., 1985	40	0.70–0.80	Emotional, instrumental, informational support and social companionship
ISSI	Henderson, Duncan-Jones, & Byrne, 1980	8/16	0.67 (C)	Focus on emotional support, close support (C), and diffuse support (D)
MOS	Sherbourne & Stewart, 1991	19	0.91–0.96	Emotional/informational, instrumental support; affection
MSPSS	Zimet, Dahlem, Zimet, & Farley, 1988	12	0.93	Satisfaction with emotional support. Three subscales combined
OARS	Blazer, 1982	6	0.82	Global emotional/instrumental support; developed for older adults
PSS	Procidano & Heller, 1983	20/20	0.90 (Fam), 0.88 (Frnd)	Emotional and informational support. Scales for family and friend support
SPS	Cutrona & Russell, 1987	24	0.65–0.76	Reassurance of worth, reliable alliance, attachment, guidance
Perceived-support measures for children and adolescents				
BSSSs	Barrera, Chassin, & Rogosch, 1993	6 (S), 1 (C)	0.90	Esteem support, guidance, companionship, etc., intimacy support (S) from parents, siblings, and friends. Includes items on conflict (C)
CISS	Wolchik, Ruehlman, Braver, & Sandler, 1989	n.a.	0.52–0.85	Interview protocol with multiple sources and ratings for support from family members, nonfamily members, peers
PSCS	Wills et al., 1996	12/3	0.76–0.85	Emotional and instrumental support from parents, parent–child conflict
SCSS	Dubow & Ullman, 1989	31	0.88 (full scale)	Emotional, instrumental, and informational support from parents, peers, and teachers, plus network assessment
Other approaches				
BSSS	Schulz & Schwarzer, 2003	52	0.63–0.83	Primarily taps emotional/instrumental support. Six subscales, various aspects
COPE	Carver, Scheier, & Weintraub, 1989	4/4	0.89 (Fam), 0.87 (Frnd)	Seeking support as a coping mechanism. Subscales for emotional support from family (Fam), friends (Frnd)
ISSB	Barrera et al., 1981	40	0.90 (full scale)	Received emotional, instrumental, informational, companionship support
TWCC	Shakespeare-Finch & Obst, 2011	21	0.86–0.92 (R); 0.84–0.86 (G)	Primarily indexes emotional/instrumental support. Subscales for Receiving (R) and Giving (G) support

Note. ASSIS = Arizona Social Support Interview Schedule; BSSS = Berlin Social Support Scales; BSSSs = Barrera Social Support Scales; CISS = Children's Inventory of Social Support; COPE = COPE Inventory; ISEL = Interpersonal Support Evaluation List; ISSB = Inventory of Socially Supportive Behavior; ISSI = Interview Schedule for Social Interaction; MOS = Medical Outcomes Study Scale; MSPSS = Multidimensional Perceived Support Scale; OARS = Older Adults Resource Schedule; PSCS = Parental Support and Conflict Scale; PSS = Perceived Support Scale for Family and Friends; SCSS = Survey of Children's Social Support; SPS = Social Provisions Scale; TWCC = Two-Way Support Scale.
[a]When multiple numbers are entered they refer to different subscales; [b]Cronbach's α.

Alternative Aspects of Social Support

The measures discussed represent major themes in support research but other aspects of social support exist, and may be relevant for particular community or clinical settings. We focus on perceived support because measures of received support such as the Inventory of Socially Supportive Behavior (ISSB; Barrera, Sandler, & Ramsay, 1981) tend to be correlated with stress and only modestly related to perceived support (Haber, Cohen, Lucas, & Baltes, 2007).

Support Seeking as a Coping Mechanism

This approach assesses the tendency to use support seeking as a coping mechanism. The COPE inventory was developed for adults and includes 4-item scales that assess support seeking from family ("When I have a problem I get emotional support from a family member") and from friends ("When I have a problem I get emotional support from a friend"). This assessment approach has been incorporated in adolescent research to index support seeking from parents and from peers. Although the coping-assessment approach is not conceptually isomorphic to the perceived-support assessment approach, it has produced some provocative results, such as the finding that parental support and peer support are related to substance use in opposite directions (e.g., Wills, Resko, Ainette, & Mendoza, 2004).

Complex Inventories

The Berlin Social Support Scales (BSSS) has the goal of assessing the type, quantity, and function of social support, with a particular emphasis on dyadic-support interaction in medically stressful situations. The 45-item measure includes subscales for perceived, provided, and received social support; need for support; support seeking; and protective buffering. This measure was initially validated on adult cancer patients and their partners but has been used in other settings. Further research with such inventories is needed to understand the convergence or divergence between assessment approaches.

Reciprocal Support Measures

While theory on social support has generally emphasized the importance of reciprocated processes (i.e., giving as well as receiving support), until recently there has not been much data directly bearing on this issue (Bolger & Amaral, 2007, and Gleason, Iida, Shrout, & Bolger, 2008, being possible exceptions). An inventory termed the Two-Way Support Scale (Shakespeare-Finch & Obst, 2011) addresses the challenge of measuring reciprocity in social support through providing brief parallel scales that index perceived availability of support (e.g., "There is someone I can talk to about the pressures in my life") and tendency to give support (e.g., "I am there to listen to other people's problems"). Data show independent effects for both the perceived- and given-support scales, hence a new direction for assessing support processes.

Online Support

In recent years there has been a transformation of social interaction patterns as young people, as well as adults, spend increasingly larger proportions of their time on e-mail, texting, and social media sites (O'Keefe & Clarke-Pearson, 2011; Valkenburg & Peter, 2007). Because social networking sites have become an important avenue for communication, individuals may have a "virtual network" in addition to a face-to-face social network. However, there has been relatively little research on measuring perceptions of support from online relationships (Huang et al., 2013). This raises intriguing questions about how the two networks overlap and whether Internet communications complement existing relationships in a "rich get richer" model (Valkenburg & Peter, 2007) versus whether heavy reliance on Internet communication detracts from the potential benefits of face-to-face social interaction (Leung, 2007; Van den Eijnden, Meerkerk, Vermulst, Spijkerman, & Engels, 2008) with adverse effects on well-being (Kross et al., 2013). This is relevant both for general populations and for persons facing serious illness, for whom the Internet can be a major source of health information and, in some cases, social support (Chou, Liu, Post, & Hesse, 2011; Hesse, Arora, Burke, & Finnery, 2008; Koch-Weser, Bradshaw, Gualtieri, & Gallagher, 2010). There have been discussions of possible dimensions of social support gained through online relationships (Mikal, Rice, Abeyta, & DeVilbiss, 2013) but the field lacks validated measures of online social support and this is a priority for future research.

Negative-Support Constructs

Social relationships may contain negative elements as well as positive ones. In addition to the social conflict dimension previously discussed, researchers have delineated negative aspects of relationships that reflect unwanted advice, intrusiveness, or overprotectiveness; failure to provide help when needed; unsympathetic or insensitive behavior; and "undermining" actions that would tend to divert a person from a positive behavior change effort (Newsom, Mahan, Rook, & Krause, 2008). There is evidence that the frequency of negative interactions is inversely related to health (Krause, Newsom, & Rook, 2008) and that excessive social pressure can have adverse effects on behavior change efforts (Rook et al., 2012; Stephens et al., 2013). Researchers should be sensitive to the potential impact of negative aspects for their area as well as to the effects of positive support. For example, Newsom et al. (2008) have a 12-item measure that assesses four aspects of negative support, and several measures discussed previously (e.g., the ASSIS, BSSS, and CSSS) include brief scales on social conflict.

Choosing a Support Measure

In choosing a measure, a researcher may consider several general questions keyed to the research goals. If stable integration in a community is hypothesized to be the primary determinant of a health outcome, a structural measure would be most relevant. If the ability to cope with stressors in personal or medical domains is a primary determinant of outcomes the researcher wishes to measure, then a functional measure would be a good choice. However, since structural and functional aspects of support both seem to relate to health status through different mechanisms (Holt-Lunstad et al., 2010), it would generally be advisable to include both types of measures in a study where this is feasible.

A researcher should examine several scales and consider their relevance to the typical problems faced by the population being assessed. Emotional support is the most broadly useful function (Wills & Shinar, 2000) and there may be settings where a brief scale of emotional support is adequate if the sample size is relatively large. However, other aspects of social support (e.g., instrumental and informational support) may make unique contributions to health status in settings where these are quite relevant to the needs of the patients and families, so measures with reliable subscales for these functions should usually be considered. When a person interacts with different social networks that each have significant implications for well-being (e.g., family, friends, medical professionals), then a measure with parallel scales for different support sources may be useful. If outcomes depend strongly on how a patient deals with specific aspects of a disease condition, then the researcher might consult recent research in the area and examine measures that tap disease-specific functions (e.g., Hanna, 2006). Selecting a measure involves several considerations (for a detailed decision protocol, see Wills & Shinar, 2000) but, above all, the items in a given measure should make sense to the researcher in line with their understanding of the population and the nature of the research goals.

Research Illustrating Use of the Measures Under Discussion

Recent years have seen a large volume of research on the effect of social support for specific populations and disease conditions (Holt-Lunstad et al., 2010; Newman & Roberts, 2013; Wills & Ainette, 2012) and the underlying psychological and physiological pathways in these effects (Eisenberger, 2013; Eisenberger & Cole, 2012; Hostinar & Gunnar, 2013; Miller, Chen, & Cole, 2009; Uchino, Bowen, Carlisle, & Birmingham, 2012). This research has generally relied on the measures discussed in this chapter. Because of the diversity of applications of social support measures, in this section we highlight recent review articles in several areas so that readers can consult studies in their particular area of interest.

For specific disease conditions, reviews have considered the effects of social support among adult diabetics (Stopford, Winkley, & Ismail, 2013) and among adolescents with type 1 diabetes (Palladino & Helgeson, 2012). Research on support has considered cancer progression (Nausheen, Gidron, Peveler, & Moss-Morris, 2009), needs of cancer patients and survivors (Luszczynska, Pawlowska, Cieslak, Knoll, & Scholz, 2013; Roland, Rodriguez, Patterson, & Trivers, 2013), and adjustment among cancer survivors (Hong, Pena-Purcell, & Ory, 2012; Park & Gaffey, 2007). Studies have addressed the role of social support in prognosis (Barth, Schneider, & Von Kanel, 2010) or recovery from heart disease (Lett et al., 2005). Studies in the neurology area have addressed benefits of social support among persons with chronic pain (Campbell, Wynne-Jones, & Dunn, 2011) and neurological injuries (Chronister, Johnson, & Berven, 2006). In psychiatric research, studies have considered the role of social support for coping with posttraumatic stress disorder (Charuvastra & Cloitre, 2008; Neria, DiGrande, & Adams, 2011; Wright, Kelsall, Sim, Clarke, & Creamer, 2013). These papers review studies in their area and point out questions that are in need of further research.

Research on children and adolescents has considered topics such as support for physical activity (Beets, Cardinal, & Alderman, 2010) or the role of social support for quality of life among adolescent cancer survivors (Decker, 2007). Other research has focused on social support processes in pregnancy (Razurel, Kaiser, Sellinet, & Epiney, 2013) or in gerontological populations (Schwarzbach, Luppa, Forstmeier, Konig, & Riedler-Heller, 2014). Several authors have considered the role of social support in health-related behaviors including eating (Shaikh, Yaroch, Nebeling, Yeh, & Resnicow, 2008; Vasnaver & Keller, 2011), substance use (Westmaas, Bontemps-Jones, & Bauer, 2010, for smoking; Groh, Jason, & Keys, 2008, for alcohol), and patient adherence to medical regimens (DiMatteo, 2004). The role of support in the work environment for reducing stress or facilitating behavior change has been considered by Albertsen, Borg, and Oldenburg (2006) and by Hausser, Mojzisch, Niesel, and Schutz-Hardt (2010). Again, research needs to clarify how social support operates to produce desirable outcomes.

Future Directions

Although social support has been an active research area, there are many questions that remain to be answered. In the following section we provide brief synopses of several issues.

1. *Structural and functional measures.* Measures of network size and perceived support are both related to health status (Holt-Lunstad et al., 2010) but are not highly correlated. This suggests that they are related to health through different pathways but there is still little research to help understand this issue. Do social networks relate to health through direct effects or through enforcing adherence to social norms about health? Does functional support actually enhance coping processes, or does it act more though perceptions of esteem and control? Designing research to include measure of postulated behavioral, affective, and biological mechanisms for effects of structural or functional support, and using statistical techniques for analyzing mediation (MacKinnon, Fairchild, & Fritz, 2006) would be very useful for helping to get at these questions.

2. *Support through online sources.* Research is needed to further our understanding of the effects of the Internet on social relationships and the significance for health outcomes. While social networking platforms allow for the opportunity to readily receive and give support, some evidence indicates that spending time on social networking sites, such as Facebook, could lead to lower subjective well-being (Kross et al., 2013). Research is needed to assist the developing technology for designing online networks so as to achieve the most favorable outcomes (Kraut & Resnick, 2012; Valente, 2012). Another outstanding question is whether there are certain aspects of online support that are unique and need to be measured differently than is possible with the existing measures of support for a face-to-face environment.

3. *Emotion and support.* Emotional support has been a central concept but there is actually little research on how emotions are involved in social support. In the act of giving or receiving support, oftentimes emotion is exchanged. Fredrickson has done long-standing work in the area of positive emotion and has created the Broaden and Build Theory (Fredrickson, 2001). This work suggests that the expression of positive emotions broadens thought repertoires leading to an increase in personal resources. Some of this work also implicates both physiological components of action (vagal tone) and the way positive emotion also impacts social connectedness (Kok & Fredrickson, 2010). Studying the interrelations of cognition, emotion, and social support is crucial and research on this question will continue to inform the field.

4. *Supportive interactions in daily life.* Perceived support must be based on memories of specific interpersonal transactions, but there is currently little research on how social support processes unfold in daily life. The approach of using ecological momentary assessment (e.g., Simons, Dvorak, Batien, & Wray, 2010; Smyth, Zawadski, Santuzzi, & Filipowski, 2014; see also Chapter 18 in this volume) to obtain repeated measures of transactions where social support may or may not have occurred (Bolger & Amaral, 2007) offer a promising avenue to broader knowledge about how social support occurs, and more such research is needed.

References

Albertsen, K., Borg, V., & Oldenburg, B. (2006). A systematic review of the impact of work environment on smoking cessation. *Preventive Medicine, 43*, 291–305. http://doi.org/10.1016/j.ypmed.2006.05.001

Barrerra, M., Jr., Chassin, L., & Rogosch, F. (1993). Effects of social support and conflict on adolescent children. *Journal of Personality and Social Psychology, 64*, 602–612. http://doi.org/10.1037/0022-3514.64.4.602

Barrera, M., Sandler, I. N., & Ramsay, T. B. (1981). Preliminary development of a scale of social support. *American Journal of Community Psychology, 9*, 435–447. http://doi.org/10.1007/BF00918174

Barth, J., Schneider, S., & Von Kanel, R. (2010). Social support in the etiology and prognosis of heart disease: Review and meta-analysis. *Psychosomatic Medicine, 72*, 229–238. http://doi.org/10.1097/PSY.0b013e3181d01611

Beets, M. W., Cardinal, B. J., & Alderman, B. L. (2010). Parental social support and the physical activity behaviors of youth: A review. *Health Education and Behavior, 37*, 621–644. http://doi.org/10.1177/1090198110363884

Berkman, L. F., Glass, T., Brissette, I., & Seeman, T. E. (2000). From social integration to health. *Social Science and Medicine, 51*, 843–857. http://doi.org/10.1016/S0277-9536(00)00065-4

Berkman, L. F., & Syme, S. L. (1979). Social networks, host resistance, and mortality: A nine-year follow-up study. *American Journal of Epidemiology, 109*, 186–204.

Blazer, D. G. (1982). Social support and mortality in an elderly community population. *American Journal of Epidemiology, 115*, 684694.

Bolger, N., & Amaral, D. (2007). Effects of support visibility on adjustment to stress. *Journal of Personality and Social Psychology, 92*, 458–475. http://doi.org/10.1037/0022-3514.92.3.458

Brissette, I., Cohen, S., & Seeman, T. E. (2000). Measuring social networks. In S. Cohen, L. Underwood, & B. Gottlieb (Eds.), *Social support measurement and intervention* (pp. 53–85). New York, NY: Oxford University Press.

Campbell, P., Wynne-Jones, G., & Dunn, K. M. (2011). The influence of social support on prognosis in spinal pain: A systematic review. *European Journal of Pain, 15*, e1–e14. http://doi.org/10.1016/j.ejpain.2010.09.011

Carver, C. S., Scheier, M. F., & Weintraub, J. K. (1989). Assessing coping strategies: A theoretically-based approach. *Journal of Personality and Social Psychology, 56*, 267283. http://doi.org/10.1037/0022-3514.56.2.267

Cauce, A. M., Reid, M., Landesman, S., & Gonzales, N. (1990). Social support in young children: Measurement and behavioral impact. In I. G. Sarason, B. R. Sarason, & G. Pierce (Eds.), *Social support: An interactional perspective* (pp. 64–94). New York, NY: Wiley.

Charuvastra, A., & Cloitre, M. (2008). Social bonds and posttraumatic stress disorder. *Annual Review of Psychology, 59*, 301–328. http://doi.org/10.1146/annurev.psych.58.110405.085650

Chou, W-Y., Liu, B., Post, S., & Hesse, B. (2011). Health-related Internet use among cancer survivors: Data from the Health Information National Trends Survey, 2003–2008. *Journal of Cancer Survivorship, 5*, 263–270. http://doi.org/10.1007/s11764-011-0179-5

Christakis, N. A., & Fowler, J. H. (2008). The collective dynamics of smoking in a large social network. *New England Journal of Medicine, 358*, 2249–2258. http://doi.org/10.1056/NEJMsa0706154

Chronister, J. A., Johnson, E. K., & Berven, N. L. (2006). Measuring social support in rehabilitation. *Disability and Rehabilitation, 28*, 75–84. http://doi.org/10.1080/09638280500163695

Clara, I. P., Cox, B. J., Enns, M., Murray, L., & Torgude, L. (2003). Confirmatory analysis of the MSPSS in clinical and student samples. *Journal of Personality Assessment, 81*, 265–270.

Cohen, S. (2004). Social relationships and health. *American Psychologist, 59*, 676–684. http://doi.org/10.1037/0003-066X.59.8.676

Cohen, S., & Lemay, E. (2007). Why would social networks be linked to affect and health practices? *Health Psychology, 26*, 410–417. http://doi.org/10.1037/0278-6133.26.4.410

Cohen, S., Mermelstein, R., Kamarck, T., & Hoberman, H. M. (1985). Measuring the functional components of social support. In I. G. Sarason & B. R. Sarason (Eds.), *Social support: Theory, research and applications* (pp. 73–94). The Hague, The Netherlands: Martinus Nijhoff.

Cohen, S., & Wills, T. (1985). Stress, social support, and the buffering hypothesis. *Psychological Bulletin, 98*, 310357. http://doi.org/10.1037/0033-2909.98.2.310

Cutrona, C. E., & Russell, D. W. (1987). The provisions of social relationships and adaptation to stress. In W. H. Jones & D. Perlman (Eds.), *Advances in personal relationships (Vol. 1*, pp. 37–67). Greenwich, CT: JAI Press.

Decker, C. L. (2007). Social support and adolescent cancer survivors: A review of the literature. *Psycho-Oncology, 16*, 1–11. http://doi.org/10.1002/pon.1073

DiMatteo, M. R. (2004). Social support and patient adherence to medical treatment: A meta-analysis. *Health Psychology, 23*, 707–218. http://doi.org/10.1037/0278-6133.23.2.207

Dubow, E. F., & Ullman, D. G. (1989). Assessing social support in school children: The Survey of Children's Social Support. *Journal of Clinical Child Psychology, 18*, 52–64. http://doi.org/10.1207/s15374424jccp1801_7

Eisenberger, N. I. (2013). An empirical review of the neural underpinnings of giving and receiving support. *Psychosomatic Medicine, 75*, 545–556. http://doi.org/10.1097/PSY.0b013e31829de2e7

Eisenberger, N. I., & Cole, S. W. (2012). Social neuroscience and health: Neurophysiological mechanisms linking social ties with physical health. *Nature Neuroscience, 15*, 669–674. http://doi.org/10.1038/nn.3086

Fowler, J. H., & Christakis, N. A. (2009). Dynamic spread of happiness in a large social network. *BMJ, 338*, 23–31.

Fredrickson, B. L. (2001). The role of positive emotions in positive psychology: The broaden-and-build theory of positive emotions. *American Psychologist, 56*(3), 218226. http://doi.org/10.1037/0003-066X.56.3.218

Fujimoto, K., Unger, J. B., & Valente, T. W. (2012). A network method of measuring affiliation-based peer influence on adolescent smoking. *Child Development, 83*, 442–451.

Gleason, M., Iida, M., Shrout, P., & Bolger, N. (2008). Receiving support as a mixed blessing. *Journal of Personality and Social Psychology, 94*, 828–838. http://doi.org/10.1037/0022-3514.94.5.824

Groh, D. R., Jason, L. A., & Keys, C. B. (2008). Social network variables in alcoholics anonymous: A literature review. *Clinical Psychology Review, 28*, 430–450. http://doi.org/10.1016/j.cpr.2007.07.014

Haber, M., Cohen, J., Lucas, T., & Baltes, B. (2007). Relation of perceived and received social support: A meta-analysis. *American Journal of Community Psychology, 39*, 133–144. http://doi.org/10.1007/s10464-007-9100-9

Hanna, K. M. (2006). Measures of diabetes-specific support for adolescents with diabetes. *Diabetes Educator, 32*, 741–750. http://doi.org/10.1177/0145721706291759

Hausser, J. A., Mojzisch, A., Niesel, M., & Schutz-Hardt, S. (2010). Research on the job demand-control (control-support) model and well-being. *Work & Stress, 24*, 1–35. http://doi.org/10.1080/02678371003683747

Henderson, S., Duncan-Jones, P., & Byrne, D. (1980). Measuring social relationships: The Interview Schedule for Social Interaction. *Psychological Medicine, 10*, 723–734. http://doi.org/10.1017/S003329170005501X

Hesse, B. W., Arora, N. K., Burke, B. E., & Finnery, R. L. J. (2008). Information support for cancer survivors. *Cancer, 112*(Suppl. 11), 2529–2540. http://doi.org/10.1002/cncr.23445

Holt-Lunstad, J., Smith, T. B., & Layton, J. B. (2010). Social relationships and mortality risk: A meta-analytic review. *PloS Medicine, 7*(7), e1000316. http://doi.org/10.1371/journal.pmed.1000316

Hong, Y., Pena-Purcell, N. C., & Ory, M. G. (2012). Outcomes of online support and resources for cancer survivors: A review. *Patient Education and Counseling, 86*, 288–296. http://doi.org/10.1016/j.pec.2011.06.014

Hostinar, C., & Gunnar, M. (2013). Directions in studying relationships as regulators of the HPA axis across development. *Journal of Clinical Child & Adolescent Psychology, 42*, 564–575. http://doi.org/10.1080/15374416.2013.804387

House, J. S., Landis, K. R., & Umberson, D. (1988). Social relationships and health. *Science, 241*, 540545. http://doi.org/10.1126/science.3399889

Hoyt, M. A., & Stanton, A. L. (2011). Unmitigated agency, social support, and psychological adjustment in men with cancer. *Journal of Personality, 79*(2), 259–278. http://doi.org/10.1111/j.1467-6494.2010.00675.x

Huang, G. C., Unger, J. B., Soto, D., Fujimoto, K., Pentz, M. A., Jordan-Marsh, M., & Valente, T. W. (2013). The impact of online and offline friendship networks on adolescent substance use. *Journal of Adolescent Health, 54*(5), 508–514. http://doi.org/10.1016/j.jadohealth.2013.07.001

Kim, H., Sherman, D. K., & Taylor, S. (2008). Culture and social support. *American Psychologist, 63*, 518–526. http://doi.org/10.1037/0003-066X

Koch-Weser, S., Bradshaw, Y. S., Gualtieri, L., & Gallagher, S. S. (2010). The Internet as a health information source: Findings from the 2007 Health Information National Trends Survey and implications. *Journal of Health Communication, 15*(Suppl. 3), 279–283. http://doi.org/10.1080/10810730.2010.522700

Kok, B. E., & Fredrickson, B. L. (2010). Upward spirals of the heart: Vagal tone reciprocally and predicts positive emotions and social connectedness. *Biological Psychology, 85*, 432436.

Krause, N., Newsom, J. T., & Rook, K. S., (2008). Financial strain, negative social interaction, and self-rated health: Evidence from two United States nationwide longitudinal surveys. *Ageing & Society, 28*(7), 1001–1023. http://doi.org/10.1017/S0144686X0800740X

Kraut, R. E., & Resnick, P. (2012). *Building successful online communities: Evidence-based social design*. Cambridge, MA: MIT Press.

Kross, E., Verduyn, P., Demiralp, E., Park, J., Lee, D. S., Lin, N., … Ybarra, O. (2013). Facebook use predicts declines in subjective well-being in young adults. *PLOS One, 8*(8), e69841. http://doi.org/10.1371/journal.pone.0069841

Lakon, C. M., & Valente, T. W. (2012). Synergy of network structure and peer influence in relation to smoking among adolescents. *Social Science and Medicine, 74*, 1407–1417. http://doi.org/10.1016/j.socscimed.2012.01.011

Lett, H. S., Blumenthal, J. A., Babyak, M., Strauman, T., Robins, C., & Sherwood, A. (2005). Social support and recovery from heart disease. *Psychosomatic Medicine, 67*, 869–878.

Leung, L. (2007). Stressful life events, motives for internet use, and social support among digital kids. *CyperPsychology and Behaviour, 10*, 204–214. http://doi.org/10.1089/cpb.2006.9967

Lewallen, A. C., Owen, J. E., Bantum, E.O., & Stanton, A. L. (2014). Language affects peer responsiveness in an online cancer support group. *Psycho-Oncology, 23*(7), 766–772. http://doi.org/10.1002/pon.3477

Luszczynska, A., Pawlowska, I., Cieslak, R., Knoll, N., & Scholz, U. (2013). Social support and quality of life in lung cancer survivors: A review. *Psycho-Oncology, 22*, 2160–2168.

Lutgendorf, S. K., De Geest, K., Bender, D., Ahmed, A., Goodheart, M. J., Dahmoush, L., … & Sood, A. K. (2012). Social influences in clinical outcomes of patients with ovarian cancer. *Journal of Clinical Oncology, 30*(23), 2885–2890. http://doi.org/10.1200/JCO.2011.39.4411

MacKinnon, D. P., Fairchild, A. J., & Fritz, M. S. (2006). Mediation analysis. *Annual Review of Psychology, 58*, 593–614. http://doi.org/10.1146/annurev.psych.58.110405.085542

Mikal, J. P., Rice, R. E., Abeyta, A., & DeVilbiss, J. (2013). Transition, stress, and computer-mediated social support. *Computers in Human Behavior, 29*, A40–A53. http://doi.org/10.1016/j.chb.2012.12.012

Miller, G., Chen, E., & Cole, S. W. (2009). Health psychology: Biologically plausible models linking the social world and physical health. *Annual Review of Psychology, 60*, 501–524. http://doi.org/10.1146/annurev.psych.60.110707.163551

Nausheen, B., Gidron, Y., Peveler, R., & Moss-Morris, R. (2009). Social support and cancer progression: A systematic review. *Journal of Psychosomatic Research, 67*, 403–415. http://doi.org/10.1016/j.jpsychores.2008.12.012

Neria, Y., DiGrande, L., & Adams, B. G. (2011). Posttraumatic stress disorder following the September 11 terrorist attacks. A review of literature. *American Psychologist, 66*, 429–446.

Newman, M. L., & Roberts, N. A. (Eds.). (2013). *Health and social relationships: The good, the bad, and the complicated*. Washington, DC: American Psychological Association.

Newsom, J. T., Mahan, T. L., Rook, K. S., & Krause, N. (2008). Stable negative social exchanges and health. *Health Psychology, 27*(1), 78–86. http://doi.org/10.1037/0278-6133.27.3.357

O'Keefe, G. S., & Clarke-Pearson, K. (2011). The impact of social media on children, adolescents, and families. *Pediatrics, 127*, 800–804. http://doi.org/10.1542/peds.2011-0054

Palladino, D. K., & Helgeson, V. S. (2012). Peer influence on self-care and symptoms in adolescents with Type 1 diabetes. *Journal of Pediatric Psychology, 37*, 591–603. http://doi.org/10.1093/jpepsy/jss009

Park, C., & Gaffey, A. E. (2007). Psychosocial factors and health behavior change in cancer survivors: An integrative review. *Annals of Behavioral Medicine, 34*, 115–134. http://doi.org/10.1007/BF02872667

Procidano, M. E., & Heller, K. (1983). Measures of perceived social support from friends and from family: Validation studies. *American Journal of Community Psychology, 11*, 1–24. http://doi.org/10.1007/BF00898416

Razurel, C., Kaiser, B., Sellenet, C., & Epiney, M. (2013). Relation between social support, coping, and maternal well-being: A review of literature. *Women & Health, 53*, 74–99. http://doi.org/10.1080/03630242.2012.732681

Roland, K. B., Rodriguez, J. L., Patterson, J. R., & Trivers, K. F. (2013). A literature review on the social support needs of ovarian cancer survivors. *Psycho-Oncology, 22*, 2408–2418. http://doi.org/10.1002/pon.3322

Rook, K. S., Luong, G., Sorkin, G., Sorkin, D. h., Newsom, J. T., & Krause, N. (2012). Ambivalent versus problematic social ties: Implications for psychological health, functional health, and interpersonal coping. *Psychology and Aging, 27*, 912–923. http://doi.org/10.1037/a0029246

Sandler, I. N., Miller, P., Short, J., & Wolchik, S. a. (1989). Social support as a protective factor for children in stress. In D. Belle (Ed.), *Children's social networks and social supports* (pp. 277–307). New York, NY: Wiley.

Schulz, U., & Schwarzer, R. (2003). Social support in coping with illness: The Berlin Social Support Scales (BSSS). *Diagnostica, 49*, 7382.

Schwarzbach, M., Luppa, M., Forstmeier, S., Konig, H., & Riedler-Heller, S. (2014). Social support and depression in later life. *International Journal of Geriatric Psychiatry, 29*, 1–21.

Shaikh, A. R., Yaroch, A. L., Nebeling, L., Yeh, M-C., & Resnicow, K. (2008). Psychosocial predictors of fruit and vegetable consumption in adults: A review of the literature. *American Journal of Preventive Medicine, 34*, 535–543. http://doi.org/10.1016/j.amepre.2007.12.028

Shakespeare-Finch, J., & Obst, P. L. (2011). The 2-Way Support Scale: Giving and receiving emotional and instrumental support. *Journal of Personality Assessment, 93*, 483–490. http://doi.org/10.1080/00223891.2011.594124

Sherbourne, C. D., & Stewart, A. L. (1991). The MOS social support survey. *Social Science and Medicine, 32*, 705714. http://doi.org/10.1016/0277-9536(91)90150-B

Simons, J. S., Dvorak, R. J., Batien, B. T. & Wray, T. B. (2010). Event-level associations between affect, alcohol intoxication, and acute dependence symptoms: Effects of urgency, self-control, and drinking experience. *Addictive Behaviors, 35*, 1045–1053. http://doi.org/10.1016/j.addbeh.2010.07.001

Smyth, J. M., Zawadski, M. J., Santuzzi, A. M., & Filipowski, K. B. (2014). Examining the effects of perceived social support on momentary mood and symptom reports in asthma and arthritis patients. *Psychology and Health, 29*, 813–831. http://doi.org/10.1080/08870446.2014.889139

Stanton, A., Revenson, T., & Tennen, H. (2007). Health psychology: Adjustment to chronic disease. *Annual Review of Psychology, 58*, 565–592. http://doi.org/10.1146/annurev.psych.58.110405.085615

Stephens, M. A. P., Franks, M. M., Rook, K. S., Iida, M., Hemphill, R. C., & Salem, J. K. (2013). Spouses' attempts to regulate day-to-day dietary adherence among patients with type 2 diabetes. *Health Psychology, 32*(10), 1029–1037. http://doi.org/10.1037/a0030018

Stopford, R., Winkley, K., & Ismail, K. (2013). Social support and glycemic control in type 2 diabetes: A review of observational studies. *Patient Education and Counseling, 93*, 549–558. http://doi.org/10.1016/j.pec.2013.08.016

Uchino, B. N. (2004). *Social support and physical health: Understanding the health consequences of relationships*. New Haven, CT: Yale University Press. http://doi.org/10.12987/yale/9780300102185.001.0001

Uchino, B. N. (2007). Social support and health: A review of physiological processes potentially underlying links to disease outcomes. *Journal of Behavioral Medicine, 29*, 377–387.

Uchino, B. N., Bowen, K., Carlisle, M., & Birmingham, W. (2012). Psychological pathways linking social support to health outcomes. *Social Science and Medicine, 74*, 949–957. http://doi.org/10.1016/j.socscimed.2011.11.023

Valente, T. W. (2012). Network interventions. *Science, 337*, 49–53. http://doi.org/10.1126/science.1217330

Valkenburg, P., & Peter, J. (2007). Adolescents' online communication and their closeness to friends. *Developmental Psychology, 43*, 267–277. http://doi.org/10.1037/0012-1649.43.2.267

Van den Eijnden, R., Meerkerk, G-J., Vermulst, A., Spijkerman, R., & Engels, C. M. E. (2008). Compulsive internet use and psychosocial well-being among adolescents. *Developmental Psychology, 44*, 655–665. http://doi.org/10.1037/0012-1649.44.3.655

Vasnaver, E., & Keller, H. H. (2011). Social influences and eating behavior in later life: A review. *Journal of Nutrition in Gerontology and Geriatrics, 30*, 2–23. http://doi.org/10.1080/01639366.2011.545038

Welin, L., Larsson, B., Sdvardsudd, K., Tigblin, B., & Tibblin, G. (1992). Social network activities and mortality. *Journal of Epidemiology and Community Health, 46*, 127–132.

Westmaas, J. L., Bontemps-Jones, J., & Bauer, J. E. (2010). Social support in smoking cessation: Reconciling theory and evidence. *Nicotine and Tobacco Research, 12*, 695–707. http://doi.org/10.1093/ntr/ntq077

Wills, T. A., & Ainette, M. G. (2012). Social networks and social support. In A. Baum, T. Revenson, & J. Singer (Eds.), *Handbook of health psychology* (2nd ed., pp. 465–492). New York, NY: Psychology Press.

Wills, T. A., & Bantum, E. O. (2012). Self-regulation and resilience among adolescents and adult cancer survivors. *Journal of Social and Clinical Psychology, 31*, 567–593. http://doi.org/10.1521/jscp.2012.31.6.568

Wills, T. A., & Cleary, S. D. (1996). How are social support effects mediated: Parental support and adolescent substance use. *Journal of Personality and Social Psychology, 71*, 937–952. http://doi.org/10.1037/0022-3514.71.5.937

Wills, T. A., Forbes, M., & Gibbons, F. X. (2014). Parental and peer support: Relations to adolescent substance use. In W. Hansen & L. Scheier (Eds.), *Parenting and teen drug use* (pp. 148–165). New York, NY: Oxford University Press.

Wills, T. A., Resko, J., Ainette, M., & Mendoza, D. (2004). Parent and peer support in adolescent substance use. *Psychology of Addictive Behaviors, 18*, 122–134. http://doi.org/10.1037/0893-164X.18.2.122

Wills, T. A., & Shinar, O. (2000). Measuring perceived and received social support. In S. Cohen, L. G. Underwood, & B. Gotttlieb (Eds.), *Social support measurement and intervention* (pp. 86–135). New York, NY: Oxford University Press.

Wolchik, S. E., Ruehlman, L. S., Braver, S. L., & Sandler, I. N. (1989). Social support for children of divorce. *American Journal of Community Psychology, 17*, 485–510. http://doi.org/10.1007/BF00931174

Wright, B., Kelsall, H. L., Sim, M., Clarke, D., & Creamer, M. (2013). Support mechanisms and vulnerabilities in relation to PTSD in veterans. *Journal of Traumatic Stress, 26*, 310–318.

Zimet, G. D., Dahlem, N. W., Zimet, S. G., & Farley, G. K. (1988). The multidimensional scale of perceived social support. *Journal of Personality Assessment, 52*, 30–41. http://doi.org/10.1207/s15327752jpa5201_2

Chapter 11
Pain and Pain Behavior

Kim E. Dixon

Psychology Service, Tuscaloosa VA Medical Center, Tuscaloosa, AL, USA

Pain is a universal experience that affects all populations across the globe. Estimates of the number of individuals in the US who suffer with chronic pain exceed 100 million (Institute of Medicine, 2011) and upwards of 20% of Australians live with persistent pain (Blyth et al., 2001). A similar prevalence rate (i.e., 19%) was noted in a large study of residents of 15 European countries and Israel (Breivik, Collett, Ventafridda, Cohen, & Gallacher, 2006). The economic toll due to medical costs, lost wages, and lost productivity is estimated as high as US $100 billion annually (Quartana, Campbell, & Edwards, 2009) and the psychological costs in terms of emotional distress and disturbances in interpersonal relationships are immeasurable. Given the tremendous burden of chronic pain, having access to accurate assessment and effective treatment is of paramount importance. This chapter reviews the theoretical foundations that guide pain assessment, delineates important domains to be included in all pain assessments, and provides examples of representative, well-validated measures relevant to each domain. Finally, important issues germane to research, clinical trials, and treatment outcomes are also discussed.

Theoretical Underpinnings of Pain Assessment

Introduction of the gate control theory of pain (Melzack & Wall, 1965) provided a broadened conceptualization of pain processing that incorporated many factors beyond the nociceptive stimulus that collectively contribute to what is ultimately experienced as pain. Besides the notable sensory-discriminative components of pain, this seminal theory drew attention to affective-motivational and cognitive-evaluative aspects as well. The biopsychosocial model of disease (Engel, 1977) that came a decade or so later also provided a fitting framework for viewing pain as a multifaceted, complex experience influenced by cognitive, affective, behavioral, and social factors (Turk & Melzack, 2011).

Melzack (1999) later introduced a more sophisticated model of pain processing, the neuromatrix model, which described the importance of genetics and an extensive neural matrix in collectively contributing to a pain experience that is unique to each individual. This neuromatrix extends throughout the somatosensory, thalamic, and limbic tracts of the brain. A recent review of neuroimaging studies of individuals with a number of chronic pain syndromes (e.g., chronic low back pain, phantom limb pain, fibromyalgia) noted structural changes and cortical reorganization throughout the areas of the brain known to be important in terms of pain processing, providing significant support for a sophisticated pain-transmitting network as described by Melzack (May, 2008).

The International Association for the Study of Pain (IASP; 1994) definition of pain acknowledges that pain is "an unpleasant sensory and emotional experience associated with actual or potential tissue damage, or described in terms of such damage" (p. 210). Because pain is a multifaceted and complex phenomenon that is inherently unique, it is rarely amenable to objective measurement. Comprehensive pain assessments should assume a biopsychosocial approach that necessarily relies heavily on subjective self-report measures of pain.

Psychologists' Role in Pain Assessment

Because as many as 80% of medical visits are directly related to pain complaints (Quartana et al., 2009), health psychologists are frequently asked to assess patients with chronic pain to identify factors that perpetuate and exacerbate pain and suffering. Identification of pertinent targets of treatment is important for tailoring an intervention to the specific needs of the patient (Heapy, Stroud, Higgins, & Sellinger, 2006), and ongoing assessment during treatment provides a means for monitoring progress and efficacy of interventions. Health psychologists also provide presurgical evaluations prior to dorsal column stimulator implants, insertion of indwelling analgesic pumps, or spinal surgery. The goal of these types of evaluations is to determine a patient's psychological suitability for surgery by assessing for variables that may negatively affect surgical outcomes (e.g., untreated mental illness, poor coping). Health psychologists may also provide assessment of individuals prior to institution of opioid therapy with a goal of identifying patients at higher risk of misuse of opioid medication (Gatchel, 2011). In research settings, health psychologists play an important role in the conduct of research aimed at exploring the many factors that contribute to the pain experience and in designing and testing assessment instruments and interventions to reduce pain and suffering.

Important Factors in Pain Assessment

At present, there is no standardized process for assessing pain; pain assessments will vary to some extent based on the patient population (e.g., infant, child, adult, patient with communication deficits), etiology (e.g., acute pain, chronic low back pain, arthritis, fibromyalgia), and purpose of the evaluation (clinical care vs. research). The sheer number of published pain assessment instruments is a testament to the challenge of capturing the multiple dimensions of pain (Breivik et al., 2008), and availability of several instruments measuring the same domain can make it difficult to determine which instruments to use. Further, access to numerous pain measures contributes to the tremendous variability in outcomes reported in the literature making comparison across studies extremely difficult and at times impossible (Turk et al., 2003). Regardless of the specific instruments selected, it is important to ensure that assessments include the sensory, affective, cognitive, and functional aspects of pain, as well as the psychosocial contributors to pain and suffering. Notable areas of consideration for all pain assessments are discussed here.

Pain Intensity

The sensory quality of pain (e.g., pain intensity) is often the only dimension of pain that is assessed in clinical settings; however, while pain intensity is a necessary part of pain assessment, in isolation it is certainly not a sufficient measure of pain. The usual methods for obtaining pain intensity ratings include visual analog scales (VAS), numeric rating scales (NRS), and verbal rating scales (VRS).

A mark placed along a 10-cm or 100-mm line represents pain intensity on a VAS. Anchors on either end typically range from *no pain* to *extreme pain*, but the actual choice of descriptors may differ slightly. The distance from no pain to the patient's mark determines the pain intensity score. VAS scores demonstrate ratio properties (Price, Bush, Long, & Harkins, 1994) and reliability and validity are well established when measuring acute pain (e.g., Bijur, Silver, & Gallagher, 2001), chronic pain (Jensen & Karoly, 2011) and experimental pain (Price et al., 1994). At face value, the 100-mm VAS would appear to have better discriminative ability than a 10-cm VAS; however, in practice patients may struggle with discriminating pain intensity above nine or 10 levels (Hjermstad et al., 2011). VAS ratings may be less reliable in patients with low literacy (Hawker, Mian, Kendzrska, & French, 2011) and patients with cognitive, visual, or motor deficits (Kahl & Cleland, 2005; Turk & Burwinkle, 2005). A clinically significant reduction in VAS ratings has been reported as 1.1 points on the 0–10 scale (Hawker et al., 2011).

NRS use a series of whole numbers generally displayed on a 0–10 scale (or 0–100) anchored with verbal descriptors of pain severity (e.g., *no pain* to *worst imaginable pain*). The psychometric properties of NRS are well documented, as is their sensitivity to change in pain intensity over time (Herr, Spratt, Mobily, & Richardson, 2004). While NRS likely do not demonstrate true ratio properties (Price et al., 1994), some reports suggest that a decrease of approximately two points on NRS is consistent with a clinically important difference in pain intensity (Farrar, Young, LaMoreaux, Werth, & Poole, 2001).

VRS differ from NRS in that they use adjectives placed uniformly along the line to reflect increasing levels of pain intensity. Similar to the VAS, most have *no pain* on the lower end of the scale and more intense pain (e.g., *extreme*) on the upper end. Each adjective is assigned a numerical value that reflects the pain intensity score. The true difference in pain intensity from one adjective to the next is unknown and may not be equal intervals of intensity (Williams, 2004), and the forced choice format may make it difficult for patients to choose a descriptor reflective of their personal and unique pain experience (Mason, Fauerbach, & Haythornthwaite, 2011). The psychometric properties of VRS are weaker than VAS or NRS (Turk & Burwinkle, 2005). However, they do seem to be sensitive to changes in pain intensity with reductions in pain from one response point to another (e.g., *severe* to *moderate*) representing a clinically significant treatment outcome (Jensen & Karoly, 2011).

The reliability and validity of single-item pain intensity measures are well established; however, use of single-item measures alone has significant drawbacks. While in general any of the above pain intensity measures are appropriate to use with most patients (Jensen & Karoly, 2011), use of NRS has been recommended for assessing cancer pain and similar recommendations for adopting use of NRS for assessing chronic pain have been proffered (Kaasa et al., 2011). It is important to note that these scales may not perform as well when used with the elderly (Chibnall & Tait, 2001) or with individuals with communication and/or significant cognitive deficits; thus, alternative assessment techniques or observational pain ratings may be more appropriate (Herr & Garand, 2001).

Stress, Coping, and Pain

Individuals vary to a great extent in their ability to cope with pain; many perceive pain as a threat, thus activating maladaptive coping strategies. The underlying cognitive and emotional schemas may adversely affect the ability to rationally interpret pain sensations and to disengage from pain-related cognitions. Catastrophizing, "an exaggerated negative mental set which comes to bear during actual or anticipated pain experience" (Sullivan et al., 2001, p. 53), is an important cognitive contributor to pain and suffering. The ongoing magnification of the threat value of pain and subsequent rumination produces an overwhelming sense of helplessness and hopelessness, further eroding the patient's perception of control over pain (Edwards, Bingham, Banthon, & Haythornthwaite, 2006; Thorn, Boothby, & Sullivan, 2002). The presence of catastrophizing predicts higher levels of reported pain, poorer overall functioning, increased disability, and significant alterations in affect and mood (Quartana et al., 2009; Sullivan et al., 2001).

It is interesting that catastrophizing may activate inflammatory processes implicated in a number of painful conditions such as fibromyalgia and arthritis (Edwards et al., 2006; Edwards et al., 2008). Catastrophizing is also related to increased activation in cortical structures associated with anticipation of pain, attention to pain, and emotional reactions to pain, over and above the effects secondary to perceptions of pain intensity (Gracely et al., 2004).

While it is clear that catastrophizing influences emotional, functional, and physiological responses to pain and predicts pain-related outcomes, questions remain about the distinctiveness of catastrophizing above depression and negative affect (Hirsh, George, Riley, & Robinson, 2005; Sullivan & D'Eon, 1990). However, a number of studies demonstrated differential effects of catastrophizing on pain outcomes over and above the effects driven by depression or negative affect (Sullivan, Bishop, & Pivik, 1995). Indeed, the presence of catastrophizing predicts depression in chronic pain patients (Tan, Jensen, Robinson-Whelen, Thornby, & Monga, 2001). Regardless, individuals who catastrophize perceive pain as *unbearable, horrible*, and *worst imaginable* exhibit low self-efficacy for dealing with pain, and may defer to powerful others to cure their pain.

There are two notable measures for assessing catastrophizing: the catastrophizing subscale of the Coping Strategies Questionnaire (CSQ; Rosenstiel & Keefe, 1983) and the Pain Catastrophizing Scale (PCS; Sullivan et al., 1995). The CSQ is a 50-item pain coping measure that assesses a variety of coping strategies including catastrophizing. It is comprised of eight subscales: six measure cognitive coping strategies (ignoring pain, reinterpretation of pain, diverting attention, coping self-statements, catastrophizing, and praying/hoping) and two assess behavioral strategies (activity levels and pain behaviors). While the CSQ is one of the most widely studied measures of pain coping (Jensen, Turner, Romano, & Karoly, 1991), and often used to assess catastrophizing, the catastrophizing subscale primarily assesses feelings of helplessness that occur with catastrophizing (Quartana et al., 2009). Further, concerns about psychometric properties of the broader instrument, including the factor structure, internal consistency, and construct validity, have also been raised (Stewart, Harvey, & Evans, 2001; Swartzman, Gwadrya, Shapirob, & Teasell, 1994). Several revisions of the CSQ, including the Coping Strategies Questionnaire-Revised (CSQ-R; Riley & Robinson, 1997), have been published. The resultant factor structure of the CSQ-R is more stable and has been replicated in several studies and preference for the CSQ-R for assessing coping in African American populations has been recommended (Hastie, Riley, & Fillingim, 2004).

The PCS provides a more thorough examination of the broader catastrophizing construct (Quartana et al., 2009). It is a brief 13-item measure developed from the catastrophizing subscale of the CSQ that assesses the frequency in which individuals experience certain thoughts and feelings when in pain (e.g., "I feel I can't go on"). Items are ranked on a scale of 0 to 4 with 0 representing *not at all* and 4 *all the time*. While the PCS provides a total score and three subscales (i.e., magnification, rumination, and helplessness), there is a high level of correlation among the subscales and questions about the stability of the factor structure have been raised (Chibnall & Tait, 2005; Quartana et al., 2009). Given these concerns, use of the total score may be more appropriate.

In a recent exploration of catastrophizing in a rehabilitation patient sample, baseline scores of 24 or better on the PCS predicted worse outcomes. Patients with scores of 14–15 after treatment reported high pain intensity scores and did not return to work. Those whose scores decreased by 38–44% were more likely to be employed and to report low pain intensity at 1-year follow-up (Scott, Wideman, & Sullivan, 2014).

Pain Anxiety/Fear of Pain

Catastrophic cognitions contribute to the development of pain-specific fear and/or anxiety, higher pain ratings, limited physical activity with deconditioning, and ultimately disability (Vlaeyen, Kole-Snijders, Rotteveel, Ruesink, & Heuts, 1995; Vlaeyen & Linton, 2000). Individuals high in pain anxiety/fear become hypervigilant and make concerted efforts to avoid or escape pain. Unfortunately, pain anxiety activates the hippocampus, produces hyperalgesia, and enhances the threat value of pain priming maladaptive behavioral responses (Ploghaus et al., 2001) arising from fear that physical activity will exacerbate pain or result in further damage or additional injury. The resultant avoidant and fearful behavior leads to deconditioning, increased disability, and poorer outcomes (Leeuw et al., 2007).

Measures have been developed to specifically assess the unique aspects of pain anxiety and fear of movement/(re)injury, including the behavioral components. One of the most often cited instruments, the Tampa Scale of Kinesiophobia (TSK; Kori, Miller, & Todd, 1990), is used to assess fear of movement/(re)injury in studies examining a wide array of persistent pain conditions. The 17-item scale assesses beliefs that activity may cause additional harm or increase pain, and that pain is a symptom of a serious medical condition. Items are scored from 1 (*strongly disagree*) to 4 (*strongly agree*) to produce a total score. While the original scale was developed in English, most subsequent psychometric studies have been done in Europe using various translations of the original scale. The reliability and validity of the TSK in European samples is generally well established (Roelofs, Goubert, Peters, Vlaeyen, & Crombez, 2004). A shortened 11-item English version (TSK-11) demonstrated good psychometric properties in a sample of chronic low back pain patients (Woby, Roach, Urmston, & Watson, 2005). Scores on the TSK, which are predicted by catastrophizing, are significantly predictive of overall disability (Vlaeyen & Linton, 2000).

The Pain Anxiety Symptom Scale (PASS; McCracken, Zayfert, & Gross, 1992) was developed from the conceptualization of fear of pain as a multidimensional response that contributes significantly to the broader pain experience. The 40-item PASS assesses three response modes for pain-related fear and anxiety: cognitive fearful thoughts and ruminations, physiological symptoms of fear manifest with pain, and avoidance and escape behaviors. The PASS produces four subscales: somatic anxiety, cognitive anxiety, fear, and escape/avoidance responses and a total score. Adequate psychometric properties were reported in the original validation study; however, concerns about the psychometrics of this and related measures have been raised (Lundberg, Grimby-Ekman, Verbunt, & Simmonds, 2011). Further refinement of the PASS resulted in a 20-item version (PASS-20) that retains adequate reliability and validity (McCracken & Dhingra, 2002).

Pain Behaviors

Overt behavioral expressions of pain include not only the expected sighing, grimacing, and/ or guarding, but also communication of pain via words, sounds or facial expressions, and activities that avoid pain such as reclining. Other pain behaviors of potential clinical importance include use of medication and pain-related health-care visits. Examination of pain behaviors is clinically important because they provide insight into coping strategies and environmental reinforcers.

While clinicians often make anecdotal observations of pain behaviors within the clinical setting, standardized methods for recording and coding pain behaviors are available (Keefe & Block, 1982). However, significant training is required, and the coding process is time consuming; thus, use of such assessment techniques is relegated primarily to research settings. Alternatively, more clinically useful measures such as the Pain Behavior Checklist (PBCL; Kerns et al., 1991) and the UAB Pain Behavior Scale (Richards, Nepomuceno, Riles, & Suer, 1982) provide more efficient and brief methods for effectively and reliably assessing pain behaviors.

The PBCL is a well-validated 17-item self-report instrument assessing the frequency in which patients engage in 25 pain behaviors categorized into four domains: distorted ambulation, facial/audible expressions, affective distress, and seeking help. Responses are scored from 0 (*never*) to 6 (*very often*). The PBCL is correlated with pain-related disability, measures of depression and anxiety, and pain interference as measured with the West Haven–Yale Multidimensional Pain Inventory (WHYMPI; Kerns et al., 1991).

The UAB Pain Behavior Scale (Richards et al., 1982) is an observational tool used to record the presence and frequency of pain behaviors (verbal and nonverbal complaints, facial grimace, standing posture, mobility, body language, use of visible support equipment, and stationary movement) and self-reported down time and medication use. The PBS produces a total score ranging from 0 to 10 with higher scores indicating more pain behaviors. Due to the brevity and ease of scoring, the PBS can be used to track changes in pain behaviors over time.

Multidimensional Pain Measures

The McGill Pain Questionnaire (MPQ; Melzack, 1975) uses a list of pain descriptors to capture the sensory, affective, and evaluative qualities of pain. Items are ranked and summed to produce a pain-rating index (PRI). The instrument includes a pain intensity scale and a line drawing of the body to record the spatial distribution of pain. The MPQ has been validated in many languages and populations and has been labeled "the leading instrument" for pain assessment (McDowell, 2006).

The stability of the original three-factor structure of the MPQ has been debated (Holroyd et al., 1992; Prieto et al., 1980); however, the overall reliability and validity are well established (Katz & Melzack, 2011). The MPQ total score correlates well with VAS ratings (Taenzer, 1983). The Short-Form MPQ (SF-MPQ; Melzack, 1987) includes 15 descriptors extracted from the original list, with the addition of the word *splitting*, that are rated on a scale of 0 to 3 (1 = *mild*, 3 = *severe*) yielding three pain scores (sensory, affective, and total score). The Present Pain Intensity (PPI) index from the original MPQ was retained and a VAS (*no pain* to *worst possible pain*) was added. The SF-MPQ is highly correlated with the Pain Rating Index (PRI) from the long-form MPQ (Dudgeon, Ranbertas, & Rosenthal, 1993; Melzack, 1987) and reliability and validity are well established (Melzack, 1987).

Another popular multidimensional pain measure is the Brief Pain Inventory (BPI; Daut, Cleeland, & Flanery, 1983). This 36-item instrument assesses the sensory dimension of the pain experience as well as what is described as a *reactive* dimension (i.e., interference in functioning). The BPI can be self-administered or administered via clinical interview in less than 15 min. The sensory dimension of pain is assessed with ratings of present pain intensity, worst pain, and least pain on a 10-point Likert scale (0=*no pain*, 10=*pain as bad as you can imagine*). A list of pain adjectives helps patients describe their pain. Items also assess the amount of pain relief after administration of analgesics and the patient's perceptions of the etiology of pain (treatment, disease, or other unrelated condition). The reactive dimension of pain is captured with items assessing the impact of pain on the patient's functioning in terms of general activity, mood, sleep, interpersonal functioning, work activities, and enjoyment of life. Although originally developed to assess cancer and other disease-related pain, the BPI has now been validated for use in a number of other pain populations (Keller et al., 2004; Tan, Jensen, Thornby, & Shanti, 2004) and it has been translated and validated in many languages and across cultures (Cleeland & Ryan, 1994). The reliability and validity are well established (Daut et al., 1983; Tan et al., 2004) and several short forms of the BPI developed for daily pain assessment have been validated (Cleeland, 1989; Mendoza, Mayne, Rublee, & Cleeland, 2006).

One of the most well researched and often cited comprehensive pain assessment measures is the WHYMPI (Kerns, Turk, & Rudy, 1985). This is a 52-item instrument with three parts (12 scales) assessing the impact of pain on the patient's life, responses of others to the patient's communication of distress and pain, and the effects of pain on daily activities. Part one includes five scales: interference, support, pain severity, self-control, and negative mood. Part two has three scales assessing patient-perceived responses of significant others to their pain: punishing responses, solicitous responses, and distracting responses. Finally, part three consists of four scales reflecting participation in common daily activities: household chores, outdoor work, activities away from home, and social activities. The WHYMPI has good psychometric properties (Kerns et al., 1985), is sensitive to change during treatment (Kerns, Turk, Holzman, & Rudy, 1986), and has been validated in both acute and persistent pain conditions. It has also been translated into a number of languages including German (Verra et al., 2012), Dutch (Lousberga et al., 1999), and Swedish (Bergström, Jensena, Linton, & Nygrena, 1999).

Pain in Special Populations

As mentioned throughout the previous sections, there are limitations for most pain assessment instruments, but additional important issues arise when assessing pain in special populations. For example, while individuals with mild to moderate levels of cognitive deficits can accurately report their pain (Chibnall & Tait, 2001), verbal descriptor scales may prove a better choice with the elderly (Herr & Mobily, 1993). For those with more significant levels of impairment, direct observation and monitoring response to medications may be preferred because proxy measures of pain that rely on ratings offered by family members or clinicians can lack validity (Herr, Bjoro, & Decker, 2006). Guarding and rubbing may be nonspecific signs in cognitively impaired patients, while grimacing is likely evidence of the presence of pain (Shega et al., 2008). Children under the age of two years, and those with developmental delays, lack the cognitive capacity to report pain (Herr et al., 2006) and there is great variability in which behaviors actually indicate pain. These examples underscore the importance of considering the idiosyncrasies of special populations when choosing assessment instruments.

Research Issues in Pain Assessment

Recent efforts to develop a recommended framework for designing, evaluating, and interpreting clinical trials of chronic pain treatment were spearheaded by the Initiative on Methods, Measurement, and Pain Assessment in Clinical Trials (IMMPACT; Dworkin et al., 2008). To make comparisons across trials possible, the IMMPACT workgroup recommended including six core outcome domains in all pain treatment trials (i.e., pain, physical functioning, emotional functioning, participant ratings of global improvement and satisfaction with treatment, symptoms and adverse events, and participant disposition) and consistent use of specific, well-validated, and psychometrically sound outcome measures for each of the previously identified assessment domains (Turk et al., 2003). The workgroup also recommended adopting a multimethod (anchor-based and distribution-based) approach to determining clinically important changes in pain trials, and provided benchmarks for determining significant changes in pain intensity, physical and emotional functioning, and global ratings of improvement (Dworkin et al., 2008). There is little doubt that adoption of the IMMPACT recommendations will enhance comparison of outcomes across studies and positively impact pain assessment and treatment.

In a similar project, The National Institutes of Health (NIH) Patient-Reported Outcomes Measurement Information System (PROMIS) Roadmap Initiative recommended standardized assessment practices for patient-reported outcomes in clinical trials relevant to a number of common medical conditions, including pain. At present, there are three item banks for pain: pain intensity, pain behaviors, and pain interference. A simple numeric rating scale is recommended to capture perceived levels of pain intensity. Pain behavior items capture both verbal (asking for assistance, verbal pain reports) and nonverbal actions (e.g., sighing, crying, resting, grimacing) that communicate to others that one is in pain (Revicki et al., 2009), and pain interference items assess the global impact of pain on daily life including alterations in sleep and enjoyment of life (Amtmann et al., 2010). The PROMIS group is also working toward determination of minimally important difference for their instruments. As is the case with the IMMPACT project, adoption of recommendations from the PROMIS initiative will no doubt improve consistency in pain trials that will serve to further our understanding of pain and its sequelae.

Conclusions and Future Directions

Pain is multiply determined and influenced by a variety of factors beyond the nociceptive stimulus, thus all aspects of pain– the sensory, affective, and cognitive/evaluative – must be assessed in order to guide treatment and determine outcomes. Equally as important to consider are important psychosocial issues such as the effects of pain on functioning, quality of life, and interpersonal relationships. Even though many of the aspects of the pain experience that portend poor outcome have been identified, there is much work to be done in terms of standardizing the way in which each is measured and interpreted. Because development of psychometrically sound and relevant assessment instruments begins with good research, the exciting and important works of IMMPACT and PROMIS are important first steps in improving our ability to accurately explore the many facets of pain.

References

Amtmann, D. A., Cook, K. F., Jensen, M. P., Chen, W-H., Choi, S. W., Revicki, D., … Lai, J-S. (2010). Development of a PROMIS item bank to measure pain interference. *Pain, 150*, 173–182. http://doi.org/10.1016/j.pain.2010.04.025

Bergström, K. G., Jensena, I. B., Linton, S. J., & Nygrena, A. L. (1999). A psychometric evaluation of the Swedish version of the Multidimensional Pain Inventory (MPI-S): A gender differentiated evaluation. *European Journal of Pain, 3*, 261–273. http://doi.org/10.1016/S1090-3801(99)90053-8

Bijur, P. E., Silver, W., & Gallagher, J. (2001). Reliability of the Visual Analog Scale for measurement of acute pain. *Academic Emergency Medicine, 8*, 1153–1157. http://doi.org/10.1111/j.1553-2712.2001.tb01132.x

Blyth, F. M., March, L. M., Brnabic, A. J. M., Jorm, L. R., Williamson, M., & Cousins, M. J. (2001). Chronic pain in Australia: A prevalence study. *Pain, 89*, 127–134. http://doi.org/10.1016/S0304-3959(00)00355-9

Breivik, H., Borchgrevink, P. C., Allen, S. M., Rossleand, L. A., Romundstad, L., Hals, E. K., … Stubhaug, A. (2008). Assessment of pain. *British Journal of Anaesthesia, 101*, 17–24. http://doi.org/10.1093/bja/aen103

Breivik, H., Collett, B., Ventafridda, V., Cohen, R., & Gallacher, D. (2006). Survey of chronic pain in Europe: Prevalence, impact on daily life, and treatment. *European Journal of Pain, 10*, 287–333. http://doi.org/10.1016/j.ejpain.2005.06.009

Chibnall, J. T., & Tait, R. C. (2001). Pain assessment in cognitively impaired and unimpaired older adults: A comparison of four scales. *Pain, 92*, 173–186. http://doi.org/10.1016/S0304-3959(00)00485-1

Chibnall, J. T., & Tait, R. C. (2005). Confirmatory factor analysis of the Pain Catastrophizing Scale in African American and Caucasian workers' compensation claimants with low back injuries. *Pain, 113*, 369–375. http://doi.org/10.1016/j.pain.2004.11.016

Cleeland, C. S. (1989). Measurement of pain by subjective report. In C. R. Chapman & J. D. Loeser (Eds.), *Issues in pain management: Advances in pain research and therapy* (Vol. 12, pp. 391–403). New York: NY, Raven Press.

Cleeland, C. S., & Ryan, K. M. (1994). Pain assessment: Global use of the Brief Pain Inventory. *Annals of the Academy of Medicine, 23*, 119–128.

Daut, R. L., Cleeland, C. S., & Flanery, R. C. (1983). Development of the Wisconsin Brief Pain Questionnaire to assess pain in cancer and other diseases. *Pain, 17*, 197–210. http://doi.org/10.1016/0304-3959(83)90143-4

Dudgeon, D., Ranbertas, R. F., & Rosenthal, S. (1993). The Short-Form McGill Pain Questionnaire in chronic cancer pain. *Journal of Pain and Symptom Management, 8*, 191–195. http://doi.org/10.1016/0885-3924(93)90126-G

Dworkin, R. H., Turk, D. C., Wyrwich, K. W., Beaton, D. Cleeland, C. S., … Zavisic, S. (2008). Interpreting the clinical importance of treatment outcomes in chronic pain clinical trials: IMMPACT recommendations. *The Journal of Pain, 9*, 105–121. http://doi.org/10.1016/j.jpain.2007.09.005

Edwards, R. R., Bingham, C. O., III, Bathon, J., & Haythornthwaite, J. A. (2006). Catastrophizing and pain in arthritis, fibromyalgia, and other rheumatic diseases. *Arthritis & Rheumatism, 55*, 325–332. http://doi.org/10.1002/art.21865

Edwards, R. R., Kronfli, T., Haythornthwaite, J. A., Smith, M. T., McGuire, L., & Page, G. G. (2008). Association of catastrophizing with Interleukin-6 responses to acute pain. *Pain, 140*, 135–144. http://doi.org/10.1016/j.pain.2008.07.024

Engel, G. L. (1977). The need for a new medical model: A challenge for biomedicine. *Science, 196*, 129–136. http://doi.org/10.1126/science.847460

Farrar, J. T., Young, J. P., Jr., LaMoreaux, L., Werth, L. L., & Poole, R. M. (2001). Clinical importance of changes in chronic pain intensity measured on an 11-point numerical rating scale. *Pain, 94*, 149–158. http://doi.org/10.1016/S0304-3959(01)00349-9

Gatchel, R. J. (2011). The importance of biopsychosocial screening before surgical intervention or opioid therapy for patients with chronic pain. In D. C. Turk & R. Melzack (Eds.), *Handbook of pain assessment* (3rd ed., pp. 444–454). New York, NY: Guilford Press.

Gracely, R. H., Geisser, M. E., Giesecke, T., Grant, M. A. B., Petzke, F. Williams, D. A., & Clauw, D. J. (2004). Pain catastrophizing and neural responses to pain among persons with fibromyalgia. *Brain, 127*, 835–843. http://doi.org/10.1093/brain/awh098

Hastie, B. A., Riley, J. L., & Fillingim, R. B. (2004). Ethnic differences in pain coping: Factor structure of the coping strategies questionnaire and coping strategies questionnaire-revised. *The Journal of Pain, 5*, 304–316. http://doi.org/10.1016/j.jpain.2004.05.004

Hawker, G. A., Mian, S., Kendzerska, T., & French, M. (2011). Measures of adult pain. *Arthritis Care & Research, 63*, S2 40–S2 52. http://doi.org/10.1002/acr.20543

Heapy, A. A., Stroud, M. W., Higgins, D. M., & Sellinger, J. J. (2006). Tailoring cognitive therapy for chronic pain: A case example. *Journal of Clinical Psychology in Session, 62*, 1345–1354. http://doi.org/10.1002/jclp.20314

Herr, K., Bjoro, K., & Decker, S. (2006). Tools for assessment of pain in nonverbal older adults with dementia: A state-of-the-science review. *Journal of Pain and Symptom Management, 31*, 170–192. http://doi.org/10.1016/j.jpainsymman.2005.07.001

Herr, K. A., & Garand, L. (2001). Assessment and measurement of pain in older adults. *Clinics in Geriatric Medicine, 17*, 457–478. http://doi.org/10.1016/S0749-0690(05)70080-X

Herr, K. A., & Mobily, P. R. (1993). Comparison of selected pain assessment tools for use with the elderly. *Applied Nursing Research, 6*, 39–46. http://doi.org/10.1016/S0897-1897(05)80041-2

Herr, K. A., Spratt, K., Mobily, P. R., & Richardson, G. (2004). Pain intensity assessment in older adults: Use of experimental pain to compare psychometric properties and usability of selected pain scales with younger adults. *The Clinical Journal of Pain, 20*, 207–219. http://doi.org/10.1097/00002508-200407000-00002

Hirsh, A., George, S., Riley, J., & Robinson, M. (2005). Sex differences and construct redundancy of the Coping Strategies Questionnaire-catastrophizing subscale. *Journal of Pain, 6*(Suppl. 1), S6 0. http://doi.org/10.1016/j.jpain.2005.01.234

Hjermstad, M. J., Fayers, P. M., Haugen, D. F., Caraceni, A., Hanks, G. W., Loge, J. H., … Kaasa, S. (2011). Studies comparing numerical rating scales, verbal rating scales, and visual analogue scales for assessment of pain intensity in adults: A systematic literature review. *Journal of Pain and Symptom Management, 41*, 1073–1093. http://doi.org/10.1016/j.jpainsymman.2010.08.016

Holroyd, K. A., Holm, J. E., Keefe, F.J., Turner, J. A., Bradley, L. A., Murphy, W. D., … O'Malley, W. B. (1992). A multi-center evaluation of the McGill Pain Questionnaire: Results from more than 1700 chronic pain patients. *Pain, 48*, 301–311. http://doi.org/10.1016/0304-3959(92)90077-O

Institute of Medicine. (2011). *Report from the Committee on Advancing Pain Research, Care, and Education: Relieving pain in America, a blueprint for transforming prevention, care, education and research*. Washington, DC: The National Academies Press.

International Association for the Study of Pain, Task Force on Taxonomy. (1994). Pain terms: A current list with definitions and notes on usage. In H. Merskey & N. Bogduk (Eds.), *Classification of chronic pain*, (2nd ed., pp. 209–214). Seattle, WA: IASP Press.

Jensen, M. P., & Karoly, P. (2011). Self-report scales and procedures for assessing pain in adults. In D. C. Turk & R. Melzack (Eds.), *Handbook of pain assessment* (3rd ed., pp. 19–35). New York, NY: Guilford Press.

Jensen, M. P., Turner, J. A., Romano, J. M., & Karoly, P. (1991). Coping with chronic pain: A critical review of the literature. *Pain, 47*, 249–283. http://doi.org/10.1016/0304-3959(91)90216-K

Kaasa, S., Apolone, G., Klepstad, P., Loge, J. H., Hjermstad, M. J., Corli, O., … Caraceni, A. (2011). Expert conference on cancer pain assessment and classification – the need for international consensus: Working proposals on international standards. *BMJ Supportive and Palliative Care, 1*, 281–287. http://doi.org/10.1136/bmjspcare-2011-000078

Kahl, C., & Cleland, J. A. (2005). Visual analogue scale, numeric pain rating scale and the McGill Pain Questionnaire: An overview of psychometric properties. *Physical Therapy Review, 10*, 123–128. http://doi.org/10.1179/108331905X55776

Katz, J., & Melzack, R. (2011). The McGill Pain Questionnaire: Development, psychometric properties, and usefulness of the long form, short form, and short form-2. In D. C. Turk & R. Melzack (Eds.), *Handbook of pain assessment* (3rd ed., pp. 45–66). New York, NY: Guilford Press.

Keefe, F. J., & Block, A. R. (1982). Development of an observational method for assessing pain behavior in chronic low back pain patients. *Behavior Therapy, 13*, 363–375. http://doi.org/10.1016/S0005-7894(82)80001-4

Keller, S., Bann, C. M., Dodd, S. L., Schein, J. Mendoza, T. R., & Cleeland, C. S. (2004). Validity of the Brief Pain inventory for documenting outcomes in noncancer pain. *Clinical Journal of Pain, 20*, 309–318. http://doi.org/10.1097/00002508-200409000-00005

Kerns, R. D., Haythornthwaite, J., Rosenberg, R., Southwick, S., Giller, E. L., & Jacob, M. C. (1991). The Pain Behavior Check List (PBCL): Factor structure and psychometric properties. *Journal of Behavioral Medicine, 14*, 155–167. http://doi.org/10.1007/BF00846177

Kerns, R. D., Turk, D. C., Holzman, A. D., & Rudy, T. E. (1986). Comparison of cognitive-behavioral and behavioral approaches to outpatient treatment of chronic pain. *Clinical Journal of Pain, 1*, 195–203.

Kerns, R. D., Turk, D. C., & Rudy, T. E. (1985). The West Haven-Yale Multidimensional Pain Inventory (WHYMPI). *Pain, 23*, 345–356. http://doi.org/10.1016/0304-3959(85)90004-1

Kori, S., Miller, R., & Todd, D. (1990). Kinesiophobia: A new view of chronic pain behavior. *Pain Management, 3*, 35–43.

Leeuw, M., Goossens, M. E. J. B., Linton, S. J., Crombez, G., Boersm, K., & Vlaeyen, J. W. S. (2007). The Fear-Avoidance Model of musculoskeletal pain: Current state of scientific evidence. *Journal of Behavioral Medicine, 30*, 77–94. http://doi.org/10.1007/s10865-006-9085-0

Lousberga, R., Van Breukelenb, G. J. P., Groenmanc, N. H., Schmidtd, A. J. M., Arntzd, A., & Wintera, F. A. M. (1999). Psychometric properties of the Multidimensional Pain Inventory, Dutch language version (MPI-DLV). *Behavior Research and Therapy, 37*, 167–182. http://doi.org/10.1016/S0005-7967(98)00137-5

Lundberg, M., Grimby-Ekman, A., Verbunt, J., & Simmonds, M. J. (2011). Pain-related fear: A critical review of related measures. *Pain Research & Treatment,* Article ID 494196. http://doi.org/1155/2011/494196

Mason, S. T., Fauerbach, J. A., & Haythornthwaite, J. A. (2011). Assessment of acute pain, pain relief, and patient satisfaction. In D. C. Turk & R. Melzack (Eds.), *Handbook of pain assessment* (3rd ed., pp. 283–293). New York, NY: Guilford.

May, A. (2008). Chronic pain may change the structure of the brain. *Pain, 137*, 7–15. http://doi.org/10.1016/j.pain.2008.02.034

McCracken, L. M., & Dhingra, L. (2002). A short version of the Pain Anxiety Symptoms Scale (PASS- 20): Preliminary development and validity. *Pain Research & Management, 7*, 45–50.

McCracken, L. M., Zayfert, C., & Gross, R. T. (1992). The Pain Anxiety Symptoms Scale: Development and validation of a scale to measure fear of pain. *Pain, 50*, 67–73. http://doi.org/10.1016/0304-3959(92)90113-P

McDowell, I. (2006). *Measuring health: A guide to rating scales and questionnaires* (3rd ed.). New York, NY: Oxford University Press. http://doi.org/10.1093/acprof:oso/9780195165678.001.0001

Melzack, R. (1975). The McGill Pain Questionnaire: Major properties and scoring methods. *Pain, 1*, 277–299. http://doi.org/10.1016/0304-3959(75)90044-5

Melzack, R. (1987). The Short-Form McGill Pain Questionnaire. *Pain, 30*, 191–197. http://doi.org/10.1016/0304-3959(87)91074-8

Melzack, R. (1999). From the gate to the neuromatrix. *Pain, Suppl. 6,* S121–S126.

Melzack, R., & Wall, P. D. (1965). Pain mechanisms: A new theory. *Science, 150*, 971–979. http://doi.org/10.1126/science.150.3699.971

Mendoza, T., Mayne, T., Rublee, D., & Cleeland, C. (2006). Reliability and validity of a modified Brief Pain Inventory short form in patients with osteoarthritis. *European Journal of Pain, 10*, 353–361. http://doi.org/10.1016/j.ejpain.2005.06.002

Ploghaus, A., Narain, C., Beckmann, C. F., Clare, S., Bantick, S., Wise, R., Matthews, P. M., … Tracey, I. (2001). Exacerbation of pain anxiety is associated with activity in a hippocampal network. *The Journal of Neuroscience, 21*, 9896–9903.

Price, D. D., Bush, F. M., Long, S., & Harkins, S. W. (1994). A comparison of pain measurement characteristics of mechanical visual analogue and simple numerical rating scales. *Pain, 56*, 217–226. http://doi.org/10.1016/0304-3959(94)90097-3

Prieto, E. J., Hopson, L., Bradley, L. A., Byrne, M., Geisinger, K. F., Midax, D., & Marchisello, P. J. (1980). The language of low back pain: Factor structure of the McGill Pain Questionnaire. *Pain, 8,* 11–19. http://doi.org/10.1016/0304-3959(80)90086-X

Quartana, P. J., Campbell, C. M., & Edwards, R. R. (2009). Pain catastrophizing: A critical review. *Expert Review of Neurotherapeutics, 9,* 745–758. http://doi.org/10.1586/ern.09.34

Revicki, D. A., Chin, W., Harnam, N., Cook, K. F., Amtmann, D., Callahan, L. F., ... Keefe, F. J. (2009). Development and psychometric analysis of the PROMIS pain behavior item bank. *Pain, 146,* 158–169. http://doi.org/10.1016/j.pain.2009.07.029

Richards, J. S., Nepomuceno, C., Riles, M., & Suer, Z. (1982). Assessing pain behavior: The UAB Pain Behavior Scale. *Pain, 14,* 393–398. http://doi.org/10.1016/0304-3959(82)90147-6

Riley, J. L., & Robinson, M. E. (1997). The Coping Strategies Questionnaire: Five factors or fiction? *Clinical Journal of Pain, 13,* 156–162. http://doi.org/10.1097/00002508-199706000-00010

Roelofs, J., Goubert, L., Peters, M. L., Vlaeyen, J. W., & Crombez, G. (2004). The Tampa Scale for Kinesiophobia: Further examination of psychometric properties in patients with chronic low back pain and fibromyalgia. *European Journal of Pain, 8,* 495–502. http://doi.org/10.1016/j.ejpain.2003.11.016

Rosenstiel, A. K., & Keefe, F. J. (1983). The use of coping strategies in chronic low back pain patients: Relationship to patient characteristics and current adjustment. *Pain, 17,* 33–44. http://doi.org/10.1016/0304-3959(83)90125-2

Scott, W., Wideman, T. H., & Sullivan, M. J. L. (2014). Clinically meaningful scores on pain catastrophizing before and after multidisciplinary rehabilitation: A prospective study of individuals with subacute pain after whiplash injury. *Clinical Journal of Pain, 3,* 183–190. http://doi.org/10.1097/AJP.0b013e31828eee6c

Shega, J. W., Rudy, T., Keefe, F. J., Perri, L. C., Mengin, O. T., & Weiner, D. K. (2008). Validity of pain behaviors in persons with mild to moderate cognitive impairment. *Journal of the American Geriatrics Society, 56,* 1631–1637. http://doi.org/10.1111/j.1532-5415.2008.01831.x

Stewart, M. W., Harvey, S. T., & Evans, I. M. (2001). Coping and catastrophizing in chronic pain: A psychometric analysis and comparison of two measures. *Journal of Clinical Psychology, 57,* 131–138. http://doi.org/10.1002/1097-4679(200101)57:1<131::AID-JCLP13>3.0.CO;2-L

Sullivan, M. J., Bishop, S. R., & Pivik, J. (1995). The Pain Catastrophizing Scale: Development and validation. *Psychological Assessment, 7,* 524–532. http://doi.org/10.1037/1040-3590.7.4.524

Sullivan, M. J., & D'Eon, J. L. (1990). Relation between catastrophizing and depression in chronic pain patients. *Journal of Abnormal Psychology, 99,* 260–263. http://doi.org/10.1037/0021-843X.99.3.260

Sullivan, M. J. L., Thorn, B., Haythornthwaite, J. A., Keefe, F., Martin, M., Bradley, L. A., & Lefebvre, J. C. (2001). *The Clinical Journal of Pain, 17,* 52–64. http://doi.org/10.1097/00002508-200112001-00012

Swartzman, L. C., Gwadrya, F.G., Shapiro, A. P., & Teasell, R. W. (1994). The factor structure of the Coping Strategies Questionnaire. *Pain, 57,* 311–316. http://doi.org/10.1016/0304-3959(94)90006-X

Taenzer, P. (1983). Postoperative pain: relationships among measures of pain, mood, and narcotic requirements. In R. Melzack (Ed.), *Pain measurement and assessment* (pp. 111–118). New York, NY: Raven Press.

Tan, G., Jensen, M. P., Robinson-Whelen, S., Thornby, J. I., & Monga, T. N. (2001). Coping with chronic pain: A comparison of two measures. *Pain, 90,* 127–133. http://doi.org/10.1016/S0304-3959(00)00395-X

Tan, G., Jensen, M. P., Thornby, J. I., & Shanti, B. F. (2004). Validation of the Brief Pain Inventory for chronic nonmalignant pain. *The Journal of Pain, 5,* 133–137. http://doi.org/10.1016/j.jpain.2003.12.005

Thorn, B. E., Boothby, J. L., & Sullivan, M. J. L. (2002). Targeted treatment of catastrophizing for the management of chronic pain. *Cognitive and Behavioral Practice, 9,* 127–138. http://doi.org/10.1016/S1077-7229(02)80006-2

Turk, D. C., & Burwinkle, T. M. (2005). Assessment of chronic pain in rehabilitation: Outcome measures in clinical trials and clinical practice. *Rehabilitation Psychology, 50,* 56–64. http://doi.org/10.1037/0090-5550.50.1.56

Turk, D. C., Dworkin, R. H., Allen, R. R., Bellamy, N., Brandenburg, N., Carr, D. B. ... Witter, J. (2003). Core outcome domains for chronic pain clinical trials: IMMPACT recommendations. *Pain, 106,* 337–345. http://doi.org/10.1016/j.pain.2003.08.001

Turk, D. C., & Melzack, R. (2011). The measurement of pain and the assessment of people experiencing pain. In D. C. Turk & R. Melzack (Eds.), *Handbook of pain assessment* (3rd ed., pp. 3–16). New York, NY: Guilford Press.

Verra, M. L, Angst, F., Staal, J. B., Brioschi, R., Lehmann, S., Aeschlimann, A., & de Bie, R. A. (2012). Reliability of the Multidimensional Pain Inventory and stability of the MPI classification system in chronic back pain. *BMC Musculoskeletal Disorders, 13*, 155. http://doi.org/10.1186/1471-2474-13-155

Vlaeyen, J. W. S., Kole-Snijders, A. M. J., Rotteveel, A. M., Ruesink, R., & Heuts, P. H. T. G. (1995). The role of fear of movement/(re)injury in pain disability. *Journal of Occupational Rehabilitation, 4*, 235–252. http://doi.org/10.1007/BF02109988

Vlaeyen, J. W. S., & Linton, S. J. (2000). Fear-avoidance and its consequences in chronic musculoskeletal pain: a state of the art. *Pain, 85*, 317–332. http://doi.org/10.1016/S0304-3959(99)00242-0

Williams, D. A. (2004). Evaluating acute pain. In R. H. Dworkin & W. S. Breitbart (Eds.), *Psychosocial aspects of pain: A handbook for healthcare providers* (pp. 79–96). *Progress in pain research and management, Vol. 27*. Seattle, WA: IASP Press.

Woby, S. R., Roach, N. K., Urmston, M., & Watson, P. J. (2005). Psychometric properties of the TSK-11: A shortened version of the Tampa Scale for Kinesiophobia. *Pain, 117*, 137–144. http://doi.org/10.1016/j.pain.2005.05.029

Chapter 12

Health Outcomes

Functional Status

Marie Johnston[1] and Diane Dixon[2]

[1]Aberdeen Health Psychology Group, Institute of Applied Health Sciences,
University of Aberdeen, UK
[2]School of Psychological Sciences and Health, University of Strathclyde, Glasgow, UK

Introduction

Research and professional practice in health psychology frequently require a measure of health or health outcome. For example, these assessments are important in planning interventions, in conducting predictive studies, or in evaluating the effects of a treatment or therapeutic intervention. This chapter addresses functional health components as identified by the World Health Organization International Classification of Functioning, Disability and Health (ICF; World Health Organization [WHO], 2001); therefore, it examines assessments of body structure and function, activity, and participation in life settings. This chapter does not deal with healthy behaviours, that is, behaviours such as eating a healthy diet or taking physical exercise that *result* in health (see Chapter 5 in this volume). However, a behaviour such as walking unaided may constitute health as it indexes functional limitations.

Other chapters in this volume deal with mental well-being (Chapter 15), physiological measures (Chapter 17), and self-assessed health (Chapter 13). Measures of quality of life (Chapter 14) have considerable overlap with measures of functional outcomes, especially those assessing health-related quality of life which typically include items assessing functional status. Quality-of-life measures aim to achieve an aggregate of valued outcomes and are more likely to have an empirical or clinical rather than theoretical basis for differentiating sub-scales.

Theoretical Background

Many different constructs such as health status, functional status, functional limitations, and activities of daily living have been used as if they are interchangeable in assessing health outcome. However, the WHO ICF (WHO, 2001) provides a commonly used conceptual framework of health outcomes. Psychological theory has been incorporated into the ICF to provide an integrated behavioural and biomedical theory of functioning and disability (Johnston & Dixon, 2013). Ware (1987) proposed that content validity of measures should be assessed against WHO definitions, referring to the precursor of the ICF. The ICF identifies three health components, each of which can be assessed on a dimension from functioning to disability. The three dimensions are: body structure and function to impairment (I), for example, bone fracture or muscle pain, activity to activity limitations (AL), for example, limitations in walking, and participation to participation restrictions (PR), that is, the ability to engage in *life situations* such as work or visiting friends. The ICF proposes that each of these components and the relationships between them influence, and are influenced by, a health condition and personal and environmental context. The ICF primarily serves to *define* the three health components and these are, therefore, the components that need to be assessed.

The differentiation of these three components was the result of a long consensus process, building on an earlier WHO model. The ICF is widely accepted and authors of previous models have promoted the use of the ICF model to provide a common, shared language (e.g., Jette, 2009), an important feature in a context where previously different words were used for the same theoretical construct and the same word was used for different constructs. For example, the word *disability* in the previous WHO model translated to *functional limitations* in other models, while the latter used the word *disability* to refer to what the WHO labelled *handicap*.

There has been some uncertainty about whether AL and PR can be differentiated in practice, and several approaches to assessment merge these two components. For example, in developing core sets of elements that should be assessed for different health conditions, Cieza and colleagues (2005) do not attempt to differentiate activity from participation. However, in qualitative studies, when people with activity limitations are asked to compare things they do, they talk spontaneously about all three health components (Dixon & Johnston, 2007), and when patients consider the potential gains from joint surgery, they spontaneously mention relief from impairment, AL, and PR in meaningful ways (Pollard, Dixon, & Johnston, 2013a). In quantitative studies, expert judges readily differentiate between items that assess impairment, AL, and PR (Dixon, Pollard, & Johnston, 2007; Pollard, Johnston, & Dieppe 2006). Further, confirmatory factor analyses of responses to health outcome questionnaires identified the three components showing that AL and PR are discriminable by individuals completing self-report questionnaires (Pollard, Johnston, & Dieppe, 2011). In evaluating measures, it is therefore important to consider how well they reflect this dominant, consensus-based, empirically supported theoretical framework.

Assessment and Measurement Issues

What Is Being Measured: The Target Construct

Many health outcome measures have arisen in clinical contexts based on clinicians' judgements of what constitutes a "good" or "bad" outcome. It is difficult to relate such measures to theoretical frameworks such as the ICF, to ensure that they are applicable to patients in other clinics, or to ensure that a full range of outcomes has been assessed. Nevertheless, such measures may have good acceptability and sensitivity in assessing change or differences between individuals in populations or contexts similar to the original. When the ICF content of measures used to assess outcomes in arthritis research was assessed using discriminant content validation methods, they were found to contain widely different percentages of items measuring I, AL, and PR, for example, 8–67% of items assessed I (Pollard et al., 2006). There is some evidence that pure measures of I, AL, and PR may be more successful in detecting specific changes following different types of intervention that have different modes of action, such as physiotherapy and pharmacotherapy (Ayis et al., 2010); these differences are hidden in global measures.

Purpose of the Measure

An assessment may be used on a single occasion, for example, to assess the need for an intervention, or on multiple occasions, for example, to assess whether an intervention is having an effect. A measure for repeated use needs to avoid biases due to recall of previous responses. Furthermore, the assessment may be used to examine change within a single individual or to compare the outcomes of an individual or group of individuals with some comparison group or norm. Clearly, measures used with a single individual need to be sensitive within the individual's range of functioning, for example, a different range may be required to assess changes in mobility in the early stages of a deteriorating condition compared with later stages; whereas a normative measure requires data about the performance of relevant populations, for example, to assess the severity of an individual's mobility problems. When a measure is used to compare groups, it must be sensitive to differences within the range of functioning of those groups.

Performance, Administered, or Self-Report Measures

While most measures used in research settings to assess health and health outcomes involve verbal responses to questions, in clinical settings measures of performance are frequently used. For example, the six-minute walk test is frequently used in heart failure (Boxer et al., 2010), while gait speed or the timed get up-and-go test has been used to screen elderly populations or to predict subsequent decline in health or falls (Viccaro, Perera, & Studenski, 2011). Such measures are restricted to observing performances at limited times and within limited settings, which may not be representative of the full range of performance. In both clinical and research settings, pedometers and accelerometers are now used to assess activity, especially walking, and can assess performance throughout the day and in diverse contexts but may not be feasible or sensitive with more limited individuals.

Performance measures and verbal response measures may be administered by a health professional, a research worker, or someone in the individual's social network, such as a partner. While these assessments may lead to bias, this can be reduced by standardising tasks and reducing the complexity of the judgements necessary, for example, by using counts rather than ratings of quality of performance.

Self-report measures are subject to all of the response biases normally found in the use of self-report, including response sets, negative affectivity, self-serving bias etc. Respondents typically overestimate how active they have been (España-Romero et al., 2014).

Measurement and Monitoring Effects

Measurement of functioning can influence functioning, an effect sometimes referred to as the *mere measurement effect*. However, there are also active processes that might lead to increased activity. For example, monitoring or self-monitoring is likely to increase activity levels partly due to the feedback and reward functions for the individual of seeing how well they are performing. In a clinical assessment situation, patients may make more strenuous efforts because they are in a less hazardous environment than the typical domestic situation so that falls are less likely to occur and less serious when they do occur. Patients may also try hard for the clinicians who have contributed to their care. However, additionally, when asked to perform a task such as an activity of daily living task, respondents may discover that they are in fact able to perform an activity that they have avoided, assuming it was beyond their capability.

Generic Versus Condition-Specific Measures

Generic measures assess health for clinical and non-clinical populations, while other measures have been developed for clinical and research use for specific conditions. For some conditions, such as arthritis and stroke, there is some consensus on a small number of core measures to be used. For other conditions, a wide range of measures are used and consensus requires an explicit process such as that published recently by the American Heart Association (Rumsfeld et al., 2013), which lists 12 measures for three cardiac conditions. While condition-specific measures may be more sensitive to change and more acceptable to people with the condition, they have the disadvantage of not allowing comparison with other clinical populations or with non-clinical populations. It is therefore a common and desirable practice to use both types of measure in research contexts.

Assessing Individuals

In clinical settings it is frequently desirable to assess an individual's level against some norm, for example, to assess need for treatment or to evaluate whether treatment has been effective. It is important that the norms used are adequate for the purpose by being based on large, relevant populations but also that comparisons with the norm are valid. In order to assert that an individual has limited functioning, they should at least be identified as an outlier of the population. Bland and Altman's (1999) method of limits of agreement allows one to assess the likely range of an obtained score for a specific measure against which an individual's score can be judged. Additionally, computational programmes are available that allow for the evaluation of single case results against population norms (e.g., see http://homepages.abdn.ac.uk/j.crawford/pages/dept/psychom.htm).

Scales and Scoring: Average, Category, Dimension, and Profile Scores

Single-item measures are best avoided as they may result in low reliability, but equally a scale with several items and a very high internal consistency may have problems of redundant and potentially burdensome items. More commonly, the measure may require the respondent or administrator to select the single item or level that best describes the level of functioning, for example, the Rankin Test (see Table 12.1). Where there is more than one item, items are usually aggregated into dimensions or categories (e.g., physical vs. mental). It is then possible to present a profile of scores for an individual or a population. Items may be aggregated according to theory of functioning or empirically based, for example, on factor analysis to identify dimensions. Alternatively, groupings may be based on scaling and measurement theory. For example, based on classic test theory, a sum or average might be used, whereas using item response theory an individual's score might be the weighting of the single item in the group of items selected as the best fit to the level of functioning.

Table 12.1. Examples of frequently used condition-specific measures of health outcomes

Condition	Key publications	Items and scales
Arthritis		
Arthritis Impact Measurement Scale (AIMS2) (AIMS2-SF)	Meenan et al., 1992; Guillemin et al., 1997	57 items. Nine subscales including several physical and social functioning (26 items)
Cancer		
EORTC-QLQ-C30 (add-on modules for different cancers)	Aaronson et al., 1993; EORTC Quality of Life Group, 2002	30 items. Five functional, three symptom, and two other scales
Functional Assessment of Cancer Therapy-General (FACT-G) (adapted for many different cancers)	Cella et al., 1993	28 items. Five subscales, including physical and functioning
Cardiovascular disease		
MacNew Questionnaire	Höfer et al., 2004. Available from: neilb@uwm.edu	27 items. Three domains, including physical. Appropriate for a wide range of cardiovascular conditions
Seattle Angina Questionnaire (for angina)	Spertus et al., 1995	19 items. Five dimensions including physical limitation and angina stability and frequency
Kansas City Cardiomyopathy Questionnaire (for heart failure)	Green et al., 2000	25 items. Four subscales including symptoms, physical limitations and social interference
Minnesota Living with Heart Failure questionnaire (for heart failure)	Rector et al., 1993; Garin et al., 2013	21 items. Includes, physical and symptom domains
Stroke		
Modified Rankin Scale (mRS)	Banks & Marotta, 2007	Choice of six grades of disability. Clinician-reported. Less evidence of sensitivity to change than other measures
Barthel Index	Shah, Vanclay, & Cooper, 1989	20 ADL items. Less evidence of sensitivity to change than other measures
COOP-WONCA charts	Lennon et al., 2011	Six diagrammatic charts, including physical fitness, daily and social activities
Back pain		
Roland–Morris Disability Index (RMDQ)	Roland & Fairbank, 2000	24 items. Based on SIP
Oswestry Disability Index (ODI)	Roland & Fairbank, 2000	Ten sections each requiring a choice
Pain		
Common Pain Grade Questionnaire	Von Korff et al., 1992; Dixon et al., 2007	Seven items. Useful in epidemiological studies. Items classified according to ICF domains

Note. ADL = activities of daily living; ICF = International Classification of Functioning, Disability and Health; SIP = Sickness Impact Profile.

Criteria for Evaluating Measures

Various authors have suggested criteria for evaluating health outcome measures (e.g., Ware, 1987) most of which are incorporated in the following sections. Many different evaluations are used and only the most commonly used generic measures have been subjected to a full range of evaluation. Usually, some form of reliability and validity are reported, concepts clarified by Lissitz and Samuelson (2007) as internal and external validity. The criteria adopted should match the purpose of the assessment.

Content

Is the measure representative and relevant to what is intended? This should be addressed before asking any respondents to complete the assessment, initially as face validity but additionally with quantitative indices of discriminant content validity (Johnston et al., 2014).

Acceptability and Feasibility

Will the proposed respondents be willing and able to complete the measure in the intended context? There may be issues of literacy levels for complex tests and of burden, especially for people who are unwell. Readability indices are readily available (see http://en.wikipedia.org/wiki/Automated_Readability_Index) and can be assessed prior to administering the measure. It is often necessary to choose between a long comprehensive measure and a short but less informative measure (e.g., compare the Sickness Impact Profile [SIP] and SF-36 in the section "Generic Measures"). Long measures may be more acceptable if they have high relevance for the population. However, in some situations, for example, in clinics or with very ill people, only short measures are possible.

Reliability

Does the measure, and different parts of the measure, always give the same result under consistent conditions? Most commonly, internal reliability is assessed using Cronbach's α to indicate internal consistency of the measure. For measures involving observer assessments, a measure of inter-rater reliability should be reported, while for assessments of stable health status, test–retest reliability is required. For each of these reliabilities, values over 0.7 are usually taken as acceptable.

Construct Validity

Does the measure show changes compatible with the underlying theory and construct? *Criterion* validity demonstrates differences between groups of respondents known to differ (e.g., inpatient vs. community residents); *concurrent* validity shows expected relationships (e.g., between health status and need for practical support); *predictive* validity indicates that the measure predicts future events or states (e.g., hospitalisation, death). *Convergent* validity indicates positive associations, while *divergent* validity indicates low or negative correlations with measures of unrelated or antithetical constructs and can be illustrated using multitrait-multimethod matrices (Campbell & Fiske, 1959). *Factor-analytic methods* can be used to evaluate the extent to which items assess the intended dimensions or constructs separately (Reise, Moore, & Haviland, 2010).

Sensitivity, Specificity, Responsiveness

Does the measure show differences between people, does it only show difference where it truly exists, and does it show change when the underlying health status changes? Lalkhen and McCluskey (2008) illustrate methods of calculating these indices. Measures should be chosen to be sensitive, specific, and responsive to change in the range of function displayed by the target groups, for example, measures that are sensitive in a general population are unlikely to be sensitive to change in people who are very disabled.

Equivalence Across Culture and Condition

An important consideration for health status measures is whether the scores obtained are equivalent for different cultures and populations. Many health status measures have been translated and adapted for different countries and conditions but interpretation depends on the scores having similar meanings. Issues in translating and adapting measures are considered in Chapter 20 of this volume. Recent developments of statistical methods to assess differential functioning of items (DIF) have demonstrated that even in widely used measures such as the SF-36 some items will give different scores for younger and older subjects or for people who are less or more deprived (Pollard et al., 2013b).

Brief Description of the Main Instruments

Useful overviews of health outcome measures are provided in several books (e.g., McDowell, 2006; Jenkinson, Fitzpatrick, Crocker, & Peters, 2013) and websites (e.g., PROQOLID by the French Mapi Research Institute, http://www.proqolid.org/search2/generic_instruments/(offset)/80; GEM by the USA National Cancer Institute, https://www.gem-beta.org/public/Home.aspx?cat=0).

Generic Measures

36-Item Short-Form Health Survey/RAND-36; MOS Short-Form Health Survey

The 36-item Short-Form Health Survey (SF-36; Ware & Sherbourne, 1992; 36 items, eight scales, two components) is probably the most widely used generic health status measure; for example, Google Scholar lists over 13,000 publications on the SF-36 for each of the years 2011 and 2012. Full details of its development and access can be found at http://www.sf-36.org/. The SF-36, developed as the Medical Outcome Study (MOS) Short-Form Health Survey, was introduced as a measure that fulfilled the WHO health definition, had good psychometric standards and low participant burden. It has 36 items, grouped into eight scales, aggregated to give two summary scores: Physical Component Score (PCS) comprising four scales (Physical Functioning [PF], Role Physical [RP], Bodily Pain [BP], General Health [GH]), and a

Mental Component Score (MCS) comprising four scales (Vitality [VT], Social Functioning [SF], Role Emotion [RE], and Mental Health [MH]). There is extensive evidence of its reliability (internal, test–retest), its validity (content, criterion, concurrent, predictive etc.), and its sensitivity to change or differentiate between groups. It was subsequently developed and licensed as SF-36 and a subsequent version SF-36v2 is now in use. The SF-36v2 made changes to the wording and response format of some items and offers both a percentage score as in the earlier version and an additional norm-based score. An example of cross-cultural validation is the Australian version provided by Hawthorne, Osborne, Taylor, and Sansoni (2007). In addition to the 36-item measures, shorter (12- and 8-item) versions are available: SF-12, SF-12v2, and SF-8.

The RAND-36 is not licensed and has identical items to the SF-36 but uses a different scoring algorithm for the Bodily Pain and General Health scales. VanderZee, Sanderman, Heyink, and de Haes (1996) evaluated the Dutch version of the RAND 36-item Health Survey in a general population sample of over 1,000 people. They found that internal consistency and convergent construct validity were high and the measure was sensitive to group differences. This measure may be useful where a validated translation is required and where the norms based on US samples are of less value.

Sickness Impact Profile

The Sickness Impact Profile (SIP; Bergner, Bobbitt, Pollard, Martin, & Gilson, 1976; 136 items, 12 categories, two dimensions) is also frequently used. Unlike the SF-36, this is a long instrument (136 items) that attempts to be comprehensive, takes 20–30 min to complete and can be self- or interviewer-administered. The items are arranged in 12 categories, nine of which can be aggregated into two dimensions: physical (consisting of ambulation, body care and movement, mobility, household, and management categories) and psychosocial (consisting of recreation and pastime, social interaction, emotion, alertness, sleep, and rest categories) or one overall score. Three categories (eating, communication, and work) are not included in the dimensions. Respondents indicate whether they are experiencing each limitation due to their health; each score is derived by adding the weightings for endorsed items, dividing by the maximum possible and multiplying by 100 to give a score ranging from 0 to 100.

While the SIP is generally found to have good psychometric properties, many have questioned the burden of responding. Some authors have proposed shortened, factor-analytic-based versions of the SIP, but this does not address the more serious problem of the scoring system, which is incompatible with the derivation of the items and can produce illogical scores (e.g., an individual with several minor limitations may score worse than someone who is severely limited). Pollard and Johnston (2001) have proposed an alternative method of administration and scoring that overcomes both problems: Items are presented within each category in a hierarchical order (rather than in a mixed order) and questioning ceases when the respondent encounters the first item on which they are limited. The item weight is then the respondent's score for that category as would be expected from the original scaling of items. Functionally limited respondents complete the fewest items and only people with very few limitations would have the burden of completing all items. Versions of the SIP with appropriate weightings have been developed for various languages and cultures, for example Patrick and Peach (1989) developed the UK version, the Functional Limitations Profile (FLP).

Nottingham Health Profile

The Nottingham Health Profile (NHP; Hunt, McKenna, McEwen, Williams, & Papp, 1981; 38 items, six scales) was developed for use in population surveys but has subsequently been used with many different populations, including clinical groups. The six scales (Physical Mobility, Energy, Pain, Sleep, Emotional Reactions, and Social Isolation) have scores ranging from 100 to 0 (0=*optimal*) and it has been translated into numerous languages. VanderZee et al. (1996) have compared it with the RAND-36 in a population sample and found the NHP to be less reliable and less sensitive to differences between people who were in relatively good health.

Functional Independence Measure

Since functional limitations are more common in older adults, many measures have been developed specifically to assess them. The Functional Independence Measure (FIM; Keith, 1987; 18 items, two scales) has two scales (Motor and Cognitive) and was developed for rehabilitation settings in Canada, but has been widely used. A review by Glenny and Stolee (2009) concluded that it out-performed other similar measures.

Aberdeen Measures of ICF Constructs

Many researchers aim to measure the ICF constructs and have used diverse existing measures (Pollard, Dixon, Dieppe, & Johnston, 2009; three scales: I, AL, PR). However, the selected measures may not validly assess ICF constructs and Cieza et al. (2005) have proposed rules for linking items to the ICF. While this process reaches some agreement about content relevant to the construct, the resulting measures may still be contaminated by measures of a different construct. This can lead to problems, for example, if the aim is to assess the impact of I on A, using measures of I that contain A items and measures of A that contain I items results in spurious associations that simply reflect measurement confound. Pollard et al. (2009) have therefore developed the Aberdeen measures of I, A, and P, starting with items that show discriminant content validity for each construct and then subjecting them to rigorous psychometric assessment involving both classic test theory and item response theory analyses. Based on these analyses, items can be selected to be sensitive and specific within the range required, resulting in scales of up to nine I, 17 A, and nine P pure items.

Performance Measures

Performance measures are frequently used in clinical situations, for example, gait speed, timed get-up-and-go (Viccaro et al., 2011), or six-minute walk (Boxer et al., 2010; Guyatt et al., 1985).

Condition-Specific Measures

In this section, the most commonly used condition-specific measures of health outcomes are described for some common clinical conditions (see Table 12.1 for details). However, these measures are rarely theoretically based and so typically assess a mixture of outcomes and only some sub-scales measure physical function. They are all available in many languages, have been extensively evaluated, and generally have evidence of good psychometric properties.

These measures are frequently used with generic measures of function as well as with measures of emotional state and quality of life.

Arthritis

Among the most commonly used arthritis outcome measure is the Arthritis Impact Measurement Scale (AIMS2; 57 items, five components, nine subscales; Meenan, Mason, Anderson, Guccione, & Kazis, 1992), which has a good percentage of items for each ICF construct (I 36%, AL 22%, PR 9%, and AL/PR 33%). It has good psychometric properties and translations in several languages are available. The short form has 26 items.

Cancer

The two most commonly used condition-specific measures are the Functional Assessment of Cancer Therapy-General (FACT-G; Cella et al., 1993) and the European Organisation for the Research and Treatment of Cancer Quality of Life Questionnaire core 30 (EORTC-QLQ-C30; Aaronson et al., 1993; EORTC Quality of Life Group, 2002). In addition, many generic measures are used, especially the MOS or SF-36, but also performance measures, such as the six-minute walk test (Mishra et al., 2012). Both the EORTC-QLQ-C30 and the FACT-G have many versions adapted for specific cancers, which give more detailed assessment of condition-specific symptoms, and for particular populations, for example, for the elderly (Wheelwright et al, 2013). Both measures perform well psychometrically and a review by Luckett et al. (2011) concluded that choosing between these two measures may be guided by availability. Nevertheless, their tables offer very useful data from a comprehensive review comparing the two measures on reliability, validity, content etc., which can be used to select a measure for a specific purpose.

Cardiovascular Disease

The most common measure appropriate for a wide range of cardiovascular conditions, and available in many languages, is the MacNew Heart Disease Questionnaire (Höfer, Lim, Guyatt, & Oldridge, 2004), which includes a physical domain. It has been carefully developed and shown to have good psychometric properties but may be superseded by the recently published HeartQoL (Oldridge et al., 2014), which has been specifically designed to allow comparison between different heart conditions.

Other condition-specific cardiovascular measures are the Seattle Angina Questionnaire (Spertus et al., 1995) and, for heart failure, both the Minnesota Living with Heart Failure Questionnaire (MLHFQ; Green, Porter, Bresnahan, & Spertus, 2000) and the Kansas City Cardiomyopathy Questionnaire (KCCQ; Rector, Kubo, & Cohn, 1993) are commonly used and available in many languages. All were listed in the measures considered as acceptable to the American Health Association (Rumsfeld et al., 2013).

Stroke

In stroke, the modified Rankin Scale (six grades) and the Barthel Index (20 items) are the most commonly used research measures (Duncan, Jorgensen, & Wade, 2000; Quinn, Dawson, Walters, & Lees, 2009) but are probably more useful in describing the sample than in evaluating change. Duncan et al. (2000) reviewed 28 stroke outcome measures and offered a classification into ICF components. More recently, Jenkinson et al. (2013) have developed the Stroke Impact Scale, which has a stronger psychometric basis but less accumulated evidence, while Lennon, Carey, Creed, Durcan, and Blake (2011) report the use of the COOP-WONCA ([Dartmouth] Primary Care Cooperative – World Organization of Colleges, Academies and Academic Associations of General Practitioners/Family Physicians) charts, which offer a very simple assessment using diagrams.

Pain

An expert panel recommended that two measures should be used to measure functional limitations in back pain: the Roland Morris Disability Index (RDQ or RMDQ; 24 items) and the Oswestry Disability Index (ODI; 10 sections; Roland & Fairbank, 2000). Both have extensive evidence of psychometric properties but the ODI may be more responsive to change in severe pain, while the RMDQ is more sensitive to change in lesser pain. Maughan and Lewis (2010) compared several outcome measures for chronic back pain and found a patient-specific measure was more responsive to change than either the ODI or the RMDQ was. A modified version of the RDMQ has recently been published (Senske & Harris, 2013). The Common Pain Grade (seven items) is useful for population studies of pain (Von Korff, Ormel, Keefe, & Dworkin, 1992) and has been classified according to ICF constructs (Dixon et al., 2007).

Comments and Conclusion

In addition to the trend towards increasing numbers of measures of functional health outcomes, two other trends are apparent that may guide future choices of instruments. First, there is an increasing requirement that measures have a theoretical basis, especially the ICF, which should be a criterion for assessing validity of measures. Second, new and additional quantitative methods of evaluating measures are becoming available due in part to clearer conceptualisation of reliability and validity, for example, discriminant content validity (Dixon et al., 2007; Johnston et al., 2014) or identifying internal and external validity (Lissitz & Samuelson, 2007), but also to the availability of more advanced statistical methods, for instance, differential functioning of items (Pollard, Johnston, & Dixon, 2012; Pollard, Johnston, & Dixon, 2013b) or bifactor methods (Reise et al., 2010). These more stringent requirements may limit the proliferation of measures, thereby making it possible to make comparisons between studies and to accumulate evidence in systematic evidence synthesis. At the simplest level, even where novel or condition-specific measures are involved it is usually desirable to include a generic measure that has a sound theoretical and psychometric basis.

References

Aaronson, N. K., Ahmedzai, S., Bergman, B., Bullinger, M., Cull, A., Duez, N. J., ... Takeda, F. (1993). The European Organization for Research and Treatment of Cancer QLQ-C30: A quality-of-life instrument for use in international clinical trials in oncology. *Journal of the National Cancer Institute, 85*, 365–376. http://doi.org/10.1093/jnci/85.5.365

Ayis, S., Arden, N., Doherty, M., Pollard, B., Johnston, M., & Dieppe, P. (2010). Applying the impairment, activity limitation, and participation restriction constructs of the ICF model to osteoarthritis and low back pain trials: A reanalysis. *Journal of Rheumatology, 37*, 1923–1931. http://doi.org/10.3899/jrheum.091332

Banks, J. L., & Marotta, C. A. (2007). Outcomes validity and reliability of the modified Rankin scale: Implications for stroke clinical trials a literature review and synthesis. *Stroke, 38*, 1091–1096. http://doi.org/10.1161/01.STR.0000258355.23810.c6

Bergner, M., Bobbitt, R. A., Pollard, W. E., Martin, D. P., & Gilson, B. S. (1976). The sickness impact profile: Validation of a health status measure. *Medical Care, 14*, 57–67. http://doi.org/10.1097/00005650-197601000-00006

Bland, J. M., & Altman, D. G. (1999). Measuring agreement in method comparison studies. *Statistical Methods in Medical Research, 8*, 135–160. http://doi.org/10.1191/096228099673819272

Boxer, R., Kleppinger, A., Ahmad, A., Annis, K., Hager, D., & Kenny, A. (2010). The 6-minute walk is associated with frailty and predicts mortality in older adults with heart failure. *Congestive Heart Failure, 16*, 208–213. http://doi.org/10.1111/j.1751-7133.2010.00151.x

Campbell, D. T., & Fiske, D. W. (1959). Convergent and discriminant validation by the multitrait-multimethod matrix. *Psychological Bulletin, 56*, 81–105. http://doi.org/10.1037/h0046016

Cella, D. F., Tulsky, D. S., Gray, G., Sarafian, B., Linn, E., Bonomi, A., ... Harris, J. (1993). The functional assessment of cancer therapy scale: Development and validation of the general measure. *Journal of Clinical Oncology, 11*, 570–579.

Cieza, A., Geyh, S., Chatterji, S., Kostanjsek, N., Űstűn, B., & Stucki, G. (2005). ICF linking rules: An update based on lessons learned. *Journal of Rehabilitation Medicine, 37*, 212–218. http://doi.org/10.1080/16501970510040263

Dixon, D., & Johnston, M. (2007). Cognitive representations of disability behaviours in people with mobility limitations: Consistency with theoretical constructs. *Disability & Rehabilitation, 30*, 126–133. http://doi.org/10.1080/09638280701256983

Dixon, D., Pollard, B. S., & Johnston, M. (2007). What does the chronic pain grade questionnaire measure? *Pain, 130*, 249–253. http://doi.org/10.1016/j.pain.2006.12.004

Duncan, P. W., Jorgensen, H. S., & Wade, D. T. (2000). Outcome measures in acute stroke trials a systematic review and some recommendations to improve practice. *Stroke, 31*, 1429–1438. http://doi.org/10.1161/01.STR.31.6.1429

EORTC Quality of Life Group. (2002). *The EORTC QLQ-C30 manuals, reference values and bibliography* [CD-ROM]. Brussels, Belgium: EORTC Quality of Life Unit.

España-Romero, V., Golubic, R., Martin, K. R., Hardy, R., Ekelund, U., Kuh, D., ... NSHD scientific and data collection teams (2014). Comparison of the EPIC Physical Activity Questionnaire with combined heart rate and movement sensing in a nationally representative sample of older British adults. *PLoS One, 9*, e87085. http://doi.org/10.1371/journal.pone.0087085

Garin, O., Ferrer, M., Pont, À., Wiklund, I., Van Ganse, E., Vilagut, G., ... Alonso, J. (2013). Evidence on the global measurement model of the Minnesota Living with Heart Failure Questionnaire. *Quality of Life Research, 22*, 2675–2684. http://doi.org/10.1007/s11136-013-0383-z

Glenny, C., & Stolee, P. (2009). Comparing the functional independence measure and the interRAI/MDS for use in the functional assessment of older adults: A review of the literature. *BMC Geriatrics, 9*, 52. http://doi.org/10.1186/1471-2318-9-52

Green, C. P., Porter, C. B., Bresnahan, D. R., & Spertus, J. A. (2000). Development and evaluation of the Kansas City Cardiomyopathy Questionnaire: A new health status measure for heart failure. *Journal of the American College of Cardiology, 35*, 1245–1255. http://doi.org/10.1016/S0735-1097(00)00531-3

Guillemin, F., Coste, J., Pouchot, J., Ghézail, M., Bregeon, C., & Sany, J. (1997). The AIMS2-SF. A short form of the arthritis impact measurement scales 2. *Arthritis & Rheumatism, 40*, 1267–1274. http://doi.org/10.1002/art.11

Guyatt, G. H., Sullivan, M. J., Thompson, P. J., Fallen, E. L., Pugsley, S. O., Taylor, D. W., & Berman, L. B. (1985). The 6-minute walk: A new measure of exercise capacity in patients with chronic heart failure. *Canadian Medical Association Journal, 132*, 919–923.

Hawthorne, G., Osborne, R. H., Taylor, A., & Sansoni, J. (2007). The SF36 Version 2: Critical analyses of population weights, scoring algorithms and population norms. *Quality of Life Research, 16*, 661–673. http://doi.org/10.1007/s11136-006-9154-4

Höfer, S., Lim, L., Guyatt, G., & Oldridge, N. (2004). The MacNew heart disease health-related quality of life instrument: A summary. *Health & Quality of Life Outcomes, 2*, 3. http://doi.org/10.1186/1477-7525-2-3

Hunt, S. M., McKenna, S. P., McEwen, J., Williams, J., & Papp, E. (1981). The Nottingham Health Profile: Subjective health status and medical consultations. Social Science & Medicine. *Part A: Medical Psychology & Medical Sociology, 15*, 221–229. http://doi.org/10.1016/0271-7123(81)90005-5

Jenkinson, C., Fitzpatrick, R., Crocker, H., & Peters, M. (2013). The Stroke Impact Scale validation in a UK setting and development of a SIS short form and SIS index. *Stroke, 44*, 2532–2535. http://doi.org/10.1161/STROKEAHA.113.001847

Jette, A. M. (2009). Beyond dueling models. *Journals of Gerontology Series A – Biological Sciences and Medical Sciences, 64*, 1175–1176. http://doi.org/10.1093/gerona/glp096

Johnston, M., & Dixon, D. (2013). Developing an integrated biomedical and behavioural theory of functioning and disability: Adding models of behaviour to the ICF framework. *Health Psychology Review, 7*, 1–39.

Johnston, M., Dixon, D., Hart, J., Glidewell, L., Schröder, C., & Pollard, B. (2014). Discriminant Content Validity (DCV): A quantitative methodology for assessing content of theory-based measures with illustrative applications. *British Journal of Health Psychology, 19*, 240–257. http://doi.org/10.1111/bjhp.12095

Keith, R. A. (1987). *The functional independence measure: A new tool for rehabilitation*. Advances in Clinical Rehabilitation, *2*, 6–18.

Lalkhen, A. G., & McCluskey, A. (2008). Clinical tests: Sensitivity and specificity. *Continuing Education in Anaesthesia, Critical Care & Pain, 8*, 221–223. http://doi.org/10.1093/bjaceaccp/mkn041

Lennon, O. C., Carey, A., Creed, A., Durcan, S., & Blake, C. (2011). Reliability and validity of COOP/WONCA functional health status charts for stroke patients in primary care. *Journal of Stroke and Cerebrovascular Diseases, 20*(5), 465–473. http://doi.org/10.1016/j.jstrokecerebrovasdis.2010.02.020

Lissitz, E. W., & Samuelson, K. (2007). A suggested change in terminology and emphasis regarding validity and education. *Educational Researcher, 36*, 437–448. http://doi.org/10.3102/0013189X07311286

Luckett, T., King, M. T., Butow, P. N., Oguchi, M., Rankin, N., Price, M. A., ... Heading, G. (2011). Choosing between the EORTC QLQ-C30 and FACT-G for measuring health-related quality of life in cancer clinical research: Issues, evidence and recommendations. *Annals of Oncology, 22*, 2179–2190. http://doi.org/10.1093/annonc/mdq721

Maughan, E. F., & Lewis, J. S. (2010). Outcome measures in chronic low back pain. *European Spine Journal, 19*, 1484–1494. http://doi.org/10.1007/s00586-010-1353-6

McDowell, I. (2006). *Measuring health: A guide to rating scales and questionnaires* (3rd ed.). Oxford, UK: Oxford University Press. http://doi.org/10.1093/acprof:oso/9780195165678.001.0001

Meenan, R. F., Mason, J. H., Anderson, J. J., Guccione, A. A., & Kazis, L. E. (1992). AIMS2: The content and properties of a revised and expanded Arthritis Impact Measurement Scales Health Status Questionnaire. *Arthritis & Rheumatism, 35*, 1–10. http://doi.org/10.1002/art.1780350102

Mishra, S. I., Scherer, R. W., Snyder, C., Geigle, P. M., Berlanstein, D. R., & Topaloglu, O. (2012). Exercise interventions on health-related quality of life for people with cancer during active treatment. *Cochrane Database of Systematic Reviews, 15*(8), CD008465. http://doi.org/10.1002/14651858.CD007566.pub2

Oldridge, N., Hofer, S., McGee, H., Conroy, R., Doyle, F., & Saner, H. (2014). The HeartQoL: Part 1. Development of a new core health-related quality of life questionnaire for patients with ischemic heart disease. *European Journal of Preventive Cardiology, 21*, 90–97. http://doi.org/10.1177/2047487312450544

Patrick, D. L., & Peach, H. (1989). *Disablement in the community*. Oxford, UK: Open University Press.

Pollard, B., Dixon, D., Dieppe, P., & Johnston, M. (2009). Measuring the ICF components of impairment, activity limitation and participation restriction: An item analysis using classical test theory and item response theory. *Health and Quality of Life Outcomes, 7*, 41. http://doi.org/10.1186/1477-7525-7-41

Pollard, B., Dixon, D., & Johnston, M. (2013a). Are the mental representations of people with osteoarthritis consistent with the international classification of functioning disability and health? *Disability & Rehabilitation, 35*(17), 1460–1465. http://doi.org/10.3109/09638288.2012.737083

Pollard, B., Dixon, D., & Johnston, M. (2013b). Does the impact of osteoarthritis vary by age, gender and social deprivation? A community study using the International Classification of Functioning, Disability and Health. *Disability & Rehabilitation, 36*(17), 1445–1451. http://doi.org/10.3109/09638288.2013.847123

Pollard, B., & Johnston, M. (2001). Problems with the Sickness Impact Profile: A theoretically-based analysis and a proposal for a new method of implementation and scoring. *Social Science and Medicine, 52*, 921–934. http://doi.org/10.1016/S0277-9536(00)00194-5

Pollard, B. S., Johnston, M., & Dieppe, P. (2006). What do osteoarthritis health outcome instruments measure? Impairment, activity limitation, or participation restriction? *Journal of Rheumatology, 33*, 757–763.

Pollard, B., Johnston, M., & Dieppe, P. (2011). Exploring the relationships between international classification of functioning, disability and health (ICF) constructs of impairment, activity limitation and participation restriction in people with osteoarthritis prior to joint replacement. *BMC Musculoskeletal Disorders, 12*, 97. http://doi.org/10.1186/1471-2474-12-97

Pollard, B., Johnston, M., & Dixon, D. (2012). Exploring differential item functioning in the Western Ontario and McMaster universities osteoarthritis index (WOMAC). *BMC Musculoskeletal Disorders, 13*, 265. http://doi.org/10.1186/1471-2474-13-265

Quinn, T. J., Dawson, J., Walters, M. R., & Lees, K. R. (2009). Functional outcome measures in contemporary stroke trials. *International Journal of Stroke, 4*, 200–205. http://doi.org/10.1111/j.1747-4949.2009.00271.x

Rector, T. S., Kubo, S. H., & Cohn, J. N. (1993). Validity of the Minnesota Living with Heart Failure questionnaire as a measure of therapeutic response to enalapril or placebo. *The American Journal of Cardiology, 71*, 1106–1107. http://doi.org/10.1016/0002-9149(93)90582-W

Reise, S. P., Moore, T. M., & Haviland, M. G. (2010). Bifactor models and rotations: Exploring the extent to which multidimensional data yield univocal scale scores. *Journal of Personality Assessment, 92*, 544–559. http://doi.org/10.1080/00223891.2010.496477

Roland, M., & Fairbank, J. (2000). The Roland–Morris disability questionnaire and the Oswestry disability questionnaire. *Spine, 25*, 3115–3124. http://doi.org/10.1097/00007632-200012150-00006

Rumsfeld, J. S., Alexander, K. P., Goff, D. C., Graham, M. M., Ho, P. M., Masoudi, F. A., ... Zerwic, J. J. (2013). Cardiovascular health: The importance of measuring patient-reported health status a scientific statement from the American Heart Association. *Circulation, 127*, 2233–2249. http://doi.org/10.1161/CIR.0b013e3182949a2e

Senske, J., & Harris, M. (2013). Initial validation of a modified version of the Roland-Morris Disability Questionnaire (RMDQ) in a general chronic pain population. *Journal of Pain, 14*, S2. http://doi.org/10.1016/j.jpain.2013.01.019

Shah, S., Vanclay, F., & Cooper, B. (1989). Improving the sensitivity of the Barthel Index for stroke rehabilitation. *Journal of Clinical Epidemiology, 42*, 703–709. http://doi.org/10.1016/0895-4356(89)90065-6

Spertus, J. A., Winder, J. A., Dewhurst, T. A., Deyo, R. A., Prodzinski, J., McDonnell, M., & Fihn, S. D. (1995). Development and evaluation of the: A new functional status measure for coronary artery disease. *Journal of the American College of Cardiology, 25*, 333–341. http://doi.org/10.1016/0735-1097(94)00397-9

VanderZee, K. I., Sanderman, R., Heyink, J. W., & de Haes, H. (1996). Psychometric qualities of the RAND 36-Item Health Survey 1.0: A multidimensional measure of general health status. *International Journal of Behavioral Medicine, 3*, 104–122. http://doi.org/10.1207/s15327558ijbm0302_2

Viccaro, L. J., Perera, S., & Studenski, S. a. (2011). Is timed up and go better than gait speed in predicting health, function, and falls in older adults? *Journal of the American Geriatrics Society, 59*, 887–892. http://doi.org/10.1111/j.1532-5415.2011.03336.x

Von Korff, M., Ormel, J., Keefe, F. J., & Dworkin, S. F. (1992). Grading the severity of chronic pain. *Pain, 50*, 133–149. http://doi.org/10.1016/0304-3959(92)90154-4

Ware, E. (1987). Standards for validating health measures: Definition and content. *Journal of Chronic Diseases, 40*, 473–480. http://doi.org/10.1016/0021-9681(87)90003-8

Ware, J. E., & Sherbourne, C. D. (1992). The MOS36-item short-form health survey (SF-36): I. Conceptual framework and item selection. *Medical Care, 30*, 473–483. http://doi.org/10.1097/00005650-199206000-00002

Wheelwright, S., Darlington, A. S., Fitzsimmons, D., Fayers, P., Arraras, J. I., Bonnetain, F., ... Johnson, C. (2013). International validation of the EORTC QLQ-ELD14 questionnaire for assessment of health-related quality of life elderly patients with cancer. *British Journal of Cancer, 109*, 852–858. http://doi.org/10.1038/bjc.2013.407

World Health Organization. (2001). *International classification of functioning, disability and health*. Geneva, Switzerland: Author.

Chapter 13
Self-Rated Health

Yael Benyamini

Bob Shapell School of Social Work, Tel Aviv University, Israel

Many health surveys begin with a simple question asking respondents to rate their health, in general. Initially, this was used mainly as an appropriate way to open an interview or questionnaire and the response was regarded mainly as a measure of morale or self-image (Friedsam & Martin, 1963) while physicians' ratings were taken to reflect true health. Self-ratings of health began attracting more attention when studies showed that they are correlated with physician ratings and also predict future ones, and not vice versa (Maddox & Douglass, 1973), and that they predict mortality over the next few years, controlling for demographics and objective information collected from individuals, physicians, and insurance claims (Mossey & Shapiro, 1982).

Since then, hundreds of studies have shown that subjective assessments of one's health predict mortality and other future health outcomes, even after controlling for a wide variety of health-related variables that are also known to affect these outcomes (Ferraro, Farmer, & Wybraniec, 1997; Idler & Benyamini, 1997; Idler & Kasl, 1995). This literature can be found under the term *self-rated health* (SRH) or similar terms, such as self-assessed health, subjective health, perceived health, or self-evaluated health. This chapter focuses on single-item measures of subjective health. For information on multi-item scales to assess health outcomes and health-related quality of life, see Chapters 12 and 14 in this volume, respectively.

What Is Self-Rated or Subjective Health?

SRH serves as a spontaneous assessment of health as well as an aspect of one's enduring self-concept (Bailis, Segall, & Chipperfield, 2003; Perruccio, Badley, Hogg-Johnson, & Davis, 2010). Qualitative (Idler, Hudson, & Leventhal, 1999) and quantitative (Benyamini, Leventhal, & Leventhal, 2003) studies suggest that it reflects physical, mental, and social health and functioning and provides an integrative summary of internal and external information on one's health (Jylhä, 2009). When judging their health, people report not only the presence or absence of disease; they are more likely to be concerned with how well they can function and what reserves they have for coping with future health adversities (Herzlich, 1973; Simon, De Boer, Joung, Bosma, & Mackenbach, 2005). Their ratings reflect severe health conditions (Benyamini, Leventhal, & Leventhal, 2000) but also non-life-threatening conditions that are likely to impair their quality of life, such as poor oral health (Benyamini, Leventhal, & Leventhal, 2004). Thus, SRH seems to capture health in its widest sense, as defined by the World Health Organization (WHO):

> Health is a state of complete physical, mental and social well-being, not merely the absence of disease or infirmity. (1947, p. 29)

Health is a positive concept emphasizing social and personal resources, as well as physical capacities. (1986, p. 1)

How Is Self-Rated Health Measured?

The two most commonly used questions ask about general or global self-rated health ("How in general would you rate your health?") and age-comparative self-rated health ("How would you rate your health in comparison to your age peers?"). People seem to adjust for their age even when not explicitly asked to do so (Leinonen, Heikkinen, & Jylhä, 1998). Social comparisons seem to be used to buffer the effects of declining physical health on SRH (Cheng, Fung, & Chan, 2007). Therefore, the comparative item may over-adjust for age, especially among older adults. Other questions that have been used are time-comparative, that is, refer to one's health in different time frames – past, current, and future (Deeg & Kriegsman, 2003; Ferraro & Wilkinson, 2013). Most studies used and analyzed single items for rating global health; a few studies combined several of these items to a multi-item scale (see Deeg & Kriegsman, 2003, and the general health subscale of the 36-Item Short-Form Health Survey; Ware & Sherbourne, 1992). By definition this is a self-rating, and thus typically not asked of proxy interviewees, yet it has also been adapted for use by laypeople, such as spouses (Ayalon & Covinsky, 2009) or interviewers (Brissette, Leventhal, & Leventhal, 2003), so that it could be compared with the self-ratings.

The response scale typically includes four or five options, such as *excellent, very good, good, fair*, and *poor* (typically used in US studies; *very good* to *very bad*, or *very poor*, is more commonly used in Europe; Jürges, Avendano, & Mackenbach, 2008). Other response scales include 7-point, 10-point, or visual analogue scales (VAS; drawn as a straight line from worst health or death to best imaginable or perfect health, or numbered from 1 to 10 or 1 to 100; Blomstedt et al., 2012; Havranek et al., 2001; Rabin & de Charro, 2001) as well as a 5-point visual scale (smiling to sad faces) alongside the verbal labels (Lennon, Carey, Creed, Durcan, & Blake, 2011).

In their statistical analyses, many studies combined some of the categories (e.g., excellent/very good; fair/poor) when there were small numbers in the end categories. Epidemiological studies often dichotomized SRH, comparing fair/poor with good and above. Although this enables a simple presentation of associations with other measures as odds ratios for poorer outcomes, it is problematic, as noted by Barger (2006): Information from the ordinal scale is discarded, thus decreasing power to detect associations with other measures and possibly undermining the validity and stability of estimated odds ratios if the cut point is not optimal.

Several studies compared different wordings of SRH and its response options: For example, a few studies compared the general and the age-comparative items (e.g., Baron-Epel & Kaplan, 2001); two studies compared a 5-point and a 7-point general SRH and an age-comparative question (Eriksson, Unden, & Elofsson, 2001; Mohseni & Lindstrom, 2007); another study compared a 5-point scale with a 0–100 VAS (Daniilidou et al., 2010). Jürges et al. (2008) compared two 5-point response scales for the general SRH question – *very good* to *very bad* and *poor* to *excellent*. The studies found some differences in the frequencies of different response options in different questions and some in the correlates of the different items (or their semantic meaning; Waller, Thalén, Janlert, Hamberg, & Forssén, 2012). In addition, age-comparative SRH is more strongly related to motivational and dispositional factors, as compared with global SRH (Mora, Orsak, DiBonaventura, & Leventhal, 2013). Global SRH was also found to be more sensitive to change at the individual and population level, compared with age-comparative SRH (Andersen, Christensen, & Frederiksen, 2007). Therefore, if one must choose, the global SRH seems to be a better choice, yet it is important to note that most of these studies concluded that the differences are minimal and the overall pattern of responses and correlations is similar, regardless of the exact wording of SRH and its response options. Moreover, the most consistent finding, of SRH as a predictor of mortality, has been reported from many dozens of studies using different wordings of the global health item and its response options, in many different languages and cultures.

Nevertheless, a few words of caution are in place here. First, the extent of congruence between different wordings may depend on the characteristics of the respondents, such as their age, gender, and disease status (Baron-Epel & Kaplan, 2001). Second, such characteristics may also affect response rates: Older people are more likely to respond to a question with a 5-point scale in which all response options are labeled as compared with a VAS or a scale with only the ends labeled (Daniilidou et al., 2010; Eriksson et al., 2001). This is important, as nonrespondents tend to have worse health than respondents (Hoeymans, Feskens, Van Den Bos, & Kromhout, 1998). Third, the lack of substantial differences may also reflect the fact that many researchers were careful to choose response scales that fit the general response tendencies in the culture they were studying. In the US, there seems to be a bias toward positive responses, so more positively worded response options are used in order to better differentiate among respondents (Bowling, 2005). In other cultures, the opposite may be true and more negatively worded options are recommended. For example, the *very poor, poor, not so good, good,* and *excellent* scale has been used with Israeli samples (Benyamini, Boyko, Blumstein, & Lerner-Geva, 2014) and additional findings suggest that such scales may also be appropriate in Eastern European cultures (Appels, Bosma, Grabauskas, Gostautas, & Sturmans, 1996). In sum, researchers should choose scales that are likely to ensure a wide spread of responses in their sample. If the study is longitudinal, it is especially important to use labels that are likely to minimize ceiling effects (e.g., *excellent* instead of *very good*, where relevant; Bowling & Windsor, 2008) and floor effects (e.g., use both *very poor* and *poor* or use *bad* instead of *poor*).

Transforming and Calibrating Self-Rated Health Scores

The interpretability and predictive validity of SRH may be improved by transformations of the scores, such as that proposed by Diehr et al. (2001). Using the probability of being healthy in the future, conditional on baseline SRH, they proposed that *excellent* be coded as 95, *very good* = 90, *good* = 80, *fair* = 30, and *poor* = 15. They also recommended coding death as 0 in longitudinal studies, in order to retain the full sample. A similar approach used the SRH category mean on a visual analogue health thermometer to recode SRH so that *excellent* = 5, *very good* = 4.5, *good* = 3.7, *fair* = 2, and *poor* = 1 (Perneger, Gayet-Ageron, Courvoisier, Agoritsas, & Cullati, 2013). Most of the vast literature on SRH to date has not employed such transformations of the raw scores (besides collapsing categories or dichotomizing the responses). However, the findings from studies that used transformed scores suggest that they explain more variance in other health measures. In addition, calibrating SRH more accurately may be particularly important in studies that rely on this measure as the sole or main instrument to assess health status.

More sophisticated statistical approaches to scaling SRH responses on the basis of other health indices have been proposed in order to enable comparisons between populations (Jürges, 2007; Lauridsen, Christiansen, & Häkkinen, 2004). These studies assume that the threshold for moving from one SRH category to another may differ according to individual and cultural characteristics and thus transformations are essential to minimize the resulting biases.

Another approach to calibrating self-assessments of health uses anchoring vignettes to resolve the problem of group differences in the thresholds used to define each SRH level. Each vignette describes a concrete level on a given domain, which respondents evaluate with the same questions and response scales as used for self-assessments. Thus, self-assessments can be scaled to take into account both perceived health status and expectations for health. This has been done simply and successfully for the narrower term of self-assessed mobility (Salomon, Tandon, & Murray, 2004), as well as for the typical SRH question (Grol-Prokopczyk, Freese, & Hauser, 2011).

Can Self-Ratings of Health Be Viewed as a Linear Measure of Health?

The nonlinear transformations of SRH suggest that this is not a linear measure of the extent of health problems, from few to many. Additional evidence supports this view. First, SRH may reflect processes of adaptation to increasing morbidity: The effects of health problems on SRH are curvilinear (Li et al., 2006), with the first disease having a stronger effect than additional ones (Galenkamp, Braam, Huisman, & Deeg, 2011). Second, positive and negative SRH are not mirror ends (Shooshtari, Menec, & Tate, 2007): The factors that people take into account when rating their health differ between those in better and in worse health, as seen from the different correlates of poor and good SRH (Schüz, Wurm, Schollgen, & Tesch-Romer, 2011) and also from direct questioning (Benyamini, Leventhal, et al., 2003). Similarly, while declines in SRH are mostly influenced by recent changes in health, improvement is a more complex phenomenon (Verropoulou, 2012).

Reliability of Self-Ratings of Health

When two items (general and age-comparative) were included, they were highly correlated (e.g, DeSalvo et al., 2006). However, most studies included only a single SRH item so internal reliability is irrelevant. More important reliability issues are its stability over time and biases that could affect the responses.

SRH has been found to be resistant to experimental mood inductions (Barger, Burke, & Limbert, 2007) and insensitive to recent acute illnesses (Benyamini, Leventhal, & Leventhal, 1999). The reproducibility of SRH over a two-week period is high, as shown by an intraclass correlation coefficient (ICC) of 0.69 for the general question and 0.85 for the age-comparative question; more than half of the respondents chose the same category as before and less than 10% moved two or more categories (DeSalvo et al., 2006). By contrast, SRH changes in response to major health events (Diehr, Williamson, Patrick, Bild, & Burke, 2001) and to changes in functional limitations (Mora, DiBonaventura, Idler, Leventhal, & Leventhal, 2008). These findings support its role as an integrative evaluation of one's health and not a momentary assessment.

Mode of administration – written questionnaire or verbal interview – and question order affect responses to the SRH question (Crossley & Kennedy, 2002). Ratings tend to be more positive when SRH is placed after rather than before a module of health questions, although the effect size is small (Bowling & Windsor, 2008). Yet another study showed differences not in the mean but in the distribution of SRH: The middle category was used less frequently when asked after other health measures (Crossley & Kennedy, 2002).

The Validity of Self-Rated Health

As Jylhä (2009) explained, "the absence of a direct objective measure of 'true health' means that there is no gold standard, no clear criterion for the validity of self-rated health" (p. 313). Nevertheless, several types of evidence support its validity: its associations with physician ratings; its correlations with other health measures; its prediction of future health outcomes; and the associations between changes in other indicators of health and changes in SRH. These are briefly reviewed in the following sections.

Comparing Self- and Physician Ratings of Health

When self-ratings were compared with physician ratings of health, in most studies over half were concordant, with more agreement seen on the higher than the lower end (e.g., Giltay, Vollaard, & Kromhout, 2011), although there are also reports of lower rates of congruence and of greater agreement on the low end (Kivinen, Halonen, Eronen, & Nissinen, 1998). The differences between physicians' and individuals' ratings may be due to physicians giving more weight to clinical measures and risk factors whereas individuals give more weight to their functioning ability and psychological status (Smith & Goldman, 2011). Physician and self-ratings are correlated and in partial agreement yet each has an independent contribution to the prediction of all-cause mortality, suggesting that they include both similar and unique information (Giltay et al., 2011). Moreover, in cases of incongruence, overestimating one's health compared with the physician's ratings is related to better survival (DeSalvo & Muntner, 2011; similar to the effect of overestimating one's health compared with disease measures; Chipperfield, 1993) so it seems important to measure SRH even when other sources of health information exist.

The Correlates of Self-Ratings of Health

SRH is related to medical conditions and to a wide variety of measures reflecting physical, psychological, cognitive, social, occupational, and financial status (Fylkesnes & Førde, 1991; Pinquart, 2001). Disability mediates the associations of physical and mental conditions with SRH (Alonso et al., 2013), which may be part of the reason that the direct associations with these conditions are weaker than the associations with more personally salient measures of functioning and vitality (Benyamini et al., 1999). A study comparing SRH with a multi-item Health Utility Index showed that they are correlated and can be substituted for one another (Barofsky, Erickson, & Eberhardt, 2004). Similarly, SRH is correlated with all subscales of the SF-36, although more strongly with physical functioning than with mental health or social functioning (Mavaddat et al., 2011). With age, the correlations of SRH with functioning and chronic diseases somewhat declines while its correlation with depression increases (although functioning is still the strongest correlate; Schnittker, 2005). Longitudinal studies uncovered reciprocal relationships between SRH and mental health status over time (Farmer & Ferraro, 1997). In sum, SRH seems to reflect both physical and mental health and in particular those aspects that are related to one's ability to carry out activities.

SRH as a Predictor of Future Health Outcomes

As mentioned, SRH has an independent contribution to the prediction of mortality over 2–28 years in representative population samples (see reviews by Benyamini & Idler, 1999; Idler & Benyamini, 1997) as well as those in specific patient groups, such as patients with heart disease (Gerber, Benyamini, Goldbourt, & Drory, 2009) or cancer (Shadbolt, Barresi, & Craft, 2002). It has also been found to predict a variety of health outcomes such as health-care utilization (Benyamini, Blumstein, Boyko, & Lerner-Geva, 2008), functional and cognitive impairment (Bond, Dickinson, Matthews, Jagger, & Brayne, 2006), incidence of chronic disease (van der Linde et al., 2013), as well as exacerbations of disease and declines in functional ability (Idler & Kasl, 1995) and recovery from major health events (Wilcox, Kasl, & Idler, 1996). These studies included large samples and adjusted for many risk factors and relevant covariates so the significant effects of SRH reflect information that is unique to this measure.

Many studies have also attempted to identify the type of SRH item that is most predictive. The findings are not entirely consistent: The global SRH item was often found to be the strongest predictor, as compared with age- or self-comparative SRH (e.g., Vuorisalmi, Lintonen, & Jylhä, 2005). Current and future SRH both predicted mortality and their combination was an even better predictor (Wang & Satariano, 2007).

Global ratings of one's health assessed by another layperson have also been found to predict mortality and their effects were independent of those of self-ratings. This was found for ratings of spouses (Ayalon & Covinsky, 2009) and interviewers (Brissette et al., 2003). Therefore, when self-ratings are unavailable, proxy ratings may also provide valid though somewhat different information (see also Jardim, Barreto, & Giatti, 2010, who reported that secondary informants gave more weight to chronic conditions in their ratings, while the elderly who were rated paid more attention to disabilities and limitations in performing activities).

Measures of Changes in SRH as Predictors of Future Health

Longitudinal studies that used SRH as a time-dependent predictor of mortality typically found that this increased its contribution, as compared with the baseline measure alone (e.g., Ferraro & Kelley-Moore, 2001; Gerber et al., 2009), which shows that changes in SRH are more sensitive predictors of future health than a single rating. In fact, there is evidence that any change, even an improvement, predicts worse health, as compared with stable good SRH (Nielsen et al., 2009). A few studies compared retrospective ratings of changes in one's health with prospective differences between SRH measures. Their findings are inconsistent: One study found prospectively measured changes in health to be superior predictors of mortality as compared with retrospectively measured changes (Erdogan-Ciftci, van Doorslaer, Bago d'Uva, & van Lenthe, 2010), while another study reported that self-assessed change in health was more strongly predictive of hospitalization than computed change in SRH (Gunasekara, Carter, & Blakely, 2012). A third study concluded that the simple current SRH question is sufficient as neither retrospective nor prospective changes in SRH improved the prediction of mortality in older adults (Galenkamp, Deeg, Braam, & Huisman, 2013).

The Limits to the Validity of Self-Rated Health

The vast literature on the predictive validity of SRH also uncovered differences between groups in this type of validity. For example, SRH has been found to be a stronger predictor of mortality among whites compared with blacks in the US (Ferraro & Kelley-Moore, 2001), men compared with women (Benyamini et al., 2000), the old compared with the old-old (Benyamini, Blumstein, Lusky, & Modan, 2003), individuals with higher versus lower education or income (e.g., Dowd & Zajacova, 2007; although the opposite was also reported; Singh-Manoux et al., 2007). Even within a group of older adults, all aged 75+ at baseline and in poor SRH (and statistically at greater risk for further health decline and mortality), those who led a more active physical and social life were at lower risk (Benyamini et al., 2011). Thus, while most people with poor SRH die earlier than most people with excellent SRH, this measure is not a perfect predictor and there is great variability within each of its categories (especially the top and bottom ones, which are limited by floor and ceiling effects). Such findings also emphasize the need to attend to group differences in SRH and its components, especially in diverse samples.

Group Differences in Self-Rated Health

Many studies have reported different responses to SRH items in groups differing in their socioeconomic status at the level of the individual (Zhang et al., 2010) or the area of residence (Foraker et al., 2011). Similarly, levels of SRH differ among groups from different ethnic or racial origins (Benyamini et al., 2014; Zhang et al., 2010) and they remain after controlling for socioeconomic status (Liang et al., 2010) or physical and psychosocial health measures (Spencer et al., 2009). Ethnic/racial and educational differences are partly mediated by health literacy (Bennett, Chen, Soroui, & White, 2009). Similarly, SRH was found to differ across countries (e.g., Babones, 2009) and these differences seem to go beyond reporting styles or differences in language or level of development (French et al., 2012). Moreover, different SRH items perform inconsistently across ethnic groups (Leung, Luo, So, & Quan, 2007). Finally, response trends to the typical SRH item across time varied even between surveys from the same country (the US; Salomon, Nordhagen, Oza, & Murray, 2009).

Thus, on the one hand, SRH is consistently found to reflect first and foremost indicators of medical and functional status, even across countries (Bardage et al., 2005). On the other hand, the many findings on group differences suggest that it may not be comparable across populations. Group differences in SRH suggest that it reflects not only actual differences in health but also social and cultural factors. These can include differences in the meaning of SRH (i.e., different referents used for judging health; Peersman, Cambier, De Maeseneer, & Willems, 2012) and/or in response styles. In fact, SRH can be decomposed into its true health component and its cultural or response style component, as shown by Jürges (2007) with data from ten European countries.

As mentioned, the predictive power of SRH also differs among different subpopulations, which suggests that there are differences among groups in the way they judge their health. Additional evidence for different meanings of SRH can be found in studies that reported interactions between group membership and health measures in their association with SRH. For example, the association between SRH and biomarkers differed by level of education: Respondents with more education had healthier levels of biomarkers for the same level of SRH (Dowd & Zajacova, 2010). Similarly, among women who rated their health as good, but not among those who reported poorer health, socioeconomic status was related to blood pressure and body mass index (Adams & White, 2006). Additional examples involve ethnicity and the associations of SRH with chronic illnesses and health-care uses (Agyemang, Denktaş, Bruijnzeels, & Foets, 2006) as well as the way in which acculturation moderates the associations between health indicators and SRH (Todorova et al., 2013). In sum, it is important to identify differences in meaning or reporting norms because they can bias cross-cultural and cross-national comparisons.

Conclusion

SRH is cheap and easy to administer. Combined with the sheer volume of research showing that SRH has an independent contribution to the prediction of mortality, it is easy to understand why such a simple question is so widely used and has intrigued researchers around the globe. As Ann Bowling wrote in a 2005 editorial: "If one question works, why use several?" Indeed, it may be valid *because* it is a single item, which reflects very elaborate processes of integration of external and internal information, that one can perform for oneself in a way that is superior to biostatistical models and formulas that try to combine such information. There is ample evidence showing that it may be valid because it is more inclusive than other health measures, may reflect trajectories of health over time, may affect health behaviors that in turn affect future health, and may reflect or affect resources that also contribute to future health (Benyamini, 2011; Idler & Benyamini, 1997). However, it is important to note the great variation across personal characteristics and group membership of the respondents. Response options must be tailored accordingly and even then, the challenge of cross-population comparisons remains. Although there are some strategies to address this challenge (Burgard & Chen, 2014), they require sophisticated statistical computations (e.g., Jürges, 2007) or are appropriate only for single-dimension ratings (e.g., mobility, cognition; Hirve et al., 2014). While these concerns require caution in using SRH to measure the health of populations, psychologists can derive important within-person information on this measure across time and can use it for the unique information it encompasses, which does not fully overlap with other indicators of health.

References

Adams, J., & White, M. (2006). Is the disease risk associated with good self-reported health constant across the socio-economic spectrum? *Public Health, 120*(1), 70–75. http://doi.org/10.1016/j.puhe.2005.05.005

Agyemang, C., Denktaş, S., Bruijnzeels, M., & Foets, M. (2006). Validity of the single-item question on self-rated health status in first generation Turkish and Moroccans versus native Dutch in the Netherlands. *Public Health, 120*, 543–550. http://doi.org/10.1016/j.puhe.2006.03.002

Alonso, J., Vilagut, G., Adroher, N. D., Chatterji, S., He, Y., Andrade, L. H., ... Kessler, R. C. (2013). Disability mediates the impact of common conditions on perceived health. *PLoS One, 8*, e65858. http://doi.org/10.1371/annotation/1b1c6fa4-a665-4241-8cdc-fad6eb6709fc

Andersen, F. K., Christensen, K., & Frederiksen, H. (2007). Self-rated health and age: A cross-sectional and longitudinal study of 11,000 Danes aged 45–102. *Scandinavian Journal of Public Health, 35*, 164–171. http://doi.org/10.1080/14034940600975674

Appels, A., Bosma, H., Grabauskas, V., Gostautas, A., & Sturmans, F. (1996). Self-rated health and mortality in a Lithuanian and a Dutch population. *Social Science and Medicine, 42*, 681–689. http://doi.org/10.1016/0277-9536(95)00195-6

Ayalon, L., & Covinsky, K. E. (2009). Spouse-rated vs self-rated health as predictors of mortality. *Archives of Internal Medicine, 169*, 2156–2161. http://doi.org/10.1001/archinternmed.2009.386

Babones, S. J. (2009). The consistency of self-rated health in comparative perspective. *Public Health, 123*, 199–201. http://doi.org/10.1016/j.puhe.2008.12.016

Bailis, D. S., Segall, A., & Chipperfield, J. G. (2003). Two views of self-rated general health status. *Social Science & Medicine, 56*, 203–217. http://doi.org/10.1016/S0277-9536(02)00020-5

Bardage, C., Pluijm, S. M. F., Pedersen, N. L., Deeg, D. J. H., Jylhä, M., Noale, M., … Otero, A. (2005). Self-rated health among older adults: A cross-national comparison. *European Journal of Aging, 2*, 149–158. http://doi.org/10.1007/s10433-005-0032-7

Barger, S. D. (2006). Do psychological characteristics explain socioeconomic stratification of self-rated health? *Journal of Health Psychology, 11*(1), 21–35. http://doi.org/10.1177/1359105306058839

Barger, S. D., Burke, S. M., & Limbert, M. J. (2007). Do induced moods really influence health perceptions? *Health Psychology, 26*(1), 85–95. http://doi.org/10.1037/0278-6133.26.1.85

Barofsky, I., Erickson, P., & Eberhardt, M. (2004). Comparison of a single global item and an index of a multi-item health status measure among persons with and without diabetes in the US. *Quality of Life Research, 13*, 1671–1681. http://doi.org/10.1007/s11136-004-0258-4

Baron-Epel, O., & Kaplan, G. (2001). General subjective health status or age-related subjective health status: Does it make a difference? *Social Science & Medicine, 53*, 1373–1381. http://doi.org/10.1016/S0277-9536(00)00426-3

Bennett, I. M., Chen, J., Soroui, J. S., & White, S. (2009). The contribution of health literacy to disparities in self-rated health status and preventive health behaviors in older adults. *The Annals of Family Medicine, 7*, 204–211. http://doi.org/10.1370/afm.940

Benyamini, Y. (2011). Editorial: Why does self-rated health predict mortality? An update on current knowledge and a research agenda for psychologists. *Psychology & Health, 26*, 1407–1413. http://doi.org/10.1080/08870446.2011.621703

Benyamini, Y., Blumstein, T., Boyko, V., & Lerner-Geva, L. (2008). Cultural and educational disparities in the use of primary and preventive health care services among midlife women in Israel. *Women's Health Issues, 18*, 257–266.

Benyamini, Y., Blumstein, T., Lusky, A., & Modan, B. (2003). Gender differences in the self-rated health-mortality association: Is it poor self-rated health that predicts mortality or excellent self-rated health that predicts survival? *Gerontologist, 43*, 396–405. http://doi.org/10.1093/geront/43.3.396

Benyamini, Y., Blumstein, T., Murad, H., & Lerner-Geva, L. (2011). Changes over time from baseline poor self-rated health: For whom does poor self-rated health not predict mortality? *Psychology & Health, 26*, 1446–1462. http://doi.org/10.1080/08870446.2011.559231

Benyamini, Y., Boyko, V., Blumstein, T., & Lerner-Geva, L. (2014). Health, cultural and socioeconomic factors related to self-rated health of long-term Jewish residents, immigrants, and Arab women in midlife in Israel. *Women & Health, 54*, 402–424. http://doi.org/10.1080/03630242.2014.897679

Benyamini, Y., & Idler, E. L. (1999). Community studies reporting association between self-rated health and mortality: Additional studies, 1995–1998. *Research on Aging, 21*, 392–401.

Benyamini, Y., Leventhal, E. A., & Leventhal, H. (1999). Self-assessments of health: What do people know that predicts their mortality? *Research on Aging, 21*, 477–500. http://doi.org/10.1177/0164027599213007

Benyamini, Y., Leventhal, E. A., & Leventhal, H. (2000). Gender differences in processing information for making self-assessments of health. *Psychosomatic Medicine, 62*, 354–364. http://doi.org/10.1097/00006842-200005000-00009

Benyamini, Y., Leventhal, E. A., & Leventhal, H. (2003). Elderly people's ratings of the importance of health-related factors to their self-assessments of health. *Social Science & Medicine, 56*, 1661–1667. http://doi.org/10.1016/S0277-9536(02)00175-2

Benyamini, Y., Leventhal, H., & Leventhal, E. A. (2004). Self-rated oral health as an independent predictor of self-rated general health, self-esteem and life satisfaction. *Social Science & Medicine, 59*, 1109–1116. http://doi.org/10.1016/j.socscimed.2003.12.021

Blomstedt, Y., Souares, A., Niamba, L., Sie, A., Weinehall, L., & Sauerborn, R. (2012). Measuring self-reported health in low-income countries: Piloting three instruments in semi-rural Burkina Faso. *Global Health Action, 5*, 84–88. http://doi.org/10.3402/gha.v5i0.8488

Bond, J., Dickinson, H. O., Matthews, F., Jagger, C., & Brayne, C. (2006). Self-rated health status as a predictor of death, functional and cognitive impairment: A longitudinal cohort study. *European Journal of Ageing, 3*, 193–206. http://doi.org/10.1007/s10433-006-0039-8

Bowling, A. (2005). Just one question: If one question works, why ask several? *Journal of Epidemiology and Community Health, 59*, 342–345. http://doi.org/10.1136/jech.2004.021204

Bowling, A., & Windsor, J. (2008). The effects of question order and response-choice on self-rated health status in the English Longitudinal Study of Ageing (ELSA). *Journal of Epidemiology and Community Health, 62*(1), 81–85. http://doi.org/10.1136/jech.2006.058214

Brissette, I., Leventhal, H., & Leventhal, E. A. (2003). Observer ratings of health and sickness: Can other people tell us anything about our health that we don't already know? *Health Psychology, 22*, 471–478. http://doi.org/10.1037/0278-6133.22.5.471

Burgard, S. a., & Chen, P. V. (2014). Challenges of health measurement in studies of health disparities. *Social Science & Medicine, 106*, 143–150. http://doi.org/10.1016/j.socscimed.2014.01.045

Cheng, S. T., Fung, H., & Chan, A. (2007). Maintaining self-rated health through social comparison in old age. *Journal of Gerontology: Psychological Sciences, 62*, P277–P285. http://doi.org/10.1093/geronb/62.5.P277

Chipperfield, J. G. (1993). Incongruence between health perceptions and health problems: Implications for survival among seniors. *Journal of Aging and Health, 5*, 475–496. http://doi.org/10.1177/089826439300500404

Crossley, T. F., & Kennedy, S. (2002). The reliability of self-assessed health status. *Journal of Health Economics, 21*, 643–658. http://doi.org/10.1016/S0167-6296(02)00007-3

Daniilidou, N. V., Gregory, S. P., Zavras, D. J., Pavi, E. A., Athanasakis, K. P., Lionis, C. D., & Kyriopoulos, J. H. (2010). Comparison between two different measures of self-rated health: A single-question measure and a visual analogue scale. *Folia Medica, 52*(1), 63–69.

Deeg, D. J., & Kriegsman, D. M. (2003). Concepts of self-rated health: Specifying the gender difference in mortality risk. *Gerontologist, 43*, 376–386. http://doi.org/10.1093/geront/43.3.376

DeSalvo, K. B., Fisher, W. P., Tran, K., Bloser, N., Merrill, W., & Peabody, J. (2006). Assessing measurement properties of two single-item general health measures. *Quality of Life Research, 15*, 191–201. http://doi.org/10.1007/s11136-005-0887-2

DeSalvo, K. B., & Muntner, P. (2011). Discordance between physician and patient self-rated health and all-cause mortality. *Ochsner Journal, 11*, 232–240.

Diehr, P., Patrick, D. L., Spertus, J., Kiefe, C. I., McDonell, M., & Fihn, S. D. (2001). Transforming self-rated health and the SF-36 scales to include death and improve interpretability. *Medical Care, 39*, 670–680. http://doi.org/10.1097/00005650-200107000-00004

Diehr, P., Williamson, J., Patrick, D. L., Bild, D. E., & Burke, G. L. (2001). Patterns of self-rated health in older adults before and after sentinel health events. *Journal of the American Geriatrics Society, 49*(1), 36–44. http://doi.org/10.1046/j.1532-5415.2001.49007.x

Dowd, J. B., & Zajacova, A. (2007). Does the predictive power of self-rated health for subsequent mortality risk vary by socioeconomic status in the US? *International Journal of Epidemiology, 36*, 1214–1221. http://doi.org/10.1093/ije/dym214

Dowd, J. B., & Zajacova, A. (2010). Does self-rated health mean the same thing across socioeconomic groups? Evidence from biomarker data. *Annals of Epidemiology, 20*, 743–749. http://doi.org/10.1016/j.annepidem.2010.06.007

Erdogan-Ciftci, E., van Doorslaer, E., Bago d'Uva, T., & van Lenthe, F. (2010). Do self-perceived health changes predict longevity? *Social Science & Medicine, 71*, 1981–1988. http://doi.org/10.1016/j.socscimed.2010.09.003

Eriksson, I., Unden, A. L., & Elofsson, S. (2001). Self-rated health. Comparisons between three different measures. Results from a population study. *International Journal of Epidemiology, 30*, 326–333. http://doi.org/10.1093/ije/30.2.326

Farmer, M. M., & Ferraro, K. F. (1997). Distress and perceived health: Mechanisms of health decline. *Journal of Health and Social Behavior, 38*, 298–311. http://doi.org/10.2307/2955372

Ferraro, K. F., Farmer, M. M., & Wybraniec, J. A. (1997). Health trajectories: Long-term dynamics among black and white adults. *Journal of Health & Social Behavior, 38*(1), 38–54. http://doi.org/10.2307/2955360

Ferraro, K. F., & Kelley-Moore, J. A. (2001). Self-rated health and mortality among Black and White adults: Examining the dynamic evaluation thesis. *Journal of Gerontology: Social Sciences, 56*, S195–S205. http://doi.org/10.1093/geronb/56.4.S195

Ferraro, K. F., & Wilkinson, L. R. (2013). Alternative measures of self-rated health for predicting mortality among older people: Is past or future orientation more important? *The Gerontologist.* http://doi.org/10.1093/geront/gnt098

Foraker, R. E., Rose, K. M., Chang, P. P., McNeill, A. M., Suchindran, C. M., Selvin, E., & Rosamond, W. D. (2011). Socioeconomic status and the trajectory of self-rated health. *Age and Ageing, 40,* 706–711. http://doi.org/10.1093/ageing/afr069

French, D. J., Browning, C., Kendig, H., Luszcz, M. A., Saito, Y., Sargent-Cox, K., & Anstey, K. J. (2012). A simple measure with complex determinants: Investigation of the correlates of self-rated health in older men and women from three continents. *BMC Public Health, 12,* 649. http://doi.org/10.1186/1471-2458-12-649

Friedsam, H. J., & Martin, H. W. (1963). A comparison of self and physicians' health ratings in an older population. *Journal of Health and Human Behavior, 4,* 179–183. http://doi.org/10.2307/2948660

Fylkesnes, K., & Førde, O. H. (1991). The Tromsø study: Predictors of self-evaluated health – has society adopted the expanded health concept? *Social Science & Medicine, 32,* 141–146. http://doi.org/10.1016/0277-9536(91)90053-F

Galenkamp, H., Braam, A. W., Huisman, M., & Deeg, D. J. (2011). Somatic multimorbidity and self-rated health in the older population. *Journals of Gerontology Series B: Psychological Sciences and Social Sciences, 66,* 380–386. http://doi.org/10.1093/geronb/gbr032

Galenkamp, H., Deeg, D. J., Braam, A. W., & Huisman, M. (2013). "How was your health 3 years ago?" Predicting mortality in older adults using a retrospective change measure of self-rated health. *Geriatrics & Gerontology International, 13,* 678–686. http://doi.org/10.1111/j.1447-0594.2012.00963.x

Gerber, Y., Benyamini, Y., Goldbourt, U., & Drory, Y. (2009). Prognostic importance and long-term determinants of self-rated health after initial acute myocardial infarction. *Medical Care, 47,* 342–349. http://doi.org/10.1097/MLR.0b013e3181894270

Giltay, E. J., Vollaard, A. M., & Kromhout, D. (2011). Self-rated health and physician-rated health as independent predictors of mortality in elderly men. *Age and Ageing, 41,* 165–171. http://doi.org/10.1093/ageing/afr161

Grol-Prokopczyk, H., Freese, J., & Hauser, R. M. (2011). Using anchoring vignettes to assess group differences in general self-rated health. *Journal of Health and Social Behavior, 52,* 246–261. http://doi.org/10.1177/0022146510396713

Gunasekara, F. I., Carter, K., & Blakely, T. (2012). Comparing self-rated health and self-assessed change in health in a longitudinal survey: Which is more valid? *Social Science & Medicine, 74,* 1117–1124. http://doi.org/10.1016/j.socscimed.2011.11.038

Havranek, E. P., Lapuerta, P., Simon, T. A., L'Italien, G., Block, A. J., & Rouleau, J. L. (2001). A health perception score predicts cardiac events in patients with heart failure: Results from the IMPRESS trial. *Journal of Cardiac Failure, 7,* 153–157. http://doi.org/10.1054/jcaf.2001.24121

Herzlich, C. (1973). *Health and illness.* New York, NY: Academic Press.

Hirve, S., Verdes, E., Lele, P., Juvekar, S., Blomstedt, Y., Tollman, S., ... Ng, N. (2014). Evaluating reporting heterogeneity in self-rated health among adults aged 50 years and above in India: An anchoring vignettes analytic approach. *Journal of Aging and Health, 26,* 1015–1031. http://doi.org/10.1177/0898264314535634

Hoeymans, N., Feskens, E. J. M., Van Den Bos, G. A. M., & Kromhout, D. (1998). Non-response bias in a study of cardiovascular diseases, functional status and self-rated health among elderly men. *Age and Ageing, 27*(1), 35–40. http://doi.org/10.1093/ageing/27.1.35

Idler, E. L., & Benyamini, Y. (1997). Self-rated health and mortality: A review of 27 community studies. *Journal of Health and Social Behavior, 38*(1), 21–37. http://doi.org/10.2307/2955359

Idler, E. L., Hudson, S. V., & Leventhal, H. (1999). The meanings of self-ratings of health: A qualitative and quantitative approach. *Research on Aging, 21,* 458–476. http://doi.org/10.1177/0164027599213006

Idler, E. L., & Kasl, S. V. (1995). Self-ratings of health: Do they also predict change in functional ability? *Journals of Gerontology: Social Sciences, 50,* S344–S353. http://doi.org/10.1093/geronb/50B.6.S344

Jardim, R., Barreto, S. M., & Giatti, L. (2010). Self-reporting and secondary informant reporting in health assessments among elderly people. *Revista de Saúde Pública, 44,* 1120–1129.

Jürges, H. (2007). True health vs response styles: Exploring cross-country differences in self-reported health. *Health Economics, 16*, 163–178. http://doi.org/10.1002/hec.1134

Jürges, H., Avendano, M., & Mackenbach, J. P. (2008). Are different measures of self-rated health comparable? An assessment in five European countries. *European Journal of Epidemiology, 23*, 773–781. http://doi.org/10.1007/s10654-008-9287-6

Jylhä, M. (2009). What is self-rated health and why does it predict mortality? Towards a unified conceptual model. *Social Science & Medicine, 69*, 307–316. http://doi.org/10.1016/j.socscimed.2009.05.013

Kivinen, P., Halonen, P., Eronen, M., & Nissinen, A. (1998). Self-rated health, physician-rated health and associated factors among elderly men: The Finnish cohorts of the Seven Countries Study. *Age and Ageing, 27*(1), 41–47. http://doi.org/10.1093/ageing/27.1.41

Lauridsen, J., Christiansen, T., & Häkkinen, U. (2004). Measuring inequality in self-reported health – discussion of a recently suggested approach using Finnish data. *Health Economics, 13*, 725–732.

Leinonen, R., Heikkinen, E., & Jylhä, M. (1998). Self-rated health and self-assessed change in health in elderly men and women – a five-year longitudinal study. *Social Science & Medicine, 46*, 591–597. http://doi.org/10.1016/S0277-9536(97)00205-0

Lennon, O. C., Carey, A., Creed, A., Durcan, S., & Blake, C. (2011). Reliability and validity of COOP/WONCA functional health status charts for stroke patients in primary care. *Journal of Stroke and Cerebrovascular Diseases, 20*, 465–473. http://doi.org/10.1016/j.jstrokecerebrovasdis.2010.02.020

Leung, B., Luo, N., So, L., & Quan, H. (2007). Comparing three measures of health status (perceived health with Likert-type scale, EQ-5D, and number of chronic conditions) in Chinese and white Canadians. *Medical Care, 45*, 610–617. http://doi.org/10.1097/MLR.0b013e3180331f58

Li, Z. B., Lam, T. H., Ho, S. Y., Chan, W. M., Ho, K. S., Li, M. P., … Fielding, R. (2006). Age- versus time-comparative self-rated health in Hong Kong Chinese older adults. *International Journal of Geriatric Psychiatry, 21*, 729–739. http://doi.org/10.1002/gps.1553

Liang, J., Quiñones, A. R., Bennett, J. M., Ye, W., Xu, X., Shaw, B. A., & Ofstedal, M. B. (2010). Evolving self-rated health in middle and old age: How does it differ across Black, Hispanic, and White Americans? *Journal of Aging and Health, 22*(1), 3–26. http://doi.org/10.1177/0898264309348877

Maddox, G. L., & Douglass, E. B. (1973). Self-assessment of health: A longitudinal study of elderly subjects. *Journal of Health and Social Behavior, 14*(1), 87–93. http://doi.org/10.2307/2136940

Mavaddat, N., Kinmonth, A. L., Sanderson, S., Surtees, P., Bingham, S., & Khaw, K. T. (2011). What determines Self-Rated Health (SRH)? A cross-sectional study of SF-36 health domains in the EPIC-Norfolk cohort. *Journal of Epidemiology and Community Health, 65*, 800–806. http://doi.org/10.1136/jech.2009.090845

Mohseni, M., & Lindstrom, M. (2007). Comparison of two items on self-rated health. *Scandinavian Journal of Public Health, 35*, 216–221. http://doi.org/10.1080/14034940600858581

Mora, P. A., DiBonaventura, M. D., Idler, E., Leventhal, E. A., & Leventhal, H. (2008). Psychological factors influencing self-assessments of health: Toward an understanding of the mechanisms underlying how people rate their own health. *Annals of Behavioral Medicine, 36*, 292–303. http://doi.org/10.1007/s12160-008-9065-4

Mora, P. A., Orsak, G., DiBonaventura, M. D., & Leventhal, E. A. (2013). Why do comparative assessments predict health? The role of self-assessed health in the formation of comparative health judgments. *Health Psychology, 32*, 1175–1178. http://doi.org/10.1037/a0032044

Mossey, J. M., & Shapiro, E. (1982). Self-rated health: A predictor of mortality among the elderly. *American Journal of Public Health, 72*, 800–808. http://doi.org/10.2105/AJPH.72.8.800

Nielsen, A. B. S., Siersma, V., Kreiner, S., Hiort, L. C., Drivsholm, T., Eplov, L. F., & Hollnagel, H. (2009). The impact of changes in self-rated general health on 28-year mortality among middle-aged Danes. *Scandinavian Journal of Primary Health Care, 27*, 160–166. http://doi.org/10.1080/02813430903020446

Peersman, W., Cambier, D., De Maeseneer, J., & Willems, S. (2012). Gender, educational and age differences in meanings that underlie global self-rated health. *International Journal of Public Health, 57*, 513–523. http://doi.org/10.1007/s00038-011-0320-2

Perneger, T. V., Gayet-Ageron, A., Courvoisier, D. S., Agoritsas, T., & Cullati, S. (2013). Self-rated health: Analysis of distances and transitions between response options. *Quality of Life Research, 22*, 2761–2768. http://doi.org/10.1007/s11136-013-0418-5

Perruccio, A. V., Badley, E. M., Hogg-Johnson, S., & Davis, A. M. (2010). Characterizing self-rated health during a period of changing health status. *Social Science & Medicine, 71,* 1636–1643. http://doi.org/10.1016/j.socscimed.2010.07.042

Pinquart, M. (2001). Correlates of subjective health in older adults: A meta-analysis. *Psychology and Aging, 16,* 414–426. http://doi.org/10.1037/0882-7974.16.3.414

Rabin, R., & de Charro, F. (2001). EQ-5D: A measure of health status from the EuroQol Group. *Annals of Medicine, 33,* 337–343. http://doi.org/10.3109/07853890109002087

Salomon, J. A., Nordhagen, S., Oza, S., & Murray, C. J. (2009). Are Americans feeling less healthy? The puzzle of trends in self-rated health. *American Journal of Epidemiology, 170,* 343–351. http://doi.org/10.1093/aje/kwp144

Salomon, J. A., Tandon, A., & Murray, C. J. (2004). Comparability of self rated health: Cross sectional multi-country survey using anchoring vignettes. *BMJ, 328,* 258. http://doi.org/10.1136/bmj.37963.691632.44

Schnittker, J. (2005). When mental health becomes health: Age and the shifting meaning of self-evaluations of general health. *Milbank Quarterly, 83,* 397–423. http://doi.org/10.1111/j.1468-0009.2005.00407.x

Schüz, B., Wurm, S., Schollgen, I., & Tesch-Romer, C. (2011). What do people include when they self-rate their health? Differential associations according to health status in community-dwelling older adults. *Quality of Life Research, 20,* 1573–1580. http://doi.org/10.1007/s11136-011-9909-4

Shadbolt, B., Barresi, J., & Craft, P. (2002). Self-rated health as a predictor of survival among patients with advanced cancer. *Journal of Clinical Oncology, 20,* 2514–2519.

Shooshtari, S., Menec, V., & Tate, R. (2007). Comparing predictors of positive and negative self-rated health between younger (25–54) and older (55+) Canadian adults: A longitudinal study of well-being. *Research on Aging, 29,* 512–554. http://doi.org/10.1177/0164027507305729

Simon, J. G., De Boer, J. B., Joung, I. M., Bosma, H., & Mackenbach, J. P. (2005). How is your health in general? A qualitative study on self-assessed health. *European Journal of Public Health, 15,* 200–208. http://doi.org/10.1093/eurpub/cki102

Singh-Manoux, A., Dugravot, A., Shipley, M. J., Ferrie, J. E., Martikainen, P., Goldberg, M., & Zins, M. (2007). The association between self-rated health and mortality in different socioeconomic groups in the GAZEL cohort study. *International Journal of Epidemiology, 36,* 1222–1228. http://doi.org/10.1093/ije/dym170

Smith, K. V., & Goldman, N. (2011). Measuring health status: Self-, interviewer, and physician reports of overall health. *Journal of Aging and Health, 23,* 242–266. http://doi.org/10.1177/0898264310383421

Spencer, S. M., Schulz, R., Rooks, R. N., Albert, S. M., Thorpe, R. J., Brenes, G. A., ... Newman, A. B. (2009). Racial differences in self-rated health at similar levels of physical functioning: An examination of health pessimism in the Health, Aging, and Body Composition Study. *Journals of Gerontology Series B: Psychological Sciences and Social Sciences, 64B*(1), 87–94.

Todorova, I. L. G., Tucker, K. L., Jimenez, M. P., Lincoln, A. K., Arevalo, S., & Falcón, L. M. (2013). Determinants of self-rated health and the role of acculturation: Implications for health inequalities. *Ethnicity & Health, 18,* 563–585. http://doi.org/10.1080/13557858.2013.771147

van der Linde, R. M., Mavaddat, N., Luben, R., Brayne, C., Simmons, R. K., Khaw, K. T., & Kinmonth, A. L. (2013). Self-rated health and cardiovascular disease incidence: Results from a longitudinal population-based cohort in Norfolk, UK. *PLoS One, 8,* e65290. http://doi.org/10.1371/journal.pone.0065290

Verropoulou, G. (2012). Determinants of change in self-related health among older adults in Europe: A longitudinal perspective based on SHARE data. *European Journal of Ageing, 9,* 305–318. http://doi.org/10.1007/s10433-012-0238-4

Vuorisalmi, M., Lintonen, T., & Jylhä, M. (2005). Global self-rated health data from a longitudinal study predicted mortality better than comparative self-rated health in old age. *Journal of Clinical Epidemiology, 58,* 680–687. http://doi.org/10.1016/j.jclinepi.2004.11.025

Waller, G., Thalén, P., Janlert, U., Hamberg, K., & Forssén, A. (2012). A cross-sectional and semantic investigation of self-rated health in the northern Sweden MONICA-study. *BMC Medical Research Methodology, 12,* 154. http://doi.org/10.1186/1471-2288-12-154

Wang, C., & Satariano, W. A. (2007). Self-rated current and future health independently predict subsequent mortality in an aging population. *Journals of Gerontology Series A: Biological Sciences and Medical Sciences, 62*, 1428–1434. http://doi.org/10.1093/gerona/62.12.1428

Ware, J. E., Jr., & Sherbourne, C. D. (1992). The MOS36-item short-form health survey (SF-36). I. Conceptual framework and item selection. *Medical Care, 30*, 473–483. http://doi.org/10.1097/00005650-199206000-00002

Wilcox, V. L., Kasl, S. V., & Idler, E. L. (1996). Self-rated health and physical disability in elderly survivors of a major medical event. *The Journals of Gerontology: Social Sciences, 51*, S96–S104. http://doi.org/10.1093/geronb/51B.2.S96

World Health Organization. (1947). *Constitution.* Geneva, Switzerland: Author.

World Health Organization. (1986). *Ottawa charter for health promotion.* Geneva, Switzerland: Author.

Zhang, W., McCubbin, H., McCubbin, L., Chen, Q., Foley, S., Strom, I., & Kehl, L. (2010). Education and self-rated health: An individual and neighborhood level analysis of Asian Americans, Hawaiians, and Caucasians in Hawaii. *Social Science & Medicine, 70*, 561–569. http://doi.org/10.1016/j.socscimed.2009.10.055

Chapter 14
Quality of Life

Karen Morgan and Hannah McGee

Royal College of Surgeons in Ireland, Dublin, Ireland

Chapter Outline

The last 40 years have seen a major upsurge of interest in quality of life (QoL) research (Barofsky, 2007), driven by an ever-growing need to evaluate and compare health interventions and to assess the impact of illness on individuals. This chapter focuses on QoL and health-related quality of life (HRQoL), discussing varying definitions and approaches to measurement including assessment tools. Recent developments, challenges, and opportunities for health psychologists researching in the area are highlighted.

Defining QoL and HRQoL

Despite the exponential increase in empirical studies of QoL, conceptual and theoretical development is limited (Joyce, Hickey, McGee, & O'Boyle, 2003). This lack of conceptual clarity has resulted in significant confusion regarding the definition of QoL (Barofsky, 2007) and contributed to the inconsistent and interchangeable use of terms such as QoL and HRQoL (McGee & Ring, 2010) and QoL and well-being (Dodge, Daly, Huyton, & Sanders, 2012). Thus, like *stress* in the past, QoL is a term in everyday vocabulary, yet there has been little consensus regarding its definition or assessment.

Early definitions of QoL highlighted that it is both subjective and individual (Joyce, 1988):

> Each person is first and foremost an individual, a somebody, a someone, a soul, a human being. Thus, it is not a large leap to define quality of life as "what the person or patient says it is." (p. 171)

Other definitions have emphasised the relative nature of QoL, defining it in terms of a gap between a current and desired state (Calman, 1984):

> Quality of life measures the difference, or the gap, at a particular period of time, between the hopes and expectations of the individual and the individual's present experiences. (p. 124)

The World Health Organization (WHO) definition acknowledges the individual, multi-dimensional, complex, and culturally bound nature of QoL, alongside the central role of health (WHOQOL Group, 1995):

> QoL is an individual's perception of their position in life in the context of the culture and value system in which they live and in relation to their goals, expectations and standards and concerns.

> It is a broad ranging concept affected in a complex way by the person's physical health, psychological state, level of independence, social relationships, and their relationship to salient features of their environment. (p. 1403)

This definition is reflected in the development of the WHO measure of QoL (WHOQOL), which will be discussed later.

The varying definitions of QoL represent different perspectives and conceptual models and therefore it is essential that studies that aim to assess QoL state which definition is being used and how the assessment tools chosen relate to this definition. Unfortunately, this is not standard practice (Taillefer, Dupuis, Roberge, & LeMay, 2003), with researchers being more concerned with how to measure rather than what to measure (McGee & Ring, 2010). In a paper on understanding the diversity of conceptions of well-being and QoL, Gasper (2010) considers both as evaluative judgements and argues these judgements are made in many different ways and according to "choices in at least six dimensions: focus of attention, values used, research instruments used, guiding purposes of the exercise, standpoint adopted and theoretical framework employed" (p. 359). Any study of QoL must consider each of these carefully.

Reflecting the challenges of defining and therefore measuring the broader concept of QoL, a pragmatic approach to assessment of QoL in health settings has been to restrict assessment to health-related aspects of an individual's life and to provide a definition of HRQoL. The rationale for creating such boundaries is that the impact of health interventions will be reflected in health-related domains. In line with this, HRQoL has been defined as representing the patient's perception of the functional effect of an illness and its consequent therapy (Schipper, Clinch, & Olweny, 1996).

Most often, HRQoL is formulated as physical, emotional, and social functioning (Patrick & Guyatt, 2013) although many measures prioritise physical health. This leads to some overlap with the assessment of functional outcomes as outlined in Chapter 12 of this volume. Gurková (2011) outlines that despite conceptual inconsistencies there is a general consensus that HRQoL includes a number of defining attributes. It is multidimensional, subjective and value-based, dynamic, tends to be defined in terms of perceived status or subjective evaluation, and involves perception of both positive and negative experiences.

The origins of HRQoL as an area of research lie in the important development of the Karnofsky score for use with cancer patients over 60 years ago (Karnofsky & Burchenal, 1949). Patients are assessed by an observer and assigned a score between 0 (*dead*) and 100 (*no evidence of disease, able to carry out normal activity and to work*). While this and related work represented an important move towards formally considering the individual patient's perspective in treatment, physician ratings of patient QoL do not engage patients in a way we would find socially acceptable today. Moreover, they tend not to concur with the patient's own assessment (Petersen, Larsen, Pedersen, Sonne, & Groenvold, 2006; Srikrishna, Robinson, Cardozo, & Gonzalez, 2009). In recent decades, it has become standard practice to ask patients to rate their own QoL. This practice has been extended beyond QoL, to include other endpoints, collectively termed patient-reported outcomes (PROs). A PRO as defined by the United States Food and Drug Administration is: "Any report of the status of a patient's health condition that comes directly from the patient, without interpretation of the patient's response by a clinician or anyone else" (U.S. Department of Health and Human Services, 2009, p. 2).

There are, importantly, some situations where proxy or surrogate ratings of QoL may be acceptable. These include situations where an individual is unable to make decisions or judgements for themselves. Where it is necessary to use a proxy or surrogate rating, it is important to consider key aspects of the situation such as who is providing the rating, the nature of their relationship to the individual whose QoL is being rated, and the level of impairment (Schiffczyk et al., 2010). It should be noted here that cognitive impairment should not necessarily be a barrier to assessing QoL (Hoe, Katona, Orrell, & Livingston, 2007; Hoe, Katona, Roch, & Livingston, 2005).

Types of HRQoL Assessment

Five main types of QoL measures have been identified: generic, disease or patient-population specific, dimension specific, individualised, and utility (Garratt, Schmidt, Mackintosh, & Fitzpatrick, 2002). This typology is presented in Table 14.1, and includes examples of assessment tools. A number of websites and online databases are available to source measures and important psychometric information. These include:

1. The Patient Reported Outcomes and Quality of Life Instruments database (PROQOLID) (http://www.proqolid.org), which currently indexes 443 HRQoL measures. Basic level access allows users to view information about the measures and to access review copies (where available).
2. The On-Line Guide to Quality of Life Assessment database (OLGA; http://www.olga-qol.com), which incorporates algorithms to help in the selection of instruments. A login is required to access the database.
3. OPTUM (http://www.optum.com), which offers questionnaires in multiple modes of administration including computerised adaptive testing (CAT). The widely used 36-Item Short-Form Health Survey (SF-36) and related surveys are available through this website.

Generic Measures

Generic measures of QoL are broad questionnaire measures that can be used across a wide range of populations and health conditions. Such measures allow comparisons within and between groups and in some cases also allow the comparison of sample values to overall population normative values. As broad measures, it is unlikely that generic measures can provide sufficient information on specific aspects of a disease, which is important in assessing the impact of disease or a treatment (O'Boyle, 2001). Therefore, many studies include both generic and disease-specific measures of HRQoL.

Some of the most commonly used generic measures of HRQoL are the Sickness Impact Profile (SIP), the Nottingham Health Profile (NHP), the SF-36, and the WHOQOL. The SIP and NHP are discussed in more detail in Chapter 12 of this volume and so are only briefly summarised here. The SIP has 136 items in 12 subscales, which are sometimes used separately. While broad-ranging it does not include assessment of pain. The NHP is a two-part measure that assesses six dimensions of health (38 items) and daily living problems (seven items). It can be used to survey health problems and also as a means of evaluating the outcome of medical and/or social interventions (Hunt et al., 1985). The NHP is more focused on disability than the SIP, and has some limitations with regard to sensitivity.

Table 14.1. Typology of QoL instruments (disease- or population-specific examples relate to cardiac patients)

Type	Focus	Examples of assessment tools
Generic	Patient or general population groups	36-Item Short-Form Health Survey (SF-36; McHorney, Ware, Lu, & Sherbourne, 1994; McHorney, Ware, & Raczek, 1993; Ware & Sherbourne, 1992)
		Nottingham Health Profile (Hunt, McEwen, & McKenna, 1985; Hunt et al., 1980)
		The World Health Organization Quality of Life (WHOQOL) measure (WHOQOL Group, 1995)
		Functional Limitations Profile (Charlton, Patrick, Matthews, & West, 1981; Patrick, Peach, & Gregg, 1982)
Disease- or patient-specific	Particular group/ diagnosis	HeartQoL (Oldridge et al., 2014a, 2014b)
		Minnesota Living with Heart Failure Questionnaire (Rector, Kubo, & Cohn, 1987)
		Seattle Angina Questionnaire (Spertus et al., 1995)
Dimension-specific	Particular component of QoL	Global Mood Scale (Denollet, 1993; Denollet & Brutsaert, 1995)
		Hospital Anxiety and Depression Scale (Zigmond & Snaith, 1983)
		The Beck Depression Inventory (BDI; Beck, Steer, Ball, & Ranieri, 1996; Beck, Ward, Mendelson, Mock, & Erbaugh, 1961)
Individual	Aspects of life determined by the individual	Schedule for the Evaluation of Individual Quality of Life (SEIQoL; Hickey et al., 1996; McGee, O'Boyle, Hickey, O'Malley, & Joyce, 1991; O'Boyle, McGee, Hickey, O'Malley, & Joyce, 1992)
		Patient Generated Index (Ruta, Garratt, Leng, Russell, & MacDonald, 1994)
Utility	Hierarchy of preferences of a particular group	EuroQoL (EQ-5D; Dolan, 1997; Kind, 1996; Shaw, Johnson, & Coons, 2005)
		Health Utilities Index (Feeny et al., 2002; Horsman, Furlong, Feeny, & Torrance, 2003; Torrance et al., 1996)

Developed in the 1990s from a large American study called the Medical Outcomes Study (MOS), the SF-36 assesses health across eight domains. With its abbreviated and adapted versions (SF-12 and SF-8), the SF-36 has become the most widely used instrument for patient-reported outcomes, with more than 41,000,000 surveys taken and over 32,000 licenses issued to date (Qualitymetric.com, 2013). An SF-10 has been developed for use with children aged 5–18 years and is scored to produce physical and psychosocial health summary measures.

The WHOQOL instruments were developed cross-culturally and reflect the organisation's commitment to a holistic view of health (Skevington, Sartorius, & Amir, 2004). The WHO-QOL-100 produces scores for domains (physical, psychological, independence, social relationships, environment, and spirituality/religion/personal beliefs) as well as for 24 facets (e.g., sleep and rest, social support, financial support). The shorter 26-item WHOQOL-BREF produces only domain scores. A 32-item WHOQOL-SRPB has been developed to assess aspects of spirituality, religiousness, and personal beliefs and a version has been developed for use with people with HIV (WHOQOL-HIV).

Most generic measures of QoL have been developed with adults and these measures are not always appropriate for use with individuals at different developmental stages, for example, children, adolescents, and older adults. Individual factors determining QoL can be expected to change over the course of the life span as priorities change. A number of generic measures have been developed for use with children and adolescents. These include KIDSCREEN and PedsQL. The KIDSCREEN instruments (a 52-item detailed HRQoL measure and the shorter KIDSCREEN-27 and KIDSCREEN-10 indexes) were developed across 13 European countries and are for use with healthy and ill children between the ages of 8 and 18 years (Ravens-Sieberer et al., 2005; The KIDSCREEN Group Europe, 2006). The 52-item measure covers 10 HRQoL domains (physical, psychological well-being, moods and emotions, self-perception, autonomy, parent relations and home life, social support and peers, school environment, social acceptance, and financial resources). Each instrument is available in a child, adolescent, and parent/proxy version. Since the measure was developed across countries it is available in several languages. The PedsQL assesses HRQoL using four multidimensional core scales assessing physical, emotional, social, and school functioning (23 items in total; Varni, Seid, & Rode, 1999). Disease-specific modules have been developed for asthma, rheumatology, diabetes, cancer, and cardiac conditions. Hence the measure, like KIDSCREEN, can be used with healthy children and adolescents as well as children with acute and chronic conditions. Also like KIDSCREEN, parent/proxy versions are available.

Another group of individuals, less clearly defined by age, for whom assessment of QoL requires tailoring, is older adults. In a burgeoning research literature on ageing, QoL is widely accepted as an indicator of successful ageing and for this reason is increasingly assessed in population studies (McGee, Morgan, Hickey, & Burke, 2011). What is notable is that older adults report more life satisfaction than younger people do (Strine, Chapman, Balluz, Moriarty, & Mokdad, 2008) even when physical decline and restrictions in daily living are experienced (Bowling, Seetai, Morris, & Ebrahim, 2007; Steverink, Westerhof, Bode, & Dittmann-Kohli, 2001). In such studies, an understanding of concepts such as *life satisfaction* and *QoL*, including choice of assessment tool, is particularly important since focusing mainly on health is likely to distort the representation of QoL. Reflecting this, large surveys of ageing such as The Irish Longitudinal Study on Ageing (TILDA) and The English Longitudinal Study of Ageing (ELSA) have used the CASP-19 (Wiggins, Higgs, Hyde, & Blane, 2004) alongside other generic measures of QoL. The CASP-19 is a 19-item measure with four subscales (Control, Autonomy, Self-Realisation, and Pleasure), developed from the theory of human needs satisfaction, and tested with adults aged 65–75 years (Wiggins et al., 2004). A number of shorter versions of the CASP have been proposed, including a 12-item version based on data from TILDA (Sexton, King-Kallimanis, Conroy, & Hickey, 2013) and a 15-item version based on ELSA (Oluboyede & Smith, 2013). Another measure developed to examine QoL among older individuals is the WHOQOL-OLD (Fang et al., 2012; Power, Quinn, & Schmidt, 2005).

Disease- or Patient-Specific Measures

Disease-specific measures may be specific to a condition (e.g., heart failure, diabetes), a certain function (e.g., sexual function), a particular problem (e.g., pain), or a population of patients (e.g., frail elderly). Such measures are designed to be more responsive to change, particularly smaller units of change that are clinically significant. They achieve this through evaluating aspects of life most affected by a condition and any treatment received. For example, measures related to arthritis tend to focus on pain and mobility. Other measures take a modular approach. The PedsQL, outlined in the previous section, has disease-specific modules for asthma, rheumatology, diabetes, cancer, and cardiac conditions. Such an approach is also taken by the EORTC QLQ-C30, a questionnaire developed to assess the QoL of cancer patients. Nineteen modules have been developed for use with patients with different types of cancer. A module has also been developed to assess QoL in older cancer patients. The EORTC QLQ-C30 has been translated into and validated in 81 languages (see http://groups.eortc.be/qol/eortc-qlq-c30).

Table 14.2 outlines a number of disease-specific measures of QoL, taking cardiac research as an example. A challenge in using instruments that are developed for use with a specific group is how to determine how different that group is, in terms of function, from other groups or the general population. The newly developed HeartQoL measure seeks to provide a basis for making between-diagnosis comparisons in the area of cardiovascular health, for example, comparing the QoL impact of a single-intervention such as cardiac rehabilitation in a mixed group such as myocardial infarction and cardiac surgery patients, or of comparing differing treatments for the same patient groups, for example, differing medication profiles for heart failure patients (Oldridge et al., 2014a, 2014b). Two other measures commonly used with cardiac patients are the Minnesota Living with Heart Failure Questionnaire (MLHFQ; Rector et al., 1987) and the Seattle Angina Questionnaire (SAQ; Spertus et al., 1995). While disease- or patient-specific measures can provide important information regarding specific illnesses and conditions, a challenge is comparing this information with information about QoL in the general population; therefore often a generic measure is used in conjunction with a disease- or patient-specific measure.

Dimension-Specific Measures

Since many of these instruments, for instance, the Hospital Anxiety and Depression Scales (HADS) will be well known in health psychology, they are not summarised here. A good reference source for scale descriptions and psychometric data are two compilations by Bowling (Bowling, 2001, 2005). See also Chapter 15 in this volume, on the assessment of psychological adjustment.

Utility- or Preference-Based Measures of HRQoL

Utility- or preference-based measures (based on utility theory) have been developed from a health economics perspective. Such measures aim to assess the value of health or health-care interventions in terms of a combination of increased QoL and length of life. The main way of combining these two variables is to calculate quality adjusted life years (QALYs). To calculate QALYs, the number of life years gained or lost as a result of an intervention is multiplied by the change in HRQoL of those treated. HRQoL is rated from 1.0 (*best possible health*) to 0 (*dead*). So if a treatment restores or maintains a person in perfect health and lengthens life by 3 years ($3 \times 1 = 3$), this would provide a gain of 3 QALYs. It is possible to calculate the cost per QALY from the cost of treatment, allowing comparison of treatments. There are a number of challenges with using QALYs. Firstly, rating HRQoL is difficult; secondly, the weights used in the calculations are derived from the general rather than a patient population; and thirdly, the nature of the calculation is inherently ageist (McGee & Ring, 2010). Despite these criticisms, QALYs remain the most popular way to combine increased quality and length of life, although other methods are available (McAlearney, Schweikhart, & Pathak, 1999). The most widely used utility measures that yield QALYs are the Health Utilities Index (HUI; Feeny et al., 2002; Horsman et al., 2003; Torrance et al., 1996) and the EuroQol-5D (EQ-5D; Dolan, 1997; Kind, 1996; Shaw et al., 2005). The HUI measures health status and HRQoL. The current version (Mark 3) assesses eight dimensions: vision, hearing, speech, ambulation, dexterity, emotion, cognition, and pain/discomfort (see http://www.healthutilities.com/). The development of the

Table 14.2. Commonly used disease-specific measures of QoL

	HeartQoL	MLHFQ	SAQ
Population focus	All types of cardiac patients, for example, angina, MI, and ischaemic heart failure	Heart failure patients	Coronary heart disease patients
Items	14 items: two subscales (physical and emotional)	21 items: two subscales (physical and emotional)	19 items: five subscales (anginal stability, anginal frequency, physical limitation, treatment satisfaction, QoL)
Administration	Self-report or interview	Self-report or interview	Self-report or interview
Reliability and validity	Initial studies (n = 6,384) report good reliability and validity (Oldridge et al., 2014b)	Recent study analysing data from eight studies (n = 3,847) supports previous research attesting to the reliability and validity of the MLHFQ. This study suggests one item to be replaced and calculation of a third specific score; Garin et al., 2013)	A number of translations and versions exist, reporting good reliability and validity (Pettersen, Reikvam, & Stavem, 2005; Yu & Liu, 2012)
Access		See http://license.umn.edu/technologies/94019_minnesota-living-with-heart-failure-questionnaire	See http://cvoutcomes.org/licenses

Note. MI = myocardial infarction; MLHFQ = Minnesota Living with Heart Failure Questionnaire; SAQ = Seattle Angina Questionnaire.

EQ-5D was informed by a review of existing measuring including the NHP and SIP. Firstly, it assesses health across five domains: anxiety/depression, mobility, pain/discomfort, self-care, and usual activities. The second part consists of a Visual Analogue Scale to measure self-perceived health on a vertical scale from 0 to 100, where 0 is the *worst imaginable health state*, and 100 is the *best imaginable health*. Utility measures are often incorporated into pharmaceutical trials as they allow for economic evaluation of an intervention in a way that other measures of QoL cannot easily do.

Individual Measures of QoL

Individual measures of QoL have at their core the assumption that QoL is subjective, relative, and above all an individual evaluation. Such measures envisage QoL as not being amenable to comprehensive representation through pre-determined questionnaire formats. One such measure is the Schedule for the Evaluation of Individual Quality of Life (SEIQoL; McGee et al., 1991; O'Boyle et al., 1992) and its short form, SEIQoL-DW (Hickey et al., 1996). The SEIQoL philosophy proposes that in an assessment of QoL the individual evaluates the current status of life areas that are important to them and that they compare this with their own set of standards concerning optimal functioning. Using the SEIQoL-DW, respondents nominate five aspects of their lives that most contribute to their QoL (these do not have to be health-related). Each area is rated for importance and assigned a relative weight. Current function in each area is then rated from *best possible* to *worst possible* (using a Visual Analogue Scale). The results can be expressed as an overall number or QoL rating. The SEIQoL has been found to be sensitive to change and research has demonstrated that health is not always listed as one of the most important domains or aspects of QoL, even among those who are chronically ill (Joyce, O'Boyle, & McGee, 1999). A recent systematic review of the SEIQoL-DW concluded the measure is a valid and feasible instrument for use even with patients experiencing severe illness, although limited conclusions could be drawn about responsiveness due to the small number of studies that examine this (Wettergren, Kettis-Lindblad, Sprangers, & Ring, 2009).

Another individual measure of QoL is the Patient-Generated Index (PGI; Ruta et al., 1994). Using the PGI, respondents name the five most important areas of life affected by their health condition and so, unlike the SEIQoL, it can only be used with patient groups (although later versions do include questions on non-health-related aspects of life). Using the PGI is a three-step process: areas are named, then they are rated in terms of how near or far their health function is from where the respondent would like it to be, and then they are assigned importance by allocating an overall fixed amount of points across them. A 12-year review found the PGI to be reliable for group comparisons; however, reported evidence for responsiveness was unclear (Martin, Camfield, Rodham, Kliempt, & Ruta, 2007).

The individual approach to assessing QoL highlights the dynamic nature of QoL by not tying respondents to predetermined aspects of life. This approach acknowledges that QoL shifts in response to developments, experiences, and changes that occur in life. This is important since it is increasingly acknowledged that QoL can be higher in patient groups than in other groups in the general population. In addition, QoL may have a relative nature for individuals, so when QoL is assessed it is not assessed in absolute terms but relative to where one might be, compared with a peer group, for example. In ageing research it is suggested that increased levels of QoL in older individuals may be due to reframing or response shift (Sprangers & Schwartz, 2000), reflecting an adaption to the ageing process. Similar adaptation may take place with chronic illness.

Conclusions

QoL and HRQoL are widely used terms despite being misunderstood and misapplied in their assessment. They capture a broad conceptual space that is seen as important in health and other settings. However, most measures currently used are based on minimal definition and focus on predetermined domains that are often overly focused on health, physical function, and symptoms. This presents a number of major research challenges including the development and application of conceptual models to elucidate both concepts. These models must acknowledge the complexity of QoL. Successful assessment is dependent upon clear research aims and definitions as well as appropriate selection of assessment methods and tools.

In sum, QoL is dynamic, and is modified by the expectations, experiences, and changes that occur in life – including and beyond health. As an enduring concept in public and professional discourse, it is an important area for further conceptual and psychometric development, in that order. As such, it is fertile ground for the focus and skill sets available within health psychology.

References

Barofsky, I. (2007). Future role of quality-of-life assessment in outcomes research. *Expert Review of Pharmacoeconomics & Outcomes Research, 7*, 427–429. http://doi.org/10.1586/14737167.7.5.427

Beck, A. T., Steer, R. A., Ball, R., & Ranieri, W. (1996). Comparison of Beck Depression Inventories-IA and -II in psychiatric outpatients. *Journal of Personality Assessment, 67*, 588–597. http://doi.org/10.1207/s15327752jpa6703_13

Beck, A. T., Ward, C. H., Mendelson, M., Mock, J., & Erbaugh, J. (1961). An inventory for measuring depression. *Archives of General Psychiatry, 4*, 561–571.

Bowling, A. (2001). *Measuring disease: A Review of disease specific quality of life measurement scales* (2nd ed.). Milton Keynes, UK: Open University Press.

Bowling, A. (2005). *Measuring health: A review of quality of life scales* (3rd ed.). Milton Keynes, UK: Open University Press.

Bowling, A., Seetai, S., Morris, R., & Ebrahim, S. (2007). Quality of life among older people with poor functioning. The influence of perceived control over life. *Age and Ageing, 36*, 310–315. http://doi.org/10.1093/ageing/afm023

Calman, K. C. (1984). Quality of life in cancer patients – an hypothesis. *Journal of Medical Ethics, 10*, 124–127. http://doi.org/10.1136/jme.10.3.124

Charlton, J. R., Patrick, D. L., Matthews, G., & West, P. A. (1981). Spending priorities in Kent: A Delphi study. *Journal of Epidemiology and Community Health, 35*, 288–292. http://doi.org/10.1136/jech.35.4.288

Denollet, J. (1993). Emotional distress and fatigue in coronary heart disease: The Global Mood Scale (GMS). *Psychological Medicine, 23*(1), 111–121. http://doi.org/10.1017/S0033291700038903

Denollet, J., & Brutsaert, D. L. (1995). Enhancing emotional well-being by comprehensive rehabilitation in patients with coronary heart disease. *European Heart Journal, 16*, 1070–1078.

Dodge, R., Daly, A P., Huyton, J., & Sanders, L. D. (2012). The challenge of defining wellbeing. *International Journal of Wellbeing, 2*, 222–235. http://doi.org/10.5502/ijw.v2.i3.4

Dolan, P. (1997). Modeling valuations for EuroQol health states. *Medical Care, 35*, 1095–1108. http://doi.org/10.1097/00005650-199711000-00002

Fang, J., Power, M., Lin, Y., Zhang, J., Hao, Y., & Chatterji, S. (2012). Development of short versions for the WHOQOL-OLD module. *Gerontologist, 52*(1), 66–78. http://doi.org/10.1093/geront/gnr085

Feeny, D., Furlong, W., Torrance, G. W., Goldsmith, C. H., Zhu, Z., DePauw, S., ... Boyle, M. (2002). Multiattribute and single-attribute utility functions for the Health Utilities Index mark 3 system. *Medical Care, 40*, 113–128. http://doi.org/10.1097/00005650-200202000-00006

Garin, O., Ferrer, M., Pont, A., Wiklund, I., Van Ganse, E., Vilagut, G., ... Alonso, J. (2013). Evidence on the global measurement model of the Minnesota Living with Heart Failure Questionnaire. *Quality of Life Research, 22*, 2675–2684. http://doi.org/10.1007/s11136-013-0383-z

Garratt, A., Schmidt, L., Mackintosh, A., & Fitzpatrick, R. (2002). Quality of life measurement: Bibliographic study of patient assessed health outcome measures. *British Medical Journal, 324*, 1417. http://doi.org/10.1136/bmj.324.7351.1417

Gasper, D. (2010). Understanding the diversity of conceptions of well-being and quality of life. *The Journal of Socio-Economics, 39*, 351–360. http://doi.org/10.1016/j.socec.2009.11.006

Gurková, E. (2011). Issues in the definitions of HRQoL. *Journal of Nursing, Social Studies, Public Health and Rehabilitation, 3–4*, 190–197.

Hickey, A. M., Bury, G., O'Boyle, C. A., Bradley, F., O'Kelly, F. D., & Shannon, W. (1996). A new short form individual quality of life measure (SEIQoL-DW): Application in a cohort of individuals with HIV/AIDS. *British Medical Journal, 313*, 29–33. http://doi.org/10.1136/bmj.313.7048.29

Hoe, J., Katona, C., Orrell, M., & Livingston, G. (2007). Quality of life in dementia: Care recipient and caregiver perceptions of quality of life in dementia: The LASER-AD study. *International Journal of Geriatric Psychiatry, 22*, 1031–1036. http://doi.org/10.1002/gps.1786

Hoe, J., Katona, C., Roch, B., & Livingston, G. (2005). Use of the QOL-AD for measuring quality of life in people with severe dementia – the LASER-AD study. *Age and Ageing, 34*, 130–135. http://doi.org/10.1093/ageing/afi030

Horsman, J., Furlong, W., Feeny, D., & Torrance, G. (2003). The Health Utilities Index (HUI): Concepts, measurement properties and applications. *Health and Quality of Life Outcomes, 1*, 54. http://doi.org/10.1186/1477-7525-1-54

Hunt, S. M., McEwen, J., & McKenna, S. P. (1985). Measuring health status: A new tool for clinicians and epidemiologists. *The Journal of the Royal College of General Practitioners, 35*, 185–188.

Hunt, S. M., McKenna, S. P., McEwen, J., Backett, E. M., Williams, J., & Papp, E. (1980). A quantitative approach to perceived health status: A validation study. *Journal of Epidemiology and Community Health, 34*, 281–286. http://doi.org/10.1136/jech.34.4.281

Joyce, C. R. B. (1988). Quality of Life: The state of the art in clinical assessment. In S. W. Walker & R. M. Rosser (Eds.), *QoL: Assessment and application* (pp. 169–179). Lancaster, UK: MPT Press.

Joyce, C. R. B., Hickey, A., McGee, H. M., & O'Boyle, C. A. (2003). A theory-based method for the evaluation of individual quality of life: The SEIQoL. *Quality of Life Research, 12*, 275–280. http://doi.org/10.1023/A:1023273117040

Joyce, C. R. B., O'Boyle, C. A., & McGee, H. (Eds.). (1999). *Individual quality of life: Approaches to conceptualisation and assessment*. Amsterdam, The Netherlands: Harwood Academic Publishers.

Karnofsky, D. A., & Burchenal, J. H. (1949). The clinical evaluation of chemotherapeutic agents in cancer. In C. M. MacLeod (Ed.), *Evaluation of Chemotherapeutic Agents* (pp. 191–205). New York, NY: Columbia University Press.

Kind, P. (1996). The EuroQoL Instrument: An index of health-related quality of life. In B. Spiker (Ed.), *Quality of life and pharmacoeconomics in clinical trials* (2nd ed., pp. 191–201). Philadelphia, PA: Lippincott-Raven.

Martin, F., Camfield, L., Rodham, K., Kliempt, P., & Ruta, D. (2007). Twelve years' experience with the Patient Generated Index (PGI) of quality of life: A graded structured review. *Quality of Life Research, 16*, 705–715. http://doi.org/10.1007/s11136-006-9152-6

McAlearney, A. S., Schweikhart, S. B., & Pathak, D. S. (1999). Quality-adjusted life-years and other health indices: A comparative analysis. *Clinical Therapeutics, 21*, 1605–1629. http://doi.org/10.1016/S0149-2918(00)80015-6

McGee, H. M., Morgan, K., Hickey, A., & Burke, H. (2011). Quality of life and beliefs about ageing. In A. Barrett, G. Savva, V. Timonen, & R. A. Kenny (Eds.), *Fifty plus in Ireland 2011: First results from The Irish Longitudinal Study on Ageing (TILDA)* (pp. 265–292). Dublin, Ireland: The Irish Longitudinal Study on Ageing.

McGee, H. M., O'Boyle, C. A., Hickey, A., O'Malley, K., & Joyce, C. R. B. (1991). Assessing the quality of life of the individual: The SEIQoL with a healthy and a gastroenterology unit population. *Psychological Medicine, 21*, 749–759. http://doi.org/10.1017/S0033291700022388

McGee, H. M., & Ring, L. (2010). Quality of life. In F. D. K. Vedhara, A. Kapten, & J. Weinman (Eds.), *Health psychology* (2nd ed.). London, UK: Wiley Blackwell.

McHorney, C. A., Ware, J. E., Jr., Lu, J. F., & Sherbourne, C. D. (1994). The MOS 36-Item Short-Form Health Survey (SF-36): III. Tests of data quality, scaling assumptions, and reliability across diverse patient groups. *Medical Care, 32*(1), 40–66. http://doi.org/10.1097/00005650-199401000-00004

McHorney, C. A., Ware, J. E., Jr., & Raczek, A. E. (1993). The MOS 36-Item Short-Form Health Survey (SF-36): II. Psychometric and clinical tests of validity in measuring physical and mental health constructs. *Medical Care, 31*, 247–263. http://doi.org/10.1097/00005650-199303000-00006

O'Boyle, C. A. (2001). Quality of life: Assessment in health settings. In J. D. Wright, N. J. Smelser, & P. B. Baltes (Eds.), *International encyclopedia of the social & behavioral sciences* (pp. 12628–12631). Amsterdam, The Netherlands: Elsevier

O'Boyle, C. A., McGee, H., Hickey, A., O'Malley, K., & Joyce, C. R. B. (1992). Individual quality of life in patients undergoing hip replacement. *Lancet, 339*, 1088–1091. http://doi.org/10.1016/0140-6736(92)90673-Q

Oldridge, N., Hofer, S., McGee, H., Conroy, R., Doyle, F., & Saner, H. (2014a). The HeartQoL: Part I. Development of a new core health-related quality of life questionnaire for patients with ischemic heart disease. *European Journal of Preventative Cardiology, 21*(1), 90–97. http://doi.org/10.1177/2047487312450544

Oldridge, N., Hofer, S., McGee, H., Conroy, R., Doyle, F., & Saner, H. (2014b). The HeartQoL: Part II. Validation of a new core health-related quality of life questionnaire for patients with ischemic heart disease. *European Journal of Preventative Cardiology, 21*(1), 98–106. http://doi.org/10.1177/2047487312450545

Oluboyede, Y., & Smith, A. B. (2013). Evidence for a unidimensional 15-item version of the CASP-19 using a Rasch model approach. *Quality of Life Research, 22*, 2429–2433. http://doi.org/10.1007/s11136-013-0367-z

Patrick, D. L., & Guyatt, G. (2013). *Patient reported outcomes esource, behavioural and social sciences research: National Institute of Health*. Retrieved from http://www.esourceresearch.org/tabid/188/default.aspx

Patrick, D. L., Peach, H., & Gregg, I. (1982). Disablement and care: A comparison of patient views and general practitioner knowledge. *The Journal of the Royal College of General Practitioners, 32*, 429–434.

Petersen, M. A., Larsen, H., Pedersen, L., Sonne, N., & Groenvold, M. (2006). Assessing health-related quality of life in palliative care: Comparing patient and physician assessments. *European Journal Cancer, 42*, 1159–1166. http://doi.org/10.1016/j.ejca.2006.01.032

Pettersen, K. I., Reikvam, A., & Stavem, K. (2005). Reliability and validity of the Norwegian translation of the Seattle Angina Questionnaire following myocardial infarction. *Quality of Life Research, 14*, 883–889. http://doi.org/10.1007/s11136-004-0802-2

Power, M., Quinn, K., & Schmidt, S. (2005). Development of the WHOQOL-old module. *Quality of Life Research, 14*, 2197–2214. http://doi.org/10.1007/s11136-005-7380-9

Qualitymetric.com. (2013). Retrieved from http://www.qualitymetric.com/WhatWeDo/GenericHealthSurveys/tabid/184/Default.aspx?gclid=CJbyi_PL_7oCFe4F4godlHYANQ

Ravens-Sieberer, U., Gosch, A., Rajmil, L., Erhart, M., Bruil, J., Duer, W., ... and the European KIDSCREEN Group. (2005). KIDSCREEN-52 quality-of-life measure for children and adolescents. *Review of Pharmacoeconomics & Outcomes Research, 5*, 353–364. http://doi.org/10.1586/14737167.5.3.353

Rector, T. S., Kubo, S. H., & Cohn, J. N. (1987). Patient's self-assessment of their congestive heart failure: Content, reliability and validity of a new measure: The Minnesota living with heart failure questionnaire. *Heart Failure, 3* 198–219.

Ruta, D. A., Garratt, A. M., Leng, M., Russell, I. T., & MacDonald, L. M. (1994). A new approach to the measurement of quality of life. The Patient-Generated Index. *Medical Care, 32*, 1109–1126. http://doi.org/10.1097/00005650-199411000-00004

Schiffczyk, C., Romero, B., Jonas, C., Lahmeyer, C., Muller, F., & Riepe, M. W. (2010). Generic quality of life assessment in dementia patients: A prospective cohort study. *BMC Neurology, 10*, 48. http://doi.org/10.1186/1471-2377-10-48

Schipper, H., Clinch, J. J., & Olweny, C. L. M. (1996). Quality of life studies: Definitions and conceptual issues. In B. Spilker (Ed.), *Quality of life and pharmacoeconomics in clinical trials* (pp. 11–23). Philadelphia, PA: Lippincott-Raven.

Sexton, E., King-Kallimanis, B. L., Conroy, R. M., & Hickey, A. (2013). Psychometric evaluation of the CASP-19 quality of life scale in an older Irish cohort. *Quality of Life Research, 22*, 2549–2559. http://doi.org/10.1007/s11136-013-0388-7

Shaw, J. W., Johnson, J. A., & Coons, S. J. (2005). US valuation of the EQ-5D health states: Development and testing of the D1 valuation model. *Medical Care, 43*, 203–220. http://doi.org/10.1097/00005650-200503000-00003

Skevington, S. M., Sartorius, N., & Amir, M. (2004). Developing methods for assessing quality of life in different cultural settings. The history of the WHOQOL instruments. *Social Psychiatry And Psychiatric Epidemiology, 39*(1), 1–8.

Spertus, J. A., Winder, J. A., Dewhurst, T. A., Deyo, R. A., Prodzinski, J., McDonell, M., & Fihn, S. D. (1995). Development and evaluation of the Seattle Angina Questionnaire: A new functional status measure for coronary artery disease. *Journal of the American College of Cardiology, 25*, 333–341. http://doi.org/10.1016/0735-1097(94)00397-9

Sprangers, M. A. G., & Schwartz, C. E. (2000). Integrating response shift into health related quality of life research: A theoretical model. In M. A. G. Sprangers & C. E. Schwartz (Eds.), *Adaptation to changing health-response shift in quality of life research* (pp. 11–23). Washington, DC: American Psychological Association.

Srikrishna, S., Robinson, D., Cardozo, L., & Gonzalez, J. (2009). Is there a discrepancy between patient and physician quality of life assessment? *Neurourology & Urodynamics, 28*, 179–182. http://doi.org/10.1002/nau.20634

Steverink, N., Westerhof, G. J., Bode, C., & Dittmann-Kohli, F. (2001). The personal experience of aging, individual resources, and subjective well-being. *Journals of Gerontology: Series B, 56*, 364–373. http://doi.org/10.1093/geronb/56.6.P364

Strine, T. W., Chapman, D. P., Balluz, L. S., Moriarty, D. G., & Mokdad, A. H. (2008). The associations between life satisfaction and health-related quality of life, chronic illness, and health behaviors among U.S. community-dwelling adults. *Journal of Community Health, 33*(1), 40–50. http://doi.org/10.1007/s10900-007-9066-4

Taillefer, M-C., Dupuis, G., Roberge, M-A., & LeMay, S. (2003). Health-related quality of life models: Systematic review of the literature. *Social Indicators Research, 64*, 293–323. http://doi.org/10.1023/A:1024740307643

The KIDSCREEN Group Europe. (2006). *The KIDSCREEN questionnaires – quality of life questionnaires for children and adolescents. Handbook.* Lengerich, Germany: Pabst Science Publishers.

Torrance, G. W., Feeny, D. h., Furlong, W. J., Barr, R. D., Zhang, Y., & Wang, Q. (1996). Multiattribute utility function for a comprehensive health status classification system. Health Utilities Index Mark 2. *Medical Care, 34*, 702–722. http://doi.org/10.1097/00005650-199607000-00004

U.S. Department of Health and Human Services. (2009). *Guidance for industry patient-reported outcome measures: Use in medical product development to support labeling claims.* Retrieved from http://www.fda.gov/downloads/drugs/guidancecomplianceregulatoryinformation/guidances/ucm193282.pdf

Varni, J. W., Seid, M., & Rode, C. A. (1999). The PedsQL: Measurement model for the pediatric quality of life inventory. *Medical Care, 37*, 126–139. http://doi.org/10.1097/00005650-199902000-00003

Ware, J. E., Jr., & Sherbourne, C. D. (1992). The MOS36-item short-form health survey (SF-36). I. Conceptual framework and item selection. *Medical Care, 30*, 473–483. http://doi.org/10.1097/00005650-199206000-00002

Wettergren, L., Kettis-Lindblad, A., Sprangers, M., & Ring, L. (2009). The use, feasibility and psychometric properties of an individualised quality-of-life instrument: A systematic review of the SEIQoL-DW. *Quality of Life Research, 18*, 737–746. http://doi.org/10.1007/s11136-009-9490-2

WHOQOL Group. (1995). The World Health Organization Quality of Life assessment (WHOQOL): Position paper from the World Health Organization. *Social Science & Medicine, 41*, 1403–1409. http://doi.org/10.1016/0277-9536(95)00112-K

Wiggins, R. D., Higgs, P. F. D., Hyde, M., & Blane, D. B. (2004). Quality of life in the third age: Key predictors of the CASP-19 measure. *Ageing and Society, 24*, 693–708. http://doi.org/10.1017/S0144686X04002284

Yu, S., & Liu, H. (2012). Development and validation of the simplified chinese version of Seattle Angina Questionnaire (SC-SAQ). *Heart, 98*(Suppl. 2), E180–E181. http://doi.org/10.1136/heartjnl-2012-302920j.62

Zigmond, A. S., & Snaith, R. P. (1983). The Hospital Anxiety and Depression Scale. *Acta Psychiatrica Scandinavica, 67*, 361–370. http://doi.org/10.1111/j.1600-0447.1983.tb09716.x

Chapter 15

Psychological Adjustment

Timothy R. Elliott[1] and Norma A. Erosa[2]

[1] Texas A&M University, College Station, TX, USA
[2] San Antonio Military Medical Center, San Antonio, NM, USA

Introduction

Psychological assessment of mental health issues in research and clinical health settings is a complex and expansive endeavor. The choice of instrumentation and the reasons for the assessment depend on the setting, the referral or research questions, the utilization of results, and who has access to the results. Increasingly, mental health issues are screened and monitored by interdisciplinary treatment teams. Mental health measures are included in large-scale outcome studies of quality of life. Consequently, mental health measures are valued by health service providers and by outcome researchers and administrators at every level of health-care service delivery – all varying in their familiarity with psychological concepts and instrumentation.

Comprehensive reviews of the many instruments used in health psychology settings already exist (e.g., McDowell, 2006). In this chapter, we briefly discuss aspects of mental health assessment in clinical health settings and in research and we comment on the instruments that are often used. We reflect on the relative strengths and shortcomings of these instruments. We then briefly explore issues that will influence future mental health assessment and related policy.

Psychological Assessment in Health Psychology Clinical Practice and Research

In general, assessment of mental health and mood in health psychology research and clinical practice serves the following purposes: (a) to assess the impact of physical illness and the psychological well-being and quality of life in patients; (b) to assess suitability for and/or potential responsiveness to treatment; (c) to identify particular areas of strength or concern to be considered by the service provider(s) in treatment planning; (d) to assess response to treatment and services, and to evaluate treatment outcomes; and (e) to assess outcomes and issues as requested by third parties concerned with legal remedies or redress.

As this list conveys, the psychological assessment of mental health issues does not serve a single stakeholder: There are multiple clients involved in health-care service provision (Sweet, Tovian, & Suchy, 2013), as well as in health psychology research. Health psychology researchers may want to examine mental health and psychological well-being in a particular group of patients; use mental health as an indicator of adjustment in illness; study the impact of a physical health condition on emotional well-being or evaluate the effectiveness of an intervention program in terms of psychological health. Health-care service providers want to know if an individual is a suitable candidate for complex and expensive procedures, and if the individual will respond well to services. Some services involve colleagues from other professions in a treatment team and information about a patient's behavioral tendencies and issues can inform their goals, objectives, and strategies for optimal outcomes. Policymakers (including health-care administrators, third-party payers, etc.) are concerned with measureable, verifiable outcomes to justify expense and continued service and to monitor quality of care and service provision. Finally, the potential for litigation and legal redress is a real and common aspect of psychological practice in several areas of care, requiring unique expertise in the assessment of issues of interest to all parties involved in the process.

Assessment strategies and instrumentation depend on the reasons for the assessment. For example, a comprehensive psychological evaluation is recommended prior to expensive, time-consuming, and intensive surgical procedures in which behavioral patterns and strict adherence to therapeutic regimens influence outcomes (e.g., organ transplantation, spinal surgeries). A comprehensive evaluation is usually warranted when psychological issues may complicate (or inform) legal decisions about malpractice or compensation for permanent, disabling injuries. In this scenario, instruments featuring indicators of malingering, response bias, and impression management are preferred. In addition, assessment of mental health and mood for research purposes depends on the specific aims of each study.

In clinical practice, time is a precious commodity for the patient and staff, and the reasons for assessment may be quite circumscribed. Interest in patient adjustment, as reflected in self-reported depression and distress, is often integral to primary care and chronic disease management programs, as well as a crucial topic in health psychology research. Brief yet reliable and valid instruments are required for this purpose.

In the following section, we review several instruments that are well suited for – and frequently used in – comprehensive evaluations, routine assessments, and mental health screenings, in monitoring mental health and studying response to treatments, and in research.

Distress, Depression, and Anxiety Measures

Measures of specific psychological problems, such as depression and anxiety, are essential elements of routine health psychology practice and research. The Symptom Checklist-90 Revised (SCL-90-R) and its shorter counterpart, the Brief Symptom Index (Derogatis & Savitz, 2000), are popular omnibus measures of distress often used to assess response to treatment. Other measures have a more specific, streamlined focus, such as the Beck Depression Inventories (now the BDI-II; Beck, Steer, & Brown, 1996) and the State-Trait Anxiety Inventory (STAI; Spielberger, Gorsuch, Lushene, Vagg, & Jacobs, 1983). These measures appear in hundreds of studies of clinical practice, outcomes, and psychometric properties in the relevant literature. In many ways, these instruments represent a gold standard for assessing these issues with self-report measures. Generally, the best instruments feature attractive psychometric properties and correspond well with diagnostic criteria and/or relevant theoretical descriptions (e.g., Beck's cognitive model of depression and anxiety; Beck, 1976). Good self-report instruments should take less time than structured diagnostic interviews and they do not require trained personnel for administration.

The Beck scales – the BDI-II and its parallel for assessing anxiety, the Beck Anxiety Inventory (BAI; Beck & Steer, 1993) – retain considerable popularity in clinical use as well as in research despite a lack of correspondence with established diagnostic criteria. Although cut-off scores exist to suggest a possible diagnosis, the items and the instructional set contribute to a respectable sensitivity but undermine their specificity to diagnostic criteria (Coyne, 1994). The BAI, for example, assesses several somatic symptoms associated with anxiety in an attempt to differentiate it from depression (Julian, 2011). The BDI-II is an excellent tool for monitoring and studying responsiveness to treatment and eventual outcomes because the items are explicitly tied to the Beck cognitive model of depression (Beck, 1976). Thus, this theoretical foundation dictates strategic treatment approaches that target each symptom assessed by the BDI-II and clinicians can reasonably monitor the effectiveness of the treatment strategy in alleviating the intensity and presence of each symptom (Persons, 2008).

The Center for Epidemiological Studies Depression Scale (CES-D; Radloff, 1977) is another popular measure that screens for depression. This 20-item, self-report, free measure has greater emphasis on the affective components of depression. However, it, too, struggles with specificity (e.g., consider the items "I was happy" and "People were unfriendly"). Consequently, these scales tend to overestimate the presence of a depressive or anxiety disorder and they do not differentiate well between a possible anxiety and depressive disorder.

Another set of measures gaining popularity provides an interesting contrast in this regard. Taken from the PRIME-MD Patient Health Questionnaire (which was first validated in a study of 3,000 obstetric-gynecological patients in several clinics; Spitzer, Kroenke, & Williams, 1999), the PHQ measures of depression (the PHQ-9; Kroenke, Spitzer, & Williams, 2001) and anxiety (the GAD-7; Spitzer, Kroenke, Williams, & Löwe, 2006) closely parallel criteria for major depressive disorder and generalized anxiety disorder, respectively. These scales are available in many languages and freely obtained at http://www.phqscreeners.com/. The GAD-7 is used to screen for anxiety and track severity. It has evidenced good utility and strong psychometric properties in primary care and community settings (Spitzer et al., 2006).

Of the two scales, the PHQ-9 is most thoroughly studied and its algorithm for determining major depressive disorder demonstrates a level of sensitivity and specificity comparable to diagnostic interview systems (Kroenke et al., 2001). It is ideal for use in primary care and family practice settings, in remote and underserved sites, and with understudied and vulnerable populations. Understandably, then, the PHQ-9 has been widely used as a screening tool for depression in several countries and across a wide array of clinical settings and health conditions (e.g., brain injury, Fann et al., 2005; spinal cord injury, Bombardier, Richards, Krause, Tulsky, & Tate, 2004). The PHQ-8 omits the suicidality item. It is recommended for use in community surveys (Kroenke et al., 2009). The PHQ-2 (Kroenke, Spitzer, & Williams, 2003) uses the first two items to screen for depression in primary care settings. A positive screen warrants a diagnostic evaluation for the possibility of a depressive syndrome (two-item "screeners" for depression lack specificity; Mitchell & Coyne, 2007).

The Hospital Anxiety and Depression Scale (HADS; Zigmond & Snaith, 1983) was developed to assess anxiety and depression disorders among medical patients, focusing on affective and cognitive symptoms and minimizing somatic aspects that can confound self-report measures in these settings (including the PHQ-9; see Hartoonian et al., 2014). The HADS has 14 items, seven each to assess depression and anxiety. It can take less than 10 min to complete and the instrument is available in several languages. Overall, the extant literature supports its psychometric properties among a wide variety of medical patients (Bjelland, Dahl, Tangen Haug, & Neckelmann, 2002) and across international boundaries (Hermann, 1997). Scores on both dimensions have demonstrated sensitivity to change. Researchers and clinicians should be aware that the anxiety component may have reduced validity among elderly patients (warranting concern about its applicability with patients who have arthritic conditions; Julian, 2011), although the depression component does not appear to share this issue (Smarr & Keefer, 2011).

Posttraumatic Stress Disorder

Clinicians as well as researchers must be aware of the possible presence of posttraumatic stress disorder (PTSD) following traumatic events and injury (Wiseman, Foster, & Curtis, 2013). Although several instruments are available to assess PTSD, two instruments warrant particular comment. The four-item Primary Care Posttraumatic Stress Disorder Screen (PC-PTSD; Prins et al., 2004) is recommended for settings in which time demands prevent a comprehensive assessment. Endorsement of any of the four items – assessing re-experiencing, emotional avoidance, behavioral avoidance, and hyperarousal – constitutes a positive result. It was the first PTSD screening instrument developed with a primary care sample. It has acceptable properties with trauma patients with some acceptable loss in sensitivity (Hanley, deRoon-Cassini, & Brasel, 2013).

The Hanley et al. study (2013) compared the PC-PTSD with the PTSD Symptom Checklist-Civilian Version (PCL-C; http://www.ptsd.va.gov/professional/assessment/adult-sr/ptsd-checklist.asp). The PCL-C has 17 items to assess specific PTSD symptoms. It has considerable reliability and validity as well as sensitivity and specificity among several Veteran samples and among survivors from motor vehicle accidents and sexual assault (Orsillo, 2001).

Personality Traits

While personality is not directly a measure of psychological adjustment or mental health, such measures are frequently used in both clinical and research settings. The Big Five model (John & Srivastava, 1999) describes dimensions or domains of personality in five factors: openness, conscientiousness, extraversion, agreeableness, and neuroticism. Research has shown that the Big Five are associated with health status, health behaviors, and health outcomes (Costa & McCrae, 1987; Goodwin & Friedman, 2006; Weiss & Costa, 2005). Neuroticism in particular has been the most researched trait. While findings are somewhat inconsistent, it has been shown to be associated with mortality and an increase in symptom reporting (Costa & McCrae, 1987; Wilson et al., 2005). Conscientiousness is another trait that has shown strong links in health and illness as well. Findings on this trait suggest that conscientiousness is related to reduced rates of mental and physical disorders among adult populations (Goodwin & Friedman, 2006) and better medication adherence (Molloy, O'Carroll, & Ferguson, 2014). Although personality traits are not assessed as heavily in health psychology practice or research, it is important to note their potential role in the field.

Comprehensive Psychological Assessment

Psychologists often rely on omnibus measures to obtain information about behavioral tendencies, issues, and general adjustment in an efficient, reliable, valid, yet comprehensive fashion. The best instruments feature indicators of response sets, test-taking attitudes, and potential malingering. The instruments in this select group include objective measures of personality: the Minnesota Multiphasic Personality Inventory (MMPI-2; Butcher, Dahlstrom, Graham, Tellegen, & Kaemmer, 1989), the various versions of the Millon Clinical Multiaxial Inventory (now the MCMI-III; Millon, 2006) and the Personality Assessment Inventory (PAI; Morey, 1991).

With a long history of use in medical settings, the MMPI may be the most frequently used instrument in clinical health psychology in many countries. Hundreds of studies have examined the MMPI profiles (and scale scores) among persons with chronic pain syndromes and this research base provides a rich empirical trove of information about differential responses to and implications for treatment and rehabilitation. The MMPI-2 is used to evaluate candidates for spinal surgery (Block, Ben-Porath, & Marek, 2013) and organ transplant surgeries (Olbrisch, Benedict, Ashe, & Levenson, 2002). It is the most frequently used multidimensional objective personality instrument in evaluations of candidates for bariatric surgery (Fabricatore, Crerand, Wadden, Sarwer, & Krausucki, 2006). Although a summary is beyond the scope of this chapter, much of the relevant literature indicates that individual characteristics assessed by the MMPI/MMPI-2 are associated with distress, functional impairment, observed pain behaviors, medication use, and return to work. Scales 1 (Hypochondriasis), 2 (Depression), and 3 (Hysteria) are sensitive to symptom over-reporting and reflect current intensity of distress, impairment, self-reported pain, and degree of comfort with a sick or disabled role (Keller & Butcher, 1991).

Two other multidimensional instruments have shown considerable utility in clinical health psychology: the MCMI-III (Millon, 2006) and the PAI (Morey, 1991). Normative data were used in developing the MMPI-2 and the PAI and both convert raw scores to scaled T scores based on norms. All versions of the MCMI, however, were normed on psychiatric patients with known diagnoses. Millon did not assume that psychopathological behaviors would be normally distributed throughout the sample (let alone people in general), although certain conditions would share specific features (e.g., schizophrenia could share paranoid tendencies). Consequently, the MCMI-III is a *criterion-referenced* measure. Psychologists must exercise great caution in using the MCMI-III with individuals who have no prior evidence of psychopathology, including personality disorder characteristics, and using the MCMI with "normal" individuals is inadvisable.

The PAI has fewer items (344) than the MMPI-2 (567). Items are written at a fourth-grade reading level and take approximately 50 min to complete. It contains four validity scales (infrequency, inconsistency, negative impression, positive impression) and 11 clinical scales (e.g., depression, somatic complaints, antisocial features, schizophrenia). The PAI also has five treatment consideration scales (e.g., aggression, treatment rejection) and two interpersonal scales (warmth, dominance) that provide clinically relevant information. Scales have a *face valid* quality and they reflect a relative intensity on each specific dimension. Unlike the MMPI-2 and the MCMI-III, PAI items were selected on theoretical and statistical grounds and the subscales have no item overlap. The lack of item overlap between scales means, for example, that high scores on the somatization scale will not affect scores on other scales, an issue that often occurs when using the MMPI-2 with medical patients who have reasonable physical and somatic concerns.

The PAI has been used to evaluate symptom clusters among persons with chronic pain syndromes (Karlin et al., 2005) and traumatic brain injury (Demakis et al., 2007), and among candidates for bariatric surgery (Corsica, Azarbad, McGill, Wool, & Hood, 2010). The Negative Impression validity scale significantly characterized individuals seeking compensation for mild traumatic brain injury (Whiteside, Galbreath, Brown, & Turnbull, 2012). The Treatment Process Index differentiated completers from noncompleters of an outpatient chronic pain treatment program, and the Treatment Rejection scale also contributed to the predictive model (Hopwood, Creech, Clark, Meagher, & Morey, 2008).

The Eysenck Personality Questionnaire (EPQ; Eysenck & Eysenck, 1975) is an established measure of personality traits and has been used for both clinical and research purposes. The EPQ takes special interest in a person's temperament, with the theory largely based on genetics and physiology. Three traits of temperament are assessed: psychoticism, extraversion, and neuroticism. Due to criticisms of low reliability to the psychoticism dimension, the EPQ-R was developed and it is the current form (EPQ-R; Eysenck, Eysenck, & Barrett, 1985).

Well-Being and Optimal Adjustment

An intense interest in quality of life as a critical outcome for persons with a chronic health condition preceded the relatively recent interest in positive psychology. Persons with chronic and debilitating conditions were often the focal point of this attention, as psychological issues among these individuals were associated with recurring and largely preventable secondary complications. Chief among the earliest instruments was the omnibus Medical Outcomes Study 36-Item Short-Form Health Survey (SF-36; Ware, Snow, Kosinski, & Gandek, 1993). Additional information about SF-36, as well as the assessment of quality of life, can be found in Chapter 14 of this volume.

More germane to our current discussion is the utility of life satisfaction and subjective well-being measures. The Satisfaction with Life Scale (SWLS; Diener, Emmons, Larsen, & Griffin, 1985) may be the most popular measure of life satisfaction. The SWLS has five items that are rated on a 1 (*strongly disagree*) to 7 (*strongly agree*) Likert-type scale. Higher scores reflect greater life satisfaction. The SWLS is free for use and is available in several languages (see http://internal.psychology.illinois.edu/~ediener/SWLS.html). In one of the largest studies to evaluate well-being scales, poor health was significantly associated with lower SWLS scores among community-residing adults ($N=5,399$; Kobau, Sniezek, Zack, Lucas, & Burns, 2010).

Resilience

There is evidence that certain "pre-injury" personality characteristics may help individuals resume prior levels of life satisfaction following disability onset (Boyce & Wood, 2011). Other work reveals that a certain percentage of individuals remain resilient throughout the first year of traumatic and severe disability, consistently reporting low levels of depression and anxiety despite the radical changes they experience (Bonanno, Kennedy, Galatzer-Levy, Lude, & Elfström, 2012). The concept of resilience may be one of the most captivating in contemporary health psychology. It is also quite elusive for clinicians. The prevailing model of resilience, and the one that has been supported across several clinical populations, identifies resilient individuals in sample-specific analytic procedures that categorize those who are consistently lower in distress over a period from those who are distressed (e.g., Bonanno et al., 2012). These studies also examine differences that may occur between resilient individuals and those who are not (such as stress appraisals, coping, mood; Bonanno, Westphal, & Mancini, 2011). Despite the empirical support for this model, it has limited utility for practitioners who want to identify resilient characteristics in psychological evaluations of individuals in clinical settings. This, in part, explains the widespread usage of the 25-item Connor-Davidson Resilience Scale (CD-RISC; Connor & Davidson, 2003). The authors describe resilience as the embodiment of "personal qualities that enable one to thrive in the face of adversity… a multidimensional characteristic that varies with context, time, age, gender and cultural origin" (Connor & Davidson,

2003, p. 76). The psychometric properties of the CD-RISC are among the best in comparisons with other available resilience measures (Windle, Bennett, & Noyes, 2011).

Yet the authors of the CD-RISC offer no real theoretical model for their concept of resilience, leaving clinicians and researchers with a relatively face-valid, self-report measure and little guidance for working with respondents who have low scores. Considerable evidence indicates that CD-RISC scores correlate with measures of distress in predictable directions (e.g., among women experiencing infertility; Sexton, Byrd, & von Kluge, 2010). Ironically, perhaps the most elegant and empirically supported theory of resilience presents psychologists with the opposite problem. A resilient personality prototype, according to the Block and Block (1980) theory of ego control and ego resiliency, develops from healthy attachment during infancy and childhood and is characterized by a capacity for effective adaptation to change and conflict. Other personality prototypes, undercontrolled and overcontrolled, develop in response to unhealthy attachments. These personality prototypes are mapped out with behavioral ratings (in studies of children; Caspi & Silva, 1995) and with self-report measures of the Big Five or other normal personality traits (e.g., the Big Five Inventory, John & Srivastava, 1999; the NEO-PI, Costa & McCrae, 1985; the Multidimensional Personality Questionnaire; Tellegen & Waller, 2008). Resilient individuals are often typified by low neuroticism and above average scores on the other factors. Undercontrolled individuals are characterized by low conscientiousness, a moderate level of neuroticism, and low agreeableness. High neuroticism, low extraversion, and average scores on the other factors characterize overcontrolled individuals.

Longitudinal research has found that behavioral ratings related to temperament of children predict emotional, behavioral, and health outcomes in adulthood (Caspi & Silva, 1995; Chapman & Goldberg, 2011). There is some evidence resilient prototypes may have a decreased cardiovascular disease risk in middle age (Chapman & Goldberg, 2011). Resilient individuals report more adaptive, proactive problem-solving styles following the onset of a severe physical disability and they report a greater sense of acceptance at medical discharge than overcontrolled individuals do (Berry, Elliott, & Rivera, 2007). Also, children with an undercontrolled personality prototype have a greater risk of injury than other children (Berry & Schwebel, 2009).

Positive Affect

Positive affect is a common characteristic of resilience across these different approaches. Positive emotionality may facilitate well-being, social ties, and motivation, and there is some indication it may be associated with brain glucose metabolism in an adaptive and perhaps protective manner (Volkow et al., 2011). Negative affectivity is associated with increased health complaints under routine and stressful conditions (Watson & Pennebaker, 1989). The Positive and Negative Affective Schedule (PANAS; Watson, Clark, & Tellegen, 1988) efficiently measures both dimensions. The PANAS has supportive psychometric properties (Crawford & Henry, 2004) and it is often included in studies of well-being (e.g., Kobau et al., 2010).

Positive and negative emotions can also be efficiently assessed with Visual Analog Scales (VAS). Separate VAS for depression, anxiety, anger, fear, and frustration can be reliably assessed on a 150-mm (or 100-mm) line with instructions to indicate along the scale the intensity of each feeling at that moment (or other time frame). Each VAS can be anchored by the descriptors *none* and *the most severe imaginable* (e.g., Harkins, Price, & Braith, 1989). The same approach is used to assess specific positive emotions (see Stern, 1997). Tactile adaptations have been made for patients in a low vision clinic (Dreer et al., 2008).

Comments and Conclusions: Promise and Participation in the Future

More changes will occur in the assessment of psychological adjustment in the clinic and in the community. The assessment of adjustment will be refined and improved, and these instruments will evaluate the success and cost effectiveness of services. Change is already in the works: The National Institutes of Health supports an ongoing project (PROMIS) to produce standardized patient-oriented outcome measures for use in research and clinical protocols (see http://www.nihpromis.org/). Measures of several dimensions discussed in this chapter are being tested in several projects (e.g., an 8-item measure of depression; Amtmann et al., 2014). PROMIS relies on item response theory to develop, evaluate, weight, and then select specific items for use with individual respondents. Ideally, these scales will be available to clinicians as well as researchers, administrators, and policymakers to promote a common understanding and dialogue about outcomes.

The PROMIS item banks will cover three broad domains: physical, mental, and social health. Psychologists will be compelled to attend more to social health, and participation, specifically, as an important health outcome. The high premium that the International Classification of Functioning, Disability and Health (World Health Organization, 2001) places on participation as an essential outcome influences much of this work. Active participation in desired pursuits may be essential to understanding quality of life among persons with chronic and debilitating conditions, as participation may effectively mediate the effects of injury severity and functional impairment to life satisfaction over time (Erosa, Berry, Elliott, Underhill, & Fine, 2014; Kalpinski et al., 2013). Psychological expertise should be involved in every aspect of item development, refinement, and evaluation in these endeavors to represent the best interests of the profession, our science, and the people we serve.

References

Amtmann, D., Kim, J., Chung, H., Bamer, A. M., Askew, R. L., Wu, S., … Johnson, K. L. (2014). Comparing CESD-10, PHQ-9, and PROMIS depression instruments in individuals with multiple sclerosis. *Rehabilitation Psychology, 59*, 220–229. http://doi.org/10.1037/a0035919

Beck, A. T. (1976). *Cognitive therapy and the emotional disorders.* New York, NY: International Universities Press.

Beck, A.T., & Steer, R.A. (1993). *Beck Anxiety Inventory Manual.* San Antonio, TX: Psychological Corporation.

Beck, A. T., Steer, R. A., & Brown, G. K. (1996). *Manual for the Beck Depression Inventory-II.* San Antonio, TX: Psychological Corporation.

Berry, J., Elliott, T., & Rivera, P. (2007). Resilient, undercontrolled, and overcontrolled personality prototypes among persons with spinal cord injury. *Journal of Personality Assessment, 89*, 292–302. http://doi.org/10.1080/00223890701629813

Berry, J. W., & Schwebel, D. C. (2009). Configural approaches to temperament assessment: Implications for predicting risk of unintentional injury in children. *Journal of Personality, 77*, 1381–1410. http://doi.org/10.1111/j.1467-6494.2009.00586.x

Bjelland, I., Dahl, A. A., Tangen Haug, T., & Neckelmann, D. (2002). The validity of the Hospital Anxiety and Depression Scale – an updated literature review. *Journal of Psychosomatic Research, 52*, 69–77. http://doi.org/10.1016/S0022-3999(01)00296-3

Block, A. R., Ben-Porath, Y. S., & Marek, R. J. (2013). Psychological risk factors for poor outcome of spine surgery and spinal cord stimulator implant: A review of the literature and their assessment with the MMPI-2-RF. *The Clinical Neuropsychologist, 27*, 81–107. http://doi.org/10.1080/13854046.2012.721007

Block, J. H., & Block, J. (1980). The role of ego control and ego resiliency in the organization of behavior. In W. A. Collins (Ed.), *The Minnesota symposium on child psychology, Vol. 13. Development of cognition, affect, and social relations* (pp. 39–101). Hillsdale, NJ: Erlbaum.

Bombardier, C. H., Richards, J. S., Krause, J. S., Tulsky, D., & Tate, D. G. (2004). Symptoms of major depression in people with spinal cord injury: Implications for screening. *Archives of Physical Medicine and Rehabilitation, 85*, 1749–1756. http://doi.org/10.1016/j.apmr.2004.07.348

Bonanno, G. A., Kennedy, P., Galatzer-Levy, I. R., Lude, P., & Elfström, M. L. (2012). Trajectories of resilience, depression, and anxiety following spinal cord injury. *Rehabilitation Psychology, 57*, 236–247. http://doi.org/10.1037/a0029256

Bonanno, G. A., Westphal, M., & Mancini, A. (2011). Resilience to loss and potential trauma. *Annual Review of Clinical Psychology, 7*, 511–535. http://doi.org/10.1146/annurev-clinpsy-032210-104526

Boyce, C. J., & Wood, A. M. (2011). Personality prior to disability determines adaptation: Agreeable individuals recover lost life satisfaction faster and more completely. *Psychological Science, 22*, 1397–1402. http://doi.org/10.1177/0956797611421790

Butcher, J. N., Dahlstrom, W. G., Graham, J. R. Tellegen, A., & Kaemmer, B. (1989). *Manual for administration and scoring. MMPI-2*. Minneapolis, MN: University of Minnesota Press.

Caspi, A., & Silva, P. A. (1995). Temperamental qualities at age three predict personality traits in young adulthood: Longitudinal evidence from a birth cohort. *Child Development, 66*, 486–498. http://doi.org/10.2307/1131592

Chapman, B. P., & Goldberg, L. R. (2011). Replicability and 40-year predictive power of childhood ARC types. *Journal of Personality and Social Psychology, 101*, 593–606. http://doi.org/10.1037/a0024289

Connor, K. M., & Davidson, J. R. T. (2003). Development of a new resilience scale: The Connor-Davidson Resilience Scale (CD-RISC). *Depression and Anxiety, 18*, 76–82. http://doi.org/10.1002/da.10113

Corsica, J. A., Azarbad, L., McGill, K., Wool, L., & Hood, M. (2010). The Personality Assessment Inventory: Clinical utility, psychometric properties, and normative data for bariatric surgery candidates. *Obesity Surgery, 20*, 722–731. http://doi.org/10.1007/s11695-009-0004-7

Costa, P. T., & McCrae, R. R. (1985). *The NEO Personality Inventory: Manual*. Odessa, FL: Psychological Assessment Resources.

Costa, P. T., & McCrae, R. R. (1987). Neuroticism, somatic complaints, and disease. *Journal of Personality, 55*, 299–316. http://doi.org/10.1111/j.1467-6494.1987.tb00438.x

Coyne, J. C. (1994). Self-reported distress: Analog or Ersatz depression? *Psychological Bulletin, 116*, 29–45. http://doi.org/10.1037/0033-2909.116.1.29

Crawford, J. R., & Henry, J. D. (2004). The Positive and Negative Affect Schedule (PANAS): Construct validity, measurement properties and normative data in a large non-clinical sample. *British Journal of Clinical Psychology, 43*, 245–265. http://doi.org/10.1348/0144665031752934

Demakis, G. J., Hammond, F., Knotts, A., Cooper, D. B., Clement, P., Kennedy, J., & Sawyer, T. (2007). The Personality Assessment Inventory in individuals with traumatic brain injury. *Archives of Clinical Neuropsychology, 22*, 123–130. http://doi.org/10.1016/j.acn.2006.09.004

Derogatis, L. R., & Savitz, K. L. (2000). The SCL-90-R and Brief Symptom Inventory (BSI) in primary care. In M. E. Maruish (Ed.), *Handbook of psychological assessment in primary care settings* (pp. 297–334). Mahweh, NJ: Lawrence Erlbaum Associates.

Diener, E., Emmons, R., Larsen, R., & Griffin, S. (1985). The satisfaction with life scale. *Journal of Personality Assessment, 49*, 71–75. http://doi.org/10.1207/s15327752jpa4901_13

Dreer, L., Elliott, T., Berry, J., Fletcher, D., Swanson, M., & McNeal, J. (2008). Cognitive appraisals, distress and disability among persons in low vision rehabilitation. *British Journal of Health Psychology, 13*, 449–456. http://doi.org/10.1348/135910707X209835

Erosa, N. A., Berry, J. W., Elliott, T. R., Underhill, A., & Fine, P. R. (2014). Predicting quality of life five years after medical discharge for traumatic spinal cord injury. *British Journal of Health Psychology, 19*, 688–700. http://doi.org/10.1111/bjhp.12063

Eysenck, H. J., & Eysenck, S. B. G. (1975). *Manual of the Eysenck Personality Questionnaire*. London, UK: Hodder and Stoughton.

Eysenck, S. B. G., Eysenck, H. J., & Barrett, P. (1985). A revised version of the psychoticism scale. *Personality and Individual Differences, 6,* 21–29. http://doi.org/10.1016/0191-8869(85)90026-1

Fann, J. R., Bombardier, C. H., Dikmen, S., Esselman, P., Warms, C. A., Pelzer, E., … Temkin, N. (2005). Validity of the Patient Health Questionnaire-9 in assessing depression following traumatic brain injury. *Journal of Head Trauma Rehabilitation, 20,* 501–511. http://doi.org/10.1097/00001199-200511000-00003

Fabricatore, A. N., Crerand, C. E., Wadden, T. A., Sarwer, D. B., & Krausucki, J. L. (2006). How do mental health professionals evaluate candidates for bariatric surgery? Survey results. *Obesity Surgery, 16,* 567–573. http://doi.org/10.1381/096089206776944986

Goodwin, R. D., & Friedman, H. S. (2006). Health status and the five-factor personality traits in a nationally representative sample. *Journal of Health Psychology, 11,* 643–654. http://doi.org/10.1177/1359105306066610

Hanley, J., deRoon-Cassini, T., & Brasel, K. (2013). Efficiency of a four-item posttraumatic stress disorder screen in trauma patients. *Journal of Trauma and Acute Care Surgery, 75,* 722–727. http://doi.org/10.1097/TA.0b013e3182a53a5f

Harkins, S., Price, D., & Braith, J. (1989). Effects of extroversion and neuroticism on experimental pain, clinical pain, and illness behavior. *Pain, 36,* 209–218. http://doi.org/10.1016/0304-3959(89)90025-0

Hartoonian, N., Hoffman, J. M., Kalpakjian, C. Z., Taylor, H. B., Krause, J. K., & Bombardier, C. H. (2014). Evaluating a spinal cord injury-specific model of depression and quality of life. *Archives of Physical Medicine and Rehabilitation, 95,* 455–465. http://doi.org/10.1016/j.apmr.2013.10.029

Hermann, C. (1997). International experiences with Hospital Anxiety and Depression Scale: A review of validation data and clinical results. *Journal of Psychosomatic Research, 42,* 17–41. http://doi.org/10.1016/S0022-3999(96)00216-4

Hopwood, C. J., Creech, S. K., Clark, T. S., Meagher, M. W., & Morey, L. C. (2008). Predicting the completion of an integrative and intensive outpatient chronic pain treatment with the Personality Assessment Inventory. *Journal of Personality Assessment, 90,* 76–80. http://doi.org/10.1080/00223890701693785

John, O. P., & Srivastava, S. (1999). The Big-Five trait taxonomy: History, measurement, and theoretical perspectives. In L. A. Pervin & O. P. John (Eds.), *Handbook of personality: Theory and research* (Vol. 2, pp. 102–138). New York, NY: Guilford.

Julian, L. J. (2011). Measures of anxiety. *Arthritis Care & Research, 63*(S11), S467–S472. http://doi.org/10.1002/acr.20561

Kalpinski, R., Williamson, M. L. C., Elliott, T. R., Berry, J. W., Underhill, A. T., & Fine, P. R. (2013). Modeling the prospective relationships of impairment, injury severity and participation to quality of life following traumatic brain injury. *BioMed Research International*, Article ID 102570.

Karlin, B. E., Creech, S. K., Grimes, J. S., Clark, T. S., Meagher, M. W., & Morey, L. C. (2005). The Personality Assessment Inventory with chronic pain patients: Psychometric properties and clinical utility. *Journal of Clinical Psychology, 61,* 1571–1585. http://doi.org/10.1002/jclp.20209

Keller, L. S., & Butcher, J. N. (1991). *Assessment of Chronic Pain Patients with the MMPI-2.* Minneapolis, MN: University of Minnesota Press.

Kobau, R., Sniezek, J., Zack, M. M., Lucas, R. E., & Burns, A. (2010). Well-being assessment: An evaluation of well-being scales for public health and population estimates of well-being among US adults. *Applied Psychology: Health and Well-Being, 2,* 272–297. http://doi.org/10.1111/j.1758-0854.2010.01035.x

Kroenke, K., Spitzer, R. L., & Williams, J. B. (2003). The Patient Health Questionnaire-2: Validity of a two-item depression screener. *Medical Care, 41,* 1284–1292. http://doi.org/10.1097/01.MLR.0000093487.78664.3C

Kroenke, K., Spitzer, R. L., & Williams, J. B. W. (2001). The PHQ-9: Validity of a brief depression severity measure. *Journal of General Internal Medicine, 16,* 606–613. http://doi.org/10.1046/j.1525-1497.2001.016009606.x

Kroenke, K., Strine, T. W., Spitzer, R. L., Williams, J. B. W., Berry, J. T., & Mokdad, A. H. (2009). The PHQ-8 as a measure of current depression in the general population. *Journal of Affective Disorders, 114,* 163–173. http://doi.org/10.1016/j.jad.2008.06.026

McDowell, I. (2006). *Measuring health: A guide to rating scales and questionnaires* (3rd ed.). New York, NY: Oxford University Press. http://doi.org/10.1093/acprof:oso/9780195165678.001.0001

Millon, T. (2006). *MCMI-III manual* (3rd ed.). Minneapolis, MN: NCS Pearson.

Mitchell, A. J., & Coyne, J. C. (2007). Do ultra-short screening instruments accurately detect depression in primary care? *British Journal of General Practice, 57*, 144–151.

Molloy, G. J., O'Carroll, R. E., & Ferguson, E. (2014). Conscientiousness and medication adherence: A meta-analysis. *Annals of Behavioral Medicine, 47*, 92–101. http://doi.org/10.1007/s12160-013-9524-4

Morey, L. C. (1991). *Personality Assessment Inventory – professional manual*. Lutz, FL: Psychological Assessment Resources.

Olbrisch, M. E., Benedict, S. M., Ashe, K., & Levenson, J. L. (2002). Psychological assessment and care of organ transplant patients. *Journal of Consulting and Clinical Psychology, 70*, 771–783. http://doi.org/10.1037/0022-006X.70.3.771

Orsillo, S. M. (2001). Measures for acute stress disorder and posttraumatic stress disorder. In M. M. Antony & S. M. Orsillo (Eds.), *Practitioner's guide to empirically based measures of anxiety* (pp. 255–307). New York, NY: Kluwer Academic/Plenum.

Persons, J. B. (2008). *The case formulation approach to cognitive-behavioral therapy*. New York, NY: Guilford.

Prins, A., Ouimette, P., Kimerling, R., Camerond, R. P., Hugelshofer, D. S., Shaw-Hegwer, J., ... Sheikh, J. I. (2004). The primary care PTSD screen (PC–PTSD): Development and operating characteristics. *Primary Care Psychiatry, 9*(1), 9–14. http://doi.org/10.1185/135525703125002360

Radloff, L. S. (1977). The CES-D scale: A self-report depression scale for research in the general population. *Applied Psychological Measurement, 1*, 385–401. http://doi.org/10.1177/014662167700100306

Sexton, M. B., Byrd, M. R., & von Kluge, S. (2010). Measuring resilience in women experiencing infertility using the CD-RISC: Examining infertility-related stress, general distress, and coping styles. *Journal of Psychiatric Research, 44*, 236–241. http://doi.org/10.1016/j.jpsychires.2009.06.007

Smarr, K. L., & Keefer, A. L. (2011). Measures of depression and depressive symptoms. *Arthritis Care & Research, 63*(S11), S454–S466. http://doi.org/10.1002/acr.20556

Spielberger, C. D., Gorsuch, R. L., Lushene, R., Vagg, P. R., & Jacobs, G. A. (1983). *Manual for the state-trait anxiety inventory*. Palo Alto, CA: Consulting Psychologists Press.

Spitzer, R. L., Kroenke, K., & Williams, J. B. (1999). Validation and utility of a self-report version of PRIME-MD: The PHQ primary care study. *Journal of the American Medical Association, 282*, 1737–1744. http://doi.org/10.1001/jama.282.18.1737

Spitzer, R. L., Kroenke, K., Williams, J. B., & Löwe, B. (2006). A brief measure for assessing generalized anxiety disorder: The GAD-7. *Archives of Internal Medicine, 166*, 1092–1097. http://doi.org/10.1001/archinte.166.10.1092

Stern, R. A. (1997). *Visual Analog Mood Scales professional manual*. Odessa, FL: Psychological Assessment Resources.

Sweet, J. J., Tovian, S. M., & Suchy, Y. (2013). Psychological assessment in medical settings. In I. B. Weiner, J. R. Graham, & J. A. Naglieri (Eds.), *Handbook of psychology, Vol. 10: Assessment psychology* (pp. 291–315). New York, NY: Wiley.

Tellegen, A., & Waller, N. G. (2008). Exploring personality through test construction: Development of the Multidimensional Personality Questionnaire. In G. J. Boyle, G. Matthews, & D. H. Saklofske (Eds.), *The Sage handbook of personality theory and assessment: Vol. II. Personality measurement and testing* (pp. 261–292). London, UK: Sage.

Volkow, N. D., Tomasi, D., Wang, G-J., Fowler, J. S., Telang, F., Goldstein, R. Z., ... Alexoff, D. (2011). Positive emotionality is associated with baseline metabolism in orbitofrontal cortex and in regions of the default network. *Molecular Psychiatry, 16*, 818–825. http://doi.org/10.1038/mp.2011.30

Ware, J., Snow, K., Kosinski, M., & Gandek, B. (1993). *SF-36 health survey: Manual and interpretation guide*. Boston, MA: The Health Institute, New England Medical Center.

Watson, D., Clark, L., & Tellegen, A. (1988). Development and validation of brief measures of positive and negative affect: The PANAS scales. *Journal of Personality and Social Psychology, 54*, 1063–1070. http://doi.org/10.1037/0022-3514.54.6.1063

Watson, D., & Pennebaker, J. (1989). Health complaints, stress, and distress: Exploring the central role of negative affectivity. *Psychological Review, 96*, 234–254. http://doi.org/10.1037/0033-295X.96.2.234

Weiss, A., & Costa, P.T. (2005). Domain and facet personality predictors of all-cause mortality among Medicare patients aged 65 to 100. *Psychosomatic Medicine, 67*, 727–733. http://doi.org/10.1097/01.psy.0000181272.58103.18

Whiteside, D. M., Galbreath, J., Brown, M., & Turnbull, J. (2012). Differential response patterns on the Personality Assessment Inventory (PAI) in compensation-seeking and non-compensation-seeking mild traumatic brain injury patients. *Journal of Clinical and Experimental Neuropsychology, 34*, 172–182. http://doi.org/10.1080/13803395.2011.630648

Wilson, R. S., Krueger, K. R., Gu, L., Bienias, J. L., Mendes de Leon, C. F., & Evans, D. A. (2005). Neuroticism, extraversion, and mortality in a defined population of older persons. *Psychosomatic Medicine, 67*, 841–845. http://doi.org/10.1097/01.psy.0000190615.20656.83

Windle, G., Bennett, K. M., & Noyes, J. (2011). A methodological review of resilience measurement scales. *Health and Quality of Life Outcomes, 9*, 8. http://doi.org/10.1186/1477-7525-9-8

Wiseman, T., Foster, K., & Curtis, K. (2013). Mental health following traumatic physical injury: An integrative review. *Injury, 44*, 1383–1390. http://doi.org/10.1016/j.injury.2012.02.015

World Health Organization. (2001). *International classification of functioning, disability and health*. Geneva, Switzerland: Author.

Zigmond, A. S., & Snaith, R. P. (1983). The Hospital Anxiety and Depression Scale. *Acta Psychiatrica Scandinavica, 67*, 361–370. http://doi.org/10.1111/j.1600-0447.1983.tb09716.x

Chapter 16
Neuropsychological Assessment

Ruchika Shaurya Prakash, Alisha L. Janssen, and Heather M. Derry

Department of Psychology, Ohio State University, Columbus, OH, USA

The burgeoning field of health psychology is rooted in the understanding and application of psychological theories and empirical findings to promote and maintain physical health (Friedman & Adler, 2011). With the growing interest and increasing understanding of the nuanced operations of the brain, the application of clinical neuropsychology to further understand aspects of physical health has become a topic of much attention. The practice of neuropsychological assessment involves creating a contextualized understanding of the cognitive profile of individuals, and studying the impact of such alterations in cognitive functioning on functional status and treatment prognosis. Thus, in contrast to the symptom-focused medical model used by physicians, neuropsychological assessment provides a framework for the understanding of cognitive decline and impairment within a person-centered context (Lezak, Howieson, & Loring, 2004).

In this chapter, our goal is to briefly introduce the field of neuropsychological assessment, specifically discussing its relevance for research and clinical practice in health psychology. We also introduce the various domains of functioning that comprise a comprehensive neuropsychological assessment. Much of this is presented using examples from the multiple sclerosis (MS) and breast cancer literatures, both of which provide substantial research-based evidence for the functional significance of cognitive impairment. The assessment of neuropsychological functioning, however, is also critical for several other chronic health conditions, such as in individuals with a variety of cardiovascular diseases, who show increased risk of cognitive impairment (Eggermont et al., 2012), resulting in poor management of the chronic disease and increased mortality rates (Zuccalà et al., 2003).

Relevance of Neuropsychological Assessment to Health Psychology

Neuropsychological assessment, a major focus of assessment among health psychologists, is primarily employed for diagnostic and treatment planning purposes (Lezak et al., 2004). Broadly defined, the study and practice of neuropsychological assessment involves the use of standardized tests to understand the profile of cognitive deficits in individuals with various health conditions. Assessment data are then considered within the context of the patient's health, disease, psychological, social, and behavioral factors in order to guide diagnostic hypotheses and aid in treatment planning.

For example, within MS, a neurodegenerative disease of the central nervous system (CNS), approximately 43–70% of individuals suffer from cognitive impairments (Rao, Leo, Bernardin, & Unverzagt, 1991). Approximately 40–80% of MS patients become unemployed within 10 years of symptom onset (Kornblith, LaRocca, & Baum, 1986), and cognitive difficulties are the single largest predictor of unemployment in this population (LaRocca, 1995). Cognitive impairment has also been linked to functional status of MS patients (Kessler, Cohen, Lauer, & Kausch, 1992), such that those with cognitive impairment participate in fewer social activities, are more prone to psychiatric illnesses, and have significant troubles in carrying out everyday household activities (Rao, Leo, Ellington et al., 1991). Differential deficits in cognition have also been associated with specific everyday limitations. For example, memory impairments are associated with difficulty in activities of daily living (Kessler et al., 1992). Similar associations between cognitive dysfunction and health-related quality of life have also been reported in individuals with breast cancer (Tchen et al., 2003), chronic heart failure (Pressler et al., 2010), and stroke (Tatemichi et al., 1994). Thus, cognitive function is a critical moderator of the influence of chronic disease on functional status.

Additionally, mounting evidence provides support for the role of cognitive impairment as an independent prognostic marker, influencing mortality rates (Goodwin, Samet, & Hunt, 1996; Zuccalà et al., 2003), treatment adherence (Stilley, Bender, Dunbar-Jacob, Sereika, & Ryan, 2010), and performance on activities of daily living (Rao, Leo, Ellington et al., 1991). For example, cancer patients undergoing surgery, chemotherapy, radiation, and/or endocrine therapy often experience cognitive dysfunction (Ahles, Root, & Ryan, 2012), which appears to improve over time after patients have completed treatment (Jim et al., 2012). In a prospective population-based study of older cancer patients, those who were cognitively impaired following diagnosis had reduced 10-year survival rates compared with those who were not cognitively impaired (Goodwin et al., 1996). Preliminary evidence also suggests that cognitive impairment can decrease breast cancer survivors' adherence to their prescribed medications (Stilley et al., 2010); with this association between cognitive function and adherence also extending to other chronic health conditions such as patients being treated for hyperlipidemia, and diabetic patients with comorbid conditions (Stilley et al., 2010). Additionally, in cross-sectional analyses examining breast cancer survivors one year after taking medical leave for cancer treatment, those with poorer neuropsychological test performance were less likely to have returned to work than those with better performance (Nieuwenhuijsen, de Boer, Spelten, Sprangers, & Verbeek, 2009).

Similarly, heart failure patients also represent a population at particularly high risk for cognitive impairment, with an odds ratio of 1.62:1 in favor of cognitive decline (Vogels, Scheltens, Schroeder-Tanka, & Weinstein, 2007). Within this population as well, the impact of cognitive dysfunction can extend beyond quality of life outcomes to predict mortality. In a large sample of heart failure patients ($n=1,113$), cognitively impaired patients were almost five times as likely to die within one year of hospital admittance, compared with cognitively preserved patients, with a significant negative correlation between cognitive functioning and in-hospital mortality rates (Zuccala et al., 2003). Because cognitive status can directly impact medical treatment effectiveness and possibly lead to increases in mortality rates, neuropsychological assessment should optimally be conducted both before and during in-patient and out-patient treatment. Given the known associations between cognitive status and health outcomes, it is thus imperative that the practice and research of health psychology include a thorough assessment of cognitive status.

Considerations for Neuropsychological Assessment With Health Populations

An essential element of psychological assessment is the integration of a patient's history and behavior with the test data, in order to address a clearly defined referral question (Graham & Naglieri, 2003). Likewise, neuropsychological assessment within clinical health psychology examines the interplay of contextual factors on cognitive test data, as well as the behavioral and psychological ramifications of such alterations in cognitive functioning.

Typical health-related, neuropsychological referral questions include whether cognitive impairment is a result of organic insult to the CNS or a product of secondary comorbidities such as anxiety or fatigue. Professionals may also want to know whether the individual's cognitive status impacts outside duties, such as returning to work or receiving and tailoring occupational rehabilitation. Neuropsychological measures may also be included as primary or secondary outcomes in behavioral intervention research trials of patients with health conditions. For example, researchers who plan to longitudinally explore subtle illness-related cognitive changes should select measurements that can detect small performance differences without substantial practice effects (Wefel, Vardy, Ahles, & Schagen, 2011). In addition, researchers may want to consider the cognitive status of participants prior to their inclusion in research trials, as cognitive impairment could impede their ability to engage in intervention tasks.

In addition to traditional psychometric guidelines (American Psychological Association, 1999), the selection of assessment tools for use in health psychology often requires further considerations. Although construct validity can be assumed when the measure has been validated in healthy controls, internal consistency and test–retest reliability estimates should be verified in disease-specific samples before implementing the measure in a clinical setting. Here, we discuss estimates of validity and reliability in MS and cancer populations, as available, for broad and domain-specific measurements. However, the health psychology assessment literature is limited by the lack of disease-specific psychometric data. Clinicians and researchers should revisit test properties for use with other medical populations not mentioned here.

Another critical issue in the selection of measures for neuropsychological assessment is the choice between fixed and flexible batteries. Comprehensive batteries, as opposed to domain-specific measurements, are appropriate for assessing fitness and progress in rehabilitation settings, progression of neurodegenerative disease, and interval testing in disorders that may present with a varying impairment pattern (Graham & Naglieri, 2003; Lezak et al., 2004). Although a flexible battery can be individually tailored, a fixed battery can ease interpretation, depending on the standardization sample available. Notably, standardized scoring for health populations is most widely available for the Wechsler assessment scales, such as the Wechsler Adult Intelligence Scale–IV (WAIS-IV) and Wechsler Memory Scale (WMS-IV). The WAIS-IV is reliable and valid in the MS population, with 65% sensitivity and 65% specificity for determining MS diagnosis using the processing speed index composite score (Ryan, Gontkovsky, Kreiner, & Tree, 2012). The use of composite scores may ease interpretation, but this method can also overlook more nuanced strengths and weaknesses within a sample. For instance, MS patients present with significantly lower processing speed index scores, but exhibit preserved verbal comprehension index scores, despite a lower overall full-scale IQ (Ryan et al., 2012). Therefore, an assessment that only reports full-scale IQ may overlook nuanced aspects of cognitive decline. Clinicians are urged to utilize the WAIS-IV analyses of strengths and weaknesses to provide a thorough conceptualization of cognitive decline profiles.

Although the WAIS-IV is a widely used battery that was originally developed for use in healthy adults, many batteries have been devised for use with specific health populations. Rao's Brief Repeatable Battery (BRB) is a well-established battery in the MS literature (Rao, 1990). This 35-min battery includes five subtests covering domains of attention and working memory, verbal memory, spatial memory, and verbal fluency. Scores can be used to form a composite, but norms are also available for subtest comparison. The composite battery is reliable and valid, but some subtests, such as the Symbol Digit Modalities Test, are more prone to practice effects than others, such as the Paced Auditory Serial Addition Test (Portaccio et al., 2010). A recent randomized controlled trial to assess the effect of a strategy-based video-game intervention on cognitive functioning in a MS sample utilized the BRB as the main outcome measure (Janssen et al., 2015). The BRB allowed for the assessment of overall intervention effectiveness on a composite score of cognitive functioning, and further analyses of individual subdomain effects revealed a significant change in visuospatial memory performance. Utilization of such population-specific fixed batteries with reliable and valid norms represents an ideal confluence of domain-specific measurement within a structured format.

Neuropsychologists may also consider strengths and limitations of different administration methods. For example, computerized assessments often lend themselves to less labor-intensive administration, can be readily reproduced, and may overcome some issues present in paper–pencil tests, such as difficulty in measuring psychomotor slowing (Cheung, Tan, & Chan, 2012). However, new bias may be introduced when using tests with patient populations who lack proficiency in use of computers. Validation and comparison with traditional neuropsychological tools is necessary prior to use.

Obtaining a measure of the individual's best performance is also essential to addressing the referral question (Lezak et al., 2004), so the impact of disease-related factors warrants careful consideration for those with chronic illnesses. A variety of common chronic health conditions can contribute to cognitive dysfunction, so the examiner should obtain medical reports about comorbid illnesses and medications, which can also affect cognition (Kelly & Doty, 1995). In addition, physical symptoms, such as pain (Hart, Martelli, & Zasler, 2000) and fatigue (Tchen et al., 2003), associated with one's illness must also be considered when conducting a neuropsychological assessment. Patients should be tested when their pain and fatigue is well managed (Hart et al., 2000), but effects of both these variables and medication (e.g., sedatives, analgesics) must be taken into account during test interpretation.

Mood state can also impact cognitive function, and those with chronic illness often experience heightened emotional distress compared with healthy adults. For example, about 25–50% individuals with MS meet criteria for major depression (Chwastiak et al., 2002). In a recent meta-analysis, depressed individuals had decreased executive function and slower processing speed than control participants (Snyder, 2013). Accordingly, neuropsychological testing is optimally accompanied by a thorough assessment of mood and psychopathology.

Assessment of Cognitive Domains

In the following sections, we highlight the cognitive domains typically included in the neuropsychological study of health psychology. We provide a broad definition of each construct, followed by a discussion of commonly used measures that assess the domain of interest. Reliability and validity data are provided when available for the MS and breast cancer populations.

Gross Assessment of Cognitive Functioning

Neuropsychological screening tools may be useful for gauging general cognitive performance under time constraints. Short screening batteries are recommended for bedside differential diagnoses assessment, and can bluntly measure the presence or absence of impairment (Graham & Naglieri, 2003; Lezak et al., 2004). However, these screening tools do not typically provide domain-specific or differential diagnostic information.

The Mini Mental Status Examination (MMSE) is widely used to rapidly screen for moderate to severe cognitive deficits, and can be performed at the bedside in under 10 min, (Folstein, Folstein, & Mchugh, 1975). A cut-off score (e.g., 24 out of 30) is traditionally used to identify cognitive impairment. However, given that age and education level strongly influence MMSE scores, employing a set cut-off score for all populations is a limitation of the MMSE (Tombaugh & Mcintyre, 1992). MMSE is not typically well suited to detect the slight cognitive changes that are present in a population such as breast cancer and does not distinguish those with mild cognitive impairment from healthy controls (Mitchell, 2009).

Given the ceiling effects of the MMSE, the High-Sensitivity Cognitive Screen (HSCS) was developed to assess mild cognitive impairment, or changes over time in higher-functioning patients (Fogel, 1991). In 20–30 min, patients complete paper-and-pencil tasks that assess memory, attention/concentration, language, visual/motor, spatial, and self-regulation and planning domains. Most items are adapted from other standardized tests, and a scoring algorithm classifies performance as normal, borderline, or abnormal (with mild, moderate, or severe impairment). The initial validation study reported good interrater reliability in a relatively small sample, but test–retest reliability was lower (< 0.8) for several items (Fogel, 1991). Despite its use in multiple cancer samples, HSCS reliability and validity data have not been consistently reported. Thus, researchers are advised to report HSCS test properties within medical samples, and to cautiously interpret data, as overestimation of deficits is possible.

Domain-Specific Measurements

We next describe domain-specific assessment tools, which can be utilized as stand-alone measures or included in comprehensive flexible assessment batteries. Although many clinical and laboratory measures exist, we discuss selected measures in this brief chapter (please see Lezak et al., 2004, for a more complete compilation).

Executive Functioning

Executive functioning is a broad construct that subsumes a variety of subdomains, with significant debate on its key facets and appropriate subdomain measures. We will employ the framework outlined by Miyake and colleagues (2000), who suggest executive functioning includes three related, yet distinct subdomains: mental set shifting, information updating, and monitoring and inhibition of pre-potent responses (Miyake et al., 2000).

Mental set-shifting taps into the ability to hold multiple attentional sets simultaneously and efficiently maneuver back and forth between them. A classic paper-and-pencil test of set-shifting ability is the Trail Making Test (TMT; Reitan, 1955). The task has two conditions: Trails A requires individuals to sequentially connect numbered or lettered circles on a worksheet, whereas Trails B requires patients to alternate between the number and letter sequences. The subtraction score (Trails B − Trails A) represents a comparatively longer time to complete Trails B, relative to Trails A, and can indicate difficulty in executive switching. The subtraction score distinguishes set-shifting abilities from deficits in motor control, especially in populations with established motor impairments (e.g., MS patients), and increases construct validity for switching deficits, compared with Trails B alone ($r^2 = .6$; Atkinson et al., 2010). Individuals with cancer and MS both appear to exhibit deficits on mental set-shifting tasks (Grigsby, Kaye, & Busenbark, 1994; Wefel et al., 2011). Age and education can influence TMT test–retest reliability (Ernst, 1987), which is relatively susceptible to practice effects after 6 weeks (Stuss et al., 2001), but is less prone to carryover effects after 6 months (Abe et al., 2004). Several other measures for mental set-shifting exist. For example, the Wisconsin Card Sorting Test (WCST) requires patients to match a series of 120 target cards to a set of reference cards according to certain attributes ("rules"), which change throughout the testing session (Grant & Berg, 1948). The WCST, however, is a one-shot test with significant practice effects, poor alternate form reliability in healthy controls (0.63 at best; Bowden et al., 1998), and poor internal validity, with a significant negative skew toward errors and perseverations (Bowden et al., 1998), so it is not particularly suitable for intervention research.

Inhibitory control involves the selection of responses based on task demands, while ignoring task-irrelevant (often pre-potent or habitual) tendencies. The Stroop task is widely used to measure inhibitory control (Stroop, 1935), over and above deficits that might be associated with processing speed, color-blindness, and reading difficulties. The primary measure of interest is the number of correct responses for the interference condition. Patients are presented with color words, printed in incongruent ink colors, and are required to name the color of the ink, thus over-riding the habitual tendency to respond to the semantic meaning of the word and leading to interference in this condition. Reliability in the MS population has been established (intraclass correlation coefficient [ICC]=0.89), and convergent validity was verified with a well-established battery of executive functioning ($R^2 = .78$; Portaccio et al., 2010).

Working memory refers to the capacity to monitor, update, and manipulate task-relevant information. Working memory can be assessed in research and clinical settings using widely available, reliable, and valid assessment tools. On the Digit-Span (Backward) task, individuals listen to digit sequences of increasing set-size, and report the numbers in reverse order. This test, which is included in the WAIS-IV and WMS-III, measures the construct of verbal working memory (Banken, 1985). Studies suggest good reliability and validity estimates for this measure (Wechsler, 1958). Another measure of working memory, commonly used in the MS literature, is the Paced Auditory Serial Addition Test (PASAT; Gronwall, 1977). This task requires patients to add a specified digit to the digit immediately preceding it. Patients complete 61 items, and digits are presented at two rates: one digit every 3 s and one digit every 2 s. The PASAT boasts well-established norms for the MS population, and is a recommended measure for clinical outcome trials (Boringa et al., 2001; Cutter et al., 1999). Although significant practice effects exist, ICCs are acceptable (0.9–0.84; Portaccio et al., 2010) and sensitivity and specificity for predicting the presence of MS are robust (74% and 65%, respectively).

Information Processing Speed

Information processing speed, or the rate at which exogenous stimuli can be processed, is a fundamental ability underlying various higher-order cognitive domains (Salthouse, 1996). The Symbol Digit Modalities Test (SDMT) is a commonly used processing speed measure (Smith, 1982). This task requires patients to view a decoding key, consisting of a series of nine symbols paired with corresponding digits. Then, a sequence of unpaired symbols is presented at the bottom of the page, and patients either write or voice the digit associated with each symbol as quickly as possible. When known visuo-motor impairments are present, the oral version might be preferable over the written format. For example, in individuals with MS, the oral SDMT is the most widely disseminated task of processing speed as it removes the variance associated with motor decrements (Drake et al., 2010). The SDMT has good test–retest reliability ($r=.98$) and better concurrent validity for diagnosis, course, and vocational status than the PASAT (Drake et al., 2010). Caution should be taken for interpretations of SDMT scores in the elderly, due to mental slowing (Salthouse, 1996).

Attention

Attention is a universal property of multiple systems (Chun, Golomb, & Turk-Browne, 2011), and thus should be considered as an influential factor on performance on most tasks. Neuropsychological tasks that tap into the broad domain of attention can be distinguished on the demands they make for divided, selective, or sustained attention processes (Chun et al., 2011).

Divided attention, or the processing of two attentional targets at once, can be measured using a variety of dual-task performance tests. These tests can consist of two simultaneous cognitive tasks, or a cognitive and motor task performed concurrently. For example, to assess dual-task fall risk in people with balance issues, patients are asked to walk while counting backward (Kressig, Beauchet, & European GAITRite Network Group, 2006). Divided attention is measured by the difference in performance between the dual-task versus single task condition. Although this measure lacks MS-specific normative data, dual-task walking assessments are reliable (ICC=0.84; Hars, Herrmann, & Trombetti, 2013) and valid prospective predictors of fall risk in older adults (Beauchet et al., 2009) and in individuals with MS (Hamilton et al., 2009). Dual-task performance can be particularly helpful in assessing functional status, which often guides decisions on return to independent living.

Selective attention directs our limited processing capacity to salient aspects of the environment, while ignoring other goal-irrelevant stimuli. The Eriksen flanker task (Eriksen & Eriksen, 1974), a commonly used selective attention task, requires individuals to selectively attend to the direction of a target arrow, while ignoring the direction of the two flanking arrows on either side. Larger reaction time values for incongruent, relative to congruent trials, indicate poorer selective attention performance (although see Lavie, 2005, for an alternative and compelling interpretation of incongruency effects in the case of the Eriksen flanker task). In a neuroimaging study, posttreatment breast cancer patients who received high-dose chemotherapy made significantly more Flanker task errors than those who did not receive chemotherapy (de Ruiter et al., 2011). A recent NIH initiative to provide widely disseminable research tools (NIH Toolbox) has established reliability (ICC=0.95), convergent validity ($r=-.48; p<.001$), and divergent validity ($r=.15; p<.01$) of this task in a sample of over 300 individuals aged 8–85 years (Weintraub et al., 2013).

Sustained attention involves continuously attending to and detecting stimuli over extended periods. For example, the visual Continuous Performance Test (CPT; Conners & Staff, 2000) requires individuals to respond when letters (targets) appear on the screen, except for the letter X (nontarget). Measures of commission (responding to nontarget stimuli) and omission (failing to respond to target stimuli) can be calculated. The manual version has been widely used for the assessment of attention-deficit/hyperactivity disorder, with well-established norms, reliability, and validity estimates (Conners & Staff, 2000). Notably, both breast cancer and MS patients exhibit preserved sustained attention capacity (Paul, Beatty, Schneider, Blanco, & Hames, 1998; Tchen et al., 2003).

Memory and Learning

Subjective memory complaints are often reported as the primary reason for referral to neuropsychological assessment (Lezak et al., 2004). Memory deficits can occur at any of three memory stages: encoding, the initial transformation of a stimulus; storage, the long-term maintenance of successfully encoded information; or retrieval, the ability to locate and bring to present awareness information from memory storage (Squire & Knowlton, 2000). Retrieval can be assessed through either free recall of encoded information or recognition, which utilizes cues to trigger the retrieval of information from storage, thus requiring less cognitive effort. Because information retention is the goal of memory assessment, these measures are especially prone to practice effects. When choosing a memory measure, the examiner should take special caution to verify test–retest reliability and use alternate test forms. A commonly used fixed battery for memory assessment with alternate form reliability is the Wechsler Memory Scale (WMS; Wechsler, 1945). Comprising seven subtests, the WMS assesses auditory memory, visual memory, visual working memory, immediate memory, and delayed memory. Although we are unable to cover the breadth of WMS tasks in this short chapter, the use of such a comprehensive battery for thorough memory assessment is encouraged when referral questions require discrimination between types of memory dysfunction.

Differentiation of memory encoding versus retrieval failure can often be accomplished using multitrial learning paradigms, such as Buschke's Selective Reminding Task (SRT; Buschke & Fuld, 1974). This task requires patients to memorize a list of 12 orally presented words over six repeated trials, while being selectively reminded of forgotten items after each trial or until all words are remembered correctly. A delayed recall trial occurs 11 min later. Early implementations of the SRT in MS patients implicated primary retrieval failure because of impaired performance on recall compared to recognition measures. However, a variant of the SRT using 12 recall trials (instead of six) revealed primary encoding decrements on initial trials, and preserved retrieval functioning on later trials due to decreased processing load (DeLuca, Barbieri-Berger, & Johnson, 1994). The test–retest reliability is fairly robust (0.62–0.73, varying by form), and construct validity and norms are well-established in the MS population (Boringa et al., 2001). Another commonly used measure within health psychology is the California Verbal Learning Test (CVLT; Delis, Kramer, Kaplan, & Ober, 2000; Woods, Delis, Scott, Kramer, & Holdnack, 2006). Test–retest reliability has been determined for a healthy sample ($r=.80–.84$; Woods et al., 2006). Cancer survivors who received chemotherapy exhibited significantly greater impairment on the CVLT compared with survivors who did not receive such treatment, suggesting that chemotherapy treatment may affect verbal memory (Ahles et al., 2002).

Multitrial learning can also be applied to assess visuospatial memory using the 10/36 spatial recall test, an adaptation of Malec's original visual spatial learning test (Malec, Ivnik, & Hinkeldey, 1991). The task requires patients to replicate a visual pattern of 10 circles on a 6×6 checkerboard (36 squares) over the course of three trials, with a delayed recall component 11 min later. Both original and adapted versions of this visual spatial learning task are reliable and valid in aging and MS populations (Boringa et al., 2001; Malec et al., 1991).

Motor Control

Thorough assessment of neuropsychological functioning includes measuring various facets of motor control. Motor speed, or the ability to complete movements at an efficient pace, can influence performance on computer tasks that measure reaction time. A commonly used test of motor speed in the MS literature is the finger-tapping task (Halstead, 1947), which requires patients to tap a key as quickly as possible for 10 s followed by a brief rest period, for a total of five blocks for each hand. Test–retest reliability estimates are robust in clinical and nonclinical populations ($r=.77$; Dikmen, Heaton, Grant, & Temkin, 1999), but can be influenced by practice (Teng et al., 1989). Additional measures of inter-tap variability and response variability can also be calculated, and can differentiate presence and levels of cognitive impairment in heart failure patients, despite no significant difference between patients and controls on overall tapping speed (Sauvé, Lewis, Blankenbiller, Rickabaugh, & Pressler, 2009).

By contrast, poor performance on paper-and-pencil tasks may be influenced by decrements in fine motor control, or the coordination of small muscle movements with visual input. Deficits in fine (movement of the fingers) and gross (movement of the limbs) motor movements can influence performance on tasks requiring motor control, over and above motor speed, such as paper-and-pencil tasks commonly employed to assess other domains of cognitive functioning. An example of a fine motor task is the nine hole peg test (Kellor, Frost, Silberberg, Iversen, & Cummings, 1971). Patients are asked to place nine pegs, one at a time, into nine holes on a board, and subsequently remove them, one at a time, as fast as possible, without losing control of the pegs or board. The time to completion is the primary dependent variable, and the task is repeated for right and left hands independently. It boasts reliable and valid norms in the MS population (Drake et al., 2010) and is included as one of the measures on the Multiple Sclerosis Functional Composite Scale (MSFC), which is a battery designed to assess progression of disease severity in individuals with MS and often used as an outcome measure for clinical trials in the MS literature (Cutter et al., 1999).

The MSFC also includes the timed 25-foot walk test as a measure of gross motor control. Gross motor control measures limb coordination involved in major body movement such as walking, balance, jumping, or reaching. In the timed 25-foot walk test, patients are asked to walk as quickly and safely as possible for 25 feet, gaining speed before the start line and continuing through the finish line, to ensure times are not affected by working up to maximum speed or slowing to stop. The composite MSFC score, which includes the PASAT, the nine hole peg test, and the timed 25-foot walk test, exhibits significant concurrent validity with other disease severity measures, and is predictive of diagnosis, disease course, and work disability, underscoring the importance of motor functioning as a marker of functional status in MS (Drake et al., 2010).

Conclusions

Neuropsychological assessment fulfills an increasingly important role within health psychology, as cognitive status can influence quality of life, vocational status, and treatment adherence. This chapter has provided a brief overview of many available instruments and considerations for neuropsychological assessment within health psychology. In examining functional status, one should also consider the ecological validity, or real-world applicability, of the selected task(s), and thus employing batteries such as the Everyday Cognition Battery (Allaire & Marsiske, 1999) to assess cognitive functioning within the context of everyday tasks such as balancing a checkbook or remembering calendar events can be helpful. Future directions in the field of neuropsychological assessment aim to increase ecological validity. The compilation and availability of validated and normed assessments (NIH toolbox; Weintraub et al., 2013) and the creation of virtual environment simulation tasks are important steps in this direction, while maintaining domain specificity. These advances can then spur the development of more applicable and targeted prevention and intervention strategies, in order to reduce the individual and societal burden of cognitive decline.

References

Abe, M., Suzuki, K., Okada, K., Miura, R., Fujii, T., Etsurou, M., & Yamadori, A. (2004). Normative data on tests for frontal lobe functions: Trail Making Test, Verbal fluency, Wisconsin Card Sorting Test (Keio version) [article in Japanese]. *No to shinkei, 56*, 567–574.

Ahles, T. A., Root, J. C., & Ryan, E. L. (2012). Cancer- and cancer treatment-associated cognitive change: An update on the state of the science. *Journal of Clinical Oncology, 30*, 3675–3686. http://doi.org/10.1200/JCO.2012.43.0116

Ahles, T. A., Saykin, A. J., Furstenberg, C. T., Cole, B., Mott, L. A., Skalla, K., … Silberfarb, P. M. (2002). Neuropsychologic impact of standard-dose systemic chemotherapy in long-term survivors of breast cancer and lymphoma. *Journal of Clinical Oncology, 20*, 485–493. http://doi.org/10.1200/JCO.20.2.485

Allaire, J. C., & Marsiske, M. (1999). Everyday cognition: Age and intellectual ability correlates. *Psychology and Aging, 14*, 627–644. http://doi.org/10.1037/0882-7974.14.4.627

American Psychological Association. (1999). *Standards for educational and psychological testing.* Washington, DC: Author.

Atkinson, T. M., Ryan, J. P., Lent, A., Wallis, A., Schachter, H., & Coder, R. (2010). Three trail making tests for use in neuropsychological assessments with brief intertest intervals. *Journal of Clinical and Experimental Neuropsychology, 32*, 151–158. http://doi.org/10.1080/13803390902881934

Banken, J. (1985). Clinical utility of considering Digits Forward and Digits Backward as separate components of the Wechsler Adult Intelligence Scale-Revised. *Journal of Clinical Psychology, 41*, 686–691. http://doi.org/10.1002/1097-4679(198509)41:5<686::AID-JCLP2270410517>3.0.CO;2-D

Beauchet, O., Annweiler, C., Dubost, V., Allali, G., Kressig, R. W., Bridenbaugh, S., … Herrmann, F. R. (2009). Stops walking when talking: A predictor of falls in older adults? *European Journal of Neurology, 16*, 786–795. http://doi.org/10.1111/j.1468-1331.2009.02612.x

Boringa, J. B., Lazeron, R. H., Reuling, I. E., Adèr, H. J., Pfennings, L. E., Lindeboom, J., … Polman, C. H. (2001). The Brief Repeatable Battery of Neuropsychological Tests: Normative values allow application in multiple sclerosis clinical practice. *Multiple Sclerosis, 7*, 263–267. http://doi.org/10.1191/135245801680209385

Bowden, S. C., Fowler, K. S., Bell, R. C., Whelan, G., Clifford, C. C., Ritter, A. J., & Long, C. M. (1998). The Reliability and Internal Validity of the Wisconsin Card Sorting Test. *Neuropsychological Rehabilitation, 8*, 243–254. http://doi.org/10.1080/713755573

Buschke, H., & Fuld, P. A. (1974). Evaluating storage, retention, and retrieval in disordered memory and learning. *Neurology, 24*, 1019–1019. http://doi.org/10.1212/WNL.24.11.1019

Cheung, Y., Tan, E., & Chan, A. (2012). An evaluation on the neuropsychological tests used in the assessment of postchemotherapy cognitive changes in breast cancer survivors. *Supportive Care in Cancer, 20*, 1361–1375. http://doi.org/10.1007/s00520-012-1445-4

Chun, M. M., Golomb, J. D., & Turk-Browne, N. B. (2011). A taxonomy of external and internal attention. In S. T. Fiske, D. L. Schacter, & S. E. Taylor (Eds.), *Annual review of psychology*, (Vol. 62, pp. 73–101). Palo Alto, CA: Annual Reviews.

Chwastiak, L., Ehde, D. M., Gibbons, L. E., Sullivan, M., Bowen, J. D., & Kraft, G. H. (2002). Depressive symptoms and severity of illness in multiple sclerosis: Epidemiologic study of a large community sample. *The American Journal of Psychiatry, 159*, 1862–1868. http://doi.org/10.1176/appi.ajp.159.11.1862

Conners, C. K., & Staff, M. H. S. (2000). *Conners' Continuous Performance Test II (CPT II V. 5)*. North Tonawanda, NY: Multi-Health Systems. Retrieved from http://www.pearsonclinical.co.uk/Psychology/ChildMentalHealth/ChildADDADHDBehaviour/ConnersContinuousPerformanceTestIIVersion5forWindows(CPTIIV5)/PDFReports/Profile.pdf

Cutter, G. R., Baier, M. L., Rudick, R. A., Cookfair, D. L., Fischer, J. S., Petkau, J., ... Willoughby, E. (1999). Development of a multiple sclerosis functional composite as a clinical trial outcome measure. *Brain, 122*, 871–882. http://doi.org/10.1093/brain/122.5.871

Delis, D. C., Kramer, J. H., Kaplan, E., & Ober, B. A. (2000). *CVLT-II*. New York, NY: The Psychological Corporation.

DeLuca, J., Barbieri-Berger, S., & Johnson, S. K. (1994). The nature of memory impairments in multiple sclerosis: Acquisition versus retrieval. *Journal of Clinical and Experimental Neuropsychology, 16*, 183–189. http://doi.org/10.1080/01688639408402629

de Ruiter, M. B., Reneman, L., Boogerd, W., Veltman, D. J., van Dam, F. S. a. M., Nederveen, A. J., ... Schagen, S. B. (2011). Cerebral hyporesponsiveness and cognitive impairment 10 years after chemotherapy for breast cancer. *Human Brain Mapping, 32*, 1206–1219. http://doi.org/10.1002/hbm.21102

Dikmen, S. S., Heaton, R. K., Grant, I., & Temkin, N. R. (1999). Test-retest reliability and practice effects of Expanded Halstead-Reitan neuropsychological test battery. *Journal of the International Neuropsychological Society, 5*, 346–356. http://doi.org/10.1017/S1355617799544056

Drake, A. S., Weinstock-Guttman, B., Morrow, S. A., Hojnacki, D., Munschauer, F. E., & Benedict, R. H. B. (2010). Psychometrics and normative data for the Multiple Sclerosis Functional Composite: Replacing the PASAT with the Symbol Digit Modalities Test. *Multiple Sclerosis, 16*, 228–237. http://doi.org/10.1177/1352458509354552

Eggermont, L. H. P., de Boer, K., Muller, M., Jaschke, A. C., Kamp, O., & Scherder, E. J. A. (2012). Cardiac disease and cognitive impairment: A systematic review. *Heart, 98*, 1334–1340. http://doi.org/10.1136/heartjnl-2012-301682

Eriksen, B. A., & Eriksen, C. W. (1974). Effects of noise letters upon the identification of a target letter in a nonsearch task. *Perception & Psychophysics, 16*, 143–149. http://doi.org/10.3758/BF03203267

Ernst, J. (1987). Neuropsychological problem-solving skills in the elderly. *Psychology and Aging, 2*, 363–365. http://doi.org/10.1037/0882-7974.2.4.363

Fogel, B. S. (1991). The High Sensitivity Cognitive Screen. *International Psychogeriatrics, 3*, 273–288. http://doi.org/10.1017/S1041610291000728

Folstein, M., Folstein, S., & Mchugh, P. (1975). Mini-Mental State – practical method for grading cognitive state of patients for clinician. *Journal of Psychiatric Research, 12*, 189–198.

Friedman, H. S., & Adler, N. (2011). The intellectual roots of health psychology. In H. Friedman (Ed.), *The Oxford Handbook of Health Psychology* (pp. 3–14). London, UK: Oxford University Press.

Goodwin, J. S., Samet, J. M., & Hunt, W. C. (1996). Determinants of survival in older cancer patients. *Journal of the National Cancer Institute, 88*, 1031–1038. http://doi.org/10.1093/jnci/88.15.1031

Graham, J. R., & Naglieri, J. A. (2003). *Handbook of psychology, assessment psychology*. Hoboken, NJ: Wiley.

Grant, D. A., & Berg, E. (1948). A behavioral analysis of degree of reinforcement and ease of shifting to new responses in a Weigl-type card-sorting problem. *Journal of Experimental Psychology, 38*, 404–411. http://doi.org/10.1037/h0059831

Grigsby, J., Kaye, K., & Busenbark, D. (1994). Alphanumeric sequencing: A report on a brief measure of information processing used among persons with multiple sclerosis. *Perceptual and Motor Skills, 78*, 883–887. http://doi.org/10.2466/pms.1994.78.3.883

Gronwall, D. M. A. (1977). Paced auditory serial-addition task: A measure of recovery from concussion. *Perceptual and Motor Skills, 44*, 367–373. http://doi.org/10.2466/pms.1977.44.2.367

Halstead, W. C. (1947). *Brain and intelligence; a quantitative study of the frontal lobes* (Vol. XIII). Chicago, IL: University of Chicago Press.

Hamilton, F., Rochester, L., Paul, L., Rafferty, D., O'Leary, C. P., & Evans, J. J. (2009). Walking and talking: An investigation of cognitive-motor dual tasking in multiple sclerosis. *Multiple Sclerosis, 15*, 1215–1227. http://doi.org/10.1177/1352458509106712

Hars, M., Herrmann, F. R., & Trombetti, A. (2013). Reliability and minimal detectable change of gait variables in community-dwelling and hospitalized older fallers. *Gait & Posture, 38*, 1010–1014. http://doi.org/10.1016/j.gaitpost.2013.05.015

Hart, R. P., Martelli, M. F., & Zasler, N. D. (2000). Chronic pain and neuropsychological functioning. *Neuropsychology Review, 10*, 131–149. http://doi.org/10.1023/A:1009020914358

Janssen, A., Boster, A., Lee, H., Patterson, B. A., & Prakash, R.S. (2015). The effects of video-game training on broad cognitive transfer in multiple sclerosis: A pilot, randomized controlled trial. *Journal of Clinical and Experimental Neuropsychology, 37*(3), 285–302. http://doi.org/10.1080/13803395.2015.1009366

Jim, H. S. L., Phillips, K. M., Chait, S., Faul, L. A., Popa, M. A., Lee, Y.-H., ... Small, B. J. (2012). Meta-analysis of cognitive functioning in breast cancer survivors previously treated with standard-dose chemotherapy. *Journal of Clinical Oncology, 30*, 3578–3587. http://doi.org/10.1200/JCO.2011.39.5640

Kellor, M., Frost, J., Silberberg, N., Iversen, I., & Cummings, R. (1971). Hand strength and dexterity. *American Journal of Occupational Therapy, 25*(2), 77–83.

Kelly, M. P., & Doty, R. E. (1995). Neuropsychological dysfunction: Research and evaluation. In P. M. Nicassio & T. W. Smith (Eds.), *Managing chronic illness: A biopsychosocial perspective* (pp. 117–162). Washington, DC: American Psychological Association.

Kessler, H., Cohen, R., Lauer, K., & Kausch, D. (1992). The relationship between disability and memory dysfunction in multiple sclerosis. *International Journal of Neuroscience, 62*(1–2), 17–34. http://doi.org/10.3109/00207459108999754

Kornblith, A., Larocca, N., & Baum, H. (1986). Employment in individuals with multiple sclerosis. *International Journal of Rehabilitation Research, 9*, 155–165. http://doi.org/10.1097/00004356-198606000-00006

Kressig, R. W., Beauchet, O., & European GAITRite Network Group. (2006). Guidelines for clinical applications of spatio-temporal gait analysis in older adults. *Aging Clinical and Experimental Research, 18*, 174–176. http://doi.org/10.1007/BF03327437

LaRocca, N. G. (1995). *Employment and multiple sclerosis*. New York, NY: National Multiple Sclerosis Society.

Lavie, N. (2005). Distracted and confused? Selective attention under load. *Trends in Cognitive Sciences, 9*(2), 75–82. http://doi.org/10.1016/j.tics.2004.12.004

Lezak, M. D., Howieson, D.B., & Loring, D. W. (2004). *Neuropsychological assessment* (4th ed.). New York, NY: Oxford University Press.

Malec, J. F., Ivnik, R. J., & Hinkeldey, N. S. (1991). Visual Spatial Learning Test. *Psychological Assessment: A Journal of Consulting and Clinical Psychology, 3*(1), 82–88. http://doi.org/10.1037/1040-3590.3.1.82

Mitchell, A. J. (2009). A meta-analysis of the accuracy of the mini-mental state examination in the detection of dementia and mild cognitive impairment. *Journal of Psychiatric Research, 43*, 411–431. http://doi.org/10.1016/j.jpsychires.2008.04.014

Miyake, A., Friedman, N. P., Emerson, M. J., Witzki, A. H., Howerter, A., & Wager, T. D. (2000). The unity and diversity of executive functions and their contributions to complex "Frontal Lobe" tasks: A latent variable analysis. *Cognitive Psychology, 41*(1), 49–100. http://doi.org/10.1006/cogp.1999.0734

Nieuwenhuijsen, K., de Boer, A., Spelten, E., Sprangers, M. A. G., & Verbeek, J. H. A. M. (2009). The role of neuropsychological functioning in cancer survivors' return to work one year after diagnosis. *Psycho-Oncology, 18*, 589–597. http://doi.org/10.1002/pon.1439

Paul, R. H., Beatty, W. W., Schneider, R., Blanco, C., & Hames, K. (1998). Impairments of attention in individuals with multiple sclerosis. *Multiple Sclerosis, 4*, 433–439. http://doi.org/10.1191/135245898678919438

Portaccio, E., Goretti, B., Zipoli, V., Iudice, A., Della Pina, D., Malentacchi, G. M., ... Amato, M. P. (2010). Reliability, practice effects, and change indices for Rao's brief repeatable battery. *Multiple Sclerosis Journal, 16*, 611–617. http://doi.org/10.1177/1352458510362818

Pressler, S. J., Subramanian, U., Kareken, D., Perkins, S. M., Gradus-Pizlo, I., Sauve, M. J., ... Shaw, R. M. (2010). Cognitive deficits and health-related quality of life in chronic heart failure. *Journal of Cardiovascular Nursing, 25*, 189–198. http://doi.org/10.1097/JCN.0b013e3181ca36fe

Rao, S. M. (1990). *A manual for the brief, repeatable battery of neuropsychological tests in multiple sclerosis*. New York, NY: National Multiple Sclerosis Society.

Rao, S., Leo, G., Bernardin, L., & Unverzagt, F. (1991). Cognitive dysfunction in multiple sclerosis. I. Frequency, patterns, and prediction. *Neurology, 41*, 685–691. http://doi.org/10.1212/WNL.41.5.685

Rao, S. M., Leo, G. J., Ellington, L., Nauertz, T., Bernardin, L., & Unverzagt, F. (1991). Cognitive dysfunction in multiple sclerosis. II. Impact on employment and social functioning. *Neurology, 41*, 692–696. http://doi.org/10.1212/WNL.41.5.692

Reitan, R. M. (1955). The relation of the Trail Making Test to organic brain damage. *Journal of Consulting Psychology, 19*, 393–394. http://doi.org/10.1037/h0044509

Ryan, J. J., Gontkovsky, S. T., Kreiner, D. S., & Tree, H. A. (2012). Wechsler Adult Intelligence Scale-Fourth Edition performance in relapsing-remitting multiple sclerosis. *Journal of Clinical and Experimental Neuropsychology, 34*, 571–579. http://doi.org/10.1080/13803395.2012.666229

Salthouse, T. A. (1996). The processing-speed theory of adult age differences in cognition. *Psychological Review, 103*, 403–428. http://doi.org/10.1037/0033-295X.103.3.403

Smith, A. (1982). *Symbol Digit Modality Test manual*. Los Angeles, CA: Western Psychological Services.

Snyder, H. R. (2013). Major depressive disorder is associated with broad impairments on neuropsychological measures of executive function: A meta-analysis and review. *Psychological Bulletin, 139*(1), 81–132. http://doi.org/10.1037/a0028727

Squire, L. R., & Knowlton, B. J. (2000). The medial temporal lobe, the hippocampus, and the memory systems of the brain. *The New Cognitive Neurosciences, 2*, 756–776.

Stilley, C. S., Bender, C. M., Dunbar-Jacob, J., Sereika, S., & Ryan, C. M. (2010). The impact of cognitive function on medication management: Three studies. *Health Psychology, 29*(1), 50–55. http://doi.org/10.1037/a0016940

Stroop, J. R. (1935). Studies of interference in serial verbal reactions. *Journal of Experimental Psychology, 18*, 643–662. http://doi.org/10.1037/h0054651

Stuss, D. T., Bisschop, S. M., Alexander, M. P., Levine, B., Katz, D., & Izukawa, D. (2001). The trail making test: A study in focal lesion patients. *Psychological Assessment, 13*, 230–239. http://doi.org/10.1037/1040-3590.13.2.230

Sauvé, M. J., Lewis, W. R., Blankenbiller, M., Rickabaugh, B., & Pressler, S. J. (2009). Cognitive impairments in chronic heart failure: A case controlled study. *Journal of Cardiac Failure, 15*(1), 1–10. http://doi.org/10.1016/j.cardfail.2008.08.007

Tatemichi, T. K., Desmond, D. W., Stern, Y., Paik, M., Sano, M., & Bagiella, E. (1994). Cognitive impairment after stroke: Frequency, patterns, and relationship to functional abilities. *Journal of Neurology, Neurosurgery & Psychiatry, 57*, 202–207. http://doi.org/10.1136/jnnp.57.2.202

Tchen, N., Juffs, H. G., Downie, F. P., Yi, Q.-L., Hu, H., Chemerynsky, I., … Warr, D. (2003). Cognitive function, fatigue, and menopausal symptoms in women receiving adjuvant chemotherapy for breast cancer. *Journal of Clinical Oncology, 21*, 4175–4183. http://doi.org/10.1200/JCO.2003.01.119

Teng, E., Wimer, C., Roberts, E., Damasio, A., Eslinger, P., Folstein, M., … Henderson, V. (1989). Alzheimer's dementia – performance on parallel forms of the Dementia Assessment Battery. *Journal of Clinical and Experimental Neuropsychology, 11*, 899–912. http://doi.org/10.1080/01688638908400943

Tombaugh, T., & Mcintyre, N. (1992). The Mini-Mental State Examination – a comprehensive review. *Journal of the American Geriatrics Society, 40*, 922–935. http://doi.org/10.1111/j.1532-5415.1992.tb01992.x

Vogels, R. L., Scheltens, P., Schroeder-Tanka, J. M., & Weinstein, H. C. (2007). Cognitive impairment in heart failure: A systematic review of the literature. *European Journal of Heart Failure, 9*, 440–449. http://doi.org/10.1016/j.ejheart.2006.11.001

Wechsler, D. (1945). *Wechsler Memory Scale*. San Antonio, TX: Psychological Corporation.

Wechsler, D. (1958). *The measurement and appraisal of adult intelligence* (4th ed., Vol. IX). Baltimore, MD: Williams & Wilkins. http://doi.org/10.1037/11167-000

Wefel, J., Vardy, J., Ahles, T., & Schagen, S. (2011). International Cognition and Cancer Task Force recommendations to harmonise studies of cognitive function in patients with cancer. *Lancet Oncology, 12*, 703–708. http://doi.org/10.1016/S1470-2045(10)70294-1

Weintraub, S., Dikmen, S. S., Heaton, R. K., Tulsky, D. S., Zelazo, P. D., Bauer, P. J., … Gershon, R. C. (2013). Cognition assessment using the NIH Toolbox. *Neurology, 80*(11 Suppl. 3), S54–S64. http://doi.org/10.1212/WNL.0b013e3182872ded

Woods, S. P., Delis, D. C., Scott, J. C., Kramer, J. H., & Holdnack, J. A. (2006). The California Verbal Learning Test – second edition: Test-retest reliability, practice effects, and reliable change indices for the standard and alternate forms. *Archives of Clinical Neuropsychology, 21*, 413–420. http://doi.org/10.1016/j.acn.2006.06.002

Zuccalà, G., Pedone, C., Cesari, M., Onder, G., Pahor, M., Marzetti, E., … Bernabei, R. (2003). The effects of cognitive impairment on mortality among hospitalized patients with heart failure. *The American Journal of Medicine, 115*, 97–103. http://doi.org/10.1016/S0002-9343(03)00264-X

Chapter 17

Biological and Physiological Measures in Health Psychology

Suzanne C. Segerstrom[1], Dorothée Out[2], Douglas A. Granger[2,3], and Timothy W. Smith[4]

[1]University of Kentucky, Lexington, KY, USA
[2]Arizona State University, Institute for Interdisciplinary Salivary Bioscience Research, Tempe, AZ, USA
[3]Johns Hopkins School of Nursing, Bloomberg School of Public Health, and School of Medicine, Baltimore, MD, USA
[4]University of Utah, Salt Lake City, UT, USA

Introduction

The interaction between psychological and physiological systems is an important facet of health psychology with a long history, perhaps dating back to ancient theories of the four humors. A modern health psychologist, rather than being concerned with whether a patient has a preponderance of black bile, might be interested in whether particular psychological characteristics correlate with biomarkers indicating disease risk, development, or progression; whether a particular psychological state can be distinguished from another state by its psychophysiological correlates; or whether a person's biological state is affecting their mental state. In all of these cases, the psychologist will be interested in assessing biological and physiological measures. These measures pose assessment challenges both familiar and unfamiliar to the average psychologist. Like other measures, biological and physiological measures must meet standards of reliability and validity; that is, they must have adequate *physiometrics* (Segerstrom & Smith, 2012). Unlike others, there are important issues of collection, storage, and contamination, for example.

The present chapter will give a necessarily brief overview of measurement in three physiological systems: the immune system, the neuroendocrine system, and the cardiovascular system. The investigator who does not have some experience with collecting biological and physiological outcomes is advised to use this information as a starting point and to seek out a collaborator or consultant with such experience. Those who do have this experience are usually willing to share it with colleagues who have interesting questions to explore. It is also important to work closely with the laboratory performing the assays to ensure that requirements regarding collection (what kind of tube should blood be drawn into?), transport (do samples need to be kept on ice en route to the lab?), and storage (should samples be stored at −20°C or −80°C?) are met.

The Immune System

Short Introduction

The immune system is a collection of organs, cells, and proteins whose missions could be described as recognizing anything in the body that is not self and destroying or neutralizing the invader (see Clark, 2008, for an accessible book-length description of the immune system). Even abnormal self (e.g., cancerous cells) can be recognized and destroyed. The grossest division in the immune system is between innate and acquired immunity. Innate immunity is phylogenetically old. It is mediated by cells including macrophages and natural killer cells that recognize nonspecific signals that something is wrong – tissue damage, for example, or infection – and respond in nonspecific ways. One of the main responses of the innate immune system is inflammation. Acute inflammation is an adaptive response that fights potential infections by drawing immune cells to the site of the problem, activating those cells to kill microbes, and promoting the initiation of healing. However, chronic inflammation – for example, due to aging or obesity – can lead to further health problems. High levels of inflammation have been linked to higher risk of a number of diseases and disorders, including heart disease, Alzheimer's disease, lymphoma, and frailty (Ershler & Keller, 2000; Papanicolaou, Wilder, Manolagas, & Chrousos, 1998; Ross, 1999).

Acquired immunity is phylogenetically newer and also more complex. It is mediated primarily by T and B lymphocytes. Each of these lymphocytes has a receptor that is specific for a particular protein fragment, or *antigen*. Therefore, one lymphocyte may recognize an antigen from a pneumococcus bacterium, whereas its neighbor recognizes an antigen from the varicella (chicken pox) virus. When such recognition occurs, the cell begins to divide or *proliferate*, creating a population of cells with the same ability to recognize the relevant antigen. Different types of lymphocytes then fight the invader in different ways. B cells manufacture *antibody*, which binds to the antigen. If bound to a virus or toxin, antibody may neutralize it. If bound to a bacterium or cell, antibody may mark it for destruction. Cytotoxic T cells cause infected cells to commit apoptosis (cell suicide). Helper T cells direct the immune system's energies in one direction or another (e.g., inflammation, antibody production, or cytotoxicity) by releasing *cytokines*, proteins that activate some facet of immunity and often inhibit others. There are a number of different kinds of helper T cells that are identified by the pattern of cytokines they release. Importantly, multiple aspects of the immune system must coordinate in order to mount an effective response. Cells of the innate immune system have to effectively present antigen to T cells in order to activate them, for example, and B cells need to receive appropriate T cell help in the form of cytokines in order to effectively activate themselves and produce antibody.

Main Outcomes: Assessment and Measurement

The functioning of the immune system can be assessed *in vivo* or *in vitro*. *In vivo* assessments typically involve administering some challenge to the immune system and then measuring the integrated outcome of that challenge, that is, the cumulative downstream effect of all of the various pieces of the immune response. This might be a desirable response, as in the T cell response to delayed-type hypersensitivity challenge, or an undesirable response, as in an allergic response. Even the same measure can have different meanings. For example, higher antibody to a vaccine is considered a desirable outcome, but higher antibody to a latent virus such as Epstein–Barr virus or cytomegalovirus indicates increased viral activation, poorer immunological control over the virus, or both (Glaser et al., 1991). Finally, it has become increasingly common to measure inflammatory markers in the blood as a measure of the degree of subclinical inflammation in the body. These inflammatory markers include the cytokines interleukin-1 (IL-1), interleukin-6 (IL-6), and tumor necrosis factor-α (TNF-α) and the acute phase protein C-reactive protein (CRP), among others. As with other kinds of assessment, immunological assessments have trade-offs, and *in vivo* tests have the advantage of ecological validity but the disadvantage that it is difficult to identify which piece of the immune response (e.g., antigen processing and presentation, cell trafficking, protein production) accounts for differences in responses to the test. Salivary markers of immune function are typically of the *in vivo* variety. Antibody and cytokines can both be measured in saliva (Granger et al., 2012); however, it should be noted that salivary antibody (IgA) is different from serum antibody (IgM and IgG) and that cytokines in the oral cavity typically reflect local rather than systemic immunological activity (Riis et al., 2014).

In vitro tests can target specific cells, proteins, or activities of the immune system. In flow cytometry, individual cells are labeled to identify their subset type, sorted, and counted with a laser. In some conditions, the numbers of cells in large subsets are clinically important (e.g., number of helper T cells in HIV). In other cases, it is smaller subsets that are relevant (e.g., number of senescent [CD28-] cytotoxic T cells in aging). The function of immune cells can also be assessed. Cytotoxicity assays typically involve incubating cytotoxic cells with their cellular targets (e.g., virally infected or tumor cell lines) and measuring the degree of target killing. Often used with natural killer cells, this assay requires careful attention to the types of cells that are present. A sample with a larger percentage of natural killer cells will have higher total cytotoxicity based on that parameter alone. Proliferative assays typically involve incubating T and/or B lymphocytes with a receptor-stimulating agent and measuring the degree to which new cells are generated. A similar technique can be used to measure the degree to which cells produce cytokines. Whereas some cytokines are relatively stable, others have short half-lives on the order of minutes. These cytokines are better measured in a production assay than in serum.

Methodological considerations that apply to many immunological measures include consideration of the physiometrics of the measure, circadian variation, reactivity to the sample collection, and variability due to laboratory supplies. First, the generalizability of immune parameters varies. Often when an investigator draws blood for the measurement of an immune parameter, she wishes to know something about the person's immune function over a larger time frame than that exact moment: Perhaps she would like to generalize from that assessment to the days or weeks around the blood draw. Unfortunately, many immune parameters are highly variable, and a single assessment may offer poor physiometrics with regard to generalizability. The percent of variance in immune parameters that is due to stable individual differences is relatively high for proinflammatory markers (37–93%), particularly when one seeks to generalize over weeks rather than months. Proliferative assays are slightly lower (48–46%), and enumerative assays can be lower still (Segerstrom & Smith, 2012). Multiple measurements (e.g., on different days) – the immunological equivalent of adding scale items – can improve reliability and generalizability.

Second, many immune parameters have circadian variation. IL-6, for example, is lowest in the morning and highest in the evening (Vgontzas et al., 2005). Therefore, it is important to attend to the time of day at which samples are taken, to take samples at the same time of day for all subjects if at all possible, and to decide on a time of day based on rational as well as practical considerations.

Third, many immune parameters are reactive to acute stress. For example, the percent of natural killer cells in peripheral blood increases dramatically with acute stress (Segerstrom & Miller, 2004). Venipuncture can itself act as an acute stressor, and for people with blood/needle anxiety, there may be significant anticipatory stress as well (Girgis, Shea, & Husband, 1988). Because of the risk of fainting as well as the effect on immune parameters, it may be desirable to exclude people with significant blood/needle anxiety from studies. Expert venipuncture decreases the time between puncture and blood collection and the amount of pain experienced by the subject. Another possibility is to place an indwelling needle and wait 30–60 min for the effects of venipuncture to wear off before collecting samples. If repeated samples are needed, so is an indwelling needle. Repeated venipuncture is not recommended!

Fourth, whether *in vivo* or *in vitro*, variability in supplies can result in significant variability in results. For example, in a study using two different kinds of antigen for delayed-type hypersensitivity skin testing (mumps and candida), with three different batches of each, there were no large differences in responses to the two kinds of antigen, but there were very large differences between batches *within* antigen type (Segerstrom & Sephton, 2010; Segerstrom & Smith, 2012). Different vaccines may have significant differences in their *antigenicity*, or degree to which they elicit an immune response, and this is particularly true of vaccines with varied components within and between years, such as the trivalent influenza vaccine. For example, within a single vaccination year (1989–1990), there were differences in antibody response to the three components of the influenza vaccine and between different forms of the vaccine (Zei, Neri, & Iorio, 1991).

Illustrations of Immunological Studies

The following are examples of innovative uses of immunological measurement in health psychology. Stone, Cox, Valdimarsdottir, Jandorf, and Neale (1987) administered daily rabbit albumin (a novel protein) orally to dental students and measured salivary antibody to the protein (IgA) three times weekly. This approach essentially constitutes an oral vaccination study, which may have clearer implications for immunocompetence than measurement of total salivary IgA. In a within-subject analysis, the investigators found that antibody response was higher when participants had less negative and more positive mood.

Cohen, Doyle, and Skoner (1999) experimentally infected subjects with influenza A virus and measured pro-inflammatory cytokine (IL-6) levels in nasal lavage. By measuring the cytokine in the compartment where the pathology was taking place, this group was able to show that inflammation mediated between psychosocial stress and illness severity. Similarly, Lutgendorf and colleagues (2005) measured natural killer cell activity in cells isolated from ovarian tumor tissue and fluids, finding that social support was associated with higher activity and distress with lower activity.

Decisions One Needs to Make When Choosing an Outcome

Perhaps the most important decision one needs to make when choosing an immunological outcome concerns the population being studied and the relevance of the parameter. In recent memory, proof-of-principle studies showing any relationship between mental states and immune parameters were of interest. However, the principle being adequately proved, one must now match the population to the parameter for maximum health relevance. The most important immune parameter in older adults (e.g., inflammation or markers of immune senescence) may be different from the most important immune parameter for children (e.g., response to vaccination or salivary IgA specific to common childhood illnesses).

This substantive decision having been made, another consideration is cost. As noted, some immune parameters may not have adequate physiometrics unless measured multiple times. Saving money by measuring immunity unreliably can result in erroneous findings (Segerstrom, Lubach, & Coe, 2006). This decision, therefore, must balance the cost of the assay, the necessary sampling frequency to achieve adequate reliability, and feasibility.

Feasibility also applies to the choice of compartment. In humans, this typically means a choice between saliva and blood, although immunity can also be measured in the skin or in the whole system, as in *in vivo* tests. It is important to recognize, however, that much immune activity takes place in compartments that are not accessible in most human studies, such as the lymph node, the bone marrow, and the spleen.

Finally, one must decide whether basal immune function or reactivity is more important. In some cases, one is interested in chronic, ongoing immune functions, such as inflammation. In others, one is interested in how the immune system responds to an immunological challenge such as vaccination. In others, one is interested in how the immune system responds to a psychological challenge such as emotion induction.

The Neuroendocrine System

Short Introduction

The endocrine system is a collection of interconnected cells, glands, and tissues that communicate via soluble chemical signaling molecules (hormones) released into the bloodstream (Nelson, 2011). The main endocrine tissues (representative secretions in parentheses) include the hypothalamus (corticotrophin-releasing hormone, growth hormone, gonadotropin-releasing hormone, oxytocin, and vasopressin), thyroid (calcitonin, thyroxine), pituitary (follicle-stimulating and luteinizing hormones, adrenocorticotropic hormone, prolactin), and pineal (melatonin) glands; as well as alimentary glands such as the liver (insulin-like growth factor), stomach (gastrin, ghrelin), duodenum (secretin), kidney (renin, calcitriol), pancreas (insulin, glucagon), and adrenal (cortisol, androgens, adrenaline, dopamine) glands. Endocrine system effects are typically slow to initiate and can last for minutes to weeks. Hormones released by the endocrine glands and tissues influence metabolism, growth and development, immune function, sleep, mood, learning and memory, and moderate behavioral and biological responsiveness to environmental influences and stress.

Within the endocrine system there are multiple subsystems (axes) that operate via positive feed-forward and negative feedback loops. Two of the major axes are the hypothalamic–pituitary–adrenal (HPA) axis and the hypothalamic–pituitary–gonadal (HPG) axis, which regulate the secretion of glucocorticoids (e.g., cortisol) and androgens (e.g., testosterone), respectively. The activity of these axes influence and are influenced by activity of each other. For example, during periods of high levels of HPA axis activity, activity of the HPG axis is suppressed. Moreover, the activity of endocrine system axes influences and is influenced by variation in central nervous and immune systems. The interconnected nature of these physiological systems highlights the importance for health psychology to incorporate multisystem measurement to examine links between physiology, emotions, behavior, and health.

In the field of health psychology, the most commonly studied components of the endocrine system are those related to the psychobiology of the stress response. This response has at least two main components. The first component involves the activation of the HPA axis and the secretion of glucocorticoids such as cortisol into the circulation. The other component involves the activation of the autonomic (and especially the sympathetic) nervous system (ANS) and the release of catecholamines such as norepinephrine into the bloodstream. Individual differences in stress-related HPA and ANS activity (i.e., acute increases or decreases in hormone levels) as well as their return to baseline levels (i.e., recovery) have been shown to reflect differential experience (e.g., adversity) and to predict a variety of outcomes related to development, behavior, and health (Nelson, 2011).

Assessment and Measurement

To capture intra- and interindividual differences in hormone secretion, there are several possible research designs and sample collection schemes. First, basal or trait-like levels can be assessed, which refer to the stable state of an individual during a resting period. Since the production and release of several hormones are influenced by moment-to-moment, diurnal, and/or monthly variation and by environmental factors and stress, multiple samples should be collected at the same time of day across a number of sampling days and aggregated across days. Second, time-dependent changes in the secretion of a hormone can be assessed through the collection of several samples before and after exposure to a discrete event. Thus, the effects of a specific event on activity of the endocrine system can be assessed; more importantly, individual differences in reactivity and recovery may predict health outcomes. A third strategy is to focus on individual differences in the secretion pattern of hormones across the day. Specific components of this diurnal rhythm, such as the awakening response for cortisol, have been associated with chronic stress and with various psychiatric and medical conditions (e.g., Chida & Steptoe, 2009; Clow, Thorn, Evans, & Hucklebridge, 2004). Finally, in studies with an ecological momentary assessment strategy (see Chapter 18 in this volume), participants collect samples in everyday contexts; after each collection, they report on their current emotions and behaviors or on the occurrence of specific events. These designs allow the researcher to link endocrine system activity to emotions, events, and behaviors in everyday contexts, which strengthens causal inference.

With regard to sample collection, endocrine activity can be measured in a variety of biological specimens, including serum/plasma, urine, and saliva samples. Saliva samples offer several advantages, as they do not require skilled professionals and special laboratory equipment; they are generally stress- and pain-free and therefore less burdensome for participants; and they allow for self- and home-based collection. Salivary biomarkers reflecting activity of components of the endocrine system include melatonin, glucocorticoids (e.g., cortisol), mineralocorticoids (e.g., aldosterone), androgens (e.g., testosterone), estrogens (e.g., estradiol, estrone, estriol), and progestogens (e.g., progesterone; for a complete list, see Granger et al., 2012). Finally, a novel approach for measuring hormones such as cortisol and testosterone is in scalp hair, which measures the average hormone exposure over a period of several months (for a study on the association with systolic heart failure, see Pereg et al., 2013).

Practical considerations for the collection of saliva samples focus on the collection materials (collecting whole saliva by passive drool is generally preferred over the use of cotton-based absorbent materials), specific instructions (with absorbent materials, the place in the mouth where the swab is placed and the collection duration should be standardized), stimulating saliva flow using, for example, sugar crystals (not recommended), and sample storage (samples should be kept cold or frozen; avoid repeated freeze–thaw cycles). It is also important to keep in mind that the integrity of the sample can be affected by food residue in the oral cavity after drinking or eating and by blood contamination due to, for example, cuts to the cheek, tongue, or gums. Finally, the use of over-the-counter and prescription medications should be documented. For a complete description of these methodological considerations, see Granger and colleagues (2012).

Main Outcomes and Illustrations of Their Use From the Literature

In an example of cortisol secretion in response to a stress reactivity paradigm, Francis, Granger, and Susman (2013) examined eating in the absence of hunger in children between 5 and 9 years old. Children first participated in a stressful public-speaking task and a difficult mental arithmetic task. Five saliva samples were collected via passive drool at baseline (samples 1 and 2) and after the stressful procedure (samples 3, 4, and 5). Total secretion of cortisol in response to the stress paradigm was associated with eating in the absence of hunger and with body mass index in older children. In an example of ecological momentary assessment, Giesbrecht, Poole, Letourneau, Campbell, and Kaplan (2013) examined diurnal cortisol secretion, psychological distress, and social support in pregnancy. At 14, 20, and 32 weeks' gestational age, pregnant women self-collected saliva samples on two consecutive days; after each collection, they rated their psychological distress. Analyses indicated that women with less effective social support showed substantial increases in cortisol when their psychological distress also increased. By contrast, women who perceived their support as effective had low levels of cortisol irrespective of their psychological distress; this decreased biological sensitivity may protect the fetus against the harmful effects of repeated increases in cortisol levels.

Decisions One Needs to Make When Choosing an Outcome

Choosing an outcome is dependent on which component of the endocrine system one is interested in and on whether the interest is in acute changes in hormone secretion versus diurnal and stable levels. Collecting saliva samples may be preferable over venipuncture, especially in vulnerable populations (e.g., clinical populations, children), when repeated sampling is needed (e.g., to examine changes in hormone secretion or to achieve adequate physiometrics), or when one is interested in everyday activities and contexts. The number of samples to be collected depends on the biomarker and the research questions, the sampling burden for the participants, the costs of collection materials and assays, and logistic and practical issues. Collection methods and specific assay protocols should always be piloted to ensure that they do not contribute to measurement error.

The Cardiovascular System

Short Introduction

The cardiovascular system comprises the heart and blood vessels, as well as the closely related neural and endocrine systems that regulate it. This system is a major focus of research and practice in health psychology, because cardiovascular diseases (CVD) are the leading cause of morbidity and mortality in most of the industrialized world (American Heart Association, 2012). Coronary heart disease (CHD) is the most common and costly form, and results from atherosclerosis in the arteries that bring blood to the heart muscle (i.e., myocardium). Atherosclerosis is a progressive process involving inflammation and fatty deposits within the walls of the major arteries, and its earliest signs can be seen in late childhood and adolescence. Atherosclerosis is a systemic disease, typically occurring simultaneously in several major arteries. Advanced atherosclerosis in coronary arteries leads to CHD, which appears as chest pain (i.e., angina), myocardial infarction (i.e., death of heart muscle due to prolonged lack of blood supply), and sudden cardiac death. Atherosclerosis in major arteries of the neck and brain (e.g., carotid arteries) contributes to occlusive stroke (i.e., the death of brain tissue), the most common form of stroke. Atherosclerosis in the major arteries descending from the heart causes peripheral arterial disease that is manifest in ischemic pain in the legs. Hypertension, or sustained elevations in blood pressure, contributes to each of these forms of CVD, as well as the second major form of stroke, in which brain blood vessels rupture (Fisher & Scheidt, 2012).

Much research and practice in health psychology addresses the modifiable behaviors that influence these forms of CVD (e.g., smoking, physical activity, diet), and measurement of preclinical endpoints figures prominently in much of this work. Other aspects of research and practice address the role of psychosocial factors related to stress in the development and course of CVD (e.g., social isolation, chronic anger and hostility, depression). In the latter focus, stress-related responses of the cardiovascular system and other systems are a major concern beyond measurement of preclinical endpoints, as these are believed to be the mechanisms linking psychosocial risk factors with the development and course of CVD. The inflammatory and neuroendocrine responses described previously are important examples, as are stress-related changes in blood pressure, heart rate, and their underlying determinants, since these are believed to contribute to the development of CVD (Steptoe & Kivimaki, 2013).

Assessment and Measurement

The clinical endpoints that define CVD (e.g., CHD, stroke, hypertension) have standard medical criteria. There is some controversy regarding the level of systolic blood pressure (SBP; pressure exerted against artery walls during a pulse) and diastolic blood pressure (DBP; pressure between pulse waves) required for the diagnosis of hypertension. Also, the diagnosis is often made on the basis of office measurements of blood pressure, but blood pressure varies considerably over time and ambulatory blood pressure measurements often have stronger associations with later signs of clinical CVD (Zanstra & Johnston, 2011). Among patients with CHD, cardiac ischemia can be assessed through a variety of clinical measures, including the electrocardiogram (ECG), in response to graded physical exercise and other challenges. These changes can also be assessed though ambulatory techniques (i.e., Holter monitoring; Fisher & Scheidt, 2012).

The presence and severity of atherosclerosis is often assessed clinically through angiography, in which dye is injected into sections of the arterial system and imaged through radiographic procedures. Given the invasiveness of this procedure, it is typically used only in instances of pressing clinical needs. Less invasive assessments of atherosclerosis include measurement of calcification in the aorta and coronary arteries, as calcium is a component of later-stage atherosclerotic lesions (Fisher & Scheidt, 2012). Atherosclerosis in arteries lying near the surface of the body, such as the carotid arteries in the neck, can be measured with ultrasound techniques, producing a measure of the thickening of the artery wall that occurs with atherosclerosis.

Atherosclerosis also reduces the elasticity of arteries, and this feature of the disease can be assessed by measuring the speed with which pulse waves travel through arteries (i.e., faster pulse wave velocity reflects less elastic artery walls seen in atherosclerosis) and the extent to which peripheral arteries dilate during increased blood flow (i.e., less flow-mediated dilation reflect less elastic arteries seen in atherosclerosis; Urbina et al., 2009).

In measuring the cardiovascular stress responses that are believed to link various sources of chronic stress and the development of CVD, measures of heart rate and blood pressure reactions to stressful stimuli (i.e., cardiovascular reactivity) and the extent to which they return to resting levels after the stressor (i.e., recovery) have been found to predict CVD (Chida & Steptoe, 2010). These measurements can be made in the laboratory in response to precisely controlled stressors or using ambulatory techniques outside the laboratory. The determinants of these cardiovascular responses are often of interest. Blood pressure reactivity, for example, can be due to increases in cardiac output (i.e., the volume of blood pumped from the heart per minute) or increases in peripheral resistance (i.e., the restriction vs. accommodating dilation of the vessels the blood moves through). Similarly, heart rate responses can be due to increases in sympathetic excitation or the withdrawal of parasympathetic inhibition of the heart. Cardiac output, peripheral resistance, and cardiac sympathetic activation can be measured noninvasively through impedance cardiography, and the degree of parasympathetic activity can be measured through analyses of changes in heart rate that are due to respiration (i.e., respiratory sinus arrhythmia, or vagal tone; Thayer, Hansen, & Johnsen, 2008).

Main Outcomes and Illustrations of Their Use From the Literature

In an example of research on both cardiovascular mechanisms assessed in the laboratory and outcomes, Carroll, Phillips, Der, Hunt, and Benzeval (2011) found that increases in blood pressure in response to a mental stressor predicted rising blood pressure over time and the development of hypertension. In a similar study using the ambulatory approach, Kamarck, Shiffman, Sutton-Simon, Muldoon, and Tepper (2012) found that high levels of psychological demand in daily experiences and concurrent levels of ambulatory blood pressure predicted progression of atherosclerosis in the carotid arteries as measured by ultrasound. Finally, in an example of clinical intervention research, Blumenthal and colleagues (2005) found that stress management treatment improved the elasticity (flow-mediated dilation) of peripheral arteries in CHD patients.

Decisions One Needs to Make When Choosing an Outcome

The selection of specific measures will depend on whether the interest is in CV outcomes or mechanisms. For outcomes, blood pressure and hypertension are straightforward, although the use of standard clinic or laboratory assessments of resting blood pressure as opposed to the more informative ambulatory method is important. For preclinical atherosclerosis, the choice among measures will be determined by a variety of factors. For example, detectable levels of coronary calcification are relatively infrequent before middle age, whereas other measures (e.g., thickening of carotid artery walls, pulse wave velocity, and flow-mediated endothelial dilation) can be used with a much broader age range – including older children and adolescents.

For research on mechanisms, a basic decision involves the greater experimental control and precision afforded by laboratory-based measures of cardiovascular reactivity versus the more realistic but "noisier" ambulatory approach. Often these two strategies are most valuable when used together across a series of studies. Finally, in some instances, the basic cardiovascular responses (i.e., changes in blood pressure and heart rate) are sufficient, but other questions justify the greater complexity and expense of measuring the underlying cardiac output and vascular resistance determinants of blood pressure responses, or the sympathetic versus parasympathetic influences on heart rate. Increasingly, parasympathetic influences on stress and cardiovascular disease are an important topic on their own, in a departure from the implicit fight-or-flight model underlying much of the research on stress and CVD (Thayer et al., 2008).

Conclusion

Assessing biological and physiological measures in health psychology poses both substantive (is this the most important parameter for my study population and research question?) and methodological (is this sample being collected correctly?) challenges. Although the reliability and generalizability of such measures are not currently assessed and reported consistently in the way that they are for psychological measures, physiometrics are equally important as psychometrics for analysis and interpretation and are gaining more attention (e.g., Out, Granger, Sephton, & Segerstrom, 2013). The cost and effort associated with assessing biomarkers may create a barrier to achieving other important methodological benchmarks in health psychology, such as larger sample sizes and more replications (O'Carroll, 2014).

Biological and physiological measures are worth the trouble, however, as they also have significant advantages. For example, they are not self-reported and therefore contribute to methodological diversity in assessment. Most important, of course, a careful consideration and assessment of these domains can provide important information about how mental states and biological states interact with and influence each other in the progression toward health or disease.

Acknowledgments

Preparation of this chapter was supported by the National Institute on Aging (K02–033629). Douglas A. Granger is Founder and Chief Scientific and Strategy Advisor at Salimetrics (Carlsbad, CA). This relationship is managed by the policies of the committees on conflict of interest at the Johns Hopkins University School of Medicine and the Office of Research Adherence and Integrity at Arizona State University.

References

American Heart Association. (2012). Heart disease and stroke statistics: 2012 update. *Circulation, 125*, e2–e220.

Blumenthal, J. A., Sherwood, A., Babyak, M., Watkins, L., Waugh, R., Georgiades, A., … Hindelighter, A. (2005). Effects of exercise and stress management training on markers of cardiovascular risk in patients with ischemic heart disease: A randomized trial. *JAMA, 293*, 1626–1634. http://doi.org/10.1001/jama.293.13.1626

Carroll, D., Phillips, A. C., Der, G., Hunt, K., & Benzeval, M. (2011). Blood pressure reactions to acute stress and future blood pressure status: Data from the 12-year follow-up of the West of Scotland Study. *Psychosomatic Medicine, 73*, 737–742. http://doi.org/10.1097/PSY.0b013e3182359808

Chida, Y., & Steptoe, A. (2009). Cortisol awakening response and psychosocial factors: A systematic review and meta-analysis. *Biological Psychology, 80*, 265–278. http://doi.org/10.1016/j.biopsycho.2008.10.004

Chida, Y., & Steptoe, A. (2010). Greater cardiovascular responses to laboratory mental stress are associated with poor subsequent cardiovascular risk status: A meta-analysis of prospective evidence. *Hypertension, 55*, 1026–1032. http://doi.org/10.1161/HYPERTENSIONAHA.109.146621

Clark, W. R. (2008). *In defense of self: How the immune system really works.* New York, NY: Oxford University Press. http://doi.org/10.1093/acprof:oso/9780195336634.001.0001

Clow, A., Thorn, L., Evans, P., & Hucklebridge, F. (2004). The awakening cortisol response: Methodological issues and significance. *Stress, 7*, 29–37. http://doi.org/10.1080/10253890410001667205

Cohen, A., Doyle, W. J., & Skoner, D. P. (1999). Psychological stress, cytokine production, and severity of upper respiratory illness. *Psychosomatic Medicine, 61*, 175–180. http://doi.org/10.1097/00006842-199903000-00009

Ershler, W. B., & Keller, E. T. (2000). Age-associated increased interleukin-6 gene expression, late-life diseases, and frailty. *Annual Review of Medicine, 51*, 245–270. http://doi.org/10.1146/annurev.med.51.1.245

Fisher, J., & Scheidt, S. S. (2012). A whirlwind tour of cardiology. In R. Allan & J. Fisher (Eds.), *Heart and mind: The practice of cardiac psychology* (pp. 17–53). Washington, DC: American Psychological Association.

Francis, L. A., Granger, D. A., & Susman, E. J. (2013). Adrenocortical regulation, eating in the absence of hunger and BMI in young children. *Appetite, 64*, 32–38. http://doi.org/10.1016/j.appet.2012.11.008

Girgis, A., Shea, J., & Husband, A. (1988). Immune and psychological responses to acute venipuncture stress. *Medical Science Research, 16*, 351–352.

Giesbrecht, G. F., Poole, J. C., Letourneau, N., Campbell, T., & Kaplan, B. J. (2013). The buffering effect of social support on hypothalamic-pituitary-adrenal axis function during pregnancy. *Psychosomatic Medicine, 75*, 856–862. http://doi.org/10.1097/PSY.0000000000000004

Glaser, R., Pearson, G. R., Jones, J. F., Hillhouse, J., Kennedy, S., Mao, H., & Kiecolt-Glaser, J. K. (1991). Stress-related activation of Epstein-Barr virus. *Brain, Behavior, and Immunity, 5*, 219–232. http://doi.org/10.1016/0889-1591(91)90018-6

Granger, D. A., Fortunato, C. K., Beltzer, K., Virag, M., Bright, M. A., & Out, D. (2012). Focus on methodology: Salivary bioscience and research on adolescence: An integrated perspective. *Journal of Adolescence, 35*, 1081–1095. http://doi.org/10.1016/j.adolescence.2012.01.005

Kamarck, T. W., Shiffman, S., Sutton-Simon, K., Muldoon, M. F., & Tepper, P. (2012). Daily psychological demands are associated with 6-year progression of carotid atherosclerosis: The Pittsburgh Healthy Heart Study. *Psychosomatic Medicine, 74*, 423–439. http://doi.org/10.1097/PSY.0b013e3182572599

Lutgendorf, S. K., Sood, A. K., Anderson, B., McGinn, S., Maiseri, H., Dao, M., ... Lubaroff, D. M. (2005). Social support, psychological distress, and natural killer cell activity in ovarian cancer. *Journal of Clinical Oncology, 23*, 7105–7113. http://doi.org/10.1200/JCO.2005.10.015

Nelson, R. J. (2011). *An introduction to behavioral endocrinology* (4th ed.). Sunderland, MA: Sinauer Associates.

O'Carroll, R. E. (2014). Health psychology interventions. *British Journal of Health Psychology, 19*, 235–239. http://doi.org/10.1111/bjhp.12082

Out, D., Granger, D.A., Sephton, S.E., & Segerstrom, S.C. (2013). Disentangling sources of individual differences in diurnal salivary α-amylase: Reliability, stability, and sensitivity to context. *Psychoneuroendocrinology, 38*, 367–375. http://doi.org/10.1016/j.psyneuen.2012.06.013

Papanicolaou, D. A, Wilder, R. L., Manolagas, S. C., & Chrousos, G. P. (1998). The pathophysiologic roles of interleukin-6 in human disease. *Annals of Internal Medicine, 128*, 127–137. http://doi.org/10.7326/0003-4819-128-2-199801150-00009

Pereg, D., Chan, J., Russell, E., Berlin, T., Mosseri, M., Seabrook, J. A., ... Van Uum, S. (2013). Cortisol and testosterone in hair as biological markers of systolic heart failure. *Psychoneuroendocrinology, 38*, 2875–2882. http://doi.org/10.1016/j.psyneuen.2013.07.015

Riis, J. L., Out, D., Dorn, L. D., Beal, S. J., Denson, L. A., Pabst, S., ... Granger, D. A. (2014). Salivary cytokines in healthy adolescent girls: Intercorrelations, stability, and associations with serum cytokines, age, and pubertal stage. *Developmental Psychobiology, 56*, 797–811. http://doi.org/10.1002/dev.21149

Ross, R. (1999). Atherosclerosis – an inflammatory disease. *New England Journal of Medicine, 340*, 115–126. http://doi.org/10.1056/NEJM199901143400207

Segerstrom, S. C., Lubach, G. R., & Coe, C. L. (2006). Identifying immune traits and biobehavioral correlates: Generalizability and reliability of immune responses in rhesus macaques. *Brain, Behavior, and Immunity, 20*, 349–358 http://doi.org/10.1016/j.bbi.2005.09.007

Segerstrom, S. C., & Miller, G. E. (2004). Psychological stress and the human immune system: A meta-analytic study of 30 years of inquiry. *Psychological Bulletin, 130*, 601–630. http://doi.org/10.1037/0033-2909.130.4.601

Segerstrom, S. C., & Sephton, S. E. (2010). Optimistic expectancies and cell-mediated immunity: The role of positive affect. *Psychological Science, 21*, 448–455. http://doi.org/10.1177/0956797610362061

Segerstrom, S. C., & Smith, G. T. (2012). Methods, variance, and error in psychoneuroimmunology research: The good, the bad, and the ugly. In S. C. Segerstrom (Ed.), *Oxford handbook of psychoneuroimmunology*. New York, NY: Oxford University Press.

Steptoe, A., & Kivimaki, M. (2013). Stress and cardiovascular disease: An update on current knowledge. *Annual Review of Public Health, 34*, 337–354. http://doi.org/10.1146/annurev-publhealth-031912-114452

Stone, A. A., Cox, D. S., Valdimarsdottir, H., Jandorf, L., & Neale, J. M. (1987). Evidence that secretory IgA is associated with daily mood. *Journal of Personality and Social Psychology, 52*, 988–993. http://doi.org/10.1037/0022-3514.52.1.56

Thayer, J. F., Hansen, A. L., & Johnsen, B. H. (2008). Non-invasive assessment of autonomic influences on the heart: Impedance cardiography and heart rate variability. In L. Leuken & L. C. Gallo (Eds.), *Handbook of physiological research methods in health psychology* (pp. 183–209). Thousand Oaks, CA: Sage.

Urbina, E. M., Williams, R. V., Alpert, B. S., Collins, R. T., Daniels, S. R., Hyaman, L., McCrindle, B. (2009). Noninvasive assessment of subclinical atherosclerosis in children and adolescents: Recommendations for standard assessment for clinical research: A scientific statement of the American Heart Association. *Hypertension, 54*, 919–950. http://doi.org/10.1161/HYPERTENSIONAHA.109.192639

Vgontzas, A. N., Bixler, E. O., Lin, H. M., Prolo, P., Trakada, G., & Chrousos, G. P. (2005). IL-6 and its circadian secretion in humans. *Neuroimmunomodulation, 12*, 131–140. http://doi.org/10.1159/000084844

Zanstra, Y. J., & Johnston, D. W. (2011). Cardiovascular reactivity in real life settings: Measurement, mechanisms, and meaning. *Biological Psychology, 86*, 98–106. http://doi.org/10.1016/j.biopsycho.2010.05.002

Zei, T., Neri, M., & Iorio, A. M. (1991). Immogenicity of trivalent subunit and split influenza vaccines (1989–90 winter season) in volunteers of different groups of age. *Vaccine, 9*, 613–617. http://doi.org/10.1016/0264-410X(91)90184-8

Part III

Assessment Methods and Issues

Chapter 18
Ecological Momentary Assessment

Derek W. Johnston

School of Psychology, University of Aberdeen, UK

Ecological momentary assessment (EMA), also known as experience sampling, is a set of techniques used to measure behaviour, thoughts, and emotions as they actually happen or very shortly afterwards in the participant's normal environment. The term was introduced by Stone and Shiffman (1994). It allows the very frequent collection of information, minimally distorted by memory and other cognitive processes, in virtually every domain of human behaviour, including health-related behaviour. This chapter addresses the main issues in applying EMA to health:

1. What is EMA and why might it be of value in health psychology?
2. How to conduct EMA.
3. Measurement frequency, duration, acceptability, and reactivity.
4. Reliability and validity of EMA measures.
5. Analysing EMA data.
6. Alternatives to EMA: back to questionnaires or forward to the day reconstruction method?

What Is Measured by EMA and Why Might It Be of Value?

EMA is frequent real-time observation and is most obviously applicable to behaviours or states that a participant is able and willing to report. However, various forms of automatic recording, such as pedometers and activity monitors, are also included in EMA. A far from exhaustive list of the health-related behaviours, emotions, and psychological processes successfully measured using EMA includes mood, perceptions of work-related stress and nursing activities (Farquharson et al., 2013; Johnston, Jones, McCann, & McKee, 2013), coping (Schwartz, Neale, Marco, Shiffman, & Stone, 1999), cognitions such as attitude and perceived control, activity, and pain (Quinn, Johnston, & Johnston, 2013; Stone et al., 2003), beliefs about heart disease and the efficacy of health care (Herber, Jones, Smith, & Johnston, 2012), daily hassles and eating (O'Connor, Jones, Conner, McMillan, & Ferguson, 2008), smoking (Henker, Whalen, Jamner, & Delfino, 2002), and alcohol consumption and drug use (Messiah, Grondin, & Encrenaz, 2011). Even potentially sensitive information such as condom use (Kiene, Tennen, & Armeli, 2008) has been acquired using EMA. In addition to self-report, objective information can be obtained from pedometers and accelerometers (Quinn et al., 2013) and ambulatory physiological recorders, which can measure heart rate, blood pressure, and more complex physiological functions (Johnston, 2012).

We can all observe, but may not accurately recall, many of our own behaviours and emotions and some aspects of our cognitive processes. We know if we have just eaten, smoked a cigarette, or drunk a beer and have some idea of what was happening just before the event and what we felt during the behaviour and afterwards. Jones & Johnston (2011) discuss the following processes that affect recall and hence bias retrospective accounts: the respondent's mood at the time of recall; the effects of attitudes and expectations; the use of heuristic strategies, such as recalling frequency of events in round numbers; and the powerful effects on recall of the most recent or most extreme events. Behaviour measured by conventional questionnaires reflects this complex process and may therefore not actually measure what really happened. While EMA may well capture a particular moment accurately, its coverage of the totality of a day, week, or month is inevitably limited and EMA may miss rare events or provide unrepresentative coverage of more common events. Nevertheless, only EMA can provide the accurate high-frequency information needed to study fast-moving processes and their determinants, correlates, and consequences. Such information is obviously important in understanding behaviour and may be essential in planning, executing, and evaluating interventions and in testing psychological theory within individuals (Johnston & Johnston, 2013).

EMA relies primarily on three forms of sampling: (1) In *signal-contingent sampling* the participant is signalled to complete a diary entry, usually by sound or vibration from some form of electronic diary. This is typically at a particular average frequency, say every 90 min with some random variation around that interval (perhaps ± 15 min) to ensure that the occurrence of the signal is not predicable (e.g., Johnston et al., 2013). (2) *Time- or interval-contingent sampling* is a simpler regime with signals at fixed intervals. This can be convenient, particularly if the EMA measure is tied to a system such as ambulatory physiological measurement (e.g., Edmondson et al., 2013), and has analytic advantages but it may be compromised by its predictability, so a participant's behaviour may be determined by the upcoming signal; a particular behaviour may be avoided, postponed, or even specially performed if it is known that a diary entry is about to be required. Interval sampling is most appropriate if the focus of study is some summary measure over a fixed time such as the amount of food eaten or exercise taken in the last hour. (3) In *event-contingent sampling* the participant provides EMA information when a specific event occurs (Jones & Johnston, 2012). This is appropriate when discrete clearly defined events of limited frequency are the main concern (e.g., smoking a cigarette, or an argument with a spouse) and is essential for detecting very rare events (fainting, a fall in an older person), but participants may fail to record an event and it is very difficult to determine if this has happened. Event-contingent sampling can be combined with signal- or interval-contingent schedules, which can provide important information on the context in which the event occurred and its consequences (Jones & Johnston, 2012).

How to Conduct EMA

EMA measurement can be done in a variety of ways but some form of electronic platform is now almost universal. Personal digital assistants (PDAs) were common and are still in use but are no longer manufactured and have been replaced by smartphones, tablets, and specially constructed devices or, for daily diaries, home-based personal computers. Environmental information can readily be acquired from GPS, sound levels, and cameras. Cognitive functions can be objectively assessed by attention and memory tasks implemented on PDA (Fahrenberg, Brugner, Foerster, & Kappler, 1999), smartphone, or specialist device such as the Prodiary (see http://www.camntech.com), although such use of real-time cognitive testing is not yet common nor extensively developed.

The advantages of a computerised device include the ease with which the format and content of the questions can be controlled and changed, control of the schedule, time stamping of all information obtained, and information on missed entries. Branching schemes for gathering information contingent on a participant's response can be implemented readily. The data are usually downloadable in a very convenient form to a standard spreadsheet or database (such as Excel or Access) for analysis. The information can be gathered in a wide variety of formats including visual analogue scales, Likert-type scales of agreement and disagreement, and other rating scales, multiple choice items, time of occurrence of an event, and counts of events. Free text can also be entered in most devices and it is possible to record speech and take pictures. The illustration in Figure 18.1 shows typical EMA PDA/smartphone screens used in a study of stress in nurses (Farquharson et al., 2013) with the free software Pocket Interview (see https://dl.dropboxusercontent.com/u/60029002/PocketInterview.zip). These illustrate the use of analogue scales, tick boxes, event sampling, and the acquisition of free-text information.

The power and flexibility of electronic diary measurements are immense and once developed they are easy to use. It is a great advantage if diaries can be easily developed by the research team, particularly when developing new protocols or in n-of-1 studies where the researcher or clinician wishes to tailor the diary to a specific participant's context. However, developing the appropriate software is not a trivial task if one cannot write computer code. Proprietary electronic devices have easy-to-use options for developing items in a variety of formats, and software packages designed to enable inexperienced users to develop their own EMA measures have been created over the years and are freely available (e.g., ESP developed by Feldman-Barrett; see http://www.experience-sampling.org/) but such freeware often fails to keep up with advances in technology. Movisens have recently developed apparently powerful and user-friendly Android EMA software that can be evaluated before purchase (see https://xs.movisens.com/). Other companies and research groups market what they claim to be suitable software or offer to develop diaries (examples include Ilumivu, http://www.ilumivu.com/, and iHabit; Runyan et al., 2013) or offer sophisticated professional programming tools (Soda, http://www10.confirmit.com/; Pendragon forms, http://www.pendragonsoftware.com/). Since smartphones are now in widespread use, many researchers use the participant's own phone.

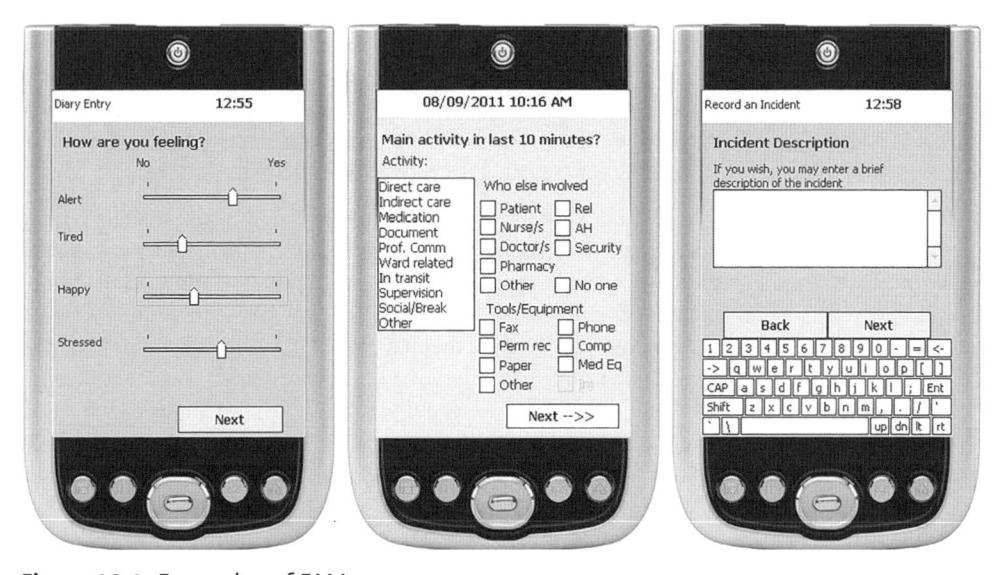

Figure 18.1. Examples of EMA screens.

This has obvious advantages of cost and availability but may require that software runs on several systems, such as iPhone and Android devices. This is a rapidly changing market and the most appropriate hardware and software available need to be assessed and rigorously tested when planning a study. Many studies are seriously delayed or even halted at this stage.

Measurement Frequency, Duration, Acceptability, and Reactivity

The frequency of measurement is dependent on the phenomena of interest and on participants' tolerance of measurement burden. Infrequent events do not require frequent measurement but may require measurement over many days or weeks, while transitory states, such as moods, may need to be sampled frequently to capture the dynamic processes involved. Increasing the frequency of measurement increases the power to detect within-person relationships, although above a certain frequency, which will vary with the behaviour being assessed, the effect of increasing the number of participants can be greater. Furthermore, the frequency of within-participant measurement has much less effect on the power needed to determine between-person effects.

Stone et al. (2003) reported good adherence and only slight interference with usual activities with 12 diary entries over a 16-hr day in a study of pain lasting for 2 weeks. Fuller-Tyszkiewicz et al. (2013) found that, over a week of EMA measurement of body satisfaction, the rate of adherence declined by only one rating (out of seven) per day but the variance in the measures reduced more markedly, raising concerns about the quality of the data as time went on. These studies suggest that a fairly high frequency of measurement (at least six times per day) can be maintained for more than a week without major problems.

EMA can be, or at least appear to be, burdensome and this could limit its acceptability to some potential participants and reduce the adherence of those who take part. Both processes could limit the usefulness of the method by limiting the populations to which findings can be generalised (a problem of external validity) or by introducing bias into the data actually recorded (an even more critical issue of internal validity). Recruitment rates provide some evidence of acceptability but are difficult to determine since the population approached may be unspecified or unknown. Sokolovsky, Mermelstein, and Hedeker (2014) found that 36.8% of over 3,600 adolescent smokers agreed to take part in a demanding longitudinal study of smoking and 94% of them actually completed the first 7 days of data collection. Serre et al. (2012) studying 260 clients at a French substance dependence clinic had a 42% acceptance rate that varied with the nature of the dependency from 31% for cannabis users to 62% for tobacco smokers.

With electronic devices it is easy to determine whether participants completed the diary entry on time. Adherence is affected by the criteria for an acceptable entry. In a recently completed study of nurse stress in which nurses were repeatedly prompted and allowed to postpone entries if the prompt came at an inconvenient time, we achieved an almost 99% completion rate although over 25% of entries were postponed for a median time of 10 min (Johnston, Johnston et al., 2013, unpublished final report). In a similar study with less prompting we obtained adherence rates that varied between 70 and 90%, depending on the hospital studied (Johnston, Jones et al., 2013). Others reported adherence rates from 68% (Sokolovsky et al., 2014) to over 90% (Stone et al., 2003).

The main issue with nonadherence is the possible biases that can be introduced. This has led to a search for predictors of missing data, which can be used to support the idea that data are missing at random and imputation procedures used. Messiah et al. (2011) studying substance use in students found that among other factors, being male and a user of multiple substances increased nonadherence as did particular times of the day or day of the week. Sokolovsky et al. (2014) found that in their adolescent smokers, adherence was better in women, those with lower negative affect, and those who smoked and drank less. In this sample, adherence was much better at home than elsewhere. They mention in passing that, unsurprisingly, monetary incentives improved adherence. Many of the factors that affect adherence will be specific to the population under study and, therefore, they can best be determined through knowledge of the population and pilot work. Allowing participants to delay a diary entry is an attractive and effective option but may introduce bias since the participant is effectively in control of the schedule.

It seems likely that EMA measurement will have an effect on behaviour given that self-monitoring is regarded as one of the most effective behaviour change techniques (Michie, Abraham, Whittington, McAteer, & Gupta, 2009), although self-monitoring in a treatment context (which usually includes other interventions) may have a different effect from EMA that is presented as a measurement technique. Measurement reactivity has not been studied extensively. The best study, by Stone et al. (2003), described previously, compared the frequency of EMA assessment and included a control group without EMA. They found no evidence of reactivity since the effects of frequency of measurement did not affect pain ratings nor did EMA influence weekly summary pain measures. Leahey, Crowther, and Mickelson (2007), also using an appropriate no-EMA control condition, could find no effect of EMA on a wide range of outcomes such as weight concerns and self-esteem. Other more recent studies have also failed to find reactivity in areas such as body image (Heron & Smyth, 2013). Overall, the evidence that EMA is a reactive measure is not compelling but it is hard to believe that repeatedly thinking about one's behaviour or emotional state (for example) will not have some effect on what is being measured.

Much of the information gathered in EMA is essentially obtained by the repeated completion of brief questionnaires and, as with conventional measures, these questionnaires should be reliable and valid. This issue has not been extensively addressed in EMA studies where there are unique challenges, the main ones being the need to limit the burden on participants. Reducing participant burden encourages the use of a small numbers of items, perhaps even single items, to measure constructs in EMA studies. Traditional psychometric considerations suggest the use of multiple items since this will increase reliability and improve coverage of the underlying construct. Diamantopoulos, Sarstedt, Fuches, Wilczynski, and Kaiser (2012), working in a marketing context and not considering EMA specifically, concluded on the basis of empirical and simulation studies that single-item scales are rarely appropriate and should be used only with great caution. They suggest that an exception may be when items in a scale are very homogeneous (they suggest Cronbach α values of more than 0.90). Attempts have been made to produce EMA versions of standard scales. Moullec et al. (2011) describe a systematic approach to reducing a French version of the 20-item Center for Epidemiologic Studies depression scale to a 4-item scale suitable for EMA use. In EMA, the repeated measurement of even a single item should ensure that overall estimates of level are reliable but individual observations may well not be. Multiple items are therefore safest and are likely to be expected by journal reviewers.

Two forms of reliability need to be considered, between- and within-person. Between-person reliability essentially provides the same internal consistency information as does Cronbach's α but includes repeated measurement in the model. The within-person reliability is perhaps more readily seen as reflecting sensitivity to change, a critical feature of EMA measurement. The current conceptually and practically simplest procedures are well described by Cranford et al. (2006) with worked examples. Drawing on generalisability theory, they use standard procedures (such as the SPPS and Stata instructions VARCOMP) to decompose the variance in EMA measures into variability across people, time, items, and their interactions. These can then be used to provide between- and within-person estimates of reliability.

Analysis

The analysis of EMA data offers a significant challenge but also the possibility of great insights into the processes that control or at least affect behaviour. The critical feature of EMA data is that they almost certainly have a hierarchical or multilevel structure with at least two levels consisting of repeated measures nested with people. More levels are possible both below people, such as repeated measures nested within days, and above, for example, hospital or clinic attended or town or country of residence. The hierarchical nature of the data should be incorporated in the analytic method in what is variously called multilevel, hierarchical, or random effects modelling. These methods were introduced into health psychology by Schwartz and Stone (1998), and their paper remains an excellent introduction. All the major statistical packages offer methods of conducting such analyses and there are also excellent stand-alone packages including HLM (http://www.ssicentral.com/hlm/) and MLwiN (http://www.bristol.ac.uk/cmm/) that are perhaps easier to use since they are focused exclusively on multilevel modelling. MLwiN is associated with very helpful documentation and online training on multilevel modelling.

The core of multilevel modelling (MLM) is to separate the variability in the data into between and within different units (people and repeated measures in the simplest case when using EMA) and to make appropriate allowance at each level for the nested structure and for factors operating at other levels. This opens up exciting possibilities that are just beginning to be exploited in health psychology. Relationships operating at the lowest level can be examined in their own right, summarised over the person, and entered as predictors at the person level, along with other person-level predictors and related back to the individual-level measures. For example, if one were to examine the relationship between self-efficacy for taking regular exercise and physical activity, one could examine whether self-efficacy predicted activity within people using repeated EMA measures of both, also whether a participant's average level of self-efficacy was related to activity or moderated the within-person relationships between self-efficacy and activity. One could also similarly relate a questionnaire measure of generalised self-efficacy to the repeated EMA measures.

Kiene et al. (2008) report an exemplary use of MLM in their study of condom use that illustrates the potential of MLM to illuminate important processes in health psychology. In a 30-day daily diary study they examined the relationship between intention to use a condom and actual condom use. Condom use was more likely when an individual's intention was higher. In addition, when the average level of an individual's intention was included in the analysis, they demonstrated that the effect of daily variations in intention was particularly high in those with high intentions to use a condom on average, that is, individuals who usually intended to use a condom were particularly likely to do so on days when their intentions are even higher than usual. Most reports focus on the fixed effects in MLM, which reflects the average effects across the sample, but differences between people can be of as much or more interest, with the degree to which an effect is present in individuals and what moderates these variable within-person effects being of great theoretical and practical importance (see Johnston, Jones et al., 2013, for an illustration).

Alternatives to EMA: Back to Questionnaire or Forward to the Day Reconstruction Method?

The relationship between EMA and retrospective/summary questionnaire measures of the same variable bears directly on the utility and validity of both types of measure. If they relate very highly then the questionnaire may be adequate for many purposes; if they relate poorly then they are assessing different things, or one or both are measuring the same thing badly. The relationship between EMA and questionnaire measures of the same construct appear modest and variable. Johnston, Jones et al. (2013) report that EMA measures of negative (NA) and positive affect (PA) assessed over 3 days in nurses at work every 90 min relate reliably but not substantially to the PANAS questionnaire measures. Solhan, Trull, Jahng, and Wood (2009) obtained slightly higher correlations between one (out of two) questionnaire measures of affective instability and variability in EMA measures of negative affect, hostility, and fear (correlations from .37 to .51) in patients with psychiatric disorders. Anestis et al. (2010) and Lavender et al. (2013) found similar relationships to Solhan et al. (2009) between EMA, NA, and questionnaire measures of affective lability in women with eating disorders. However, average NA did not relate to questionnaire NA. Edmondson et al. (2013) found that single items assessing anxiety/tension and anger/hostility correlated .25 and .22 with the Spielberger trait anxiety score and the Cook–Medley total hostility score, respectively. Schwartz et al. (1999) assessed coping by EMA and both the WOC and Daily Hassles coping inventories. Despite the EMA measures being closely modelled on the questionnaires, the relationships between EMA mean levels and the questionnaires were low.

The comparative power of EMA and questionnaires in predicting behaviour is critical but rarely examined. Henker et al. (2002) showed that EMA measures of anxiety predicted smoking in adolescents better than a standardised anxiety questionnaire. Kamarck, Muldoon, Shiffman, and Sutton-Tyrrell (2007) found that real-time measures of demand and control predicted arterial deterioration but the widely used Job Content Questionnaire (Karasek et al., 1998) did not. In people with bulimia nervosa (Anestis et al., 2010) or anorexia nervosa (Lavender et al., 2013), EMA measures of affective lability were as good or better than a similar questionnaire in correlating with interview measures of the eating disorders and correlated much more highly with EMA measures of bulimia or days of restricted eating.

One of the strengths of EMA is that it offers the promise of accurate information on behaviour minimally contaminated by memory or complex cognitive processes. Questionnaires in which participants summarise their experiences over a long period (recently, last week, last month) are almost certainly biased but they also capture the person's current considered view of their behaviour and their beliefs about their experience. Remembered experience can be a better predictor of future action or intentions than actual experience, as Wirtz, Kruger, Scollon, and Diener (2003) showed in a study of people's experience of holidays and future holiday plans. While people's actual experience on holiday, measured repeatedly using standard EMA methods, did predict their subsequent recollections of the holiday, the actual experience was a poorer predictor of intention than their remembered experience and contributed no additional information.

Remembered experience is heavily influenced by the most striking "peak" event and the last part of an event. Redelmeier, Katz, and Kahneman (2003) have shown that making the final minute of a colonoscopy more pleasant (by extending the final less painful procedure for a few minutes) leads to the whole procedure being recalled as more pleasant (although the EMA measures showed it to have been more painful overall) and to increase the likelihood that patients return for a repeat investigation. EMA provides information on what actually happened and the dynamics of behaviour lacking in questionnaire measures. This might be essential in planning an intervention. For example, if snacking occurs after a particular event at work or in a particular environment then a programme directed at reducing snacking could focus on that event or suggest ways of avoiding the critical environment or dealing with it differently.

There are good reasons to believe that the predictive power of EMA and questionnaires will not be similar and certainly no reason to believe that EMA will invariably be better. Predicting or changing behaviour determined by a complex decision process, such as a holiday plan or intention to leave a job, may require retrospective questionnaires that may be better at capturing some of the evidence that people use to make their decision. Outcomes that relate to what one actually does, such as physical activity, weight and eating, or stress and arterial state, may well be predicted better by EMA measures than by retrospective accounts.

In 2004, Kahneman, Kruger, Schkade, Schwarz, and Stone introduced the day reconstruction method (DRM) as a possibly less burdensome alternative to EMA. In the DRM participants retrospectively divide their day into what they see as sensible units, such as *having breakfast, commuting, taking kids to school, at work* etc. and then rate their feelings retrospectively over these units. It is believed that the use of specific, hopefully homogeneous, units of behaviour assessed shortly after they occurred minimises the biases of conventional questionnaires. A critical question is how well DRM relates to EMA, the gold standard for momentary measurement.

There are two important issues in relating the two methods: the similarity in average values obtained and the degree to which they track each other over time. Dockray et al. (2010) compared DRM and a paper-and-pencil-based EMA over a working day and a leisure day in university employees. The levels of happiness and tiredness were similar using both methods and they showed similar average changes over time. The correlation of average levels of happiness and tiredness between methods was reasonably high (ranging from .61 to .72) although the correlations at individual time points were much lower (averaging .46–.54). Dockray et al. (2010) did not report directly on the within-person correlation of EMA and DRM. Blysma, Taylor-Clift, and Rottenberg (2011) compared EMA and DRM in the assessment of PA and NA in people with depression and controls. EMA and DRM average values over a day correlate reasonably highly (correlations from .60 to .80) but average levels of PA and NA were lower for DRM than for EMA. However, neither Dockray et al. nor Blysma et al. report on the within-person correlation of EMA and DRM measures. Kim, Kikuchi, and Yamamoto (2013) examined the within-person tracking of fatigue, depression, and anxiety of EMA and DRM, and found that correlations were significant but low, ranging from .31 to .52. This led them to suggest that DRM is not appropriate for accurate tracking of mood over time, although average levels correlated highly in the same study (H. Kikuchi, personal communication, November 19, 2013).

A factor that may reduce the relationship over time between EMA and DRM is that EMA samples behaviour at one moment while DRM deals with episodes that could last for some time. Kim et al. (2013) introduced an episode-based form of EMA in which participants completed EMA entries for periods that they considered discrete episodes at the time. The poor tracking of EMA and DRM mood was still found when episode-based EMA was used and they obtained only limited correspondence in time and duration between the episodes determined in real time (by EMA) and retrospectively by DRM. It is likely that EMA will remain the gold standard for the measurement of momentary behaviour. If, however, EMA is not available or inappropriate, perhaps because EMA cannot be used in a particular environment, or if accurate high-frequency information is not required and average levels of the measure of interest are adequate, then DRM is well worth considering.

Overview

EMA is now an established technique in health psychology. It is the best method of obtaining frequent accurate information on peoples' behaviour, emotions, and thoughts on a huge range of health-related issues. It is acceptable to many, can be implemented on widely available and commonly used devices such as smartphones, and can be integrated with other forms of automatic data collection and sources of environmental information. EMA is not invariably better than traditional retrospective questionnaires but provides unique information that can complement, and on occasion replace, other methods.

References

Anestis, M. D., Selby, E. A., Crosby, R. D., Wonderlich, S. A., Engel, S. G., & Joiner, T. (2010). A comparison of retrospective self-report versus ecological momentary assessment measures of affective lability in the examination of its relationship with bulimic symptomatology. *Behaviour Research and Therapy, 48*, 607–613. http://doi.org/10.1016/j.brat.2010.03.012

Blysma, L. M., Taylor-Clift, A., & Rottenberg, J. (2011). Emotional reactivity to daily events in major and minor depression. *Journal of Abnormal Psychology, 129*, 155–167. http://doi.org/10.1037/a0021662

Cranford, J. A., Shrout, P. E., Ida, M., Rafaeli, E., Yip, T., & Bolger, N. (2006). A procedure for evaluating sensitivity to within-person change: Can mood measures in dairy studies detect change reliably. *Personality and social Psychology Bulletin, 32*, 917–929. http://doi.org/10.1177/0146167206287721

Diamantopoulos, A., Sarstedt, M., Fuches, C., Wilczynski, P., & Kaiser, S. (2012). Guidelines for choosing between multi-item and single-item scales for construct measurement: A predictive validity perspective. *Journal of the Academy of Marketing Science, 40*, 434–449. http://doi.org/10.1007/s11747-011-0300-3

Dockray, S., Grant, H., Stone, A. A., Kahneman, D., Wardle, J., & Steptoe, A. (2010). A comparison of affect ratings obtained with ecological momentary assessment and the day reconstruction method. *Social Indicator Research, 99*, 269–283. http://doi.org/10.1007/s11205-010-9578-7

Edmondson, D., Shaffer, J. A., Chaplin, W. F., Burg, M. M., Stone, A. A., & Schwartz, J. E. (2013). Trait anxiety and trait anger measured by ecological momentary assessment and their correspondence with traditional trait questionnaires. *Journal of Research in Personality, 47*, 843–852. http://doi.org/10.1016/j.jrp.2013.08.005

Fahrenberg, J., Brugner, G., Foerster, F., & Kappler, C. (1999). Ambulatory assessment of diurnal changes with a hand held computer: Mood, attention and morningness-eveningness. *Personality and Individual Differences, 26*, 641–656. http://doi.org/10.1016/S0191-8869(98)00160-3

Farquharson, B., Bell, C., Johnston, D., Jones, M., Schofield, P., Allan, J., … Johnston, M. (2013). Nursing stress and patient care: Real-time investigation of the effect of nursing tasks and demands on psychological stress, physiological stress, and job performance: Study protocol. *Journal of Advanced Nursing, 16*, 1624–1635.

Fuller-Tyszkiewicz, M., Skouteris, H., Richardson, B., Bloe, J., Holmes, M., & Mills, J. (2013). Does the burden of experience sampling method undermine data quality in body imagine research? *Body Image, 10*, 607–613. http://doi.org/10.1016/j.bodyim.2013.06.003

Henker, B., Whalen, C. K., Jamner, J. D., & Delfino, R. J. (2002). Anxiety, affect and activity in teenagers: Monitoring daily life with electronic diaries. *Journal of the American Academy of Child and Adolescent Psychiatry, 41*, 660–670. http://doi.org/10.1097/00004583-200206000-00005

Herber, O. R., Jones, M. C., Smith, K., & Johnston, D. W. (2012). Assessing acute coronary syndrome patients' cardiac-related beliefs, motivation and mood over time to predict non-attendance at cardiac rehabilitation. *Journal of Advanced Nursing, 68*, 2778–2788.

Heron, K. E., & Smyth, J. M. (2013). Is intensive measurement of body image reactive? A two-study evaluation of ecological momentary assessment suggests not. *Body Image, 10*, 35–44. http://doi.org/10.1016/j.bodyim.2012.08.006

Johnston, D. W. (2012). Ambulatory monitory. In M. D. Gellman & J. R. Turner (Eds.), *Encyclopedia of behavioral medicine* (pp. 77–79). New York, NY: Springer.

Johnston, D. W., & Johnston, M. (2013). Useful theories should apply to individuals. *British Journal of Health Psychology, 18*, 469–473. http://doi.org/10.1111/bjhp.12049

Johnston, D. W., Jones, M. C., McCann, C. K., & McKee, L. (2013) Stress in nurses: Stress-related affect and its determinants examined over the nursing day. *Annals of Behavioural Medicine, 45*, 348–356. http://doi.org/10.1007/s12160-012-9458-2

Johnston, M., Johnston, D. W., Jones, M. C., Ricketts, I., Schofield, P., Allan, J., … Bell, B. (2013). *Nursing stress and patient care: Real-time investigation of the effect of nursing tasks and demands on psychological stress, physiological stress, and job performance. Final report (Grant CZH/4/640).* Edinburgh, UK: Chief Scientist Office.

Jones, M. C., & Johnston, D. (2011). Understanding phenomena in the real world: The case for real time data collection in health services research. *Journal of Health Services Research and Policy, 16*, 172–176. http://doi.org/10.1258/jhsrp.2010.010016

Jones, M. C., & Johnston, D. W. (2012). Does clinical incident seriousness and receipt of work-based support influence mood experienced by nurses at work? A behavioural diary study. *International Journal Nursing Studies, 48*, 978–987. http://doi.org/10.1016/j.ijnurstu.2012.02.014

Kahneman, D., Kruger, A. B., Schkade, D. A., Schwartz, N., & Stone, A. A. (2004). A survey method for characterizing daily life experience: The day reconstruction method. *Science, 306*, 1776–1780. http://doi.org/10.1126/science.1103572

Kamarck, T. W., Muldoon, M. F., Shiffman, S. S., & Sutton-Tyrrell, K. (2007). Experiences of demand and control during daily life are predictors of carotid athersosclerotic progression among health men. *Health Psychology, 26*, 324–332. http://doi.org/10.1037/0278-6133.26.3.324

Karasek, R., Brisson, C., Kawakami, N., Houtman, I., Bongers, P., & Amick, B. (1998). The Job Content Questionnaire (JCQ): An instrument for internationally comparative assessments of psychosocial job characteristics. *Journal of Occupational Health Psychology, 3*, 322–355. http://doi.org/10.1037/1076-8998.3.4.322

Kiene, S. M., Tennen, H., & Armeli, S. (2008). Today I'll use a condom, but who knows about tomorrow: A daily process study of variability in predictors of condom use. *Health Psychology, 27*, 463–472. http://doi.org/10.1037/0278-6133.27.4.463

Kim, J. M., Kikuchi, H., & Yamamoto, Y. (2013). Systematic comparison between ecological momentary assessment and day reconstruction method for fatigue and mood states in health adults. *British Journal of Heath Psychology, 18*, 155–167. http://doi.org/10.1111/bjhp.12000

Lavender, J. M., de Young, K. P., Anestis, M. D., Wonderlich, S. a., Crosby, R. D., Engel, S. G., … le Grange, D. (2013). Associations between retrospective versus ecological momentary assessment of emotion and eating disorder symptoms in anorexia nervosa. *Journal of Psychiatric Research, 47*, 1514–1520. http://doi.org/10.1016/j.jpsychires.2013.06.021

Leahey, T. M., Crowther, J. H., & Mickelson, K. D. (2007). The frequency, nature, and effects of naturally occurring appearance-focused social comparisons. *Behavior Therapy, 38*(2), 132–143. http://doi.org/10.1016/j.beth.2006.06.004

Messiah, A., Grondin, O., & Encrenaz, G. (2011). Factors associated with missing data in an experience sampling investigation of substance use determinants. *Drug and Alcohol Dependence, 114*, 153–158.

Michie, S., Abraham, C., Whittington, C., McAteer, J., & Gupta, S. (2009). Effective techniques in healthy eating and physical activity interventions: A meta-regression. *Health Psychology, 28*, 690–701. http://doi.org/10.1037/a0016136

Moullec, G., Maiano, C., Morin, A. J. S., Monthuy-Blanc, J., Rosello, L., & Ninot, G. (2011). A very short visual analog form of the Center for Epidemiologic Studies Depression Scale (CES-D) for the idiographic measurement of depression. *Journal of Affective Disorders, 1218*, 220–234. http://doi.org/10.1016/j.jad.2010.06.006

O'Connor, D. B., Jones, F., Conner, M., McMillan, B., & Ferguson, E. (2008). Effects of daily hassles and eating style on eating behavior. *Health Psychology, 27*(1S), S20–S31. http://doi.org/10.1037/0278-6133.27.1.S20

Quinn, F., Johnston, M., & Johnston, D. W. (2013). Testing an integrated behavioural and biomedical model of disability in N-of-1 studies with chronic pain. *Psychology & Health, 28*, 1391–1406. http://doi.org/10.1080/08870446.2013.814773

Redelmeier, D. A., Katz, J., & Kahneman, D. (2003). Memories of colonoscopy: A randomized trial. *Pain, 104*, 187–194. http://doi.org/10.1016/S0304-3959(03)00003-4

Runyan, J. D., Steenbergh, T. A., Bainbridge, C., Daugherty, D. A., Oke, L., & Fry, B. N. A. (2013). Smartphone ecological momentary assessment/intervention "App" for collecting real-time data and promoting self-awareness. *Plos One, 8*, e71325. http://doi.org/10.1371/journal.pone.0071325

Schwartz, J. E., & Stone, A. A. (1998). Strategies for analyzing ecological momentary assessment data. *Health Psychology, 17*, 6–16. http://doi.org/10.1037/0278-6133.17.1.6

Schwartz, J. E., Neale, J., Marco, C., Shiffman, S. S., & Stone, A. A. (1999). Does trait coping exist? A momentary assessment approach to the evaluation of traits. *Journal of Personality and Social Psychology, 77*, 360–369. http://doi.org/10.1037/0022-3514.77.2.360

Serre, F., Fatseas, M., Debrabant, R., Alexandre, J.-M., Auriacombe, M., & Swendsen, J. (2012). Ecological momentary assessment in alcohol, tobacco, cannabis and opiate dependence: A comparison of feasibility and validity. *Drug and Alcohol Dependence, 126*, 118–123. http://doi.org/10.1016/j.drugalcdep.2012.04.025

Sokolovsky, A. W., Mermelstein, R. J., & Hedeker, D. (2014). Factors predicting compliance to ecological momentary assessment among adolescent smokers. *Nicotine and Tobacco Research, 16*(3), 351–358. http://doi.org/10.1093/ntr/ntt154

Solhan, M. B., Trull, T. J., Jahng, S., & Wood, P. K. (2009). Clinical assessment of affective instability: Comparing EMA indices, questionnaire reports, and retrospective recall. *Psychological Assessment, 21*, 425–436. http://doi.org/10.1037/a0016869

Stone, A. A., & Shiffman, S. (1994). Ecological momentary assessment (EMA) in behavorial medicine. *Annals of Behavioral Medicine, 16*, 199–202.

Stone, A. A., Broderick, J. E., Schwartz, J. E., Shiffman, S., Litcher-Kelly, L., & Calvanese, P. (2003). Intensive momentary reporting of pain with an electronic diary: Reactivity, compliance, and patient satisfaction. *Pain, 104*, 343–351. http://doi.org/10.1016/S0304-3959(03)00040-X

Wirtz, D., Kruger, J., Scollon, C. N., & Diener, E. (2003). What to do on spring break? The role of predicted, on-line, and remembered experience in future choice. *Psychological Science, 14*, 520–524. http://doi.org/10.1111/1467-9280.03455

Chapter 19

Reporting Behaviour Change Interventions and Techniques

Susan Michie and Caroline E. Wood

UCL Centre for Behaviour Change, University College London, UK

In this chapter we outline the need for behavioural science to develop and implement an agreed, shared standard and method for the reporting of complex behaviour change interventions. We discuss the use of behaviour change techniques (BCTs) as a reliable methodology for the specification of interventions and illustrate this with examples from current research and practice.

Preventable behaviours, such as smoking, physical inactivity, eating unhealthy diets, and excessive alcohol consumption, have been identified as the leading causes of morbidity and mortality (Lozano et al., 2012; Mokdad, Marks, Stroup, & Gerberding, 2004; Murray et al., 2013; National Institute for Health and Care Excellence [NICE], 2007). Progress in tackling major health problems such as these requires behaviour change in those who are at risk from ill health, those with a chronic or acute illness, and health professionals and others responsible for delivering effective, evidence-based public health and health care. Interventions to change behaviour are therefore fundamental to promoting the uptake of healthy behaviours and the implementation of effective clinical practice (NICE, 2014). *Behaviour change interventions* refer to coordinated sets of activities designed to change specified behaviour patterns, such as prescribing behaviours, adherence behaviours, and screening attendance (Michie, Churchill, & West, 2011).

Behaviour change interventions are typically complex and comprise several potentially interacting active components (Craig et al., 2008). This complexity can make them challenging to accurately replicate in research, to synthesise across studies in evidence reviews, and to translate into practice. Thus, to inform the development of more effective health behaviour change interventions and to enhance the understanding of their mechanisms of action, it is crucial that researchers report interventions with clarity and detail. We require a reporting method that would enable us to have a clearer understanding of *what* was delivered in the intervention (i.e., the active ingredients) and *how* it was delivered, that is, who delivered, to whom, how often, for how long, in what format, and in what context (Davidson et al., 2003; Hoffmann, Erueti, & Glasziou, 2013; Michie, Fixsen, Grimshaw, & Eccles, 2009). This clarity is also needed to advance behavioural science, as evidence accumulation about behaviour change can only occur if scientists know exactly what was delivered in a particular intervention (Michie & Johnston, 2012, 2013; Rothman, 2004). Studies of published trials reports show that poor descriptions render 40–89% of interventions non-replicable. Thus, precise and reliable description of intervention content is an important step in reducing the waste that is evident in the current research process (Glasziou et al., 2014; Macleod et al., 2014). There are at least three potential benefits of implementing a more rigorous approach for specifying intervention content:

(1) Promotion of the accurate replication of interventions and control conditions in comparative effectiveness research;
(2) Specification of intervention content to facilitate faithful implementation of (a) intervention protocols in research and (b) interventions found to be effective; and
(3) Extraction and synthesis of information about intervention content in systematic reviews.

Promoting Accurate Replication of Interventions and Control Conditions in Comparative Effectiveness Research

Replicating interventions is a key activity in accumulating scientific knowledge and investigating generalisability across behaviours, populations, and settings. However, published descriptions of both behavioural and biomedical interventions frequently omit essential information; one analysis found that 67% of drug intervention descriptions were adequate compared with only 29% of non-pharmacological interventions (Glasziou, Meats, Heneghan, & Shepperd, 2008). When secondary data analyses take place to identify types of interventions that are effective, many are too poorly specified to be included (Michie, Abraham, Whittington, McAteer, & Gupta, 2009). This leads to confusion and uncertainty amongst researchers and practitioners and may result in low confidence in their abilities to accurately replicate interventions (Michie, Hardeman, et al., 2008).

To address this problem, a guide for reporting the essential minimum data for interventions was developed, drawing on existing checklists and relevant literature evaluated and synthesised in a consensus exercise involving 90 international experts from many disciplines (Hoffmann et al., 2014). The result is the Template for Intervention Description and Replication (TIDieR), a 12-item checklist covering intervention name, why (rationale), what (materials), what (procedure), who provided, how, where, when and how much, tailoring, modifications, how well (planned), how well (actual). The guide contains a brief explanation and cross-disciplinary examples for each item and can be used to guide the writing of intervention reports and may also be of value to journal editors and reviewers.

TIDieR is a significant step forward in reporting interventions. To complement this, a more fine-grained method is required to specify and report the content or active ingredients of interventions. These are the techniques with potential, in the right circumstances, to bring about changes to behaviour. In both intervention protocols and published reports, these active ingredients are often described in partial or vague terms. This is illustrated in a study of 152 Cochrane review trials of behavioural support for smoking cessation that found that only 44% of the techniques specified in the treatment manuals were specified in the published reports (Lorencatto, West, Stavri, & Michie, 2012).

Specifying Intervention Content for Faithful Implementation of Interventions

An under-specified intervention cannot be delivered with fidelity (i.e., as documented in the research protocol). This limits both the replication of interventions in the effort to accumulate evidence and the implementation of effective interventions. Poor fidelity to intervention protocols when practitioners try to implement the intervention in clinical practice has been documented in many areas (Borrelli, 2011). On average, fewer than half the techniques specified in treatment manuals were found to be delivered in a study of behavioural support for smoking cessation (Lorencatto, West, Bruguera, & Michie, 2014) and in a study of interventions to increase physical activity amongst a sedentary population with a family history of type 2 diabetes (Hardeman et al., 2007); the percentages were 41% and 42%, respectively.

Extracting and Synthesising Information on Intervention Content in Systematic Reviews

Evidence about behaviour change intervention effectiveness is accumulating slowly (NICE, 2007, 2014). Systematic reviews have been conducted across a wide range of behaviours and populations, as can be found in the Cochrane Collaboration library (http://www.thecochranelibrary.com/) and guidance provided by NICE (http://guidance.nice.org.uk/) and serve as a useful guide for health providers seeking the most effective interventions to bring about behaviour change. These reviews tend to report modest effects from very heterogeneous interventions and evaluation methods. This has limited the extent to which there are clear patterns of results and indications that one specific method or technique should be favoured over another. The essential elements of behaviour change interventions are frequently omitted from intervention descriptions. Titles and abstracts of published interventions have been found to mention the active components of the intervention in only 56% of published descriptions compared with over 90% in pharmacological interventions (McCleary, Duncan, Stewart, & Francis, 2013). This creates difficulties for evidence synthesis.

To date, we do not have a full understanding of what accounts for variability in effectiveness across interventions. Lack of a methodology for unpacking the "black box" of intervention content has limited progress in developing more effective interventions and reliably implementing effective ones (Craig et al., 2008; NICE, 2014). The absence of an agreed methodology also means that systematic reviewers develop their own systems for classifying content and synthesising intervention outcomes (Albarracín et al., 2005; Hardeman et al., 2007; Mischel, 2012; West, Walia, Hyder, Shahab, & Michie, 2010). This does not enhance evidence accumulation.

Guidance for Reporting Interventions

In the last decade, several guidance documents have clarified best practice in reporting intervention construction, content, and delivery. For example, CONSORT (Moher, Schulz, & Altman, 2003) advises researchers to report the precise details of the intervention as actually administered, and the TREND statement (Des Jarlais, Lyles, & Crepaz, 2004) emphasises the reporting of the theories used and full description of comparison and intervention conditions. The CONSORT statement has since been updated and extended to enable application to different study designs, interventions, and data (e.g., Boutron, Moher, Altman, Schulz, & Ravaud, 2008; Campbell, Piaggio, Elbourne, & Altman, 2012). More recently, the TIDieR checklist has been developed by incorporating guidance from statements such as CONSORT and TREND, to guide the writing of intervention reports (Hoffmann et al., 2014).

The existing guidance has been pivotal to improving the clarity and structure of intervention reporting and as such has been endorsed by many journals. The WIDER (Workgroup for Intervention Development and Evaluation Research) group has had some success in encouraging journal editors to ensure that transparent and accessible intervention descriptions are available before publication of intervention outcomes (Albrecht, Archibald, Arseneau, & Scott, 2013). However, descriptions of intervention content (i.e., the active ingredients) often still lack sufficient detail to allow replication.

The UK Medical Research Council's (MRC) guidance for developing and evaluating complex interventions called for the specification of the active ingredients as a necessary step for investigating how interventions exert their effect and therefore for designing more effective interventions and applying them appropriately across group and setting (Craig et al., 2008).

The detailed specification of interventions is important for both basic and applied behaviour science (Davidson et al., 2003; Hoffmann et al., 2013; Moher et al., 2003; Proctor, Powell, & McMillen, 2013). Further, a well-specified intervention is essential before evaluation of effectiveness is worth undertaking. Progress has been made in improving how intervention content is reported. However, if descriptions are to be communicated effectively and successfully replicated, a shared and standardised method of classifying intervention content is needed (Michie, Abraham, et al., 2011). In the absence of such a methodology, the same techniques may be reported with different labels (e.g., *self-monitoring* may be labelled *daily diaries*), or the same labels may be applied to different techniques (e.g., *behavioural counselling* may involve *educating patients or feedback, self-monitoring, and reinforcement*; Michie, Johnston, Francis, Hardeman, & Eccles, 2008).

Behaviour Change Technique (BCT) Taxonomies

One approach taken by researchers to develop a standardised method for reporting the content of interventions to change behaviour has been to specify the potentially active ingredients in terms of BCTs (Abraham & Michie, 2008; Albarracín et al., 2005; Hardeman, Griffin, Johnston, Kinmonth, & Wareham, 2000). By BCT, we mean an observable, replicable, and irreducible component of an intervention designed to alter or redirect causal processes that regulate behaviour (e.g., feedback, self-monitoring, reinforcement; Michie, Abraham, et al., 2011; Michie & Johnston, 2013). BCTs can be used alone or in combination and in a variety of formats. BCTs have been presented in structured lists, or *taxonomies* (Stavri & Michie, 2012). The BCTs have standardised labels, clear definitions and examples to specify the active content of interventions so that any given BCT will always be described by the same label and that label will always be used to describe the same BCT.

The first cross-domain BCT taxonomy was developed by Abraham and Michie (2008) and comprised 26 BCTs. Abraham and Michie's 26-item taxonomy showed good inter-coder reliability (i.e., the extent to which coders agreed on the presence/absence of BCTs) in identifying 22 BCTs and four BCT packages across 221 intervention descriptions in papers and manuals. More specifically, this work demonstrated the feasibility of specifying intervention content according to BCTs and provided a model by which researchers and practitioners could begin to ascertain which techniques, or combination of techniques, are associated with effective behaviour change.

The taxonomy has been widely used internationally to report interventions, synthesise evidence (Dombrowski et al., 2010; Dusseldorp, van Genugten, van Buuren, Verheijden, & van Empelen, 2014; Michie, Abraham, et al., 2009; Michie, Jochelson, Markham, & Bridle, 2009; Quinn, 2010), and design interventions (Araujo-Soares, McIntyre, MacLennan, & Sniehotta, 2009; Cahill & Lancaster, 2008; Michie, Hardeman, et al., 2008). Additionally, it has been used to assess the extent to which published reports reflect intervention protocols (Lorencatto et al., 2012) and to assess fidelity of delivery (Lorencatto et al., 2014). Abraham and Michie's taxonomy has also enabled the specification of professional competences for delivering BCTs (Dixon & Johnston, 2012; Michie, Churchill, et al., 2011) and has formed the basis for a national training programme (West & Michie, 2013; see http://www.ncsct.co.uk). Guidance has also been developed for incorporating BCTs in text-based interventions (Abraham, 2012).

Taxonomies of BCTs have since been developed to enable specification of BCTs across a number of different behavioural domains. For example, physical activity and healthy eating (Dombrowski et al., 2010; Michie, Abraham, et al., 2009), smoking cessation (Michie, Churchill, et al., 2011; West, Evans, & Michie, 2011; West et al., 2010), excessive alcohol consumption (Michie et al., 2012), sexually transmitted infections (Abraham, Good, Huedo-Medina, Warren, & Johnson, 2012; Albarracín et al., 2005), and changing professional behaviour (Ivers et al., 2012).

The development of BCT taxonomies has been accompanied by a progressive increase in comprehensiveness and clarity; however, this work has been conducted by only a few research groups. For the BCT methodology to maximise scientific advance, there is a need for collaborative work to develop agreed labels and definitions and reliable procedures for their identification across behaviours, disciplines, and countries. Given the number of BCTs that have been identified, it is also necessary to start exploring ways in which we can group BCTs to make the taxonomy more memorable and useable (Stavri & Michie, 2012). Previously, taxonomies have existed either in the form of an unstructured list or were linked to, or structured, according to categories judged to be the most appropriate by the authors, for example, theory (Abraham & Michie, 2008; Albarracín et al., 2005) and theoretical mechanism (Dixon & Johnston, 2012). Science and practice will be served by an agreed method for identifying BCTs and grouping them to make the method easier to use and more reliable.

The Behaviour Change Technique Taxonomy v1 (BCTTv1)

With these factors in mind, a three-year project, funded by the UK Medical Research Council, developed such a method. It engaged the input from a total of 400 researchers, practitioners, and policymakers all of whom were active in investigating, reviewing, designing, or delivering behavioural interventions. The result is a comprehensive, cross-domain, hierarchically structured list of clearly defined BCTs: Behaviour Change Technique Taxonomy v1 (BCTTv1; Michie, Abraham, et al., 2011; Michie et al., 2013). The project involved seven studies that developed and tested BCTTv1 as an appropriate and acceptable tool for improving specification of complex behaviour change interventions. In this next section, we summarise the findings from each study.

Developing a Comprehensive List of BCTs

The aim of this study was to develop an extensive, agreed list of BCTs used in behaviour change interventions. First, a list of distinct BCT labels and definitions was systematically developed using Delphi methods, building on a preliminary list of six published taxonomies (Abraham et al., 2012; Abraham & Michie, 2008; Dixon & Johnston, 2012; Michie, Abraham, et al., 2009; Michie, Hyder, Walia, & West, 2011; Michie et al., 2012). The list was then refined following feedback from the study's multi-disciplinary International Advisory Board of 30 behaviour change experts (see http://www.ucl.ac.uk/health-psychology/BCTtaxonomy/collaborators.php). BCTs were added, divided, and removed and their labels and definitions refined to capture the smallest components compatible with retaining the proposed active ingredients with the minimum of overlap. This resulted in 93 distinct BCTs, BCT Taxonomy v1 (BCTTv1; Michie et al., 2013). Development of BCTTv1 comprised a series of consensus exercises involving 35 experts in delivering and/or designing behaviour change interventions. These experts were drawn from a variety of disciplines including psychology, behavioural medicine, and health promotion and from seven countries. The resulting BCTs therefore have relevance among experts from varied behavioural domains, disciplines, and countries and potential relevance to the populations from which they were drawn.

Exploring the Structure of BCTTv1

The 93-item taxonomy poses problems for the easy recall of, and ready access to, the BCTs and thus its speed and accuracy of use. This study therefore aimed to provide a structure for the list to increase its ease of use, and to compare a pragmatic bottom-up method with a theoretical top-down method for generating this structure. Its objectives were to: (a) develop a hierarchical structure within BCTTv1 using an open-sort task (bottom-up method), (b) identify whether BCTs could reliably be linked to theoretical domains using a closed-sort task (top-down method), and (c) identify any overlap between the bottom-up and top-down groupings.

Participants created an average of 15.11 groups ($SD=6.11$, range 5–24 groups). BCTs relating to reward and punishment and cues and cue responses were perceived as markedly different to other BCTs. Fifty-nine of the BCTs were reliably allocated to 12 of the 14 theoretical domains; 47 were significant and 12 were of borderline significance. There was a significant association between the 16 bottom-up groupings and the 13 top-down groupings, $\chi^2=437.80$, $p<.001$. Thirty-six of the 208 bottom-up × top-down pairings (i.e., 16 × 13) showed greater overlap than expected by chance. However, only six combinations achieved satisfactory evidence of similarity. The bottom-up method, resulting in 16 groupings had some overlap with the theory-driven groupings. The moderate overlap between the groupings indicates some tendency to implicitly conceptualise BCTs in terms of the same theoretical domains. Further research into understanding the nature of this overlap will aid the conceptualisation of BCTs in terms of theory and application.

Training to Code Intervention Descriptions Using BCTTv1

Satisfactory inter-coder reliability has been demonstrated in using BCT taxonomies for shorter, specific behaviour categories amongst coders with varying amounts of training (Abraham et al., 2012; Abraham & Michie, 2008; Michie, Ashford, et al., 2011; Michie, Hyder, et al., 2011; Michie et al., 2012). For a BCT taxonomy to be reliably applied, it needs to have intrinsic clarity and structure *and* to be used by those with adequate skills.

The process of coding intervention descriptions into BCTs is a highly skilled task requiring familiarity with the BCT labels and definitions and the ability to make a series of complex interpretative judgments. This requires an effective programme of coder training to ensure a sufficient level of skills to demonstrate reliability and validity of identifying BCTs. Reliability can be measured by the extent to which coders agree with each other on the presence and absence of BCTs in intervention descriptions (inter-coder agreement) and validity can be measured by the extent to which coders agree with expert judgement about BCTs present and absent. In this study, two programmes of user training were developed, 1-day workshops and distance group-tutorials. Effectiveness was evaluated in terms of whether training enhanced coding reliability, validity, confidence in identifying BCTs, and the proportion of trainees reaching the accepted standard of competence. Both methods of training improved coding competence, trainee agreement with experts (i.e., validity; both $p<.001$), and trainee confidence in identifying the BCTs (workshops, $p<.001$; tutorials, $p<.05$). Training did not improve agreement between trainees about which BCTs were present and absent in the descriptions. Training was evaluated positively by trainees.

Assessing the Reliability and Validity of BCTTv1

The aim of this study was to investigate the reliability and validity of BCTTv1. Reliability was assessed by inter-coder and test–retest reliability (measured at two time points 1 month apart) in coding intervention descriptions into BCTs, and validity was assessed by the extent to which this coding agreed with experts (consensus reached by the BCTTv1 study team as to which BCTs were present). We calculated PABAK (prevalence- and bias-adjusted κ; Byrt, Bishop, & Carlin, 1993) to assess agreement between coders. In addition, we also calculated the AC1 statistic (Gwet, 2012) and tested whether the two statistics gave different measurements of inter-coder agreement. Finally, we investigated trained coders' confidence in identifying BCTs in intervention descriptions and whether descriptions varied in the ease with which BCTs could be identified.

In all, 80 of 93 defined BCTs were identified by at least one trained coder and 22 BCTs were identified in 16 or more of 40 descriptions. Thus coders made extensive use of BCTTv1, justifying the large number of BCTs included. Good inter-coder reliability was observed across 80 BCTs; 64 (80%) achieved mean PABAK scores of 0.70 or greater and 59 (74%) achieved mean scores of 0.80 or greater. There was good within-coder agreement between time 1 and time 2 thus demonstrating good test–retest reliability. Good validity was demonstrated for the 15 BCTs identified by experts; trained coder agreement with expert coding was good (i.e., PABAK >0.70) for 14 of the 15 BCTs. Coders' confidence in their BCT identifications varied across BCTs and increased from time 1 to time 2.

Inter-coder reliability was good across all of the intervention descriptions ($M=0.87$, $SD=0.05$). Only 4 of 40 descriptions had PABAK scores below 0.80 (mean PABAK for the four descriptions $=.76$, $SD=0.04$). All four intervention descriptions were from protocols published in 2010 by BMC Public Health. Results showed that the PABAK and AC1 statistics generated very similar assessment of inter-coder reliability for the majority of BCTs; they only differed for the most frequently occurring BCTs with PABAK generating lower scores than AC1.

Since its development, BCTTv1 has been widely applied by researchers and practitioners to specify, evaluate, and synthesise behaviour change interventions targeting a range of behaviours, for example, to increase young adults' condom use intentions and behaviour (Newby, French, Brown, & Lecky, 2013), to reduce decline of physical activity during pregnancy (Currie et al., 2013), to evaluate a national sexual health and relationships education package (Dale, Raftery, & Locke, 2014), and to improve oral hygiene behaviours (Schwarzer, Antoniuk, & Gholami, 2015). The final group of studies sought to explore whether BCTTv1 can improve the quality of behaviour change intervention reporting.

Using BCTTv1 to Report Behaviour Change Interventions

In three different study designs, 166 participants (writers) watched videos of behaviour change interventions and wrote descriptions of the active content delivered, with and without BCTTv1 provision and with and without training. The first two studies (both randomised controlled trials) examined provision of BCTTv1 without training, and the effects of training plus provision of BCTTv1 compared with a control group receiving neither the taxonomy nor training. A within-person design was used to assess change in the quality of descriptions before and after training. Writers provided with BCTTv1 for the task evaluated usability and acceptability of using BCTTv1 to write descriptions. Twelve raters (untrained in BCTTv1) assessed description quality in terms of clarity and replicability, and 12 coders (trained in BCTTv1) coded the descriptions for BCTs.

Provision of the taxonomy alone did not improve quality. Training writers resulted in descriptions that were rated to be of poorer quality in one study but training improved description quality in the within-person study. The taxonomy improved agreement between coders on the presence of BCTs. More work is being undertaken to develop guidance for using BCTTv1 to describe the content of behaviour change interventions in written reports.

Future Developments

The work discussed in this chapter is a step towards the objective of developing agreed methods that permit and facilitate the aims of CONSORT and UK MRC guidance of precise reporting of complex behavioural interventions. BCT taxonomies lay the foundation for the reliable and systematic specification of behaviour change interventions. Their use significantly increases the possibilities of identifying the active ingredients within intervention components, the conditions under which they are effective and the possibilities of replicating and implementing effective interventions. The BCTTv1 (Michie, Abraham, et al., 2011; Michie et al., 2013) is foundational for long-term goals of developing a comprehensive, hierarchical, reliable, and generalisable BCT taxonomy that can be applied, and possibly extended, to many different types of intervention, including organisational and community interventions.

We recommend that coders already trained in the use of BCTTv1 regularly review training materials and check their own reliability. To give coders further practice and experience in applying relevant learning principles to coding BCTs, and in order to train new coders using BCTTv1, we have developed an interactive online training course that can be accessed via the BCT Taxonomy project website (http://www.ucl.ac.uk/health-psychology/BCTtaxonomy/). The course trains coders on frequently used BCTs from the taxonomy over a number of tutorial sessions and practice coding tasks. This allows trainees to apply newly acquired knowledge and skills. They also have access to a social support network to foster continued and effective learning. To further increase usability of the taxonomy, a digital version of BCTTv1 available as a smartphone and tablet application has been developed. Users can download this version via a link on the website.

It is anticipated that further refinement and development of BCTTv1 will occur as a result of its use and feedback from trainees, primary researchers, systematic reviewers, and practitioners. A system has already been set up on the website to receive this feedback and a multidisciplinary, international team is being established to guide the development of BCTTv2.

BCTTv1 is a methodological tool for specifying intervention content and does not, itself, make links with theory. Further research is needed to link BCTs to theories of behaviour change, for both designing and evaluating theory-based interventions. Publications have suggested links between BCTs and domains of theoretical constructs (Abraham, 2012; Michie, Johnston, Francis, & Hardeman, 2005). A methodology for linking BCTs to theoretical constructs is currently being developed and evaluated in a multi-disciplinary and internationally supported project led by Michie and funded by the MRC Methodology Board. Details of this project are available on the BCT Taxonomy project website. This project will begin to develop a behaviour change ontology, linking BCTs, theoretical mechanisms of action, modes of delivery, and context. This will allow the investigation, and building, of an evidence base of interactions within this ontology and of their impact on outcomes. This will be a step change in advancing behavioural science research.

Meanwhile, a guide to developing behaviour change interventions has been published. This guide provides a systematic method for selecting BCTs on the basis of a theoretical analysis of the target behaviour in context, using the theoretical domains framework (Cane, O'Connor, & Michie, 2012; Michie, Johnston, Abraham, et al., 2005) and/or the behaviour change wheel (Michie, van Stralen, & West, 2011). This book is aimed at researchers, practitioners, policymakers, organisational change consultants and systems scientists, and all those involved in designing behaviour change interventions (Michie, Atkins, & West, 2014). *The Behaviour Change Wheel Guide* will be available via the website of University College London's Centre for Behaviour Change (http://www.ucl.ac.uk/behaviour-change).

Conclusion

BCT taxonomies can be used to reliably specify the active content of complex behaviour change interventions in standard terms that can be understood across discipline and country. BCTTv1 is an extensive, hierarchically organised taxonomy of 93 distinct BCTs (with clear definitions and examples) that offers a reliable and useable method for specifying the active content of interventions. The process of building a shareable consensus methodology is likely to be an ongoing, iterative process, involving collaborative input from international advisors and networks. The increasing standardisation and communication of methods, and wide collaborations and networks to achieve this, are steps forward in advancing the science of behaviour change.

References

Abraham, C. (2012). Mapping change mechanisms and behaviour change techniques: A systematic approach to promoting behaviour change through text. In C. K. Abraham & M. Kools (Eds.), *Writing health communication: An evidence-based guide* (pp. 89–98). London, UK: Sage.

Abraham, C., Good, A., Huedo-Medina, T., Warren, M., & Johnson, B. (2012). Reliability and utility of the SHARP Taxonomy of Behaviour Change Techniques. *Psychology & Health, 27*, 1–2.

Abraham, C., & Michie, S. (2008). A taxonomy of behavior change techniques used in interventions. *Health Psychology, 27*, 379–387. http://doi.org/10.1037/0278-6133.27.3.379

Albarracín, D., Gillette, J. C., Earl, A. N., Glasman, L. R., Durantini, M. R., & Ho, M.-H. (2005). A test of major assumptions about behavior change: A comprehensive look at the effects of passive and active HIV-prevention interventions since the beginning of the epidemic. *Psychological Bulletin, 131*, 856–897 http://doi.org/10.1037/0033-2909.131.6.856

Albrecht, L., Archibald, M., Arseneau, D., & Scott, S. D. (2013). Development of a checklist to assess the quality of reporting of knowledge translation interventions using the Workgroup for Intervention Development and Evaluation Research (WIDER) recommendations. *Implementation Science, 8*, 52. http://doi.org/10.1186/1748-5908-8-52

Araujo-Soares, V., McIntyre, T., MacLennan, G., & Sniehotta, F. F. (2009). Development and exploratory cluster-randomised opportunistic trial of a theory-based intervention to enhance physical activity among adolescents. *Psychology and Health, 24*, 805–822. http://doi.org/10.1080/08870440802040707

Borrelli, B. (2011). The assessment, monitoring, and enhancement of treatment fidelity in public health clinical trials. *Journal of Public Health Dentistry, 71*(Suppl. 1), S52–S63. http://doi.org/10.1111/j.1752-7325.2011.00233.x

Boutron, I., Moher, D., Altman, D., Schulz, K., & Ravaud, P. (2008). Methods and processes of the CONSORT Group: Example of an extension for trials assessing nonpharmacologic treatments. *Annals of Internal Medicine, 148*, W60–W66. http://doi.org/10.7326/0003-4819-148-4-200802190-00008-w1

Byrt, T., Bishop, J., & Carlin, J. B. (1993). Bias, prevalence and kappa. *Journal of Clinical Epidemiology, 46*, 423–429. http://doi.org/10.1016/0895-4356(93)90018-V

Cahill, K. M., & Lancaster, T. (2008). Workplace interventions for smoking cessation. *Cochrane Database of Systematic Reviews, CD003440*(4), 70.

Campbell, M., Piaggio, G., Elbourne, D., & Altman, D. (2012). Consort 2010 statement: Extension to cluster randomised trials. *BMJ, 345*.

Cane, J., O'Connor, D., & Michie, S. (2012). Validation of the theoretical domains framework for use in behaviour change and implementation research. *Implementation Science, 7*, 37. http://doi.org/10.1186/1748-5908-7-37

Craig, P., Dieppe, P., Macintyre, S., Michie, S., Nazareth, I., & Petticrew, M. (2008). Developing and evaluating complex interventions: The new Medical Research Council guidance. *British Medical Journal, 337*, 979–983. http://doi.org/10.1136/bmj.a1655

Currie, S., Sinclair, M., Murphy, M., Madden, E., Dunwoody, L., & Liddle, D. (2013). Reducing the decline in physical activity during pregnancy: A systematic review of behaviour change interventions. *Plos One, 8*(6), e66385. http://doi.org/10.1371/journal.pone.0066385

Dale, H., Raftery, B., & Locke, H. (2014). Behaviour change and sexual health: SHARE programme evaluation. *Health Education, 114*(1), 2–19. http://doi.org/10.1108/HE-12-2012-0056

Davidson, K. W., Goldstein, M., Kaplan, R. M., Kaufmann, P. G., Knatterud, G. L., Orleans, C. T., … Whitlock, E. P. (2003). Evidence-based behavioral medicine: What is it and how do we achieve it? *Annals of Behavioral Medicine, 26*(3), 161–171. http://doi.org/10.1207/S15324796ABM2603_01

Des Jarlais, D. C., Lyles, C., & Crepaz, N. (2004). Improving the reporting quality of nonrandomized evaluations of behavioral and public health interventions: The TREND statement. *American Journal of Public Health, 94*(3), 361–366. http://doi.org/10.2105/AJPH.94.3.361

Dixon, D., & Johnston, M. (2012). *Health behavior change competency framework: Competences to deliver interventions to change lifestyle behaviors that affect health*. Edinburgh, UK: Scottish Government.

Dombrowski, S. U., Sniehotta, F. F., Avenell, A., Johnston, M., MacLennan, G., & Araújo-Soares, V. (2010). Identifying active ingredients in complex behavioural interventions for obese adults with obesity-related co-morbidities or additional risk factors for co-morbidities: a systematic review. *Health Psychology Review, 6*(1), 7–32. http://doi.org/10.1080/17437199.2010.513298

Dusseldorp, E., van Genugten, L., van Buuren, S., Verheijden, M. W., & van Empelen, P. (2014). Combinations of techniques that effectively change health behavior: Evidence from meta-CART analysis. *Health Psychology, 33*, 1530–1540. http://doi.org/10.1037/hea0000018

Glasziou, P., Altman, D., Bossuyt, P., Boutron, I., Clarke, M., Julious, S., … Wager, E. (2014). Reducing waste from incomplete or unusable reports of biomedical research. *The Lancet, 383*, 267–276. http://doi.org/10.1016/S0140-6736(13)62228-X

Glasziou, P., Meats, E., Heneghan, C., & Shepperd, S. (2008). What is missing from descriptions of treatment in trials and reviews? *BMJ, 336*(7659), 1472–1474. http://doi.org/10.1136/bmj.39590.732037.47

Gwet, K. L. (2012). *Handbook of inter-rater reliability: The definitive guide to measuring the extent of agreement among multiple raters*. Gaithersburg, MD: Advanced Analytics Press.

Hardeman, W., Griffin, S., Johnston, M., Kinmonth, A., & Wareham, N. (2000). Interventions to prevent weight gain: A systematic review of psychological models and behaviour change methods. *International Journal of Obesity and Related Metabolic Disorders, 24*, 131–143. http://doi.org/10.1038/sj.ijo.0801100

Hardeman, W., Michie, S., Fanshawe, T., Prevost, T., McLoughlin, K., & Kinmonth, A. (2007). Fidelity of delivery of a physical activity intervention: Predictors and consequences. *Psychology & Health, 23*(1), 11–24. http://doi.org/10.1080/08870440701615948

Hoffmann, T., Erueti, C., & Glasziou, P. (2013). Poor description of non-pharmacological interventions: Analysis of consecutive sample of randomised trials. *BMJ, 347*.

Hoffmann, T. C., Glasziou, P. P., Boutron, I., Milne, R., Perera, R., Moher, D., ... Michie, S. (2014). Better reporting of interventions: Template for intervention description and replication (TIDieR) checklist and guide. *BMJ, 348*.

Ivers, N., Jamtvedt, G., Flottorp, S., Young, J. M., Odgaard-Jensen, J., French, S. D., ... Oxman, A. D. (2012). Audit and feedback: Effects on professional practice and healthcare outcomes. *Cochrane Database of Systematic Reviews, 6*, CD000259. http://doi.org/10.1002/14651858.CD000259.pub3

Lorencatto, F., West, R., Bruguera, C., & Michie, S. (2014). A method for assessing fidelity of delivery of telephone behavioral support for smoking cessation. *Journal of Consulting and Clinical Psychology, 82*, 482–491. http://doi.org/10.1037/a0035149

Lorencatto, F., West, R., Stavri, Z., & Michie, S. (2012). How well is intervention content described in published reports of smoking cessation interventions? *Nicotine & Tobacco Research, 15*, 1273–1282. http://doi.org/10.1093/ntr/nts266

Lozano, R., Naghavi, M., Foreman, K., Lim, S., Shibuya, K., Aboyans, V., ... Memish, Z. A. (2012). Global and regional mortality from 235 causes of death for 20 age groups in 1990 and 2010: A systematic analysis for the Global Burden of Disease Study 2010. *Lancet, 380*, 2095–2128. http://doi.org/10.1016/S0140-6736(12)61728-0

Macleod, M., Michie, S., Roberts, I., Dirnagl, U., Chalmers, I., Ioannidis, J., ... Glasziou, P. (2014). Biomedical research: Increasing value, reducing waste. *Lancet, 383*, 101–104. http://doi.org/10.1016/S0140-6736(13)62329-6

McCleary, N., Duncan, E. M., Stewart, F., & Francis, J. J. (2013). Active ingredients are reported more often for pharmacologic than non-pharmacologic interventions: An illustrative review of reporting practices in titles and abstracts. *Trials, 14*, 146. http://doi.org/10.1186/1745-6215-14-146

Michie, S., Abraham, C., Eccles, M., Francis, J., Hardeman, W., & Johnston, M. (2011). Strengthening evaluation and implementation by specifying components of behaviour change interventions: A study protocol. *Implementation Science, 6*, 10. http://doi.org/10.1186/1748-5908-6-10

Michie, S., Abraham, C., Whittington, C., McAteer, J., & Gupta, S. (2009). Effective techniques in healthy eating and physical activity interventions: A meta-regression. *Health Psychology, 28*, 690–701. http://doi.org/10.1037/a0016136

Michie, S., Ashford, S., Sniehotta, F., Dombrowski, S., Bishop, A., & French, D. (2011). A refined taxonomy of behaviour change techniques to help people change their physical activity and healthy eating behaviours: The CALO-RE taxonomy. *Psychology & Health, 26*, 1479–1498. http://doi.org/10.1080/08870446.2010.540664

Michie, S., Atkins, L., & West, R. (2014). *The behaviour change wheel: A guide to designing interventions*. London, UK: Silverback Publishing.

Michie, S., Churchill, S., & West, R. (2011). Identifying evidence-based competences required to deliver behavioural support for smoking cessation. *Annals of Behavioral Medicine, 41*(1), 59–70. http://doi.org/10.1007/s12160-010-9235-z

Michie, S., Fixsen, D., Grimshaw, J., & Eccles, M. (2009). Specifying and reporting complex behaviour change interventions: The need for a scientific method. *Implemention Science, 4*, 40. http://doi.org/10.1186/1748-5908-4-40

Michie, S., Hardeman, W., Fanshawe, T., Toby Prevost, A., Taylor, L., & Kinmonth, A. (2008). Investigating theoretical explanations for behaviour change: The case study of ProActive. *Psychology & Health, 23*(1), 25–39.

Michie, S., Hyder, N., Walia, A., & West, R. (2011). Development of a taxonomy of behaviour change techniques used in individual behavioural support for smoking cessation. *Addictive Behaviors, 36*, 315–319. http://doi.org/10.1016/j.addbeh.2010.11.016

Michie, S., Jochelson, K., Markham, W., & Bridle, C. (2009). Low-income groups and behaviour change interventions: A review of intervention content, effectiveness and theoretical frameworks. *Journal of Epidemiology and Community Health, 63*, 610–622. http://doi.org/10.1136/jech.2008.078725

Michie, S., & Johnston, M. (2012). Theories and techniques of behaviour change: Developing a cumulative science of behaviour change. *Health Psychology Review, 6*(1), 1–6. http://doi.org/10.1080/17437199.2012.654964

Michie, S., & Johnston, M. (2013). Behaviour change techniques. In M. Gellman & J. R. Turner (Eds.), *Encyclopeadia of behavioural medicine* (pp. 182–187). London, UK: Springer.

Michie, S., Johnston, M., Abraham, C., Lawton, R., Parker, D., & Walker, A. (2005). Making psychological theory useful for implementing evidence based practice: A consensus approach. *Quality & Safety in Health Care, 14*(1), 26–33. http://doi.org/10.1136/qshc.2004.011155

Michie, S., Johnston, M., Francis, J., & Hardeman, W. (2005, November). *Behaviour change interventions: Developing a classification system (workshop)*. Paper presented at the Annual Scientific Meeting of the UK Society of Behavioural Medicine, London, UK.

Michie, S., Johnston, M., Francis, J., Hardeman, W., & Eccles, M. (2008). From theory to intervention: Mapping theoretically derived behavioural determinants to behaviour change techniques. *Applied Psychology, 57*, 660–680. http://doi.org/10.1111/j.1464-0597.2008.00341.x

Michie, S., Richardson, M., Johnston, M., Abraham, C., Francis, J., Hardeman, W., … Wood, C. (2013). The behavior change technique taxonomy (v1) of 93 hierarchically clustered techniques: Building an international consensus for the reporting of behavior change interventions. *Annals of Behavioral Medicine, 46*(1), 81–95. http://doi.org/10.1007/s12160-013-9486-6

Michie, S., van Stralen, M., & West, R. (2011). The behaviour change wheel: A new method for characterising and designing behaviour change interventions. *Implementation Science, 6*, 42. http://doi.org/10.1186/1748-5908-6-42

Michie, S., Whittington, C., Hamoudi, S., Zarnani, F., Tober, G., & West, R. (2012). Identification of behaviour change techniques to reduce excessive alcohol consumption. *Addiction, 107*, 1431–1440. http://doi.org/10.1111/j.1360-0443.2012.03845.x

Mischel, W. (2012, May). *Presidential address*. Paper presented at the Association for Psychological Science Annual Convention, Washington, DC.

Moher, D., Schulz, K., & Altman, D. (2003). The CONSORT statement: Revised recommendations for improving the quality of reports of parallel-group randomised trials. *Clinical Oral Investigations, 7*(1), 2–7.

Mokdad, A. H., Marks, J. S., Stroup, D. F., & Gerberding, J. L. (2004). Actual causes of death in the United States, 2000. *Journal of the Americal Medical Association, 291*, 1238–1245. http://doi.org/10.1001/jama.291.10.1238

Murray, C. J. L., Richards, M. A., Newton, J. N., Fenton, K. A., Anderson, H. R., Atkinson, C., … Davis, A. (2013). UK health performance: Findings of the Global Burden of Disease Study 2010. *The Lancet, 381*, 997–1020. http://doi.org/10.1016/S0140-6736(13)60355-4

Newby, K., French, D., Brown, K., & Lecky, D. (2013). Increasing young adults' condom use intentions and behaviour through changing chlamydia risk and coping appraisals: Study protocol for a cluster randomised controlled trial of efficacy. *BMC Public Health, 13*, 528. http://doi.org/10.1186/1471-2458-13-528

National Institute for Health and Care Excellence (NICE). (2007). *Behaviour change: The principles for effective interventions (PH6)*. London, UK: Author.

National Institute for Health and Care Excellence (NICE). (2014). *Behaviour change: The principles for effective interventions (PH6)*. London, UK: Author.

Proctor, E., Powell, B., & McMillen, J. (2013). Implementation strategies: Recommendations for specifying and reporting. *Implementation Science, 8*, 139. http://doi.org/10.1186/1748-5908-8-139

Quinn, F. (2010). *On integrating biomedical and behavioural approaches to activity limitation with chronic pain: Testing integrated models between and within persons*. Unpublished doctoral dissertation. University of Aberdeen, UK.

Rothman, A. J. (2004). "Is there nothing more practical than a good theory?": Why innovations and advances in health behavior change will arise if interventions are used to test and refine theory. *International Journal of Behavioral Nutrition and Physical Activity, 1*(1), 11.

Schwarzer, R., Antoniuk, A., & Gholami, M. (2015). A brief intervention changing oral self-care, self-efficacy, and self-monitoring. *British Journal of Health Psychology, 20*, 56–67. http://doi.org/10.1111/bjhp.12091

Stavri, Z., & Michie, S. (2012). Classification systems in behavioural science: Current systems and lessons from the natural, medical and social sciences. *Health Psychology Review, 6*(1), 113–140. http://doi.org/10.1080/17437199.2011.641101

West, R., Evans, A., & Michie, S. (2011). Behavior change techniques used in group-based behavioral support by the English stop-smoking services and preliminary assessment of association with short-term quit outcomes. *Nicotine & Tobacco Research, 13*, 1316–1320. http://doi.org/10.1093/ntr/ntr120

West, R., & Michie, S. (2013). Carbon monoxide verified 4-week quit rates in the English Stop Smoking Services before versus after establishment of the National Centre for Smoking Cessation and Training. *Smoking in Britain, 1*, 3.

West, R., Walia, A., Hyder, N., Shahab, L., & Michie, S. (2010). Behavior change techniques used by the English Stop Smoking Services and their associations with short-term quit outcomes. *Nicotine & Tobacco Research, 12*, 742–747. http://doi.org/10.1093/ntr/ntq074

Chapter 20
Cultural Adaptation of Measures

Sofía López-Roig and María-Ángeles Pastor

Miguel Hernández University, Department of Health Psychology, Elche, Spain

Introduction

The internationalization of science promotes the adaptation of instruments from one language and cultural context to another, where the language may be the same or different. As a consolidated field, health psychology offers possibilities for the interchange of knowledge. Moreover, improvements can be made in testing hypotheses and confirming and modifying theories by achieving external validity through different socio-cultural contexts. These issues require culturally adapted instruments. In fact, cultural adaptation of instruments and their international use is one of the most important areas in psychology assessment (Evers et al., 2013; Muñiz, Elosua, & Hambleton, 2013).

Nowadays there are many validated instruments in the health psychology area and most have been originally developed in English-speaking countries. Therefore, the main work consists in adapting instruments from this language to others. However, even in countries or areas sharing the same language, it is also necessary to adapt measures from one culture to another (e.g., English in North America and Britain, Spanish in South America and Spain, French in France and Canada or other countries) or between different cultural communities within a single country (Beaton, Bombardier, Guillemin, & Bosi Ferraz, 2000; Guillemin, Bombardier, & Beaton, 1993; Hambleton, 2005).

There are many guidelines, methods, and procedures for translating and adapting tests and psychological instruments, including different empirical- and theory-based recommendations (Acquadro, Conway, Hareendran, & Aaronson, 2008; Beaton et al., 2000; Guillemin et al., 1993; Hambleton, Merenda, & Spielberger, 2005; International Test Commission [ITC], 2010; Matsumoto & Van De Vijver, 2011; Muñiz et al., 2013; Two et al., 2010; Wild et al., 2005; Wild et al., 2009). Acquadro et al. (2008) conducted a literature review on the methods for linguistic validation used for Health Related Quality of Life questionnaires. They concluded that a multistep approach involving a centralized review process was a common feature but each group proposed its own sequence of translation and weighted each step differently. Furthermore, they found no empirical evidence on the superiority of one specific method over another. As each test adaptation project can be seen as unique, we cannot find a single and complete standardized procedure. However, there are important recurring themes to take into account such as non-literal translations, cultural features, the construct relevance, and validation procedures (Matsumoto & Van De Vijver, 2011).

The ITC (http://www.intestcom.org) has been working for decades in this field and has recently reviewed their principles for test translation and adaptation according to 20 guidelines grouped in six main areas: Precondition, test development, confirmation, administration, score scales and interpretation, and documentation (Muñiz et al., 2013). In this chapter, we deal with different steps related mainly to instrument development (translation and adaptation) and confirmation (empirical study of adaptation) areas, considering also the proposals of scientific guidelines for generic and health-specific measures.

Methodological Issues

Cultural adaptation implies the modification of a previously validated measure in another language and/or context by searching for linguistic and psychological similarities. Both domains are important for a quality adapted measure. The former refers to text aspects, such as semantic equality, comprehensibility, readability, and style. Psychological issues involve the pragmatics of language in a cultural context perspective to guarantee the same meaning in both cultural contexts. Adaptation maximizes psychological similarity (Van de Vijver & Poortinga, 2005).

According to the ITC, before starting the adaptation process, we should consider legal issues related to the use of the instrument, such as intellectual property questions, and we should also consider the construct measured by the instrument. We should ask whether the construct is relevant or makes sense in the new target population and whether the construct could show a reasonable level of overlap between both the original and the target version (Beaton et al., 2000; Hambleton, 2005; Matsumoto & Van de Vijver, 2011; Muñiz et al., 2013).

Development of Instruments: Translation and Adaptation

Linguistic and Cultural Adaptation

Forward and backward judgmental designs are used to adapt measures (for an overview Hambleton, 2005; Matsumoto & Van de Vijver, 2011). Both designs require independent translators to adapt the instrument to the target language. Authors recommend using at least two independent translators, in order to contrast and resolve different points and avoid preferences or peculiarities (Guillemin et al., 1993; Hambleton, 2005). Selection and training of translators is a main issue. They should be competent in the language of interest and preferably be familiar with both the source and target cultures and not just the languages. It is also desirable that one of them has knowledge in the adaptation of instruments and the objectives and concepts involved (Beaton et al., 2000; Guillemin et al., 1993). Translators should provide written reports on their versions.

In *forward-translation design*, after at least two target versions are provided by independent translators, another translator judges the equivalences between the target language versions. After he/she detects errors and divergent interpretations (in items, answer scales, or instructions) and drafts the report, a final target version is produced by another person or committee. In *back-translation design*, other translators take each of the target language versions and translate them back to the source language. This step requires translators without knowledge of the original instrument who independently produce as many back-translations as translations. Translators and back-translators should translate into their mother tongue. In all steps, written reports are provided by each translator. At this stage, the original and back-translated versions are judged on their equivalence by another person or committee (Beaton et al., 2000; Guillemin et al., 1993; Hambleton, 2005). The original and a final back-translated version might not show a high level of coincidence. The reason being that cultural equivalence needs to ensure a fully comprehensible translation, maintaining the concept while also fitting the cultural target context (Guillemin et al., 1993; ITC, 2010; Muñiz et al., 2013).

Where possible, the final review should be performed by a committee of experts (e.g., translators, representatives of the target group, methodologists, and experts in the construct measured) participating and judging the adaptation in an iterative depuration process (Guillemin et al., 1993; Hambleton, 2005; Muñiz et al., 2013). The committee will be able to detect both misunderstandings and failures to adapt to the target cultural context and ambiguity in the source version. Furthermore, they will be able to work with unexpected meanings or interpretations in the final versions (Beaton et al., 2000; Guillemin et al., 1993). External and independent experts in the construct measured can also evaluate the representativeness and relevance of items to support evidence for *face validity* in the new translation version. They can also apply matching and rating tasks and several *content validity* indexes to establish the content congruence (Sireci & Faulkner-Bond, 2014).

Appropriate translation and adaptation processes involve semantic, idiomatic, experiential, and conceptual equivalence (Beaton et al., 2000; Guillemin et al., 1993).

Semantic equivalence in the meaning of words requires special attention to vocabulary and grammar (e.g., verbal modes, adverbs, prepositions). For example, the passive voice is common in English but less so in other languages; or in other language versions of instruments such as the French, German, or Spanish, the present perfect is replaced by the simple present (Le Gal et al., 2010).

To achieve *idiomatic* equivalence, expressions and colloquialisms from the original version usually need to be substituted by another equivalent expression in the target language. Words and expressions have to show similar frequencies and level of difficulty, readability, grammar usage, and writing style and have to be comparable in both versions (Van de Vijver & Poortinga, 2005). For example, "Do you feel blue?" – blue in most non-English-speaking countries is just a colour.

Experiential equivalence implies that the situations evoked by the source version have correspondence in the target version. In that sense, it is advisable to take into account emotions, behaviours, and thoughts (Van de Vijver & Poortinga, 2005). The greater the distance between source and target group, the greater the differences of a specific culture's conceptualization of a particular experience. For example, instruments developed in industrialized countries might need some adaptation in other industrialized countries, whereas in other contexts, such as rural areas, completely new measures may be required (Jayawickreme, Atanasov, Goonasekera, & Foa, 2012).

Item contents, especially referring to experiences, feelings, skills, behaviours, or activities, need to be commonplace and familiar for the target population. For instance, people differ in their expressions of pain or distress, which can range from words describing universal symptoms and emotions to local culturally acceptable terms (Bass, Bolton, & Murray, 2007). In the case of *feeling blue* or *feeling down*, describing the experience of sadness, we should find expressions in the target version sensitive enough to capture the emotion (Van de Vijver & Poortinga, 2005; Jayawickreme et al., 2012). For example, in Spanish the meaning is frequently expressed as *feeling sad* or *under the weather*.

Quite often, items referring to daily life experience may have a good translation in the intended language and yet make no sense in the target group because they do not reflect meaningful experiences. Some activities, situations, or tasks depicted in the source measure must be replaced by others similarly representative in the repertoire of the target groups (Hambleton, 2005). For example, in our Spanish adaptation of the West Haven–Yale Multidimensional Pain Inventory-Part III (MPI; Kerns, Turk, & Rudy, 1985) for rheumatic patients (Pastor, López-Roig, Rodríguez-Marín, Terol, & Sánchez, 1995), *work in the garden* (item 6) was unusual in a Spanish context. It was replaced by *looking after the plants*. In adaptations of American health status instruments *walk several blocks* is changed to *walk more than one kilometre* because the original expression is meaningless in some European countries; or it is necessary to delete *dryer* from *to do laundry with washer and dryer* because that machine is not used in some countries (Le Gal et al., 2010).

Finally, *conceptual* equivalence refers to the connection of words and expressions with the construct. Sometimes words and expressions have different conceptual meanings in different cultures. A quality adapted version implies a good validity of the concept explored, which means that events have to be related to the concept in the target population. For instance, the meaning of *family* would differ between cultures with different concepts (i.e., nuclear vs. extended family). In some countries, *friend* refers to someone very close, and when the aim of the item is to discriminate the capacity to recognise acquaintances ("I have difficulty locating a friend in a crowd of people"), it has to be replaced by "somebody I know" or "a familiar person" (Le Gal et al., 2010). In some cultural groups, *brother* or *cousin* can mean more than *relatives* (Guillemin et al., 1993). Similarly, *leisure activities* could also mean very different behaviours and experiences.

When equivalent words and expressions do not exist or are not meaningful in the target language, *de-centring* is a useful strategy (Hambleton, 2005). It involves simply using equivalent material in both source and target language. That is possible when source and target versions are developed at the same time, as in the case of measures intended for use in international assessments (Guillemin et al., 1993; Hambleton, 2005). De-centring is also applied in the adaptation of an instrument and it implies the removal of culture-specific items and their replacement with culturally more appropriate stimulus materials, which changes the source instrument. One option could be to specify on the one hand the part of the construct that is common across groups, and on the other the corresponding specific parts in each group (Van de Vijver & Poortinga, 2005).

As mentioned before, in all of this process, item formats, answer scales, and instructions must be taken into consideration. For example, the answer scales should reflect the same concept and the same distance between scores in both versions. Thus, attention should be paid to the configuration of the Likert-type response scales with these contents (Hambleton, 2005). Notions of time and amount are often difficult to express in any language (Le Gal et al., 2010). For instance, expressions such as *the past week* or *the last week* have to be occasionally replaced by *the past seven days* in order to avoid problems in the interpretation of the time period (Le Gal et al., 2010).

Sometimes it is not possible to achieve scale similarities because of differences in response styles. In specific groups we can find a tendency to give extreme scores depending on the rating scale anchor (Van de Vijver & Poortinga, 2005) or difficulties in answering due to a lack of familiarity with the specifications of the extreme scores. For example, in our Spanish adaptation of the Chronic Pain Self-Efficacy Scale (Martín-Aragón et al., 1999), the original response scale which ranged from 10 to 100 was changed to 0 to 100. We also introduced broader instructions than the original, including an example of how to answer.

Pilot Study

A pilot study in the target population will complete the adaptation process. A field test will allow the research team to identify other flaws that are manifest in the actual conditions under application. Furthermore, the field test helps to address construct and method equivalence. It does not necessarily involve a large sample but is qualitatively representative of the target intended population.

We can elicit information from participants in order to identify items that give problems in practice, to elucidate their correct understanding, and to provide explanations of answers and thus explore equivalence of interpretations between versions. People are invited to answer with free-response questions about the meaning of items in a face-to-face interview format.

In the aforementioned Spanish adaptation of WHYMPI-II (Significant Others scale), for example, the item *express frustration at me* (item 7) was deleted in our Spanish version after a pilot study because, on the one hand, patients did not understand the meaning and always required additional explanations and, on the other, participants reported it did not represent a life event with their significant others. Furthermore, the answer scales of the first part of the instrument were also modified by always putting the same extremes (*not at all–extremely*) rather than the different ones for each question, as in the original version, because it was more comprehensible for responders.

A structured way of gathering information on item problems is the use of think-aloud methods. This cognitive interview technique allows researchers to assess how participants interpret and respond to the items by asking them to think aloud and verbalize their thought processes as they completed the items. An example is the validation of the Aberdeen Measures of Impairment, Activity Limitation and Participation Restriction (Ab-IAP; Horwood, Pollard, Ayis, McIlvenna, & Johnston, 2010). The authors employed a standardized classification scheme based on cognitive psychology models in order to identify four types of response problems (comprehension, retrieval, judgment, response) and subsequently added two more types: *struggled* to answer an item and *insufficient information*. Quantitative and thematic analysis allowed them to identify where and how the items failed to achieve their measurement purpose (Horwood et al., 2010).

Confirmation: Empirical Study of Adaptation

Testing for equivalence of measures is important for psychological research and particularly for cross-cultural research. The aim of the complete adaptation process is to achieve the best possible level of linguistic, cultural, conceptual, and metric equivalence between versions (Muñiz et al., 2013).

Cross-cultural research distinguishes four hierarchical levels of equivalence or measurement invariance and each one requires confirmation of the previous one. The basic level, functional equivalence, ensures that the construct exists in the target group; structural equivalence establishes that both source and target instruments measure the same psychological construct; metric equivalence implies the same measurement unit across groups; and scalar equivalence refers to the identical origin of measurement scales across groups. Empirical evidence throughout the entire process is needed to identify and control the construct, method, or item biases that may account for non-equivalence in the target population (Elosua & Iliescu, 2012; Milfont & Fischer, 2010; Muñiz et al., 2013).

Functional equivalence, and in part structural equivalence, must be addressed in the previous stage, mainly by means of qualitative methods (a set of rational-analytic and empirical procedures such as judgmental procedures, content analysis, and interviews). This is a prerequisite of the complete testing of structural equivalence and the study of metric and scalar equivalence as well as other psychometric studies. Quantitative methods using statistical techniques are applied in this confirmation stage. Research has to be conducted to replicate the same hypothesis tested by the instrument in the previous source context (American Educational Research Association [AERA], American Psychological Association, & National Council on Measurement in Education, 1999; ITC, 2010).

Firstly, good qualitative and quantitative selection of study samples is essential. Secondly, it is necessary to select from the wide range of statistical methods, in order to accumulate evidence to support the use of an assessment instrument for its intended purposes (AERA et al., 1999). This stage can be performed in different studies, each involving specific aims (establishing the validity, reliability, items equivalence, among others). Comparisons should be made with the corresponding results in the source group.

Data Collection Designs

Three data collection designs have been proposed (Hambleton, 2005). In the first one, a bilingual target sample takes both versions (or one of the two versions at random). This approach is useful for investigating convergence validity (but it does not ensure an equivalent application to the monolingual target population). The second design consists of source-language monolinguals taking both the original and back-translated versions. Item equivalence is identified by comparing both performances of each item (but data are not really collected from the target-language version, which is the original aim). The third option uses two samples: source and target language monolinguals, respectively; participants in each sample take the corresponding language version. This system is useful for work on item equivalence in the two groups (but taking account that there may be other explanations for the differences related to actual cultural differences; Hambleton, 2005). Each option has advantages and weaknesses and a combination is preferable. In practice, most of the adaptation studies have only used the monolingual target sample to analyse and compare results with previous data from the source instrument.

Validity Evidence Based on Internal Structure

Evidence on structural equivalence requires confirmation that an adapted instrument shows the same internal structure as in the source population, in terms of patterns of correlations among the items and test components (ITC, 2010). Several methods are available to evaluate whether the structure of an original instrument is consistent with the translated version: multidimensional scaling (MDS), principal component analysis, exploratory factor analysis (EFA), and confirmatory factor analysis (CFA; Sireci, Patsula, & Hambleton, 2005). Factor analytic techniques compare dimensionality based on theoretical and empirical information about the internal structure of the test (underlying dimensions and item-to-factor relationships, i.e., factor loadings). EFA and MDS do not require specifying test structure a priori. CFA and MDS allow simultaneous multiple group analysis (Milfont & Fischer, 2010).

CFA models are one of the most widely used methods to test for measurement invariance and to evaluate method effects. The model of relationships between item responses and latent variables is specified a priori for the target population, according to the model in the original population. There is large number of goodness-of-fit indexes to judge model fit and several models for application (e.g., bifactorial model; for an overview, see Rios & Wells, 2014).

It is possible to find that an adapted instrument shows the same dimensions as in the source group (the same item responses to measure the same factor) although the loadings of items on factors differ from the original. Such findings could indicate either that those groups differ somewhat cross-culturally or that there are problems related to the adaptation process. This conceptual level is the most basic and necessary level of equivalence that must be demonstrated, as it indicates that the intended meaning is retained across versions (Van de Vijver & Poortinga, 2005).

Another possibility is to find metric equivalence, which involves similarity of factor loadings across groups. This measurement unit of the scales allows for indirect comparisons as the score intervals are equal across groups (Van de Vijver & Poortinga, 2005). Cross-cultural measures are often used to develop direct score comparisons. They require not only conceptual and metric but also scalar equivalence. This means that there are similar intercepts across groups, and therefore the scales of the latent construct share the same origin (Van de Vijver & Poortinga, 2005). This highest level of equivalence means that differences or similarities between direct scores among persons from different cultural groups can be meaningfully interpreted. CFA provides evidence of how an instrument should be scored (Milfont & Fischer, 2010; Rios & Wells, 2014).

Although biases might have been controlled for, we can find non-equivalent structure between versions, in terms of non-equivalent factor structure, or non-equivalent items. Both cases may be useful in researching content validity of scores reported for each population separately, as well as in providing specific and useful information about the target population (ITC, 2010). For example, the factorial structure of the Pain Locus of Control (Toomey, Lundden, Mann, & Abashian, 1988) traditionally includes three dimensions (*internal, external powerful others*, and *external chance*). As a result of the splitting of *external chance* into *chance* and *fate* factors, in our adaptation process for Spanish fibromyalgia syndrome patients, analysis showed four dimensions. This result fits in with the importance of fate in Spanish culture (Pastor et al., 1990).

As another example, in a study conducted to replicate in UK and Spanish students the motivational factor structure for studying medicine, results of the CFA in target samples did not support the original three-factor structure. However, subsequent EFA showed a very similar factor structure in both the UK and Spain, which explained an adequate amount of variance in both cases. Thus, in order to obtain a motivational measure suitable for cross-cultural comparisons, only the items that had a significant loading for three factors in the target and source samples were retained. The result was a common measure made up of ten items, only four items fewer than the original scale (Pastor et al., 2009). This kind of result acts as a stimulus to further research on how the measures work in other cultural contexts.

In the study of *equivalence of items* both classical and modern methods have been developed to identify item bias. Item analysis from the classical test theory (CTT) approach is based on correlational data (factor loadings in EFA, item to total correlations, item-to-other variables correlation, and reliability analysis). Item response theory (IRT) is a useful approach for solving measurement problems as it overcomes the disadvantages of CTT (i.e., dependency on number of items and sample size). IRT models allow for item invariance across groups and measurement error estimation across the ability level and across persons. Hence, it allows us to see whether an item is functioning at the same level of difficulty in both versions and it does not depend on the sample used to test the measure. Differential item functioning (DIF) methods evaluate invariance for each item individually. DIF clarifies whether differences on an item between groups are due to item bias or actual group differences. An item is biased when it is unrelated to the purpose of the instrument. DIF identifies items that score differentially across groups that have similar performance in the measure. Several methods can be selected depending on data (dichotomous or polytomous) or multivariate matching: delta plot, standardization, Mantel–Haenszel, logistic regression, and other methods based on IRT. All these procedures are applied to compare source and target groups that are assumed to be matched on the content measured by the test (Sireci, 2011). After detecting DIF in one item, we need to explore possible explanations related either to language or cultural issues such as poor translation, unfamiliarity of content or format, differential difficulty or relevance when adapted to the target population. For example, DIF can be the result of diverse cultural conditions such as social deprivation (Pollard, Dixon, & Johnston, 2013).

Reliability Analysis

Reliability is not an intrinsic property of a measure or a scale, but a psychometric property of a specific sample's responses to a measure administered under specific conditions (AERA et al., 1999). Reliability coefficients should be reported for each scale in each specific sample. From CTT, there are many statistical indexes whose selection depends on the reliability design (equivalent measures, internal consistency, or test–retest), the response metric (quantitative, ordinal, or nominal), and the reliability level (consistency or agreement). In particular Cronbach's α is the most often reported and the most well-known estimator of reliability (Osburn, 2000). Reliability coefficients are also useful to evaluate scores of individuals, as the standard error of measurement derives in part from the sample-level reliability coefficient and standard deviation (Green, Chen, Helms, & Henze, 2011). In another vein, unexpected results (e.g., differences in test–retest change across versions), could reflect method bias such as instrument (e.g., differential familiarity with response procedure, differential response styles) or administration bias (e.g., differential familiarity with stimulus material, differences in administration conditions, ambiguous instructions, interviewer effects).

Validity Based on the Relations to Other Variables

To complete the study of construct equivalence, in addition to testing structural equivalence, we should compare the relationships between instrument scores and other variables hypothesized as related to the construct measured. In that sense, we can expect a similar pattern of significant correlations with other measures of the construct, and low correlations with measures of unrelated constructs, across versions (Sireci et al., 2005). Reliability coefficients help to correct these convergent and divergent validity tests by means of the correction of coefficients for attenuation. It allows us to estimate the likely magnitude of correlations under similar measurement conditions as if one or both measures had yielded scores that were perfectly reliable (Green et al., 2011; Osburn, 2000).

The hypothesis about relations to other variables can also be studied by means of a multitrait–multimethod matrices design (Sireci et al., 2005). This construct validity method implies the administration of the adapted measure and other instruments assessing the same construct through different evaluation methods, together with other measures of unrelated construct also using different evaluation methods. Structural equation methods can be used to analyse multitrait–multimethod matrices. It also helps to control the assessment method effects, which could be one of method bias in applying the new instrument (Sireci et al., 2005).

Other approaches aim to demonstrate relations of measure to: a gold standard, in order to test if the measure provides the same results (criterion validity); or a result, such as a health outcome, a treatment response, or a patients' profile (predictive validity); or its sensitivity to detect changes overtime as a result of a treatment. As mentioned, different studies can be developed involving these specific aims.

Other Issues

New conceptualizations of sources of validity include evidence based on testing consequences and on response processes, both important as their absence may threaten the representativeness and relevance of a measure (AERA et al., 1999). The former provides evidence on whether the instrument actually achieves the intended goals, purposes, and outcomes and considers the intended and unintended consequences of its administration. In that sense we should show, for instance, that the instrument has the same viability (good cost/benefit ratio) as in the source population, in terms of time, effort, inconvenience, or failed expectations. Furthermore, it is necessary to demonstrate the collateral benefits of its application in the new context (e.g., improvement in health outcomes or health system processes such as diagnosis or treatment; Viladrich & Doval, 2011).

The response process could provide problems that may actually alter other sources of evidence, such as evidence based on test content. They occur when the test items elicit varieties of response other than those intended (Padilla & Benítez, 2014). Differential familiarity with item response procedures (e.g., item and response formats) and differential response style (e.g., trend acquiescence, social desirability, extremity tendency) are the two main sources of instrument bias and differential item functioning related to response process problems. Methods for obtaining this type of validity evidence deal with the quantitative analyses of responses (atypical response patterns, participation response rates, missing value analysis, distribution responses) and other procedures linked to either the psychological processes (e.g., think aloud, focus group, and cognitive interviews) or indirect information (eye tracking, response times; Johnson, Shavitt, & Holbrook, 2011; Padilla & Benítez, 2014).

Manuals for adapted instruments should include adequate information on the translation and adaptation processes, the equivalence between the original and the adapted form, and the interpretation of scores (normative and criteria interpretation, and, where relevant, cut-off scores). It is also necessary to provide sufficient information on aims, methods, and results of each stage of the cultural adaptation work. Good descriptions of the instrument modifications in each and all of its components are especially important in adaptation. All these areas are important for completing the quality of the adaptation process and ensuring future research studies, as in the development process of an original instrument (Elosua & Iliescu, 2012; Green et al., 2011).

Studies Illustrating the Cultural Adaptation Use

In scientific literature it is frequent to meet with experts' consensus on relevant areas and measures regarding health outcomes. There is a broad agreement for using standardized outcome measures in order to test the efficacy of both biomedical and psychological clinical trials and practice. In this domain, the successive workshops and meetings of the group for the Initiative on Methods, Measurement and Pain Assessment in Clinical Trials (IMMPACT; http://www.immpact.org) or the group for Outcomes Measures in Rheumatoid Arthritis Clinical Trials (OMERACT; http://www.omeract.org) are especially noteworthy. Obviously, these consensuses increase the need for culturally adapted instruments for comparisons and scientific advance.

For example, the adaptation of six measures included in the OMERACT consensus for fibromyalgia (Choy et al., 2009; Mease et al., 2005; Mease et al., 2009) has been developed for 12 European languages in order to ensure their linguistic equivalence with the original English version (Le Gal et al., 2010). The measures were: FIQ (Fibromyalgia Impact Questionnaire), BDI-II (Beck Depression Inventory-II), STAI (State–Trait Anxiety Inventory), MFI (Multidimensional Fatigue Inventory), MASQ (Multiple Ability Self-Report Questionnaire), and PGIC (Patient Global Impression of Change). Le Gal et al. (2010) followed the *Guidelines for the Process of Cross-Cultural Adaptation* published by Guillemin et al. (1993) and Beaton et al. (2000) looking for semantic, idiomatic, experiential, and conceptual equivalence of the different target versions with the original. Authors included in the process: (a) two independent forward translations, (b) consensus between them, (c) one independent backward translation, (d) comparison of this backward version with the original, and (e) a pilot study of the final version. The pilot study included two activities: the review of that final version by a clinician expert, and face-to-face interviewing with five native speakers, subjects of each country for checking comprehension and acceptability of the instrument. The results related to this process were analysed to produce the last final version. At the beginning of this process, authors contacted developers of each instrument asking for information about the concepts investigated in the correspondent instrument. Furthermore, they asked for the developers' inputs for some translation decisions and for their permission to make the proposed changes in the target version of the instrument.

Another example is the work on the Illness Perception Questionnaire (IPQ; Weinman, Petrie, Moss-Morris, & Horne, 1996). It illustrates a process in which the measure of a construct is developed and then its cultural adaptation extends to a variety of countries and illness contexts. IPQ assesses cognitive representation of illness, based on the common-sense model of self-regulation of health and illness (Leventhal, Brissette, & Leventhal, 2003). A revised version (IPQ-R; Moss-Morris et al., 2002) and a brief version (B-IPQ; Broadbent, Petrie, Main, & Weinman, 2006) have been developed from the original instrument. The IPQ website (http://www.uib.no/ipq) shows the three IPQ questionnaires, references, and explanations of how to use and score them. Furthermore, there are translated versions for different languages and conditions, mainly for people with chronic illnesses but also for the evaluation of cognitive representation of illness in healthy people. One of the examples of a linguistic and cultural adaptation is the study of the IPQ-R and the BIPQ for the Spanish population (Pacheco-Huergo et al., 2012). The authors developed a complete procedure to establish conceptual and linguistic equivalence with the original questionnaires. They proceeded in three phases: double forward-translation, pilot study, and double back-translation, including one consensus meeting of a committee in each phase and a final meeting with one of the authors of the original questionnaire (Pacheco-Huergo et al., 2012). Moreover, there are many empirical studies with different aims related to psychometric proprieties and validity evidence of IPQ, especially for the IPQ-R and BIPQ versions. As a result, dimensions of cognitive illness representations have empirical evidence and their predictive power in the terms proposed by the model has confirmation in different illnesses and contexts.

Comments and Conclusions

An instrument needs adequate psychometric properties to be selected for its adaptation across cultures. The new version must show that the instrument has psychological similarity in the new context. The first stage consists of the linguistic and cultural adaptation of the measure to the new language and context. The second stage comprises a series of studies to test how the instrument works in the target populations and to test the same hypotheses that were contrasted in the original instrument. Thus, it is vital to design the whole process carefully, following international guidelines. It is necessary to provide an adequate report of the aims, methods, and results of each stage of the cultural adaptation work.

References

Acquadro, C., Conway, K., Hareendran, A., & Aaronson, N. (2008). Group for the European Regulatory Issues and Quality of Life Assessment (ERIQA). Literature review of methods to translate health-related quality of life questionnaires for use in multinational clinical trials. *Value in Health, 11*, 509–521. http://doi.org/10.1111/j.1524-4733.2007.00292.x

American Educational Research Association (AERA), American Psychological Association, & National Council on Measurement in Education. (1999). *Standards for educational and psychological testing.* Washington, DC: American Psychological Association.

Bass, J. K., Bolton, P. A., & Murray, L. K. (2007). Do not forget culture when studying mental health. *Lancet, 370*, 918–919. http://doi.org/10.1016/S0140-6736(07)61426-3

Beaton, D., Bombardier, C., Guillemin, F., & Bosi Ferraz, M. (2000). Guidelines for the process of cross-cultural adaptation of self-report measures. *Spine, 25*, 3186–3191. http://doi.org/10.1097/00007632-200012150-00014

Broadbent, E., Petrie, K. J., Main, J., & Weinman, J. (2006). The Brief Illness Perception Questionnaire. *Journal of Psychosomatic Research, 60*, 631–637. http://doi.org/10.1016/j.jpsychores.2005.10.020

Choy, E. H., Arnold, L. M., Clauw, D. J., Crofford, L. J., Glass, J. M., Simon, L. S., ... Mease, P. J. (2009). Content and criterion validity of the preliminary core dataset for clinical trials in fibromyalgia syndrome. *Journal of Rheumatology, 36*, 2330–2334. http://doi.org/10.3899/jrheum.090368

Elosua, P., & Iliescu, D. (2012). Test in Europe: Where we are and where we should go. *International Journal of Testing, 12*, 157–175. http://doi.org/10.1080/15305058.2012.657316

Evers, A., Muñiz, J., Hagemeister, C., Høstmælingen, A., Lindley, P., Sjöberg, A., & Bartram, D. (2013). Assessing the quality of tests: Revision of the EFPA review model. *Psicothema, 25*, 283–291.

Green, C. E., Chen, C. E., Helms, J. E., & Henze, K. T. (2011). Recent reliability reporting practices in psychological assessment: Recognizing the people behind the data. *Psychological Assessment, 23*(3), 656–669. http://doi.org/10.1037/a0023089

Guillemin, F., Bombardier, C., & Beaton, D. (1993). Cross-cultural adaptation of health-related quality of life measures: Literature review and proposed guidelines. *Journal of Clinical Epidemiology, 46*, 1417–1432. http://doi.org/10.1016/0895-4356(93)90142-N

Hambleton, R. K. (2005). Issues, designs and technical guidelines for adapting tests into multiple languages and cultures. In R. K. Hambleton, P. F. Merenda, & C. D. Spielberger (Eds.), *Adapting educational and psychological tests for cross-cultural assessment* (pp. 3–39). London, UK: Erlbaum.

Hambleton, R. K., Merenda, P. F., & Spielberger, C. D. (Eds.). (2005). *Adapting educational and psychological tests for cross-cultural assessment.* London, UK: Erlbaum.

Horwood, J., Pollard, B., Ayis, S., McIlvenna, T., & Johnston, M. (2010). Listening to patients: using verbal data in the validation of the Aberdeen Measures of Impairment, Activity Limitation and Participation Restriction (Ab-IAP). *BMC Musculoskeletal Disorders, 11*(1), 182. http://doi.org/10.1186/1471-2474-11-182

International Test Commission. (2010). *International test commission guidelines for translating and adapting tests.* Retrieved from http://www.intestcom.org

Jayawickreme, N., Atanasov, P., Goonasekera, M. A., & Foa, E. B. (2012). Are culturally specific measures of trauma-related anxiety and depression needed? The case of Sri Lanka psychological assessment. *American Psychological Association, 24*, 791–800.

Johnson, T. P., Shavitt, S., & Holbrook, A. L. (2011). Survey response styles across cultures. In D. Matsumoto & F. J. R. Van De Vijver (Eds.), *Cross-cultural research methods in psychology* (pp. 130–175). New York, NY: Cambridge University Press.

Kerns, R. D., Turk, D. C., & Rudy, T. E. (1985). The West Haven-Yale Multidimensional Pain Inventory (WHYMPI). *Pain, 23*, 345–356. http://doi.org/10.1016/0304-3959(85)90004-1

Le Gal, M., Mainguy, Y., Le Lay, K., Nadjar, A., Allain, D., & Galissié, M. (2010). Linguistic validation of six patient-reported outcomes instruments into 12 languages for patients with fibromyalgia. *Joint Bone Spine, 77*, 165–170. http://doi.org/10.1016/j.jbspin.2010.01.005

Leventhal, H., Brissette, I., & Leventhal, E. A. (2003). The common-sense model of self-regulation of health and illness. In L. D. Cameron & H. Leventhal (Eds.), *The self-regulation on health and illness behaviour* (pp. 42–65). London, UK: Routledge.

Matsumoto, D., & Van De Vijver, F. J. R. (Eds.). (2011). *Cross-cultural research methods in psychology*. New York, NY: Cambridge University Press.

Martín-Aragón, M., Pastor, M. A., Rodríguez-Marín, J., March, M. J., Lledó, A., López-Roig, S., & Terol, M. C. (1999). Percepción de Autoeficacia en Dolor Crónico. Adaptación y Validación de la Chronic Pain Self-efficacy Scale [Self-efficacy perception in chronic pain. Adaptation and validation of the Chronic Pain Self-efficacy Scale]. *Revista de Psicología de la Salud, 11*, 53–76.

Mease, P., Arnold, L. M., Choy, E. H., Clauw, K. J., Crofford, L. J., Glass, J. M., …Williams, D. A. (2009). Fibromyalgia syndrome module at OMERACT 9: Domain construct. *Journal of Rheumatology, 36*, 2318–2329. http://doi.org/10.3899/jrheum.090367

Mease, P., Clauw, D. J., Arnold, L. M., Goldenberg, D. L., Witter, J., Williams, D. A., …Crofford, L. J. (2005). Fibromyalgia syndrome. *Journal of Rheumatology, 32*, 2270–2277.

Milfont, T. L., & Fischer, R. (2010). Testing measurement invariance across groups: Applications in cross-cultural research. *International Journal of Psychological Research, 3*(1), 111–121.

Moss-Morris, R., Weinman, J., Petrie, K. J., Home, R., Cameron, L. D., & Buick, D. (2002). The Revised Illness Perception Questionnaire (IPQ-R). *Psychology & Health, 17*, 1–16. http://doi.org/10.1080/08870440290001494

Muñiz, J., Elosua, P., & Hambleton, R. K. (2013). Directrices para la traducción y adaptación de los tests: segunda edición [International Test Commission guidelines for test translation and adaptation: 2nd edition]. *Psicothema, 25*, 151–157.

Osburn, H. G. (2000). Coefficient alpha and related internal consistency reliability coefficient. *Psychological methods, 5*, 343–355. http://doi.org/10.1037/1082-989X.5.3.343

Pacheco-Huergo, V., Viladrich, C., Pujol-Ribera, E., Cabezas-Peña, C., Núñez, M., Roura-Olmeda, P., … del Val, J. L. (IPQ-R Group). (2012). Percepción en enfermedades crónicas: validación lingüística del Illness Perception Questionnaire Revised y del Brief Illness Perception Questionnaire para la población española [Perception of chronic illness: Linguistic validation of the Illness Perception Questionnaire Revised and the Brief Illness Perception Questionnaire for a Spanish population]. *Atención Primaria, 44*, 280–287. http://doi.org/10.1016/j.aprim.2010.11.022

Padilla, J. L., & Benítez, I. (2014). Validity evidence base on response processes. *Psicothema, 26*, 136–144.

Pastor, M. A., López, S., Rodríguez-Marín, J., Sánchez, S., Salas, E., & Pascual, E. (1990). Expectativas de control sobre la experiencia de dolor: adaptación y análisis preliminar de la Escala Multidimensional de Locus de Control de Salud [Control expectancies in pain experiences: Adaptation and preliminary analysis of the Multidimensional Health Locus of Control Scale]. *Revista de Psicología de la Salud, 2*(1–2), 91–111.

Pastor, M. A., López-Roig, S., Sánchez, S., Hart, J., Johnston, M., & Dixon, D. (2009). Measuring motivation to do medicine cross-culturally: Development of the International Motivation to do Medicine scale (IMMS). *Escritos de Psicología, 2*, 3–9.

Pastor, M. A., López-Roig, S., Rodríguez-Marín, J., Terol, M. C., & Sánchez, S. (1995). Evaluación multidimensional del dolor crónico en enfermos reumáticos [Multidimensional assessment of chronic pain in rheumatic illnesses]. *Revista de Psicología de la Salud, 7*, 79–106.

Pollard, B., Dixon, D., & Johnston, M. (2013). Does the impact of osteoarthritis vary by age, gender and social deprivation? A community study using the International Classification of Functioning, Disability and Health. *Disability and Rehabilitation, 36*, 1445–1451. http://doi.org/10.3109/09638288.2013.847123

Rios, J., & Wells, C. (2014). Validity evidence based on internal structure. *Psicothema, 26*, 108–116.

Sireci, S. G. (2011). Evaluating test and survey items for bias across languages and cultures. In D. Matsumoto & F. J. R. Van De Vijver (Eds.), *Cross-cultural research methods in psychology* (pp. 216–240). New York, NY: Cambridge University Press.

Sireci, S. G., & Faulkner-Bond, M. (2014). Validity evidence based on test content. *Psicothema, 26*, 100–107.

Sireci, S. G., Patsula, L., & Hambleton, R. K. (2005). Statistical methods for identifying flaws in the test adaptation process. In R. K. Hambleton, P. F. Merenda, & C. D. Spielberger (Eds.), *Adapting educational and psychological tests for cross-cultural assessment* (pp. 93–117). London, UK: Erlbaum.

Toomey, T. C., Lunden, T. E., Mann, J. D., & Abashian, S. (1988, November). *The pain locus of control scale: a comparison of chronic pain patients and the normals.* Paper presented at the Annual Joint Meeting of American/Canadian Pain Societies, Toronto, Canada.

Two, R., Verjee-Lorenz, A., Clayson, D., Dalal, M., Grotzinger, K., & Younossi, Z. M. (2010). A methodology for successfully producing global translations of patient reported outcome measures for use in multiple countries. *Value in Health, 13*, 128–131. http://doi.org/10.1111/j.1524-4733.2009.00585.x

Van de Vijver, F. J. R., & Poortinga, Y. H. (2005). Conceptual and methodological issues in adapting tests. In R. K. Hambleton, P. F. Merenda, & C. D. Spielberger (Eds.), *Adapting educational and psychological tests for cross-cultural assessment* (pp. 39–63). London, UK: Erlbaum.

Viladrich, C., & Doval, E. (2011). Pruebas basadas en el proceso de respuesta [Tests based on the response process]. In C. Viladrich & E. Doval (Eds.), *Medición: Fiabilidad y validez.* (pp. 139–155). Bellaterra, Spain: Laboratori d'Estadística Aplicada i Modelització (UAB).

Weinman, J., Petrie, K., Moss-Morris, R., & Horne, R. (1996). The Illness Perception Questionnaire: A new method for assessing the cognitive representation of illness. *Psychology & Health, 11*, 431–435. http://doi.org/10.1080/08870449608400270

Wild, D., Eremenco, S., Mear, I., Martin, M., Houchin, C., Gawlicki, M., … Molsen, E. (2009). Multinational trials – recommendations on the translations required, approaches to using the same language in different countries, and the approaches to support pooling the data: The ISPOR patient-reported outcomes translation and linguistic validation good research practices task force report. *Value in Health, 12*, 430–440. http://doi.org/10.1111/j.1524-4733.2008.00471.x

Wild, D., Grove, A., Martin, M., Eremenco, S., McElroy, S., Verjee-Lorenz, A., … Erikson, P. (2005). Principles of good practice for the translation and cultural adaptation process for patient-reported outcomes (PRO) measures: Report of the ISPOR task force for translation and cultural adaptation. *Value in Health, 8*, 94–104. http://doi.org/10.1111/j.1524-4733.2005.04054.x

Chapter 21
Assessment in Children

Deborah Christie

Department of Child and Adolescent Psychological Services,
University College London Hospitals, London, UK

Introduction

Health psychology has an important role in research and in supporting healthy behaviours. However, the management of chronic illness in children is usually located in paediatric services in general or specialist hospitals or community settings. Despite this dichotomy both health and clinical psychologists are concerned with understanding reasons for poor doctor–family communication, poor adherence, cognitive difficulties, management of sleep or behavioural difficulties, chronic fatigue and/or chronic pain, obesity, difficulty coping with chronic illness, and stress management in relation to illness.

Challenges Specific to Assessment of Children and Adolescents

There are a number of general challenges for both research and clinical assessments. The first is the selection of age-appropriate instruments that are acceptable, reliable, and valid for the target population. For a full discussion of selection criteria, please see Chapter 1 in this volume.

It is essential to keep in mind the different needs of young children, children, and adolescents in terms of a general approach to assessment at each developmental stage. Young children (pre-school) need to have their attention engaged at all times using items such as puppets or toys that capture their attention. They also need to feel safe and comfortable to ensure they can respond as independently from their parents as possible. This is to try and ensure that the younger child is giving their own responses rather than the parent responding on their behalf. School-age children are slightly easier to work with as they will be familiar with sitting at a desk and completing paper-and-pencil type tests; however, monitoring the time taken to complete assessments is important in order not to exceed their attention span. For adolescents, helping them to understand the reason for the assessment can help engage them in the process; however, avoiding being too "cool" may be important so as not to appear patronising.

The second issue is informed consent. Children and adolescents should be included in decision making regarding clinical interventions or participation in research protocols. The doctrine of informed consent only has a limited application in paediatrics. Young people over 16 years of age are considered to have appropriate decisional capacity and legal empowerment and can give informed consent to medical care or research participation. For young people under

16, parents or other surrogates provide informed permission for diagnosis and treatment of children *with the assent of the child whenever appropriate*. Seeking assent should help the child or young person achieve a developmentally appropriate awareness of the nature of his or her condition or reason for the research. They should be told what they can expect with tests and treatment(s). There should be an assessment of their understanding of the situation and the factors influencing how they are responding (including whether there is inappropriate pressure to accept testing or therapy; American Academy of Pediatrics, 1995; Angst & Deatrick, 1996).

Another area that is different in children is the degree to which confidentiality can be offered. Rules about confidentiality must be clarified with children, young people, and parents at the beginning of conversations. For younger children and young people under 16 it may not be possible or appropriate to keep information confidential. Research protocols should also clarify what information will be communicated to general practitioners or parents. A principle should be that unless we are concerned about risk or harm we should be able to keep conversations confidential.

A significant difference in assessing children and young people is that they rarely choose to participate in research or make a referral themselves. This is usually the decision of an adult (doctor or parent). Many children and young people are therefore brought to the psychologist by frustrated or worried parents rather than choosing to come. Families are also sent to psychologists with no clear understanding of why the referral has been made. It is often the doctor who has concerns about the child and/or the families' ability to manage their medical condition.

For very young children unable to complete a questionnaire themselves, it may be necessary to rely on a parent completing a report on behalf of the child. Proxy reports must be considered with care. Parents will often over-report particular symptoms or have a very different perspective to the child (Vetter, Bridgewater, & McGwin, 2012).

It is also important to note that responses may be affected by the way these measures are administered. There do not appear to be any differences between web- or paper-based administration (Young et al., 2009) although the wish to please the interviewer may lead to an underestimation of emotional/behavioural difficulties in both self-reported and interview-based questionnaires (Horsch, McManus, Kennedy, & Edge, 2007).

The importance of patient-centred consultations have been well-recognised and described in adult medical consultations (see Chapter 6 in this volume on patient–physician communication). This focuses on the patient's needs and involves the doctor listening to what the patient wants before decisions are made. For children, however, the "patient" is rarely on their own and will be accompanied by a parent or carer. Being involved in the process of choosing a treatment can be difficult with younger children, children with learning difficulties, or teenagers who are unwilling to participate in conversations about their care. Engaging with teenagers requires a particular therapeutic style and as a result for many children and young people the consultation becomes essentially doctor-centred. The consultation is between the doctor and the parents and therefore experienced by the patient as directive, with the child or young person having a limited role, if any, in the decision-making process.

There are a vast number of measures available but questionnaires are only screening measures and should not be used as a primary diagnostic tool. Questionnaires are not infallible or diagnostic, but are screening tools to help health-care professionals, families, and young people think about whether additional assessment and support is needed (Canning & Kelleher, 1994).

They can be incorporated into the assessment as a way of evaluating the progress and outcome of a treatment programme in an individual or evaluating an intervention programme. For very young children, observation can be used to help describe their actions, roles, and behaviour. Observational techniques are generally underused in health-care research. Collection of observational data focuses on natural settings. They span research paradigms and qualitative approaches and help illustrate what children do in different situations and how behaviours might change in response to different situations and at different times. Whilst observing may appear to be an intrinsically simple approach it is also important to consider how the sample to be observed is selected as well as ensuring all individuals have given consent to how data is collected (e.g., recorded or videoed) as well as how it will be analysed and used.

Main Areas of Assessment and Specific Recommended Instruments

Developmental Level

If there are concerns about the young person's level of understanding, it may be helpful to complete a developmental assessment and/or a formal assessment of cognitive skills. An IQ assessment can highlight possible global or specific learning difficulties as well as highlight specific cognitive difficulties associated with chronic illness or neurodevelopmental disorders such as dyspraxia, dyslexia, Tourette's syndrome, autism, or Asperger's syndrome. Profiles might include non-verbal learning difficulties with high verbal IQ compared with low non-verbal IQ or low processing speed or working memory. For young people with verbal delay and possible autism or pervasive developmental disorders, the theory of mind test (TOM) may be helpful in children aged 5–12 years (Muris et al., 1999). Theory of mind should improve as children get older. Internal consistency of the TOM is high (0.92–0.98) with good inter-rater reliability (> 0.87). The TOM correlated positively and significantly with performance on several other theory of mind tasks.

Cognitive Skills

Formally measuring cognitive skills requires an understanding of the difference between achievement (accomplished skills) and aptitude (measure of potential). It is important to select measures that are reproducible and consistent (reliability) as well as to ensure the measurement of the right thing (validity). For children under the age of 3 years, checklists of developmental tasks can be completed with parents to assess the extent to which a child passes or fails an item that the majority of children of a particular age can complete. The Vineland is a survey-based interview to assess intellectual and developmental delay from birth to 90 years with specific versions for birth to 5 years 11 months and from 3 years to 21 years 11 months. It is completed by the parent or caregiver and also has teacher rating forms. It has high internal consistency for each domain: communication (0.84–0.93), daily living skills (0.86–0.91), socialisation (0.84–0.93), motor skills (0.77–0.90), and maladaptive behaviour (0.85–0.91; Sparrow, Cicchetti, & Balla, 2005).

The Griffiths Mental Development Scales (GDMS) focus on motor skills and early pre-symbolic language skills and measure the rate of development of infants and young children from birth to 2 years (internal consistency 0.91–0.97) and 2 years to 8 years (internal consistency > 0.70). All items in the six subscales are representative of their content domain and relevant to the construct being measured (Luiz et al., 2006).

Verbal and non-verbal areas of intellectual functioning (including attention and memory, quantitative ability) from the ages of 2 years 6 months to 16 years can be assessed by the Wechsler Intelligence Tests for children (Wechsler, 2002, 2004).

Memory and Learning

Memory and learning (difficulties) in younger children can be assessed using the Children's Memory Scale (Cohen, 2011). Concerns about attention can be assessed using the The Test of Every day Attention in Children (T-EACH; Manly et al., 2001).

Higher-Order Cognitive Skills

Higher-order cognitive skills (executive function) related to frontal lobe development include initiating and planning, self-monitoring and adjusting progress, inhibiting wrong responses, starting, finishing, and changing from one activity to another, and flexible thinking. The Delis–Kaplan Executive Function System (D-KEFS) can be used on subjects aged 8–89 years and is sensitive to the detection of brain damage (Delis, Kaplan, & Kramer, 2006).

The Behavioural Assessment of the Dysexecutive Syndrome in children (BADS-C) assists in early identification of deficits in executive functioning in children aged 7–16 years. It also includes a Dysexecutive Questionnaire for Children (DEX-C). Poor scores on the BADS-C are associated with increased reporting of the presence of difficulties and higher ratings of severity (Engel-Yeger, Josman, & Rosenblum, 2009).

A Note of Caution

Most of these tests have been developed in the US or UK for an English-speaking population. Cultural issues are important to keep in mind when interpreting test scores since limited exposure to written and spoken English in the home will make interpretation of scores difficult. Test results for young people from different cultural backgrounds should be interpreted with caution (Cummins, 1980). There are some instruments that have been adapted to a number of languages and cultures; however, finding someone appropriate to administer these in the relevant language may be an issue (for more information on cultural adaptation of measures, see Chapter 20 in this volume).

Standard IQ tests are also unable to discriminate the children at the very bottom or top of the ability range and therefore are inappropriate for very high or low functioning children (Hessl et al., 2009).

Emotional Health and Well-Being

Behavioural difficulties, depression, and anxiety are common symptoms in childhood and adolescence. A number of questionnaires can be used to obtain a quantitative measure of potentially problematic behaviour and emotional functioning, which can be used both as part of a baseline for clinical treatment but also in a research context to ensure homogeneity in interventional research.

The Child Behaviour Checklist (CBCL; Achenbach, 1991, 1992) can be used to measure internalising (e.g., anxious, depressive) behaviours and externalising (e.g., aggressive, hyperactive) behaviours that may be associated with a range of emotional and behavioural difficulties in children and young people aged between 1 year 6 months and 18 years. The checklist is made up of two sections: The first section contains 20 items assessing competence and the second section consists of 120 items to assess emotional and behavioural difficulties in the past 6 months. The checklist can be filled out by parents, caregivers, teachers, and young people and discriminates between demographically similar referred and non-referred children ($p \leq .01$).

The Strengths and Difficulties Questionnaire (SDQ; Goodman, 1997) is a behavioural screening questionnaire for children aged between 3 and 16 years. There are parent and teacher versions and also a youth self-report version for young people aged 11+. The SDQ is made up of 25 items divided between five scales: emotional difficulties, behavioural difficulties, hyperactivity, peer relationship difficulties, and pro-social behaviours. More recent versions also contain an impact supplement that can be used to assess the impact of identified difficulties on the young person's life (Goodman, 1999). The SDQ can help identify risks of developing an emotional, behavioural, or inattention disorder in young people. SDQ scores above the 90th percentile predict the probability of independently diagnosed psychiatric disorders.

The Development and Well-Being Assessment (DAWBA; Goodman, Ford, Richards, Gatward, & Meltzer, 2000) is an online survey designed to generate ICD-10 and DSM-IV psychiatric diagnoses in 5- to 17-year-olds. The web-based measure can be completed by young people (aged 11–17 years) as well as by their parents and teachers. Information from different informants is drawn together to predict the likely diagnosis or diagnoses, generating six probability bands, ranging from a probability of less than 0.1% of having the relevant diagnosis to a probability of over 70% of having the relevant diagnosis. In clinical situations, experienced clinical raters can decide whether to accept or overturn the computer diagnoses (or lack of diagnoses) by reviewing additional interview data.

The Beck Youth Inventories, Second Edition (Beck, Beck, Jolly, & Steer, 2005) are for use with children and adolescents between the ages of 7 and 18. There are five self-report scales that can be used on their own or together. Each inventory contains 20 statements about thoughts, feelings, or behaviours associated with depression, anxiety, anger, disruptive behaviour, and self-concept. The five inventories are the Beck Depression Inventory for Youth (BDI-Y), Beck Anxiety Inventory for Youth (BAI-Y), Beck Anger Inventory for Youth (BANI-Y), Beck Disruptive Behaviour Inventory for Youth (BDBI-Y), and Beck Self-Concept Inventory for Youth (BSCI-Y).

The Mood and Feelings Questionnaire (MFQ; Angold, Costello, Pickles, & Winder, 1987) is made up of a series of 34 short-statement items to detect clinical depression in children aged between 13 and 18 years. Parent and teacher versions have 33 items. Both versions have high internal consistency ($\alpha = 0.95$). There is a short form for parents and children with 13 items in each.

The Multiscore Depression Inventory for adolescents (and adults; MDI; Berndt, 1986) is a self-report tool made up of 118 true/false statements designed to identify indicators of depression in young people aged 13 and over. Subscales include low energy level, cognitive difficulty, and guilt. The Multiscore Depression Inventory for Children (MDI-C) is for use with children aged between 8 and 12 years and is made up of 79 true/false statements (Berndt &

Kaiser, 1996). Subscales include anxiety, self-esteem, sad mood, instrumental helplessness, social introversion, low energy, pessimism, and defiance.

The Child Depression Inventory (CDI) is a 27-item self-report tool designed to measure cognitive, affective, and behavioural indicators of depression in young people between the ages of 7 and 17 years (Carey, Faulstich, Gresham, Ruggiero, & Enyart, 1987). Subscales include negative mood/physical symptoms, negative self-esteem, interpersonal problems, and ineffectiveness. Construct and discriminant validity is reasonable and able to distinguish between non-referred and clinical subjects. However, it did not distinguish depressed youth from youth diagnosed with conduct disorder.

The Reynolds Child Depression Scale (RCDS; Reynolds, 1989) for ages 8– 2 and the Reynolds Adolescent Depression Scale (2nd ed., RADS-2) for ages 11–20 are self-report scales made up of 30 items designed to screen for different categories of depressive symptoms. The last item consists of five faces from *happy* to *sad*.

The Children's Depression Rating Scale–Revised (CDRS-R; Poznanski & Mokros 1996) has become the most widely used rating scale for assessing severity of depression and change in depressive symptoms for clinical research trials in children and adolescents with depression. The CDRS-R was originally developed as a rating scale for children aged 6–12 years. It is a 17-item scale, with items ranging from 1 to 5 or 1 to 7 (possible total score from 17 to 113), rated by a clinician via interviews with the child and parent. A score of ≥ 40 is indicative of depression, whereas a score of ≤ 28 is often used to define remission (minimal or no symptoms).

The Center of Epidemiological Studies Depression Scale modified for children (CES-DC) is a 20-item self-report rating scale to measure current level of depressive symptoms and can be completed by children between the ages of 6 and 17 (Weissman, Orvaschel, & Padian, 1980). The scale shows ability to distinguish between depressed and non-depressed children and adolescents.

The WHO-5 Well-Being Index is a short questionnaire containing five positively worded statements designed to capture a young person's emotional well-being over the previous two weeks. It offers the possibility to screen for mood changes at regular intervals and in general practice. This web-based questionnaire may offer new and faster opportunities to identify pathological changes in emotional well-being and lead to earlier therapeutic interventions (http://www.who-5.org; Bech, 2004).

Anxiety

A well-used measure of anxiety is the State-Trait Anxiety Inventory for Children (STAIC). This self-report tool is made up of 20 items to assess temperament-based (trait) anxiety and 20 items to assess current level (state) anxiety in children aged between 8 and 14 years (Spielberger, 1973). The STAIC discriminated between adolescents with substance use disorder and conduct disorder, anxiety disorder, and adolescents with no psychiatric disorder ($p<.0001$; Kirisci, Clark, & Moss, 1996).

The Spence Children's Anxiety Scale (SCAS; Spence, 1998) is for children aged 8–12 years. It is an indicator of anxious rather than depressive symptoms and consists of 38 items that reflect anxiety and six positive filler items. It has high internal consistency ($\alpha = 0.92$) and good test–retest reliability at 6 months (0.60).

The Multidimensional Anxiety Scale for Children Second Edition (MASC2 Self-report and MASC 2 Parent; March, 2013) is a revised version of the MASC (March, Parker, Sullivan, Stallings, & Conners, 1997). It has self-report and parent-completed forms for children and young people aged 8–19 years. Both forms have 50 items that distinguish between the presence of important anxiety symptoms. The MASC2 aids in the early identification, diagnosis, treatment planning, and monitoring of anxiety-prone youth. Both rating forms can be administered using online or paper-and-pencil formats. There is also a 10-item short form that is designed for repeated testing.

Quality of Life

Quality of life (QoL) is an integrative construct of "physical and emotional well-being, level of independence, social relationships and their relationship to salient features of their environment" (WHOQOL Group, 1995, p. 1405). Medical treatment can significantly impact upon health-related QoL (Gill & Feinstein, 1994). In addition to symptom-based outcome measures, understanding the impact of clinical interventions and treatment outcomes can be enhanced by an understanding of quality of life outcomes (see Chapter 14 in this volume). However, there are challenges to identifying QoL constructs that are meaningful for both adults and children. The limited ability of younger children to think about the future (Atance & O'Neill, 2001) influences their ability to rate or give a value to their life in the future in contrast to rating their life in the present. Responses of young children are also influenced by language development, concrete thinking, and developmental level (Christie, 2006). Historically, asking young children to draw, complete stories or sentences, or describe pictures has been used to assess emotions, perceptions of social relationships, and future thinking, although the psychometric validity, reliability, and sensitivity of this approach has been challenged (Lilienfeld, Wood, & Garb, 2000). Reported QoL may be significantly influenced if a child has experienced long-term illness and treatment. Eiser and Morse (2001) provide an extensive review of measures of QoL. Another more recent review of measures to assess QoL of children and youth was published by King, Schwellnuss, Russell, Shapiro, and Aboelele (2005).

Specific Conditions

Sleep

Sleep disorders can occur in physically well children and adolescents (Noland, Price, Dake, & Telljohann, 2009). Sleep disturbance may also be a corollary of neurodevelopmental disorders (Jan et al., 2008) or affected by health conditions such as overweight (Seicean et al., 2007), pain (Bruni, Galli, & Guidetti, 1999), or depression or anxiety (Cho, Kim, & Lee, 2013). Treatment regimens may contribute to sleep disruption (e.g., parents of children with diabetes doing hourly finger pricks to check blood sugars during the night). The Children's Sleep Habits Questionnaire (CSHQ; Owens, Spirito, & McGuinn, 2000) can be used to document sleep habits in younger children. For adults, the Sleep Hygiene Index has good psychometric properties but has not been evaluated with adolescents (Cho et al., 2013).

Chronic Fatigue and Chronic Pain

Four to 15% of the adolescent population will develop fatigue, with or without pain. Fatigue and pain cause a vicious spiral of decreasing physical activity and fitness. This leads to deconditioning, fatigue, and paradoxically an increase in pain. For some young people the body becomes hypersensitive to touch, symptoms can get worse and may start to spread to different parts of the body. The symptoms create high levels of distress and anxiety in young people as well as stress and concern for their families. They also compromise successful negotiation of independence and disrupt school attendance as well as other physical and social activities. The most useful scale for measuring fatigue is the Chalder Fatigue Scale (Chalder et al., 1993). This has been used extensively on adults and adolescents (Morriss, Wearden, & Mullis, 1998). Friedberg and Jason (2002) have also written a guide to selecting a fatigue rating scale. A relatively recent evidence-based review of paediatric pain measures looked at 17 measures that included self-report of pain intensity, questionnaires and diaries, and behavioural observations. The review evaluates the different instruments for assessing paediatric pain (Cohen et al., 2008) for particular purposes (e.g., research, clinical work; see also Chapter 11 in this volume).

Obesity and Overweight

The Impact of Weight on Quality of Life – Kids (IWQOL-Kids; Kolotkin et al., 2006) is a 27-item self-report scale designed for use with adolescents aged 11–19 years. Each item begins with the phrase, "Because of my weight," and contains five response options, ranging from *always true* to *never true*. In addition to a total score, there are scores on four domains: physical comfort, body esteem, social life, and family relations. It has good internal consistency (ranging from 0.88 to 0.95 for scales, and 0.96 for total score). It is sensitive to differences among BMI groups and between clinical and community samples as well as being responsive to weight loss/social support interventions. It is also available as a parent proxy form and exists in a number of different languages (see http://www.qualityoflifeconsulting.com/iwqol-lite.html).

Adherence

Self-Reports and Diaries

Self-report is convenient, easy, and inexpensive; however, it tends to produce an exaggerated estimate of adherence in both children and adults (see also Chapter 7 in this volume). Children will be adamant they are taking their medication when their physical status clearly indicates they are not. Parents will also be compelled to tell you that they are adequately supervising or providing treatment when they may be doing it much less. Disease-specific self-report questionnaires or interview schedules assess self-perceptions of adherence to self-care recommendations over a period of time. Respondents retrospectively rate how well they have adhered with regimen recommendations on a scale with higher scores indicating better adherence. These more structured measures appear to produce more honest responses than just asking "are you taking your medication?" A more accurate and precise way to assess adherence is completing a diary describing all behaviour over a 24-hr period (in person or over the phone) that the young person has been involved in rather than just asking about time spent on medical adherence. The diary allows one to look at the frequency and activity patterns as well as mood. The diary can also be used to look at the different behaviours of siblings where one child has a chronic illness and the other is healthy as well as how parents behave with each sibling (Johnson et al., 1986).

Physician Ratings

Ratings completed by health-care providers can also be used to quantify regimen adherence. However, a major limitation of this approach is the provider's knowledge of prior adherence behaviours, thereby introducing a bias into their ratings.

Quittner, Modi, Lemanek, Levers-Landis, and Rapoff (2008) have published a review of 18 evidence-based adherence measures for paediatric chronic illness. These included self-report/ structured interviews, daily diary procedures, and electronic monitoring. Only four met the criteria for *well-established* (e.g., at least two research teams have published sufficient information evaluating the measure and establishing its strong psychometric properties). These were the Self-Care Inventory (SCI; La Greca, Swales, Klemp, & Madigan, 1988), the Diabetes Regimen Adherence Questionnaire (DRAQ; Brownlee-Duffeck et al., 1987), and the 24-hr recall interview (Johnson et al., 1986), which are all for children and adolescents with diabetes, and the Disease Management Interview for Cystic Fibrosis (DMI-CF; Quittner et al., 2000)

Conclusion

The use of psychological questionnaires can contribute to the assessment and treatment of children and adolescents. In clinical settings, however, the questionnaire should be seen as part of a wider assessment, which is integral to the medical treatment, and not a last resort when the medical team runs out of options. However, a questionnaire should never be used by unqualified staff as a cheap alternative to a comprehensive clinical interview delivered by a qualified clinician. It is important for researchers to understand the clinical meaning of a questionnaire and to consider how to use the data at an individual level, should clinical difficulties be reported by the young person participating in the research project. Whilst questionnaires are rarely diagnostic, scores above accepted cut-off levels need to be reviewed and thought about carefully with relevant members of the team.

It is beyond the scope of a single chapter to list all questionnaires available for the assessment of health and health difficulties in children and adolescence. A small amount of time on the Internet will produce a vast number of questionnaires and structured measures designed to assess and screen for the majority of difficulties. A careful review of the questionnaire characteristics will enable a decision to be made as to the suitability of a particular questionnaire rather than just selecting the one that everyone else uses. The selection of an appropriate instrument is a challenge and should be considered carefully to ensure that it will enhance the assessment and engagement process in both clinical and research settings.

References

Achenbach, T. (1991). *Manual for the Child Behavior Checklist/4–18 and 1991 profile*. Burlington, VT: University of Vermont Department of Psychiatry.
Achenbach, T. (1992). *Manual for the Child Behavior Checklist/2–3 and 1992 profile*. Burlington, VT: University of Vermont Department of Psychiatry.

American Academy of Pediatrics, Committee on Bioethics. (1995). Informed consent, parental permission, and assent in pediatric practice. *Pediatrics, 95*, 314–317.

Angold, A., Costello, E., Pickles, E., & Winder, F. (1987). *The development of a questionnaire for use in epidemiological studies of depression in children and adolescents*. London, UK: Medical Research Council.

Angst, D. B., & Deatrick, J. A. (1996). Involvement in health care decisions: Parents and children with chronic illness. *Journal of Family Nursing, 2*, 174–194. http://doi.org/10.1177/107484079600200205

Atance, M., & O'Neill, D. K. (2001). Episodic future thinking. *Trends in Cognitive Sciences, 5*, 533–539. http://doi.org/10.1016/S1364-6613(00)01804-0

Bech, P. (2004). Measuring the dimensions of the psychological general well-being by the WHO-5. *QoL Newsletter, 32*, 15–16.

Beck, A., Beck, J., Jolly, J., & Steer, R. (2005). *Beck Youth Inventories – second edition for children and adolescents (BYI-II)*. London, UK: Pearson Education.

Berndt, D. J. (1986). *Multiscore Depression Inventory (MDI) manual*. Los Angeles, CA: Western Psychological Services.

Berndt, D., & Kaiser, C. F. (1996). *Multiscore Depression Inventory for Children (MDI-C)*. Los Angeles, CA: Western Psychological Services.

Brownlee-Duffeck, M., Peterson, L., Simonds, J. F., Goldstein, D., Kilo, C., & Hoette, S. (1987). The role of health beliefs in the regimen adherence and metabolic control of adolescents and adults with diabetes mellitus. *Journal of Consulting and Clinical Psychology, 55*, 139–144 http://doi.org/10.1037/0022-006X.55.2.139

Bruni, O., Galli, F., & Guidetti, V. (1999). Sleep hygiene and migraine in children and adolescents. *Cephalalgia, 19*(25, Suppl.), 57–59.

Canning, E. H., & Kelleher, K. (1994). Performance of screening tools for mental health problems in chronically ill children. *Archives of Pediatric and Adolescent Medicine, 148*, 272–278. http://doi.org/10.1001/archpedi.1994.02170120116029

Carey, M. P., Faulstich, M. E., Gresham, F. M., Ruggiero, L., & Enyart, P. (1987). Children's Depression Inventory: Construct and discriminant validity across clinical and non-referred (control) populations. *Journal of Consulting and Clinical Psychology, 55*, 755–761. http://doi.org/10.1037/0022-006X.55.5.755

Chalder, T., Berelowitz, G., Pawlikowska, T., Watts, L., Wessely, S., Wright, D., & Wallace, E.P. (1993). Development of a fatigue scale. *Journal of Psychosomatic Research, 37*, 147–153. http://doi.org/10.1016/0022-3999(93)90081-P

Christie, D. (2006). Cognitive, emotional and behavioural development. In M. Bellman & E. Peile (Eds.), *The normal child* (pp. 73–82), London, UK: Elsevier.

Cho, S., Kim, G. S., & Lee, J. H. (2013). Psychometric evaluation of a sample of patients with chronic pain. *Health and Quality of Life Outcomes, 11*(1), 213. http://doi.org/10.1186/1477-7525-11-213

Cohen, L. L., Lemanek, K., Blount, R. L., Dahlquist, L. M., Lim, C. S., Palermo, T. M., ... Weiss, K. E. (2008). Evidence-based assessment of pediatric pain. *Journal of Pediatric Psychology, 33*, 939–955. http://doi.org/10.1093/jpepsy/jsm103

Cohen, M. J. (2011). Children's memory scale. In J. Kreutzer, J. DeLuca, & B. Caplan (Eds.), *Encyclopedia of clinical neuropsychology* (pp. 556–559). New York, NY: Springer.

Cummins, J. (1980). Psychological assessment of immigrant children: Logic or intuition? *Journal of Multilingual and Multicultural Development, 1*(2), 97–111. http://doi.org/10.1080/01434632.1980.9994005

Delis, D. C., Kaplan, E., & Kramer, J. H. (2006). Delis Kaplan Executive Function System (D-KEFS). *Applied Neuropsychology, 13*, 275–279.

Eiser, C., & Morse, R. (2001). A review of measures of quality of life for children with chronic illness. *Archives of Disease in Childhood, 84*, 205–211. http://doi.org/10.1136/adc.84.3.205

Engel-Yeger, B., Josman, N., & Rosenblum, S. (2009). Behavioural Assessment of the Dysexecutive Syndrome for Children (BADS-C): An examination of construct validity. *Neuropsychological Rehabilitation, 19*, 662–676. http://doi.org/10.1080/09602010802622730

Friedberg, F., & Jason, L. A. (2002). Selecting a fatigue rating scale. *The CFS Research Review, 35*, 7–11.

Gill, T. M., & Feinstein, A. R. (1994). A critical appraisal of the quality of quality-of-life measurements. *Journal of the American Medical Association, 272*, 619–626. http://doi.org/10.1001/jama.272.8.619

Goodman, R. (1997). The Strengths and Difficulties Questionnaire: A research note. *Journal of Child Psychology and Psychiatry, 38*, 581–586. http://doi.org/10.1111/j.1469-7610.1997.tb01545.x

Goodman, R. (1999). The extended version of the Strengths and Difficulties Questionnaire as a guide to child psychiatric caseness and consequent burden. *Journal of Child Psychology and Psychiatry, 40*, 791–801. http://doi.org/10.1111/1469-7610.00494

Goodman, R., Ford, T., Richards, H., Gatward, R., & Meltzer, H. (2000). The Development and Well-Being Assessment: Description and initial validation of an integrated assessment of child and adolescent psychopathology. *Journal of Child Psychology and Psychiatry, 41*, 645–655. http://doi.org/10.1111/j.1469-7610.2000.tb02345.x

Hessl, D., Nguyen, D. V., Green, C., Chavez, A., Tassone, F., Hagerman, R. J., … Hall, S. (2009). A solution to limitations of cognitive testing in children with intellectual disabilities: The case of fragile X syndrome. *Journal of Neurodevelopmental Disorders, 1*(1), 33–45. http://doi.org/10.1007/s11689-008-9001-8

Horsch, A., McManus, F., Kennedy, P., & Edge, J. (2007). Anxiety, depressive, and posttraumatic stress symptoms in mothers of children with type 1 diabetes. *Journal of Trauma and Stress, 20*, 881–891. http://doi.org/10.1002/jts.20247

Jan, J. E., Owens, J. A., Weiss, M. D., Johnson, K. P., Wasdell, M. B., Freeman, R. D., & Ipsiroglou, R. S. (2008). Sleep hygiene for children with neurodevelopmental disabilities. *Pediatrics, 122*, 1343–1350. http://doi.org/10.1542/peds.2007-3308

Johnson, S. B., Silverstein, J., Rosenbloom, A., Carter, R., & Cunningham, W. (1986). Assessing daily management in childhood diabetes. *Health Psychology, 5*, 545–564. http://doi.org/10.1037/0278-6133.5.6.545

King, S., Schwellnus, H., Russell, D., Shapiro, L., & Aboelele, O. (2005). *Assessing quality of life of children and youth with disabilities: A review of available measures*. CanChild Centre for Childhood Disability Research. Retrieved from www.canchild.ca/en/canchildresources/assessingqualityoflife.asp

Kirisci, L., Clark, D. B., & Moss, H. B. (1996). Reliability and validity of the State-Trait Anxiety Inventory for Children in adolescent substance abusers: Confirmatory factor analysis and item response theory. *Journal of Child & Adolescent Substance Abuse, 5*(3), 57–69. http://doi.org/10.1300/J029v05n03_04

Kolotkin, R. L., Zeller, M., Modi, A. C., Samsa, G. P., Quinlan, N. P., Yanovski, J. A., … Roehrig, H. R. (2006). Assessing weight-related quality of life in adolescents. *Obesity, 14*, 448–457. http://doi.org/10.1038/oby.2006.59

La Greca, A. M., Swales, T., Klemp, S., & Madigan, S. (1988). Self care behaviors among adolescents with diabetes [Abstract]. In N. B. Anderson (Ed.), *Ninth Annual Sessions of the Society of Behavioral Medicine, Boston, MA*. Knoxville, TN: Society of Behavioral Medicine.

Lilienfeld, S. O., Wood, J. M., & Garb, H. N. (2000). The scientific status of projective techniques. *Psychological Science in the Public Interest, 1*, 27–66.

Luiz, D., Barnard, A., Knosen, N., Kotras, N., Horrocks, S., McAlinden, P., … O'Connell, R. (2006). *Griffiths Mental Development Scales – extended revised: 2 to 8 years*. London, UK: Pearson Education.

Manly, T., Anderson, V., Nimmo-Smith, I., Turnder, A., Watson, P., & Robertson, I. H. (2001). The differential assessment of children's attention: The Test of Everyday Attention for Children (TEA-Ch): Normative sample and ADHD performance. *Journal of Child Psychology and Psychiatry, 42*, 1065–1081. http://doi.org/10.1111/1469-7610.00806

Morriss, R., Wearden, A., & Mullis, R. (1998). Exploring the validity of the Chalder Fatigue scale in chronic fatigue syndrome. *Journal of Psychosomatic Research, 45*, 411–417. http://doi.org/10.1016/S0022-3999(98)00022-1

March, J. S. (2013). *Multidimensional Anxiety Scale for Children – 2nd Edition (MASC-2)*. North Tonawanda, NY: Multi-Health Systems.

March, J. S., Parker, J. D., Sullivan, K., Stallings, P., & Conners, C. K. (1997). The multidimensional anxiety scale for children (MASC): Factor structure, reliability and validity. *Journal of the American*

Academy of Child and Adolescent Psychiatry, 36, 554–565. http://doi.org/10.1097/00004583-199704000-00019

Muris, P., Steerneman, P., Meesters, C., Merckelbach, H., Horselenberg, R., van den Hogen, T., & van Donger, L. (1999). The TOM Test: A new instrument for assessing theory of mind in normal children and children with pervasive developmental disorders. *Journal of Autism and Developmental Disorders, 29*(1), 67–80. http://doi.org/10.1023/A:1025922717020

Noland, H., Price, J. H., Dake, J., & Telljohann, S. K. (2009). Adolescents' sleep behaviors and perceptions of sleep. *Journal of School Health, 79*, 224–230. http://doi.org/10.1111/j.1746-1561.2009.00402.x

Owens, J. A., Spirito, A., & McGuinn, M. (2000). The Children's Sleep Habits Questionnaire (CSHQ): Psychometric properties of a survey instrument for school-aged children. *Sleep, 23*, 1043–1052.

Poznanski, E., & Mokros, H. (1996). *Children's Depression Rating Scale–Revised (CDRS-R)*. Los Angeles, CA: WPS.

Quittner, A. L., Modi, A. C., Lemanek, K. L., Levers-Landis, C. E., & Rapoff, M. A. (2008). Evidence-based assessment of adherence to medical treatments in pediatric psychology. *Journal of Pediatric Psychology, 33*, 916–936. http://doi.org/10.1093/jpepsy/jsm064

Quittner, A. L., Drotar, D., Ievers-Landis, C. E., Seidner, D., Slocum, N., & Jacobsen, J. (2000). Adherence to medical treatments in adolescents with cystic fibrosis: The development and evaluation of family-based interventions. In D. Drotar (Ed.), *Promoting adherence to medical treatment in childhood chronic illness: Interventions and methods* (pp. 340–364). Hillsdale, NJ: Erlbaum.

Reynolds, W. M. (1989). *Reynolds Child Depression Scale*. Odessa, FL: Psychological Assessment Resources.

Seicean, A., Redline, S., Seicean, S., Kirchner, H. L., Gao, Y., Sekine, M., ... Storfer-Isser, A. (2007). Association between short sleeping hours and overweight in adolescents: Results from a US Suburban High School survey. *Sleep and Breathing, 11*, 285–293. http://doi.org/10.1007/s11325-007-0108-z

Sparrow, S. S., Cicchetti, D. V., & Balla, D. A. (2005). *Vineland Adaptive Behavior Scales* (2nd ed.). London, UK: Pearson Education.

Spence, S. H. (1998). A measure of anxiety symptoms among children. *Behavior Research and Therapy, 36*, 545–566. http://doi.org/10.1016/S0005-7967(98)00034-5

Spielberger, C. D. (1973). *Manual for the state-trait anxiety inventory for children*. Palo Alto, CA: Consulting Psychologists Press.

Vetter, T. R., Bridgewater, C. L., & McGwin, G., Jr. (2012). An observational study of patient versus parental perceptions of health-related quality of life in children and adolescents with a chronic pain condition: Who should the clinician believe? *Health and Quality of Life Outcomes, 10*, 85. http://doi.org/10.1186/1477-7525-10-85

Wechsler, D. (2002). *Wechsler Preschool and Primary Scale of Intelligence – third edition*. San Antonio, TX: Psychological Corporation.

Wechsler, D. (2004). *Wechsler Intelligence Scale for Children – fourth edition*. London, UK: Pearson Assessment.

Weissman, M. M., Orvaschel, H., & Padian, N. (1980). Children's symptom and social functioning self-report scales: Comparison of mothers' and children's reports. *Journal of Nervous Mental Disorders, 168*, 736–740. http://doi.org/10.1097/00005053-198012000-00005

WHOQOL Group. (1995). The World Health Organization quality of life assessment (WHOQOL): Position paper from the World Health Organization. *Social Science and Medicine, 41*, 1403–1409. http://doi.org/10.1016/0277-9536(95)00112-K

Young, N. L., Varni, J. W., Snider, S. McCormack, A., Sawatzky, B., Scott, M., ... Nicholas, D. (2009). The Internet is valid and reliable for child-report: An example using the Activities Scale for Kids (ASK) and the Pediatric Quality of Life Inventory (PedsQL). *Journal of Clinical Epidemiology, 62*, 314–320. http://doi.org/10.1016/j.jclinepi.2008.06.011

Chapter 22

Qualitative Assessment

Felicity L. Bishop and Lucy Yardley

Department of Psychology, University of Southampton, UK

In recent decades there has been increasing recognition of qualitative methods as essential means of assessment in health psychology. A wide variety of methods are available to researchers who want to capture and interpret qualitative data and we introduce some key methods in this chapter. Typically, qualitative data are verbal or textual (i.e., words) and are collected by talking to people individually or in groups. Such data are often detailed and complex and the researcher must engage in rigorous analytic procedures to interpret them. Traditionally, qualitative researchers have taken an open-ended inductive approach to assessing phenomena, allowing subjects and issues to arise that had not been anticipated by the investigator. This approach makes qualitative assessment particularly suitable for assessing phenomena that have not been investigated previously – for systematically describing and conceptualising these phenomena, and for generating hypotheses about their dimensions and relationships to their context. When qualitative assessment focuses on the way in which meaning is constructed, it has the potential to challenge investigators' fundamental assumptions about the nature of what they are measuring – for example, qualitative approaches can elucidate what different people may mean by terms and concepts that are often taken for granted, such as *illness* or *benefit*. Qualitative assessment is also particularly useful for understanding phenomena that need to be understood in their real-world context, such as the effects of clinical interventions in practice. Since qualitative assessment involves in-depth study of a small number of cases, it is a suitable method for assessing phenomena that are exceptional or difficult to gain access to. Qualitative methods thus provide insights that cannot be derived using quantitative methods alone.

To understand the strengths (and limitations) of qualitative methods relative to quantitative methods, it is necessary to appreciate the different assumptions made by each approach. In general, quantitative methods are associated with a post-positivist epistemology while qualitative methods are associated with a social constructionist epistemology. Post-positivist researchers use experimental designs to control and manipulate variables, striving for objective measurement in order to discover general laws that govern human behaviour. Social constructionist researchers see knowledge as intimately embedded in values, language, and culture; they therefore believe that objective knowledge of social psychological phenomena is impossible and aim instead to achieve critical and/or contextual interpretations that improve our understandings or inspire change.

Because of their post-positivist underpinnings, quantitative methods of assessment have high internal validity – they are designed to provide an accurate, precise, objective, and replicable measurement of a pre-selected variable of interest. But the price for high internal validity is loss of ecological validity – the extent to which it is possible to generalise to more complex real-world settings in which the variables of interest may vary, evolve, and interact in subtle and complex ways. For example, a quantitative measure may accurately assess a construct but may fail to detect crucial contextual influences on that construct, while important variations in participant meanings and perspectives may be missed when questionnaire responses are aggregated for statistical analysis. By contrast, qualitative methods strive to maximise ecological validity by describing and analysing phenomena in their real-world, socio-linguistic context (Camic, Rhodes, & Yardley, 2003).

Since the goal of qualitative assessment is ecological rather than internal validity, appropriate methods of establishing validity must be employed (Yardley, 2000). The assessment must be thorough and competent, which means that the investigators should be suitably skilled and the data collection and analysis must have sufficient depth and breadth to achieve its aims. The assessment should be coherent and transparent, so that it is clear to others what was done, the rationale, and how conclusions were reached. In addition, a good qualitative assessment should demonstrate sensitivity to how findings may be influenced by the context of the study; relevant influences could include the participants and the investigator, the local setting where the assessment takes place, the wider socio-linguistic influences on what is said and experienced, and the theoretical context of the study. A variety of specific techniques can be employed to increase and establish validity (Yardley, 2008), such as developing a coding manual and paper trail to document the analysis process, and combining and comparing the findings from different assessment approaches (triangulation).

In summary, qualitative assessment rests on different fundamental assumptions to those underpinning quantitative methods, can be used in situations where quantitative assessment is not appropriate or feasible, and can answer questions that quantitative methods cannot address.

Data Collection Methods

The aim of qualitative data collection is generally to understand the diverse perspectives of participants and the subjective, socio-cultural, and linguistic contexts and processes shaping the views they express. To achieve this aim, it is necessary to use flexible open-ended methods of collecting data, which allow participants to express themselves in ways that are not strictly controlled by the researcher. For example, a questionnaire designed to collect quantitative data would assess the impact of pain using questions constructed to measure pre-defined dimensions, with a limited set of response categories; for example, "How often did pain limit your normal activities this week?" (*never/sometimes/frequently*). By contrast, a qualitative approach would be to ask a more open-ended question that permits the respondent to define and discuss the dimensions most important to them; for example, "How does your pain currently affect your life?" The quantitative approach relies on the researcher being able to correctly anticipate and accurately assess all the most relevant dimensions of the topic – and choosing a particular response to tick seldom captures the complexity of participants' experiences. The qualitative approach allows the issues most salient to participants to emerge from the data and to be explained in depth, in the context of the participants' wider values and lifestyle.

Interviews and Focus Groups

Interviews and focus groups are the most commonly used methods of eliciting the viewpoint of participants in qualitative assessment (Joffe & Yardley, 2004). Both methods typically employ a series of planned semi-structured questions to prompt the participants to talk about various aspects of the topic of investigation, followed up by specific probes to explore each aspect in more detail, and neutral prompts to encourage participants to elaborate ("That's interesting, can you tell me more?"). Other methods of collecting qualitative data include observation in real-world contexts (e.g., consultations) and sampling existing texts (e.g., patient leaflets or online patient forums) or visual images (e.g., food advertisements).

Asking Questions

Excellent interpersonal and communication skills are required for both interviewing and leading focus groups; the investigator must learn how to be an attentive, sensitive, and non-judgemental listener, to give the interviewee or focus group participants the opportunity and the confidence to express themselves freely. The design of questions is also crucial in order to elicit rich data without overly constraining participant responses. It is important to avoid leading questions that are likely to bias answers in a particular direction and closed questions that can be answered by a word or phrase, and so will not generate rich data. For example, the question "Did you find the treatment helpful?" will tend to yield the uninformative and potentially biased answer "Yes"! Participants are usually most frank and expansive when giving an account of a personal experience, so it can be helpful to word questions so as to elicit personal stories; for example, "Can you tell me all about your first experience of ...?" A common temptation is to construct very detailed questions or abstract questions about psychological processes rather than experiences, in an attempt to elicit data that directly addresses your hypotheses or concerns. However, this type of interrogation can be intimidating to respondents, may overly influence what they say, and often leads to participants giving short, socially desirable answers.

Qualitative Sampling

Because qualitative data collection is resource intensive it is rarely possible to gather – and indeed analyse – data from a large enough sample to be statistically representative of a wider population. However, since the aim of qualitative research is to understand differences between people and contexts there is no expectation that findings could or should be representative of a "typical" population – instead, the intention is to derive insights into variations in perspectives and experiences. Consequently, purposive rather than random sampling is used to ensure that people and contexts are selected that may represent the range of variation likely to be most relevant to the topic assessed. For example, if views and experiences are likely to be affected by gender, age, and treatment outcome then the sample should include men, women, people of different ages, and people with good and bad treatment outcomes. The size of the sample needed is determined empirically by the point at which saturation is reached, that is, interviewing further people does not generate any important new themes. If the target population is very homogeneous then saturation may be reached with a small sample (e.g., 8–10 people). If purposive sampling is used to select groups of people likely to have different views, then sufficient numbers of people should be sampled in each category to provide some confidence that the views expressed are not unique to a few individuals who may be unusual.

Validity and Reflexivity

A common concern among researchers more accustomed to quantitative assessment is that qualitative data will not be objective, and could be influenced by participant self-presentation or by the perspective of the researcher. These influences on the data are unavoidable (whether the data is qualitative or quantitative), and so qualitative data collection should be reflexive about how the data is likely to be affected, that is, should be sensitive to and open about this issue. For example, if people who have designed or carried out an intervention interview the participants, then the investigators' natural enthusiasm is likely to lead to under-reporting of negative views. The interview techniques described in the section "Asking Questions" can help to reduce the influence of the researcher on the data, and audio-recording and transcribing of all that is said is employed to maximise the transparency and completeness of the data; this is the first step in creating a thorough paper trail linking what participants said to the findings of the analysis (see later sections). *Respondent validation* can also be appropriate for some projects, particularly those seeking to represent participants' views. This technique entails researchers sharing their findings with participants to ensure the researchers' interpretation still resonates with or rings true to participants.

Ethical Issues

Because of the personal contact with participants and the focus on socio-cultural influences on research, qualitative researchers are particularly attentive to ethical issues. The data generated by qualitative assessment often contain contextual details that could identify the participant even when the text has been anonymised for analysis. For example, if the participants are patients or health professionals from a small clinic and the hospital is named in the paper then clinicians and relatives might be able to recognise participants' accounts in a publication. It is therefore essential to obtain explicit consent for using quotations, and it may be necessary to check that participants are happy for potentially sensitive text excerpts to be reported. Criteria for assessing the quality of qualitative research, such as the widely used Critical Appraisal Skills Programme (CASP) checklist (CASP, 2010), provide useful reminders of ethical and other issues to consider when engaging in qualitative data collection.

Data Analysis Methods

Qualitative analysis typically begins before data collection has finished. This is so that initial findings or observations can inform subsequent data collection: Unlike quantitative assessment, which often proceeds in distinct stages, qualitative assessment often uses iterative designs. Because qualitative data is often rich and detailed, during data analysis researchers repeatedly read and/or listen to the data in order to become very familiar with it. Verbal data (such as that collected from interviews or focus groups) are usually transcribed word-for-word to produce a written record of the interaction to work with during analysis. Systematic and rigorous coding techniques are used to identify patterns in the data. These patterns are then interpreted and presented in answer to a research question, using selected examples of raw data to illustrate the analytic claims.

Data analysis methods can be classified in different ways. One relevant dimension is epistemology, as different epistemological assumptions lead us to interpret qualitative data in different ways. Some approaches are somewhat flexible and can be carried out from different epistemological standpoints; these include thematic analysis and grounded theory. Other approaches are more closely linked with particular assumptions about the social world and how we can generate knowledge; these include interpretative phenomenological analysis (IPA) and discourse analysis. *Interpretive* approaches focus on participants' talk as a means through which researchers can access their participants' subjective experiences. IPA tends to focus in this way on the subjective meanings that are represented in participants' talk. *Constructionist* approaches emphasise the social nature and functions of participants' talk. For example, discourse analysis focuses on how language itself shapes subjective experience and achieves social actions such as excusing or blaming. In the rest of this section, we briefly describe a few specific approaches to qualitative data analysis and discuss how they can be applied in health psychology.

Thematic Analysis

Thematic analysis is an accessible and flexible approach to qualitative data analysis that has become popular in health psychology and related disciplines. Thematic analysis typically involves working inductively to generate low-level codes that describe data, before combining these codes to form more abstract categories and themes that summarise common ideas and patterns in the dataset as a whole. So thematic analysis can be used to assess and describe themes that occur in data obtained from multiple participants and to analyse and interpret the relationships among themes. For example, thematic analysis could be used in health psychology to assess an intervention from the perspective of recipients (e.g., Tonkin-Crine, Bishop, Ellis, Moss-Morris, & Everitt, 2013). Such an analysis could identify effects of the intervention that the researchers had not anticipated in advance and explore how the intervention was received in the broader context of people's lives. Rather than establishing whether an intervention worked, qualitative assessment using thematic analysis would provide detailed insight into how and why the intervention worked for different people. The findings would thus be valuable for improving the intervention for future recipients. Braun and Clarke (2006) describe one approach to thematic analysis, using worked examples and providing clear guidance on different phases of data analysis.

Content Analysis

Content analysis provides a means to quantify qualitative data; it can be used to describe the prevalence of different themes in a large qualitative dataset or to compare the frequency of themes in subsets of data obtained from different groups of participants. Content analysis is well suited to describing and summarising written or verbal data, such as patient information leaflets, websites, or interviews (e.g., Alexander et al., 2014; Bishop, Adams, Kaptchuk, & Lewith, 2012). When carrying out content analysis, thematic coding is used to identify categories or themes, which are then counted and can be analysed using statistical techniques (Joffe & Yardley, 2004). Because content analysis interprets the prevalence of codes or themes in a dataset it is important to demonstrate that coding is reliable. This can be done by having two researchers independently apply a coding frame to the same data and calculating inter-rater agreement using Cohen's κ.

Interpretative Phenomenological Analysis (IPA)

IPA is an explicitly phenomenological approach to qualitative assessment: It seeks to understand what something is like from the perspective of participants and to explore how people make sense of lived experience (Smith, Flowers, & Larkin, 2009). IPA is particularly well-suited to idiographic work, which focuses on very small numbers of individuals and seeks to describe and understand their experiences in depth. Health psychologists could use IPA, for example, to produce a detailed analytic account of what it is like to live with or to be diagnosed with a specific long-term condition and how patients make sense of their condition (e.g., Mistry & Simpson, 2013; Osborn & Smith, 1998). Such a study might have specific practical implications for diagnostic processes as well as broader implications for how we theorise illness experience. Other phenomenological approaches such as descriptive phenomenology and hermeneutic phenomenology also seek to describe and/or interpret subjective experience from the perspective of the individual. Langdridge (2007) introduces, reviews, and compares different phenomenological research methods for psychology.

Grounded Theory

Grounded theory is perhaps the most established approach to qualitative assessment. Grounded theory provides a method for developing novel theories that explain and/or make predictions about social phenomena and are *grounded* in data collected from naturalistic settings. It is known for its constant comparison approach, in which the researcher compares and contrasts elements such as data excerpts, participants, codes, and the categories that emerge during the analytic process. Other key features of grounded theory include postponing a detailed literature review until later in the project, working iteratively between data collection and analysis so that early findings inform subsequent interviews, and using detailed rigorous coding and sampling techniques such as *open coding* and *theoretical sampling*. Grounded theory researchers begin with a very open question that they refine based on initial data and analysis before proceeding through additional phases of data collection and analysis to develop a theory that includes a *core category* and captures the main story in their data. Grounded theory is particularly useful when seeking to understand new topics or topics that are poorly theorised and is best used to address process-oriented *how* questions. For example, health psychologists might use grounded theory to develop new understandings of how people make health-related decisions (e.g., Cooper Robbins, Bernard, McCaffery, Brotherton, & Skinner, 2010). Grounded theory was originally developed by sociologists Glaser and Strauss (1967). Since then, multiple versions of grounded theory have been developed that differ in important characteristics, including epistemology and approaches to data analysis (Charmaz, 1990; Strauss & Corbin, 1998). These different versions of grounded theory are not interchangeable; it is therefore important to be clear about which version one is using and why (Bryant & Charmaz, 2007).

Discourse Analysis

Discourse analysis refers to a set of approaches to qualitative data that include, among others, discursive psychology (Edwards & Potter, 1992), Foucauldian discourse analysis (Arribas-Ayllon & Walkerdine, 2008), and critical discourse analysis (Fairclough, 2010). Discourse analysis often involves the detailed close study of naturally occurring data such as recorded conversations or written documents. Unlike interpretive approaches that treat participants' talk as directly reporting their subjective experience, discourse analysis focuses on language itself. One approach focuses on how language provides the interpretative frameworks that shape our subjective and collective experiences. This style of discourse analysis can be used to assess how different ways of talking about the same health topic promote different interpretations and opportunities for action (e.g., Sloan, Gough, & Conner, 2009). For example, an assessment of a patient education campaign might explore the discourses used (words, metaphors etc.) to examine how health risks are constructed or portrayed (e.g., as social or individual problems) and how this makes particular actions and subjective experiences possible for patients who are exposed to the campaign. Another approach to discourse analysis focuses on how language is used to perform social acts (e.g., Wiggins, 2009). This style of discourse analysis can be used to assess how health-related actions such as prescribing an intervention or resisting a diagnosis are accomplished through language. For example, discourse analysis could be used to assess the advice given by telemedicine services. A discourse analysis of calls to a helpline might explore how callers express health concerns and how call-takers respond, a detailed analysis of which could be used to develop training for call-takers.

Framework Analysis

In comparison to the primarily inductive approaches described earlier, qualitative methods are sometimes used deductively. Framework analysis (Ritchie & Spencer, 1994) can be used deductively, when one already has a very clear idea of the specific topics of interest at the start of a project. This approach involves coming up with a set of codes (a *framework*) in advance and then applying it to qualitative data. The framework might be based on existing theory, specific objectives of the research, or the interview questions (e.g., Barlow, Edwards, & Turner, 2008; Hind et al., 2009). For example, health psychologists could use framework analysis to assess the content of illness perceptions according to established dimensions in a novel condition or population.

Qualitative Software

Most approaches to qualitative analysis can be conducted either by hand or with the assistance of specially designed tools known as computer-assisted qualitative data analysis software or CAQDAS (Lewins & Silver, 2009). Examples of CAQDAS include NVivo and Atlas.ti. These tools can help researchers to analyse not only textual data (such as interviews and documents) but also visual data (such as photographs or drawings). They can greatly facilitate data management and coding processes, allowing fast retrieval of quotations and enabling researchers to quickly compare different elements of a dataset. CAQDAS can also help to produce an audit trail documenting how the researcher got from the raw data to the final conclusions. However, CAQDAS does not do the thoughtful analytic work required for qualitative assessment, and care is needed to ensure the analysis is implemented appropriately for the chosen method; the quality of the analysis is determined by the skill of the analyst, not the software.

Illustrations of Qualitative Assessment

Qualitative research is particularly useful for providing a fresh perspective that can challenge the status quo and/or generate novel theory. Three studies in psycho-oncology illustrate how different qualitative approaches offer new ways of thinking about established concepts in relation to coping with cancer. Quantitative research assesses participants' attitudes and behaviours on pre-defined constructs such as *positive thinking* derived from existing psychological theory. Qualitative techniques can take a broader focus, exploring patients' lived experiences within particular socio-cultural contexts. Wilkinson and Kitzinger (2000) used focus groups to explore how women with breast cancer discuss *thinking positive*. They took a discursive approach to data analysis and showed how thinking positive functions as a figure of speech or idiom, which is typically rather vague and ambiguous: When women talk about thinking positively they are not reporting on their use of a psychological coping strategy. Instead, such talk has implications in the immediate context of a discussion. For example, describing oneself as thinking positive can close down descriptions of difficult and emotional experiences and enable women to discuss their suffering. In the focus groups, women described many different negative thoughts and feelings around their experiences of cancer. These accounts of negative emotions can be difficult for other people to respond to conversationally and so often women also included positive idioms such as, "I'm the positive thinking type of person, and so you've just got to, you know, get on" (Wilkinson & Kitzinger, 2000, pp. 805–806), which made it easier for conversations to continue. Furthermore, Wilkinson and Kitzinger showed how the phrase *thinking positive* was not used to describe a natural response to cancer but as an exhortation to respond in a particular manner that is deemed morally desirable in our culture. This study thus challenged traditional notions of positive thinking as a coping strategy whose measurement using self-report tools is unproblematic.

Horgan, Holcombe, and Salmon (2011) took as their starting point the evidence that some women experience positive change or personal growth following a diagnosis of breast cancer. Explaining that little is known about *how* such positive emotional changes come about, they undertook a grounded theory study to explore this process. They interviewed a diverse range of women aged 32–75 years who had been diagnosed with breast cancer 3 months to 28 years earlier, some in each cancer stage from 0 to IV. Data collection and analysis proceeded iteratively; early interviews were very open, while later interviews were more focused on developing and testing out interpretations from earlier interviews. The resulting theory describes how different positive changes are brought about by reflecting on different aspects of illness experience. Reflecting on the management of breast cancer fostered increased self-confidence, while reflecting on physical and emotional suffering fostered transformative changes in priorities and increased spirituality and empathy for others who may be suffering. Factors that promoted and delayed these processes of reflection and positive change were also identified and their clinical implications discussed. This study used grounded theory to generate a new understanding of how reflecting can foster personal growth after cancer diagnosis, opening up new lines of inquiry for future research on adjustment processes.

Willig (2011) provides a way to think about the relationship between a focus on discourse (as in Wilkinson & Kitzinger, 2000) and a focus on women's experiences (as in Horgan et al., 2011). Using a Foucauldian approach to discourse analysis, Willig (2011) describes currently dominant discourses around cancer and examines how these make available certain ways of experiencing and living with a cancer diagnosis while hiding or mitigating against other possibilities. For example, enduring discourses around positive thinking, fighting the cancer "enemy," and behavioural causes of cancer position patients as individually culpable and morally responsible to do everything possible to secure victory (i.e., survival). These discourses constrain opportunities for patients to confront their mortality, to engage with and receive social support for suffering, and to share control over and responsibility for events. This study exemplifies how qualitative research can help us to traverse the gap between the socio-cultural and the phenomenological, by tracing the implications of socio-cultural resources for individual subjective experience.

The ability of qualitative research to challenge assumptions and pre-conceptions can also be valuable in applied research. Research into older people's views of fall prevention programmes provides an example (Yardley et al., 2006). Clinicians and interventionists tend to assume that older people will be motivated to take part in fall prevention programmes by their awareness and fear of the potentially serious consequences of falling for them. To find out what does motivate older people to engage with fall prevention programmes, older people in six countries were interviewed, sampling very different contexts; the sample included men and women of different ages, with differing levels of education, living alone or with family, in good and poor health, who had or had not been offered, started, or completed an intervention. Despite the variety of older people who took part, a very clear and unexpected message emerged. Older people were not primarily motivated to take up fall prevention programmes by the negative reason of avoiding fall risk, but were attracted by positive benefits such as remaining strong, confident, and independent. Indeed, most participants rejected the stigmatising identity of being at risk of falling, even if they had had a serious fall. These findings have important implications for maximising the reach of fall prevention programmes, which have since successfully been re-branded as programmes to maintain strength and fitness.

Qualitative research can also play a crucial role in optimising the accessibility and acceptability of an intervention. A good example is the extensive qualitative usability testing carried out in one study (Rotondi et al., 2007) to determine how to make a health information website accessible to people with seriously impaired cognitive abilities. Using a variety of methods of data collection, 98 participants were asked their views of various elements or aspects of the website, or were observed trying to use it. This was an iterative process; modifications were made on the basis of early feedback and then evaluated with new users. The findings had important implications for making websites as widely accessible and easy to use as possible. For example, the hierarchical menu typical of many websites makes heavy demands on abstract thinking and memory; a design that is easier for people to use when they have problems with attention, memory, or fatigue is a flat structure where the user can always return to the homepage by just one click on a clearly labelled button.

Qualitative process studies can also complement quantitative assessment in the evaluation of interventions. While standardised quantitative assessment is required for accurately assessing change in a randomised controlled trial, qualitative methods can provide important insights into the possible reasons for trial outcomes. For example, in a trial comparing treatments for back pain, the Alexander Technique achieved better outcomes than an exercise prescription. Since the interventions differed in numerous ways it was important to analyse what aspects of each intervention might be responsible for the different outcomes. Interviews carried out with participants in each intervention arm (Yardley et al., 2010) revealed that participants who had learned the Alexander Technique felt that it made sense, could be practiced while carrying out everyday activities or relaxing, taught them skills for managing back pain, and was an enjoyable experience – whereas the exercise prescription seemed to lack a clear and novel rationale, and could provoke pain. In addition, much less personal attention and support was reported by participants receiving the exercise prescription. These findings are important because they suggest that the non-specific factors that can affect patient expectancies, adherence, and outcome were enhanced in the Alexander Technique and could have influenced trial outcomes. These findings also have potentially useful implications for improving the acceptability and credibility of other treatments for back pain.

Future Directions

Qualitative assessment continues to evolve with new approaches to data collection and analysis. Creative adaptations that can enhance qualitative data collection include walking interviews (in which participants are interviewed while walking), which can help elicit participants' experiences of place and environment (Van Cauwenberg et al., 2012), and photo-elicitation techniques, where participants take photographs to be discussed with the interviewer (Hodgetts, Radley, Chamberlain, & Hodgetts, 2007). New approaches to the analysis of qualitative data include media framing analysis (Shaw & Giles, 2009), which directs researchers to examine key features of media reports such as framing, characterization, reader identification, and narrative form, and thus can be used to analyse media coverage of health topics.

Recently, some researchers have begun to adopt more deductive, theory-based qualitative approaches. For example, existing theories may be used as the basis for generating questions, and/or data analysis may involve mapping data onto categories corresponding to the constructs of existing theories (e.g., Gallacher, May, Montori, & Mair, 2011). These approaches can be useful for ensuring that all constructs believed on a priori grounds to be relevant are covered, and for generating detailed information about user views relevant to the implementation of a particular theory in a specific context. However, a crucial limitation of theory-based approaches is that they diminish the unique potential of qualitative research to reveal unexpected new insights, or to challenge the researcher's assumptions. One solution to this problem may be to commence data collection with some inductive, open-ended questions to allow participants to express what is most salient to them in their own way, followed up by theory-based questions to ensure comprehensive coverage of the topic.

Qualitative assessment techniques are also being combined in interesting and novel ways. One approach is *pluralism* in qualitative research, which involves combining different qualitative methods (Frost et al., 2010). Another approach is *mixed-methods* research that combines qualitative and quantitative methods in a single project or programme of research (Yardley & Bishop, 2008). While some forms of mixed-methods research have a long tradition (e.g., using qualitative methods to develop items for quantitative questionnaires), others are still being developed and becoming established (e.g., using qualitative methods to help interpret the results of quantitative studies). In mixed-methods research the strengths and limitations of qualitative techniques can be used to complement those of quantitative techniques. Mixed-methods research can thus facilitate more comprehensive assessment in health psychology.

References

Alexander, A. B., Stupiansky, N. W., Ott, M. A., Herbenick, D., Reece, M., & Zimet, G. D. (2014). What parents and their adolescent sons suggest for male HPV vaccine messaging. *Health Psychology, 33*, 448–456. http://doi.org/10.1037/a0033863

Arribas-Ayllon, M., & Walkerdine, V. (2008). Foucauldian Discourse Analysis. In C. Willig & W. Stainton-Rogers (Eds.), *The Sage handbook of qualitative research in psychology* (pp. 91–108). London, UK: Sage.

Barlow, J., Edwards, R., & Turner, A. (2008). The experience of attending a lay-led, chronic disease self-management programme from the perspective of participants with multiple sclerosis. *Psychology & Health, 24*, 1167–1180. http://doi.org/10.1080/08870440802040277

Bishop, F. L., Adams, A. E. M., Kaptchuk, T. J., & Lewith, G. T. (2012). Informed consent and placebo effects: A content analysis of information leaflets to identify what clinical trial participants are told about placebos. *PLoS One, 7*, e39661. http://doi.org/10.1371/journal.pone.0039661

Braun, V., & Clarke, V. (2006). Using thematic analysis in psychology. *Qualitative Research in Psychology, 3*, 77–101. http://doi.org/10.1191/1478088706qp063oa

Bryant, A., & Charmaz, K. (2007). *The Sage handbook of grounded theory*. London, UK: Sage.

Critical Appraisal Skills Programme (CASP). (2010). *Making sense of evidence about clinical effectiveness: 10 questions to help you make sense of qualitative research*. Retrieved from http://www.caspinternational.org/mod_product/uploads/CASP_Qualitative_Studies%20_Checklist_14.10.10.pdf

Camic, P. M., Rhodes, J. E., & Yardley, L. (Eds.). (2003). *Qualitative research in psychology: Expanding perspectives in methodology and design*. Washington, DC: American Psychological Association. http://doi.org/10.1037/10595-000

Charmaz, K. (1990). 'Discovering' chronic illness: Using grounded theory. *Social Science & Medicine, 30*, 1161–1172. http://doi.org/10.1016/0277-9536(90)90256-R

Cooper Robbins, S. C., Bernard, D., McCaffery, K., Brotherton, J. M. L., & Skinner, S. R. (2010). 'I just signed': Factors influencing decision-making for school-based HPV vaccination of adolescent girls. *Health Psychology, 29*, 618–625. http://doi.org/10.1037/a0021449

Edwards, D., & Potter, J. (1992). *Discursive psychology*. London, UK: Sage.

Fairclough, N. (2010). *Critical discourse analysis: The critical study of language* (2nd ed.) Harlow, UK: Pearson Education.

Frost, N., Nolas, S. M., Brooks-Gordon, B., Esin, C., Holt, A., Mehdizadeh, L., & Shinebourne, P. (2010). Pluralism in qualitative research: The impact of different researchers and qualitative approaches on the analysis of qualitative data. *Qualitative Research, 10*, 441–460. http://doi.org/10.1177/1468794110366802

Gallacher, K., May, C. R., Montori, V. M., & Mair, F. S. (2011). Understanding patients' experiences of treatment burden in chronic heart failure using normalization process theory. *Annals of Family Medicine, 9*, 235–243. http://doi.org/10.1370/afm.1249

Glaser, B. G., & Strauss, A. (1967). The discovery of grounded theory. In B. G. Glaser & A. Strauss (Eds.), *The discovery of grounded theory* (pp. 1–18). London, UK: Weidenfeld and Nicolson.

Hind, D., O'Cathain, A., Cooper, C. L., Parry, G. D., Isaac, C. L., Rose, A., ... Sharrack, B. (2009). The acceptability of computerised cognitive behavioural therapy for the treatment of depression in people with chronic physical disease: A qualitative study of people with multiple sclerosis. *Psychology & Health, 25*, 699–712. http://doi.org/10.1080/08870440902842739

Hodgetts, D., Radley, A., Chamberlain, K., & Hodgetts, A. (2007). Health inequalities and homelessness: Considering material, spatial and relational dimensions. *Journal of Health Psychology, 12*, 709–725. http://doi.org/10.1177/1359105307080593

Horgan, O., Holcombe, C., & Salmon, P. (2011). Experiencing positive change after a diagnosis of breast cancer: A grounded theory analysis. *Psycho-Oncology, 20*, 1116–1125. http://doi.org/10.1002/pon.1825

Joffe, H., & Yardley, L. (2004). Content and thematic analysis. In D. Marks & L. Yardley (Eds.), *Research methods for clinical and health psychology* (pp. 56–68). London, UK: Sage.

Langdridge, D. (2007). *Phenomenological psychology: Theory, research and method*. Harlow, UK: Pearson Prentice Hall.

Lewins, A., & Silver, C. (2009). *Choosing a CAQDAS package, a working paper* (6th ed.). Retrieved from http://caqdas.soc.surrey.ac.uk/QUICworkingpapers.html

Mistry, K., & Simpson, J. (2013). Exploring the transitional process from receiving a diagnosis to living with motor neurone disease. *Psychology & Health, 28*, 939–953. http://doi.org/10.1080/08870446.2013.770513

Osborn, M., & Smith, J. A. (1998). The personal experience of chronic benign lower back pain: An interpretative phenomenological analysis. *British Journal of Health Psychology, 3*, 65–83. http://doi.org/10.1111/j.2044-8287.1998.tb00556.x

Ritchie, J., & Spencer, L. (1994). Qualitative data analysis for applied policy research. In A. Bryman & R. G. Burgess (Eds.), *Analyzing qualitative data* (pp. 173–194). London, UK: Routledge.

Rotondi, A. J., Sinkule, J., Haas, G. L., Spring, M. B., Litschge, C. M., Newhill, C. E., ... Anderson, C. M. (2007). Designing websites for persons with cognitive deficits: Design and usability of a psychoeducational intervention for persons with severe mental illness. *Psychological Services, 4*, 202–224. http://doi.org/10.1037/1541-1559.4.3.202

Shaw, R. L., & Giles, D. C. (2009). Motherhood on ice? A media framing analysis of older mothers in the UK news. *Psychology & Health, 24*, 221–236. http://doi.org/10.1080/08870440701601625

Sloan, C., Gough, B., & Conner, M. (2009). Healthy masculinities? How ostensibly healthy men talk about lifestyle, health and gender. *Psychology & Health, 25*, 783–803. http://doi.org/10.1080/08870440902883204

Smith, J. A., Flowers, P., & Larkin, M. (2009). *Interpretative phenomenological analysis: Theory, method and research*. London, UK: Sage.

Strauss, A., & Corbin, J. (1998). *Basics of qualitative research* (2nd ed.). Thousand Oaks, CA: Sage.

Tonkin-Crine, S., Bishop, F. L., Ellis, M., Moss-Morris, R., & Everitt, H. (2013). Exploring patients' views of a Cognitive Behavioral Therapy-based website for the self-management of irritable bowel syndrome symptoms. *Journal of Medical Internet Research, 15*, e190. http://doi.org/10.2196/jmir.2672

Van Cauwenberg, J., Van Holle, V., Simons, D., Deridder, R., Clarys, P., Goubert, L. ... Deforche, B. (2012). Environmental factors influencing older adults' walking for transportation: A study using walk-along interviews. *International Journal of Behavioral Nutrition and Physical Activity, 9*, 85. http://doi.org/10.1186/1479-5868-9-85

Wiggins, S. (2009). Managing blame in NHS weight management treatment: Psychologizing weight and 'obesity'. *Journal of Community & Applied Social Psychology, 19*, 374–387. http://doi.org/10.1002/casp.1017

Wilkinson, S., & Kitzinger, C. (2000). Thinking differently about thinking positive: A discursive approach to cancer patients' talk. *Social Science & Medicine, 50*, 797–811. http://doi.org/10.1016/S0277-9536(99)00337-8

Willig, C. (2011). Cancer diagnosis as discursive capture: Phenomenological repercussions of being positioned within dominant constructions of cancer. *Social Science & Medicine, 73*, 897–903. http://doi.org/10.1016/j.socscimed.2011.02.028

Yardley, L. (2000). Dilemmas in qualitative health research. *Psychology & Health, 15*(2), 215–228. http://doi.org/10.1080/08870440008400302

Yardley, L. (2008). Demonstrating validity in qualitative psychology. In J. A. Smith (Ed.), *Qualitative psychology* (2nd ed., pp. 235–251). London, UK: Sage.

Yardley, L., & Bishop, F. (2008). Mixing qualitative and quantitative methods: A pragmatic approach. In C. Willig & W. Stainton-Rogers (Eds.), *The Sage handbook of qualitative research in psychology* (pp. 352–369). London, UK: Sage.

Yardley, L., Bishop, F. L., Beyer, N., Hauer, K., Kempen, G. I. J. M., Piot-Ziegler, C., … Rosell, A. (2006). Older people's views of falls prevention interventions in six European countries. *The Gerontologist, 46*, 650–660. http://doi.org/10.1093/geront/46.5.650

Yardley, L., Dennison, L., Coker, R., Webley, F., Middleton, K., Barnett, J., … Little, P. (2010). Patients' views of receiving lessons in the Alexander Technique and an exercise prescription for managing back pain in the ATEAM trial. *Family Practice, 27*, 198–204. http://doi.org/10.1093/fampra/cmp093

Part IV
Conclusion

Chapter 23

Assessment: Moving Beyond Association to Explanation and Intervention

Howard Leventhal[1], Danielle E. McCarthy[1], Emily Roman[1], and Elaine A. Leventhal[2]

[1]Institute for Health and Department of Psychology, Rutgers University, New Brunswick, NJ, USA
[2]Department of Medicine, Robert Wood Johnson Medical School, Rutgers University, New Brunswick, NJ, USA

Introduction

You have entered an auto dealership to consider purchasing the latest vehicle for personal transportation. The motto, "The future is now!" adorns the walls. The sales person greets you and exclaims, "You look like you are ready to move into the future of technologically driven, personal transportation." Gazing longingly at the sleek vehicle you reply, "It looks cool, but how does it work? And what would I have to do to make sure it gets where I want to go?" The effusive reply, "We've run multiple regression models on thousands of potential customers and given your scores on self-efficacy, conscientiousness, and positive and optimistic approaches to life, the multiple R is .8 for getting where you want to go for a trip less than 300 miles and is still an amazing .7 for trips up to a 1,000 miles! Those are remarkable numbers. They might edge up a bit if you drop 20 pounds, and complete a few weeks of strength training to ease entry and exit." How would you respond? Would you ask, "Can it get where I want to go 100% of the time rather than 64% or 49% of the time? Are there garages and mechanics around the country who understand how it works to make repairs if needed?" If the answer to either question is *No*, would you buy the car?

As absurd as the above scenario may seem, it mirrors to a considerable degree the current offerings of behavioral health research. Multiple R's in the ranges cited would dazzle reviewers and editors and many hundreds of articles published during the past three decades present far less robust relationships between predictors and outcomes than our fictitious example. Factors such as social support (Berkman, Glass, Brissette, & Seeman, 2000; Uchino, 2009), ethnicity (Karlsen & Nazroo, 2002), gender and age (McDonough & Walters, 2001; Samaras, Chevalley, Samaras, & Gold, 2010), personality (e.g., conscientiousness; Boog & Roberts, 2004), personal competency (Sheer, 2014; Smith, Wallston, & Smith, 1995), and affective traits and states (Moussavi et al., 2007) have been used to predict behavioral and medical outcomes such as quality of life (Lerner & Levine, 1994), treatment adherence (DiMatteo,

Lepper, & Croghan, 2000), use of emergency care (Aminzadeh & Dalziel, 2002), re-hospitalization (Kansagara, et al., 2011), and mortality. In many, though not all instances, the predictors and many of the outcome measures are assessed using multi-item scales to ensure reliability (Cortina, 1993) and validity. Collections such as *Measuring Health* (McDowell, 2006) and chapters in this volume attest to the care and concern for assessment of health outcomes, as do volumes on the assessment of predictors (Blalock, 1972; Boog & Roberts, 2004; Sheer, 2014). Rules for assessment of reliability and validity are amply cited in method sections describing the instruments used in descriptive studies and experimental studies.

Problems arising from the rigid application of rules for reliability and validity have not gone unnoticed. Ensuring a high coefficient α (Blalock, 1972) by increasing scale length can create problems for respondents, leading to assessment reactivity, lackadaisical responding, or social conformity (Kerkhofs & Lindeboom, 1995; Streiner & Norman, 2008). The emphasis on reliability was questioned decades ago by Meehl and colleagues who did not see internal consistency as an essential prior to validity (Cronbach & Meehl, 1955). The debate has current relevance as investigators adopt a "trans-diagnostic approach" that calls for assessment of specific cognitive and behavioral components (e.g., hopelessness, anhedonia) previously buried within instruments for assessing diagnostic categories, for example, depressive disorders (American Psychiatric Association, 2000).

We have benefited from the development of an array of reliable and valid instruments to assess moderators and mediators proven to be reliable and valid predictors of health behaviors (e.g., smoking), treatment adherence, bio-markers (e.g., HbA1c, blood pressure), and hard health outcomes (e.g., mortality). Indeed, assessing outcomes through valid self-reports (e.g., adherence; Thompson, Kulkarni, & Sergejew, 2000) posed a challenge that has been managed with considerable success. Our enthusiasm for substantial beta weights in multiple regressions in cross-sectional and longitudinal data does not, however, negate the simple fact that correlation does not equal causation. This is not to claim these findings are useless; identifying associations between such factors and outcomes indicates where a problem exists, that mortality and diseases are affecting specifiable sets of individuals at particular places and times. In our view, it is important to remember that these findings do not describe the causal mechanisms and processes underlying these associations.

Assessment and Analysis of Mediation: Challenges and Approaches

Recognizing the problem raises the following critical question: "How can we examine the mechanisms linking predictors and outcomes in regression models?" No matter how reliable and valid our assessments of external predictors or moderators and outcomes, both our science and practice are limited if we do not model the mediating processes connecting predictors to outcomes. For example, socioeconomic status has been linked to various health outcomes with little evidence of the mechanisms that connect them (Alder et al., 1994). Given the typical size of these associations, for example, odds ratios of 1.5 to 2.5, it is clear that at least some study participants do very well on the health outcomes although they score low scores on the predictors, while others with high predictor scores do poorly. The question of course is whether the low-scoring individuals achieving positive outcomes are doing the same or different things from those scoring high, and vice versa. We may be able to identify subgroups for whom the positive association between predictor and outcome holds (i.e., identify a moderator), but this will advance our understanding only a little unless we are able to link that to a process (i.e., mediated moderation). This would allow psychologists to solve more interesting questions and tailor interventions for different groups based on the particular mechanism effecting change.

As we move from description to intervention, we need conceptual models that tell us more than that intervention X1 affects the behavior of 72% of patients who score high on factor A and have poor health outcomes. We need to assess the mechanisms and processes leading to positive and negative health outcomes if we are to create settings in which people can discover and take actions needed to reach favorable outcomes. In short, we may travel better in the future by managing underlying mechanisms rather than traveling the route laid out by regression models suggesting that we have 64% or 49% possibility of getting where we want to go if, by good fortune, the correlations describe causal relationships.

Assessment and Analysis of Mediation: Current Approaches

As we focus on interventions to assist people, both well and ill, to modify behavior so as to enhance health and quality of life, studies using regression analysis to identify moderators and one or two mediators of outcomes will prove less useful. Rather than repeat studies relating known predictors to outcomes, we need to conceptualize and assess the mechanisms and processes that define pathways from interventions and moderators of treatment response to health outcomes. The shift will demand: (a) multidisciplinary theory to guide the substance and methods for assessment and to establish time frames for assessment essential for causal inferences; (b) varied methodologies, for example, focus groups and intensive interviews, descriptive multivariable longitudinal studies, randomized controlled trials (RCT), and dynamic modeling; and (c) integration of the assessments from various methods to represent the sequence of events defining pathways from predictors/moderators to outcomes. We will briefly consider the extent to which current approaches meet these demands and will then outline future challenges.

Structural Models: A Step Toward Identifying Health Behavior Processes

Baron and Kenny's (1986) application of path analysis (Blalock, 1964; Wright, 1960) or structural modeling (SEM) to behavioral research encouraged the conceptualization and assessment of factors active in direct and indirect pathways between predictors (including interventions and moderators) and outcomes. Most importantly, SEM allowed investigators to determine which pathways remained in a structural model and which predictors failed to connect directly or indirectly with outcomes. For example, a recent study of treatment adherence (Phillips, Leventhal, & Leventhal, 2011) identified a direct pathway to resolution of a health problem through recall of information about self-treatment, ways to monitor progress, and likely outcomes provided by the clinician. There was also an indirect pathway from the communication of self-management procedures to adherence and problem resolution one month later. Provider communication and patient recall of that communication had beneficial effects on patient self-management. Patient ratings of satisfaction with the encounter, by contrast, were strongly, negatively related to problem resolution. Patients who reported that their provider was more empathic and understanding were more likely to report high levels of satisfaction with the encounter, but this predicted lower odds of problem resolution. There was no direct relation between provider empathy and adherence. These data are important because they suggest that specific provider behaviors have opposing effects that we can detect with proper assessment. By differentiating pathways linking provider behavior and patient outcomes, SEM provides guidelines for developing interventions.

Although the Phillips et al. findings are consistent with theory (common-sense model; Leventhal, Breland, Mora, & Leventhal, 2010; Leventhal, Weinman, Leventhal, & Phillips, 2008) and previously published research (Michie, Miles, & Weinman, 2003), there is room for criticism of its measures, given the modest evidence for the reliability and validity of the scales assessing moderators (common-sense self-regulation; attentiveness to emotional needs), mediators (adherence), and outcomes (reported problem resolution and need for follow-up care). Investigators must find a difficult balance between selection of reliable and valid measures while also finding brief, low-burden assessments that permit deeper investigation of treatment-response processes. A deeper investigation would involve examining patient self-management at home, assessing self-management challenges, and carefully assessing patient strategies that lead to favorable or unfavorable outcomes. Measures of these processes may be mixed quantitative and qualitative approaches and may be idiosyncratic. They will need to be as brief and efficient as possible, even at the cost of reliability. Improving the quality of instruments can still be melded into studies whose primary goal is modeling and assessing patients' decisions to initiate and embed health behaviors in their daily routines, and identify factors that supported these actions. This latter focus will generate the conceptual framework for advancing research and practice.

Increasing the Tools for Assessment

In recognition of the need to examine a wider range of outcomes and mediating processes, the National Institute of Health created the PROMIS initiative (National Institutes of Health, 2014, http://www.nihpromis.org). PROMIS provides an ever-expanding bank of long and short forms (single-item versions in some cases) of scales that can be used to assess moderators, mediators, and outcomes for behavioral health research. Current reliability and validity data are available online. The value of the bank is enhanced as a number of scales assess components of concepts previously assessed with global measures and some assess mediators little attended to in prior research. The great majority of scales in PROMIS are multi-item self-report scales and relatively few address specific factors nested in the dynamic mechanisms actively linking predictors and outcomes.

Capturing Change to Delineate Pathways to Outcomes

Imagine that we are planning an RCT to improve treatment adherence for the management of blood glucose for patients with type 2 diabetes. Assume that we have two broad objectives for our diabetes intervention: to generate replicable outcomes (e.g., lowering HbA1c), and to enhance the probability of successful dissemination to clinical practice. To meet these objectives, we may want to play it safe and select established measures of key constructs (e.g., self-efficacy) that have been validated in broad or diverse populations. This may lead us to an impressive R in a multiple regression. However, these established scales may fail to detect critical processes at work in some participants. For example, some people may report low self-efficacy regarding diabetes management, but may still manage well because they seek and accept help from others (e.g., a spouse) in management (e.g., devising healthy menus, prompting exercise, monitoring, or medication use). Others may not think about confidence or self-management because they have so woven management into their daily routine that reflection on this is unnecessary. Knowledge of these key processes to successful self-management of diabetes would be lost using a conventional approach. Subtle differences across samples in the number of people using such successful but unmeasured processes may contribute to frequent failures to replicate (Derogatis, Meyer, & Dupkin, 1976; Segraves, Schoenberg, Zarins, Knopf, & Camic, 1981; Simon, 2012). Lack of knowledge of the variables that unfold over time and define mediating pathways is the gateway to replication failure when the procedures are implemented in different settings and populations.

The key issue is whether we can conduct an RCT that: (a) assesses pathways connecting the intervention to the outcome; (b) illustrates change trajectories by assessing multiple factors at multiple time points; and (c) is based on a theoretical model capable of guiding the selection and timing of assessments across different levels of description, that is, from disease process and treatment to patient expectations in a social context. These requirements will affect what we assess and how and when we do so. These standards will neither be easily nor completely met. What can we draw upon to move forward?

Devices for Assessment

Assessment of multiple factors over multiple time points suggests looking for measures other than multi-item scales with high internal consistency; our aim is to find and construct brief measures that will meet criteria for measurement invariance across time, test–retest reliability, and, most importantly, validity. Fortunately, we can draw on a number of approaches for rapid recording of responses at multiple time points such as *momentary assessments* (Stone & Shiffman, 1994), *experience sampling* (Hektner, Schmidt, & Csikszentmihalyi, 2007), and *ambulatory assessment* (Fahrenberg, Myrtek, Pawlik, & Perrez, 2007; for further information on ecological momentary assessments, see Chapter 18 in this volume). If we assume that the individual's physical and social environment creates opportunities and barriers to adherence and desired outcomes, we can search the National Institutes of Health's Basic Behavioral and Social Science Opportunity Network (National Institutes of Health, Data and Statistics, 2009) and search for tools useful for assessing environmental variables in real time. Electronically activated audio-recording to sample environmental sounds (Mehl, Robbins, & Deters, 2012) is a tool that can detect whether a study participant is alone, with others, speaking, or laughing. Such observations can be linked to reports of thoughts or moods and reports and observations of behaviors. Small, lightweight, low-cost video recorders are also available. These can be attached to users and generate hour-long recordings in naturalistic settings. Records of behavioral sequences could provide investigators and patients with the observations needed to detect times and places for inserting procedures for disease management into daily life (Brooks et al., 2014). These measures may not be free of bias (given that they capture a participant rather than observer perspective), but they may assess change processes and intervention opportunities better than conventional approaches.

Data recording at the biomedical level is also poised for a digital revolution. Devices for assessing blood pressure, heart rate, and cardiac irregularities will be miniaturized and technology for monitoring blood glucose through the skin is promised in the near future (Tura, Maran, & Pacini, 2007). Such data may be used for real-time or delayed tele-monitoring (Tildesley, Po, & Ross, 2015) and linked to real-time recording of variables in the patient's natural environment. To the extent we can code and analyze data from this array of data-capture devices and integrate diverse kinds of data, we may be able to study the antecedents and consequences of behavior change interventions in new ways.

Integrating Data Across Levels

Now that we have the technology to assess biological, psychological, and social/contextual change processes in descriptive or intervention studies, we need the analytical tools to integrate these data. We will need to develop, test, and refine complex models of feed-back and feed-forward pathways of interacting mechanisms. These models will guide assessments at every level (multiple or single items of mood or action; interval or ratio scales; indices or rates of change in blood glucose). The timing of assessment will be critical. Without appropriate measures at appropriate times, we cannot draw models depicting causal pathways from externals (moderators; interventions) through mediators to outcomes. Behavior will be at the center of the model, linking effects of environmental variables and somatic experience (symptoms and function) on decisions, actions, and their consequences. A strong model will also suggest pathways by which action alters the underlying biological processes and biomedical markers. This may suggest ways to enhance interventions and improve health.

Time Frames for Disease/Risk and Treatment/Interventions

What would multilevel, multimodal assessment look like in our hypothetical blood glucose control? Capturing causal linkages is typically approached by assessing dependent variable Y at t_1, introducing X at t_2, and assessing Y at t_3, assuming that the intervening X determines change in Y from t_1 to t_3 when the change differs from that in a control condition in the absence of X. Given a p value less than .05, or better yet less than .001, and rigorous adherence to randomization, investigators are prone to conclude that X caused the change in Y, forgetting that the statistical test has simply given them the opportunity to reject the null hypothesis that the intervention and control conditions do not differ. Causation can only be assumed if the relationship is based on a theoretically specified pathway, in a biologically plausible manner and timeframe. Imagine that in our diabetes RCT, we randomly assign patients to an active demonstration of exercise effects on blood glucose, or a discussion control. The way we design the demonstration is critical, particularly with regard to timing. If a blood glucose reading is taken at t_1, immediately before a 30-min exercise session at t_2, then the timing of t_3 blood glucose testing will determine not just the magnitude, but also the direction of the exercise intervention effect. If t_3 is within 2 hrs of t_1, glucometer readings will likely be higher than at t_1. If t_3 is at least 2 hrs after t_1, however, the opposite will be true, and blood glucose will fall at t_3. In this way, consideration of causal models informed by biomedical knowledge is critical. Getting the timing wrong could lead participants to think that exercise increases diabetes risk because it increases blood glucose, and could lead patients to conclude that nothing makes sense and undermine motivation for behavioral change. The degree of change in blood glucose from t_1 to t_3 may vary considerably across people, and across trials within people, in addition to varying across time intervals. It is critical to keep this variability in mind when designing assessments and analyzing data (see also Chapter 17 in this volume, for further information on biological and physiological measures).

The aforementioned example of the confusion that can arise when patients assess their blood glucose suggests that the intervention in our hypothetical trial will need to address the targets people use to evaluate the efficacy of their actions and take into account at least three sets of time frames: (a) individual differences in the temporal changes in disease and treatment; (b) patient beliefs, expectations, and perceptions, respecting what and when to observe to evaluate the efficacy of their behavior, essential for predicting adherence; and (c) the information on targets and time frames that patients share with practitioners, other patients, family, and friends. All three temporal issues are critical for replication in different places and populations and for dissemination to clinical practice.

Time Frames for Disease and Treatment

Timing for assessing the effects of treatment and behavioral change will vary by the assessed target. For example, serum blood glucose levels (SMBG) are highly variable measures of the moment. HbA1c, a measure of the proportion of glucose-attached hemoglobin within the red cells, changes far more slowly, for example, over 3- to 6-month time frames. Important systemic clinical changes, for example, vascular changes and ulcer formation, kidney damage, etc., may not occur until many years after onset of diabetes. Time lines for assessing the effects of interventions also vary: The effects of insulin are measureable quickly; metformin, frequently prescribed for type 2 diabetes, acts rapidly although less quickly than insulin; the response to both in terms of SBMG depends upon dosage. Dietary intervention, for example, substituting rapidly metabolized carbohydrates for those that require more metabolic energy, may dampen rapid rises of blood glucose (SMBG) but replacement foods may also elevate readings in the short term and differences between the two diets in assessment of HbA1c may take months to detect. Rates of change and time frames for assessment are also highly variable among individual patients.

Patient Expectations Regarding Targets and Time Frames

Our example on the mixed, correct, and incorrect conclusions patients can draw from blood glucose levels and exercise makes clear the importance of assessing patient expectations as to when to check and what they should see when evaluating the effects of their behavior on disease risk. In addition to medical biomarkers, patients may monitor symptoms to assess treatment progress, for example, clinicians hear complaints of dizziness as a marker of both hypo- and hyperglycemia. Identifying and assessing these subjective markers and patient expectations regarding their rates of change are important as they may cue behaviors that are inconsistent with those called for by objective indicators. As symptom and functional changes are internal, they are immediately and often continually available, giving them greater weight than objective indicators in many instances. Regardless of their source, the amounts and rates of change in these targets will affect appraisals of treatment efficacy and the patients' perceptions of disease risk. Assessment may also need to determine if patients use a single time frame (e.g., expecting immediate effects across diverse indicators) or a set of marker-appropriate time frames (e.g., immediate changes in SBMG or dizziness, quarterly changes in Hb1Ac) to assess treatment benefit. Pairing marker-specific expectations with strategy-specific action plans (e.g., developing a routine for medication and another for exercise) will foster automatic, habitual adherence over the long term (Phillips & Chapman, 2011). The expectations and actions involved in these processes may vary by the individual patient's cultural background, age, health literacy, and disease- or treatment-specific beliefs.

Shared Targets and Time Frames

The interplay between patients and practitioners respecting targets and temporal expectations represents the third area for assessment. Did the provider (or experimental intervener) discuss targets and time frames for subjective or biomarker changes in response to treatment? Conversations may or may not address these issues for different treatment targets and may vary across patients. However, even if providers follow a protocol for such discussions, we do not know how patients hear, comprehend, recall, or act on these unless we assess these steps after exposure (Ley, 1977).

The Translational Process: Assessment for Dissemination

Although our brief review of targets and time frames for assessment may seem excessively detailed and specific to diabetes, it is an important step toward meeting the two objectives of our hypothetical RCT. Having a model that describes how one moves from the intervention to an outcome is an essential first step for identifying pathways. A model that defines and calls for assessment of specific pathways allows interventionists to anticipate how changes in contexts and participant populations will alter the impact of their intervention; action based on this understanding will increase the probability of replication. The second objective, to generate procedures that can be disseminated to clinical practice, requires assessment of expectations and perceptions of actions, targets, and time frames for change among all trial participants (i.e., investigators, lay and patient participants, and practicing clinicians). Not all clinical trials require the conceptualization and assessment of this array of factors. There may be little need for assessment of patient expectations and perceptions in clinical trials comparing the potency of two antiseptics to avoid infection, or two levels of blood transfusion to avoid hypoxemia during surgery under anesthesia. If, however, there is concern that the interventions may have varying postoperative effects on behavior, patient expectations and practitioner communication may need to be assessed. For most behavioral trials, dissemination requires understanding how participants see their roles and the effects of these situational self-definitions on performance. If self-definitions of trial participants differ sharply from those of patients in clinical settings, and these differences affect behaviors critical for treatment adherence, trial results will not generalize to practice.

In preparing the design of our trial and selecting instruments for assessment, it will be helpful to remember that "behavioral intervention research cannot become a cumulate science – until intervention studies can answer not only IF the intervention changed behavior, but also HOW it changed behavior and WHICH intervention components were most effective in changing behavior" (Riley & Rivera, 2014, p. 234). We can also learn from innovations in clinical trial design and data modeling to achieve the goals of our RCT.

Efficient Research Designs

A recent innovation in clinical trial design is the multiphase optimization strategy (MOST) for the development of interventions (Collins, Trail, Kugler, Baker, & Mermelstein, 2014). The objective of MOST is to conduct one or more efficient, preliminary, screening studies to "identify one of the best combinations of components" for an intervention rather than design studies to identify "the single best combination" of intervention components against a single control. Collins et al. (2014) include excellent tables allowing readers to assimilate a range of issues including assessment of effect sizes for single modules and data sets are available online (http://methodology.psu.edu/ra/most) allowing readers to play with these ideas. MOST is a reasonable antecedent for planning large (fully powered) RCTs to test behavioral interventions to enhance diabetes self-management. The MOST team rejects efforts to identify the single best combination of intervention modules as doing so would require a massive RCT with "intervention arms corresponding to each viable combination"; 64 conditions with six intervention modules. They recommend fractional factorial designs as a partial solution, as these designs can reduce the number of conditions by half (Collins et al., 2014, p. 240). In our diabetes trial, we seek to lower blood glucose levels through multiple interventions (i.e., medication, an exercise intervention, a dietary intervention, self-monitoring training). We also want to explore treatment interactions (i.e., does medication have less of a benefit in people who achieve stable lifestyle change). The intervention in our RCT will be complex and assessment will extend over variable time frames with multiple indicators (e.g., intensive SBMG monitoring for brief periods, longer-term eating and physical activity, distal HbA1C or physical health outcomes).

A fractional factorial design may generate considerable knowledge about mediators of intervention effects on outcomes, despite not looking at all possible treatment component combinations as a full factorial design would. MOST's aim of selecting "one of the best combinations" may, in our judgment, lead some investigators to focus too quickly on outcomes (e.g., HbA1c three months post intervention), rather than on the dynamic processes in the pathway leading to improved HbA1c. An advantage of assessing mediators rather than distal outcomes is that the mediator is more proximal in the pathway to desired behavioral outcomes and therefore can be more useful in identifying nonresponders who may benefit from intensified or different interventions (e.g., adaptive interventions). Ideally, the mediator would be linked in specific ways to the intervention and the outcome. Self-efficacy is a commonly studied mediator that is not closely linked in this way. We need to understand the ways in which specific components (e.g., an exercise intervention) induced changes in self-efficacy, and how these changes came about (what experiences were critical). We also need to understand which specific behaviors mediate self-efficacy relations with distal outcomes.

We need data and models specifying the likely different pathways to adherence to medication, physical activity, and diet change that lead to avoidance of remote, adverse consequences of diabetes. Though all three sets of actions are useful for controlling blood glucose, there are many reasons for a patient to rely on one and ignore the others. Taking medication is both simpler and provides more immediate and intelligible feedback than changing diet and physical activity. On the other hand, patients may be concerned with the timing for using medication (before meals when eating alone is quite different than when eating with others) and with side effects, leading them to focus on other behavioral pathways. Some patients may be motivated to change diet and activity in the hope of stopping medication, while other patients may find it too difficult to change diet and physical activity and simply give up. Each of these pathways requires conceptualization and assessment of the factors underlying decisions, actions, and changes in action over time. Assessing these pathways may be more complex in low-income populations where diabetes is highly prevalent and the environmental factors create barriers for adherence to particular paths, for example, lack and cost of diabetes-appropriate foods in low-income areas (Breland, McAndrew, Gross, Leventhal, & Horowitz, 2013).

Theoretical models enriched with data would allow investigators to anticipate the time at which specific transitions would occur along pathways such as those outlined previously. The models would suggest what modules to test, and when and how to introduce them to maximize the possible impact on the behavioral system at various points in time. Identifying transitions involves consideration of the patient's experience of disease and treatment and how these processes affect communication with family and friends. Such communication may then feedback to patient decisions that impact mediating variables (e.g., self-efficacy) and outcomes (e.g., treatment adherence, seeking care and advice for diet, physical activity). If our theory addresses how and when behaviors and treatment affect the biological aspects of disease, it should suggest specific combinations of modules and sequences and timing for introducing the modules and conducting assessments. Whether this would reduce the number of modules and assessment for testing is moot at this point in time; MOST, however, points to an important preliminary step for our hypothetical, fully powered RCT.

Novel Data Analytic Approaches

A recent article adopts a "control systems engineering approach for adaptive behavioral interventions" to the management of pain and sleep for fibromyalgia (Deshpande, Rivera, Younger, & Nandola, 2014, p. 275). The article described important features of dynamical systems modeling, such as the use of difference equations to represent the unfolding temporal effects of an intervention (naltrexone) on pain and sleep quality. Intervention effects are assessed with 100-point scales appropriate for dynamic models, instead of the 5-, 7-, or 10- point scales typical in regression analysis. One might go a step further and ask whether ratio scales with true 0 points, might yield further benefits (Stevens, 1951). Participants in this demonstration study were randomly assigned either to placebo-naltrexone or naltrexone-placebo and reported on pain and sleep quality multiple times. Dynamical systems models may help identify important feedback loops and control systems in health behavior. In designing our hypothetical trial, we also need to consider how well dynamical systems modeling can be incorporated into a MOST design and we need to consider possible dissemination implications of repeating assessments to model dynamical systems.

Although dynamic modeling could be incorporated at specific time points in a fully powered RCT, an integration of dynamic modeling with MOST would be the most informative first step toward the development of any trial including our own. For example, we would examine how patients implement and automate medication, diet change, and physical activity, by recording actions and self-monitored glucose values in real time in the home environment. The value of integrating this within MOST is that it allows us to assess in real time the effects of specific modules on how patients use behaviorally generated feedback; this information would help select modules effective for assisting patients traveling a pathway to improved blood glucose management and see how patients discover ways to automate behavior for long-term adherence.

For example, our study of asthma in the elderly showed that patients who automate their use of corticosteroids by placing an inhaler in the bathroom and using it on awakening were 4 times more adherent than patients who did not use such a routine (Brooks et al., 2014). To understand the conditions under which diabetic patients make similar discoveries, we might attach digital devices to a small set of participants in our MOST trial, and instruct them to talk aloud and video their morning movements as they explore different placements for their diabetes medication. The data could tell us whether the medication is taken as prescribed, that is, before rather than after eating, and integrated into the morning routine (e.g., by being placed right next to the coffee maker used every morning). These recordings would allow us to examine how patients exposed to the MOST module chose places to keep and use their medication and compare their search processes to patients unexposed to MOST; we could also observe how the unexposed are inconsistent in placement and nonadherent. The data would increase our understanding as to how we can assist patients discover procedures, a different level of understanding than simply identifying existent, effective procedures. The approach also could be used to evaluate modules to assist patients with readjusting diets and physical activity. For example, digital audio and video devices could be attached to a subset of patients to record their behavior and thoughts as they move about the supermarket to search for, select, and purchase diabetes-safe foods. Recording could be repeated during food preparation, and when they sit down to eat. The data could suggest how the MOST modules affected procedures and decisions leading to changes in food preferences and overcoming barriers to change at each step from purchase through preparation (and negotiation with other family eaters) to eating.

Designs and assessment for dynamic modeling of blood glucose monitoring to regulate diet and physical activity would require study designs similar to those for fibromyalgia; both involve continuous monitoring before and after specific activities, adjustment of behavior in light of results, and observing the effects of behavioral change on food and activity preferences and glucose values. Exposure to specific antecedent modules would be critical in preparing patients to make sense of and adjust their behaviors to glucose readings as the response of the biological system often appears random. We could also design a module that would prepare and allow patients to connect wirelessly with a nurse or diabetes educator for sharing and discussing glucose readings in real time.

Focus group and intensive interviews with individual patients are an alternative to dynamic designs. The advantages, not relying on complex technology, are offset, however, by the limitations of self-reports such as failure to attend, identify, and recall factors that facilitated and interfered with initiating and automating action, and possible biases created by efforts to paint a positive picture of oneself. Directing discussions and interviews to specific transitions can improve the utility of these data, and combining directed interviewing with digital recording (e.g., having patients respond to video and/or auditory recording of their online behavior) might produce details useful for conceptualizing and understanding transitions in pathways and improving modules for RCT. Useful evidence on behaviors for transitioning pathways can be elicited by having highly successful self-managing patients suggest how they would advise other patients having difficulty with specific aspects of adherence (e.g., know what to buy, how to persuade family members to tolerate their gastronomic needs; Tannenbaum et al., 2015). This procedure is similar to that used to study expertise in chess (Chase & Simon, 1973). Each of these approaches poses the challenge of designing novel approaches to assessment that record processes of theoretical and practice importance.

The assessment process used in dynamic modeling, as in the fibromyalgia study and our proposal for modeling blood glucose, poses issues for dissemination that may go unrecognized. The problems involve differences in communication between experimenters and participants and that between practitioners and patients. Dynamic modeling assessment in the fibromyalgia study enlisted the patient as a member of the study team; the patients were asked to serve as faithful recorders of pain and sleep under each of two conditions, medication or no medication. In this research context, participants are likely basing their expectations as to when the drug should work to study-specific variables, rather than their own knowledge or experiences. Likewise, participants are less likely to stop using a medication when their expectations of the medication effects are not met, because of the influence of the trial context. The experimental context of dynamic modeling may therefore differ dramatically from the traditional clinical practice where patients are often left to supplement the physicians' targets with their own (e.g., symptoms), and time frames for evaluating treatment efficacy may be vague or noncommunicated.

The experimental and clinical contexts are radically different in terms of environment, relationship, and communication. Failure to assess how patients perceive their roles, what they look for to evaluate treatment efficacy, when they make their observations, and what they do in response to feedback ignores critical features of the context essential for dissemination. Not assessing and addressing these perceptions in clinical practice can open a massive gap between the research environment and clinical practice and become a recipe for failure in dissemination.

Concluding Comments

Our chapter's primary goal is to broaden our view of the assessment process by freeing assessment from the rules of reliability and validity linked to regression modeling and the randomized, clinical trial. Multi-item scales with high reliability are gold standards when multiple regression analysis dominates data analysis; this is the case whether data are cross-sectional or longitudinal. Regression-based designs and findings are important for identifying the occasions and individuals with health problems in particular physical and social contexts. The data also point to factors that may affect behaviors involved in seeking treatment and treatment outcomes. Despite its many contributions, a regression-focused approach does not provide a detailed view of the mechanisms and causal pathways in health behavior and self-management. The pathways linking somatic changes (symptoms and dysfunction), cognitive self-appraisals (shaped by observation and experience), social communication, self-care attempts and outcomes, consultation with others, or use of medical care and interventions are complex (Cameron, Leventhal, & Leventhal, 1993).

The rules and procedures for generating reliable and valid instruments are important for any behavioral research program, but they are only part of the game and need to be viewed in context. Specifically, regression-based approaches are most efficient and effective for assessment of predictors (including risk/protective factors, interventions, and moderators) and outcomes with relatively few repetitions of the latter, but insufficient for describing processes intervening between, that is, for defining mediating pathways. If our objective is to create assessment instruments to generate data that is replicable and useful for dissemination to public health and clinical practice, we need to select varied study designs, tools for assessment, and methods of analysis. And we need to use these methods wisely. We need to integrate methods, so each is designed to illuminate specific features of the system underlying specific health outcomes. Nesting assessment in a single-design format and a single approach to statistical analysis will not meet these objectives.

We also emphasized the importance of theory, of models with multilevel concepts (i.e., concepts that have perceptual and behavioral referents and abstract, hierarchical features and verbal labels), and the posit mechanisms that connect these concepts over time. Theory is essential for forming hypotheses, generating interventions, informing measures, and designing assessment (including target constructs and timeframes). Although the literature abounds with specialized hypotheses, there are few relatively comprehensive theoretical models. Many separate models that strive to be comprehensive share common features (i.e., variables that may have different names yet serve similar purposes), and share common assumptions about process. Although no current theory or model is complete and "correct" in all features, theory is an essential guide for examining the pathways between predictors and outcomes; theory is essential for replicability and dissemination. As we continue to examine mechanisms and processes between start points and outcomes, and the feedback within and across conceptual levels, new concepts will appear, old ones will be refined, and relationships and dynamics will be better understood. We will have better theories, better practice, and hopefully better health outcomes and richer quality of life.

References

Alder, N. E., Boyce, T., Chesney, M. A., Cohen, S., Folkman, S., Kahn, R. L., & Syme, S. (1994). Socioeconomic status and health: The challenge of the gradient. *American Psychologist, 49*, 15–24. http://doi.org/10.1037/0003-066X.49.1.15

American Psychiatric Association. (2000). *Diagnostic and statistical manual of mental disorders: DSM-IV-TR* (4th ed.). Washington, DC: Author.

Aminzadeh, F., & Dalziel, W. B. (2002). Older adults in the emergency department: A systematic review of patterns of use, adverse outcomes, and effectiveness of interventions. *Annals of Emergency Medicine, 39*, 238–247. http://doi.org/10.1067/mem.2002.121523

Baron, R., & Kenny, D. (1986). The moderator–mediator variable distinction in social psychological research: Conceptual, strategic, and statistical considerations. *Journal of Personality and Social Psychology, 51*(6), 1173. http://doi.org/10.1037/0022-3514.51.6.1173

Berkman, L., Glass, T., Brissette, I., & Seeman, T. (2000). From social integration to health: Durkheim in the new millenium. *Social Science & Medicine, 51*, 843–857. http://doi.org/10.1016/S0277-9536(00)00065-4

Blalock, H. M., Jr. (1964). *Causal Inferences in nonexperimental research*. Chapel Hill, NC: University of North Carolina Press.

Blalock, H. M., Jr. (1972). *Social statistics* (2nd ed.). New York, NY: McGraw-Hill.

Boog, T., & Roberts, B. (2004). Conscientiousness and health-related behaviors: A meta-analysis of the leading behavioral contributors to mortality. *Psychological Bulletin, 130*, 887–919. http://doi.org/10.1037/0033-2909.130.6.887

Breland, J., McAndrew, L., Gross, R., Leventhal, H., & Horowitz, C. (2013). Challenges to healthy eating for peaople with diabetes in a low-income, minority neighborhood. *Diabetes Care, 36*, 2895–2901. http://doi.org/10.2337/dc12-1632

Brooks, T., Leventhal, H., Wolf, M., O'Conor, R., Morillo, J., Martynenko, M., … Federman, A. (2014). Strategies used by older adults with asthma for adherence to inhaled corticosteriods. *Journal of General Internal Medicine, 29*, 1506–1512. http://doi.org/10.1007/s11606-014-2940-8

Cameron, L., Leventhal, E., & Leventhal, H. (1993). Symptom representations and affect as determinants of care seeking in a community-dwelling, adult sample population. *Health Psychology, 12*, 171–179. http://doi.org/10.1037/0278-6133.12.3.171

Chase, W., & Simon, H. (1973). Perception in chess. *Cognitive Psychology, 4*, 55–81. http://doi.org/10.1016/0010-0285(73)90004-2

Collins, L., Trail, J., Kugler, K., Baker, T. P., & Mermelstein, R. (2014). Evaluating individual intervention components: Making decisions based on the results of a factorial screening experiment. *Translational Behavioral Medicine, 4*, 238–251. http://doi.org/10.1007/s13142-013-0239-7

Cortina, J. (1993). What is coefficient alpha? An examination of theory and applications. *Journal of Applied Psychology, 78*, 98–104. http://doi.org/10.1037/0021-9010.78.1.98

Cronbach, L., & Meehl, P. (1955). Construct validity in psychological tests. *Psychological Bulletin, 52*, 281–302. http://doi.org/10.1037/h0040957

Derogatis, L., Meyer, J., & Dupkin, C. (1976). Discrimination of organic versus psychogenic impotence with the DSFI. *Journal of Sex and Marital Therapy, 2*, 229–240. http://doi.org/10.1080/00926237608405325

Deshpande, S., Rivera, D., Younger, J., & Nandola, N. (2014). A control systems engineering approach for adaptie behavioral interventions: Illustration with a fibromyalgia intervention. *Translational Behavioral Medicine, 4*, 275–289. http://doi.org/10.1007/s13142-014-0294-8

DiMatteo, R., Lepper, H., & Croghan, T. (2000). Depression is a risk factor for noncompliance with medical treatment: Meta-analysis of the effects. *Archives of Internal Medicine, 24*, 2101–2107. http://doi.org/10.1001/archinte.160.14.2101

Fahrenberg, J., Myrtek, M., Pawlik, K., & Perrez, M. (2007). Ambulatory assessment – monitoring behavior in daily life settings: A behavioral-scientific challenge for psychology. *European Journal of Psychological Assessment, 23*, 206–213. http://doi.org/10.1027/1015-5759.23.4.206

Hektner, J., Schmidt, J., & Csikszentmihalyi, M. (2007). *Experience sampling method: Measuring the quality of everyday life*. Thousand Oaks, CA: Sage.

Kansagara, D., Englander, H., Salanitro, A., Kagen, D., Theobald, C., Freeman, M., & Kripalani, S. (2011). Risk prediction models for hospital readmission: A systematic review. *Journal of the American Medical Association, 306*, 1688–1698. http://doi.org/10.1001/jama.2011.1515

Karlsen, S., & Nazroo, J. (2002). Relation between racial discrimination, social class, and health among ethnic minority groups. *American Journal of Public Health, 92*, 624–631. http://doi.org/10.2105/AJPH.92.4.624

Kerkhofs, M., & Lindeboom, M. (1995). Subjective health measures and state dependent reporting errors. *Econometrics and Health Economics, 4*, 221–235. http://doi.org/10.1002/hec.4730040307

Lerner, D., & Levine, S. (1994). Health-related quality of life: Origins, gaps, and directions. In G. F. Albrecht, *Advances in medical sociology: Quality of life in health care* (Vol. 5, pp. 43–65). Greenwich, CT: JAI Press.

Leventhal, H., Breland, J., Mora, P., & Leventhal, E. (2010). Lay representations of illness and treatment: A framework for action. In A. Steptoe (Ed.), *Handbook of behavioral medicine* (pp. 137–154). New York, NY: Springer.

Leventhal, H., Weinman, J., Leventhal, E., & Phillips, L. (2008). Health psychology: The search for pathways between behavior and health. *Annual Review of Psychology, 59*, 477–505. http://doi.org/10.1146/annurev.psych.59.103006.093643

Ley, P. (1977). Psychological studies of doctor-patient communication. In S. Rachman (Ed.), *Contributions to medical psychology* (pp. 9–42). Oxford, UK: Pergamon.

McDonough, P., & Walters, V. (2001). Gender and health: Reassessing patterns and explanations. *Social Science and Medicine, 52*, 547–559. http://doi.org/10.1016/S0277-9536(00)00159-3

McDowell, I. (2006). *Measuring health: A guide to rating scales and questionnaires* (3rd ed.). New York, NY: Oxford University Press. http://doi.org/10.1093/acprof:oso/9780195165678.001.0001

Mehl, M., Robbins, M., & Deters, F. (2012). Naturalistic observation of health-relevant social processes: The electronically activated recorder methodology in psychosomatics. *Psychosomatic Medicine, 74*, 410–417. http://doi.org/10.1097/PSY.0b013e3182545470

Michie, S., Miles, J., & Weinman, J. (2003). Patient-centeredness in chronic illness: What is it and does it matter? *Patient Education and Counseling, 51*, 197–206. http://doi.org/10.1016/S0738-3991(02)00194-5

Moussavi, S., Chatterji, S., Verders, E., Tandon, A., Patel, V., & Ustun, B. (2007). Depression, chronic diseases, and decrements in health: Results from the World Health Surveys. *The Lancet, 370*, 851–858. http://doi.org/10.1016/S0140-6736(07)61415-9

National Institutes of Health. (2009). *Data and statistics*. Retrieved from http://oppnet.nih.gov/resources-data-statistics.asp

National Institutes of Health. (2014). *PROMIS: Dynamic tools to measure health outcomes from the patient perspective*. Retrieved from http://www.nihpromis.org

Phillips, A., & Chapman, G. (2011). Consistent behavior development: Is a personal-rule or a deliberation-based strategy more effective. *The Journal of General Psychology, 138*, 243–259. http://doi.org/10.1080/00221309.2011.592872

Phillips, L., Leventhal, H., & Leventhal, E. A. (2011). Physicians' communication of the common-sense self-regulation model results in greater reported adherence than physicians' use of interpersonal skills. *British Journal of Health Psychology, 17*, 1–14.

Riley, W., & Rivera, D. (2014). Methodologies for optimizing behavioral interventions: Introduction to special section. *Translational Behavioral Medicine, 4*, 234–237. http://doi.org/10.1007/s13142-014-0281-0

Samaras, N., Chevalley, T., Samaras, D., & Gold, G. (2010). Older patients in the emergency department: A review. *Annals of Emergency Medicine, 56*, 261–269. http://doi.org/10.1016/j.annemergmed.2010.04.015

Segraves, R., Schoenberg, H., Zarins, C., Knopf, J., & Camic, P. (1981). Discrimination of organic versus psychological impotence with DSFI: A failure to replicate. *Journal of Sex and Marital Therapy, 7*, 230–238. http://doi.org/10.1080/00926238108405807

Sheer, V. (2014). A meta-synthesis of health-related self-efficacy instrumentation: Problems and suggestions. *Journal of Nursing Measurement, 22*, 77–93. http://doi.org/10.1891/1061-3749.22.1.77

Simon, D. (2012). Replication: Where do we go from here? *The Psychologist, 25*, 349–350.

Smith, M., Wallston, K., & Smith, C. A. (1995). The development and validation of the perceived health competence scale. *Health Education Research, 10*, 51–64. http://doi.org/10.1093/her/10.1.51

Stevens, S. (1951). Mathematices, measurement and psychophysics. In S. Stevens (Ed.), *Handbook of experimental psychology* (pp. 1–49). New York, NY: Wiley.

Stone, A., & Shiffman, S. (1994). Ecological momentary assessment (EMA) in behavioral medicine. *Annals of Behavioral Medicine, 16*, 199–202.

Streiner, D., & Norman, G. (2008). *Health measurement scales: A practical guide to their development and use*. New York, NY: Oxford University Press. http://doi.org/10.1093/acprof:oso/9780199231881.001.0001

Tannenbaum, M., Leventhal, H., Yu, J., Breland, J., Walker, E., & Gonzalez, J. (2015). Successful self-management among non-insulin-treated adults with Type 2 diabetes: A self-regulation perspective. *Diabetes Medicine*. Advance online publication. http://doi.org/10.1111/dme.12745

Thompson, K., Kulkarni, J., & Sergejew, A. (2000). Reliability and validity of a new Medication Adherence Rating Scale (MARS) for the psychoses. *Schizophrenia Research, 5*, 241–247. http://doi.org/10.1016/S0920-9964(99)00130-9

Tildesley, H., Po, M., & Ross, S. (2015). Internet blood glucose monitoring systems provide lasting glycemic benefit in type 1 and 2 diabetes: A systematic review. *Medical Clinics of North America, 99*, 17–33.

Tura, A., Maran, A., & Pacini, G. (2007). Non-invasive glucose monitoring: Assessment of technologies and devices according to quantitative criteria. *Diabetes Research and Clinical Practice, 77*, 16–40. http://doi.org/10.1016/j.diabres.2006.10.027

Uchino, B. (2009). Understanding the links between social support and physical health: A life-span perspective with emphasis on the separability of perceived and received support. *Perspectives on Psychological Science, 4*, 236–255. http://doi.org/10.1111/j.1745-6924.2009.01122.x

Wright, S. (1960). Path coefficients and path regressions: Alternative or complementary concepts? *Biometrics, 16*, 189–202. http://doi.org/10.2307/2527551

Chapter 24

Measurement Issues in Health Psychology

Marie Johnston[1], Yael Benyamini[2], and Evangelos C. Karademas[3]

[1]Aberdeen Health Psychology Group, Institute of Applied Health Sciences, University of Aberdeen, UK
[2]Bob Shapell School of Social Work, Tel Aviv University, Israel
[3]Department of Psychology, University of Crete, Greece

Each domain of measurement in health psychology adopts standards of what constitutes good measurement and identifies problems or criticisms of current measurement. However, these standards and issues vary somewhat across domains. The aim of this chapter is to draw together methodological issues that are emphasised in various chapters of the book. Some issues have been addressed more fully in certain measurement domains than others. However, it may be that every domain can learn something from the other domains; therefore, we have attempted to summarise issues that researchers and practitioners might wish to bear in mind.

What to Measure

Link to Theory

The decision to measure a specific construct in a research or practice setting is usually based on an explicit or implicit theory of how that construct is important for the current or future endeavour. Even when there is no explicit theory, the decision that a construct is important enough to measure is likely to be based on some implicit reasoning, for example, that this construct predicts some valued outcome or that this construct defines the processes underlying a successful outcome. Researchers and/or practitioners might find it beneficial to make that theory explicit as it may guide the measurement process, for example, the timing and type of measures, other constructs that should be measured. Where theory is explicit, especially where a formal one is involved, the theory will guide aspects of the process. For example, if the theory suggests that behaviour change will occur due to changes in beliefs, then it is important to assess change in these beliefs earlier than the assessment of behaviour change; if the theory suggests that two constructs work together, then one should measure both constructs unless there is a reason to believe that one of these constructs does not operate or does not vary in the specific context. Additionally, some form of theory is necessary in order to evaluate the validity of a measure – how can one investigate whether it measures what it is intended to measure if one lacks clarity about what the intended construct is?

Standard Measures of Theoretical Constructs May Restrict Measurement

While standard measures of specific theoretical constructs are immensely useful, they may also trap the user by the ease of their use. First, they may encourage a measure that omits an aspect of the construct that may have relevance in the proposed context; second, their use may result in other measures of the construct being ignored; and third, their ease of use may result in other constructs being overlooked. For example, current measures of theory of planned behaviour constructs, such as behavioural intention, emphasise strength of agreement that one has the intention, whereas other aspects of intention, such as the direct estimation of frequency of intention, are also valid but rarely measured (Johnston et al., 2014). Further, since the introduction of the Illness Perceptions Questionnaire (IPQ) and its revision (Moss-Morris et al., 2002; Weinman, Petrie, Moss-Morris, & Horne, 1996), reviews of support for the common sense self-regulation model (Leventhal, Meyer, & Nerenz, 1980) have typically not included other assessments of illness representations (e.g., Hagger & Orbell, 2003) although other assessments are also possible (Diefenbach & Leventhal, 1996). Also, applications of social cognitive theory (Bandura, 1986, 1997) frequently measure only self-efficacy, the construct that has clear guidelines about how it should be measured, while omitting to measure outcome expectancies or other constructs within the theory. We should therefore be aware that while readily available measures may help to coordinate research efforts by making measurement simple, they may restrict investigations unnecessarily.

Overlapping Constructs and Measures

Some constructs have overlapping theoretical content and it is therefore impossible to develop distinct measurement. For example, the assessment of certain personality traits, such as neuroticism, may be confounded with the assessment of physical and mental health. Also, *quality of life* may incorporate *functional health outcomes* and *psychological adjustment*. In the long term this is a challenge to theoretical development to establish how the constructs might be related. In the short term, one is faced with the same measure being used to assess different constructs: For example, the Short-Form Health Survey (SF-36) may be used without adjustment as an index of health status, functional outcomes, or quality of life.

Using Old Measures to Assess New Constructs

Measures that were developed to assess one construct are frequently used to measure another, more recent or pertinent construct. This is very common when theory moves on and pre-existing measures continue to be used: When the International Classification of Functioning, Disability, and Health (ICF; World Health Organization, 2001) was published, many authors simply asserted that existing measures were appropriate but closer analyses indicated that they typically contained a mixture of ICF constructs (Pollard, Dixon, Dieppe, & Johnston, 2009). Kaplan, Riley, and Mabry (2014) warn of this danger in using existing big data, as the measures used in these data sets may not correspond exactly to the construct that the current investigator wishes to study.

Generic Versus Specific Measures

An important issue in health research is whether to use a measure that is applicable to a wide range of populations or one that is specific to the current focus. In particular, does one need measures specific to each health condition or health-care situation? This is an obvious question when measuring health outcomes such as functional limitations, but also health-related quality of life where specific measures have been developed for diverse health conditions or diseases of particular physiological systems (e.g., the MacNew Heart Disease Questionnaire for cardiovascular diseases; Höfer, Lim, Guyatt, & Oldridge, 2004).

Additionally, many psychological constructs relating to health conditions have been assessed by both generic and specific measures. For example, the well-established COPE (Carver, Scheier & Weintraub, 1989) and the Revised Ways of Coping (RWOC; Vitaliano, Russo, Carr, Maiuro, & Becker, 1985) are generic measures of coping that can be applied to any situation whether health-related or not, whereas measures have been developed to assess coping with specific health conditions or healthcare situations involving stressful medical procedures, for example, the Pain Coping Strategies Questionnaire (Rosenstiel & Keefe, 1983) and the Coping with Infertility Questionnaire (Benyamini et al., 2008). Similarly, anxiety may be assessed using a generic measure such as the State–Trait Anxiety Inventory (STAI) or the Hospital Anxiety and Depression Scale (HADS), but it may also be assessed with respect to a particular condition such as cancer (e.g., the Mental Adjustment to Cancer [MAC]; Watson et al., 1988) or undergoing a specific procedure (e.g., the Post-Imaging Distress Questionnaire to assess anxiety during magnetic resonance imaging; Dantendorfer et al., 1997).

In addition to the obvious benefit of being available "off the shelf," generic measures have the advantage that they allow evaluation of findings against norms, comparison over conditions and assimilation of data into the wider corpus of knowledge. Specific measures have to be developed for each specific situation and may as a result be less fully developed and evaluated; however, they are likely to be more sensitive and more acceptable to users in their specific situation and may provide more useful practical feedback. Thus, there may be situations in which the investigator uses either generic or specific measures, but frequently it will be advisable to use both a specific and a generic measure.

Idiographic Versus Standardised Measures

Standardised measures have considerable advantages over personally tailored measures as they allow valid comparisons to be made between individuals and between groups of people. If the measures have norms, it is possible to assess how far an individual or group of individuals is from the normative population using standard scores or, for individuals, to use methods developed for comparing single respondents with norms (Crawford & Garthwaite, 2006). However, there are also situations in which one needs more personally tailored measures that incorporate content specific to the individual. For example, in assessing quality of life, the Schedule for the Evaluation of Individual Quality of Life (SEIQOL) methods (McGee, O'Boyle, Hickey, O'Malley, & Joyce, 1991) enable the individual to identify their personal criteria for quality of life and assess their quality of life against these criteria; similarly, the Patient-Generated Index (Ruta, Garratt, Leng, Russell, & MacDonald, 1994) assesses health outcomes using the individual's criteria. Both of these measures generate scores that can be compared across individuals.

In a different context, there are situations where it is important to compare an individual with themselves, for example, examining how they change over time or in response to an intervention. Ecological momentary assessment (EMA; see Chapter 18 in this volume) frequently uses measures tailored to the individual and this may be particularly important in making the very frequent assessments acceptable to respondents. However, using truly idiographic assessments, it may be difficult to assess psychometric properties, such as the validity of the measures, and it is not possible to make comparisons with norms.

How to Measure

Assessment Versus Measurement

While these two words are frequently used interchangeably, *assessment* suggests that responses are being judged against some criterion, perhaps in order to reach some decision, for example, about treatment, and that the judgement may be based on a qualitative or a quantitative evaluation. *Measurement* implies the attribution of numerical values to reflect quantities of an underlying construct and may be used in making an assessment.

Types of Measurement

While a large number of measures in health psychology involve self-report questionnaires, it is important to bear in mind other forms of measurement that are less susceptible to some of the measurement problems of self-report. For example, performance measures such as those used in assessing executive function or physical activity (see Chapters 5 and 12 in this volume) can involve either observation of performance or some automated electronic measurement. Observed performance measures or proxy reports by someone close to the target person are restricted to settings in which observation is possible. Electronic measures are limited both by the range of functions that can be detected and by the problems that arise when they malfunction or are tampered with. As a result of these problems, O'Carroll and Chambers (Chapter 7 in this volume) suggest that in the assessment of adherence to medication regimens, self-report is likely to be as good as these more complex methods.

Constructing and Using Multi-Item Scales

Creating a new measure is not something that should be undertaken lightly and one should consider adapting existing measures if possible. Creating a new measure involves: (a) clear definition of the construct to be measured; (b) creation of a representative set of items (stems and response formats) with face validity, intelligibility, and appropriateness for the intended population; (c) assessment of quantitative content validity of items in order to select items for further testing (e.g., using discriminant content validity [DCV] methods; Johnston et al., 2014); (d) preliminary assessments of internal consistency, sensitivity, and validity in the target population leading to further selection of items; and (e) finally, full, reportable psychometric evaluation. When an existing measure is being used or adapted to a new population, it also requires the latter two stages and users should report the results obtained with the new population.

The psychometric assessment depends on the measurement theory adopted. The most common approach to measurement in health psychology is classical test theory, which assumes that each item is an equal assessment of the underlying construct. Psychometric evaluation involves assessment of internal consistency (e.g., using Cronbach's α or McDonald's ω coefficient) and validity (e.g., using statistical methods, such as factor analyses and structural equation modelling).

Other theories of measurement have also been used. For example, the Sickness Impact Profile is based on Thurstone scaling in which only one item within a given scale represents the true measure for a given individual, and it is the weight of that item that is their score; in this form of scaling it is inappropriate to add the scores over the items of the scale, and doing so can create illogical scoring (Pollard & Johnston, 2001). Item response theory (IRT) is widely used as a theory of measurement that identifies the item that most clearly represents an individual, and using methods such as Rasch (Rasch, 1960; Bond & Fox, 2001) or Mokken scaling (Mokken, 1971; Sijtsma, Debets, & Molenaar, 1990) indicates the degree of difficulty or position on the underlying dimension of the item.

Neither Thurstone scaling nor IRT make the assumption of classical test theory that items are equivalent. Clinimetrics takes this one stage further, selecting items for inclusion in the scale by their capacity to add to the predictive value. Examples are the Apgar score (Apgar, 1953) used to assess the viability of newborns or cardiac risk scores; the latter may involve items as disparate as genetic risk, blood pressure, and smoking (e.g., Bosley, Newcombe, & Dauncey, 1981). No attempt is made to achieve internal consistency, nor are items ordered in degree of difficulty. Clinimetric measures are evaluated in terms of the reliability of their predictions.

Response Formats and Scoring Items

Measures vary widely in the response format, the number of items, and the scoring of items. Many health psychology measures use verbal rating scales, such as *not at all, somewhat, extremely*, or *rarely, sometimes, often*, or *not at all confident to extremely confident*, or the popular format of Likert ratings from *strongly agree* to *strongly disagree*. These ratings address different facets of the construct (amount, frequency, confidence, intensity) and it is important to ensure that the appropriate facet is measured. Verbal scales depend on the respondent's interpretation, for example, what may be considered *sometimes* by one person may be thought *often* by another.

Gigerenzer and Edwards (2003) have argued for the use of responses that represent something realistic using direct estimation methods. For example, expressing snacking intentions as the number of intended snacks in a given period followed by assessment of snack eating gives a quantitative estimate of the intention–behaviour gap (Allan, Johnston, & Campbell, 2011), while estimating the number of persons one intends to give advice to (Hart, 2006) or the number of days one intends to delay before taking appropriate clinical actions (Smith et al., 2013) provides more information than a verbal scale of agreement. The content validity of direct estimation methods can be assessed and have been found to have as great content validity as the Likert format responses (Johnston et al., 2014).

Single-item measures are generally frowned upon as they may be less reliable than multi-item measures, but it may also be argued that in a multi-item scale with very high internal consistency each additional item does not add to the reliability of measurement. In some situations, such as high frequency assessment in EMA, it may only be possible to use single items but investigators would be wise to establish the psychometrics of the single item used prior to embarking on an intensive phase of data collection. In addition, certain single items may provide more information than a multi-item scale because they provide a better overall subjective assessment of a complex concept, as compared with detailed scales. Robins, Hendin, and Trzesniewski (2001), who provided evidence for the validity of a single-item measure of global self-esteem, suggested that it may have evoked an existing schema that is chronically accessible by adulthood. In the health area, a prominent example is self-rated health (Chapter 13 in this volume), typically measured with a single item that provides an integrative subjective summary of a multitude of health-related factors.

There is also debate about the number of response choices, some suggesting 5-point scales, others proposing 7-point, 9-point, or more, while visual analogue scales (VAS) allow for an infinite number of points. On the one hand, one is seeking to improve discriminations to achieve more sensitive measurement and ensure variance for statistical analyses; but on the other hand, there is likely to be a limit on the number of choices that respondents can handle reliably, and increasing the number of choices may simply add noise. While results are inconsistent, Weng (2004) found that poorer test–retest reliability was obtained with fewer response options on Likert-type scales. Context and piloting will be important in making the decision: Fewer choices may be appropriate for respondents who are less motivated, less educated, or older (e.g., Daniilidou et al., 2010) while more choices may be possible with highly motivated participants. In EMA or other studies where participants respond frequently, respondents have more opportunity to learn the response format and it is important that current responses are not unduly influenced by recall of previous responses; for these situations, more choices, and especially VAS, are normally used.

A further issue is the use of anchors for numerical points. It is well recognised that the use of verbal labels as anchors results in more numerous responses at the labelled points. Labelling each response point has been found to result in greater test–retest reliability than only labelling endpoints of Likert scales and it would appear that labelling all points should be preferred. However, this consistency may be the result of recalling previous responses that may be undesirable when one is assessing change. Recently, Au and Lorgelly (2014) examined the use of anchoring vignettes in self-rated health and suggest that they may improve consistency of responses.

Response Bias

Some forms of response bias common to all self-report questionnaires have not been fully resolved and continue to be a problem. Anchoring, the tendency to respond closer to anchor points, can be seen as a form of response bias and research on methods of reducing this bias have not proved fruitful (Epley & Gilovich, 2006). Attempts to deal with extreme responding by reversing some items have led to problems when negatively worded items are misinterpreted. The bias of central responding is typically dealt with by using an even number of response choices and this format is commonly used except for Likert-type responses of agreement where the option *neither agree nor disagree* is usually provided.

Two important forms of response bias in health psychology are negative affectivity (NA) and response shift. NA can result in spurious relationships between variables if each is biased by the tendency to see the world in a negative light (Watson & Pennebaker, 1989). Investigators may choose to allow for this bias by co-varying a measure of NA such as the Positive and Negative Affect Schedule (PANAS; Watson, Clark, & Tellegen, 1988). Response shift occurs when respondents recalibrate the standard they use in making a judgement of a health outcome: For example, a person with a deteriorating condition may rate their quality of life by considering comparison with others having the condition, whereas, prior to onset of the condition, they might have rated their quality of life relative to other people in general. Investigators can allow for this using a "then-test," which asks respondents on the later occasion to rate not only how they are at that time, but also how they were on the previous occasion; Schwartz and Sprangers (2010) offer guidelines on this method.

Another form of bias is related to the order of the measure items. Although this problem in not frequently addressed, Knäuper and Schwarz (2004) stressed that the order of items within a scale may affect responses. Likewise, Standing and Shearson (2010) found that not only an assessment bias may be introduced by the item order, but also that this may interact with other aspects of measurement, such as the response format. Therefore, the item order should concern researchers and practitioners, especially when instruments that are new or with unclear properties are used. Bias may also be caused by the order in which a measure is included within a questionnaire or if the respondent has seen the questionnaire before: For example, different levels of anxiety may be found if the anxiety measure precedes or follows other measures or if it is being completed for the first time (Johnston, 1999).

Further, a specific form of response bias refers to symptoms recall and report, especially when symptoms are assessed retrospectively. Skelton, Loveland, and Yeagley (1996) found that recalling a specific symptom from the past may magnify the perceived intensity of this symptom in the present. As the authors point out, symptom recall is sensitive to the context provided by memory. Thus, researchers and practitioners should pay attention to the assessment context in which the report takes place.

Finally, a more recently identified source of bias is the potential of the semantic structure of questionnaires to shape responses. Arnulf, Larsen, Martinsen, and Bong (2014) found that the results of tests of organisational theory could be replicated using information from the semantic structure of the questionnaires alone, that is, without any data from respondents. If replicated, these results are challenging for questionnaire measures as they suggest either some form of response bias due to the words used, or that language has incorporated the theories being tested.

Translation Versus Adaptation

Many of the commonly used measures in health psychology have been translated into several languages. For a measure to have equivalence in several languages requires considerably more than translation, and many additional steps are required to achieve the context and culture equivalence (see Chapter 20 in this volume). While this is obvious for some measures, such as measures of functional outcomes, it may easily be forgotten when the language is unchanged but the culture may be different, for example, in using English language questionnaires developed in the US with respondents in the UK. For example, Patrick and Peach (1989) have shown that the Sickness Impact Profile required an adaptation and it was renamed the "Functional Limitations Profile."

Evaluating Measures

In evaluating a new or existing measure, several issues need to be addressed, but clearly content validity and sensitivity to change will always be important.

User's Objectives

Researchers and practitioners should, first of all, be clear as to what they intend to measure (e.g., in terms of specifically defined key variables) and then match their purposes with the characteristics and the objectives of the measure. An extensive search for the appropriate measure may be needed. A lack of clarity about the objective of the user is a major obstacle for choosing the right measure, as well as for a successful assessment.

Content validity has been defined as the extent to which a measure, including both item stems and the response formats, is relevant and representative of the intended construct (Haynes, Richard, & Kubany, 1995). It can be considered as *internal validity* since it mainly requires assessment of the apparent content, contrasted with *external validity*, more usually termed *construct validity*, which requires data from respondents (Lissitz & Samuelson, 2007). Content validity is considered to be necessary before construct validity can be established; in other words, unless the measure contains items relevant to the construct, finding that it relates to other measures, as would be expected, is not adequate evidence of construct validity.

Relevance has typically been assessed as face validity, but this is an unreliable, unreportable, non-transparent subjective process and would now be seen as insufficient. Transparent quantitative indices have been developed and should be reported. For example, the Content Validity Index (CVI; Polit, Beck, & Owen, 2007; Rico, Dios, & Ruch, 2012) uses judges' ratings to reach a decision about relevance with a cut-off for each item. More recently, DCV methods have been developed that give a quantitative estimate of the extent to which an item is relevant for the intended construct and also an estimate of the extent to which it is discriminable and distinct from other competing or overlapping constructs (Johnston et al., 2014). The important feature of both CVI and DCV is that they can and should be undertaken at an early stage in the development and/or adoption of a measure and can be achieved with responses from expert judges *before* requiring responses from the intended participants.

While these quantitative indices may take representativeness into account, they mainly indicate whether the items are representative of the construct. However, it is still possible that the full range of the construct has not been represented.

Appropriateness for the Intended Population

In addition to the general considerations, one would wish to assess whether the proposed measure was appropriate for the intended population and context. For performance measures this will require information about the likely range of performance of the participants, for example, a measure of walking ability would include different distances for a fit versus a disabled population, and might be different for patients before and after successful orthopaedic surgery.

For self-report measures and questionnaires, achieving appropriateness is likely to require piloting of the measure, perhaps using think-aloud methods to assess comprehension, recall, judgement, and consistency of responses (Broadbent, Kaptein, & Petrie, 2011; Horwood, Pollard, Ayis, McIlvenna, & Johnston, 2010). Estimates of intelligibility (Friedman & Hoffman-Goetz, 2006) may be relevant especially when the target respondents have low educational levels (readability indices are available at http://en.wikipedia.org/wiki/Automated_Readability_Index). It may also prove useful to establish that the measure is working with the target population as anticipated in the measure development and prior evidence and evaluation of differential item functioning (DIF; e.g., Pollard, Dixon, & Johnston, 2014) can indicate whether items are leading to inappropriate conclusions for the current population.

Acceptability and Feasibility

Measures need to be acceptable to the target population and this is a consideration in achieving content validity (see "User's Objectives" section). Specific measures are likely to be more acceptable than generic measures as they will seem more relevant in the context. Nevertheless, even acceptable measures may not be feasible, for example, if the respondent is too ill or if the clinical context does not allow enough time. Piloting is important to ensure acceptability and feasibility.

Evaluation by Classical Test Theory (CTT) or by Item Response Theory (IRT)

As noted in Chapter 1 of this volume, CTT and IRT make different assumptions about items. CTT assumes every item is equivalent to every other in assessing the construct whereas IRT assumes that items will vary in their level of difficulty and sensitivity to change in the underlying attribute. Reliability as discussed here is essential in CTT but less appropriate for IRT where Rasch or Mokken scaling will be more appropriate for assessing how well the items function in measuring the construct.

Both methods may be used in selecting items or evaluating a measure. For example, when both methods were used in measures of functional limitations, each identified problems with the same items (Pollard et al., 2009), but this may not always be the case.

Reliability is assessed as internal consistency, inter-rater reliability, test–retest reliability, and equivalent (or alternative) forms reliability. Health psychology typically reports internal consistency but more attention might additionally be paid to the latter three types of reliability, each assessed using familiar measures such as correlation coefficients to assess the concordance between sets of scores. While internal consistency has commonly been reported using Cronbach's α, this may be unsuitable where items have very different response formats. In this case, variance or sensitivity, and alternatives including ω values have been suggested as more appropriate (Peters, 2014; Dunn, Baguley, & Brunsden, 2014)

Construct validity refers to whether a measure shows changes compatible with the underlying theory and construct. It is an overarching type of validity that includes criterion validity, concurrent validity, predictive validity, and convergent validity (see Chapter 1 in this volume). Factor-analytic methods can be used to evaluate the extent to which items assess the intended dimensions or constructs separately.

Sensitivity to Change

Measures should be chosen to be sensitive, specific, and responsive to change. Lalkhen and McCluskey (2008) illustrate methods of calculating indices of sensitivity, specificity, and responsiveness to change. However, on some occasions the minimally detectable change may be of little value and minimally important change should define the necessary range of sensitivity (de Vet et al., 2006). Methods of assessing cross-sectional differences and longitudinal change are discussed by Crosby, Kolotkin, and Williams (2003).

Differential Functioning of Items

Items that measure a construct successfully in one population may be misleading with a different population. For example, in the context of mood measurement an item such as "I cry a lot" may be endorsed at a higher level in women than in men, with the result that women may appear to have lower mood (Covic, Pallant, Conaghan, & Tennant 2007). Similarly, people of different ages respond differently to items of the SF-36 (Pollard, Johnston, & Dixon, 2013) and to the HADS (Cameron, Crawford, Lawton, & Reid, 2013) with the result that differences between older and younger people arising due to problems with the questionnaire may be misinterpreted as differences in the underlying constructs. When a measure is used with a new population, it will be valuable to assess DIF.

Using Measures

Within or Between Individuals

The choice and evaluation of measures will be different for studies that seek to compare individuals from those that aim to investigate changes within an individual. Many theoretical frameworks in health psychology describe within-person processes but are frequently tested between individuals (Johnston & Johnston, 2013). For example, if the investigation is conducted as a basis for designing an intervention, then evidence of within-person processes will be necessary; if the aim is to find persons for whom an intervention is necessary, then a between-persons analysis may be appropriate. Finding support for a hypothesis in a between-persons study does not indicate that the same result will hold true within-persons, and vice versa.

Within-person investigations for research or clinical purposes often require a high frequency of measures, as in EMA (see Chapter 18 in this volume). Then it will be necessary to minimise the number of items but increase their acceptability and content validity compared with the requirements of a between-person study. A within-person study may also reduce the problem of response biases if one assumes that the person will have stable biases.

If a measure is used to compare an individual with norms for the measure, care needs to be taken over the skewness of distributions, establishing confidence limits and estimating power. These issues are addressed in detail by Crawford and Garthwaite (2006), while Crawford's website (http://homepages.abdn.ac.uk/j.crawford/pages/dept/SingleCaseMethodology.htm) supplies programmes that can be used to conduct the analyses.

Adaptive Testing Using IRT

IRT can provide information about the difficulty of each item and therefore about the appropriate range for sensitive measurement for a specific person or population. In addition, items can be selected systematically to identify the appropriate range for sensitive measurement. So, instead of requiring the respondents to answer every question, a small number of strategically chosen items can systematically approach the degree of difficulty that reflects the respondent's position on the scale. This process is illustrated for scales measuring the impact of headache by Ware, Bjorner, and Kosinski (2000), and can be particularly valuable where it is important to reduce respondent burden.

Clinical or Statistical Significance

Jacobson and colleagues have been influential in arguing that statistical significance is not enough and that in the health domain one is looking for differences or changes that reflect important differences (Jacobson, Roberts, Berns, & McGlinchey, 1999). Crosby et al. (2003) summarise methods of assessing meaningful change in terms of cut-offs established as a number of standard deviations from the scores of a target population. In this respect, some researchers have proposed a half standard deviation as the minimally important difference (MID), at least regarding health-related quality of life (Norman, Sloan, & Wyrwich, 2003). Although not applicable to every case, this value might serve as a basis of evaluating clinically significant changes or a treatment effect. Finally, Rouquette et al. (2014) describe IRT-based methods of establishing minimally important differences.

Routine Assessments

There are some situations in which measures are collected routinely rather than with the aim of answering a specific question. For example, such data may be collected in clinical settings or in national data sets. Routine assessments can be useful in describing a population, how it changes over time, or whether a new intervention changes outcomes. For instance, the Smoking Toolkit Study (http://www.smokinginengland.info/) has provided such information about smoking in England, for example, about changes over time, patterns in sub-groups of the population, the effects of introducing the smoking ban in public places, and changes following the introduction of electronic cigarettes.

Where possible, routine assessments should use standard measures and should certainly use measures that have stood the test of careful evaluation. Otherwise the data collected will be of little value beyond the local situation.

Portfolios

Researchers or practitioners may take advantage of the existing portfolios of measures. However, as Marks (2004) notes, portfolios are a mixed blessing. They provide, especially to young scientists, a useful toolbox with measures ready to use in a rather easy way. On the other hand, the measures included in a portfolio might not be of the same quality. They may also constrain the researcher's scope to what is in the box. Therefore, portfolios should be used with caution and in addition to a thorough search of other available measures.

Conclusion

We have come a long way since early efforts to measure health to the far more elaborate methods of assessing complex constructs and variables that are of interest to health psychologists. This progress has been illustrated in all the chapters of this book, together with the acknowledgement that assessing health-related variables is an ongoing procedure, an "under construction" area. Much has been achieved and there are already some useful ways to assess what we want or need to assess. Nevertheless, we can be sure that even finer ways will be developed and far more be achieved in the future.

The progress in three interrelated areas, that is, psychological theories, measurement and assessment, and research design and statistics, will guide the development of more accurate, reliable, and valid measures. This, in turn, will contribute to the advancement of research, theory, and practice. As we noted at the beginning of Chapter 1 in this book, effective measurement and assessment are a prerequisite for the development of more successful theories and applications, and vice versa.

In addition, the interaction and collaboration with researchers and practitioners from other psychology specialties and other disciplines will set the context for the evolution of measurement and assessment, probably in directions that will surprise us. It should not escape our attention that the interaction with different types of knowledge and practice has been the fuel of the maturation of health psychology and its progress, and so it will probably be in the future.

Throughout the pages of this book, experts from different areas have managed to present in a concise and inclusive way the existing knowledge about assessment in an extended area of topics from stress and coping, to health cognition and behaviours, and to quality of life. Not an easy task, considering the rapid growth in the available assessment tools and methods. Furthermore, in almost all chapters, and especially in those of Part III of this book ("Assessment Methods and Issues", Chapters 18, 19, 20, 21, and 22 in this volume), several important assessment-related issues and novel approaches have been addressed.

Still, despite all the progress in assessment presented in this book, it is important to make a final note. A researcher or practitioner has to ask, first of all, what they want to know or understand, and what they want to measure. Then, define it in the most clear and exact way possible. And, finally, try hard to find the most accurate, reliable, and valid way to assess it. They also need to divert efforts from easy but low-quality paths (e.g., ready-to-use but invalid instruments). Although this may not always be an easy task, one should not give up the effort to ask and find what one really has in mind, and try to do so the best way one can. We hope this book will be of help towards this direction.

References

Allan, J. L., Johnston, M., & Campbell, N. (2011). Missed by an inch or a mile? Predicting the size of intention–behaviour gap from measures of executive control. *Psychology & Health, 26*, 635–650.

Apgar, V. (1953). A proposal for a new method of evaluation of the newborn infant. *Current Researches in Anesthesia and Analgesia, 32*, 260–267.

Arnulf, J. K., Larsen, K. R., Martinsen, Ø. L., & Bong, C. H. (2014). Predicting survey responses: How and why semantics shape survey statistics on organizational behaviour. *PLoS ONE, 9*, e106361. http://doi.org/10.1371/journal.pone.0106361

Au, N., & Lorgelly, P. K. (2014). Anchoring vignettes for health comparisons: An analysis of response consistency. *Quality of Life Research, 23*, 1721–1731. http://doi.org/10.1007/s11136-013-0615-2

Bandura, A. (1986). *Social foundations of thought and action: A social cognitive theory*. Englewood Cliffs, NJ: Prentice-Hall.

Bandura, A. (1997). *Self-efficacy: The exercise of control*. New York, NY: Freeman.

Benyamini, Y., Gefen-Bardarian, Y., Gozlan, M., Tabiv, G., Shiloh, S., & Kokia, E. (2008). Coping specificity: The case of women coping with infertility treatments. *Psychology & Health, 23*, 221–241. http://doi.org/10.1080/14768320601154706

Bond, T. G., & Fox, C. M. (2001). *Applying the Rasch model: Fundamental measurement in the human sciences*. Mahwah, NJ: Erlbaum.

Bosley, A. R. J., Newcombe, R. G., & Dauncey, M. E. (1981). Maternal smoking and APGAR score. *The Lancet, 317*, 337–338. http://doi.org/10.1016/S0140-6736(81)91963-2

Broadbent, E., Kaptein, A. A., & Petrie, K. J. (2011). Double Dutch: The 'think-aloud' Brief IPQ study uses a Dutch translation with confusing wording and the wrong instructions. *British Journal of Health Psychology, 16*, 246–249. http://doi.org/10.1111/j.2044-8287.2011.02021.x

Cameron, I. M., Crawford, J. R., Lawton, K., & Reid, I. C. (2013). Differential item functioning of the HADS and PHQ-9: An investigation of age, gender and educational background in a clinical UK primary care sample. *Journal of Affective Disorders, 147,* 262–268. http://doi.org/10.1016/j.jad.2012.11.015

Carver, C. S., Scheier, M. F., & Weintraub, J. K. (1989). Assessing coping strategies: A theoretically based approach. *Journal of Personality and Social Psychology, 56,* 267–283. http://doi.org/10.1037/0022-3514.56.2.267

Covic, T., Pallant, J. F., Conaghan, P. G., & Tennant, A. (2007). A longitudinal evaluation of the Center for Epidemiologic Studies-Depression scale (CES-D) in a rheumatoid arthritis population using Rasch analysis. *Health and Quality of Life Outcomes, 5,* 41. http://doi.org/10.1186/1477-7525-5-41

Crawford, J. R., & Garthwaite, P. H. (2006). Methods of testing for a deficit in single case studies: Evaluation of statistical power by Monte Carlo simulation. *Cognitive Neuropsychology, 23,* 877–904. http://doi.org/10.1080/02643290500538372

Crosby, R. D., Kolotkin, R. L., & Williams, G. R. (2003). Defining clinically meaningful change in health-related quality of life. *Journal of Clinical Epidemiology, 56,* 395–407. http://doi.org/10.1016/S0895-4356(03)00044-1

Daniilidou, N. V., Gregory, S. P., Zavras, D. J., Pavi, E. A., Athanasakis, K. P., Lionis, C. D., & Kyriopoulos, J. H. (2010). Comparison between two different measures of self-rated health: A single-question measure and a visual analogue scale. *Folia Medica, 52*(1), 63–69.

Dantendorfer, K., Amering, M., Bankier, A., Helbich, T., Prayer, D., Youssefzadeh, S., ... Katschnig, H. (1997). A study of the effects of patient anxiety, perceptions and equipment on motion artifacts in magnetic resonance imaging. *Magnetic Resonance Imaging, 15,* 301–306. http://doi.org/10.1016/S0730-725X(96)00385-2

de Vet, H. C., Terwee, C. B., Ostelo, R. W., Beckerman, H., Knol, D. L., & Bouter, L. M. (2006). Minimal changes in health status questionnaires: Distinction between minimally detectable change and minimally important change. *Health and Quality of Life Outcomes, 4,* 54. http://doi.org/10.1186/1477-7525-4-54

Diefenbach, M. A., & Leventhal, H. (1996). The common-sense model of illness representation: Theoretical and practical considerations. *The Journal of Social Distress and the Homeless, 5,* 11–38. http://doi.org/10.1007/BF02090456

Dunn, T. J., Baguley, T., & Brunsden, V. (2014). From alpha to omega: A practical solution to the pervasive problem of internal consistency estimation. *British Journal of Psychology, 105,* 399–412. http://doi.org/10.1111/bjop.12046

Epley, N., & Gilovich, T. (2006). The anchoring-and-adjustment heuristic: Why the adjustments are insufficient. *Psychological science, 17,* 311–318. http://doi.org/10.1111/j.1467-9280.2006.01704.x

Friedman, D. B., & Hoffman-Goetz, L. (2006). A systematic review of readability and comprehension instruments used for print and web-based cancer information. *Health Education & Behavior, 33,* 352–373. http://doi.org/10.1177/1090198105277329

Gigerenzer, G., & Edwards, A. (2003). Simple tools for understanding risks: from innumeracy to insight. *British Medical Journal, 327,* 741–744.

Hagger, M. S., & Orbell, S. (2003). A meta-analytic review of the common-sense model of illness representations. *Psychology and Health, 18,* 141–184. http://doi.org/10.1080/088704403100081321

Hart, J. (2006). *Health behaviour advice: Cognitive and educational influences* (Unpublished doctoral dissertation). University of Aberdeen, UK.

Haynes, S. N., Richard, D., & Kubany, E. S. (1995). Content validity in psychological assessment: A functional approach to concepts and methods. *Psychological Assessment, 7,* 238–247.

Höfer, S., Lim, L., Guyatt, G., & Oldridge, N. (2004). The MacNew heart disease health-related quality of life instrument: A summary. *Health & Quality of Life Outcomes, 2,* 3. http://doi.org/10.1186/1477-7525-2-3

Horwood, J., Pollard, B., Ayis, S., McIlvenna, T., & Johnston, M. (2010). Listening to patients: Using verbal data in the validation of the Aberdeen Measures of Impairment, Activity Limitation and Participation Restriction (Ab-IAP). *BMC Musculoskeletal Disorders, 11,* 182. http://doi.org/10.1186/1471-2474-11-182

Jacobson, N. S., Roberts, L. J., Berns, S. B., & McGlinchey, J. B. (1999). Methods for defining and determining the clinical significance of treatment effects: Description, application, and alternatives. *Journal of Consulting and Clinical Psychology, 67*, 300–307. http://doi.org/10.1037/0022-006X.67.3.300

Johnston, D. W., & Johnston, M. (2013). Useful theories should apply to individuals. *British Journal of Health Psychology, 18*, 469–473. http://doi.org/10.1111/bjhp.12049

Johnston, M. (1999). Mood in chronic disease: Questioning the answers. *Current Psychology, 18*, 71–87 http://doi.org/10.1007/s12144-999-1017-z

Johnston, M., Dixon, D., Hart, J., Glidewell, L., Schröder, C., & Pollard, B. (2014). Discriminant Content Validity (DCV): A quantitative methodology for assessing content of theory-based measures with illustrative applications. *British Journal of Health Psychology, 19*, 240–257. http://doi.org/10.1111/bjhp.12095

Kaplan, R. M., Riley, W. T., & Mabry, P. L. (2014). News from the NIH: Leveraging big data in the behavioural sciences. *Translational Behavioural Medicine, 4*, 229–231. http://doi.org/10.1007/s13142-014-0267-y

Knäuper, B., & Schwarz, N. (2004). Why your research may be out of order. *The Psychologist, 17*, 28–33.

Lalkhen, A. G., & McCluskey, A. (2008). Clinical tests: Sensitivity and specificity. *Continuing Education in Anaesthesia, Critical Care & Pain, 8*, 221–223. http://doi.org/10.1093/bjaceaccp/mkn041

Leventhal, H., Meyer, D., & Nerenz, D. R. (1980). The common sense representation of illness danger. In S. Rachman (Ed.), *Contributions to medical psychology* (Vol. 2, pp. 17–30). New York, NY: Pergamon.

Lissitz, E. W., & Samuelson, K. (2007). A suggested change in terminology and emphasis regarding validity and education. *Educational Researcher, 36*, 437–448. http://doi.org/10.3102/0013189X07311286

Marks, D. F. (2004). Questionnaires and surveys. In D. F. Marks & L. Yardley (Eds.), *Research methods for clinical and health psychology* (pp. 122–144). London, UK: Sage.

McGee, H. M., O'Boyle, C. A., Hickey, A., O'Malley, K., & Joyce, C. R. B. (1991). Assessing the quality of life of the individual: The SEIQoL with a healthy and a gastroenterology unit population. *Psychological Medicine, 21*(3), 749–759. http://doi.org/10.1017/S0033291700022388

Mokken, R. J. (1971). *A theory and procedure of scale analysis*. The Hague, The Netherlands: Mouton. http://doi.org/10.1515/9783110813203

Moss-Morris, R., Weinman, J., Petrie, K. J., Horne, R., Cameron, L. D., & Buick, D. (2002). The revised Illness Perception Questionnaire (IPQ-R). *Psychology & Health, 17*, 1–16. http://doi.org/10.1080/08870440290001494

Norman, G. R., Sloan, J. A., & Wyrwich, K. W. (2003). Interpretation of changes in health-related quality of life. *Medical Care, 41*, 582–592. http://doi.org/10.1097/00005650-200305000-00007

Patrick, D. L., & Peach, H. (1989). *Disablement in the community*. Oxford, UK: Oxford University Press.

Peters, G.-J. Y. (2014). The alpha and the omega of scale reliability and validity. *The European Health Psychologist, 16*, 56–69.

Pollard, B., Dixon, D., Dieppe, P., & Johnston, M. (2009). Measuring the ICF components of impairment, activity limitation and participation restriction: An item analysis using classical test theory and item response theory. *Health and Quality of Life Outcomes, 7*, 41. http://doi.org/10.1186/1477-7525-7-41

Pollard, B., Dixon, D., & Johnston, M. (2014). Does the impact of osteoarthritis vary by age, gender and social deprivation? A community study using the International Classification of Functioning, Disability and Health. *Disability & Rehabilitation, 36*, 1445–1451. http://doi.org/10.3109/09638288.2013.847123

Pollard, B., & Johnston, M. (2001). Problems with the Sickness Impact Profile: A theoretically-based analysis and a proposal for a new method of implementation and scoring. *Social Science and Medicine, 52*, 921–934. http://doi.org/10.1016/S0277-9536(00)00194-5

Pollard, B., Johnston, M., & Dixon, D. (2013). Exploring differential item functioning in the SF-36 by demographic, clinical, psychological and social factors in an osteoarthritis population. *BMC Musculoskeletal Disorders, 14*, 346. http://doi.org/10.1186/1471-2474-14-346

Polit, D. F., Beck, C. T., & Owen, S. V. (2007). Is the CVI an acceptable indicator of content validity? Appraisal and recommendations. *Research in Nursing & Health, 30*, 459–467. http://doi.org/10.1002/nur.20199

Rasch, G. (1960). *Probabilistic models for some intelligence and attainment tests*. Copenhagen, Denmark: Danmarks Paedogogiske Institut.

Rico, E. D., Dios, H. C., & Ruch, W. (2012). Content validity evidences in test development: An applied perspective. *International Journal of Clinical and Health Psychology, 12*, 449–460.

Robins, R.W., Hendin, H. M., & Trzesniewski, K. H. (2001). Measuring global self-esteem: Construct validation of a single-item measure and the Rosenberg Self-esteem Scale. *Personality and Social Psychology Bulletin, 27*, 151–161. http://doi.org/10.1177/0146167201272002

Rosenstiel, A. K., & Keefe, F. J. (1983). The use of coping strategies in chronic low back pain patients: Relationship to patient characteristics and current adjustment. *Pain, 17*, 33–44. http://doi.org/10.1016/0304-3959(83)90125-2

Rouquette, A., Blanchin, M., Sébille, V., Guillemin, F., Côté, S. M., Falissard, B., & Hardouin, J. B. (2014). The Minimal Clinically Important Difference determined using Item Response Theory Models: An attempt to solve the issue of the association with baseline score. *Journal of Clinical Epidemiology, 67*, 433–440. http://doi.org/10.1016/j.jclinepi.2013.10.009

Ruta, D. A., Garratt, A. M., Leng, M., Russell, I. T., & MacDonald, L. M. (1994). A new approach to the measurement of quality of life. The Patient-Generated Index. *Medical Care, 32*, 1109–1126. http://doi.org/10.1097/00005650-199411000-00004

Schwartz, C. E., & Sprangers, M. A. (2010). Guidelines for improving the stringency of response shift research using the then-test. *Quality of Life Research, 19*, 455–464.

Sijtsma, K., Debets, P., & Molenaar, I.W. (1990). Mokken scale analysis for polychotomous items: Theory, a computer program and an empirical application. *Quality and Quantity, 24*, 173–188. http://doi.org/10.1007/BF00209550

Skelton, J. A., Loveland, J. E., & Yeagley, J. L. (1996). Recalling symptom episodes affects reports of immediately-experienced symptoms: Inducing symptom suggestibility. *Psychology and Health, 11*, 183–201. http://doi.org/10.1080/08870449608400252

Smith, S., Fielding, S., Murchie, P., Johnston, M., Wyke, S., Powell, R., ... Campbell, N.C. (2013). Reducing the time before consulting with symptoms of lung cancer: A randomised controlled trial in primary care. *British Journal of General Practice, 63*, e47–e54. http://doi.org/10.3399/bjgp13X660779

Standing, L. G., & Shearson, C. G. (2010). Does the order of questionnaire items change subjects' responses? An example involving a cheating survey. *American Journal of Psychology, 12*, 603–614.

Vitaliano, P. P., Russo, J., Carr, J. E., Maiuro, R. D., & Becker, J. (1985). The Ways of Coping Checklist: Revision and psychometric properties. *Multivariate Behavioral Research, 20*(1), 3–26. http://doi.org/10.1207/s15327906mbr2001_1

Ware, J. E., Bjorner, J. B., & Kosinski, M. (2000). Practical implications of item response theory and computerized adaptive testing: A brief summary of ongoing studies of widely used headache impact scales. *Medical Care, 38*(9 Suppl.), II73–II82.

Watson, D., Clark, L. A., & Tellegen, A. (1988). Development and validation of brief measures of positive and negative affect: The PANAS scales. *Journal of Personality and Social Psychology, 54*, 1063–1070. http://doi.org/10.1037/0022-3514.54.6.1063

Watson, M., Greer, S., Young, J., Inayat, Q., Burgess, C., & Robertson, B. (1988). Development of a questionnaire measure of adjustment to cancer: The MAC scale. *Psychological Medicine, 18*, 203–209. http://doi.org/10.1017/S0033291700002026

Watson, D., & Pennebaker, J. W. (1989). Health complaints, stress, and distress: Exploring the central role of negative affectivity. *Psychological Review, 96*(2), 234–254. http://doi.org/10.1037/0033-295X.96.2.234

Weinman, J., Petrie, K. J., Moss-Morris, R., & Horne, R. (1996). The illness perception questionnaire: A new method for assessing the cognitive representations of illness. *Psychology & Health, 11*, 431–445. http://doi.org/10.1080/08870449608400270

Weng, L. J. (2004). Impact of the number of response categories and anchor labels on coefficient alpha and test-retest reliability. *Educational and Psychological Measurement, 64*, 956–972. http://doi.org/10.1177/0013164404268674

World Health Organization. (2001). *International classification of functioning, disability and health*. Geneva, Switzerland: Author.

Contributors

Michael G. Ainette
Department of Psychology
Dominican College
Orangeburg, NY
USA
E-mail michael.ainette@dc.edu

Erin O'Carroll Bantum
University of Hawaii Cancer Center
Honolulu, HI
USA
E-mail ebantum@cc.hawaii.edu

Yael Benyamini
Bob Shapell School of Social Work
Tel Aviv University
Tel Aviv
Israel
E-mail benyael@post.tau.ac.il

Felicity L. Bishop
Department of Psychology
University of Southampton
Southampton
UK
E-mail f.l.bishop@soton.ac.uk

Julie A. Chambers
Department of Psychology
University of Stirling
Stirling
UK
E-mail j.a.chambers@stir.ac.uk

Linda D. Cameron
School of Social Sciences, Humanities, and the Arts
University of California
Merced, CA
USA
E-mail lcameron@ucmerced.edu

Deborah Christie
University College Hospital
London
UK
E-mail deborah.christie@uclh.nhs.uk

Mark Conner
School of Psychology
University of Leeds
Leeds
UK
E-mail m.t.conner@leeds.ac.uk

Heather M. Derry
Department of Psychology
Ohio State University
Columbus, OH
USA
E-mail derry.12@osu.edu

Diane Dixon
School of Psychological Sciences and Health
University of Strathclyde
Glasgow
UK
E-mail diane.dixon@strath.ac.uk

Kim E. Dixon
Psychology Service
Tuscaloosa VA Medical Center
Tuscaloosa, AL
USA
E-mail kim.dixon@va.gov

Arturo Durazo
School of Social Sciences, Humanities, and the Arts
University of California
Merced, CA
USA
E-mail adurazo2@ucmerced.edu

Timothy R. Elliott
Department of Educational Psychology
Texas A&M University
College Station, TX
USA
E-mail timothyrelliott@tamu.edu

Norma A. Erosa
San Antonio Military Medical Center
San Antonio, TX
USA
E-mail erosa17@gmail.com

Eamonn Ferguson
School of Psychology
University of Nottingham
Nottingham
UK
E-mail eamonn.ferguson@nottingham.ac.uk

Benjamin H. Gottlieb
Department of Psychology
University of Guelph
Guelph, ON
Canada
E-mail bgottlie@uoguelph.ca

Douglas A. Granger
Institute for Interdisciplinary Salivary
Bioscience Research
Arizona State University
Tempe, AZ
USA
E-mail dgrange2@jhu.edu

Martin Hagger
Faculty of Health Sciences
Curtin University
Bentley, Perth, WA
Australia
E-mail martin.hagger@curtin.edu.au

Kelly B. Haskard-Zolnierek
Department of Psychology
Texas State University
San Marcos, TX
USA
E-mail kh36@txstate.edu

Alisha L. Janssen
Department of Psychology
Ohio State University
Columbus, OH
USA
E-mail aljanssen4@gmail.com

Marie Johnston
Aberdeen Health Psychology Group
Institute of Applied Health Sciences
University of Aberdeen
Aberdeen
UK
E-mail m.johnston@abdn.ac.uk

Derek W. Johnston
School of Psychology
University of Aberdeen
Aberdeen
UK
E-mail d.johnston@abdn.ac.uk

Evangelos C. Karademas
Department of Psychology
University of Crete
Rethymnon
Greece
E-mail karademas@uoc.gr

Elaine A. Leventhal
Professor Emeritus
Department of Medicine
Robert Wood Johnson Medical School
Rutgers University
New Brunswick, NJ
USA
E-mail eleventh@ifh.rutgers.edu

Howard Leventhal
Institute for Health
Department of Psychology
Rutgers University
New Brunswick, NJ
USA
E-mail hleventhal@ifh.rutgers.edu

Sofía López-Roig
Department of Health Psychology
Miguel Hernández University
Elche
Spain
E-mail slroig@umh.es

Aleksandra Luszczynska
Trauma, Health, & Hazards Center
University of Colorado at Colorado Springs
Colorado Springs, CO
USA
E-mail aluszczy@uccs.edu

Danielle E. McCarthy
Department of Psychology and Institute for Health
Rutgers University
New Brunswick, NJ
USA
E-mail demccart@rci.rutgers.edu

Hannah McGee
Royal College of Surgeons in Ireland
Dublin
Ireland
E-mail hmcgee@rcsi.ie

Susan Michie
UCL Centre for Behaviour Change
University College London
London
UK
E-mail s.michie@ucl.ac.uk

Karen Morgan
Royal College of Surgeons in Ireland
Dublin
Ireland
E-mail kmorgan@rcsi.ie

Ronan E. O'Carroll
Department of Psychology
University of Stirling
Stirling
UK
E-mail ronan.ocarroll@stir.ac.uk

Daryl B. O'Connor
School of Psychology
University of Leeds
Leeds
UK
E-mail d.b.oconnor@leeds.ac.uk

Dorothée Out
Institute of Educational Sciences
and Family Studies
Leiden University
Leiden
The Netherlands
E-mail dout@fsw.leidenuniv.nl

María-Ángeles Pastor
Department of Health Psychology
Miguel Hernández University
Elche
Spain
E-mail mapastor@umh.es

Ruchika Shaurya Prakash
Department of Psychology
Ohio State University
Columbus, OH
USA
E-mail prakash.30@osu.edu

Emily Roman
Institute for Health
Department of Psychology
Rutgers University
New Brunswick, NJ
USA
E-mail emily.roman@rutgers.edu

Holly M. Rus
School of Social Sciences, Humanities, and the Arts
University of California
Merced, CA
USA
E-mail hrus@ucmerced.edu

Ralf Schwarzer
Institute for Positive Psychology and Education
Faculty of Health Sciences
Australian Catholic University
Strathfield, NSW
Australia
E-mail ralf.schwarzer@acu.edu.au

Suzanne C. Segerstrom
Department of Psychology
University of Kentucky
Lexington, KY
USA
E-mail scsege0@uky.edu

Timothy W. Smith
Department of Psychology
University of Utah
Salt Lake City, UT
USA
E-mail tim.smith@psych.utah.edu

Summer L. Williams
Department of Psychology
Westfield State University
Westfield, MA
USA
E-mail swilliams@westfield.ma.edu

Thomas A. Wills
University of Hawaii Cancer Center
Honolulu, HI
USA
E-mail twills@cc.hawaii.edu

Caroline E. Wood
UCL Centre for Behaviour Change
University College London
London
UK
E-mail caroline.wood@ucl.ac.uk

Lucy Yardley
Department of Psychology
University of Southampton
Sothampton
UK
E-mail l.yardley@soton.ac.uk

Subject Index

24-hr recall 61
25-foot walk test 221

A

abstinence violation effect 33
AC1 statistic 258
accelerometer 64, 241
acceptability 161, 165, 328, 329
activities of daily living (ADL) 164
activity limitations (AL) 161
adherence 140, 244, 245
    – measures 89
    – pharmacy-based 68
    – to medical advice 86, 88, 89
adolescents 136, 278
alcohol 34, 38, 241
ambulatory assessment 234, 235
anchoring 325
angina 164, 169
antibody 228, 229, 230
anxiety 281, 283
Apgar score 11, 324
applicability 7
appraisal
    – cognitive 106
    – primary 105, 112, 113, 120
    – secondary 105, 112, 113, 120
arthritis 164, 169
Arthritis Impact Measurement Scale (AIMS2) 169
assent 279
atherosclerosis 234, 235
attention 281
attitude 21, 24

B

barriers 20, 28, 35
Barthel Index 169
behavioral
    – difficulties 281
    – intention 40
    – intervention 312, 314
    – perceived behavioral control (PBC) 20, 23
behavior change
    – intervention effectiveness 254
    – interventions 252
    – ontology 260
    – wheel 260

behavior change techniques (BCTs) 255
    – competences for delivering 256
    – identification
        – reliability and validity of 257
    – labels 256, 257
    – links to theoretical constructs 260
    – taxonomies 255
        – Behaviour Change Technique Taxonomy v1 (BCTTv1) 256, 257, 259
        – Behaviour Change Technique Taxonomy v2 (BCTTv2) 259
        – taxonomy project 259
benefit 20, 28
biological markers 66
    – assessment of 89
biopsychosocial model 5
blood 229, 230
    – diastolic blood pressure (DBP) 234
    – pressure 89, 234, 235, 241
    – systolic blood pressure (SBP) 234
body satisfaction 244
buffering 138

C

California Verbal Learning Test (CVLT) 220
cancer 164, 218, 220
    – breast cancer 213, 214, 217, 219
    – needs of cancer patients 140
cardiovascular diseases (CVD) 164, 169, 233
cardiovascular system 227, 233
catastrophizing 150
catecholamines 232
causal attribution 53
central responding 325
change
    – responsiveness 328
    – sensitivity to 326, 328
    – specificity 328
children 136, 278
cholesterol 89
chronic conditions 87
clinimetrics 11, 324
coding 293, 295, 296
coding competence 258
cognition 241

cognitive
- functions 242
- skills 280
- status 214, 215
cognitive appraisal theory 46
coherence 54
common-sense model (CSM) 45, 46, 47, 52, 54, 56, 86, 274
communication
- instrumental/task-oriented 74
- instrumental/test-oriented 80
- nonverbal 74
- physician–patient 73, 74, 75, 80
- socioemotional/affective 74, 80
community
- integration in a 139
computer-assisted qualitative data analysis software (CAQDAS) 296
condom use 39, 241
confidentiality 279
consent 278
CONSORT 254
constructionist approaches 294
Consumer Assessment of Healthcare Providers and Systems (CAHPS) 78
content analysis 270, 294
Continuous Performance Test (CPT) 219
coping 138, 140, 149
- approach 121
- avoidant 121
- classes of 121
- cognitive 122
- COPE Inventory 123, 322
- Coping Checklist (CC) 123
- Coping Inventory for Stressful Situations (CISS) 123
- Coping Strategies Questionnaire (CSQ) 124, 150
- Coping Strategy Indicator (CSI) 123
- Coping with Infertility Questionnaire 322
- effectiveness of 127
- measures 122
- mode of 121
- Pain Coping Strategies Questionnaire 322
- proactive 126
- Revised Ways of Coping Checklist (RWOC) 322
- self-efficacy 126
- situational 120

core sets 161
coronary heart disease (CHD) 234
cortisol 107, 231, 232, 233
Critical Appraisal Skills Programme (CASP) 193
Cronbach α 245
cues to action 20
cultural
- beliefs 49
- differences 133
- issues 281
culturally sensitive medicine 82
cut-offs 330
cytokines 228, 229

D

day reconstruction method (DRM) 247, 248
dental hygiene 38
depression 281, 283
detection behaviors 40
diabetes 94, 308, 310, 311, 312, 313, 314
diary 285
- daily 107, 110, 113
- electronic 243
dietary behaviors 36
differential item functioning (DIF) 166, 272, 273, 327, 329
dimensionality 270
direct estimation 324
direct observation 89
disability 161, 164
- Roland Morris Disability Index (RDQ) 170
discourse analysis 295, 297
discriminant content validity (DCV) 9, 161, 323, 327
drug use 241
dual-task performance tests 219
dynamic modeling 307, 314, 315

E

ecological momentary assessment (EMA) 64, 122, 323, 324, 325, 329
- episode-based 248
- software
  - Ilumivu 243
  - Movisens 243
  - Pendragon 243
electrocardiogram (ECG) 234
electronic devices 99
electronic measures 323
electronic pill-devices 89, 92

endocrine system 231
epistemology 290, 293
equivalence
– conceptual 267, 268, 274
– cultural 326
– functional 269, 270
– metric 269, 271
– scalar 269, 270, 271
– structural 269, 270, 272
Eriksen flanker task 219
ethical issues 293
European Organisation for Research and Treatment of Cancer (EORTC) 164
European Organisation for Research and Treatment of Cancer Quality of Life Questionnaire core 30 (EORTC-QLQ-C30) 169, 193
evidence synthesis 255
executive functioning 217, 218, 281
explanatory models
– Barts Explanatory Model Inventory (BEMI) 50, 52
– Explanatory Model Interview Catalogue (EMIC) 48, 49, 50, 59
– Kleinman's Explanatory Models Approach 48, 50, 55
– Short Explanatory Model Interview (SEMI) 49, 50

F
factor analysis 10, 165
– confirmatory (CFA) 10
– exploratory (EFA) 10
fatigue 285
Fear-Avoidance Beliefs Questionnaire 55
feasibility 165, 328
fight-or-flight reaction 103
finger-tapping task 221
focus groups 291, 296
free association 34
Functional Independence Measure (FIM) 168
functional limitations 160
Functional Limitations Profile (FLP) 167, 326
functional status 213, 214, 219, 221

G
gate control theory 147
general adaptation syndrome (GAS) 103
gold standard 92, 99, 100

grounded theory 293, 295, 297
guidelines 265, 266, 274

H
hassles 106, 111
– daily 106, 110, 241
health 131
– behavior 88
– belief model 20
– global self-reports of health behavior 61
– mental 11
– motivation 20
– outcomes 86
– perceived 175
– practitioner assessment 89
– self-assessed 175
– self-rated 325
– Short-Form Health Survey-10 (SF-10) for Children 192
– Short-Form Health Survey (SF-36) 166, 169, 176, 191, 321, 329
– subjective 175
Health Utilities Index (HUI) 194
heart disease 241
– recovery from 140
heart failure 164, 169
HeartQoL 194
heart rate 235, 241
High-Sensitivity Cognitive Screen (HSCS) 217
HIV 94
hormones 231, 232
Hospital Anxiety and Depression Scale (HADS) 194, 322, 329
hypertension 234
hypothalamic–pituitary–adrenal (HPA) axis 107, 231
hypothalamic–pituitary–gonadal (HPG) axis 231

I
identity 45
illness
– Assessment of Illness Risk Representations (AIRR) 51, 54, 56
– Asthma Illness Representation Scale 55
– beliefs about 86
– Brief Illness Perception Questionnaire (B-IPQ) 51, 53, 274
– chronic 86, 274

- Illness Cognition Questionnaire (ICQ) 51, 54, 56
- Illness Perception Questionnaire (IPQ) 12, 274, 321
- Illness Perception Questionnaire-Revised (IPQ-R) 51, 52, 53, 54, 56, 274
- McGill Illness Narrative Interview (MINI) 49, 50, 52
- Meaning of Illness Questionnaire (MIQ) 54
- Meaning of Illness Questionnaire (MIQ) (Revised) 51
- narrative 45
- perceptions 45
- representation attitudes
  - cause 45
  - coherence 46, 53
  - consequences 45, 53, 54
  - control 53
  - control/cure 45
  - emotional representation 53
  - identity 52
  - timeline 45, 53
- representations 45, 46, 47, 48, 55, 86
- Revised Illness Perception Questionnaire-Healthy Version 53
- risk 46, 47
- risk representations 54, 55, 57

imagery 47, 48, 54, 55, 57
immune parameters 230
immune system 227, 228
impairment 161
inflammation 228, 229, 231, 234
intention 20, 23
intentional nonadherence 94
interactional analysis system 75
inter-coder reliability 255
internal consistency 8, 9, 324, 328
International Classification of Functioning, Disability and Health (ICF) 160, 168, 169, 170
interpretative phenomenological analysis (IPA) 293, 294
interventions
- content 255
- descriptions, coding of 257
- design of 255
- fidelity of delivery 256
- reporting of 255
- specification of 255

interviews 291, 297, 298
item response theory (IRT) 9, 10, 11, 163, 324, 328, 329, 330

K
KIDSCREEN 193
- KIDSCREEN-10 193
- KIDSCREEN-27 193

L
learning 220, 281
life events 106, 110, 111, 112
Likert scale 324, 325

M
measurement invariance 269, 270
measures
- Aberdeen 168
- condition-specific 163, 164
- functional 132
- generic 163
- portfolios of 330
- single-item 324, 325
- social participation 134
- social support 137
- structural 132

Medical Interview Satisfaction Scale (MISS) 78
Medical Outcome Study (MOS) 166, 169
medication adherence 88, 89, 94, 99, 100, 323
Medication Event Monitoring System (MEMS) 99
medication possession ratio (MPR) 89, 99
memory 220, 281
Mental Adjustment to Cancer scale (MAC) 124, 322
mental model 45, 52
mere measurement effect 89, 162
methodology 124
minimally important difference (MID) 330
Mini Mental Status Examination (MMSE) 217
Minnesota Living with Heart Failure Questionnaire (MLHFQ) 194
Minnesota Multiphasic Personality Inventory (MMPI) 204, 205
mixed methods 299
Mokken scale 9, 10, 324, 328
motor control 221
multi-item scales 306, 308, 309, 316
multilevel modelling (MLM) 246

multiphase optimization strategy (MOST) 312, 313, 314
Multiple Sclerosis Functional Composite Scale (MSFC) 221
multiple sclerosis (MS) 213, 214, 215, 216, 218, 219, 221

N

negative affectivity (NA) 325
network mapping 135
network measure 134
neuroendocrine responses 234
neuroendocrine system 227
neurological injuries 140
neuromatrix model 147
neuropsychological assessment 213, 215, 216
nine hole peg test 221
nonadherence 245
– intentional 86, 88, 92, 100
– nonintentional 86, 88, 92, 94, 100
nonverbal 75
norms 163, 329
– subjective 21, 26
Nottingham Health Profile (NHP) 168, 191
numeric rating scales (NRS) 149
nursing 241
nutrition 37

O

obesity 285
observation 280, 292
open-ended questions 291, 299
order of items 326
Oswestry Disability Index (ODI) 170
outcomes
– clinical 89, 100
– functional health 321
– outcome expectancies 25, 33, 34
– Outcomes Measures in Rheumatoid Arthritis Clinical Trials (OMERACT) 274
overweight 285

P

Paced Auditory Serial Addition Test (PASAT) 218, 219, 221
pain 164, 170, 244, 267, 285
– anxiety 151
– assessment 274
– behaviors 152
– Brief Pain Inventory (BPI) 153
– chronic 268
– Common Pain Grade 170
– Initiative on Methods, Measurement, and Pain Assessment in Clinical Trials (IMMPACT) 154
– intensity 148
– McGill Pain Questionnaire (MPQ) 152
– Pain Anxiety Symptom Scale (PASS) 151
– Pain Behavior Checklist (PBCL) 152
– Pain Catastrophizing Scale (PCS) 150
– Pain Coping Strategies Questionnaires 322
– UAB Pain Behavior Scale 152
– West Haven–Yale Multidimensional Pain Inventory (WHYMPI) 152
participation restrictions (PR) 161
patient adherence 74, 75
patient-centred consultations 279
Patient-Generated Index (PGI) 196, 322
Patient-Reported Outcomes Measurement Information System (PROMIS) 154
patient-reported outcomes (PROs) 190
patient satisfaction 73, 74, 75, 80
Patient Satisfaction Questionnaire 78
pedometers 241
PedsQL 193
perceived control 241
perceptual style
– blunting 127
– monitoring 127
performance 162
personal control over prevention 54
personal digital assistant (PDA) 242, 243
personality 105, 111, 204, 205, 206, 207
phenomenology 295
physical activity 37, 140
physician ratings 286
physiological recorders 241
physiometrics 227, 229, 231, 233, 236
pill-count 89, 99
Positive and Negative Affect Schedule (PANAS) 325
Post-Imaging Distress Questionnaire 322
post-positivism 290
Posttraumatic Stress Disorder (PTSD) 140, 204
pregnancy 140
principle of compatibility 22
processing speed 218, 219
Protection Motivation Theory 20

proxy
- ratings 180
- report 279
psychological
- adjustment 321
- assessment 201, 204
psychometric properties 272
pulse wave velocity 235

Q
qualitative methods 290
quality adjusted life years (QALYs) 194
quality of care 78
quality of life (QoL) 11, 189, 214, 221, 284, 321
- EuroQol
  - EuroQol-5D (EQ-5D) 194
- health-related (HRQoL) 189
- questionnaires 265
- RAND-36 Measure of Health-Related Quality of Life 167
- Schedule for the Evaluation of Individual Quality of Life (SEIQoL) 195, 322
- World Health Organization Quality of Life Assessment (WHOQOL) 190, 192
  - WHOQOL-100 192
  - WHOQOL-BREF 192
  - WHOQOL-HIV 192
  - WHOQOL-OLD 193
  - WHOQOL-SRPB 192
questionnaire
- semantic structure 326

R
randomized controlled trial (RCT) 307
Rankin Scale 169
Rasch model 9, 10, 324, 328
reactivity 235
readability 165
readability indices 327
recovery 235
reflexivity 292
reliability 8, 9, 10, 22, 165, 245, 328
- alternative form 9
- coefficients 272
- inter-rater 9
- test–retest 9
resources 120
response
- bias 162, 325, 326, 329
- shift 325

responsiveness 166
risk
- behavior 35
- causal 54
- identity 54
- timeline 54
Roter Interaction Analysis System (RIAS) 75, 80

S
saliva 230, 231, 232, 233
sampling 292
- event-contingent 242
- interval-contingent 242
- signal-contingent 242
saturation 292
screening 88, 279
Seattle Angina Questionnaire (SAQ) 194
Selective Reminding Task (SRT) 220
self-care 88, 89, 94
self-efficacy 20, 31, 321
- volitional 37
self-monitoring 162, 245
self-regulation 86, 87
- theory 45
self-report 92, 94, 99, 162, 285, 323, 325
semi-structured questions 291
sensitivity 8, 10, 166, 328
severity 28
Sickness Impact Profile (SIP) 164, 167, 191, 324, 326
signal detection theory (SDT) 11
single case 163
six-minute walk test 162, 168, 169
sleep 284
smartphone 243
smoking 35, 241
- cessation 39
- Smoking Toolkit Study 330
social
- cognitive theory (SCT) 21, 31, 321
- conflict 139
- constructionist 290
- Social Readjustment Rating Scale 106
- support 120, 131
  - among adult diabetics 140
  - reciprocity in 138
specificity 166
State–Trait Anxiety Inventory (STAI) 322
stress 103, 119, 230
- appraisal 105, 111, 112
- buffering of 132

– perceived 105, 109
– Perceived Stress Scale (PSS) 109
– transactional model of 105
– work-related 241
stroke 169
Stroke Impact Scale 170
structural modeling (SEM) 307
substance use 140
support
– companionship 132
– emotional 132, 135
– from online relationships 139
– groups 135
– instrumental 132, 135
– perceived 136
– seeking 138
– sources of 133
susceptibility 20
– perceived 27
Symbol Digit Modalities Test (SDMT) 218, 219

T

Tampa Scale of Kinesiophobia (TSK) 151
Template for Intervention Description and Replication (TIDieR) 253, 254
test
– classical test theory (CTT) 10, 11, 163, 323, 328
– development 266
– test–retest reliability 258
– translation 266
testosterone 231, 232
thematic analysis 294
theoretical domains framework 260
theory of mind 280
theory of planned behavior 20, 321
think-aloud 327
Thurstone scaling 324
Time-Line Follow-Back (TLFB) 61
Trail Making Test (TMT) 217, 218
trainee confidence 258
training 257
translation 326
– back-translation 266, 274
– forward-translation 266, 274
treatment
– adherence 214, 221
– beliefs about 86
TREND statement 254

U

ultrasound 234, 235
uplifts 106, 110
urine assay 89

V

validity 8, 9, 10, 22, 292, 324
– concurrent 165
– construct 9, 10, 165, 327, 328
– content 9, 10, 11, 267, 271, 324, 326, 327, 328, 329
– Content Validity Index (CVI) 327
– convergent 165
– convergent construct 9
– criterion 10, 165, 328
– discriminant construct 10
– discriminant content 165, 170
– divergent 165
– ecological 290
– external 327
– face 267, 327
– internal 327
– predictive 165, 328
verbal rating scales (VRS) 149
visual analogue scales (VAS) 99, 149, 325
visual spatial learning test 220
vulnerability
– perceived 27

W

walking 162
wearable camera 65
Wechsler Adult Intelligence Scale (WAIS) 215, 216, 218
Wechsler Memory Scale (WMS) 215, 218, 220
West Haven–Yale Multidimensional Pain Inventory-Part III (MPI) 268
Wisconsin Card Sorting Test (WCST) 218
within-person investigations 329
Workgroup for Intervention Development and Evaluation Research (WIDER) 254

Also available in the series
Psychological Assessment – Science and Practice

Vol. 1
Tuulia M. Ortner, Fons J. R. van de Vijver (Eds.)
Behavior-Based Assessment in Psychology
Going Beyond Self-Report in the Personality, Affective, Motivation, and Social Domains
2015 (July), vi + 232 pages
ISBN 978-0-88937-437-9
US $63.00 / £36.00 / €44.95

Vol. 3
Karl Schweizer, Christine Di Stefano (Eds.)
Principles and Methods of Test Construction
Standards and Recent Advances
2016 (March), vi + 330 pages
ISBN 978-0-88937-449-2
US $69.00 / £39.00 / €49.95

For more information and further volumes, please see www.hogrefe.com
Prices subject to change.